SECESSION

The end of the Cold War brought about new secessionist aspirations and the strengthening and re-awakening of existing or dormant separatist claims everywhere. The creation of a new independent entity through the separation of part of the territory and population of an existing State raises serious difficulties as to the role of international law. This book offers a comprehensive study of secession from an international law perspective, focusing on recent practice and applicable rules of contemporary international law. It includes theoretical analyses and a scrutiny of practice throughout the world by eighteen distinguished authors from Western and Eastern Europe, North and Sub-Saharan Africa, North and Latin America, and Asia. Core questions are addressed from different perspectives, and in some cases with divergent views. The reader is also exposed to a far-reaching picture of State practice, including some cases which are rarely mentioned and often neglected in scholarly analysis of secession.

MARCELO G. KOHEN is Professor of International Law at the Graduate Institute of International Studies, Geneva.

SECESSION

International Law Perspectives

Edited by
MARCELO G. KOHEN

CAMBRIDGE
UNIVERSITY PRESS

CAMBRIDGE
UNIVERSITY PRESS

University Printing House, Cambridge CB2 8BS, United Kingdom

Cambridge University Press is part of the University of Cambridge.

It furthers the University's mission by disseminating knowledge in the pursuit of education, learning and research at the highest international levels of excellence.

www.cambridge.org
Information on this title: www.cambridge.org/9780521849289

First published 2006
First paperback edition 2012

A catalogue record for this publication is available from the British Library

ISBN 978-0-521-84928-9 Hardback

CONTENTS

*In French, with abstract in English.

CONTRIBUTORS

Georges Abi-Saab, Honorary Professor, Graduate Institute of International Studies, Geneva; Member of the *Institut de Droit international*

Frida Armas Pfirter, Professor, Faculty of Law, Austral University, Buenos Aires

Théodore Christakis, Professor, Faculty of Law, University of Grenoble

Andrew Clapham, Professor of International Law, Graduate Institute of International Studies, Geneva

Olivier Corten, Professor, Faculty of Law, Free University of Brussels

Christian Dominicé, Honorary Professor, Graduate Institute of International Studies and Law Faculty, University of Geneva; Member and former Secretary-General of the *Institut de Droit international*

John Dugard, Professor, University of Leiden; Member of the International Law Commission; Member of the *Institut de Droit international*

Patrick Dumberry, Member of the Quebec Bar, Attorney at Lalive & Partners, Geneva

Marcelo G. Kohen, Professor of International Law, Graduate Institute of International Studies, Geneva

Silvina González Napolitano, Professor of International Law, Catholic University of Argentina; Associate Professor, University of Buenos Aires

Georg Nolte, Professor, Institute of International Law, University of Munich

Fatsah Ouguergouz, Secretary of the International Court of Justice, The Hague

Photini Pazartzis, *Professeur agregée*, Faculty of Law, National and Capodistrian University of Athens

David Raič, Deputy Director and Senior Programme Coordinator, Hague Institute for the Internationalisation of Law.

Antonello Tancredi, Professor of International Law, Faculty of Law, University of Palermo

Djacoba Liva Tehindrazanarivelo, PhD in International Law and Guest-Lecturer, Graduate Institute of International Studies, Geneva; Lecturer, Faculty of Law, University of Neuchâtel

Li-ann Thio Associate Professor, Faculty of Law, National University of Singapore

Christian Tomuschat, Professor, Faculty of Law, Humboldt-University of Berlin; Member of the *Institut de Droit international*

Andreas Zimmermann, Professor, Director of the Walther-Schücking-Institute for International Law, University of Kiel

PREFACE

The early origin of this book derives from a workshop on International Law and Secession that I organised at the Graduate Institute of International Studies in Geneva in March 2000. Some of the contributors were present and many enthusiastically supported the idea of publishing a comprehensive analysis of the phenomenon of secession from an international law perspective, without any preconceived views or any hidden political agendas. On the basis of a list of topics I had suggested at that time, invitations to contribute were subsequently addressed to scholars from different legal and cultural backgrounds as well as regional origins. The result is a list of eighteen contributors hailing from Western and Eastern Europe, North and Sub-Saharan Africa, North and Latin America, and Asia. Diversity also finds its expression by the existence of four chapters in French with summaries in English.

This volume is divided into two parts, the first encompassing a theoretical analysis of the issue and the second, a scrutiny of regional practice. As the fourteen chapters show, both aspects are interwoven. The reader will find specific analysis of particular situations in both parts of the book. Similarly, authors of the chapters devoted to the study of regional practice also arrive at theoretical conclusions through the examination of cases of secession and separatism in their respective regions, including the way regional institutions or systems approach the problem. Core questions are addressed from different perspectives – and in some cases with divergent views – in several chapters. Although the purpose of this book is not to describe every case of real or potential secession, the reader will be exposed to a far-reaching picture of practice in all regions of the world, including cases rarely mentioned and often neglected in the scholarly analysis of this topic.

I am extremely grateful to Yasmin Naqvi (teaching and research assistant and Ph.D. candidate at the Graduate Institute of International Studies) and Divvya Vorburger-Rajagopalan (Ph.D. candidate at the Graduate Institute of International Studies), for their editorial work with the

English texts and the preparation of the list of cases and international instruments referred to in this volume, and to Liva Djacoba Tehindrazanarivelo (*chargé d'enseignement invité* at the Graduate Institute of International Studies), who edited the French texts and substantially contributed to the preparation of the bibliography included in the volume. My sincere appreciation also goes to all the contributors, for sharing their knowledge of the topics covered and for the serious work they have each put into their chapters.

In general, developments which took place up to January 2005 were taken into consideration. Authors, including the editor, are exclusively responsible for any statements of fact and opinions expressed in their respective contributions.

M. G. K.
Geneva, 2 February 2005

TABLE OF CASES

PCIJ cases

ICJ cases

ECHR cases

ECJ cases

ICTY cases

International arbitration and other cases

Domestic case law

Canada

Cyprus

France

Greece

Italy

The Netherlands

New Zealand

Pakistan

Russia

Rhodesia (South Africa)

United Kingdom

United States of America

TABLE OF INTERNATIONAL INSTRUMENTS

Treaties

Security Council Resolutions

General Assembly Resolutions

Other UN/League of Nations Resolutions, Declarations and Projects

Commission of Human Rights Resolutions

African Resolutions and Decisions

EC/EU and CSCE/OSCE Resolutions/Declarations

Asian Resolutions/Declarations

National Constitutions and Domestic Legislation

Internal agreements and non-state actors' statements

ABBREVIATIONS

A/RES/ . . .	General Assembly Resolution
AADI	*Annuaire africain de droit international*
ACDI	*Annuaire de la Commission du droit international*
ADI	*Anuario de Derecho Internacional*
AFDI	*Annuaire français de droit international*
AfYIL	*African Yearbook of International and Comparative Law*
AJIL	*American Journal of International Law*
AHR	*The American Historical Review*
ALR	*Arizona Law Review*
ASDI	*Annuaire suisse de droit international*
ASICL	African Society of International and Comparative Law
ASIL	American Society of International Law
ASR	*African Security Review*
AsYIL	*Asian Yearbook of International Law*
AUILR	*American University International Law Review*
Australian JIA	*Australian Journal of International affairs*
Australian JIL	*Australian Journal of International Law*
Berkeley JIL	Berkeley Journal of International Law
BJIL	*Berkeley Journal of International Law*
Boston UILJ	*Boston University International Law Journal*
Boston CLR	*Boston College Law Review*
Boston CICLR	*Boston College International and Comparative Law Review*
BYIL	*The British Year Book of International Law*
CADHP	Commission africaine des droits de l'homme et des peuples
Canadian B. L. J.	*Canadian Business Law Journal*
Canadian J. L. J.	*Canadian Journal of Law and Jurisprudence*

Canadian J. L. S.	*Canadian Journal of Law and Society*
Canadian J. P. S.	*Canadian Journal of Political Science*
Caribbean L. R.	*Caribbean Law Review*
CBR	*The Canadian Bar Review*
CEDH	Cour européenne des droits de l'homme
CEET	*Communist Economies and Economic Transformation*
CERD	Comité (ONU) pour l'élimination du racisme et de la discrimination
CIJ, Recueil	Recueil des arrêts et avis consultatifs de la Cour internationale de Justice
CJIL	*Chinese Journal of International Law*
CJTL	*Columbia Journal of Transnational Law*
CLR	*Columbia Law Review*
Columbia HRLR	*Columbia Human Rights Law Review*
Columbia JTL	*Columbia Journal of Transnational Law*
Cornell I. L. J.	*Cornell International Law Journal*
CPJI	Cour permanente de Justice internationale
CWRJIL	*Case Western Reserve Journal of International Law*
CYIL	*Canadian Yearbook of International Law*
DAI	Documents d'actualités internationales
Denver J. I. L. P.	*Denver Journal of International Law and Policy*
Dickinson J. I. L.	*Dickinson Journal of International Law*
DJLS	*Dalhousie Journal of Legal Studies*
DLR	*Dalhousie Law Review*
Duke J. C. I. L.	*Duke Journal of Comparative and International Law*
EJIL	*European Journal of International Law*
Emory I. L. R.	*Emory International Law Review*
EPIL	*Encyclopedia of Public International Law*
FF	*Feuille Fédérale* (Switzerland)
FULJ	*Fordham Urban Law Journal*
FYIL	*Finnish Yearbook of International Law*
Georgia JICL	*Georgia Journal of International and Comparative Law*
HILJ	*Harvard International Law Journal*
HJPLP	*Hamline Journal of Public Law and Policy*
HLR	*Hawaii Law Review*
Houston J. I. L.	*Houston Journal of International Law*

HRLJ	*Human Rights Law Journal*
ICJ Reports	Reports of judgements and advisory opinions of the International Court of Justice
ICLQ	*International and Comparative Law Quarterly*
IJIL	*Indian Journal of International Law*
IJMGR	*International Journal on Minority and Group Rights*
ILC	International Law Commission
ILM	International Legal Materials
ILR	*International Law Reports*
IRRC	*International Review of the Red Cross*
JAH	*The Journal of American History*
JIA	*Journal of International Affairs*
JPR	*Journal of Peace Research*
LCP	*Law and Contemporary Problems*
Liverpool L. R.	*The Liverpool Law Review*
LJIL	*Leiden Journal of International Law*
L.N.T.S.	League of Nations Treaty Series
Loyola LAICLR	*Loyola of Los Angeles International & Comparative Law Review*
Maryland J. I. L. T.	*Maryland Journal of International Law and Trade*
Max Planck UNYB	*Max Planck Yearbook of United Nations Law*
McGill L. J.	*McGill Law Journal*
Melbourne U. L. R.	*Melbourne University Law Review*
Michigan J.I.L.	*Michigan Journal of International Law*
MLR	*The Modern Law Review*
Moscow J. I. L.	*Moscow Journal of International Law*
MVHR	*The Mississippi Valley Historical Review*
Nat. J. Const. L.	*National Journal of Constitutional Law*
NILR	*Netherlands International Law Review*
NYIL	*Netherlands Yearbook of International Law*
NYILR	*New York International Law Review*
NYLSJICL	*New York Law School Journal of International and Comparative Law*
NYUJILP	*New York University Journal of International Law and Politics*
OHLJ	*Osgoode Hall Law Journal*
Osgood Hall L. J.	Osgood Hall Law Journal
PCIJ	Permanent Court of International Justice

Polish Q. I. A.	*Polish Quarterly of International Affairs*
PSILR	*Pennsylvania State International Law Review*
QLR	*Queen's Law Review*
RADIC	*Revue africaine de droit international et comparé*
RBDC	*Revue belge de droit constitutionnel*
RBDI	*Revue belge de droit international*
RDI	*Revue de droit international*
RDISDP	*Revue de droit international, de sciences diplomatiques et politiques*
Recueil des cours	*Recueil des cours de l'Académie de droit international de La Haye* / Collected Courses of the Hague Academy of International Law
RFDA	*Revue française de droit administratif*
RFDC	*Revue française de droit constitutionnel*
RGDIP	*Revue générale de droit international public*
RIAA	Report of International Arbitration Awards
Rivista	*Rivista di diritto internazionale*
RJEUL	*Revue juridique d'étudiants de l'Université Laval*
RJPIC	*Revue juridique et politique, indépendance et coopération*
ROJU	*Recueil officiel du Canton du Jura*
R. Québécoise D.I	*Revue Québécoise de Droit International*
RSA	*Recueil des sentences arbitrales*
RSJB	*Revue de la Société des juristes bernois*
RSJU	*Recueil systématique du Canton du Jura*
RUDH	*Revue universelle des droits de l'homme*
SAYIL	*South-African Yearbook of International Law*
SCT	*Studies in Conflict and Terrorism*
SJEAA	*Stanford Journal of East Asian Affairs*
SJICL	*Singapore Journal of International and Comparative Law*
SJIL	*Stanford Journal of International Law*
SLR	*Stanford Law Review*
S/RES/ . . .	UN Security Council Resolution (French texts)
Stetson L. R.	*Stetson Law Review*
St Louis U. L.J.	*Saint Louis University Law Journal*

STLR	*South Texas Law Review*
St. TLR	*Saint Thomas Law Review*
Suffolk T. L. R.	*Suffolk Transnational Law Review*
Temple I. C. L. J.	*Temple International and Comparative Law Journal*
Texas I. L. J.	*Texas International Law Journal*
Tulane J. I. C. L.	*Tulane Journal of International and Comparative Law*
Tulsa J. C. I. L.	*Tulsa Journal of Comparative and International Law*
TWQ	*Third World Quarterly*
UBCLR	*University of British Columbia Law Review*
UCLR	*The University of Chicago Law Review*
U.Haw.L. R.	*University of Hawaii Law Review*
UKMIL	United Kingdom Materials on International Law
UNCIO	United Nations Conference on International Organizations
U. New Brunswick L. J.	*University of New Brunswick Law Journal*
UN GA Res.	Resolution of the United Nations General Assembly
UN SC Res.	Resolution of the United Nations Security Council
UNSWLJ	*The University of New South Wales Law Journal*
U. Penn. JIEL	*University of Pennsylvania Journal of International and Economic Law*
UTLJ	*University of Toronto Law Journal*
UWAus.LR	*University of Western Australia Law Review*
Vanderbilt J. T. L.	*Vanderbilt Journal of Transnational Law*
VJIL	*Virginia Journal of International Law*
VLR	*Vermont Law Review*
VRU	*Verfassung und Recht in Ubersee* / Law and Politics in Africa, Asia and Latin America
WILR	*Wisconsin International Law Journal*
WSULR	*Western State University Law Review*
YEL	*Yearbook of European Law*
YHRDLJ	*Yale Human Rights & Development Law Journal*
YJIL	*The Yale Journal of International Law*

YLJ	*Yale Law Journal*
ZaöRV	*Zeitschrift für ausländisches öffentliches Recht und Völkerrecht*
ZöR	*Zeitschrift für öffentliches Recht*

INTRODUCTION

MARCELO G. KOHEN

The relationship between secession and international law is a subject that has long attracted the interest of jurisprudence. The emergence of a new State to the detriment of an older sovereign entity disrupts the composition of international society and challenges the very foundations of its main actors. At the time of the creation of the new independent States in the Americas during the eighteenth and nineteenth centuries, the idea of – and consequently, the term – 'decolonisation' did not exist. Hence, the process of what was the first phenomenon of independence of colonies from their European metropolises took the form of secession. In other words, these new States were not created as a result of the existence of any right to independence under international law. Their existence came into being as a matter of fact and of recognition by the other members of the more limited community of States of the time.

This approach drastically changed during the United Nations era. Decolonisation, the most important means of creation of new States during the second half of the twentieth century, was not viewed by the international legal order as a case of secession. One of the reasons for this is summarised in the Declaration of Principles of International Law embodied in UNGA Resolution 2625 (XXV): 'the territory of a colony or other non-self-governing territory has, under the Charter, a status separate and distinct from the territory of the State administering it'.[1] The other reason lies in the emergence of the principle of self-determination as a right of all peoples. For the first time in history, international law contained a rule granting a right to some communities, those which qualified as 'peoples', to create their own independent States. In spite of this completely new phenomenon, secession remained – actually or potentially – as another important way to create States in the contemporary world.

[1] See Andreas Zimmermann's chapter 'Secession and the Law of State Succession' in this volume.

The end of the Cold War brought about new secessionist aspirations and the strengthening and re-awakening of existing or dormant separatist claims in nearly all regions of the world. An observer can be struck by this renewed zeal to create new sovereign States in a world that is more and more interdependent. Apparently, we are facing two simultaneous contradictory phenomena. Globalisation implies, by definition, the losing of competencies by States, the transfer of their power either to the top (as supranational or integration processes show) or to the bottom (mainly through decentralisation, deregulation and privatisation policies within the State adopted by governments nearly all over the world). As an explanation of this paradox, Zygmunt Bauman has advanced the argument that, 'it was the *demise* of state sovereignty, not its triumph, that made the idea of statehood so tremendously popular'.[2]

The growth of UN membership from its original 51 member States in 1945 to 149 in 1984 was essentially due to decolonisation. The increase in this figure from 151 in 1990 to 191 at present has been essentially due, broadly speaking, to secession. Indeed, even if one accepts the controversial qualifications of the collapse of the Soviet Union and the Socialist Federal Republic of Yugoslavia as cases of dissolution, there is no doubt that these processes of dissolution at least began with secessionist attempts made by some components of both former federations.

I. Secession: broad and strict conceptions

There are different perceptions in legal – as well as political – theories about the phenomenon of secession. Not surprisingly, authors of this collective work adopted or had in mind different perspectives. Some of them followed a broad notion of secession, including in their analyses all cases of separation of States in which the predecessor State continues to exist in a diminished territorial and demographic form. Situations of dismemberment of States, in which the predecessor State ceases to exist, were also envisaged. The case of the Socialist Federal Republic of Yugoslavia obviously attracted much scrutiny, in particular with regard to its legal qualification as a case of secession or dissolution. Other authors also considered situations related to processes of decolonisation.

[2] Z. Bauman, *Globalization: The Human Consequences* (Cambridge: Polity Press, 1998), p. 64.

Most of the contributors adopted a more restricted perception. This is also the view followed by the editor. In the narrower sense of the concept, secession is the creation of a new independent entity through the separation of part of the territory and population of an existing State, without the consent of the latter. Yet, secession can also take the form of the separation of part of the territory of a State in order to be incorporated as part of another State, without the consent of the former. When a new State is formed from part of the territory of another State with its consent, it is a situation of 'devolution' rather than 'secession'.[3] This presupposes an agreement between both entities and, as such, is not a source of conflict, at least with regard to the existence of the new State itself.

The lack of consent of the predecessor State is the key element that characterises a strict notion of secession. At the same time, this factor explains why secession is so controversial in international law. On the one hand, the absence of agreement is a source of dispute between the new and the 'parent' State. On the other hand, for want of consent of the latter, the newly formed entity has to find a legal justification for its creation elsewhere. Conversely, the parent State will presumably attest that this justification does not exist in international law and that, on the contrary, the international legal order protects itself against attempts to dismantle it, such as those processes constituting secession. This situation provides a rough summary of the whole picture of the legal implications of secession in international law. The present study, although focusing upon situations of secession, will also address examples of devolution as a way to contrast both processes and the legal consequences thereof.

II. International law: its increasing role regarding secession

Not surprisingly, existing States have shown themselves to be 'allergic' to the concept of secession at all times. Their representatives even carefully avoided the very use of the term 'secession' when involved in codifying the rules of State succession, preferring to speak about 'separation of part of a State'.[4] This aversion is not simply terminological. It is evidence that

[3] For a classification of the different categories of creation of States in the contemporary world see: M. G. Kohen, 'Création d'Etats en droit international contemporain', *Bancaja Euromediterranean Courses of International Law* 6 (2002) 571–4.

[4] The 1978 Vienna Convention on Succession of States in respect of Treaties did not even distinguish under this heading between true cases of separation (i.e. devolution and secession) and those of dissolution. See its article 34. Cf. articles 17, 30 and 40 of the 1983 Vienna Convention on Succession of States in respect of State Property, Archives and Debts.

States are not willing to allow even a potential consideration that secession is a situation governed by international law, even after the success of a secessionist State.

The creation of States has traditionally been perceived as a matter of fact. For most authors, international law does not impact upon this process, and is limited to taking note of the existence of a new sovereign entity, with all the legal consequences attached to it, i.e. the existence of rights and obligations in the international realm. Even as recently as 1991, the arbitration commission of the Peace Conference for Yugoslavia (known as the Badinter Commission) insisted that 'the existence or disappearance of the State is a question of fact'.[5] As a result of this view, which foresees an insignificant role for international law in this field, very little legal theory on the creation of States emerged. Instead, legal scholarship was concerned mainly with the attitude of the rest of international society with regard to the arrival of a new entity, i.e., recognition.[6] James Crawford's reference book *The Creation of States in International Law* constituted the exception to this state of affairs. The study not only dealt with the question, but it also demonstrated that international law had much to say in the matter.[7]

At the end of the Cold War, some of the new States which emerged were created on the basis of international law. In other words, the international legal system played the role of a 'midwife', providing legal justification for the creation of new States. This was particularly the case for Namibia in 1990 and East Timor in 2002. Micronesia and Palau achieved their statehood in 1990 and 1994 respectively, when the Security Council put an end to these last trust territories. However, the role of international law in the creation of those States was not new; it was just the continuation of the process of decolonisation of the 1960s and 1970s and probably represented the last remnants of that process. To some extent, the independence of Eritrea in 1993 could also be included in the list of States created by operation of international law, since the territory had been incorporated into Ethiopia by the UN General Assembly, under the condition that

[5] *ILM* 31 (1992) 1495.

[6] After the creation of new States following the First World War, some courses at The Hague Academy of International Law dealt with the question, laying stress nevertheless upon political rather than legal considerations, or essentially focusing upon recognition. Cf. R. Erich, 'La naissance et la reconnaissance des Etats', *Recueil des cours* 3 (1926) 431–505. By contrast, legal literature related to recognition of States is abundant. The two major works on this are: H. Lauterpacht, *Recognition in International Law* (Cambridge: Cambridge University Press, 1947) and J. Verhoeven, *La reconnaissance internationale dans la pratique contemporaine* (Paris: Pedone, 1975).

[7] J. Crawford, *The Creation of States in International Law* (Oxford: Clarendon Press, 1979).

the territory would hold an autonomous status within a federation,[8] a condition not respected by the parent State. The other cases of new States which emerged after the end of the Cold War, which represented the larger number of new States, did not benefit from international legal backing. Apparently, these States came into being as 'a matter of fact', a situation which international law, it seems, neither sanctions nor prevents. Olivier Corten's chapter on the existence of a 'gap' in international law with regard to secession addresses this problem. He comes to the conclusion that international law's 'neutrality' in this respect is less and less evident, since the mechanisms to protect States from disruption are even stronger today than before.

The traditional view was that secessionist movements, when not under foreign control, were a purely internal affair. According to this view, which is reflected in some chapters of this volume, international law neither encourages secessionism nor prohibits it. Secessionism was a matter of fact: if the secessionist forces were able to impose the existence of a new State, then the international legal system was to record the fact of the existence of this new entity.

The key element for distinguishing between those situations where international law played a direct role by providing a legal justification for the creation of the new State, and those situations where international law did not play such a role, is the status of the territory in question. In the former situations, the territories in question had an international status, such as former mandates, trusteeships, non-self-governing territories or territories having been placed under the sovereignty of an existing State by an international organisation, as was in the case of Eritrea. In the latter situations, the creation of the new sovereign entities was made to the detriment of the territory of an existing independent State. Situations of agreed dissolution, unification or devolution do not create major problems with regard to the very fact of the coming into being of the new States. It is essentially secession that is problematic from the legal perspective. This is shown not only by the cases of unilateral proclamations of independence of the former Yugoslav and Soviet republics, but also by other such proclamations that have not been followed by the effective existence of new States, as in the case of Kosovo, Chechnya, Bougainville, Somaliland, Anjouan, South Sudan, North Ossetia or Abkhazia, to mention a few.

[8] GA Res. 390 (V) of 2 December 1950. See the discussion of this case in the chapters by Tomuschat and Ouguergouz/Tehindrazanarivelo in this volume.

The main interest in the legal analysis of secession from the viewpoint of time is at the moment of the emergence of the new State. In other words, the essential questions at issue concern whether there exists a right to secession and the role of the fundamental principles of international law in supporting or opposing the creation of a new independent entity, as well as the impact of the so-called principle of effectiveness and of recognition in this process. International law also determines certain legal consequences pertaining to the situation after secession. Questions related to the respect for human and minority rights, democracy, and other issues such as respect for boundaries, play a persuasive role in whether or not new States are accepted as members of the international society in recent times. These are not questions that are specifically related to cases of secession but interest all situations where new States are created. As such, there are no specific rules deriving from these fields that apply to a secessionist State. Conversely, the question arises whether secession deserves a particular treatment with regard to some problems related to State succession, such as succession to treaties concluded by the predecessor State, nationality of the inhabitants of the seceding State, distribution of property, debts and archives. Andreas Zimmermann's chapter deals with these aspects of the problem, showing the supplementary difficulties that secession brings in the field of State succession, in particular, when no agreement between the predecessor and the successor State is reached.

III. The impact of fundamental principles of international law

For States, respect of their territorial integrity is paramount. This is a consequence of the recognition of their equal sovereign character. One of the essential elements of the principle of territorial integrity is to provide a guarantee against any dismemberment of the territory. It is not only the respect of the territorial sovereignty, but of its *integrity*. This explains, for instance, why support for secessionist movements, or a colonial power's decision to keep part of the territory of a colony after its independence, can be considered violations of the territorial integrity of the State or the people concerned. It is beyond doubt that this rule plays a fundamental role in international relations and, as a mutual obligation, it requires all States to respect each other's territories. It is a guarantee against eventual *external* breaches, or, in other words, threats against the territorial sovereignty coming from abroad. But does this obligation also apply to internal secessionist movements?

At first sight, territorial integrity cannot be invoked as a legal argument to oppose secessionist movements, since these do not constitute subjects of international law, as explained by Georges Abi-Saab in his conclusion. In other words, the principle applies to actions coming from abroad, not to threats emanating from inside a State. However, a perusal of recent practice appears *prima facie* as contradictory in this regard. On the one hand, no reference to the respect of the territorial integrity of the Socialist Federal Republic of Yugoslavia (SFRY) was mentioned in the numerous resolutions and declarations adopted at the moment of Slovenia and Croatia's unilateral proclamations of independence, followed by other components of that federal State. In the case of Eritrea, not only did the UN not evoke Ethiopia's territorial integrity, but it actively participated in the organisation of the referendum. On the other hand, in the cases of Bosnia and Herzegovina, Georgia, Azerbaijan, Comoros and Kosovo, among others, the international community addressed all parties involved in those internal conflicts – and consequently secessionist movements also – reminding them of the obligation to respect the territorial integrity of the States concerned and warning in some cases that any entity unilaterally declared in contravention to the principle would not be accepted.[9]

This seeming contradiction can nevertheless be explained in legal terms. As mentioned, the case of Yugoslavia was held by the Arbitration Commission and the UN to be one of dissolution and not of secession. By definition, the territorial integrity principle is not at issue if a State is dissolving: the State in question will not exist any more. The case of Eritrea, for its part, was one in which its special status of autonomy conferred by the UN was not respected by the State into which the territory was incorporated. Conversely, all the cases where an express reference to the respect of territorial integrity was made involved secessionist movements trying to

[9] See in particular SC Res. 787 (1992) concerning Bosnia and Herzegovina, in which the Security Council '[s]trongly reaffirms its call on all parties and others concerned to respect strictly the territorial integrity of Bosnia and Herzegovina, and affirms that any entities unilaterally declared or arrangements imposed in contravention thereof will not be accepted'. Similarly, SC Res. 971 (1995), which 'calls upon the parties to intensify efforts . . . to achieve an early and comprehensive political settlement of the conflict, including on the political status of Abkhazia, *fully respecting the sovereignty and territorial integrity of the Republic of Georgia*' (emphasis added). Among others, cf. for Georgia, SC Resolutions 876 (1993), 896 (1994) and 906 (1994); for Azerbaijan, SC Resolutions 882 (1993), 853 (1993), 874 (1993) and 884 (1993); for Comoros, the Agreement of Addis Abeba of 13 December 1997 in: 4 *Documents d'actualité internationale*, (Paris: La documentation française, 1998), p. 143 and for Kosovo, cf. SC Resolutions 1160 (1998), 1199 (1998), 1203 (1998) and 1244 (1999).

obtain independence through forcible means. This practice reveals a trend to enlarge the scope of application of the principle of respect of territorial integrity to cases where secessionist movements resort to force. This practice prefigures the position of international law to acknowledge the creation of new States only when this occurs through peaceful means.

The principle of the prohibition of the use of force in international relations seems to appear unrelated to the problem of secession, with the obvious exception of foreign military intervention for the purpose of creating a new State, as occurred in the case of the Turkish Republic of Northern Cyprus. Again, it must be stressed that struggle against forcible colonial rule is not at issue here.[10] The traditional cases, in which a central government and a secessionist movement are involved in a violent conflict, are not candidates for the application of the rule prohibiting the use of force. In these cases, the violence used does not amount to a use of force in international relations, but is governed within the domestic sphere of a given State, as stressed by Olivier Corten and Georges Abi-Saab. Forcible repression, armed struggle or terrorism within the boundaries of one State are not governed by *ius ad bellum*, but by the domestic law of the State concerned. This means, on the one hand, that central authorities can resort to the legitimate exercise of forcible means and, on the other hand, that resort to violent measures by separatist movements has no legal ground. Contrary to what happened in the context of decolonisation, international law has not recognised a right to use force for secessionist movements, even in circumstances of grave violations of human rights against minorities or other groups, as the case of Kosovo demonstrates.[11] As a matter of course, human rights must be respected in all cases of repression of separatist struggle, as must humanitarian law if the confrontation reaches the level of an internal armed conflict. The case of Chechnya is an example in which these considerations are applicable.[12] Andrew

[10] On this aspect, see G. Abi-Saab, 'Wars of National Liberation in the Geneva Conventions and Protocols', *Recueil des cours* 165 (1979-IV) 366–374.

[11] In the above mentioned resolutions (note 9), the Security Council 'condemn[ed] all acts of violence by any party, as well as terrorism in pursuit of political goals by any group or individual, and all external support for such activities in Kosovo, including the supply of arms and training for terrorist activities in Kosovo' and '*Insist[ed]* that the Kosovo Albanian leadership condemn all terrorist actions, *demand[ed]* that such actions cease immediately and *emphasize[d]* that all elements in the Kosovo Albanian community should pursue their goals by peaceful means only'.

[12] In the Declaration of 11 December 1999, in Helsinki, 'The European Council does not question the right of Russia to preserve its territorial integrity nor its right to fight against terrorism. However, the fight against terrorism cannot, under any circumstances,

Clapham's contribution addresses the particular case in which secessionist movements resort to force, sometimes using terrorist methods, and focuses on problems of qualification in the application of anti-terrorist rules.

The principle of self-determination, when applicable, can lead to the creation of new States. There are not two different rights to self-determination, one internal and the other external, but two aspects of a single right.[13] If the application of the principle in the context of colonial or foreign rule is no longer controversial, the essential point for the discussion on secession is whether the principle has any relevance in existing States. Christian Tomuschat's chapter concludes that a narrow conception of self-determination prevails in international law. In the editor's view, practice shows that the international legal definition of 'peoples' acknowledges the existence of only one people where there exists a State. The exception is furnished by those cases in which the State defines itself as constituted by a plurality of peoples having the right to self-determination and hence to separate.[14] This is the case, at present, of the constitutions of Ethiopia, and Serbia and Montenegro. This view is not espoused by some contributors (e.g., Clapham, Dugard/Raič), who consider, as does the Canadian Supreme Court, that '"a people" may include a portion of the population of an existing state'.[15] Practice, however, shows that a clear distinction among three different categories of human communities is made in international law, each having their corresponding rights: peoples, minorities and indigenous populations. Only peoples have the right to self-determination. The last two groups form part of the first, broader group: the peoples. To speak about national minorities within States makes no sense if those minorities are also considered 'peoples'. By definition, a minority cannot but be identified within a wider human community. Sociological or other definitions of 'peoples' must not be confused with the definition under international law, with which they may or may not coincide. In this particular field, it should also be stressed that the recognition by the international community through the relevant UN organs that a given human community constitutes a 'people' is also

warrant the destruction of cities, nor that they be emptied of their inhabitants, nor that a whole population be considered as terrorist.' Available at: http://europa.eu.int/abc/doc/off/bull/en/9912/p000031.htm.

[13] Cf., however, the chapter on the practice in Africa and the Asia-Pacific regions.

[14] For the editor's analysis of self-determination, see M. G. Kohen, *Possession contestée et souveraineté territoriale* (Paris: P.U.F., 1997), pp. 407–23, as well as 'Création d'Etats en droit international contemporain', pp. 583–9 and 594–6.

[15] *ILM* 37 (1998) 1370, para. 124.

important, as the practice in the field of decolonisation shows.[16] To some extent, recognition with regard to peoples can play a constitutive role, contrary to the situation with regard to the creation of States.

A very controversial issue debated at some length in this book is the scope of the so-called 'safeguard clause' embodied in the Friendly Relations Declaration and repeated in subsequent instruments.[17] For some of the contributors, such as Tomuschat, Dugard/Raič, Ouguergouz/Tehindrazanarivelo and Thio, the interpretation of this clause leads to the legal acceptance of a 'remedial secession', at least as a measure of last resort. If a State is not behaving in the manner prescribed by the Friendly Relations Declaration, then the part of the population being discriminated against could have its right to self-determination recognised, the State acting in contradiction with this right losing the protection of its territorial integrity to this extent. Like other authors in this book (e.g., Tancredi, Corten, and Christakis), the editor does not share this view which, according to him, is not in conformity with the rest of the Declaration's chapter on self-determination. The 'safeguard clause' was originally drafted with situations such as South Africa and Rhodesia in mind, without any intention to extend recognition to any 'secession' rights to the majority of the South African and Zimbabwean peoples, as victims of racist regimes. Curiously enough, it was Pretoria's minority regime which encouraged a 'secessionist' policy, through the creation of Bantustan 'independent' States (Transkei, Ciskei, Bophuthatswana and Venda).

In addition, the interpretation of the safeguard clause as allowing 'remedial secession' would lead, as a consequence of the violation of the internal dimension of self-determination, to the loss of the territory of the State whose government is acting in this way. This is tantamount to saying that when a national, religious or linguistic minority is seriously discriminated

[16] 'The validity of the principle of self-determination, defined as the need to pay regard to the freely expressed will of peoples, is not affected by the fact that in certain cases the General Assembly has dispensed with the requirement of consulting the inhabitants of a given territory. Those instances were based either on the consideration that a certain population did not constitute a "people" entitled to self-determination or on the conviction that a consultation was totally unnecessary, in view of special circumstances.' *Western Sahara, Advisory Opinion, ICJ Reports* 1975, p. 33, para. 59.

[17] 'Nothing in the foregoing paragraphs [related to self-determination] shall be construed as authorising or encouraging any action which would dismember or impair, totally or in part, the territorial integrity or political unity of sovereign and independent States conducting themselves in compliance with the principle of equal rights and self-determination of peoples . . . and thus possessed of a government representing the whole people belonging to the territory without distinction as to race, creed or colour'.

against, then it becomes a 'people'. It seems that the more appropriate way to address the issue of serious violations of human rights, either collective or individual, is rather through the restoration of the respect of such rights. These kinds of violations are often due to the existence of a particular government following discriminatory policies. By definition, this can be a temporary situation. By contrast, a radical 'solution' such as secession is permanent, or at least, lasting. As a matter of course, the situation is different if the State itself recognises its composition by a plurality of people entitled to the right to self-determination, as is mentioned above.

Georg Nolte's chapter addresses the impact of intervention, both by the UN and third States. The principle of non-intervention in matters that essentially fall within the domestic jurisdiction of a State imposes on third States and international organisations the obligation not to support any attempt made by a group to create a new State from the territory of an existing State. This is the reason why support to secessionist movements from abroad can also be considered as a breach of this principle.[18] The gravest cases of this intervention may also take the form of a violation of the prohibition of the use of force, as well as the principle of the respect of territorial integrity. The cases of Northern Cyprus and Bangladesh seem emblematic in this regard. Contrary to the former example, the latter is a case of an accomplished secession. This case is extensively discussed in the present book and different interpretations are provided by Tomuschat, Nolte, Dugard/Raič, Tancredi and Thio. Irrespective of the views followed, the case of Bangladesh could show that the principle of non-intervention is unable to prevent the creation of a new State if this is the final result. This could either be a striking demonstration that the creation of States is a pure question of fact or that what is essential is recognition of the new State by the international community, irrespective of the legal conditions that led to its creation. Another perspective is that the principle of non-intervention is not properly applied in international relations, and that double standards are followed in this field, as well as in others. For the editor, a careful study of the case shows that the independence of Bangladesh was proclaimed on 26 March 1971, that it was Pakistan that first resorted to force against India on 3 December 1971, and that the latter country recognised Bangladesh's independence three days later. No doubt, the defeat of the Pakistani Army by India opened the way for the

[18] As the Court stated in the *Nicaragua case*, support to peoples in the context of their struggle against colonialism is not concerned by this principle (*Case Concerning Military & Paramilitary Actions in and Against Nicaragua, (Nicaragua v. United States of America) ICJ Reports* 1986, p. 14, at p. 108, para. 206).

affirmation of Bangladesh as an independent State, but it would be an exaggeration to consider that the creation of this State was due to the Indian intervention. To some extent, the creation of a new State outside the application of the principle of self-determination, as was in the case of Bangladesh, is also evidence of what was advanced above with regard to the existence of one people within a State. Ultimately, it is the success of a 'non-people' human community in the creation of a new State that transforms this community into a 'people'.

IV. Secession between effectiveness and recognition

John Dugard/David Raič's chapter deals in depth with problems related to the recognition of States and to the existence of an obligation not to recognise entities in some circumstances. The authors come to the conclusion that collective recognition can be a useful instrument for the creation of States but collective non-recognition can in turn be used to obstruct secession as well. Undoubtedly, recognition by the parent State paves the way for an established confirmation of the existence of the new entity, although this is not a *conditio sine qua non* for that existence.[19] The Baltic States' independence was generally accepted, and consequently these States became members of the UN, once the USSR itself recognised their independence. Ethiopia's recognition of the right of Eritrea to become independent also contributed to make this case non-controversial in the end. Conversely, the proclaiming of independence by Croatia and Slovenia respectively, and later by Bosnia and Herzegovina, was recognised at the international level, including through UN membership, even against the will of the still existent Yugoslavian central government. A similar situation had previously occurred with the international recognition of Bangladesh before recognition by Pakistan.

Recent practice regarding international recognition could lead to the conclusion that the traditional view of it as having a declaratory and not a constitutive effect must be reviewed. It could be that co-opting by the international community is the way to admit new States into international society in contemporary times. UN admission would be the ultimate stage of this co-optation. However, a perusal of recent practice illustrates that this is not the case. Some States have lived outside the UN without any

[19] Contrary to the opinion defended by Viktor Bruns as arbitrator in the *Deutsche Continental Gas Gesellschaft v. Etat polonais* case, n° 1877, Mixed German-Polish Arbitral Tribunal Rec. TAM, 9, 336, 1 August 1929; reprinted in *ZaöRV* 2/1–2 (1930), p. 34.

controversy about their existence as such. One of the last members to join the UN, Switzerland, is a striking case in this regard. More relevant are the cases of recently created States that did not immediately become UN members, such as the former Yugoslavian Republic of Macedonia and the Federal Republic of Yugoslavia (now Serbia and Montenegro). Their admission to the UN was problematic for different reasons, although their statehood was not at issue. Moreover, a new State has no obligation to become a member of the Organization and the latter makes admission conditional on fulfilment of criteria other than simply being a State. The cases of Palestine and the so-called Democratic Saharaoui Arab Republic are also interesting in this regard, even though they are not concerned with secession. These entities benefit from wide international recognition and are even members of regional organisations (the League of Arab States and the African Union, respectively). This remarkable fact has not transformed them into States, even if they are entitled to the right to be constituted as States. The starkest evidence is provided by their authorities: they act at the international level through their national liberation movements, rather than through the 'State' apparatus. Thus, international recognition is not the decisive criterion for secession. It essentially remains a political choice.

Christakis' chapter examines the place traditionally attributed to effectiveness for the creation of States through secession. It shows that the maxim '*ex factis ius oritur*' is seriously contradicted by the more prominent '*ex iniuria ius non oritur*'. The Canadian Supreme Court rightly summarised the distinction between legality and effectiveness: 'A right is recognized in law: mere physical ability is not necessarily given status as a right. The fact that an individual or group can act in a certain way says nothing at all about the legal status or consequences of the act. A power may be exercised even in the absence of a right to do so, but if it is, then it is exercised without legal foundation.'[20] Effective control is essential, although not decisive. Legality requires a minimum of effectiveness in order for an entity to be able to be considered as a new sovereign entity. This fact still requires further scrutiny, in order properly to ascertain its consistency with the relevant rules. In his conclusion, Georges Abi-Saab develops his view of the State as a *legal fact*. There cannot be an automatic translation of a *de facto* situation into a *de iure* one. An apparently successful secession still has to pass the international law test. No-one denies the effective control over territory and population by organised entities such as the TRNC or Somaliland, even if, with regard to the former, the

[20] *ILM* 37 (1998) 1367, para. 106.

question of the independence of that entity arises. Notwithstanding their effectiveness, they do not constitute States. The reason is that their consideration as States would fly in the face of fundamental principles of international law. Legality is another essential condition for the creation of States and secession does not escape this requirement.[21]

V. Secession as a process

Secession is not an instant fact. It always implies a complex series of claims and decisions, negotiations and/or struggle, which may – or may not – lead to the creation of a new State. This process is mostly conducted domestically, but international involvement – or at least concern – is more and more frequent. Tancredi's chapter analyses the international law requirements and discusses different positions taken in this regard, and concludes that international law sets up a 'due process' that guides the creation of States in case of secession. This process includes three rules addressed to the secessionist movement's authorities. There must be: 1) no foreign direct or indirect military support, 2) consent of the majority of the local population expressed through referendum and 3) respect of the *uti possidetis* principle. According to the author, this process does not deal with the substance of the State creation, but only with the procedure, in other words, how the secessionist State is created and not whether it exists. Following this perspective, even if some of the 'procedural rules' are not respected, this is not tantamount to saying that the newly created State does not exist. In the editor's view, if the creation of a State is due to foreign armed intervention, no matter how effective the so-called State's 'constitutive elements' are, the entity in question is not a State. The non-recognition by third States is not in this case the reason for the non-existence, but another consequence of the violation of international obligations having a peremptory character. This does not mean, however, that the authorities of the entity in question, or even the entity itself, would not be responsible on the international plane. The fact of not being a State does not necessarily mean that it does not constitute a *de facto* entity to which certain international rules are applicable. Moreover, some of these requirements are essential conditions determining the very existence of a State, whereas others do not arise prior to but only after the creation of a new State, that is, only if secession is successful. An example of the former type of rule is the prohibition of the use of force by States. Of the latter

[21] For a challenge to this view, see Tancredi's chapter in this volume.

type of rule, the *uti possidetis* principle may be cited. The perception of the impact of this principle in secessionist situations is largely misleading. *Uti possidetis*, as a customary rule providing for the respect of territorial limits as they exist at the moment of independence, does not come into issue during the process of secession. Furthermore, the principle does not even grant a prospective right to the territory of the would-be State. Not until the new State actually exists may it claim the respect of the existing limits at the time of its independence, if no agreement modifies them.[22]

It is worth comparing secession as a process leading to the creation of a new sovereign entity at the international level with the constitutional procedures for the creation of new entities within federal States. Interestingly enough, in the latter situation, the creation of new federated entities cannot be accomplished – putting aside the situation of incorporation of new territories – except to the detriment of the territorial and demographic elements of the other existing federated members. Christian Dominicé's chapter presents an exhaustive analysis of such a situation: the creation of the Canton of Jura in Switzerland in 1978, through its separation from the Canton of Bern. It explains the requirement of referenda both at the local and the federal levels, and a double majority from the whole Swiss people and from the constitutive cantons of Switzerland. Other federal constitutions also require the agreement of both the interested federated members and the federal legislative body.[23]

In the context of decolonisation, international law offers a striking procedural example for the creation of States. The UN, essentially through the General Assembly, played the key role by determining which were the territories that had to be decolonised and how this was to be done, limiting the competences of the colonial powers during that process and controlling the way those territories were administrated. In some cases, it organised referenda and decided what options would be offered, and even administered territories during the interim period preceding the exercise of self-determination. Another procedural example of the creation of a State is the 'Road Map to a Permanent Two-State Solution to the Israeli-Palestinian Conflict', which determines step by step the emergence of Palestine as an independent State.

Secessionist attempts may also face procedures under constitutional law or in domestic legislation as well as those contained in bilateral agreements

[22] In chapter 1 of this volume, Christian Tomuschat shares this perspective. Theodore Christakis in his chapter espouses another view.

[23] See, for example, article 29 of the Federal Republic of Germany's Fundamental Law, and articles 13 and 75, paragraph 15, of Argentina's Constitution.

for resolving internal conflicts, in some cases with international participation. Examples of the former type of procedures are the constitutional provisions of St. Christopher and Nevis, Uzbekistan, Ethiopia, and Serbia and Montenegro, the legislation of 3 April 1990 enacted by the USSR Supreme Soviet during the Gorbachev era to 'implement' (rather to render inapplicable) the Constitutional provision allowing secession to the Socialist Soviet Republics, and the legislation passed by Canada's House of Commons on 15 March 2000, following the Supreme Court's advisory opinion of 20 August 1998. Patrick Dumberry's chapter carefully comments upon the latter. In other cases, generally in the context of violent internal conflicts, governments and separatist movements may sign an agreement which includes the possibility of secession if a future referendum goes in favour of such a change. The 11 January 2005 agreement concerning southern Sudan is a recent example.

As far as referenda are concerned, recent practice shows that the expression of the will of the populations concerned is a necessary condition for the establishment of a new State. It is not, however, a sufficient condition to create a new State or to establish a right to the creation of a new State.[24] The cases of Anjouan and Somaliland provide striking examples of this legal situation. In spite of the fact that 99.88 per cent and 97 per cent of the populations voted for independence on 26 October 1997 and 31 May 2001 respectively,[25] neither entity constitutes an independent State. The reason for this, despite the population's choice, lies in the absence of a right of the entities being part of a State to become independent by their own will on the one hand, and, on the other, the fact that these populations do not constitute 'peoples'. The principle of self-determination has not transformed federal States into confederal ones.

VI. Regional practices

The second part of this book contains a detailed analysis of the practices regarding secession in different regions of the world, as well as the significant case of the Canton of Jura within Switzerland mentioned above.

[24] Cf. J. Crawford, 'State Practice and International Law in Relation to Secession', *BYIL* 69 (1998) 116.

[25] See A. Oraison, 'L'obligation de non-reconnaissance de l'Etat d'Anjouan: les problèmes posés par la nouvelle balkanisation de la République fédérale islamique des Comores', *RDISDP* 76 (1998) 164; United Nations, *Report of the Secretary-General on the Situation in Somalia*, 11 October 2001, UN doc. S/2001/963, p. 3, para. 18.

Photini Pazartis addresses European practice, focusing on secessionist movements of the 1990s. Secession in Europe is neither a novelty nor a problem of the past. Some separatist movements largely remain confined as political minorities within the populations concerned, in some cases resorting to terrorism as a way to achieve their goals. In other cases, such groups try to follow peaceful procedures towards eventual secession. The 'Ibarretxe Plan' adopted by the Basque Parliament on 30 December 2004,[26] although proposing a 'free association' with Spain, basically amounts to a way to open the door to future independence. It has no chance to be implemented as a new statute for the Basque Community, since it fails to conform with the Spanish Constitution, given its reference to the Basques as a 'people' and to their right to self-determination. For its part, Kosovo remains a crucial test for the future UN attitude towards secession in general. By adopting the policy it has, the Organization has created the basis for a potential conflict. On the one hand, it has not relinquished its constant defence of the territorial integrity of Serbia and Montenegro. On the other hand, it administers the territory in such a way that renders any factual re-integration of the territory to the Serbian or the federal structure extremely difficult.

Fatsah Ouguergouz and Djacoba Tehindrazanarivelo examine the rich African practice, both at the national and the regional level. They analyse the creation of States following the boundaries inherited from the colonial period, which cut across ethnic realities, and come to the conclusion that, despite the institutional revulsion towards secession, the African Charter on Peoples and Human Rights potentially foresees such a possibility in case of violation of the internal dimension of self-determination. It is arguable whether ethnic factors are better indicators for identifying candidates for self-determination than the peoples who lived within the limits of the colonial units, whose struggle for independence was fought precisely against colonial rule without ethnic distinctions. For the reasons mentioned above, it remains to be proved that secession is the way to solve the democratic and human rights problems of many African States. The Charter of the African Union, as stressed by the authors, emphasises internal respect of democratic principles and territorial integrity, and goes well beyond any other international organisation's constitutive instrument, by expressly recognising a right to humanitarian intervention under certain serious conditions.

[26] E. Legebiltzarra / P. Vasco, Nuevo Estatuto de Euskadi, available at: http://www.nuevoestatutodeeuskadi.net

Li-ann Thio extensively presents the Asian and Pacific cases of actual or potential secession, both past and present. These regions probably have experienced the largest range of secession practices in the world, from the peaceful and quite exemplary case of the separation of Singapore from Malaysia, the successful secession of Bangladesh, to the current multiple and often violent separatist attempts, particularly in South and East Asia and in the Pacific. Her chapter demonstrates that Bangladesh remains a rather exceptional case, that no other secessionist movement gained recognition either in the regions concerned or at the universal level, and that the promotion of autonomy and economic development is the more common reaction at the State and regional level.

Looking at North American practice, Patrick Dumberry distinguishes the manner in which secession was treated in the United States of America in the nineteenth century and in Canada at the end of the twentieth and the beginning of the present century. Focusing on this last case, he contrasts provincial and federal legislative attitudes with regard to Quebec, after an advisory opinion delivered by the Canadian Supreme Court that clearly illustrates the absence of a right to secession under domestic or international law on the one hand, and the requirement to negotiate between the provincial and the federal authorities over any possible modification of the Canadian Constitution in order to allow the separation of Quebec, if this is the clear wish of its population, on the other hand. The outcome of these negotiations cannot be determined beforehand. In other words, there exists an obligation to negotiate, but the law does not impose any particular result. In the editor's view, this obligation may have constitutional grounds, but not necessarily any under international law. If a central government is not obliged to negotiate under its domestic law, there are no rules in international law compelling it to do so in the face of a secessionist will on the part of one of its components or part of its population. Neither human rights nor an emergent principle of democratic governance can be invoked to impose on a State the obligation to negotiate its partition. The State's obligation from the international law perspective is to ensure democratic participation in public affairs to all its citizens within its internal structures. From the political viewpoint, nevertheless, a negative posture of a central government to addressing the issue democratically raised by part of its population can have an important impact in the perception of this situation by third States.

Frida Armas Pfirter and Silvina González Napolitano deal with Latin American practice, an often neglected region when it comes to doctrine dealing with secession. It is mainly a nineteenth century practice, the last case of secession having taken place in 1904 with Panama's separation from Colombia. Their chapter illustrates that this has been the most stable region with regard to the phenomenon under scrutiny from the beginning of the twentieth century. Previous practice is extremely rich as it provides successive and complex examples of unification, separation and dissolution. Surprisingly, up till now, no particular attention was generally given by authors dealing with the cases of the SFRY and USSR to the practice of this region in order to compare these cases with those of the Federal Republic of Central America and Great Colombia. The latter are striking cases of dissolution that were performed not by a single act but through a process. Another lesson of the Latin American practice is that the separation of States mostly occurred through peaceful means and by agreement with the parent State.

VII. International law increasingly regulates secession

Generally applicable rules as well as practice compel the revisiting of traditional conceptions about the relationship between secession and international law. As opposed to the traditional view, it is suggested that in some cases international law prevents secession, in other cases authorises it, and in yet others – the remaining situations only – it neither permits nor interdicts secession. In the two latter cases, however, when secession actually occurs, international law imposes certain rules with regard to the procedural aspects of the creation of States, the territorial scope, governance, human rights and State succession.

The cases in which international law prevents secession concern situations where the secessionist action violates its fundamental principles. Even if the so-called State 'constitutive elements' are effectively fulfilled by an entity, it will not constitute a State if it was created through the use of force by another State, or by its intervention, or if the forcible secessionist attempt is considered as a threat to international peace and security, leading the Security Council to invoke the principle of territorial integrity. In such cases, international law prevents the desired outcome of the secessionist forces. As a result, entities created in such a way are unable to become States.

In other cases, secession must be authorized under international law. These cases are the following:

1) Territory incorporated into a State by a decision of the UN General Assembly under certain conditions. If these conditions are not respected, separation then becomes a legal possibility. This was the situation of Eritrea.

2) Entities illegally incorporated into a State. Their separation from the annexing State does not constitute any breach of the territorial integrity of the latter. Such a state of affairs could be perceived as the restoration of the legal situation. This was the case of the Baltic States in 1991, whose independence became effective even before the collapse of the Soviet Union at the end of the same year.
3) States expressly recognising a right to secession in domestic law or acknowledging that they are constituted by a plurality of peoples having the right to self-determination. This recognition falls within matters of international concern. Hence, a non-respect of the relevant domestic rules by the central government can open the way for a legal secession from the international law viewpoint. For some, this was the situation of the SFRY. At present, this kind of constitutional provision exists in Ethiopia, Serbia and Montenegro, St. Christopher and Nevis, and Uzbekistan.

To state that in the remaining situations there will be no separation unless the parent State agrees is tantamount to invoking a general prohibition of secession in international law. As Corten demonstrates, this is not the case. What can be advanced is that forcible attempts at secession have a strong possibility of being considered as threats to international peace and security.[27] For the rest, no international law rule prevents a political movement or an entity within a State from seeking secession through non-forcible means.

This view of the relationship between international law and secession in the contemporary world is in conformity with the legal trends inaugurated by the UN Charter. A considerable number of the two hundred or so States existing today were created through the participation of the international community, especially through the process of decolonisation. International law is more and more 'interventionist' in the creation of new States. On the one hand, international law serves to promote the creation of new States through the operation of the principle of self-determination; on the other hand, outside the context of self-determination, it lays down rather strict requirements for a new State to come into being. In the view of the editor, the principle of legality, i.e., the conformity of a fact with the legal order, has become a significant 'constitutive element' in the creation of new States.

[27] See Georg Nolte's chapter 'Secession and External Intervention' in this volume.

PART I

The Foundations of International Law and Their Impact on Secession

1

Secession and self-determination

CHRISTIAN TOMUSCHAT

I. Introduction: the concept of people

A discourse on the relationship between secession and self-determination starts out with a big question mark. According to all the relevant texts dealing with self-determination, all 'peoples' are the holders of this right. The Declaration on the Granting of Independence to Colonial Countries and Peoples,[1] the starting point for the rise of self-determination as a principle generating true legal rights, derived its moral force from the generality of its statement that 'all peoples have the right to self-determination'. Although primarily designed to foster the decolonization process, its drafters had to enlarge its scope *ratione personae* in order to make the proposition more attractive to the world at large. In fact, a few years later, the formulation of common Article 1(1) within the two International Covenants on human rights left no doubt that the wording in the Declaration on the Granting of Independence to Colonial Countries and Peoples[2] was intended fully to mean what the text seemed to convey, namely, that all peoples, without any discrimination, enjoy the right of self-determination. This is also the message of the Friendly Relations Declaration,[3] which lacked any predominant anti-colonial overtones, having been conceived as an instrument particularizing the basic principles laid down in the Charter of the United Nations as they apply to the international community in its entirety.

The dilemma of legal construction becomes evident when, in attempting to define the concept of people, one simply equates the concept in its juridical sense as contemplated by the instruments just referred to above

[1] GA Res. 1514 (XV) of 14 December 1960.

[2] There is a slight difference only in that Res. 1514 (XV) speaks of the right 'to' self-determination, whereas the two Covenants employ the words 'right of self-determination'.

[3] GA Res. 2625 (XXV) of 24 October 1970.

with the concept of people in the ethnic sense. No matter how much care may be taken to circumscribe the objective and subjective characteristics of a people in a somewhat restrictive fashion, it is clear that the majority of the States of this globe would then be composed of different peoples[4] which would each have – individually and without any coordination – a right of self-determination.[5] Knowing that the substance of self-determination invariably implies the right to establish a sovereign and independent State – in addition to the other choices: free association or integration with an independent State or the emergence into any other political status[6] – no-one would have to engage in difficult legal argument to draw the conclusion that the right to secession constitutes a necessary component of the right to self-determination. A people living in a State from which it wishes to break loose in order to establish its own State has no other procedure at hand, if no commonly agreed settlement can be reached. Yet, the ease with which secession would be available as a consequence of such merry jurisprudence would unavoidably pave the way to chaos and anarchy. In particular, all the large federal States of this globe would have to see this legal set-up as an arrangement for their premature death inasmuch as, in the texts referred to, the right of self-determination has been stipulated without any preconditions: it exists and can be activated at any moment, subject only to the will of the ethnic community concerned. But also other States with a tradition of centralization would be at the mercy of claims for independent statehood by minority groups of their population. Even France might have to fear an erosion of its national territory as a result of secessionist claims by Alsatians, Bretons or Corsicans. Already at first glance, these potential consequences

[4] Only four nations seem to be ethnically homogeneous, see A. Cassese, 'Self-Determination Revisited', in *Liber Amicorum Eduardo Jiménez de Aréchaga*, Vol. I (Montevideo: F.C.U., 1994), p. 229.

[5] Thus, Y. Dinstein, 'Is there a Right to Secede', *ASIL Proceedings* 1996, p. 299, at p. 302, writes: '. . . a people unhappy about its political status within the bounds of an existing State – federal as much as unitary – is entitled to secede and create a new State'; also: Cassese, *Self Determination*, p. 241. See also J. Duursma, *Fragmentation and the International Relations of Micro-States. Self-determination and Statehood* (Cambridge: Cambridge University Press, 1996), p. 80: '. . . all peoples, as defined by objective and subjective factors, have a full right of self-determination, that is a free choice of internal and external self-determination.' For a similar line of reasoning see J. Klabbers and R. Lefeber, 'Africa: Lost between Self-Determination and *Uti Possidetis*', in Brölmann *et al.* (eds.), *Peoples and Minorities in International Law* (Dordrecht *et al.*, 1993), p. 37.

[6] See GA Res. 1541 of 15 December 1960, Principle VI; GA Res. 2625 (XXV) of 24 October 1970, Principle of equal rights and self-determination of peoples, para. 4.

seem to militate against an extensive understanding of the notion of 'peoples'.

It is difficult to find out from a perusal of the relevant texts what connotation the drafters attached to that notion. It can of course be presumed that, as representatives of States, they did not wish to ring the death-knell for their masters.[7] Very few people deliberately dig their own grave. But the enigma remains unresolved. How can the two propositions: that all 'peoples' have a right to self-determination, and that self-determination includes the right to the establishment of a sovereign State, be reconciled to fit reasonably well into the edifice of present-day international law?

During the period of decolonization, the legal position was fairly simple. All the peoples under colonial rule were considered as a unit together with the territories which the colonial powers had fixed either through treaties with other competing powers or by internal orders under their domestic law.[8] In each case, the human beings concerned were more or less treated as an appurtenance of the territory where they lived. Essentially, this method ran against the idea of self-determination, according to which humans should be able freely to decide to which polity they wish to belong.

It goes without saying that the present study will be conducted in accordance with legal methods, even though political science too has contributed a wealth of interesting ideas to the understanding of the legitimacy of secession. Writings by Allen Buchanan,[9] Lea Brilmayer[10] and Diane F. Orentlicher,[11] for instance, have shed new light on the context

[7] It results from the *travaux préparatoires* relating to the Charter that a right of secession was rejected at the founding conference of San Francisco, see 'summary report of sixth meeting of Committee', I/1, conclusion A, *UNCIO*, Vol. VI, 15 May 1945, p. 296.

[8] See, for instance, Cassese, *Self Determination*, p. 237; T. Franck, 'Postmodern Tribalism and the Right to Secession', in Brölmann, *Peoples and Minorities*, p. 3; K. Ginther, 'Selbstbestimmung in Europa', in W. Karl (ed.), *In memoriam Herbert Miehsler. Gedächtnisvorlesungen an der Universität Salzburg 1987–1996* (Köln *et al.*, 1998), p. 149, at p. 163; H. Quane, 'The United Nations and the Evolving Right to Self-Determination', *ICLQ* 47 (1998), p. 537, at p. 570; R. C. A. White, 'Self-Determination: Time for a Re-Assessment?' *NILR* 28 (1981), p. 147, at p. 150.

[9] A. Buchanan, *Secession: The Morality of Political Divorce from Fort Sumter to Lithuania and Quebec* (Boulder, Colorado: Westview Press, 1991), p. 174; A. Buchanan, 'The International Institutional Dimension of Secession', in P. B. Lehning (ed.), *Theories of Secession* (London/New York 1998), p. 227.

[10] L. Brilmayer, 'Secession and Self-Determination: A Territorial Interpretation', *YJIL* 16 (1991), pp. 177–202.

[11] D. F. Orentlicher, 'Separation Anxiety: International Responses to Ethno-Separatist Claims', *YJIL* 23 (1998), pp. 1–78.

within which secession may be encountered and justified from a philosophical viewpoint. However, most of these reflections remain confined to an astonishingly narrow framework of abstract ideas. In general, writers focusing on the *problématique* from the viewpoint of political theory attempt to clarify the question whether claims for secession may be seen as a direct offspring of democratic values. On the other hand, one finds very little about the disturbances caused by each and every historical process of secession. Almost invariably, whenever a right to secession has to be invoked, failing consent between the two partners, one of whom wishes to divorce, violent methods are resorted to. For that reason alone, secession qualifies as a complex process, the pros and cons of which must be carefully weighed before a definitive judgment can be given.

II. The relevant sources

We shall, first of all, resort to the classic method of examining the available sources one by one. It will be seen that the debate relating to secession touches upon issues of great methodological complexity.

A. Treaty law

The relevant treaty law consists of no more than common Article 1 of the two Covenants. Apart from an unconvincing study by Daniel Turp, who, as defender of a possible secession of Québec from Canada has put forward the thesis that a right to secession is inherent in the text of that provision,[12] no-one else has contended that the Covenants might have clarified the legal position. The *travaux* are quite inconclusive. Curiously enough, during the deliberations in the Commission on Human Rights, Yugoslavia presented an amendment to the effect that self-determination includes 'the right to secede and to establish a politically and economically independent State',[13] and similar proposals were made by the United States.[14] But these suggestions were not adopted. The relevant UN document summarizing the debates indicates that this was due to a feeling that 'any numeration of the components of the right of self-determination was likely to be incomplete'.[15] At the same time, this inference from a single voice in the debate of the Commission on Human Rights is certainly to be viewed more as an enlightened guess than as an accurate description

[12] D. Turp, 'Le droit de sécession en droit international public', *CYIL* 20 (1982), pp. 24–78.

[13] UN doc. E/CN.4/L.22, see M. J. Bossuyt, *Guide to the* 'Travaux Préparatoires' *of the International Covenant on Civil and Political Rights* (Dordrecht *et al.*, 1987), p. 34.

[14] *Ibid.* [15] *Ibid.*

of what prompted delegates to show some reluctance vis-à-vis an explicit mention of secession.

B. Customary law

1. Practice

Turning to customary law, it would be necessary, following the classic approach as prescribed by article 38(1)(b) of the Statute of the International Court of Justice (ICJ), to identify first a practice susceptible of supporting a rule mirroring that factual pattern, and second an *opinio juris* transferring the relevant empirical findings from the factual to the normative realm. In the following, it will be shown that very few factual clues can be gleaned. Although it must be admitted that secession could never be a routine occurrence to be observed on a daily basis involving hundreds of cases, the scarcity of the phenomenon is striking. Thus, the few examples carry little weight in comparison with all the instances where the territorial unity of existing States is maintained and preserved notwithstanding major grievances which a minority may hold against the majority of the population.

In Africa, the configuration of the maps as it has emerged from the fifties to the seventies of the last century, when almost all of the African nations obtained their independence, has remained remarkably stable over many decades now. Certainly one of the main reasons is the resolution adopted by the Organization of African Unity at its Cairo meeting in July 1964[16] whereby the African Heads of State agreed on the binding character of the frontiers fixed by the former colonial powers. No claims derived from ethnic ties between communities formerly belonging together but now divided by State boundaries were recognized as allowing to challenge the existing boundary lines. It is this approach that the ICJ took in its judgment on the *Frontier Dispute* between Burkina Faso and Mali.[17] This decision has generally put an end to any kind of territorial irredentism which could have engulfed Africa in endless wars, in addition to the armed conflicts which have erupted on other grounds.[18] *Uti possidetis* has thus become the leading maxim for the territorial delimitation of Africa, relegating self-determination in that respect to an insignificant, inferior place.

[16] *OAU Assembly Resolution AHG/Res. 16 (I)* adopted in Cairo in 1964 by the Heads of African States, 6–10 July 1999.

[17] Judgment of 22 December 1986, *ICJ Reports* 1986, p. 554, at p. 567 para. 25.

[18] See also the judgment of the ICJ in the *Case concerning the Land and Maritime Boundary between Cameroon and Nigeria, 10 October 2002*, pp. 401–16, paras. 200–25.

There is only one major departure from the application of the *uti possidetis* principle, namely Eritrea.[19] But the case of Eritrea has specific characteristics which make it unsuitable as a general precedent for supporting the proposition that distinct ethnic communities enjoy a right of self-determination and hence of secession if they are part of a State dominated by another ethnic group. According to Resolution 390 A (V) of 2 December 1950, the former Italian colony of Eritrea was to be established as 'an autonomous unit federated with Ethiopia under the sovereignty of the Ethiopian Crown'.[20] In consonance with this basic premise, the resolution provided that 'the Eritrean Government shall possess legislative, executive and judicial powers in the field of domestic affairs'.[21] Within a few years, however, the central government of Ethiopia set aside the autonomy of the province and in 1962 brought about the dissolution of the regional parliament, thereby violating the commitments undertaken vis-à-vis the United Nations. In spite of this breach of binding rules governing the status of the province, the civil war which followed the *de facto* abolition of the entrenched autonomy found little encouragement with the Organization of African Unity and the United Nations. Eventually, Ethiopia itself recognized the legitimate claims of the Eritreans after dictator Menghistu had been toppled in 1991. A referendum was held in April 1993, under international supervision, which gave overwhelming support to the claim for national independence. Immediately thereafter, in May 1993, Eritrea was admitted as a new member of the United Nations. In sum, the whole process of secession was oriented towards remedying the wrong suffered by the population as a consequence of the Ethiopian decision to do away with the autonomy they had been promised to enjoy. Even under these conditions, however, the international community remained reluctant to acknowledge the claims of the Eritrean population for independence as a legitimate exercise of a right to self-determination.

It is well known, on the other hand, that the endeavours of the Ibo population in south-eastern Nigeria to establish a State of Biafra failed, ending in bloodshed and death.[22] Independence was declared on 30 May 1967, and the definitive surrender of the Biafran forces occurred on 12 May 1970.

[19] For a detailed account see A. Tancredi, 'Secessione e diritto internazionale', *Rivista* (1998), pp. 673–737. Cf. also the analysis of this case in the introduction and in chapter 10 of this volume.

[20] Para. 1, GA Res. 390 A (V) of 2 December 1950.

[21] *Ibid.*, para. 2.

[22] On the secessionist attempt by Biafra see, for instance, T. D. Musgrave, *Self-Determination and National Minorities* (Oxford, 1997), p. 197; Tancredi, 'Secessione e diritto internazionale', pp. 701–4, and F. Ouguergouz / D. Tehindrazanarivelo's contribution to this volume.

Although the Ibos displayed all the features which, from an ethnic viewpoint, one would consider as being the constitutive elements of a 'people', the entity they had indeed brought into being under the name of Biafra was recognized by a few States only.[23] At the regional and at the world-wide level, the secessionist forces did not receive any assistance. The Organization of African Unity stated that the situation in Nigeria was 'an internal affair the solution of which is primarily the responsibility of Nigerians themselves',[24] and the United Nations totally abstained from dealing with the conflict. Not even in the General Assembly, which has always viewed itself as the promoting force for self-determination, did a debate take place, and the Secretary-General of the epoch, U Thant, made the famous statement:

'As far as the question of secession of a particular section of a State is concerned, the United Nations attitude is unequivocal. As an international organization, the United Nations has never accepted and does not accept and I do not believe will ever accept the principle of secession of a part of its member States.'[25]

It is abundantly clear, therefore, that international practice from Africa, the continent where the greatest number of incongruities between ethnic lines and State boundary lines can be observed, strongly speaks against acknowledging a right of secession being enjoyed by ethnic groups. In fact, in countries like Nigeria, where roughly 250 linguistic and ethnic groups exist, and Cameroon, where the number of indigenous languages rises to more than 120, the application of that legal proposition would lead to nonsensical results through infinite fragmentation which could hardly be stopped at any given point if no additional criteria were introduced, such as the viability of a potential State entity. Yet, the available texts do not mention such additional requirements – quite obviously because it was never thought that the assertion of self-determination could end up in such a chaotic state of affairs. This, again, confirms that the presumed premise – the existence of an unlimited right of secession for every ethnic group – must be wrong.

Contrary to Biafra, Bangladesh – the former East Pakistan – was able to gain its independence due, in particular, to massive support received from India.[26] The secessionist movement, spearheaded by the Awami

[23] Tanzania, Gabon, Ivory Coast, Zambia, Haiti.

[24] *ILM* 6 (1967), p. 1243.

[25] *UN Monthly Chronicle* 7 (1970), p. 36.

[26] On the secession of Bangladesh see L. Buchheit, *Secession. The Legitimacy of Self-Determination*, (New Haven/London 1978), p. 198; Musgrave, *Self-Determination and National Minorities*, p. 189; Tancredi, 'Secessione e diritto internazionale', pp. 704–10.

League, had been unleashed in March 1971 by a brutal governmental policy of repression throughout the country, involving the arrest, torture and killing of political leaders, as well as the indiscriminate killing of civilians. The United Nations remained silent regarding the issue of self-determination,[27] confining itself to demanding that the troops of India and Pakistan be withdrawn from each other's territory.[28] The conflict ended after a few months, in December 1971, with the capitulation of the Pakistani forces deployed in the eastern part of the country. Thereafter, Bangladesh existed *de facto* as a viable State and was eventually admitted to the United Nations in September 1974, after China had abstained from casting another veto. No great legal debate took place on the issue of a right to secession. What brought about the recognition of the new entity by the international community was simply the principle of effectiveness. Bangladesh had emerged as an uncontested new State on the international stage.

It is not possible, within the limited space allocated to this contribution, to give a comprehensive overview of all the other relevant instances of the last decades. It suffices to point out that the demise of the Soviet Union can hardly serve as an example for the successful vindication of the right to self-determination. It is certainly true that during the turbulent years from 1988 to 1991 the Soviet Union lost a large belt of its former component States in the south and in the west, thus being territorially reduced to Russia.[29] Yet all the States which obtained their sovereign independence reached this goal by virtue of the consent which the Soviet Government, at least tacitly, gave to the auto-dissolution of its empire. In the preamble of the Agreement Establishing the Commonwealth of Independent States, the founding members of the Soviet Union, Belarus, Russia and Ukraine noted that the Soviet Union 'as a subject of international law, and a geopolitical reality no longer exists'.[30] Quite obviously, the leaders of the Soviet Union realized that the collapse of socialism was tantamount to the disappearance of the sole common ideology which had held the disparate elements of the huge empire together. Therefore, insisting on the unity of

[27] See Buchheit, *Secession*, p. 209.

[28] GA Res. 2793 (XXVI) of 7 December 1971; SC Res. 307 of 21 December 1971.

[29] For a detailed account of the process see T. Schweisfurth, 'Das Recht der Staatensukzession: Die Staatenpraxis der Nachfolge in völkerrechtliche Verträge, Staatsvermögen, Staatsschulden und Archive in den Teilungsfällen Sowjetunion, Tschechoslowakei und Jugoslawien', *Berichte der Deutschen Gesellschaft für Völkerrecht* 35 (1996), p. 49, at p. 56.

[30] Of 8/21 December 1991, *ILM* 31 (1992), p. 143.

the all-encompassing Union would have entailed useless and interminable armed conflict.

The Baltic States were embedded in a different context. Even the Soviet Union eventually had to acknowledge that in 1940 these States had been annexed against the wishes of their populations and therefore contrary to international law.[31] Restoring these States as sovereign entities was therefore an act of restitution, required by the rules of international responsibility. Indeed, Estonia, Latvia and Lithuania all maintain that they kept their identity as States under international law, notwithstanding a foreign occupation which lasted for half a century. Again, therefore, the Baltic resurrection cannot be adduced as evidence for the existence of a general right of peoples to claim independent statehood by virtue of the right of self-determination.[32]

On the other hand, the armed conflict in Chechnya provides ample proof that the international community flatly denies a right to self-determination of ethnic groups included in the population of a sovereign State. It goes without saying that Russia, which has been fighting the Chechen uprising for more than a decade, is not willing to let the Chechens and Chechnya leave Russia. At the same time, the international community has not raised any objections against this legal viewpoint. Russia has been criticized time and again for not respecting the rules of humanitarian law, but no voices can be perceived which would suggest that the Chechens have a legal right to secession.[33] In any event, Chechnya does not appear on the agenda of any of the UN bodies. If international law granted a right of self-determination to every ethnic community that qualifies as a people – and the Chechens certainly meet all the necessary requirements on account of their language, their history and their common understanding of being a nation separate from the Russian people – this silence would hardly be understandable.

[31] On 24 December 1989 the Congress of People's Deputies of the Soviet Union condemned the annexation of the Baltic States as having been 'in conflict with the sovereignty and independence of a number of third countries', see T. Gazzini, 'Considerations on the Conflict in Chechnya', *HRLJ* 17 (1996), p. 93, at p. 96 (with further references to sources).

[32] See, in particular, R. Mullerson, 'The Continuity and Succession of States, by Reference to the Former USSR and Yugoslavia', *ICLQ* 42 (1993), p. 473, at pp. 480–1; R. Yakemtchouk, 'Les républiques baltes en droit international. Echec d'une annexion opérée en violation du droit des gens', *AFDI* 37 (1991), p. 259, at p. 276.

[33] See Gazzini, 'Conflict in Chechnya', p. 96; T. D. Grant, 'A Panel of Experts for Chechnya: Purposes and Prospects in Light of International Law', *VJIL* 40 (1999), p. 115, at p. 175. Somewhat confused is the article by R. Kherad, 'De la nature juridique du conflit tchétchène', *RGDIP* 104 (2000), pp. 143–79.

The developments in the former Yugoslavia are also ambiguous, to say the least.[34] They had strong underpinnings in the constitutional law of the Socialist Federal Republic of Yugoslavia (SFRY). Yugoslavia had been founded as the Kingdom of the Serbs, Croats and Slovenes. In the introductory part of the constitution of the SFRY of 1974, under the heading 'Basic Principles' it was explicitly stated that the component States had a right of secession.[35] Although, because of its generality, the precise status of that proposition was not free from doubt,[36] the attempts by the Serb leadership to destroy the federal structure of Yugoslavia in the period preceding the declarations of independence by Croatia and Slovenia in June 1991 could be viewed as an implicit denunciation of the constitutional pact underlying the carefully balanced architecture of the State.[37] In other words, the process of disintegration of the SFRY was based on specific grounds which had little to do with the assertion of a general right of secession under general international law.[38]

The particular status conferred on the former Yugoslav province of Kosovo may be seen in a different light. Security Council Resolution 1244 (1999), adopted at the end of NATO's air operations against rump Yugoslavia, the Federal Republic of Yugoslavia (FRY), amounted to serious interference with the sovereign rights of the country. The FRY was made to withdraw all its military, police and paramilitary forces from Kosovo; and instead, under UN auspices, an international 'civil and military presence' (UNMIK and KFOR) was established. No effective governmental powers were left to the FRY. The resolution provided that Kosovo would enjoy 'substantial autonomy and meaningful self-administration'.[39] Chapter VII of the UN Charter empowers the Security Council with extensive competencies to impose its will on States members of the world Organization.

[34] For a detailed account of the events see Schweisfurth, 'Das Recht der Staatensukzession', pp. 68–82.

[35] 'The nations of Yugoslavia, proceeding from the right of every nation to self-determination, including the right of secession . . .'.

[36] B. Bagwell, 'Yugoslavian Constitutional Questions: Self-Determination and Secession of Member Republics', *Georgia J. I. C. L.* 21 (1991), p. 489, at p. 508–10.

[37] In fact, in its first opinion of 29 November 1991, *ILM* 31 (1992), p. 1494, at p. 1497, the Arbitration Committee of the Conference on Yugoslavia noted 'that the Socialist Federal Republic of Yugoslavia is in the process of dissolution'.

[38] Same appraisal by A. Pellet, 'Quel avenir pour le droit des peuples à disposer d'eux-mêmes?', in *Liber Amicorum Jiménez de Aréchaga*, p. 255. But see P. Radan, 'Secessionist Self-Determination: The Cases of Slovenia and Croatia', in R. Petkovic *et al.*, *International Law and the Changed Yugoslavia* (Belgrade: 1995), p. 69; D. Raic, *Statehood and the Law of Self-Determination* (The Hague *et al.*: Kluwer, 2002), p. 362.

[39] Preamble, para. 11, SC Res. 1244 of 10 June 1999.

But these powers were designed to maintain and safeguard international peace and security. Never before had the Security Council exerted its mandate in such a draconian fashion, imparting instructions on how the internal constitutional order of a sovereign State should be framed.[40] It might be argued, on the other hand, that Resolution 1244 emphasizes explicitly 'the sovereignty and territorial integrity' of the FRY.[41] However, determinations on the constitutional structure of a given territory cannot be conceived of as transitional measures subject at any time to review and possible repeal. If the Security Council takes the view that, in order to secure stable conditions in Kosovo, a substantial measure of internal autonomy is indispensable, it remains bound by the logic of its initial decision. It cannot freely shed the legal construction which it has brought into being, in the light of changing political circumstances.

Consequently, the question of how Resolution 1244 may be justified cannot be avoided. At first glance, consent would appear to provide the most plausible answer. It is stated explicitly in the preamble that the FRY accepted the principles of a paper presented in Belgrade on 2 June 1999, around which the resolution was drafted.[42] Yet, one may have serious doubts as to whether this acceptance holds the key to resolving all the issues involved. Obviously, the government of the FRY acted under pressure. NATO's air operation would have continued if it had not consented to withdrawing its troops and renouncing the exercise of its governmental powers over the province for an indefinite period of time. Additionally, it should be observed that the Security Council is certainly not entitled to adopt and enforce decisions which are incompatible with the requirements of Chapter VII by invoking consent expressed by the State concerned.[43] What remains as a possible justification is the right of self-determination. It should be noted that Resolution 1244 carefully avoids mentioning this word. Nowhere does it appear in the text. Implicitly,

[40] On these aspects see M. Ruffert, 'The Administration of Kosovo and East-Timor by the International Community', *ICLQ* 50 (2001), p. 613, at pp. 627–30; G. Seidel, 'A New Dimension of the Right of Self-Determination in Kosovo?', in C. Tomuschat (ed.), *Kosovo and the International Community. A Legal Assessment* (The Hague *et al.*: Kluwer, 2002), p. 203; C. Stahn, 'Constitution Without a State? Kosovo Under the United Nations Constitutional Framework for Self-Government', *LJIL* 14 (2001), pp. 531–61; C. Tomuschat, 'Yugoslavia's Damaged Sovereignty over the Province of Kosovo', in G. Kreijen (ed.), *State, Sovereignty and International Governance. Liber Amicorum Judge Kooijmans* (Oxford: 2002), p. 323.

[41] Preamble, para. 10 of SC Res. 1244 of 10 June 1999.

[42] Preamble, para. 9, *ibid.*

[43] For a cogent criticism of the expansive understanding of the role which the Security Council has manifested in recent years see G. Arangio-Ruiz, 'On the Security Council's "Law-Making"', *Rivista* 83 (2000), pp. 609–725.

however, it permeates the entire texture of the resolution. Autonomy for a given human community cannot be invented by the Security Council without any backing in general international law. In conclusion, Security Council Resolution 1244 can be deemed to constitute the first formalized decision of the international community recognizing that a human community within a sovereign State may under specific circumstances enjoy a right of self-determination.[44]

A short glance at East Timor should round off our enquiry as to whether practice exists which might indicate that self-determination can be understood in the wide sense suggested by those who equate the ethnic concept of 'people' with the legal concept enshrined in the same word. East Timor was annexed by Indonesia against the wishes of the East Timorese themselves who, as a 'colonial people', undoubtedly enjoyed a right of self-determination under General Assembly Resolution 1514 (XV).[45] In that regard, the claims of the East Timorese people for independent statehood very closely resembled the claims of the Baltic peoples.[46] Consequently, by withdrawing its troops and opening the way for a referendum on the future of the territory, Indonesia did no more than comply with its duty of restoration under the rules of international responsibility.[47]

The conclusion to be drawn from the preceding considerations is very simple: practice as one of the two prongs on which a rule of customary international law must be founded is totally lacking as far as the suggested rule is concerned, i.e., that ethnic groups within States – even if they may claim to qualify as 'peoples' – are *ipso jure* holders of a right of secession.

2. *Opinio juris*

In fact, the conclusion just drawn is confirmed by a search for clues as to the existence of a corresponding *opinio juris*. GA Resolution 2625 (XXV) emphasizes the principle of national unity, departing from that proposition in view of instances only where the government of the country concerned does not represent the entire people but mirrors discrimination

[44] Attention is also drawn to the advisory opinion of the Supreme Court of Canada on *Secession of Quebec*, 20 August 1998, *ILM* 37 (1998), p. 1340, at p. 1373, where the Court held that the population of a Canadian province may, under special circumstances, enjoy a right to secession.

[45] This was acknowledged by the ICJ in the *East Timor (Portugal v. Australia) case*, *ICJ Reports* 1995, p. 90, at pp. 102–4, paras. 29, 31 and 37.

[46] We do not agree with the analysis by J. Charney, 'Self-Determination: Chechnya, Kosovo, and East Timor', *Vanderbilt J. T. L.* 34 (2001), p. 455, at pp. 4465–7, who sees a parallel between Kosovo and East Timor.

[47] See SC Res. 1272 of 25 October 1999.

based on race, creed or colour.[48] The conditioning of national unity by a significant reservation was not only meant to apply to processes of decolonization. Indeed, it was re-affirmed in two documents of great importance, the Declaration of the UN World Conference on Human Rights held in Vienna in June 1993[49] and the GA Declaration on the Occasion of the Fiftieth Anniversary of the UN,[50] where the non-discrimination clause was even extended to distinctions of 'any kind'. Although for a right to secession to arise, the threshold indicated by these resolutions must certainly be higher; a mere lack of representativeness of a government would not suffice to bring about a right to secession as a form of a right of resistance. The phrase employed rightly conveys the idea that exceptional circumstances are capable of sustaining a claim for secession – circumstances which may roughly be summarized as a grave and massive violation of the human rights of a specific group in a discriminatory fashion. This is the situation which Lee Buchheit has called 'remedial secession',[51] a term which has found wide acceptance in the legal literature. According to our judgment, the only major controversy which still rages among legal writers centres on this concept. Whereas one group adheres to this concept, viewing secession as a kind of *ultima ratio* if a given human community suffers unbearable persecution,[52] other authors draw attention to the fact that all three resolutions mentioned constitute

[48] Principle of self-determination, para. 7, GA Res. 2625 (XXV) of 24 October 1970.

[49] *ILM* 32 (1993), p. 1663, at p. 1665, para. 2.

[50] GA Res. 50/6 of 24 October 1995, para. 1.

[51] Buchheit, *Secession*, p. 222.

[52] See, for instance, Franck, 'Postmodern Tribalism', p. 13; K. Doehring, 'Self-Determination', in B. Simma (ed.), *The Charter of the United Nations* (Oxford: Oxford University Press, 1994), p. 56; H. Hannum, 'Rethinking Self-Determination', *VJIL* 34 (1993), p. 1, at pp. 45–7 (stressing that a right of secession will arise only in the most extreme circumstances); J. Heintze, *Selbstbestimmungsrecht und Minderheitenrechte im Völkerrecht* (Baden-Baden, 1994), p. 88; K. Henrard, *Devising an Adequate System of Minority Protection. Individual Human Rights, Minority Rights and the Right to Self-Determination* (The Hague: Martinus Nijhoff Publishers, 2000), p. 290; D. Murswiek, 'The Issue of a Right of Secession – Reconsidered', in C. Tomuschat (ed.), *Modern Law of Self-Determination* (Dordrecht *et al.*: 1993), p. 21; Musgrave, *Self-Determination and National Minorities*, p. 209; V. P. Nanda, 'Self-Determination under International Law: Validity of Claims to Secede', *CWRJIL* 13 (1981), p. 257, at p. 269; S. Oeter, 'Selbstbestimmungsrecht im Wandel', *ZöR* 52 (1992), p. 741, at p. 765; Raic, *Statehood*, p. 313; O. Schachter, 'Micronationalism and Secession', in *Recht zwischen Umbruch und Bewährung. Festschrift für Rudolf Bernhardt* (Berlin *et al.*, 1995), p. 179; S. Simon, *Autonomie im Völkerrecht. Ein Versuch zum Selbstbestimmungsrecht der Völker* (Baden-Baden, 2000), p. 69; G. J. Simpson, 'The Diffusion of Sovereignty: Self-Determination in the Post-Colonial Age', *SJIL* 32 (1996), p. 255, at pp. 283–5; J. Stromseth, 'Self-Determination, Secession and Humanitarian Intervention by the United Nations', *ASIL Proceedings* 1992, p. 370, at p. 371; C. Tomuschat, 'Self-Determination in a Post-Colonial World', in Tomuschat, *Modern Law of Self Determination*, p. 1; White,

no more than soft law and that practice transferring them into the realm of hard law is conspicuously lacking.[53]

In the practice of the General Assembly of the United Nations, a narrow concept of self-determination prevails. Self-determination is dealt with as a matter concerning solely the territories which – on the most diverse grounds – have been left behind in the march that has led the great majority of the former colonies to independence. Thus, for instance, during its fifty-fifth session in 2000, the General Assembly adopted reports of the Special Political and Decolonization Committee (Fourth Committee) and individual resolutions on Western Sahara,[54] New Caledonia,[55] and Tokelau,[56] as well as a comprehensive resolution on American Samoa, Anguilla, Bermuda, the British Virgin Islands, the Cayman Islands, Guam, Montserrat, Pitcairn, St. Helena, the Turks and Caicos Islands and the United States Virgin Islands.[57] Furthermore, in adopting reports of its Third Committee, it adopted a resolution on the right of the Palestinian people to self-determination[58] – which, in spite of its extremely fair wording, was opposed not only by Israel, but also by the United States – as well as a general resolution on the 'Universal realization of the right of peoples to self-determination'.[59] Explicitly, this resolution seeks to provide support to 'peoples under colonial, foreign or alien occupation' and to 'sovereign peoples and nations'.[60] No trace can be found of concern with

'Self Determination', at pp. 161, 164. In the *Loizidou* case, European Court of Human Rights, judgment of 18 December 1996, *Reports of Judgments and Decision* 1996-VI, p. 2216, judges Wilhaber and Ryssdal, in a concurring opinion, *ibid.*, p. 2241, pronounced themselves strongly in favour of a right of secession of a minority victim of massive discrimination.

53 R. Higgins, 'Postmodern Tribalism and the Right to Secession', in Brölmann, *Peoples and Minorities*, p. 29; Quane, 'United Nations', p. 564; Tancredi, 'Secessione e diritto internazionale', p. 756. See also Klabbers/Lefeber, 'Africa', p. 53, who maintain that the 'oppression theory' could be approved only according to a 'natural law interpretation of self-determination'.

54 GA Res. 55/141 of 8 December 2000.

55 GA Res. 55/142 of 8 December 2000.

56 GA Res. 55/143 of 8 December 2000.

57 GA Res. 55/144 of 8 December 2000.

58 GA Res. 55/87 of 4 December 2000. In the SC Res. 1387 of 12 March 2002, preamble, para. 2, the Security Council affirmed 'a vision of a region where two States, Israel and Palestine, live side by side within secure and recognized borders'.

59 GA Res. 55/85 of 4 December 2000. Parallel to these enactments, a resolution on the 'Implementation of the Declaration on the Granting of Independence to Colonial Countries and Peoples' was adopted without reference to a Main Committee, GA Res. 55/47 of 29 November 2000. In its advisory opinion of 9 July 2004, the ICJ 'observes that the existence of a "Palestinian people" is no longer in issue' (*Legal Consequences of the Construction of a Wall in the Occupied Palestinian Territory, Advisory Opinion, ICJ. Reports* 2004, p. 183, para. 118).

60 *Ibid.*, preamble, paras. 2, 3.

oppressed communities within any of the member States of the world Organization. Not even Kosovo is focused upon in any one of the resolutions, whereas in 1999 the situation prevailing in that territory had been mentioned as a human rights problem.[61]

It should also be noted that indigenous peoples, who undoubtedly are peoples in the ethnic and cultural sense, have never been recognized as holders of a right to self-determination involving secession. The draft declaration on the rights of indigenous populations drawn up by the Sub-Commission on the Promotion and Protection of Human Rights,[62] which mentions self-determination,[63] has now been pending since 1994 before the Commission on Human Rights. But it emerges from the report of the working group entrusted by the Commission with finalizing the draft for adoption that disagreement on the issue of self-determination is the principal issue preventing agreement.[64]

The practice of the General Assembly is all the more important since the intensification of the principle of self-determination, which marked the UN system as from 1960 when Resolution 1514 (XV) was adopted, which was due mainly to the pressure engendered by the 'world parliament', with its dominance of third world countries. Essentially, self-determination is a child of the General Assembly (GA). In the eyes of the GA, however, and also of the Commission on Human Rights, external self-determination as a right to establish an independent State does not exist for ethnic communities which constitute integral elements of a sovereign State and are thus able to take part in the conduct of public affairs of that State. Legal doctrine overwhelmingly shares this view.[65]

C. *The relevance of* uti possidetis

Many times, the stability and intangibility of existing boundary lines is also presented as a consequence of the principle of *uti possidetis*. Thus,

[61] GA Res. 54/183 of 17 December 1999.

[62] UN doc. E/CN.4/1995/2, reprinted in *ILM* 34 (1995), p. 546.

[63] See C. Tomuschat, 'International Law: Ensuring the Survival of Mankind on the Eve of a New Century', *Recueil des Cours* 281 (1999), p. 252.

[64] UN doc. E/CN.4/2001/85, paras. 56–115.

[65] See, for instance, A. Cassese, *Self-Determination of Peoples. A Legal Reappraisal* (Cambridge, 1995), p. 61; Franck, 'Postmodern Tribalism', p. 16; A. Kiss, 'The Peoples' Right to Secession', *HRLJ* 7 (1986) 165, at 168; G. J. Simpson, 'The Diffusion of Sovereignty: Self-Determination in the Post-Colonial Age', *SJIL* 32 (1996) 255, at 264; A. Pellet, 'Quel avenir pour le droit des peuples', p. 255; Tomuschat, 'Self-Determination in a Post-Colonial World', p. 16.

a recent monograph portrays *uti possidetis* as the main obstacle to secessionist claims for independent statehood.[66] To be sure, the ICJ has greatly contributed to this understanding by placing in its judgment in the *Frontier Dispute* case, *uti possidetis* as a necessary criterion for the interpretation of the principle of self-determination.[67] Closer analysis cannot share that appraisal of the legal position. *Uti possidetis* is important when a State becomes independent. Its boundaries will be determined by the previous boundaries as they exist at that moment.[68] Thereafter, a State which has emerged from colonial rule is a State like any other State. After having served its purpose, the principle of *uti possidetis* becomes irrelevant. Whether the territory of a new State may change by increasing or decreasing in size is determined by the rules which are applicable on a world-wide scale. Among these rules are also those which govern the issue of legitimate secession.[69]

III. Remedial secession – a concept of positive international law?

Given the scarcity of available practice, there is not only a possibility, but indeed a firm need to ask whether the concept of remedial secession, although it has broad support in the legal literature, can be deemed to exist as a concept rooted in positive international law. The example of Kosovo constitutes, to date, an isolated occurrence of intervention by the international community to secure the rights of an ethnic group suffering from persecution based on racial grounds. Can the lessons to be drawn from Kosovo be generalized, or will Kosovo remain a unique *rocher de bronze*, with no real chance of being emulated in the near future?

It is here that the methodological issue comes in, revealing its decisive importance. According to its origins, customary international law is

[66] J. Castellino, *International Law and Self-Determination. The Interplay of the Politics of Territorial Possession with Formulations of Post-Colonial 'National' Identity* (The Hague *et al.*: 2000), p. 132.

[67] *ICJ Reports* 1986, p. 554, at p. 567, para. 25.

[68] M. Kohen, *Possession contestée et souveraineté territoriale* (Paris: P.U.F., 1997), p. 445: 'L'uti possidetis signifie la succession par l'Etat nouvellement indépendant au territoire de l'ancienne division administrative où il s'est établi'. Higgins, 'Postmodern Tribalism and the Right to Secession', p. 34, likewise sets the record straight in stating: '*Uti possidetis* is the principle . . . whereby states become independent within their colonial boundaries . . .'. Ambiguous is the statement in Opinion No. 2 of the Arbitration Commission of the Conference on Yugoslavia, 11 January 1992, *ILM* 31 (1992), p. 1497, at p. 1498, para. 1: 'it is well established that . . . the right to self-determination must not involve changes to existing frontiers at the time of independence (*uti possidetis juris*) except where the States concerned agree otherwise'.

[69] See Kohen, *Possession*, p. 429.

dependent on solid empirical foundations. As stressed by Article 38(1)(b) of the Statute of the ICJ, custom needs – as the primary of its two component elements – a general practice. Traditionally, international lawyers have been looking around for bits and pieces of the required practice, referring to judicial decisions, diplomatic notes, treaties etc. Having filled the basket of research with their findings, they attempted to explain that the data thus collected could be galvanized in a general legal concept, covering the situation at hand.

Today, however, this traditional method is not the only one generally acknowledged as corresponding to the *lex artis.* Not only individual writers, but also recognized institutions of the international community, such as the ICJ or the International Criminal Tribunal for the former Yugoslavia, resort to other methods of law-finding. Inasmuch as the international community establishes certain elementary principles by consecrating them in such momentous instruments as the Charter of the United Nations or the Treaty on European Union (article 6), such principles must be heeded and implemented. They cannot be dismissed as having to yield whenever 'serious' legal business is at issue. In the case of *Nicaragua v. United States,*[70] the ICJ held, without much attention to practice, that the principles of non-use of force and of non-intervention had crystallized as customary law. Clearly, the commitment of States to protect human rights and fundamental freedoms belongs also to the determinative centre-pieces of the present-day legal order. Whenever governmental action in a given State amounts to a 'consistent pattern of gross and reliably attested violations of human rights',[71] the international community is called upon to respond by taking remedial action in favour of the human beings under threat. Of course, genocide on racial grounds counts among the worst forms of such a pattern of violations. To deny members of a given ethnic group any form of participation in the conduct of the public affairs of the country concerned is another serious form of a violation, the relevance of which largely transcends national boundaries – all the more so since discrimination in the political field is often co-terminous with discrimination and even persecution over the whole breadth of human activities.

What response the international community can provide in such instances is an issue which requires careful examination. Human rights activists have manifested their conviction that in case of breach of *jus cogens* rules or *erga omnes* obligations, any constraints derived from the

[70] *ICJ Reports* 1986, p. 14, at pp. 98–109.

[71] This is the language of ECOSOC Res. 1503 (XLVIII), 27 May 1970.

principle of national sovereignty could be brushed aside. In particular, it has been suggested that, in such instances, the principle of universal jurisdiction should apply for the purposes of criminal prosecution,[72] that jurisdiction to hear civil reparation claims should be acknowledged without any regard to the *lex loci delicti commissi*,[73] that neither immunities of States[74] nor the immunity of individuals discharging high governmental functions[75] should bar claims brought against them, etc. It is certainly correct that all of these possible legal consequences of the commission of a (grave) breach deserve close scrutiny. At the outset, however, it should be pointed out that each and every potential sanction must be considered on its own merits. It would be totally wrong to contend that in case of a breach of *jus cogens* norms or *erga omnes* obligations, the orthodox rules do not command any respect. *Jus cogens* and *erga omnes* are not magic words; they do not provide the justification for completely ignoring the traditional framework of rules whose epicentre is sovereign equality.[76] The right solution is a different one. It consists of exploring the suitability of an envisioned method of furthering the goal to be achieved, without dealing a lethal blow to the framework which secures the viability of international law as a system, the principles and rules of which are recognized by all the members of the international community. Even the United States has carefully circumscribed the conditions under which claims may

[72] See for instance C. Enache-Brown and A. Fried, 'Universal Crime, Jurisdiction and Duty: The Obligation of *Aut Dedere Aut Judicare* in International Law', *McGill L. J.* 43 (1998), p. 603, at p. 612; C. C. Joyner, 'Arresting Impunity: The Case for Universal Jurisdiction in Bringing War Criminals to Accountability', *LCP* 59 (1996), p. 152, at pp. 165–70; V. D. van der Vyver, 'Universal Jurisdiction in International Criminal Law', *SAYIL* 24 (1999), p. 107, at p. 114.

[73] This is the philosophy which underlies the U.S. Alien Tort Claims Act, 28 U.S.C. § 1350.

[74] See judgment of the Greek Supreme Court in *Prefecture of Voiotia v. Federal Republic of Germany*, summary in *AJIL* 95 (2001), with comment by M. Gavouneli, *ibid.*, at pp. 201–4. Recently, the Highest Greek Special Tribunal ruled in a judgment of 17 September 2002 that the principle of State immunity still exists as a general rule of international law which excludes legal actions by private persons before the courts of another State. See our critical comments: 'Current Issues of Responsibility under International Law', *Bancaja Euromediterranean Courses of International Law* IV (2000), p. 515, at pp. 566–73. In the United States, many writers have welcomed non-respect of State immunity as directed by recent domestic legislation. See, for instance, C. M. Cerna, 'Hugo Princz v. Federal Republic of Germany: How Far Does the Long-Arm Jurisdiction of US Law Reach?', *LJIL* 8 (1995), pp. 377–93; Roht-Arriaza, N., 'The Foreign Sovereign Immunities Act and Human Rights Violations: One Step Forward, Two Steps Back?', *BJIL* 16 (1998), pp. 71–84.

[75] See on this issue the judgment of the ICJ in *Arrest Warrant of 11 April 2000*, 14 February 2002, *ICJ Reports 2002*, p. 11.

[76] See our comments in Tomuschat, 'Ensuring the Survival of Mankind', pp. 85–8.

be brought against a State 'designated as a sponsor of terrorism' under the Effective Death Penalty Act of 1996.[77]

In this perspective it should be noted that, in our contemporary epoch, sovereign equality of States has lost its monopoly as the central pillar of the edifice of international law. As any other branch of the law, international law is designed to preserve international peace and security and the well-being of individual human beings. Indeed, the UN Charter mentions promoting and encouraging respect for human rights and fundamental freedoms as one of the guiding purposes of the world Organization (article 1(3)). Consequently, if a State strays from this path, not just by negligence but on account of a deliberate policy, it may forfeit the protection it enjoys by virtue of international law. To be sure, the interests at issue must be carefully balanced. In the present context, the relevant question is whether the international community, which for its part has many options to pursue, wishes to remain the only actor entitled to take remedial action by way of countermeasures or open criticism in formalized procedures, as practised in particular in the fora of the United Nations, or whether it grants a certain space of independent action to the actual victims of oppressive policies. Our conclusion is put forward without any hesitation. Within a context where the individual citizen is no more regarded as a simple object, international law must allow the members of a community suffering structural discrimination – amounting to grave prejudice affecting their lives – to strive for secession as a measure of last resort after all other methods employed to bring about change have failed.

It is at this juncture that the debate on a right to secession and the debate on the admissibility of humanitarian intervention[78] converge to

[77] *ILM* 36 (1997), p. 759.

[78] We may confine ourselves to referring to the voices collected in our earlier publication: Tomuschat, 'Ensuring the Survival of Mankind', pp. 224–6. From the later publications see, in particular, J.-F. Flauss, 'La primarité des droits de la personne: licéité ou illicéité de l'intervention humanitaire', in Tomuschat, *Kosovo and the International Community*, p. 87; T. M. Franck, *Recourse to Force. State Action Against Threats and Armed Attacks* (Cambridge: Cambridge University Press, 2002), p. 135; F. Francioni, 'Of War, Humanity and Justice: International Law After Kosovo', *Max Planck UNYB* 4 (2000), pp. 107–26; C. Gray, *International Law and the Use of Force* (Oxford, 2000); H. Neuhold, 'Collective Security After 'Operation Allied Force', *Max Planck UNYB* 4 (2000), p. 73, at pp. 98–103; N. K. Tsagourias, *Jurisprudence of International Law. The Humanitarian Dimension* (Manchester, 2000); R. Uerpmann, 'La primauté des droits de l'homme: licéité ou illicéité de l'intervention humanitaire', in Tomuschat, *Kosovo and the International Community*, p. 65.

cover the same ground.[79] The controversy about the pros and cons of humanitarian intervention cannot be reopened here. We have already expressed our conviction that in extreme circumstances humanitarian intervention must be acknowledged not only as morally defensible, but also as legally justified. It appears that the grounds with the potential to justify the assertion of a right of secession are exactly the same as those which members of the international community may invoke in their quest to assist an oppressed minority against a tyrannical government. There can be no doubt that a response by the members of the victim group themselves will have a far higher degree of legitimacy than a strategy planned and carried out by some powerful third nations who can always be suspected of pursuing selfish interests. On the basis of this deductive reasoning, remedial secession should be acknowledged as part and parcel of positive law, notwithstanding the fact that its empirical basis is fairly thin, but not totally lacking: as pointed out, the events leading to the establishment of Bangladesh and the events giving rise to Kosovo as an autonomous entity under international administration can both be classified as coming within the purview of remedial secession.

IV. The consequences of lawful resort to secession

A. The relationship between a secessionist movement and the affected State

The actual consequences of the recognition of a right to secession will normally be fairly limited. All empirical data suggest that the oppressor State itself will not feel bound to heed the argument advanced by its opponents that they enjoy a right of secession which they now wish to assert. On the contrary, the threat to start a secessionist movement will normally increase the repression suffered by the population concerned. In such instances, the international community should not lightly accept any allegation that 'acts of terrorism' are being committed by the victims. Unfortunately, however, confrontations of that kind, more often than not, end up in a vicious circle of violence and counter-violence. In any event, a right of resistance will never be a remedy exclusively handled

[79] Interestingly enough, in 1973, T. Franck and N. S. Rodley, in 'After Bangladesh: The Law of Humanitarian Intervention by Military Force', *AJIL* 67 (1973), pp. 275–305, discussed Bangladesh's secession exclusively from the viewpoint of humanitarian intervention (by India). For a joint consideration of both issues see C. Tomuschat, 'The Right of Resistance and Human Rights', in UNESCO (ed.), *Violations of Human Rights: Possible Rights of Recourse and Forms of Resistance* (Paris, 1984), p. 13.

by lawyers and their specific techniques of argument and persuasion. Therefore, the question centres on whether and to what extent third parties are permitted to support a minority group in its quest for independent statehood.

B. *Intervention by the Security Council*

It goes without saying that the Security Council enjoys wide discretion in taking measures to defuse a situation of tension threatening international peace and security. Invariably, an attempt to break away from an existing State by armed means will meet the requirements of Article 39 of the UN Charter. In the Kosovo crisis, the Security Council indeed made use of its powers by adopting Resolution 1244. Given the air operations which NATO carried out against Yugoslavia, there was no doubt that the conflict between the Kosovars and the government of the FRY had an international dimension. On the other hand, it is well-known from the recent practice of the Council that even internal occurrences, which lack any trans-boundary effect proper, can be characterized as threatening international peace and security.[80] Thus, intervention by the Security Council poses no legal, but only political, problems.

C. *Intervention by third States*

An assessment of the right of third States to support a secessionist movement raises greater difficulties. Different situations must be distinguished in that regard.

a) First of all, a secessionist movement may press ahead without being able to invoke paragraph 7 of the self-determination section of GA Resolution 2625 (XXV). In such instances, international law does not pass a negative judgment on the conduct of any of the two parties involved. Internal strife, including initiatives for secession from an existing State, is not prohibited as such by international law.[81] All the parties to an armed

[80] See, in particular, SC Res. 794 of 3 December 1992 on Somalia, and SC Res. 841 of 16 June 1993 on Haiti.

[81] On this issue, there exists broad consensus in the legal literature. See, for instance, Franck, 'Postmodern Tribalism', p. 13; Higgins, 'Postmodern Tribalism and the Right to Secession', p. 33; Klabbers/Lefeber, 'Africa', p. 53; Musgrave, *Self-Determination and National Minorities*, p. 193. See also the contribution of Olivier Corten to this volume as well as Georges Abi-Saab's conclusion. Cf. however the nuance suggested by Marcelo Kohen in his introduction.

conflict have to do is respect the rules of humanitarian law. If a secessionist movement is successful, the new entity established as a result will be recognized as a State if it fulfils the minimum requirements of statehood. The criterion of effectiveness will take precedence over any considerations of legitimacy. Third party intervention in favour of the insurgents would be unlawful. In *Nicaragua v. United States*, the ICJ manifested its attachment to the orthodox theory according to which a government may request assistance from other countries, whereas the insurgents may not be supported by outside forces.[82]

b) The situation is different when a group suffering from persecution can invoke the rule enunciated in paragraph 7 (see above para. a)). Given the special circumstances set out in that provision, the group concerned would legitimately pursue its aim of obtaining independent statehood, which necessarily means that the State from which it would seek to secede would engage in unlawful conduct by trying to repress the secessionist movement. Consequently, the inference is to be drawn that third States would be entitled to provide any kind of support short of military means. Whether third States might go beyond that threshold by intervening militarily is an issue which must be answered with the utmost care. International peace and security should not be sacrificed light-handedly. Again, an analogy with the rules on humanitarian intervention would appear to provide the most reliable answer. Essentially, the conditions upon which the permissibility of humanitarian intervention depends, and the conditions under which a group suffering grave discrimination may invoke a right to self-determination and secession, must be the same, i.e., if one affirms the lawfulness of humanitarian intervention. The only difference lies in the political aims of the affected population. While, in the case of humanitarian intervention, the international community is primarily and almost exclusively concerned with the fate of the victims, a group claiming a right to secession pursues a definite political project, namely the establishment of its own State. Such groups are a step ahead of a population which simply wishes to see the repression to which it is exposed brought to a halt.

V. Conclusion

The above considerations have attempted to present the legal framework within which self-determination and secession are situated. Nobody

[82] *ICJ Reports* 1986, p. 14, at p. 102.

should, however, be blind to realities. Secession generally raises deep-seated emotional responses. In a vicious circle of breaches of the law and reactions thereto, an armed conflict centring around secession can easily spin out of control. It would therefore be extremely helpful to have a procedure under which the controversial issues could be resolved by means other than resort to armed force.[83] Currently, there are no chances that such a procedure might materialize soon. This means that the UN Security Council will, for the time being, remain the decisive international institution whose expertise and intelligence will decide whether a conflict of secession may be settled peacefully or whether it will end in massive bloodshed.

[83] See the contribution of Antonello Tancredi in this volume.

2

Secession, terrorism and the right of self-determination

ANDREW CLAPHAM

I. Anti-terrorism treaties and secessionist struggle

One of the historical obstacles confronting the achievement of an internationally agreed definition of terrorism, as a crime under international law, has been support by some governments for the legitimacy of the use of force by peoples subjected to oppressive regimes. This support has extended into the negotiation of international treaties aimed at defining terrorist acts as crimes, and determining forms of international co-operation to punish such crimes. A clear illustration of such support can be found in the Convention of the Organisation of the Islamic Conference (OIC) on Combating International Terrorism of 1999:

> Article 2(a) Peoples' struggle including armed struggle against foreign occupation, aggression, colonialism, and hegemony, aimed at liberation and self-determination in accordance with the principles of international law shall not be considered a terrorist crime.

This definition of what is not a terrorist crime, of course only applies in the context of this particular Convention, but other non-universal Conventions include similar exclusions. Consider the 1999 OAU Convention on the Prevention and Combating of Terrorism 1999:

> Article 3(1) Notwithstanding the provisions of Article 1, the struggle waged by peoples in accordance with the principles of international law for their liberation or self-determination, including armed struggle against colonialism, occupation, aggression and domination by foreign forces shall not be considered as terrorist acts.

Lastly, consider also Article 2 of the Arab Convention on the Suppression of Terrorism 1998:

> All cases of struggle by whatever means, including armed struggle, against foreign occupation and aggression for liberation and self-determination, in accordance with the principles of international law, shall not be regarded as an offence. This provision shall not apply to any act prejudicing the territorial integrity of any Arab State.

The last sentence makes it clear, that should there be any doubt, a secessionist struggle within any existing Arab State could not be the sort of armed struggle which would be excluded from the definition of terrorist acts covered by the Convention.

Protecting those who use force in the context of certain liberation struggles has been a traditional concern of those who have won their nationhood through struggle against colonialism, racism and alien domination. As is well known, many such struggles involved acts which today would be classed as terrorism. This short essay examines the current state of international law and asks: do secessionist fighters inevitably engage in terrorist acts within the emerging crimes of terrorism under international law? And what role does the right to self-determination play in such a context? The two treaties that we will concentrate on are significant beyond their immediate application since, as we shall see, they contain definitions of terrorist offences that are applied in numerous other anti-terrorism treaties.

II. The Terrorist Bombing Convention of 1997

The terrorism Conventions cited above represent some of the most recent instruments for international cooperation and build into their framework, the earlier various terrorism conventions which define terrorist acts as crimes under international law. These earlier treaties were adopted in response to specific incidents. One of the most comprehensive is the 1997 Terrorist Bombing Convention introduced following the 1996 truck bomb attack on US service personnel in Dhahran, Saudi Arabia.[1] Other bombs had exploded at that time in Sri Lanka, England and Israel.[2] The treaty, unlike the terrorist treaties referred to above, made no exception for those engaged in liberation struggles. This treaty has been in force since 23 May 2001 and has been ratified by states such as Kenya, Israel, India, the United States and the Russian Federation.

[1] S. M. Witten, 'The International Convention for the Suppression of Terrorist Bombings', *AJIL* 92 (1998), pp. 774–81.

[2] *Ibid*, p. 774.

Recent bombings therefore, fall within its scope and illustrate how the meaning of 'terrorist' in this context, although disputed at the political level and in the draft UN Comprehensive Convention,[3] is actually already quite comprehensive for the purposes of this regime. Beyond the treaty regime, it seems likely that the Terrorist Bombing Convention has indirectly determined what counts as terrorism in international law and politics. More concretely, acts falling within the scope of the Convention will be terrorist acts not only for the purposes of action under this Convention but also with regards to the International Convention for the Suppression of the Financing of Terrorism (1999) and the other framework Conventions which annex the Bombing Convention such as the Inter-American Convention Against Terrorism (2002) and the European Convention on the Suppression of Terrorism (1977), taken together with the amending Protocol (2003),[4] as well as the Conventions of the OAU, OIC and Arab League, mentioned as the start of this essay.

The assumption which links attacks on 'innocent civilians' to acts of terrorism is not borne out when we examine the text of the Terrorist Bombing Convention. First, there is no particular focus on civilian targets, clearly inappropriate, considering the incidents which were uppermost in the minds of at least the US delegation at the time of drafting. The Convention covers all attacks on public places, this would include a military building or other military objective.[5] In other words, an attack during a secessionist struggle by the rebels on the government's military headquarters could fall within the scope of the Convention. Unlike the African, Arab and Islamic Conventions, there is no protected category of those fighting for self-determination. There is, however, a relevant exclusion clause which removes certain acts in armed conflict from the scope of the Convention. We now examine this clause in detail.

[3] The details of the competing draft articles can be found in 'Report of the Ad Hoc Committee established by the General Assembly Resolution 51/210 of 17 December 1996', *General Assembly Official records*, Sixth session, (28 January–1 February 2002), Fifty-seventh Session Supplement No. 37 UN Doc. (A/57/37). See also A/58/37 and subsequent reports.

[4] Not in force at the time of writing.

[5] Article 2 reads: 'Any person commits an offence within the meaning of this Convention if that person unlawfully and intentionally delivers, places, discharges or detonates an explosive or other lethal device in, into or against a place of public use, a State or government facility, a public transportation system or an infrastructure facility: (a) With the intent to cause death or serious bodily injury; or (b) With the intent to cause extensive destruction of such a place, facility or system, where such destruction results in or is likely to result in major economic loss.'

A. *The armed conflict exception*

The armed conflict exception reads as follows:

Article 19

> 1. Nothing in this Convention shall affect other rights, obligations and responsibilities of States and individuals under international law, in particular the purposes and principles of the Charter of the United Nations and international humanitarian law.
> 2. The activities of armed forces during an armed conflict, as those terms are understood under international humanitarian law, which are governed by that law, are not governed by this Convention, and the activities undertaken by military forces of a State in the exercise of their official duties, inasmuch as they are governed by other rules of international law, are not governed by this Convention.

Thus this exclusion, according to Witten, 'excludes the activities of armed forces (which would include both armed forces of states and subnational armed forces), so long as those activities are engaged in during an "armed conflict", where such activities are governed by laws of war'.[6] He goes on to suggest this 'carve-out' could be appropriately construed by reference to the exclusion in Article 1(2) of the 1977 Protocol II to the Geneva Conventions and this is, in fact, the 'understanding' registered by the United States.[7] Article 1(2) of Protocol II specifies that the Protocol does not apply 'to situations of internal disturbances and tensions, such as riots, isolated and sporadic acts of a similar nature, as not being armed conflicts'. However, defining one exception by another exception does not tell us what is meant by 'armed conflict'.

One might first consider in this context, the Statute of the International Criminal Court. This Statute has built in thresholds for the application of war crimes law in internal armed conflict in Articles 8(2)(c)(d)(e)(f). However, these thresholds may not be that helpful in the definition of an armed conflict for the Terrorist Bombings Convention, as they could

[6] Witten, 'International Convention', p. 780. Witten participated as a member of the US delegation during the drafting of this Convention. He gives of course the usual disclaimer that the views in the article are not necessarily those of the US Government.

[7] '(1) EXCLUSION FROM COVERAGE OF TERM "ARMED CONFLICT". The United States of America understands that the term "armed conflict" in Article 19 (2) of the Convention does not include internal disturbances and tensions, such as riots, isolated and sporadic acts of violence, and other acts of a similar nature. (2) MEANING OF TERM "INTERNATIONAL HUMANITARIAN LAW". The United States of America understands that the term "international humanitarian law" in Article 19 of the Convention has the same substantive meaning as the law of war.'

be seen simply as jurisdictional thresholds; and the Statute has not yet been ratified by a number of key States. Perhaps the best known and universally applicable definition can be found in the *Tadic* judgment of the International Criminal Tribunal for the Former Yugoslavia:

> we find that an armed conflict exists whenever there is a resort to armed force between States or protracted armed violence between governmental authorities and organized armed groups or between such groups within a State. International humanitarian law applies from the initiation of such armed conflicts and extends beyond the cessation of hostilities until a general conclusion of peace is reached; or, in the case of internal conflicts, a peaceful settlement is achieved. Until that moment, international humanitarian law continues to apply in the whole territory of the warring States or, in the case of internal conflicts, the whole territory under the control of a party, whether or not actual combat takes place there.[8]

Should an armed conflict satisfy this definition, then secessionist fighters (the organized armed groups) would not fall within the scope of the Terrorist Bombing Convention. Of course, certain acts would still be violations of the laws of war and could be prosecuted as such in certain jurisdictions. For example Article 4(2)(d) of Protocol II to the Geneva Conventions outlaws acts of terrorism against those not taking a direct part in hostilities.[9]

B. *The military forces of the State exception*

Although the term 'armed forces' is not defined in the Convention, the term 'military forces of a state' is defined in a wide way, thus excluding civilians working in support of the armed forces from the reach of the Convention and hence indirectly from the wider definition of 'terrorist'. Of course humanitarian law, human rights law and the law of state responsibility will continue to apply to acts undertaken by State officials. Violations of the relevant norms will continue to be violations of international

[8] *Decision On The Defence Motion For Interlocutory Appeal On Jurisdiction*, 2 October 1995, para. 70.

[9] For a prosecution of the 'war crime of terror' see *Prosecutor v Galić, C. Judgment of the International Criminal Tribunal for the Former Yugoslavia, 5 December 2003, Case No. IT-98-29-T*, paras. 63–138 (finding the defendant responsible for the crime of terror against the civilian population in Sarajevo). See further H. P. Gasser, 'Prohibition of Terrorist Acts in International Humanitarian Law', *IRRC* 253 (1986), pp. 200–12; H. P. Gasser, 'Acts of Terror, "Terrorism" and International Humanitarian Law' *IRRC* 847 (2002), pp. 547–70.

law; they will simply not be defined as offences under the Terrorist Bombing Convention.

Article 1(4) reads:

> 'Military forces of a State' means the armed forces of a State which are organized, trained and equipped under its internal law for the primary purpose of national defence or security, and persons acting in support of those armed forces who are under their formal command, control and responsibility.

Again, the exclusion from the scope of the Bombing Convention should not be understood as excluding acts committed by the military from the scope of terrorism. The law of war, as we saw above, prohibits acts of terrorism against those taking no part in hostilities. In addition, 'Acts or threats of violence the primary purpose of which is to spread terror among the civilian population are prohibited.'[10]

C. *Struggle short of armed conflict*

It seems from the above that armed forces on either side of an armed conflict as understood in international humanitarian law would not fall within the scope of the convention during an armed conflict. What if the struggle does not reach the level of an armed conflict? Would the secessionist bombings be covered? (We know that the bombings carried out by the regular armed forces and associated civilians are not covered as terrorist offences.) Here, a rather traditional exclusion clause has been inserted in a way that leaves the bombing covered with regards to some treaty obligations and excluded with regard to others. Article 3 reads:

> This Convention shall not apply where the offence is committed within a single State, the alleged offender and the victims are nationals of that State, the alleged offender is found in the territory of that State and no other State has a basis under article 6, paragraph 1, or article 6, paragraph 2, of this Convention to exercise jurisdiction, except that the provisions of articles 10 to 15 shall, as appropriate, apply in those cases.

[10] Protocol II, Article 13(2), and see also Protocol I, with regard to international armed conflicts, which provides 'Acts or threats of violence the primary purpose of which is to spread terror among the civilian population are prohibited' Article 51(2). The Fourth Geneva Convention for the Protection of Civilians also includes the following injunction, Article 33: 'Collective penalties and likewise all measures of intimidation or of terrorism are prohibited.'

In effect, this means that a secessionist accused of a Convention terrorist bombing with no transnational element and who is captured in the State where the bombing took place is not covered by certain provisions which oblige States to submit the case to its prosecutorial authorities. This is, in a way, not surprising. However, the provisions on mutual assistance and the human rights of the detainee do apply. It would be fair to conclude, therefore, that a secessionist suspected of a bombing (even with no transnational element) comes within this terrorism Convention and can in legal terms therefore be described as a Convention terrorist upon conviction.

D. Conclusion regarding the Terrorist Bombing Convention

So in a secessionist struggle that has risen to the level of an armed conflict, whether or not the people enjoyed the right to self-determination, the Terrorist Bombing Convention does not apply to the Military forces of the State or the armed forces of an organized armed group. Whether the bomb was used against military or civilian targets is irrelevant for the purposes of this Convention. In a struggle short of armed conflict, suspected bombers from the secessionist side fall within the scope of the Convention and can be extradited or prosecuted abroad under the 'extradite or prosecute' provisions in the treaty. Where the secessionist's acts take place in the State of the secessionist's nationality and the victims are all nationals of that State then the extradition and jurisdictional provisions do not apply, but the acts can still fall within the scope of the Terrorist Bombing Convention. In the context of this recent treaty, the tricky issue of the licence to use force in the struggle for self-determination has been eclipsed. The justness of the secessionist struggle is more or less irrelevant in this context. Even certain states that have supported a self-determination exclusion in other contexts have now ratified the Convention, including States such as Pakistan, Yemen, Algeria, Libya, and Sudan.

III. The Hostage-taking Convention

This earlier Convention employs slightly different wording as compared to the Bombing Convention, but the differences are worth considering if we want a full picture of the extent to which secessionist campaigns can be relabelled 'terrorism' under international law. The Convention preamble refers to 'acts of taking of hostages as manifestations of international terrorism'.[11]

With regard to the armed conflict exception, the 'carve out' is different and needs some explanation:

Article 12 reads:

> In so far as the Geneva Conventions of 1949 for the protection of war victims or the Additional Protocols to those Conventions are applicable to a particular act of hostage-taking, and in so far as States Parties to this Convention are bound under those conventions to prosecute or hand over the hostage-taker, the present Convention shall not apply to an act of hostage-taking committed in the course of armed conflicts as defined in the Geneva Conventions of 1949 and the Protocols thereto, including armed conflicts mentioned in article 1, paragraph 4, of Additional Protocol I of 1977, in which peoples are fighting against colonial domination and alien occupation and against racist regimes in the exercise of their right of self-determination, as enshrined in the Charter of the United Nations and the Declaration on Principles of International Law concerning Friendly Relations and Co-operation among States in accordance with the Charter of the United Nations.

On a textual reading, it seems that two conditions are necessary for a hostage taking to be excluded from the Convention under this provision. First, the humanitarian law treaties have to actually apply, that is, they must not only be applicable under their terms, but also have been ratified by the relevant parties. Second, the actual hostage taking has to fall within the grave breaches regime which creates 'extradite or prosecute' obligations under the treaties. The purpose of this clause seems to be that a hostage-taker falling within the general scope of the hostages treaty will either be covered by the hostages treaty or be prosecuted under the relevant provisions of international humanitarian law. There is no exception for armed conflict or the armed forces of a State as we had in the Bombing Convention. Hostage taking is always illegal, it is only a question of which regime is used to extradite or prosecute. The label may change from 'act of terrorism' to 'grave breach' / 'war crime', but there is no exception for secessionists, whether or not they are struggling for self-determination.

How would a secessionist struggle be viewed in the application of this article? On a strict reading, internal armed conflicts do not give rise to

[11] International Convention against the Taking of Hostages, 1979, in force 3 June 1983, preambular paragraph 5.

'extradite or prosecute' obligations under the treaties, therefore secessionists would be covered only by the Hostages Convention. With regard to self-determination struggles covered by Article 1(4) of Protocol 1, as explained in Article 12 above, the secessionists would have to be subjected to colonial domination, alien occupation or a racist régime. Much has been written about the scope of these terms;[12] to the extent that they reflect categories in customary international law, their content may develop over time. For present purposes, Article 12 seems to suggest that the Protocol Article 1(4) has to apply as a treaty obligation. In this case, that means that the relevant State must be a party to the Protocol and the secessionist 'authority' must have made a declaration under Article 96(3) of the Protocol. There are no secessionist conflicts where this regime currently applies as international law and it is unlikely that any secessionist movement will today be able to easily deposit a declaration as it would probably meet with objections from the depositary or the States parties. Furthermore, States which could be considered by some to be the sites of secessionist or liberation movements have refrained from ratifying the Protocol or have done so with reservations.[13]

IV. Definitions of terrorism beyond the international terrorism treaties

In this section, we will examine recent judgments concerning the banning of certain organizations as terrorist organizations in the United Kingdom. We shall consider the challenge by a number of political groups to the proscription of 21 organizations under the UK's Terrorism Act.[14] The

[12] See in particular G. Abi-Saab, 'The Legal Nature of Wars of National Liberation' *Recueil des Cours* 165 (1979-IV) 363–445; A. Cassese, 'Wars of National Liberation and Humanitarian Law' in C. Swinarski (ed), *Studies and Essays in Honour of Jean Pictet* (The Hague: Nijhoff, 1984), p. 322; J. J. Lambert, *Terrorism and Hostages in International law: A Commentary of the Hostages Convention 1979*, (Cambridge: Grotius, 1990), p. 293.

[13] See the UK Reservation: (d) Re: ARTICLE 1, paragraph 4 and ARTICLE 96, paragraph 3 'It is the understanding of the United Kingdom that the term "armed conflict" of itself and in its context denotes a situation of a kind which is not constituted by the commission of ordinary crimes including acts of terrorism whether concerted or in isolation.

'The United Kingdom will not, in relation to any situation in which it is itself involved, consider itself bound in consequence of any declaration purporting to be made under paragraph 3 of Article 96 unless the United Kingdom shall have expressly recognised that it has been made by a body which is genuinely an authority representing a people engaged in an armed conflict of the type to which Article 1, paragraph 4, applies. (. . .)', Corrected Letter of 28 January 1998 sent to the Swiss Government by Christopher Hulse, HM Ambassador of the United Kingdom.

[14] (Proscribed Organisations) Order 2001, SI 2001 No. 1261.

challenge in *R (The Kurdistan Workers Party and others)* v. *Secretary of State for the Home Department* contended that on the one hand, the primary legislation, i.e. the Terrorism Act 2000, the Order, and the procedure which was used in making the order are incompatible with human rights under Articles 10, 11 and 14 of the European Convention on Human Rights. Under the UK Human Rights Act of 1998, the High Court can issue a Declaration of Incompatibility with regard to this legislation. On the other hand, the complaint included a challenge by individual applicants that the proscription of the organization and the criminal offences created by the Terrorism Act constitute a disproportionate interference with their rights to freedom of expression and association under Articles 10 and 11 of the ECHR as incorporated in the Human Rights Act 1998.

The Terrorism Act adopts a definition of terrorism which departs from any of the treaty-based or UN definitions adopted at the international level. The definition at the national level may itself give rise to compatibility problems with international law. Section 1 of the Terrorism Act 2000 states:

> 1. (1) In this Act 'terrorism' means the use or threat of action where-
>   (a) the action falls within subsection (2),
>   (b) the use or threat is designed to influence the government or to intimidate the public or a section of the public, and
>   (c) the use or threat is made for the purpose of advancing a political, religious or ideological cause.
>
> (2) Action falls within this subsection if it-
>   (a) involves serious violence against a person,
>   (b) involves serious damage to property,
>   (c) endangers a person's life, other than that of the person committing the action,
>   (d) creates a serious risk to the health or safety of the public or a section of the public, or
>   (e) is designed seriously to interfere with or seriously to disrupt an electronic system.
>
> (3) The use or threat of action falling within subsection (2) which involves the use of firearms or explosives is terrorism whether or not subsection (1)(b) is satisfied.
>
> (4) In this section-
>   (a) 'action' includes action outside the United Kingdom,
>   (b) a reference to any person or to property is a reference to any person, or to property, wherever situated,
>   (c) a reference to the public includes a reference to the public of a country other than the United Kingdom, and

(d) 'the government' means the government of the United Kingdom, of a Part of the United Kingdom or of a country other than the United Kingdom.

(5) In this Act a reference to action taken for the purposes of terrorism includes a reference to action taken for the benefit of a proscribed organisation.

This can be compared with Article 2 of the International Convention for the Financing of Terrorism which defines terrorism as:

1. Any person commits an offence within the meaning of this Convention if that person by any means, directly or indirectly, unlawfully and wilfully, provides or collects funds with the intention that they should be used or in the knowledge that they are to be used, in full or in part, in order to carry out:
   (a) An act which constitutes an offence within the scope of and as defined in one of the treaties listed in the annex; [this includes the two terrorism treaties discussed above] or
   (b) Any other act intended to cause death or serious bodily injury to a civilian, or to any other person not taking an active part in the hostilities in a situation of armed conflict, when the purpose of such act, by its nature or context, is to intimidate a population, or to compel a Government or an international organization to do or to abstain from doing any act.

The national law definition is clearly wider than the international framework definition. For the purposes of the present essay, we shall concentrate on the effects of the criminalization of the organization and the effect they claim this criminalization is having on their individual rights. Twenty one organizations were proscribed in a single order. Once an organization has been proscribed under this procedure, it is an offence under the Act for a person to belong to or profess to belong to such an organization or invite support for such an organization (Sections 11 and 12(1)) or take part in arrangements for a meeting of three or more persons in support of such an organization (12(2)) or address such a meeting in order to encourage support for the organization (12(3)). It is an offence for a person to wear in a public place an article which raises a reasonable suspicion that he is a member or supporter of a proscribed organization. In other words, wearing an organization's badge is an offence. This carries a maximum of six months in prison. It is also an offence to invite others to provide money for the purposes of the proscribed organization. This carries a maximum of 14 years imprisonment (Sections 15, 16 and 1(5)).

Part of the challenge mounted by the proscribed organizations at the national level concerned the fact that the legislation does nothing to protect the rights of those taking up arms against oppressive regimes or in the legitimate exercise of their right to self-determination. The groups involved in this challenge come from Iran, Turkey, and Kashmir. Let us leave aside for the moment the tricky issue of whether these groups actually enjoy any international rights of self-determination. For the purposes of the present discussion it is sufficient to imagine that there could be entities representing peoples entitled to the right of self-determination who could find their rights curtailed or impinged through the application of this legislation. The legislation relies on the exercise of 'Executive discretion' to ensure that not all groups would be subject to the legislation. But the issue remains, what if the legislation were to affect the right of self-determination, perhaps for a group where the Executive were less sympathetic at the political level. In fact, in the ILC's recent Commentary to their 'Articles on Responsibility of States for Internationally Wrongful Acts' the Commission stated that the right of self-determination was not only customary but also a peremptory norm of international law (*ius cogens*), which we know gives rise to obligations for all States in the world.

So far, relatively few peremptory norms have been recognized as such. But various tribunals, national and international, have affirmed the idea of peremptory norms in contexts not limited to the validity of treaties. Those peremptory norms that are clearly accepted and recognized include the prohibitions of aggression, genocide, slavery, racial discrimination, crimes against humanity and torture, and the right of self-determination.[15]

Later on, the Commentary again lists the peremptory norms of international law and finishes the list in the following way:

> Finally, the obligation to respect the right of self-determination deserves to be mentioned. As the International Court noted in the *East Timor* case, '[t]he principle of self-determination . . . is one of the essential principles of contemporary international law,' which gives rise to an obligation to the international community as a whole to permit and respect its exercise.[16]

[15] Commentary to Article 26, para 5. Report of the *ILC*, GAOR, Supp. No. 10 (A/56/10), p. 208 (footnotes omitted).

[16] Commentary to Article 40, para 5. Report of the *ILC*, GAOR, Supp. No. 10 (A/56/10), p. 284. The Commentary's footnote at this point reads: '*East Timor (Portugal v. Australia), ICJ Reports* 1995, p. 90, at p. 102, para. 29. See Declaration on Principles of International Law concerning Friendly Relations and Cooperation among States in accordance with the Charter of the United Nations, G. A. Res. 2625 (XXV) of 24 October 1970, fifth principle.'

The fact that the right of self-determination is a peremptory norm means that there can be no derogation from this right[17] and that all States are prohibited from rendering aid or assistance in maintaining a situation caused by a serious breach of such a norm.[18]

Whether or not the UK courts will recognize an interpretation of the right of self-determination which legitimizes the right to resort to military force,[19] the new Articles on State Responsibility strongly suggest that States are prohibited from rendering aid or assistance in maintaining a situation caused by a serious breach of such a norm.[20] A State would have to give serious attention to any action that might assist a state forcibly repressing the right to self-determination. Preventing the people entitled to self-determination from organizing at the political level is not military or economic assistance but could be seen to undermine the right to self-determination under customary international law.

In his *International Law*, Antonio Cassese summarizes the legal situation:

> [t]hird States are legally authorized to support peoples entitled to self-determination, by granting them any assistance short of dispatching armed troops. Conversely, they must refrain from aiding and abetting oppressor States. Furthermore, they are entitled to claim respect for the principle from States denying self-determination.[21]

Turning to treaty law, the right of self-determination is contained in the two human rights Covenants. Common Article 1 of the International Covenant on Civil and Political Rights (1966) and of the International Covenant on Economic Social and Cultural Rights states in part:

17 1969 Vienna Convention on the Law of Treaties, Article 53.

18 Article 41 of the Draft Articles on State Responsibility adopted by the International Law Commission in 2001.

19 Consider the interpretation by A. Cassese, *Self-Determination of Peoples: A Legal Reappaisal* (Cambridge: Grotius, 1995) that states: 'liberation movements have been given a *legal entitlement* that is less than a *right* proper but more than the *absence of any authorization whatsoever.* This position can be best expressed by holding that liberation movements, although they do not possess a *legal right* to enforce their substantive right to self-determination by resort to war, nevertheless have a *legal license* to do so.' (At p. 153, and see p. 154 for internal self-determination.) See also p. 200, and p. 195 for a reference to the legitimation of the use of force by the organization representing the people entitled to the right to self-determination in situations where this is forcibly denied them. In *International Law*, 2nd edn (Oxford: Oxford University Press, 2005), p. 63, he states: 'self-determination has resulted in granting to liberation movements a legal license to use force for the purpose of reacting to the forcible denial of self-determination by a colonial State, an occupying Power, or a State refusing a racial group equal access to government'.

20 Article 41 of the Draft Articles on State Responsibility adopted by the International Law Commission in 2001.

21 Cassese, *International Law*, p. 62.

> 1(1) All peoples have the right of self-determination. By virtue of that right they freely determine their political status and freely pursue their economic, social and cultural development.
>
> 1(3) The States Parties to the present Covenant, including those having responsibility for the administration of Non-Self-Governing and Trust Territories, shall promote the realization of the right of self-determination, and shall respect that right, in conformity with the provisions of the Charter of the United Nations.

According to the UN Human Rights Committee 'The obligations exist irrespective of whether a people entitled to self-determination depends on a State party to the Covenant or not. It follows that all States parties to the Covenant should take positive action to facilitate realization of and respect for the rights of peoples to self-determination.'[22]

The right of self-determination was not a central feature of the two judgments that the UK Courts delivered concerning the challenge by the proscribed organizations. In the first judgment the Court stated:[23]

> 47. The starting point is the very broad definition of 'terrorism' in s.1 of the 2000 Act and the very broad power of proscription in s.3. The Act permits the proscription of organisations that would never be proscribed in practice, including organisations which are fighting against undemocratic and oppressive regimes and, in particular, those which have engaged in lawful armed conflict in the exercise of the internationally recognised right to self-determination of peoples (where the United Kingdom is bound in international law to recognise the right and to refrain from offering material support to states engaged in the suppression of the exercise of the right by military or other coercive means). The fact that the power of proscription extends wider than the use that Parliament can have intended to be made of it provides the strongest support for the requirement that intelligible criteria be laid down for the exercise of the Secretary of State's discretion and for effective Parliamentary and judicial scrutiny. The explicit assumption on which the legislation depends is that the Secretary of State will not proscribe certain organisations even though they meet the statutory criteria in ss.1 and 3. There is, however, no clear indication in the legislation or in any published policy of the Secretary of State as to the basis on which the Secretary of State is to distinguish between one organisation and another.

[22] General Comment 12, para. 6 (1984). UN Doc HRI/GEN/1/Rev.4, p. 91.

[23] Case Nos.: CO/2587/2001, CO/4039/2001 and CO/878/2002, Neutral citation no.: [2002] EWHC 644 (Admin) *The Queen (on the application of the Kurdistan Workers' Party and Others)* v. *Secretary of State for the Home Department*; *The Queen (on the application of the People's Mojahedin Organisation of Iran and Others) v. Secretary of State for the Home Department; The Queen (on the application of Nisar Ahmed) v. Secretary of State for the Home Department.*

> 59. The court's special attention is drawn by the claimant to the international law situation and factual circumstances of Jammu and Kashmir, which it is submitted were matters that Parliament was unable properly to consider but which render the proscription of the LeT disproportionate and discriminatory compared with other organisations which have not been proscribed. In particular, it is said that the LeT does not call for the armed overthrow of the Government of India in Kashmir, but campaigns for the right to a plebiscite; this is a campaign for the fulfilment of the international law right to self-determination; the LeT's military activities are directed exclusively against the Indian regime's military/security apparatus and to the disputed territory of Kashmir; they have never targeted civilians and have never posed any threat to the UK or to British nationals overseas; and independent human rights organisations have documented consistent human rights abuses and violations of fundamental tenets of democratic rule in Kashmir. Further, in relation to discrimination in breach of Article 14, it is submitted that the relevant class is of organisations capable of being proscribed as terrorist organisations and that no adequate justification has been advanced for the difference of treatment between the LeT and organisations such as the Northern Alliance in Afghanistan which have not been proscribed.

The Court therefore left open the possibility that should the Executive proscribe 'organisations which are fighting against undemocratic and oppressive regimes and, in particular, those which have engaged in lawful armed conflict in the exercise of the internationally recognised right to self-determination of peoples,' there might be international obligations on the UK. The arguments presented by the Government had simply dismissed the right to self-determination as irrelevant in the context of terrorism.

> 57. In the Secretary of State's letter of 31 August 2001 refusing to deproscribe the LeT, it is stated:
>
> In reaching his decision the Home Secretary has taken full account of the submission made on behalf of your client. This includes the assertion that Lashkar e Tayyaba is not a terrorist organisation but a legitimate freedom movement. The Home Secretary does not accept, however, that any perceived right to self-determination justifies the terrorist actions of LT, or any other terrorist organisation. The Government condemns all acts of terrorism, whatever the source or motivation . . .

This Court rejected the challenges before it and, on appeal, The Proscribed Organizations Appeal Commission referred in its judgment to the argument regarding self-determination whereby the UK legislation could catch 'those whose struggles are widely regarded as legitimate'; but the Appeal Commission felt no need to go further into this aspect of the challenge. Nor did the Appeal Commission consider that the restrictive definition of terrorism contained in the international treaties should restrict the application of anti-terrorism laws at the national level.

> 42. The appellants contend that the definition of terrorism is 'excessively wide'; it relates to actions outside the United Kingdom as well as within it; where the object of intimidation is the public or Government it extends to countries other than the United Kingdom as well as the United Kingdom itself. It is apt to cover a group of environmental protestors who cut down GM crops or hack into websites. It was argued that it goes beyond the essence of 'terrorism' as defined in international law, by including acts of violence against non-civilians even in situations of active conflict (see Article 2(1)(b) of the International Convention for the Suppression of Financing of Terrorism, United Nations General Assembly Resolution 54/109 December 1999). (We should note that it was correctly accepted in argument that there is not a 'definition' of 'terrorism' in international law, that the General Assembly Resolution relied on was not binding on States in international law and only dealt with one aspect of 'terrorism' and that there were legally binding instruments, such as Security Council Resolution 1373 (2001) adopted on 28 September 2001, which clearly used a wider concept of 'terrorism' than that for which the appellants contended.) It would include organisations which have the political support of the United Kingdom of the day, which for that reason would not be proscribed. The Iraqi Kurds were given as an example of such an organization in the course of debate in the House of Commons. It will also include those whose struggles against repressive regimes are widely regarded as legitimate, for example the African National Congress in its struggle against apartheid and those struggling to establish democracy or self-determination against repressive regimes guilty of widespread violation of human rights.[24]

The Security Council's Counter Terrorism Committee is operating with an understanding which similarly reflects this admitted subjectivity. It would seem quite capable of covering secessionist movements of all stripes. The former Chair of the Security Council's Counter Terrorism Committee, Ambassador Greenstock, has explained the approach of this political body:

[24] Proscribed Organisations Appeal Commission, *PMOI, Nisar Ahmed v. Secretary of State for the Home Department*, Appeal PC/001/2002, 15 November 2002.

> Our job is to help raise the capability of every Member State to deal with terrorism on its territory. For the Committee, terrorism is what the members of the Committee decide unanimously is terrorism.[25]

So the restrictive definition of terrorism used in the international terrorism conventions does not necessarily determine the scope of terrorism in national law or at the level of the Security Council. What we can say after this brief examination of the UK challenge is that a group fighting a recognized struggle for self-determination may, in some circumstances, garner support from that internationally recognized right. In such a situation, anti-terrorism measures at the national level which, actually rather than potentially, penalized acts which are legal under the law of armed conflict could place the state in violation of its international obligations with regard to the right of self-determination. So far the UK Courts have not recognized any of the groups which have challenged their proscription as having this sort of international legitimacy. The fact that other groups which might have such legitimacy have not been proscribed has not been seen as legally relevant in the context of the challenge by the proscribed groups.

V. Concluding summary

1. Under the regime established by the Terrorist Bombing Convention, a secessionist bombing suspect who is a member of the armed forces of the secessionist group can avoid the scope of the Convention only where the struggle takes the form of an armed conflict. In other cases, such a bombing will be classed as an offence within the Terrorist Bombing Convention. In addition, if the fighting is in the context of an armed conflict, any bombings that target civilians will be war crimes and could be tried as such in the International Criminal Court, should that Court have jurisdiction.
2. Under the Hostages Convention regime, a secessionist hostage-taker can not avoid the scope of the Convention under normal circumstances. Exceptionally, should the secessionist movement qualify as a people 'fighting against colonial domination and alien occupation and against racist régimes in exercise of their right of self-determination,'

[25] *The Counter-terrorism Committee*, pamphlet produced by the Permanent Mission of the United Kingdom to the United Nations, New York. Available at: http://www.fco.gov.uk/servlet/Front?pagename = OpenMarket/Xcelerate/ShowPage = Pageid = 1033555909926.

and it successfully registers a declaration under article 96(3) of Protocol I, and the State they are fighting against also accepts the obligations in Protocol I by becoming a party to the treaty without relevant reservations, then the hostage-taking will most likely count as a grave breach and will be prosecuted under the grave breaches regime as a war crime. Again if the International Criminal Court has jurisdiction, the secessionist hostage-taking could be prosecuted in that Court as a war crime. In this case it would be as a war crime committed in an internal armed conflict, Article 8(2)(c)(iii), as the ICC does not recognize the internationalization of self-determination struggles in the same way as Protocol I.

3. Anti-terrorism measures taken at the national level may go beyond the terrorist conventions in their definition of terrorism. In the UK, the legislation which enables the proscription of terrorist organizations has left little room for any explicit exception for secessionist groups struggling for self-determination. Where this has been challenged, the problem has been assumed to be academic, as the Executive retains enough discretion to refuse to proscribe an organization engaged in a legitimate struggle for self-determination.
4. The scope of self-determination is notoriously difficult to discern. There may be a hard core of legal content, but even that could develop according to the expectations placed in the concept by secessionist movements. Other essays in this volume deal with the scope of self-determination. We have considered self-determination to the extent that it may affect the rules regarding counter-terrorism measures. Even as the scope of the international law covering terrorism is expanding, this scope remains determined in part by the scope of the right of self-determination. In the post-colonial world, it seems likely that secessionist groups will inherit the loudest claims to self-determination. Like terrorism, self-determination is hardly a static concept, and it seems likely that these two terms will continue to evolve in ways which demand a detailed understanding of their complex interaction. We end by simply recalling the caution urged by James Crawford:

> But this does not mean that the only 'peoples' relevant for international purposes are the whole people of each state. International lawyers should resist the conclusion that a widely-used term is to be stipulatively and narrowly defined, in such a way that it reflects neither normal usage nor the

self-perception and identity of diverse and long-established human groups. That would make the principle of self-determination into a cruel deception: it may be so, but the presumption is to the contrary, and our function should be to make sense of existing normative language, corresponding to widely-regarded claims of right, and not to retreat into a self-denying legalism.[26]

[26] J. Crawford, 'The Right of Self-Determination in International Law': Its Development and Future' in Alston, P., (ed.), *Peoples' Rights* (Oxford: Oxford University Press, 2001), p. 7.

3

Secession and external intervention

GEORG NOLTE

I. Introduction

Secession attempts sometimes provoke external interventions. Such interventions can take various forms. They can take place by armed force, by economic coercion, or by political means, such as by means of recognition. Interventions can also originate from different actors. They can be undertaken by the United Nations, by another international organization, by a State or a group of States, or by Non-State actors. This article does not cover all possible forms of external intervention within secession processes, rather it concentrates on describing some general rules of international law that are applicable in such situations and on providing a few pertinent examples from international practice. The focus will be on the role of the United Nations (section II) and on armed intervention by third States, both at the invitation of the government concerned and without (section III).

Secession, as a legal term, means the – not necessarily forceful – breaking away of an integral part of the territory of a State and its subsequent establishment as a new State. This chapter, however, only deals with the rules that apply to a narrower concept of secession. Thus, we are not concerned with conflicts about internationally disputed territories, e.g. the cases of the Baltic States, Kashmir, Palestine, East-Timor, or the divided States such as China, Germany, Korea, Yemen. Cases of domestic conflict which merely contain a remote possibility that they will turn into a serious secession attempt such as the Basque country, Corsica and Scotland are also beyond the scope of the present work. However, since external interventions usually take place before secession is actually achieved, it is necessary to consider cases in which a serious secession attempt has been undertaken. This includes those cases in which the goal of secession has been openly proclaimed by recognized leaders of the population of the part of the State territory in question. On the other hand, conflicts in which local leaders merely demand autonomy within the existing State, as has long been the case for Kurdistan,[1] and more recently, the former Yugoslav Republic of Macedonia,[2] do not fall into this category. Furthermore, only those cases of external intervention are considered which are acknowledged as such, as opposed to covert military operations or other external aid.[3] Lastly, neither does this chapter concern itself with cases in which a peaceful demand for secession has merely been politically 'accompanied' by third States e.g., thus far, Serbia and Montenegro.

II. Intervention by the United Nations

The main task of the United Nations is to maintain or restore international peace and security. To fulfil this task, the Organization has been endowed with certain powers. These include decisions by the Security Council under Chapters VI and VII of the UN Charter and recommendations by the General Assembly. At the same time, Article 2(7) of the United Nations Charter provides a limited prohibition for the Organization to intervene in the domestic affairs of member States.

The United Nations (UN) Charter was not written with secession conflicts in mind. It established a comprehensive prohibition on the use of force by States and corresponding institutional machinery by which responsibility for the maintenance or restoration of peace and security is to be exercised. Under the Charter, secession conflicts are, as a general rule, domestic conflicts which may give rise to threats to the peace and have the potential to develop into international conflicts. Thus, secession conflicts are not considered to be a special category as per UN law, and the powers of the United Nations apply equally to all situations concerning international peace and security, independent of whether such situations arise from a disputed claim to secession, a regular inter-State conflict, or any other domestic conflict.

1 L. C. Buchheit, *Secession – The Legitimacy of Self-Determination* (New Haven: Yale University Press, 1978), p. 160.

2 Statement by the Political Leader of the Militant UCK on 7 April 2001, Ali Ahmeti, *Archiv der Gegenwart* 2001, p. 44913; see also SC Res. 1345 of 21 March 2001; SC Res. 1373 of 28 September 2001; Statement by the President of the Security Council of 7 March 2001, S/PRST/2001/7; Statement by the President of the Security Council of 13 August 2001, S/PRST/2001/20.

3 Buchheit, *Secession*, p. 158, mentions the case of support of the Kurdish insurgency in Iraq by Iran and the United States which may have merely served the purpose of weakening Iraq as a State.

Since the early 1990s, a series of resolutions of the Security Council has led to a broadened understanding of the term 'threat to the peace', which is the prerequisite under Article 39 of the Charter for the taking of enforcement measures by the Security Council.[4] Secession conflicts have played a distinct role in the process of gradually extending the concept of 'threat to the peace'. As a result of which, Security Council Resolution 713 (1991), which ordered an arms embargo against Yugoslavia, is sometimes cited as one of the milestones in this process.[5] The more important resolutions in this context,[6] however, did not concern secession processes. The case of Resolution 794 (1992) concerning Somalia, in particular, has shown that such a 'threat to the peace' can arise from 'the magnitude of the human tragedy', and need not depend on substantial trans-boundary effects.

Thus, the treatment of secession conflicts by the political UN organs seems to be characteristic only in respect to their anti-secessionist attitude concerning the eventual political resolution of such conflicts. Another aspect which merits some attention is whether Article 2(7) of the Charter still contains significant legal limitations to UN intervention in secession conflicts.

A. *The anti-secessionist attitude of the political UN organs*

The first major modern case in which the powers of the United Nations to intervene in a secession conflict were put to the test was the Katanga aspect of the Congo operation.[7] Although this case was closely linked to the decolonization process, it was technically a secession conflict. In addition, it was a formative event for the attitude of the United Nations towards secession conflicts. It was within days after the internationally agreed proclamation of independence by the Congo, that the leader of the province of Katanga, Moïse Tschombé, declared the independence

[4] J. A. Frowein and N. Krisch, 'Article 39', *in* B. Simma, (ed.), *The Charter of the United Nations – A Commentary* (Oxford University Press, 2nd edn, 2002), p. 718.

[5] T. M. Franck, 'Fairness in the International Legal and Institutional System', *Recueil des Cours* (1993-III), p. 211.

[6] SC Res. 748 of 31 March 1992; SC Res. 794 of 3 December 1992; SC Res. 875 of 16 October 1993.

[7] See G. Abi-Saab, *The United Nations Operation in the Congo 1960–1964* (Oxford: Oxford University Press, 1978); R. Simmonds, *Legal Problems Arising from the United Nations Military Operations in the Congo* (The Hague: Martinus Nijhoff, 1968); T. M. Franck and J. Carey (eds.), *The Legal Aspects of the United Nations Action in the Congo* (New York: Oceana Publications, 1963).

of that part of the country. His move was part of a more general power struggle in and about the Congo which prompted the Security Council to send the peacekeeping mission ONUC to help the Congolese central government maintain and restore public order and to bring about the withdrawal of Belgian forces which in the meantime had intervened in Katanga.

Initially, the position of UN Secretary-General Hammarskjöld and the Security Council had been to insist on the difference between the presence of Belgian troops which ostensibly justified the presence of UN forces, on the one hand, and the domestic problem of the relation between the central government of the Congo and the breakaway province of Katanga, on the other, which was initially considered an internal affair.[8] However, after more than a year of chaotic power struggles among Congolese factions and the withdrawal of the Belgian forces, the Security Council passed Resolution 169 (1961) which deplored 'specifically secessionist activities and armed action now being carried out by the provincial administration of Katanga with the aid of external resources and foreign forces'. If read in combination with previous resolutions, this resolution provided a basis for the ultimately successful ONUC operations in 1962/63 to bring the Katanga secession to an end. Indeed, as Buchheit has put it rather cautiously: 'in retrospect, the United Nations action in the Congo stands as a major precedent against an international recognition of secessionist legitimacy in circumstances similar to those surrounding the Congo at independence'.[9]

Since then, the anti-secessionist attitude of the United Nations has not changed significantly. Thus, when fighting erupted in the former Yugoslav Republic of Macedonia in 2001, between fighters from the ethnic Albanian minority and government forces, the spectre of yet another secession conflict was raised. The Security Council reacted not only by condemning the violence as such, but also by 'reaffirming its commitment to the sovereignty and territorial integrity of . . . the former Yugoslav Republic of Macedonia'. The Security Council noted that 'such violence has support from ethnic Albanian extremists outside these areas and constitutes a threat to the security and stability of the wider region'.[10] In almost all other secession conflicts, the Security Council has insisted on a political solution on the basis of the sovereignty and territorial

[8] Note of the Secretary General, UN Doc. S/4417/Add. 6 (1960); Buchheit, *Secession*, p. 146.
[9] Buchheit, *Secession*, p. 151.
[10] SC Res. 1345 of 21 March 2001.

integrity of the State concerned, such as in Cyprus,[11] Armenia/Azerbaijan (Nagorno-Karabakh),[12] Georgia (Abkhazia),[13] Bosnia and Herzegovina,[14] and Yugoslavia (Kosovo).[15] The General Assembly has adopted a similar attitude.[16] The only notable exception to this rule appears to be the early phase of the disintegration of Yugoslavia. In its first Resolution 713 (1991) relating to the Yugoslav conflict, the Security Council merely insisted on a 'peaceful and negotiated outcome of the conflict'.

B. *The United Nations and its duty of non-intervention*[17]

In practice, the UN organs have generally respected Article 2(7) of the Charter in regard to secession conflicts. This can be confirmed by a closer analysis of this non-intervention clause in light of the Organization's practices with respect to certain issues which are typically present in secession conflicts.

1. The main elements of Article 2(7)

The purpose of Article 2(7) of the Charter is to protect the sovereignty of the member States.[18] The concept of sovereignty has, however, been questioned in recent years.[19] States and UN organs, on the other hand,

[11] SC Res. 367 of 12 March 1975; SC Res. 1251 of 29 June 1999 ('Calling . . . upon all States to respect the . . . territorial integrity of the Republic of Cyprus, and . . . to refrain from . . . any attempt at partition of the island or its unification with any other country').

[12] SC Res. 874 of 14 October 1993.

[13] SC Res. 1393 of 31 January 2002 ('. . . which must include a settlement of the political status of Abkhazia within the State of Georgia').

[14] SC Res. 752 of 15 May 1992; SC Res. 1357 of 21 June 2001.

[15] SC Res. 1244 of 10 June 1999.

[16] See e.g. GA Res. 56/106 of 7 February 2002 (Somalia); GA Res. 55/116 of 4 December 2000 (Sudan); GA Res. 48/114 of 20 December 1993 (Azerbaijan).

[17] For a more elaborate treatment of this particular issue see G. Nolte, 'Article 2 (7)', *in* B. Simma (ed.), *The Charter of the United Nations – A Commentary* (Oxford University Press, 2nd edn, 2002), p. 148.

[18] *Case Concerning Military and Paramilitary Activities In and Against Nicaragua, ICJ Reports* 1986, p. 14, at p. 107, para. 205; R. Jennings and A. Watts (eds.), *Oppenheim's International Law* (Harlow, Essex: Longman Group UK Limited, vol. I, part 2, 9th edn, 1992), p. 428.

[19] See e.g. A. Rosas, 'The Decline of Sovereignty: Legal Perspectives', *in* J. Iivonen (ed.), *The Future of the Nation State in Europe* (Aldershot: E. Elgar Pub. 1993), p. 131, at p. 149; C. Schreuer, 'The Waning of the Sovereign State: Towards a New Paradigm for International Law', *EJIL* 4 (1993), pp. 447–71; R. Higgins, A. M. Slaughter, T. M. Franck, S. R. Ratner, C. Chinkin, Panel on 'The End of Sovereignty', *ASIL Proceedings* 88 (1994), pp. 71–87; A. van Staden and V. Vollaard, 'The Erosion of State Sovereignty: Towards a Post-territorial

have continued to insist on the importance of the principle.[20] In any case, sovereignty does not mean complete independence or absolute power over internal matters.[21] It can be understood more formally as independence within the limits of international law.[22] It can also be conceived more substantively as mentioned in the 1970 Declaration on Friendly Relations among States in which the General Assembly has consensually adopted a definition of 'sovereign equality' according to which 'all States enjoy the rights that are inherent in full sovereignty', and 'each State has the right freely to choose and to develop its political, social, economic and cultural systems'.[23] Today, neither a purely formal nor a fully substantive understanding of sovereignty is generally accepted or appropriate.[24] Moreover, it has recently been stressed that sovereignty implies not only rights for States but also responsibilities.[25]

The term 'to intervene' in Article 2(7) has been given a broad and also a narrow interpretation.[26] The drafters thought that the concept of intervention was so broad that it would even include discussions and recommendations with regard to domestic matters.[27] Under classical international law, however, the term 'intervention' has been most commonly defined as 'dictatorial interference', thus implying the use of force or a

World?', *ibid.*, p. 165 at p. 169; G. Fox, and B. Roth, 'Introduction: The Spread of Liberal Democracy and its Implications for International Law', *in* G. Fox, and B. Roth (eds.), *Democratic Governance and International Law*, (Cambridge: Cambridge University Press, 2000), p. 1; H. Stacy, 'Relational Sovereignty' *SLR* 55 (2003), pp. 2029–45.

20 See e.g. SC Res.1271 of 22 October 1999; SC Res. 1101 of 28 March 1997; SC Res. 1525 of 30 January 2004; SC Res. 1511 of 13 October 2003; SC Res. 1500 of 14 August 2003; GA Res. 58/189 of 22 December 2003; GA Res. 52/119 of 12 December 1997.

21 *An Agenda for Peace*, 'Report of the Secretary-General', A/47/277-S/24111, 17 June 1992, at p. 5, para. 17; *The Responsibility to Protect*, 'Report of the International Commission on Intervention and State Sovereignty', December 2001, http://www.dfait-maeci.gc.ca/iciss-ciise/pdf/Commission-Report.pdf (last visited May 11, 2004), p. 7 para 1.32 and p. 12 para 2.7; Higgins et al., 'The End of Sovereignty', p. 71; Fox, Roth, *Democratic Governance*; Stacy, 'Relational Sovereignty', pp. 2029– 45.

22 *Nationality Decrees in Tunis and Morocco, 1923, P C I J, Series B, No. 4*, p. 24; H. Steinberger, 'Sovereignty', *in* R. Bernhardt (ed.), *Encyclopedia of Public International Law*, vol. 4, (Amsterdam: North Holland, 2000), p. 518.

23 GA Res. 2625 (XXV) of 24 October 1970.

24 Nolte, 'Article 2 (7)', p. 151.

25 *The Responsibility to Protect*, 'Report of the International Commission on Intervention and State Sovereignty'.

26 G. Guillaume, 'Article 2 Paragraphe 7', *in* J. P. Cot & A. Pellet, *La Charte des Nations Unies*, (Paris Economica, 2nd edn., 1991), p. 149; B. Conforti, *The Law and Practice of the United Nations*, (The Hague: Kluwer, 1996), p. 146.

27 L. Preuss, 'Article 2, Paragraph 7 of the Charter of the United Nations and Matters of Domestic Jurisdiction', *Recueil des Cours* (1949-I), pp. 579–83.

similar form of 'imperative pressure'.[28] This narrow definition of intervention, however, hardly leaves any field of application for Article 2(7).[29] It should also be borne in mind that the concept of intervention in general international law expanded in the course of the debates which led to the proclamation of the Declaration on Friendly Relations among States in 1970. According to the Declaration, intervention comprises not only 'armed intervention' but also 'all other forms of interference or attempted threats against the personality of the State or against its political, economic and cultural elements'.[30] This was confirmed by the International Court of Justice in the Nicaragua judgment.[31] Although there have since been intense debates about possible new exceptions to what would otherwise be a prohibited intervention, particularly with respect to humanitarian intervention after the Kosovo intervention of 1999,[32] no further efforts have been made to narrow the general definition of intervention, as embodied in the Friendly Relations Declaration. The 2001 *Report on Intervention and State Sovereignty*, a rather representative assessment of the legal situation and policy options after the Kosovo intervention of 1999, emphasized that 'it should be the Security Council which should be making the hard decisions in the hard cases about overriding State sovereignty', thereby leaving intact the traditional understanding of intervention.[33] This state of general international law also affects the interpretation of the term 'to intervene' in Article 2(7).[34]

[28] H. Lauterpacht, 'The International Protection of Human Rights', *Recueil des Cours* (1947-I), p. 19; Preuss, 'Article 2, Paragraph 7 of the Charter of the United Nations', pp. 611.

[29] Conforti, *The Law and Practice of the UN*, p. 146; Preuss, 'Article 2, Paragraph 7 of the Charter of the United Nations', p. 606.

[30] GA Res. 2625 (XXV) of 24 October 1970.

[31] *Case concerning Military and Paramilitary Activities In and Against Nicaragua, ICJ Reports* 1986, p. 14, at p. 107, para. 205; G. Abi-Saab, 'Some Thoughts on the Principle of Non-Intervention', *in* K. Wellens (ed.), *International Law: Theory and Practice* (The Hague: M. Nijhoff Publishers, 1998), p. 231.

[32] See e.g. A. Cassese, '*Ex iniuria ius oritur*: Are We Moving towards International Legitimation of Forcible Humanitarian Countermeasures in the World Community?', *EJIL* 10, (1999), pp. 23–30; B. Simma, 'NATO, the UN and the Use of Force: Legal Aspects', *EJIL* 10 (1999), pp. 1–22; M. G. Kohen, 'L'emploi de la force et la crise du Kosovo: vers un nouveau désordre juridique international', *RBDI 32* (1999), pp. 122–48; F. Tesón, *Humanitarian Intervention: An Inquiry into Law and Morality*, (Irvington-On-Hudson: Transnational, 2nd edn, 1997), p. 146; G. Nolte, 'Kosovo und Konstitutionalisierung: Zur humanitären Intervention der NATO-Staaten', *ZaöRV* 59 (1999), pp. 941–60.

[33] *The Responsibility to Protect*, 'Report of the International Commission on Intervention and State Sovereignty', no. 6.14, p. 49.

[34] Nolte, 'Article 2 (7)', p. 154.

The key concept of Article 2(7) is, however, the term 'domestic jurisdiction'. The leading pronouncement on this concept is the judgment by the Permanent Court of International Justice in the case of *Nationality Decrees in Tunis and Morocco*. In this case the Court declared that matters solely within the domestic jurisdiction of a State are such 'matters which are not, in principle, regulated by international law' and 'with respect to which States, therefore, remained sole judge'. It continued with its famous dictum: 'The question whether a certain matter is or is not solely within the jurisdiction of a State is an essentially relative question; it depends on the development of international relations.'[35]

The decisive question in this context is not whether the State concerned is or is not competent under international law to take a particular action, but whether the action is governed in some respect by rules of international law.[36] This means that the concept of 'domestic jurisdiction' circumscribes areas which, taking into account the situation at hand, are not even *prima facie* affected by rules of international law. The development of international law after the Second World War has led to the coverage of so many fields by (consensual or customary) rules of international law that the definition of the 'matters under domestic jurisdiction' by the Permanent Court no longer leaves much room for such a concept.[37] This becomes clear when we look at the issues which are typically raised by secession conflicts.

2. Issues

Secession conflicts typically raise issues of self-determination, human rights and the Charter rules relating to the maintenance or restoration of peace and security. It is in these areas where the scope of Article 2(7) has been particularly eroded by practice.

a. Self-determination In the early years of the UN, a number of States have held that the manner in which a State applied the principle of self-determination fell essentially within its domestic jurisdiction. It was asserted that nothing could be more clearly within the domestic jurisdiction of a State than its own composition and political structure.[38] Over the years, however, support grew for the arguments speaking against this

[35] *Nationality Decrees in Tunis and Morocco, 1923, PCIJ, Series B, No. 4*, p. 24.

[36] Ibid., at p. 26; Nolte, 'Article 2 (7)', p. 156.

[37] Nolte, 'Article 2 (7)', p. 158.

[38] UN Repertory of Practice I, Suppl. 1, para. 160 (GA (X), Plen., 530th mtg., paras. 111 and 112).

interpretation. It was maintained that if Article 2(7) had an overriding effect, many provisions of the Charter would become meaningless.[39] It was also argued that self-determination was linked to human rights, which sufficed to remove it from domestic jurisdiction.[40] Ultimately, widespread agreement has developed that Article 2(7) is inapplicable as far as the principle of self-determination applies.[41]

b. Human rights The same is true with respect to human rights. According to former UN Secretary-General Boutros-Ghali, human rights are a concern not only of the United Nations, but of all actors on the global scene.[42] It is unquestionably true that States have vastly reduced their sphere of unfettered decision-making by agreeing to a large number of human rights declarations and treaties and by participating in the formation of a considerable body of customary international human rights law.[43] In addition, the sphere of domestic jurisdiction with respect to human rights has been significantly reduced for all States because the 'basic rights of the human person' have acquired the status of *ius cogens* as well as of customary international law.[44]

c. Maintenance of international peace and security The major issues concerning the question of whether a situation relating to international peace and security could fall within the domestic jurisdiction of a State are: internal conflicts, conflict prevention, and peacekeeping operations.[45] All of these issues can arise in secession conflicts.

The possible limits of the Security Council's powers under Chapter VII cannot be discussed with reference to Article 2(7) but rather with respect to Articles 39 and 24 of the Charter. Article 2(7) does, on the other hand, apply to all other activities of UN organs, in particular to those

[39] UN Repertory of Practice I, Suppl. 1, para. 160 (GA (X), Plen., 529th mtg., para. 175).

[40] UN Repertory of Practice I, Suppl. 2, para. 172 (GA (XI), 1st Com., 838th mtg., para. 20; 852nd mtg., para. 37).

[41] A. Cassese, *Self-Determination of Peoples* (Cambridge: Cambridge University Press, 1995), p. 174; Nolte, 'Article 2(7)', p. 163.

[42] UN Doc. GAOR A/51/PV.78 of 10 December 1996, p. 3.

[43] B. Simma, 'Human Rights', *in* C. Tomuschat (ed.), *The United Nations at Age Fifty* (The Hague: Kluwer, 1995), p. 263; D. McGoldrick, 'The Principle of Non-Intervention: Human Rights', *in* V. Lowe, and C. Warbrick (eds.), *The United Nations and the Principles of International Law* (London: Routledge, 1994), p. 94.

[44] *Barcelona Traction, Light and Power Co. Case, ICJ Reports* 1970, p. 3, at p. 32, para. 33; *United States Diplomatic and Consular Staff in Tehran Case, ICJ Reports* 1980, p. 42, para. 91.

[45] Nolte, 'Article 2 (7)', p. 164.

under Chapter VI and Article 99 of the Charter, as long as such activities are directed towards the resolution of internal conflicts which involve violations of, or threats to, human rights. These activities do not, however, concern matters which are essentially within the domestic jurisdiction of any State. This is a consequence of the development of the interpretation of Article 2(7) since 1945, especially in the area of human rights.[46] It is true that after the Kosovo intervention, a number of States have reinforced their insistence on the principles of sovereignty and non-intervention.[47] Those States, however, primarily object to unilateral uses of force, and not so much to the activities of UN organs.[48] One exception is the position which India took during the Kosovo crisis when it insisted that, since Kosovo was a recognized part of Yugoslavia, the United Nations had, under application of Article 2(7), no role in the settlement of domestic political problems of the country.[49] However, since the Security Council Resolutions 1199 and 1203 had previously defined the situation in Kosovo as a threat to international peace and security in the region, this meant that the situation could no longer be a matter which was exclusively within the domestic jurisdiction of a State. Even if the Security Council had not defined the situation under Chapter VII as a threat to the peace, Article 2(7) would not have applied because of the verifiable massive violations of human rights that were being perpetrated.[50]

The General Assembly has demanded in recent years that UN activities in the fields of early warning, good offices, and non-military measures to prevent disputes from escalating into conflicts should respect, *inter alia*, the principle of non-intervention.[51] The Security Council

[46] Secretary-General Kofi Annan, UN Press Release SG/SM/6613, 26 June 1998, p. 2.

[47] See e.g. SC Meeting 4950 of 22 April 2004, S/PV. 4950 (Resumption 1), p. 17 (Namibia); SC Meeting 4933, of 25 March 2004, S/PV. 4933 p. 23 (Russian Federation); Statement by the President of the Security Council of 25 February, 2004, S/PRST./2004/3; SC Meeting 4903 of 26 January 2004, S/PV. 4903 (Resumption 1), p. 18 (India), p. 22 (Morocco); SC Meeting 4899 of 23 January 2004, S/PV. 4899, p. 32 (Côte d'Ivoire); SC Meeting 4072 of 29 November 1999, S/PV. 4072, p. 14 (China), p. 15 (Russian Federation), p. 22 (Brazil), p. 32 (Libya), p. 35 (UAE), p. 41 (Sudan), p. 45 (Belarus).

[48] SC Meeting 4072 of 29 November 1999, S/PV. 4072, p. 7 (France).

[49] SC Meeting 3988 of 24 March 1999, S/PV. 3988, p. 16 (India).

[50] See Report of the UN Secretary-General of 17 March 1999, (S/1999/293); Letter of 26 February 1999 From the Secretary-General Addressed to the President of the Security Council, (S/1999/214); Report of the UN Secretary General Prepared Pursuant to Resolutions 1160 (1998), 1199 (1998) and 1203 (1998) of the Security Council of 30 January 1999, (S/1999/99).

[51] E.g. GA Plenary Meeting 51/219 of 18 December 1996; GA Plenary Meeting 47/120 of 18 December 1992 (An Agenda for Peace).

debate on the prevention of armed conflict which was held in the aftermath of the Kosovo conflict has made it clear that this is a question of degree. During this debate the delegate of the Netherlands claimed that the Council 'could not avoid addressing the internal situation of States wherever negative developments were apt to degenerate into large-scale atrocities and massive dislocation of civilians' and that this could not be rejected on grounds of domestic jurisdiction.[52] China, on the other hand, insisted that in cases in which a country's sovereignty would be concerned, preventive measures could only be taken upon request or with the consent and cooperation of the country or parties concerned.[53] These two statements are not necessarily incompatible. Disagreement mainly exists over the necessary proximity of the danger for the rights and values which are protected by international law. Since most States have expressed their support for 'a culture of prevention', it appears that the Kosovo crisis has ultimately resulted in a widespread agreement that the powers of the United Nations organs to initiate and undertake measures of conflict prevention outside Chapter VII without violating Article 2(7) are rather wide.[54] Since this agreement has been formed with a (potential) secession conflict in mind, it applies to such conflicts in particular.

The same is true for the good offices of the UN Secretary-General. Although some States insist that the Secretary-General's good offices require the consent of the States concerned, others consider that the Secretary-General possesses freedom of action in this respect.[55] In practice, the Secretary-General needs the willingness of the parties concerned to cooperate rendering the insistence on consent somewhat superfluous.[56] How far the Secretary-General may go when exercising this function is not only a question of the subject-matter at hand but also again a matter of degree. Again, the discussion of preventative measures after the Kosovo conflict seems to have reflected a widespread understanding that the powers of the Secretary-General are very broad.

52 SC Meeting 4072 of 29 November 1999, p. 28 (The Netherlands).

53 SC Meeting 4072 of 29 November 1999, p. 14 (China).

54 See *The Responsibility to Protect*, 'Report of the International Commission on Intervention and State Sovereignty', p. 35 para. 3.1, p. 38 para. 3.19.

55 GA Report of the Committee for Programme and Coordination of 13 September 1996, (A/51/16 (Part II)), paras. 20 and 46 at (k).

56 T. M. Franck and G. Nolte, 'The Good Offices of the Secretary-General', *in* A. Roberts and B. Kingsbury (eds.), *United Nations – Divided World*, 2nd edn (Oxford: Clarendon Press; New York: Oxford University Press, 2nd edn, 1993), pp. 143–82, at p. 174.

Finally, peacekeeping is an area in which the United Nations directly exercises powers within member States. In its annual reports on 'Comprehensive Review of the whole Question of Peacekeeping Operations in all their Aspects', the Special Committee of the General Assembly on Peacekeeping Operations regularly 'stresses that peacekeeping operations should strictly observe the principles and purposes enshrined in the Charter' and, in particular, 'that respect for the principles of sovereignty, territorial integrity and political independence, and non-intervention in matters that are essentially within the domestic jurisdiction of any State is crucial to . . . peacekeeping operations'.[57] Such statements show that Article 2(7) is still insisted upon in principle. The reports by the Special Committee, however, do not evince substantial practical issues on which Article 2(7) has been invoked. This is true even for the Kosovo and the East Timor missions, which have been endowed with the most extensive and complex mandates to date.[58]

III. Armed intervention by States or groups of States without UN authorization

Armed interventions in secession conflicts without UN authorization by other States, or groups of States have been comparatively rare. In fact, full-blown violent secession conflicts are themselves comparatively rare. This is true, in particular, for Africa, where most violent internal conflicts have taken place in recent years.[59] Third States have not openly intervened militarily in African secession conflicts. This appears to be true even for the Cuban troops which supported the government of Ethiopia during and after the conflict with Somalia over the Ogaden region in 1978.[60] In Latin America there have been virtually no violent secession conflicts, and in Asian countries there have been only very few.

[57] GA Report 54/839 of the Special Committee on Peacekeeping Operations of 20 March 2000, para. 51.

[58] GA Report 54/839 of the Special Committee on Peacekeeping Operations of 20 March 2000; S. Chesterman, *You, the People – The United Nations, Transitional Administration, and State Building* (Oxford: Oxford University Press, 2004) p. 126; J. Cerone, 'Minding the Gap: Outlining KFOR Accountability in Post-Conflict Kosovo', *EJIL* 12 (2001), pp. 469; H. Strohmeyer, 'Collapse and Reconstruction of a Judicial System: The United Nations Missions in Kosovo and East Timor', *AJIL* 95 (2001), p. 46; M. J. Matheson, 'United Nations Governance of Postconflict Societies', *AJIL* 95 (2001), p. 76; J. Klabbers, 'Redemption Song? Human Rights Versus Community-Building in East Timor', *LJIL* 16 (2003), p. 367.

[59] See Nigeria/Biafra, Ethiopia/Eritrea, Somalia/Ogaden, Somalia/Somalialand, and Sudan.

[60] K. Somerville, *Foreign Military Intervention in Africa* (London: Pinter Publishers; New York: St. Martin's Press), p. 136.

The point of departure for the legal analysis has been formulated by the International Court of Justice in the Nicaragua judgment. In this case the Court pronounced:

> Indeed, it is difficult to see what would remain of the principle of non-intervention in international law if intervention, which is already allowable at the request of the government of a State, were also to be allowed at the request of the opposition.[61]

Two important precedents confirm this *dictum* for secession conflicts, the cases of Northern Cyprus (1974) and Sri Lanka (1987). Following a military coup by Greek officers which called into question the internationally guaranteed constitutional framework of Cyprus, Turkey sent in troops on 20 July 1974 which occupied the northern part of the island.[62] Although this intervention was clearly designed to support the Turkish-speaking minority on the island, it was only on 15 November 1983 that a separate 'Turkish Republic of Northern Cyprus' was officially declared. Both the invasion and the declaration of independence were immediately denounced by the UN Security Council as a violation of the sovereignty of the Republic of Cyprus[63] and as an invalid attempt to create a new State.[64] Since the existence of the northern entity clearly depends on the presence of Turkish troops, these resolutions imply a continuing condemnation by the international community of States of the intervention and its objectives.

In 1987, Turkey critically compared both the universal rejection of its intervention in Northern Cyprus and the non-recognition by other States of the Northern Cypriot entity with the general acceptance of the intervention of Indian troops in Sri Lanka. In response, India and Sri Lanka pointed out that the critical difference lay in the invitation of the Indian troops by the Sri Lankan government.[65] When the Indian troops arrived in 1987, the conflict in Sri Lanka had already developed into a full-blown civil war between large parts of the Tamil minority and the

[61] *Case concerning Military and Paramilitary Activities In and Against Nicaragua, ICJ Reports* 1986, p. 14, at p. 126, para. 246.

[62] See generally, T. Oppermann, 'Cyprus', *in* Bernhardt (ed.), *Encyclopedia of Public International Law*, Vol. I (Amsterdam: Elsevier Science Publishers B. V., 1992), p. 923 with further references.

[63] SC Res. 353 of 20 July 1974.

[64] SC Res. 541 of 18 November 1983.

[65] See Letter dated 17 December 1987 from the Permanent Representative of India to the United Nations Addressed to the President of the Security Council (S/19354) and Letter dated 17 December 1987 from the Chargé d'Affaires A. I. of the Permanent Mission of Sri Lanka to the United Nations Addressed to the President of the Security Council (S/19355).

central government which was supported by the 70 per cent Singhalese majority of the population.[66] Not least because this conflict affected the Indian province of Tamil Nadu, India developed a serious interest in its resolution. In 1987, the governments of India and Sri Lanka agreed that a substantial number of Indian troops would implement and, if necessary, enforce a peace plan together with or even against the Tamil rebels.[67] After an initial phase of cooperation, Indian troops undertook a large-scale offensive which led to a temporary recapture of the northern parts of Sri Lanka, including its third-largest city, Jaffna. Interestingly, the Indo-Sri Lankan Accord and the subsequent operations by Indian troops were never criticized by other States.[68] To the contrary, during the military operations, the fourty-five member States of the Commonwealth praised the Accord as an act of highest Statesmanship.[69] Ultimately, however, the Indian intervention was not successful and the Indian troops were withdrawn in 1990.

The *dictum* of the International Court of Justice and the precedents of Northern Cyprus and Sri Lanka create a strong *prima facie* case that external armed interventions, at least in secession conflicts, are legal when carried out at the invitation of a government, while they are illegal when undertaken at the request of the separatists. This can be confirmed by a closer analysis of the pertinent principles of international law:

A. *Armed intervention at the invitation of the government*

The legality of armed intervention at the invitation of the government has never been entirely free of doubt.[70] Such interventions mainly raise concerns about their compatibility with the rules relating to the status

[66] See A. J. Bullion, *India, Sri Lanka and the Tamil Crisis 1976–1994* (London, New York: Pinter, 1995), p. 39.

[67] See the Agreement to Establish Peace and Normalcy in Sri Lanka of 29 July 1987, *ILM* 26 (1987), p. 1175; S. K. Hennayake, 'The Peace Accord and the Tamils in Sri Lanka', *Asian Survey* 29 (1989), pp. 401–15.

[68] G. Nolte, *Eingreifen auf Einladung – Zur völkerrechtlichen Zulässigkeit des Einsatzes fremder Truppen im internen Konflikt auf Einladung der Regierung* (Intervention upon Invitation – Use of Force by Foreign Troops in Internal Conflicts at the Invitation of a Government under International Law) (Berlin, New York: Springer, 1999), p. 529; Bullion, *India, Sri Lanka and the Tamil Crisis*, p. 115.

[69] Documented *in Survey of Current Affairs* 17 (1987), p. 347; *The Round Table* 77 (1988), p. 84.

[70] See Nolte, *Eingreifen auf Einladung*, p. 29.

of the inviting government, the use of force, non-intervention, and self-determination. The scant practice which relates specifically to secession conflicts militates in favour of the acceptability of this ground for intervention:

1. Status of the inviting government

Some have questioned the permissibility of interventions by foreign forces at the invitation of a government by arguing that a government which is challenged by a force that has obtained the control of at least some part of the territory of the State has lost the necessary representativeness to act in the name of the State.[71] If such a government were to be regarded merely as one of the parties to a violent conflict it would indeed be difficult to establish why this government should have the privilege of being able to procure military aid for itself from abroad. International law, however, has traditionally accorded the challenged government the privilege to speak and act in the name of the State as long as it has not lost effective control to such an extent that the prospect for the re-establishment of its authority has become marginal.[72] It is open to debate whether this traditional position is still fully valid in light of the more recent practice of the United Nations of regarding and treating the 'parties' of an internal conflict in many respects on an equal footing. Be that as it may, the issue does not arise in the same way in secession conflicts. In such conflicts, the position of the central government is challenged only with regard to a certain territory. Third States typically continue to treat the central government as the government of the State as such. It is only when the separatist forces have succeeded in establishing a stabilized *de facto* regime, such as in situations of divided States such as China, Germany (until 1990), Yemen (until 1990) that a prohibition on the use of force and, *a fortiori*,

[71] A. Tanca, *Foreign Armed Intervention in Internal Conflict* (Dordrecht, Boston: M. Nijhoff Publishers, 1993), p. 22; W. E. Hall and A. P. Higgins (eds.), *A Treatise on International Law* (Oxford: The Clarendon Press, 1924; reprint of 8th edn, Buffalo: William S. Hein Co., 2001), p. 347.

[72] See the contributions by O. Corten and Th. Christakis to this volume; see also L. Doswald-Beck, 'The Legal Validity of Military Intervention by Invitation of the Government', *BYIL* 56 (1985), p. 197; S. Talmon, 'Recognition of Governments: An Analysis of the New British Policy and Practice', *BYIL* 63 (1992), pp. 253 and 263; M. J. Peterson, *Recognition of Governments: Legal Doctrine and State Practice, 1815–1995* (Houndmills, Basingstoke, Hampshire: Macmillan; New York: St. Martin's Press, 1997), p. 42.

on inviting foreign troops for combat purposes against a *de facto* regime, applies.[73]

2. Use of force

Article 2(4) of the UN Charter prohibits the use of force by one State against another. Traditionally, the consent of the government of a State to the operation of foreign troops on its territory has generally been viewed as excluding the element of intergovernmental constraint which is necessary for Article 2(4) to apply.[74] It is true that the prohibition of the use of force has been extended to *de facto* regimes which, technically, implies a limited prohibition for governments which are confronted with such regimes to invite foreign troops to fight on their behalf.[75] It is also true that in recent years the regular condemnation of the use of force in internal conflicts by the Security Council has led some authors to reflect on whether Article 2(4) could be extended to cover such conflicts as well.[76] Such an extension of the rule would obviously affect the scope of permissible interventions upon invitation. So far, however, such tendencies have not matured into law and practice,[77] and there are good reasons why this has been the case. Such a rule would, after all, raise a whole host of difficult questions, including the determination of its threshold (necessary level of organized violence, e.g. terror attacks), the applicability of the right of self-defence, the recognition of exceptions for 'just' causes ('revolution', self-determination), and the responsibility of the United Nations to police the extended prohibition.

Another possible way to apply Article 2(4) to interventions upon invitation would be to consider transfrontier operations of foreign troops as a 'use of force in . . . international relations'. Such an approach could draw some support from certain formulations in the Friendly Relations

[73] J. A. Frowein, 'De facto Régime', *in* Bernhardt (ed.), *Encyclopedia of Public International Law*, Vol. I (Amsterdam: Elsevier Science Publishers B. V., 1992), p. 966.

[74] H. Kelsen, *Principles of International Law* (New York, Rinehart, 1952), p. 32; A. Cassese, 'Return to Westphalia? Considerations on the Gradual Erosion of the Charter System', *in* A. Cassese (ed.), *The Current Legal Regulation of the Use of Force* (Dordrecht, Boston: M. Nijhoff/Kluwer Academic Publishers, 1986), p. 506.

[75] See Frowein, 'De facto Régime'.

[76] See D. Wippman, 'Change and Continuity in Legal Justifications for Military Intervention in Internal Conflict', *Columbia HRLR* 27 (1996), p. 435; J. A. Frowein, 'Globale und regionale Friedenssicherung nach 50 Jahren Vereinte Nationen', *Zeitschrift für Schweizerisches Recht* 114 (1995), p. 269.

[77] See Nolte, *Eingreifen auf Einladung*, p. 204.

Declaration which are, albeit, mere variants of the principles of non-intervention and of self-determination (see below 3 and 4).[78]

This leaves the danger of an 'escalation of conflicts' as an argument which is specific to the prohibition on the use of force.[79] While this danger played an important role for many States during the Cold War, leading them to assert a broad interpretation of the rule against force and a narrow interpretation of its exception(s), it has played a surprisingly small role in the discussion of the use of force in internal conflicts. This may be connected with the fact that many developing countries at the time asserted the right of liberation movements to use force and receive armed support, a position which was required in order to emphasize the danger of escalation.[80] After the end of the Cold War, the danger-of-escalation-argument has lost much of its force.

3. Non-intervention

The principle of non-intervention between States is time honoured and its existence is well established. Its precise meaning and contours have, nevertheless, always been subject to dispute. Since 1945, the principle of non-intervention derives both from customary international law and from Article 2(1) of the UN Charter.[81] Its ambiguity, however, extends to the question of intervention upon invitation. The classical definition of intervention as 'dictatorial interference' would suggest the permissibility of interventions upon invitation, since acts which are conditioned upon the will of a recognized government can hardly be considered 'dictatorial' – a term that suggests autonomous and arbitrary decision-making. On the other hand, the definition of intervention by the authoritative General Assembly Declarations, of 1965 on Inadmissibility of Intervention, and of 1970 on Friendly Relations, seems to suggest the contrary. It describes one aspect of the duty of non-intervention as follows 'no State shall . . . interfere in civil strife of another State'.[82] This formulation appears to express a duty of third States to remain neutral towards any party to an internal conflict, including the government.

[78] GA Res. 2625 (XXV) of 24 October 1970: 'the duty to refrain from . . . participating in acts of civil strife . . . when the acts . . . involve a threat or use of force' and 'the duty to refrain from any forcible action which deprives peoples . . . of the principle of equal rights and self-determination . . .'

[79] Cassese, *The Current Legal Regulation*, p. 516.

[80] Nolte, *Eingreifen auf Einladung*, p. 216.

[81] *Case concerning Military and Paramilitary Activities In and Against Nicaragua, ICJ Report* 1986, p. 106, para. 202.

[82] GA Res. 2131 (XX) of 21 December 1965 and GA Res. 2625 (XXV) of 24 October 1970.

A closer analysis of the General Assembly Declarations of 1965 and 1970 is still of some importance today, because these Declarations represent the high tide of a broad understanding of the principle of non-intervention. Their drafting histories reveal two important points; the first is the disagreement which ensued at the time on whether the seemingly comprehensive formulation 'interference in civil strife' would indeed cover interventions upon the invitation of a government. In 1965, a number of Western States – with the notable exception of the United Kingdom[83] and some of their allies in the developing world – insisted that such interventions would remain legal even under such a broadly formulated prohibition,[84] and only very few States contradicted them.[85] The discrepancy between the broad prohibitory formulation and the more permissive picture which emerges from the debate can be explained by the political situation at the time, when, following the Stanleyville operation and the intervention in the Dominican Republic, the developing countries and the socialist States were exerting strong pressure to secure a broadly phrased prohibition, but were willing to acquiesce in an exception which was compatible with their notions of sovereignty and which could also prove useful for themselves.

The second important point is that the pertinent contributions to the debates of 1965 and 1970 clearly did not have secession conflicts in mind but rather struggles for power over the central government. This is an important point since, at the time, struggles for control of the central government were seen as a form of choice by the people of a State over its political status, a choice which, in principle, should remain uninfluenced from the outside. Secession conflicts, on the other hand, did not possess

[83] Report of the Special Committee on Principles of International Law concerning Friendly Relations and Co-operation Among States, A/5746, p. 116, para. 205.

[84] GAOR 18th Sess., 6th Com., 808th mtg., SR, 147, para. 24 (USA); GAOR 20th Sess., 1st Com., 1405th mtg., SR, 317, para. 19 (Belgium); GAOR 20th Sess., 1st Com., 1405th mtg., SR, 319, para. 43 (France); GAOR 20th Sess., 1st Com., 1422nd mtg., SR, 433, para. 43 (Italy); GAOR 20th Sess., 1st Com., 1422nd mtg., SR, 431, para. 32 (Austria); GAOR 18th Sess., 6th Com., 814th mtg., SR, 183, para. 45 (Greece); A/AC.119/SR.28, para. 6 (Argentina); GAOR 20th Sess., 1st Com., 1398th mtg., SR, 265, para. 31 (Thailand); GAOR 20th Sess., 1st Com., 1398th mtg., SR, 266, paras. 40 (Argentina); GAOR 20th Sess., 1st Com., 1402th mtg., SR, 293, paras. 21 and 23 (Kenya); GAOR 20th Sess., 1st Com., 1402th mtg., SR, 295, para. 36 (Cote d'Ivoire); GAOR 20th Sess., 1st Com., 1406th mtg., SR, 328, para. 32 (Jamaica); GAOR 20th Sess., 1st Com., 1400th mtg., SR, 280, para. 40 (Congo).

[85] GAOR 18th Sess., 6th Com., 804th mtg., SR, 121, para. 28 (Chile); 813th mtg., SR, 175, para. 13 (Albania); 820th mtg., SR, 221, para. 32 (Cuba); 822th mtg., SR, 230, para. 8 (Cyprus); GAOR 21st Sess., 6th Com., 935th mtg., SR, 212, para. 30 (Indonesia); see also Nolte, *Eingreifen auf Einladung*, p. 172.

the same legitimacy.[86] The drafting histories of the Declarations of 1965 and 1970 therefore clearly suggest that the broadly phrased prohibition to intervene in the civil strife of another State did not apply to intervention in secession conflicts by foreign troops at the invitation of the government concerned.

Interestingly, the General Assembly Declaration on the Inadmissibility of Intervention of 1981 no longer included the phrase 'no State shall . . . interfere in civil strife of another State' but only iterated 'the duty to refrain from any . . . military activity in the territory of another State without its consent'.[87] Although the Declaration of 1981 is less authoritative than the 1970 Declaration on Friendly Relations, the opposition to the Western States did not relate to this particular aspect.

After 1990, the principle of non-intervention played a lesser role in General Assembly resolutions, and efforts to define it more precisely have more or less subsided.[88] Although there have been new debates about its meaning and parameters, in particular with respect to election monitoring and humanitarian intervention, no fresh debates on the legality of intervention in internal conflicts at the invitation of a government as such have taken place. This is perhaps not surprising, given the fact that no major controversial cases of such interventions have occurred since 1990 (see below 5) with respect to such interventions in secession conflicts. In addition, the concept of 'sovereignty' leaves room for interventions upon invitation in both its formal and its substantive understanding. This is true, in particular, for interventions upon invitation in secession conflicts. By definition, such interventions at the invitation of the government aim at preserving the sovereignty and territorial integrity of the State. Even at a time when the call for a comprehensive prohibition of all forms of intervention was at its height, in principle, this form of intervention was insisted upon as being legal. Even up to the present day, it seems that the invitation of foreign troops by a government undergoing secession conflicts does not violate the principle of non-intervention.

86 See e.g. Report of the Special Committee on Principles of International Law concerning Friendly Relations and Co-operation among States, GAOR 24th Sess., 1969, Suppl. No. 19 (A/7619), 43, para. 121 (Kenya).

87 GA Res. 36/103 of 9 December 1981.

88 The principle of non-intervention has been invoked from time to time (e.g. GA Res. 48/83 of 16 December 1993), but no attempts at a new comprehensive definition have been undertaken. GA Res. 50/439 of 18 September 1995 (Cuba); GA Res. 58/70 of 7 January 2004; see The Responsibility to Protect, *supra* note 21, p. 31, para. 4.13; p. 47, para. 6.2; J. I. Levitt, 'The Responsibility to Protect: A Beaver without a Dam?', *Michigan JIL* 25 (2003), p. 153.

4. Self-determination

The right of self-determination is the right of all peoples 'freely to determine, without external interference, their political status'.[89] If all forms of violent political conflict which affect the political status of a people were regarded as an exercise of the right to self-determination, this right would clearly preclude the power of a government to invite foreign forces to combat secessionist forces. Some authors have indeed alleged that some States exercise their right to self-determination 'by ballot', others 'by bullet'.[90] Such a proposition may have contained some truth during the time of the Cold War. After 1990, however, violent internal conflicts are no longer regarded as one of several equally acceptable forms of self-determination, but rather as an undesirable form of domestic conflict resolution. This coincides with the advances in classical liberal and democratic theories on the international arena which see the core of the right of self-determination in the creation of a common (or majority) popular will by way of regular and peaceful procedures.[91]

Even if the right to self-determination were to include the right of a people to determine their political status 'by bullet', this would not necessarily mean that foreign interventions in secession conflicts upon invitation of the government are illegal. Secession conflicts, after all, are not about the political system within the framework of the State, but rather about whether a particular State should continue to exist in its previous form. It is clearly not the purpose of the principle of self-determination to shield every violent secession conflict from interventions at the invitation of the central government. This could only be the case if and as far as the right of self-determination would include a right to secession. During the Cold War, most States and the legal literature opposed the extension of the concept of a 'people' entitled to self-determination to other groups than those under colonial domination, alien occupation/subjugation or those subject to systematic racial discrimination.[92] This attitude was based mainly on the practical difficulty of conceiving of a concept of a 'people' which was not identical with the citizens of a State or a group under

89 Declaration on Friendly Relations: GA Res. 2625 (XXV) of 24 October 1970.

90 J. Dugard, *International Law – A South African Perspective* (Kenwyn, Juta & Co, 1994), p. 325; L. Doswald-Beck, 'Legal Validity of Military Intervention', p. 200.

91 M. Koskenniemi, 'National Self-Determination Today: Problems of Legal Theory and Practice', *ICLQ* 43 (1994), pp. 241–66.

92 A. Cassese, *Self-Determination of Peoples* (Cambridge: Cambridge University Press, 1995), pp. 59 and 102; C. Tomuschat, 'Self-Determination in a Post-Colonial World' *in* C. Tomuschat (ed.), *Modern Law of Self-Determination* (Dordrecht: M. Nijhoff Publishers, 1993), p. 11; Koskenniemi, 'National Self-Determination', p. 43.

colonial domination, or alien occupation or subjugation, and the concern that an imprecise and potentially unlimited right to secession would lead to the violent disintegration of many States. The International Court of Justice, conscious of this danger, proclaimed that the essential requirement of stability had to be taken into account when interpreting the principle of self-determination.[93] Thus, during the Cold War, States and the great majority of legal observers did not recognize that a secessionist part of the population – except colonial peoples and those under alien occupation or subjugation – could invoke the right to self-determination. This led to the conclusion that the invitation of foreign troops by a government with the purpose of combating secessionist forces did not violate the principle of self-determination.[94]

After the Cold War, the circumstances of the break-up of Yugoslavia, and in particular the recognition by the Badinter Commission of a limited right to self-determination for sub-State groups,[95] have given rise to debates about whether a right to secession should now be recognized.[96] Later cases however, such as Nagorno-Karabakh, Abkhazia, and Chechnya, have demonstrated that the attitudes of States and the great majority of writers on the subject have not changed. In these cases, the discrimination against parts of the population has been at least as pronounced as in the cases of Slovenia and Croatia. In addition, States have not questioned the right of governments to put an end to violent secession attempts by force. They have rather insisted on the respect for the principle of proportionality and other humanitarian rules in the conduct of hostilities. It would therefore go too far to deduce from the recognition of a limited right of self-determination for sub-State groups, a new limitation on the permissibility in principle to use force against violent secession attempts.

It is not entirely excluded that there exists a right of secession in extreme circumstances in which the coexistence of different groups within a State would obviously be impossible in the long run. Such circumstances, however, are hard to fathom and they have, thus far, not been recognized,

93 *Burkina Faso v. Mali*, *ICJ Reports* 1986, p. 567, para 25.

94 Doswald-Beck, 'Legal Validity of Military Intervention', p. 56; A. Randelzhofer, 'Article 2(4)', *in* B. Simma (ed.), *The Charter of the United Nations – Commentary* (Oxford: Oxford University Press, 2nd edn, 2002), p. 121.

95 'Badinter Arbitration Committee, Opinion No. 2, 3', *EJIL* 3 (1992), p. 184.

96 J. Crawford, 'State Practice and International Law in Relation to Unilateral Secession', available at http://canada.justice.gc.ca/en/news/nr/1977/factum/craw.html; R. McCorquodale, 'Self-Determination: A Human Rights Approach', *ICLQ* 43 (1994), p. 883; D. P. Haljan, 'Negotiating Quebec Secession', *RBDI* 31 (1998), pp. 191–216.

even in the cases of Biafra, Kosovo, or in Bosnia and Herzegovina. Therefore, even today, the right of self-determination does not, for all practical purposes, include a right to secession and therefore does not preclude the intervention by foreign troops in a secession conflict at the invitation of a government, except perhaps in the remote theoretical case in which no peaceful solution is imaginable even in the long term.[97]

5. Practice of intervention upon invitation of the government in secession conflicts

The preceding analysis is confirmed by the few cases of interventions by foreign troops in secession conflicts at the invitation of the central government. One example is the intervention in 1995 by regular Croatian forces at the official invitation of the government of Bosnia and Herzegovina to fight the Bosnian Serb forces in the UN protected zone of Bihac and surrounding areas of northwestern Bosnia.[98] This Croatian intervention led to the collapse and widespread retreat of Bosnian-Serb forces and thereby initiated, together with air attacks by NATO forces, the end of the Bosnian civil war, as was later confirmed by the Dayton Accords. The value of this precedent for establishing the permissibility of an intervention in civil wars at the invitation of the government, however, is limited. While the Croatian operation was undertaken in full accordance with the government of Bosnia and Herzegovina, this government certainly did not possess the full capacity to legalize this operation, since Chapter VII resolutions of the UN Security Council contained limitations on the powers of any government. And while it is true that the Croatian intervention was initially not criticized in the UN bodies, and only very mildly after it had achieved its purpose,[99] the lack of disagreement at the time can also be explained by the fact that the Croatian intervention served the goals of those resolutions and almost all UN member States.

Minor interventions by foreign troops at the invitation of the government against secessionist forces have occurred in micro-States; when insurgents attempted to establish the independence of Union Island, which is a part of the Caribbean State of St. Vincent and the Grenadines in

[97] Nolte, *Eingreifen auf Einladung*, p. 248.

[98] See Report of the Secretary-General S/1995/650 of 3 August 1995; Letter of the Secretary-General S/1995/666 of 7 August 1995.

[99] Security Council Presidential Statement of 3 August 1995.

1979, the government of that country called in troops from Barbados, not to fight the rebels, but to assist with the maintenance of internal security.[100] A similar situation occurred one year later in connection with the decolonization of Vanuatu (New Hebrides). When rebels tried to force the independence of the Vanuatu island of Santo, the newly established government of Vanuatu called in several hundred British and French troops. When these troops failed to crush the rebellion, additional troops from Papua New Guinea were called in.[101] These interventions in St. Vincent and the Grenadines and in Vanuatu did not provoke measurable international reactions. They have little value as a precedent, since the scale of the conflict was limited and the operations closely resembled a police action.

B. Armed intervention against the central government

The practice of armed intervention in secession conflicts against the will of the central government can be subdivided into those before 1945, those during the Cold War, and those after 1990.

1. Interventions before 1945

Before 1945, a number of armed interventions against the (central) government took place, aimed at bringing about secession. Successful examples include the support by France of the American War of Independence after 1776, the intervention in 1827 by France, Great Britain and Russia in favour of the Greek independence movement, the naval blockade imposed on Antwerp in support of the Belgian revolution of 1830, the US intervention in Cuba of 1898 which resulted in Cuban independence and, finally, the US intervention in 1903 which enabled the secession of Panama from Colombia.[102] These interventions occurred when international law did not yet recognize a general prohibition on the use of force and the principle of self-determination. In addition, it was only during the course of the nineteenth century that the principle of non-intervention gradually developed, as proclaimed by Great Britain, against the claims of the Post-Napoleonic Holy Alliance, and ultimately accepted as a general

[100] Keesings Contemporary Archives 1980, p. 30180.

[101] Keesings Contemporary Archives 1980, p. 30641.

[102] See T. M. Franck and N. Rodley, 'After Bangladesh: The Law of Humanitarian Intervention by Military Force', *AJIL* 67 (1973), pp. 277–85; M. Hartwig, 'Panama Canal', *in* Bernhardt (ed.), *Encyclopedia of Public International Law*, vol. 3, (Amsterdam, North Holland, 2000), p. 878, at 879.

rule according to which armed intervention was prohibited save for certain exceptions.[103] Such exceptions, however, were many, and they included interventions to save human lives. Officially, it was primarily this concern, and not the intention to bring about secession, that was ultimately emphasised as a justification by the intervening powers in the cases of Greece (1827) and Cuba (1898).[104]

The rule on non-intervention began to change during the inter-war period. This was not, however, due to a significant practice of armed intervention in secession conflicts but rather the result of developments with respect to the general rules on the use of force and non-intervention. On a universal level, the Covenant of the League of Nations and the Kellogg-Briand Pact led to substantial restrictions on the right of States to use force. On the regional level, the 1933 Good-Neighbour Policy of the United States of America towards the Latin American States included the recognition by the United States of a comprehensive prohibition on intervention.[105] Neither development had been influenced by previous secession conflicts owing to the post World War I issue of minority rights, the general problem of inter-State wars and the specific experience of the robust exercise of US hegemony over many Latin American States that were more pressing at that time.

2. Trends and practice during the Cold War

During the first forty-five years of its existence, the development of the United Nations system and its rules on the use of force and armed intervention was under the influence of two phenomena which pushed the system in opposite directions. The Cold War with its proxy wars and its threat of nuclear catastrophe led most States to insist on comprehensive and clear-cut prohibitions on the use of force and intervention, including third-party interventions in civil wars and secession conflicts. This was expressed by the Declarations of 1965 on Inadmissibility of Intervention and of 1970 on Friendly Relations between States,[106] as well as by the reactions of most States on armed interventions in internal conflicts by

[103] R. J. Vincent, *Non-Intervention and International Order* (Princeton University Press, 1974), p. 19; A. J. Thomas, and A. Thomas, *Non-Intervention* (Dallas: Southern Methodists University Press, 1956), p. 3.

[104] Franck and Rodley, 'After Bangladesh', pp. 280 and 285.

[105] G. H. Hackworth, *Digest of International Law*, vol. 2 (Washington: U.S. Gov. Print. Off., 1941), p. 327; O. C. Stoetzer, *The Organisation of American States*, (Westport: Praeger, 2nd edn, 1993), p. 20.

[106] GA Res. 2131 (XX) of 21 December 1965 and GA Res. 2625 (XXV) of 24 October 1970.

the two super-powers.[107] On the other hand, during the long process of decolonization, a doctrine of 'wars of national liberation' was asserted by many States and legal observers which implied that colonial peoples and peoples under alien occupation or subjugation had the right to use armed force against the colonial or occupation power.[108] This doctrine implied that national liberation movements, the recognized leaders of colonial and other peoples, would have the right to invite external military aid against the administrative powers. If accepted, this doctrine would have constituted an important exception to the rule that external armed intervention against the government is prohibited. Resistance to this doctrine by the Western States led to an ambiguous formulation in the Declaration on Friendly Relations (which only refers to 'aid'), and the disagreement eventually subsided in the eighties,[109] although the Israeli/Palestinian conflict remained one of self-determination on the UN agenda.

The divergent trends which characterized the period of the Cold War show that international law under the Charter has the potential of being both strict and absolute with respect to third-party intervention in secession conflicts and of developing large-scale exceptions. Depending on whether the emphasis is laid on the stability of the international order or on the justice of a particular cause, the result is different. Since both basic Cold War phenomena of the super-power conflict and decolonization have nearly disappeared, it would theoretically have been possible to interpret the situation after 1990 as *tabula rasa*, at least with respect to secession conflicts. It must be borne in mind, however, that the basic phenomenon which characterizes the situation since 1990, namely, ethnic conflict, was already present, both in practice and in the minds of the actors, since the early days of the United Nations.

During the Cold War the most important case of an armed intervention by a State in a secession conflict against the government was the intervention by India in 1971 in East-Pakistan.[110] This is a modern case in the sense that it had little to do with decolonization or the super-power rivalry. It rather concerned, to a substantial extent, democratic representation,

[107] Nolte, *Eingreifen auf Einladung*, p. 261.

[108] H. A. Wilson, *International Law and the Use of Force by National Liberation Movements* (Oxford: Clarendon Press, 1988), p. 94.

[109] A. Cassese, *Self-Determination of Peoples*, (Cambridge: Cambridge University Press, 1995), p. 199; H. J. Uibopuu, 'Wars of National Liberation', *in* Bernhardt (ed.), *Encyclopedia of Public International Law*, vol. 4 (Amsterdam: North Holland, 2000), p. 1408; see also G. Abi-Saab, 'Wars of National Liberation', *Recueil des Cours* (1979-II), pp. 353–445.

[110] See Franck and Rodley, 'After Bangladesh'.

refugee flows and gross human rights violations. The elections in Pakistan had led to the victory of the Awami League, a movement which demanded substantial autonomy for East-Pakistan against the intransigent West-Pakistani leadership. The situation deteriorated after the West-Pakistan dominated central government employed troops to suppress the autonomy movement and armed radicals. The crack-down resulted in large-scale killings, gross human rights violations and a refugee flow of nearly ten million into neighbouring India. India itself had a number of motives for intervening in East-Pakistan, including serious concerns that its eastern provinces would be destabilized by the refugee flow, the desire to see its main rival country on the subcontinent weakened by partition, and possibly humanitarian concerns. India's military intervention in December 1971 quickly led to the collapse of the Pakistani army and the establishment of effective control by the newly created Awami-League government which proclaimed the independence of Bangladesh.[111]

Until today, the Indian intervention in East-Pakistan is one of the rare cases of armed intervention in which the motive to bring about secession played an important role. This motive was not, however, acknowledged by India. India defended its intervention on grounds of self-defence in direct response to (pre-emptive) air strikes launched by Pakistan, as well as the refugee problem, and, at one particular moment, by invoking humanitarian concerns on grounds that the action was necessary for the protection of Bengalis from gross and persistent violations of human rights by the Pakistani army.[112] It has, however, been reported that India later retracted its 'pro-humanitarian interventionist' statements.[113] Finally, India argued that Bangladesh had become a victim of colonial rule, and was a non-self-governing territory.[114] Some legal observers justified the intervention as lawful assistance to a people struggling for their right to self-determination.[115] In the Security Council, however, several countries highlighted the secessionist aspects of the intervention and condemned

[111] See R. Sisson, and L. Rose, *War and Secession – Pakistan, India, and the Creation of Bangladesh* (Berkely: University of California Press, 1990), p. 206.

[112] UN Doc. S/PV.1606 of 4 December 1971, p. 86; S/PV. 1608 of 6 December 1971, p. 141; *UN Monthly Chronicle* (1972), p. 25.

[113] M. Akehurst, 'Humanitarian Intervention', *in* H. Bull (ed.), *Intervention in World Politics* (Oxford: Clarendon Press, 1984), p. 96; Tesón, *Humanitarian Intervention*, p. 207, contests this interpretation.

[114] UN Doc. S/PV.1606 of 4 December 1971, pp. 78 and 86.

[115] Tesón, *Humanitarian Intervention*, p. 206; K. Doehring, *Völkerrecht* (Heidelberg: C. F. Müller, 1999), p. 340.

aid given by one State to secessionist movements in another.[116] China, in particular, condemned the secessionist motives behind the intervention and compared the case of Bangladesh to that of Manchukuo.[117] Other States stressed respect for the unity and territorial integrity of Pakistan.[118] The debate in the United Nations and among legal writers ended somewhat inconclusively with respect to the legality of the intervention as such because of the self-defence argument. It did result, however, in a reaffirmation of the illegality of intervention with the purpose of bringing about secession and, despite some dissent from academia, of intervention with the purpose of saving human lives.[119] Although Security Council Resolution 307 (1971) did not specifically condemn the Indian intervention, it nevertheless contained an implicit rejection of the legality of the intervention.

3. Trends and practice after 1990

After the end of the Cold War, more armed interventions by third States against the (central) government have occurred which, with perhaps one exception, have not exhibited the tendency to alter the broad prohibition. The conflict between Azerbaijan and Armenia over Nagorno-Karabakh started before the demise of the Soviet Union, and later the Security Council, while criticizing only invasions 'by local Armenian forces', reaffirmed the 'respect for sovereignty and territorial integrity of all States in the region'.[120] The secession conflict in Moldova over Transnistria has certainly been heavily influenced by the presence and, at one point, even the operation of the remaining Russian troops against the forces of the central government. In this case, however, Russia has never openly supported the claim of Transnistria for independence and has engaged in credible negotiations over troop withdrawal and reconciliation.[121] The secession conflict

[116] Argentina, UN Doc. S/PV.1608 of 6 December 1971, p. 141; Saudi Arabia, *ibid.*, pp. 225–31.

[117] UN Doc. S/PV.1608 of 6 December 1971, p. 120.

[118] Syrian Arab Republic, UN Doc. S/PV.1606 of 4 December 1971, p. 245.

[119] See I. Brownlie, 'Thoughts on Kind-Hearted Gunmen', *in* R. B. Lillich (ed.), *Humanitarian Intervention and the United Nations* (Charlottesville: University Press of Virginia, 1973), p. 139; T. Farer, 'Humanitarian Intervention: The View from Charlottesville', *in* Lillich, *ibid.*, p. 157; Franck and Rodley, 'After Bangladesh', p. 302; Tesón, *Humanitarian Intervention*, p. 208.

[120] See e.g. SC Res. 822 of 30 April 1993; on the Nagorno-Karabach conflict generally, see T. Portier, *Conflict in Nagorno-Karabach, Abkhasia and South Ossetia: A Legal Appraisal* (The Hague: Kluwer, 2001).

[121] A. Williams, 'Conflict Resolution after the Cold War: the Case of Moldova', *Review of International Studies* 25 (1999), pp. 71–86; W. Hill, 'Making Istanbul a Reality: Moldova,

in Georgia over Abkhazia is said to have been influenced by Russian troops in favour of the Abkhaz side. Russia, however, has never acknowledged official involvement.[122] Finally, the secession conflict in Bosnia and Herzegovina between the Bosnian-Croats and the Serbs has been influenced by support from the Federal Republic of Yugoslavia in favour of the Serbs. This support, however, has been regularly condemned as illegal by the Security Council and has not consisted of operations by regular military forces but of lesser means.[123]

The only armed intervention in a secession conflict against the government which may have affected the applicable rules of international law is the Kosovo intervention by NATO countries. Characteristically, however, the intervening countries did not conceive the conflict as a secession attempt but as a 'humanitarian catastrophe' which necessitated the immediate application of armed force against a regime which grossly violated human rights, created a huge refugee flow and appeared to be engaged in a campaign of 'ethnic cleansing'.[124] This is not the place to engage in a discussion of the legality of humanitarian intervention after Kosovo.[125] It should be noted, however, that the NATO States made it clear that their campaign did not support secessionist goals.[126]

The attitude of the NATO States towards the Kosovo conflict conforms to that of most States with respect to secession conflicts. Even so-called 'kinship-States' usually take the position that they do not favour armed conflict or calling the territorial integrity of the State concerned into question. Thus, when armed clashes erupted in 2001 in Macedonia between fighters from the Albanian minority and government troops, the Albanian

Russia, and withdrawal from Transdniestria', *Helsinki Monitor* 13 (2002), pp. 129–45; Agreement on Withdrawal of Russian Forces from Moldova, incorporated in OSCE Final Act of 19 November 1999 of the Conference of the State Parties to the Treaty on Conventional Armed Forces in Europe, URL: http://www.osce.org/docs/english/1990–1999/cfe/cfefinact99e.htm (last visited May 10, 2004).

122 D. Trofimor, 'The Conflict in Abchasia: Roots', *in* Ehrhardt, Kreikemeyer and Zagorski (eds.), *Crisis Management in the CIS: Whither Russia?* (Baden-Baden: Nomos, 1995), p. 75.

123 SC Res. 752 of 15 May 1992; SC Res. 757 of 30 May 1992; SC Res. 787 of 16 November 1992; SC Res. 820 of 17 April 1993; SC Res. 838 of 10 June 1993.

124 See Statements by Canada, France, Germany, the United Kingdom and the United States, *in* H. Krieger (ed.), *The Kosovo Conflict and International Law* (Cambridge: Cambridge University Press, 2001), at pp. 390, 393, 399, 408 and 415.

125 See the contributions cited in footnote 32, and R. Uerpmann, 'La primauté des droits de l'homme: licéité ou illicéité de l'intervention humanitaire' *in* C. Tomuschat (ed.), *Kosovo and the International Community* (The Hague: Kluwer, 2002), p. 65.

126 See Statements by the Contact Group, France, Germany, Greece, and USA, in Krieger, *Kosovo Conflict*, pp. 121, 395, 402, 404 and 416.

Foreign Minister repeatedly stressed that Albania rejected the use of violence to achieve political goals and that 'the issues dealing with the framework of the national rights of communities in any country should be solved in a political manner and within the institutional framework of these countries'.[127]

IV. Conclusion

As regards external intervention, secession conflicts are not a separate legal category. The United Nations organs can address them within the hardly noticeable limits of Article 2(7) of the Charter as threats to the peace (Article 39) or as situations which are likely to endanger the maintenance of international peace and security (Chapter VI). Third States are bound, in particular, by the principles of the non-use of force, non-intervention and self-determination when they contemplate intervening by force in a secession conflict. The most important legal distinction in this context is whether a State intervenes on the side of the recognized government of the State concerned or on the side of its opponents. In practice, however, States have rarely intervened in secession conflicts with the express purpose of influencing the secession process in one direction. This is certainly due to the prevailing attitude in the international community that secession is disfavoured. Other justifications, such as humanitarian intervention, evacuation of nationals abroad and counter-terrorist operations are currently pertinent, but they apply equally to non-secession situations.

[127] Letter to the UN Security Council of 22 March 2001, www.mfa.gov.al/news/2001/22mar2001.htm; see also Press Statement of 15 March 2001, www.mfa.gov.al/news/2001/15mar2001.htm.

4

The role of recognition in the law and practice of secession

JOHN DUGARD AND DAVID RAIČ

I. Introduction

Recognition and secession are closely associated. Recognition has provided the *imprimatur* of statehood to seceding entities for over two hundred years. Early secessions were, however, generally portrayed as assertions of independence from colonial empires or unions rather than as secessions. As international law until recent times did not exalt respect for existing boundaries into a well-nigh absolute rule, secessions were anticipated, if not approved, as a natural consequence of decolonisation and the restructuring of States to correspond to historical realities and ethnic needs. Recognition served as the instrument for the validation of claims to statehood on the part of new entities by existing member States of the community of nations. In exercising their discretion to grant or withhold recognition, States were concerned with the requirements of effective government, independence, absence of control by another State and the ability on the part of the claimant State to conduct foreign affairs with existing States, and not with the question whether the emergence of a new State violated the territorial integrity of the State from which it sought to secede. The main prohibition on recognition was to be found in the rule against premature recognition. This probably explains why neither of the leading English-language treatises on recognition – Hersch Lauterpacht's *Recognition in International Law* (1947) and Ti-Chian Chen's *The International Law of Recognition* (1951) – treats secession as a topic worthy of separate attention in the context of recognition.

The position has changed radically since the end of decolonisation. Existing boundaries have become virtually sacrosanct, in both decolonised States and those that precede the age of decolonisation, and any attempt to redraw boundaries is viewed as a violation of the principle of territorial integrity, which is seen in some quarters to have assumed the character of a peremptory norm. Recognition of a new State that emerges from the territory of an existing State, without the consent of the latter, is in most circumstances viewed as a violation of international law. No longer is the question *when* may States recognise seceding entities, in order to avoid the prohibition on premature recognition, but *whether* they may do so at all. Recognition as an instrument of validation of secession has become a rare phenomenon as the States that comprise today's community of nations, with few and insignificant exceptions, all claim to be non-colonial, sovereign, independent States whose territorial integrity and existing boundaries must be respected in all circumstances.

Secession has become an accursed concept among nations, and the role of recognition of new States greatly reduced. Conversely, non-recognition, the instrument by which States collectively or unilaterally express their disapproval of territorial change, has become more important and more widely practised. The present study seeks to examine this state of affairs.

A preliminary point must be made however. The question of the legitimacy of recognition of a secessionary claim and a subsequently established State cannot be adequately answered without an analysis of a directly related question, namely, whether international law contains any rules which, if violated, form a bar to the acquisition of statehood by an otherwise fully effective entity and result in an obligation not to recognise the entity as a State. As will be seen later, international law does contain such rules, as, for instance, the prohibition of aggression. The question is, however, whether these legal effects apply in the case of unilateral secession as well. This means that the analysis of the question of the legitimacy of recognition of secessionary entities as States requires a discussion of the question whether the modern law of self-determination contains any rules regarding the legitimacy of secession. It can not *a priori* be excluded that the answer to the question of the legitimacy of recognition of secessionist claims depends on the answer to such questions as whether international law prohibits unilateral secession under all circumstances, whether a right of unilateral secession does not exist under international law or whether international law recognises such a right in specific circumstances only. Therefore, and notwithstanding the analysis of regional practice in the field of secession in other chapters in this book, this study will, of necessity, briefly deal with the question of the legitimacy of unilateral secession, using the analysis and conclusions reached in that context as stepping stones for approaching the principal issue: the legitimacy of recognition of secessionist claims by the international community.

Accordingly, this chapter will first describe the rules governing the recognition and non-recognition of States. Secondly, it will consider the rules governing the secession of States and the question whether they include a right to secede in any circumstances. Thirdly, it will examine the recognition and non-recognition practice of States in secessionist situations, with special emphasis on the post-1960 period, that is, following the adoption by the General Assembly of the United Nations of the Declaration on the Granting of Independence to Colonial Countries and Peoples, Resolution 1514 (XV), which sought to balance the competing values of self-determination and territorial integrity. Considerations of time and space prevent an exhaustive study of this practice. Instead, special cases have been selected to illustrate the manner in which recognition is withheld or granted. Fourthly, this chapter will evaluate the role of recognition and non-recognition in a world committed to self-determination and human rights, but hostile to territorial change.

II. Recognition: the basic rules, practices and principles

The traditional criteria for statehood, as described in the Montevideo Convention of 1933,[1] are a permanent population, a defined territory, a government that is in effective control of its territory and independent of any other authority, and a capacity to enter into relations with other States. More recently, since human rights and self-determination have become more important in international law, it has been suggested that for a new entity to succeed in a claim for statehood, it should meet the standards and expectations of the international community on these subjects. This development was given support by the Guidelines on the Recognition of New States in Eastern Europe and in the Soviet Union issued by the European Community in 1991,[2] and later extended to Yugoslavia, which sought to make recognition of States dependent on compliance with international norms relating to self-determination, respect for human rights and the protection of minorities.

In the absence of any international authority charged with the task of determining whether an entity claiming to be a State *in fact* complies with the above requirements, it is for each State or international organisation to make such a determination on the available factual information and

[1] See Article 1 of the 1933 Montevideo Convention on the Rights and Duties of States, 165 *L.N.T.S.*, p. 19.

[2] *BYIL* 62 (1991), p. 559; *ICLQ* 41 (1992), p. 477.

on its own assessment of whether the new entity should be admitted to the community of nations. This determination is known as recognition.

Recognition may be either unilateral or collective. In the former case an individual State, already accepted as a State by the community of nations, recognises that another entity, claiming to be a State, meets the requirement of statehood and is therefore to be regarded as a State, with the rights and duties attached to statehood. Collective recognition occurs when a group of States, such as the European Community or the United Nations, recognises the existence of a claimant State directly, by an act of recognition, or indirectly, by the admission of the State to the organisation in question.

A. *Unilateral recognition*

Different views are held on the purpose and consequences of unilateral recognition. Two principal schools of thought dominate this debate: the constitutive, and the declaratory. According to the constitutive school, the recognition of a claimant entity as a State creates or constitutes the State.[3] Recognition therefore becomes an additional requirement of statehood. The declaratory school, on the other hand, maintains that an entity becomes a State on meeting the factual requirements of statehood and that recognition by other States simply acknowledges (declares) 'as a fact something that has hitherto been uncertain'.[4]

The main objection to the constitutive view is, if the claimant State is recognised by State A and not by State B, it is in effect both a State and a non-State. North Korea was for many years recognised as a State by the Soviet Union, China and some fifty other States, while it remained unrecognised by the United States, the United Kingdom and many other States. Was it a State? Or was it a State only for those States that recognised it? Clearly such uncertainty is undesirable.

What Hersch Lauterpacht described as the 'grotesque spectacle'[5] of an entity being a State for some States and not for others could be avoided if States were to recognise entities as soon as they complied with the requirements of statehood set out in the Montevideo Convention. Thus H. Lauterpacht contended that, once these requirements had been met,

[3] See H. Kelsen, 'Recognition in International Law: Theoretical Observations', *AJIL* 35 (1941), p. 605.

[4] J. L. Brierly, *Law of Nations*, 6th edn (Oxford University Press, 1963), p. 139.

[5] H. Lauterpacht, *Recognition in International Law* (Cambridge: Cambridge University Press, 1947), p. 78.

> [t]he existing States are under the duty to grant recognition. In the absence of an international organ competent to ascertain and authoritatively to declare the presence of the requirements of full international personality, States already established fulfil that function in their capacity as organs of international law. In thus acting they administer the law of nations. This legal rule signifies that in granting or withholding recognition States do not claim and are not entitled to serve exclusively the interests of their national policy and convenience regardless of the principles of international law in the matter.[6]

Unfortunately Lauterpacht's contention is not supported by State practice. States do not regard themselves as being under a legal duty to recognise entities as States once they comply with the requirements of statehood. In most cases they do recognise States that meet these requirements, so recognition is not an arbitrary process. On the other hand, it is essential to appreciate that political considerations do influence the decision and may prompt a State to recognise an entity prematurely or to refuse to grant it recognition.

The political nature of recognition has prompted support for the declaratory school[7] which accepts that an entity that meets the requirements of statehood becomes a State regardless of recognition. This may be true in the case of a State which has been recognised by some States but not by others. It is, however, difficult to maintain that an entity that has received recognition by none or very few States, such as the Turkish Republic of Northern Cyprus or South Africa's Bantustan States of Transkei, Bophuthatswana, Venda or Ciskei, can claim to be a State, as it cannot demonstrate its capacity to enter into relations with other States and thus from a functional point of view cannot be described as a State.[8]

[6] Ibid., p. 6.

[7] The Badinter Arbitration Commission, charged with the task of monitoring compliance with the European Community's guidelines for the recognition of States following the dissolution of Yugoslavia, found that 'the existence or disappearance of the State is a question of fact; that the effects of recognition by other States are purely declaratory': Opinion 1 in *ILR* 92, p. 162.

[8] In *Caglar v Billingham (Inspector of Taxes)* the Tribunal stated: 'In view of the non-recognition of the Turkish Republic of Northern Cyprus by the whole of the international community other than Turkey we conclude that it does not have functional independence as it cannot enter into relations with other States', ILR 108, p. 545, para. 182. *Sed contra*, see M. Shaw, *International Law* 5th edn (Cambridge University Press, 2003), p. 371, who states that if an entity were totally unrecognised 'this would undoubtedly hamper the exercise of its rights and duties . . . but it would not seem in law to amount to a decisive argument against statehood itself', p. 245.

In the final resort,[9] therefore, recognition does have a role to play in the creation of a State. This explains the complexity of the constitutive versus declaratory debate. Most 'declaratorists' are compelled to acknowledge the need for at least some recognition on the part of existing States as a precondition of statehood.[10]

B. *Collective recognition*

In recent years, the European Community (now European Union) has sought to speak with one voice on the recognition of new States in Europe.[11] This is a wise policy that has helped to produce some consistency in recognition practice in Europe. Here, States have exercised their individual right of recognition collectively in a manner which does not depart substantially from traditional recognition practice. More controversial is the question whether admission to the United Nations constitutes recognition.

Membership in the United Nations is limited to States only. This is clear from Articles 3 and 4, and it is reaffirmed by numerous other references to 'State' in the Charter which indicate that the rights and obligations contained in the Charter are linked to statehood.[12] Once a State is admitted to the United Nations, its acceptance as a State for all purposes is assured. This explains the alacrity with which claimant States seek admission to the United Nations, as illustrated by the hasty admission of Slovenia, Croatia, and Bosnia-Herzegovina in May 1992, in order to confirm their separation from Yugoslavia. Today, apart from Israel whose statehood is still denied by some Arab States, all members of the United Nations are accepted as States despite the fact that several probably would not have received widespread recognition by individual States had they been left to make a determination of statehood in accordance with the traditional criteria. Thus it is fair to conclude that many States have achieved statehood by admission to the United Nations and that this procedure for recognition co-exists alongside the traditional method of unilateral

[9] H. Bull, *The Anarchical Society* (London: Macmillan, 1977), wrote that a community that claims to be sovereign 'but cannot assert this right in practice, is not a State properly so called', p. 8.

[10] J. Crawford, *The Creation of States in International Law* (Oxford: Oxford University Press 1979), p. 74.

[11] For example, in the cases of Croatia, Slovenia, Bosnia-Herzegovina and Macedonia: *ICLQ* 41 (1992), p. 471; *ICLQ* 42 (1993), p. 433.

[12] Articles 2(4)–(7); 11(2): 33, 35(2); 43(3); 50; 52(3); 53(1)–(2); 59; 79; 80(1); 81; 9(2); 107; 110(1)–(4).

recognition. Any description of the law of recognition that fails to take account of this development cannot lay claim to be an accurate reflection of State practice.[13]

The claim that admission to the United Nations constitutes or confirms the existence of a State has important implications for the debate between 'constitutivists' and 'declaratorists'. The main criticisms directed at the constitutive school are, first, the anomalous situation that arises where a State is recognised by State A but not by State B, and is therefore both an international person and not an international person at the same time, and, secondly, the fact that the constitutive doctrine gives individual States the arbitrary power to recognise an entity as a State or to withhold recognition. Both these weaknesses in the 'constitutivist' position are remedied by the collective recognition of States through the United Nations. If all member States within the United Nations recognise each other's existence as States – with the above-mentioned exception of Israel by some Arab States – it follows logically that the 'grotesque spectacle'[14] of an entity being a State for some States but not for others is no longer a practical possibility. Furthermore, the arbitrary and subjective individual State decision is replaced by collective decision of the United Nations.

C. *Collective non-recognition*[15]

The United Nations plays an important role in the admission of new States to the international community by the process of collective recognition. Conversely, it may block the acceptance of a State by means of collective non-recognition.

The doctrine of non-recognition of entities claiming statehood has its origins in the non-recognition of the puppet State of Manchukuo. When Japan invaded the Chinese province of Manchuria in 1932 and set up the State of Manchukuo, the Secretary of State of the United States, Mr Henry Stimson, declared that the United States would not recognise Manchukuo on the ground that it had been created in violation of the Pact of Paris of 1928, in which States renounced war. This was followed by a resolution of the Assembly of the League of Nations, calling upon its members not to recognise Manchukuo.[16] Jurisprudentially, the

[13] J. Dugard, *Recognition and the United Nations* (Cambridge: Grotius, 1987); but see D. Raič, *Statehood and the Law of Self-Determination* (Dordrecht: Kluwer, 2002), pp. 39–47.

[14] Lauterpacht, *Recognition in International Law*, p. 78.

[15] *See* generally Dugard, *Recognition and the United Nations*.

[16] *Ibid.*, pp. 29–35.

doctrine of non-recognition is founded on the principle of *ex injuria jus non oritur*.[17] When this doctrine of non-recognition was first expounded, the idea that there were peremptory norms or *jus cogens* was undeveloped. Today, it is accepted that there are certain basic norms upon which the international order is founded and that these are peremptory and may not be derogated from under any circumstances. The modern law of non-recognition takes cognisance of this development. An act in violation of a norm having the character of *jus cogens* is illegal and is therefore null and void. This applies to the creation of States and to the acquisition of territory. States are under a duty not to recognise such acts under customary international law and in accordance with the general principles of law. This has been confirmed by the International Law Commission in its Draft Articles on the Responsibility of States for Internationally Wrongful Acts of 2001.[18] Resolutions of the Security Council and the General Assembly are, from a jurisprudential perspective, declaratory in the sense that they confirm an already existing duty on States not to recognise such situations. In practical terms, such resolutions are essential, as they provide certainty by substituting, for the decision of an individual State, a collective determination of illegality and nullity.

In accordance with this doctrine, the United Nations has directed States not to recognise claimant States created on the basis of aggression (e.g., the Turkish Republic of Northern Cyprus[19]), systematic racial discrimination and the denial of human rights (e.g., South Africa's Bantustan States[20]) and the denial of self-determination (e.g., Katanga[21] and Rhodesia[22]).

III. Secession in international law[23]

In its external dimension, political self-determination is implemented through the formation of an independent State, or through integration in or association with an independent State. Secession is a means by which

[17] Lauterpacht, *Recognition in International Law*, p. 420.

[18] Articles 40 and 41. See, too, the commentary on Article 41(2): 'Report of the International Law Commission', 53rd session, G.A.O.R. 50th session, Supplement No. 10 (A/56/10) 286–289.

[19] SC Res. 541 of 18 November 1983 and SC Res. 550 of 11 May 1984.

[20] See Dugard, *Recognition and the United Nations*, pp. 98–108. J. Dugard, *International Law. A South African Perspective* 2nd edn (Capetown: Juta, 2000), pp. 445–61.

[21] Dugard, *Recognition and the United Nations*, pp. 86–90.

[22] *Ibid.*, pp. 90–8.

[23] See Raič, *Statehood and the Law of Self-Determination*, pp. 308–97.

external self-determination may be achieved.[24] Secession may be defined as the separation of part of the territory of a State carried out by the resident population with the aim of creating a new independent State or acceding to another existing State.[25] Unilateral secession is the separation of part of the territory of a State which takes place in the absence of the prior consent of the previous sovereign.[26] The 'right' of unilateral secession under international law therefore refers to the right of a people to separate a part of the territory of the parent State on the basis of that people's right of self-determination. The potential holder of any right of secession would therefore be a subgroup within a State which is the subject of the right of self-determination.

One will search in vain for an explicit prohibition of unilateral secession in international instruments. The same is true for the explicit recognition of such a right. The only international instruments which contain a reference, and then only implicit, to a right of secession are the 1970 Declaration on Principles of International Law concerning Friendly Relations and Cooperation among States in accordance with the Charter of the United Nations,[27] and the 1993 Vienna Declaration and Programme of Action adopted by the World Conference on Human Rights on 25 June 1993.[28] The former Declaration states in Paragraph 7 of Principle V, after affirming that all peoples have the right of self-determination, that

> [n]othing in the forgoing paragraphs shall be construed as authorising or encouraging any action which would dismember or impair, totally or in part, the territorial integrity or political unity of sovereign and independent States conducting themselves in compliance with the principle of equal rights and self-determination of peoples as described above and thus possessed of a government representing the whole people belonging to the territory without distinction as to race, creed or colour.

[24] Secession is thus but one such means. Other means are, for instance, dissolution (peaceful or consensual) and merger/union.

[25] C. Haverland, 'Secession', in: *Encyclopedia of Public International Law*, Vol. 10 (Amsterdam: Elsevier Science Publishers B.V., 1987), p. 384.

[26] Crawford, *The Creation of States in International Law*, p. 246.

[27] GA Res. 2625 (XXV) of 24 October 1970, (hereinafter 'Friendly Relations Declaration').

[28] A/CONF.157/23 (25 June 1993). Paragraph I(2) of this Declaration states: '[n]othing in the forgoing paragraphs shall be construed as authorising or encouraging any action which would dismember or impair, totally or in part, the territorial integrity or political unity of sovereign and independent States conducting themselves in compliance with the principle of equal rights and self-determination of peoples as described above and thus possessed of a government representing the whole people belonging to the territory without distinction *of any kind*' (emphasis added).

The text of the Friendly Relations Declaration regarding the principle of self-determination was the subject of much discussion in the Special Committee on Principles of International Law Concerning Friendly Relations and Co-operation Among States which was established by the General Assembly in 1968. As the title of the Declaration suggests, the instrument is primarily concerned with 'Friendly Relations and Co-Operation *Among States*'.[29] Because of this, it must be assumed that the negative formulation in Paragraph 7 that the principle of self-determination 'shall not be construed as authorising or encouraging any action which would dismember or impair, totally or in part, the territorial integrity or political unity of sovereign and independent States [. . .]' was intended to be addressed to third States. It may be argued therefore *a contrario* that third States would be entitled to support a people which attempts to secede, even if such support would eventually lead to the infringement of the territorial integrity of the target State. But this would only be permissible if the target State does not conduct itself in compliance with the right of self-determination of the people concerned, and such support would have to be in accordance with the other principles contained in the Friendly Relations Declaration.[30]

At the outset, it must be emphasised that Paragraph 7 was accepted against the background of intensive discussions in the Special Committee with regard to the existence or non-existence of a right of secession under international law. These discussions therefore must be taken into consideration for an understanding of the scope and meaning of the paragraph. Although the text of the paragraph may be interpreted in several ways, it is clear that it does not exclude a right of secession. It may therefore be argued that the provision is either neutral with respect to secession or, albeit implicitly, acknowledges the legitimacy of secession under certain circumstances, including the denial of internal self-determination and/or a serious violation of fundamental human rights. The latter position has been accepted by many scholars.[31]

On the basis of the discussions in the Special Committee, it can be concluded that Paragraph 7 implicitly endorses the legitimacy of

[29] Emphasis added.

[30] See Para. 2 of the General Part of the Friendly Relations Declaration.

[31] A. Cassese, *Self-Determination of Peoples: A Legal Reappraisal* (Cambridge: Cambridge University Press, 1995), p. 118. To the same effect see, e.g., F. L. Kirgis Jr., 'The Degrees of Self-Determination in the United Nations Era', *AJIL* 88 (1994), p. 304, at pp. 305–6; S. R. Chowdhury, 'The Status and Norms of Self-Determination in Contemporary International Law' in: H. Meijers and E. W. Vierdag (eds.), *24 Essays on International Law and Relations in Honour of A. J. P. Tammes* (Sijthoff & Noordoff, 1977), p. 72, at p. 80.

secession in the case of unrepresentative or discriminatory governments. Here, the argument would run as follows. The permissibility of 'action' by third States which may 'dismember or impair the territorial integrity' of the parent State must be linked to the justifiability of secession. While it was not the object of the Friendly Relations Declaration to address the existence of a right of secession under international law, the issue is indirectly dealt with in Paragraph 7 in the context of the permissibility of 'action' by third States in those cases where the right to self-determination is seriously violated by the parent State. This circumstance is determinative of the legitimacy of the secession attempt and would raise the situation to the level of international concern. This, in turn, would permit third State 'action' – including recognition – in support of that attempt. The *travaux préparatoires* with respect to the principle of self-determination in the Friendly Relations Declaration contain support for this argument.[32]

It may thus be argued that Paragraph 7 of the Friendly Relations Declaration implicitly acknowledges a *qualified* right of secession within the framework of the legality of inter-State conduct. In effect this means that the justifiability of the attempt at secession by a people is made dependent on the legitimacy and conduct of the government of the parent State and this must be taken into consideration in determining the lawfulness of third State action in support of that people's right of self-determination. Paragraph 7 therefore limits the general obligation contained in Paragraph 8 that '[e]very State shall refrain from any action aimed at the partial or total disruption of the national unity and territorial integrity of any other State or country'. Because a right of secession will come into existence only if the right of self-determination can not be exercised internally, this line of reasoning suggests that, at a certain point, the right of internal

[32] See, e.g., Statement of the Soviet Union, A/AC.125/SR.106 (1969), para. 62; Statement of Yugoslavia, A/AC.125/SR.40 (1966), para. 10; Statement of the Netherlands, A/AC.125/SR.107 (1969), para. 85. See also Statement of Kenya, A/AC/125/SR.69 (1967), para. 22, '[s]elf-determination must not be used as a licence for the fragmentation or emasculation of sovereign States exercising their sovereignty under conditions of equal rights for all their people. As set out in the Charter, the principle did not sanction an *unjustifiable* claim to secession by a minority group which traditionally formed part of an independent sovereign State' (emphasis added)); Statement of Ghana, A/AC.125/SR.68 (1967), para. 12; Statement of the United States, A/AC.125/SR.44 (1966), para. 12 ('no rational international legal order could exist if the Charter were taken to sanction an *unlimited* right of secession by indigenous peoples from sovereign and independent States' (emphasis added)).

self-determination converts into a right of external self-determination. Until that point, however, the exercise of the right of self-determination is limited by the right of territorial integrity of States.[33] This means that while the obligation to respect the principle of territorial integrity is addressed to third States, the principle is linked to the interpretation, and hence the exercise, of the right of self-determination, which must normally be implemented within the external boundaries of the parent State. This conclusion is supported by subsequent practice. In the Organisation for Security and Cooperation in Europe (OSCE) Charter of Paris, for instance, the participating States declare:

> We reaffirm the equal rights of peoples and their right to self-determination in conformity with the Charter of the United Nations and with the relevant norms of international law, including those relating to territorial integrity of States.

The fact that this provision must be interpreted not only as an obligation for third States to respect the principle of territorial integrity, but also as a *limitation* on the exercise of self-determination by peoples is made clear in the 'Declaration on the Situation in Yugoslavia' issued by the European Community on 5 July 1991:

> [The Community and its member States] stress again that it is only for the peoples of Yugoslavia themselves to decide on the country's future . . . The Community and its member States call for a dialogue . . . between all parties on the future of Yugoslavia, which should be based on . . . the right of peoples to self-determination in conformity with . . . the relevant norms of international law, including those relating to territorial integrity of States (Charter of Paris).[34]

The text is clear that the implementation of the right of self-determination by 'the peoples of Yugoslavia' must be in conformity with the principle of territorial integrity. This does not mean that 'the peoples of Yugoslavia' as such are regarded as the (additional) addressees of the principle of territorial integrity. What it means is that the scope and implementation

[33] See, e.g., F. Capotorti, 'Cours Général de Droit International Public', *Recueil des Cours* IV (1994), p. 13, at p. 36.

[34] Reprinted in S. Trifunovska (ed.), *Yugoslavia Through Documents. From its Creation to its Dissolution* (Brill Academic Publishers, 1994), p. 310. An identical formulation is used in the so-called Brioni Accord which was concluded between the Yugoslav parties and which provided for a three-month suspension of the proclamations of independence of Croatia and Slovenia. Reprinted in *ibid.*, p. 312.

of the right of self-determination must be *interpreted* in the light of the fundamental principle of territorial integrity of States under international law, which necessarily excludes the thesis that self-determination includes an absolute right of unilateral secession.

Paragraph 7 of Principle V of the Friendly Relations Declaration, and the almost identical provision in the 1993 Vienna Declaration, therefore reflect, albeit implicitly, a general principle that the right of self-determination is limited by the right of territorial integrity of States. This means that States are entitled to resist attempts at unilateral secession by peoples within their borders if they are carried out in the absence of special circumstances which serve to legitimise such claims. However, the right of territorial integrity is in its turn limited by international law. It must be exercised in conformity with that State's obligations under, *inter alia*, the law of self-determination, the law concerning human rights and humanitarian law.

Consequently, if the penultimate paragraph of the Friendly Relations Declaration implicitly acknowledges the existence of a right of unilateral secession for peoples within existing States, it is necessarily a qualified right. A people is only entitled to secede from an existing State under certain exceptional circumstances for the purpose of safeguarding that people's collective identity and the fundamental individual rights of its members, as well as to restore its freedom. If such circumstances do not exist, the principle of territorial integrity is to prevail, which means that the right of self-determination must be exercised *within* the external boundaries of the parent State. Thus, where the parent State respects the right of internal self-determination of a people and the human rights of its members, any act of unilateral secession aimed at the implementation of the right of self-determination externally would amount to an abuse of that right and a violation of the law of self-determination. The view that a right of secession exists under certain exceptional circumstances will be referred to in this study as 'the qualified secession doctrine'.[35]

The existence of such a qualified right of secession has received strong support in the legal literature.[36] It also enjoys support in judicial

[35] See Raič, *Statehood and the Law of Self-Determination*, pp. 324–32.

[36] See, e.g., Capotorti, 'Cours Général', p. 36; K. Doehring, 'Self-Determination' in: B. Simma (ed.), *The Charter of the United Nations, A Commentary* (Oxford: Oxford University Press, 1994), p. 56, at pp. 66; R. Emerson, 'The Logic of Secession', *YLJ* 29 (1979–80), p. 802 at pp. 808–9; T. M. Franck, 'Opinion Directed at Question 2 of the Reference re Secession of Quebec in *Amicus curiae*, 1997' in: *Rapports d'experts de l'amicus curiae*,

decisions and opinions. The Commission of Rapporteurs in the Aaland Island dispute denied the existence of any absolute entitlement to secession by a minority, but it did not rule out a right of secession under all circumstances:

> The separation of a minority from the State of which it forms part and its incorporation in another State can only be considered as an altogether exceptional solution, a last resort when the State lacks either the will or the power to enact and apply just and effective guarantees [of religious, linguistic, and social freedom].[37]

A more recent judicial decision with respect to the question of secession has been given by the African Commission on Human and Peoples' Rights in *Katangese Peoples' Congress* v. *Zaire*.[38] In 1992, the President of the Katangese Peoples' Congress, the only political party representing the people of Katanga, submitted a communication under Article 65(5) of the African Charter on Human and Peoples' Rights in which the Commission was requested to recognise the Katangese Peoples' Congress as a liberation movement and the right of the Katangese people to secede from Zaire. The Commission first observed that the right of self-determination was applicable in this case and subsequently clarified that that right could be

pp. 10–11, para. 2.13; M. N. Shaw, 'Re: Order in Council P. C.', 1996–1497 of 30 September 1996, Aug. 1997, Supplément au dossier, in: *ibid.*, pp. 18–19, paras. 44, 46, 49–50; J. A. Frowein, 'Self-Determination as a Limit to Obligations Under International Law' in: C. Tomuschat (ed.), *Modern Law of Self-Determination* (Dordrecht: Martinus Nijhoff, 1993), p. 211, at p. 48; J. Klabbers and R. Lefeber, 'Africa: Lost Between Self-Determination and *Uti Possidetis*' in: C. Brölmann, *et al.* (eds.), *Peoples and Minorities in International Law* (Boston/London: Dordrecht, 1993), p. 37; P. H. Kooijmans, 'Tolerance, Sovereignty and Self-Determination', *NILR* XLII (1996), p. 211, at p. 215; R. McCorquodale, 'Self-Determination: A Human Rights Approach' *ICLQ* 43 (1994), p. 857, at pp. 880–1; S. Oeter, 'Selbstbestimmungsrecht im Wandel: Überlegungen zur Debatte um Selbstbestimmung, Sezessionsrecht und 'vorzeitige' Anerkennung', *ZaöRV* 52 (1992), p. 741 at pp. 764–5; D. Murswiek, 'The Issue of a Right of Secession – Reconsidered', in: Tomuschat, *Modern Law of Self-Determination*, p. 21, at pp. 26–7; U. Umozurike, *Self-Determination in International Law* (Hamden, CT: Archon Books, 1972), p. 199; 'Conclusions and Recommendations of the Conference of Independent Legal Experts from the CIS Member-states' on *The Problem of Self-Determination and Secession in Contemporary International Law*, Moscow, 12–14 July 2000, para. II (d). But see J. Crawford, 'State Practice and International Law in Relation to Secession', *BYIL* 69 (1998), pp. 87–117; 'Conclusions and Recommendations' of *America's Regional Conference (of Independent Legal Experts) on Secession and International Law*, Santa Clara, 31 Jan.–2 Feb. 2001, para. 10.

[37] The Aaland Islands Question, LN Doc. B7.21/68/106, 1921, at p. 28.

[38] African Commission on Human and Peoples' Rights, Communication 75/92, Katangese Peoples' Congress *v.* Zaire; Decision taken at its 16th Session, Banjul, The Gambia, 1994.

exercised in a variety of ways, including 'independence, self-government, federalism, confederalism, unitarism or any other form of relations that accords with the wishes of the people, but fully cognizant of other recognised principles such as sovereignty and territorial integrity'.[39] It then continued:

> The Commission is obligated to uphold the sovereignty and territorial integrity of Zaire, a member of the OAU and a party to the African Charter on Human and Peoples' Rights. In the absence of concrete evidence of violations of human rights to the point that the territorial integrity of Zaire should be called to question and in the absence of evidence that the people of Katanga are denied the right to participate in government as guaranteed by Article 13(1) of the African Charter, the Commission holds the view that Katanga is obliged to exercise a variant of self-determination that is compatible with the sovereignty and territorial integrity of Zaire.[40]

An *a contrario* reading of the decision makes it clear that the Commission was of the opinion that in the case of serious violations of human rights and a denial of internal self-determination the Katangese people would be entitled to exercise a form of self-determination which would lead to the disruption of the territorial integrity of Zaire. In the absence of such conditions, the Commission held that according to the international law of self-determination, Katanga was under an obligation to implement the right of self-determination internally.

A more cautious approach was adopted by the Supreme Court of Canada in *Reference re Secession of Quebec*. The Court summarised its findings as follows:

> [T]he international law right to self-determination only generates, at best, a right to external self-determination in situations of former colonies; where a people is oppressed, as for example under foreign military occupation; or where a definable group is denied meaningful access to government to pursue their political, economic, social and cultural development. In all three situations, the people in question are entitled to a right to external self-determination because they have been denied the ability to exert internally their right to self-determination.[41]

There is therefore considerable support for both the position that the right of self-determination is limited by the right of territorial integrity of

[39] *Ibid.*, at para. 26.

[40] *Ibid.*, at paras. 27–8. See also the analysis in chapter 9 of this volume.

[41] Reference re Secession of Quebec, Supreme Court of Canada, *ILM* 37 (1998), p. 1340, at p. 1373, para. 138.

States and the position that the right of self-determination encompasses a qualified right of secession. Within the framework of the qualified secession doctrine there is general agreement on the constitutive parameters for a right of secession:[42]

(a) There must be a people which, though forming a numerical minority in relation to the rest of the population of the parent State, forms a majority within a part of the territory of that State.
(b) The State from which the people in question wishes to secede must have exposed that people to serious grievances (*carence de souveraineté*), consisting of either
  (i) a serious violation or denial of the right of internal self-determination of the people concerned (through, for instance, a pattern of discrimination), and/or
  (ii) serious and widespread violations of fundamental human rights of the members of that people;
(c) There must be no (further) realistic and effective remedies for the peaceful settlement of the conflict.

An act of unilateral secession that does not fulfil these conditions is an abuse of right and unlawful as a violation of the law of self-determination. State practice[43] indicates that statehood will be denied and recognition withheld if an entity has been created in violation of the law of self-determination.[44] In other words, the obligation of respect for the right of self-determination, including the prohibition of abuse of this right, has entered the law of statehood and may now be seen as a constitutive condition for statehood. This means that recognition of an otherwise effective territorial entity which has been created in violation of the right of self-determination is in itself unlawful because it constitutes a violation of the prohibition of premature recognition and of the principle of non-intervention (an aspect of the principle of territorial integrity).

On the other hand, if the conditions for a right of secession are met (and the traditional criteria for statehood satisfied), there is a legitimate expectation on the part of the seceding entity that it will be recognised

[42] See Raič, *Statehood and the Law of Self-Determination*, p. 332.
[43] As in the cases of Southern Rhodesia, Katanga and Abkhazia.
[44] Crawford, *The Creation of States in International Law*, pp. 105–106; Dugard, *Recognition and the United Nations*, pp. 97–98; J. E. S. Fawcett, 'Security Council Resolutions on Rhodesia', *BYIL* 41 (1965–1966), p. 103, at pp. 112–13; Raič, *Statehood and the Law of Self-Determination*, pp. 151–158, 418–426.

as a State by the international community. There is, however, no general obligation on States to recognise such a claim under the law of self-determination.[45]

IV. Recognition and secession: the practice of States

Recognition has played an important role in the validation of claims to statehood for over two hundred years. The best examples of this are to be found in the recognition of entities seeking to secede from their colonial rulers. Thus recognition helped to secure the independence of the United States of America from Britain[46] and the Latin-American States from Spain.[47] Secessions unconnected with decolonisation were also validated by recognition or obstructed by the failure to obtain recognition. In 1831, Belgium forcibly seceded from its union with the Netherlands and secured its independence by means of a collective act of recognition by the European Great Powers.[48] Conversely, the Confederacy failed to obtain the desired recognition to validate its secession from the United States.[49] Probably the best example of the validation of secession by recognition before World War I occurred in the case of Panama. Here the United States' recognition of Panama's secession from Colombia in 1903, with the threat that force would be used to prevent Colombia from reasserting its sovereignty over Panama, was soon followed by recognition from France, China, Germany and Austria-Hungary.[50] Undoubtedly this recognition, later admitted by the United States to be premature,[51] secured the independence of Panama – and, in due course of time, the construction of the Panama Canal!

As shown in Section 3, the rules relating to secession have changed dramatically since 1903 when the United States was able to grant

[45] See R. Lefeber and D. Raič, 'Frontiers of International Law, Part One: The Chechen People' *LJIL* 9 (1997) p. 1, at p. 6; Raič, *Statehood and the Law of Self-Determination*, pp. 428–429.

[46] France's recognition of the United States in 1778 undoubtedly contributed to the success of the American Revolution: Lauterpacht, *Recognition in International Law*, pp. 8, 36, 50.

[47] Lauterpacht, *Recognition in International Law*, pp. 13–16, 18–21; T. C. Chen, *The International Law of Recognition* (London: Stevens & Sons, Ltd., 1951), pp. 79–82.

[48] Lauterpacht, *Recognition in International Law*, pp. 10, 68.

[49] *Ibid.*, pp. 17, 21.

[50] J. B. Scott, 'The Treaty between Colombia and the United States', *AJIL* 15 (1921), p. 430. See the analysis of this case in chapter 12 of this volume.

[51] In 1921 the United States paid $ 25,000,000 to Colombia to settle the dispute between the two countries on this issue: *ibid.*

recognition to Panama without consideration of the territorial integrity of Colombia, the principle of *uti possidetis* or the question whether the people of Panama constituted a people for the purpose of self-determination. Since 1960, and the adoption of Resolution 1514 (XV) on the Granting of Independence of Colonial Countries and Peoples, there have been few successful secessions. Conversely, the sanction of non-recognition has been employed in secessionist situations to invalidate claims to statehood.

V. Recognition practice since 1960

A. *Unsuccessful secessions*

Since 1960, many attempts at secession have failed. In such cases failure is evidenced by the absence of recognition on the part of a sufficient number of States to ensure acceptance by the international community.

Africa is replete with examples of failed secession. In Southern Sudan, the criteria for the exercise of the qualified right of secession have probably been met, but the principle of territorial integrity has prevailed. The conflicts in the Democratic Republic of Congo, Angola and Somalia all have a secessionist character, but, again, self-determination has been subordinated to the principle of territorial integrity. The clearest African secessionist failure was that of Biafra, in which a rebellious province of Nigeria waged a bitter secessionist war from 1967 to 1970.[52] Five States – Tanzania, Gabon, Ivory Coast, Zambia and Haiti – recognised Biafra, largely for humanitarian reasons, but failed to enter into diplomatic relations with her. Although Biafra probably met the criteria for secession, the Organization of African Unity invoked the principles of national unity and territorial integrity to justify its support for the Nigerian central government,[53] and the United Nations abstained from involvement in the conflict on the ground that it was essentially an African problem.[54]

[52] See M. G. Kaladharan Nayar, 'Self-Determination beyond the Colonial Context: Biafra in Retrospect', *Texas I. L. J* 10 (1995), p. 321; D. A. Ijalaye, 'Was Biafra at any time a State in International Law?', *AJIL* 65 (1971), p. 551.

[53] *Ibid.*, pp. 555–6.

[54] S. A. Tiewul, 'Relations between the United Nations Organization and the Organization of African Unity in the Settlement of Secessionist Conflicts', *HILJ* 16 (1975), pp. 259, at pp. 289–90.

Recognition of secession has not been forthcoming in Asia or the Pacific region. Hence the non-recognition of Bougainville's attempted secession from Papua New Guinea[55] and the discouragement of the secession of Aceh from Indonesia.[56]

The Kosovo conflict clearly has a secessionist flavour, but both NATO and the United Nations have determined that the legitimate grievances of the Albanian Kosovars are to be resolved in a manner that does not end its association with the Federal Republic of Yugoslavia (now Serbia and Montenegro).[57] Chechnya too is a case of failure of secession because of the withholding of recognition.[58] An interesting example of non-recognition of an attempted secession in Eastern Europe that receives little attention is that of Abkhazia. This case has been selected for special consideration as it illustrates the reluctance of States, individually or collectively, to recognise the independence of a secessionist entity that fails to meet the criteria for the exercise of a right to secession.

[55] On 17 May 1990 Bougainville declared its independence from Papua New Guinea, an assertion of independence which remained unrecognised, despite the fact that the Bougainville government exercised considerable control over the island at least until February 1993. At that time the army of Papua New Guinea gained control over the capital of Bougainville. However, as fighting continued in the following years it became clear that the army of Papua New Guinea was unable to win the war. Violence only came to an end with the signing of a peace agreement between Papua New Guinea and Bougainville on 26 January 2001. The agreement provides for the holding of a referendum on independence which should be held between 10 and 15 years from the election of the first autonomous government of Bougainville. The autonomous government must be elected within 12 months of the signing of the agreement. Thus, this agreement recognises both the right of internal and external self-determination of the people of Bougainville, but excludes, for a period of ten years, the exercise of external self-determination through unilateral secession. See, generally, *Bougainville: The Peace Process and Beyond*, Canberra, Commonwealth of Australia (1999), Australia Parliament, Joint Standing Committee on Foreign Affairs, Defence, and Trade; M. Rafiqul Islam, 'Secession Crisis in Papua New Guinea: The Proclaimed Republic of Bougainville in International Law', *U. Haw. L. R* 13 (1991), p. 453.

[56] Cf. the analysis of these cases in chapter 10 of this volume.

[57] SC Res. 1160 of 31 March 1998, para. 5. See also SC Res. 1199 of 23 September 1998, preamble, para. 12; SC Res. 1203 of 24 October 1998, preamble, para. 8; SC Res.1244 of 10 June 1999, preamble, para. 11. See, generally, M. Vickers, *Between Serb and Albanian: a History of Kosovo* (New York / London: Columbia University Press, 1998); N. Malcolm, *Kosovo: A Short History* (London, 1998).

[58] See, generally, J. Charney, 'Self-Determination: Chechnya, Kosovo and East-Timor', *Vanderbilt T. I. L* 34 (2001), p. 455; T. N. Tappe, 'Chechnya and the State of Self-Determination in a Breakaway Region of the Former Soviet Union: Evaluating the Legitimacy of Secessionist Claims', *Columbia JTL* 10 (1995), p. 255; W. T. Atrokov, 'The Khasavyurt Accords: Maintaining the Rule of Law and Legitimacy of Democracy in the Russian Federation Amidst the Chechen Crisis', *Cornell I. L. J* 32 (1999), p. 367.

1. The Republic of Abkhazia[59]

In the tenth century, the territory that is today Abkhazia became part of the united feudal State of Georgia. Abkhazia broke away in the seventeenth century to become an independent principality. In 1864, Tsarist Russia crushed North Caucasian resistance and formally annexed Abkhazia. The majority of Moslem Abkhazians were deported by Russia to the Ottoman Empire as a punishment for their resistance to the Russian occupation of Abkhazia.[60] On 4 March 1921, the Abkhazian Soviet Republic was formed, which possessed full republican status in the Soviet Union. In December 1921, under pressure from the central government of the Soviet Union, a special 'contract of alliance' was signed between Abkhazia and Georgia, by which Abkhazia became part of the Georgian Soviet Socialist Republic while it retained its status as Union republic. On 1 April 1925, the Abkhazian Constitution was adopted which enshrined its republican status with treaty ties to Georgia. However, under Stalin, the status of Abkhazia was reduced to an autonomous republic within Georgia. In the course of the 1930s, large numbers of Georgians were resettled in the region, which explains why the Abkhazians in Abkhazia, prior to the hostilities in the 1990s, were a numerical minority in their own homeland, comprising only 18 per cent of the area's population, while Georgians constituted the largest ethnic group (46%), in addition to Russians (16%), Armenians (15%) and others (5%). Under Stalin's rule, a period of 'Georgianisation' took place in the late 1940s and early 1950s. The Abkhazian language was banned from administration and publication and the Abkhazian alphabet was changed to a Georgian base. In 1953, following the death of Stalin, this policy changed and the Abkhazians were rehabilitated and compensated with over-representation in local offices. In 1978, the Abkhaz launched a campaign to separate the Autonomous Republic of Abkhazia from the Georgian Soviet Socialist Republic and to incorporate it in the Russian

[59] The analysis in this section is largely based on detailed studies on Abkhazia such as T. Potier, *Conflict in Nagorno-Karabakh, Abkhazia and South Ossetia, A Legal Appraisal* (Kluwer Law Publications, 2001); A. Khachikian, 'Multilateral Mediation in Intrastate Conflicts: Russia, the United Nations, and the War in Abkhazia', in: M. C. Greenberg, J. H. Barton and M. E. McGuinness (eds.), *Words Over War, Mediation and Arbitration to Prevent Deadly Conflict* (Rowman & Littlefield Publishers, 2000), p. 15; S. N. MacFarlane, 'Conflict Resolution in Georgia', in: H. G. Ehrhart and A. Schnabel (eds.), *The Southeast European Challenge: Ethnic Conflict and the International Response* (Hamburg: Nomos Verlagsgesellleschaft, 1999), p. 117. See also Raič, *Statehood and the Law of Self-Determination*, pp. 379–86.

[60] This explains why Abkhazians in modern Abkhazia are predominantly (Orthodox) Christians.

Federative Socialist Republic. Although rejected by Russia, this resulted in significant concessions to the Abkhaz, including disproportionate representation in the Supreme Soviet of Abkhazia.

Abkhazian fears of renewed Georgianisation and the concomitant desire for secession were provoked by the rise of Georgian nationalism at the end of the 1980s. On 25 August 1990, the Abkhazian Supreme Soviet, in the absence of its Georgian deputies, voted in favour of independence and, like virtually all autonomous republics of the former Soviet Union, declared the state sovereignty of the Abkhazian Autonomous Soviet Republic (ASR). At the same time, the Abkhazians declared their willingness to enter into negotiations with the Georgian government for the formation of a federal constitutional structure which would preserve Georgia's territorial integrity.[61] The Abkhazian decision was declared invalid by Georgia the following day.

The year 1991 saw the demise of the Soviet Union. The turmoil which accompanied the Soviet Union's collapse provided a breeding ground for increasing internal unrest in Georgia. Georgia was the only republic which boycotted the all-Union referendum on the future of the USSR, but polling stations were opened in South Ossetia and Abkhazia. In December 1991, a new parliament was elected in Abkhazia on the basis of a two-chamber system, in which 28 of the 65 seats were allocated to Abkhazians, 26 to Georgians and 11 to other nationalities. Within months, the new parliament was paralysed because decisions taken by a majority were repeatedly rejected by the Georgian deputies. This inevitably led to inter-ethnic tensions.

In a referendum on 31 March 1991, on the question whether Georgian independence should be restored on the basis of the Act of Independence of 26 May 1918, an overwhelming majority of those who participated voted in favour of independence.[62] Subsequently, on 9 April 1991, the Georgian Supreme Soviet approved a decree for the restoration of Georgia's independence on the basis of the 1918 Act, and on 26 May 1991 Gamsakhurdia was elected as executive President. The period from April until December was characterised by firm opposition to Gamsakhurdia, which culminated in an armed conflict between the opposition and those who supported the President. Eventually Gamsakhurdia fled Georgia in January 1991. Following this *coup d'état*, the Georgian Military Council reinstated Georgia's 1921 constitution which did not recognise Abkhazia's

[61] Potier, *Conflict in Nagorno-Karabakh*, p. 10.

[62] 'Georgia', *The European World Year Book* (1994), p. 1231.

status as a separate entity within Georgia. In March 1992, the former Minister of Foreign Affairs of the Soviet Union, Eduard Shevardnadze, returned to Georgia, and the new regime declared all laws adopted during Soviet times to be null and void. At this time the Chairman of the Abkhazian legislature, Ardzinba, proposed a draft treaty to the Georgian State Council which would have provided for federative relations between Georgia and Abkhazia. The proposal was ignored and, in response, on 23 July 1992, the Abkhazian Supreme Soviet declared Abkhazia's sovereignty as the 'Republic of Abkhazia', reinstating the Constitution of 1925. This step was not, however, intended as a proclamation of independence, as the 1925 Constitution provided for a federative relationship between 'two equal republics'. The reinstatement of the 1925 Constitution was intended as a temporary measure, filling a constitutional vacuum, to protect Abkhazia's hitherto autonomous political status.[63] On 14 August 1992, the Georgian government dispatched units of the National Guard to Abkhazia, which prompted armed resistance by Abkhazian militia. Several reasons for the Georgian step were provided, but eventually it became clear that the purpose was to suppress the growing Abkhazian secessionist movement. Georgian troops took control of the capital city of Sukhumi and Russian President Yeltsin pledged support for Georgia's territorial integrity. In the period between January and June 1993, the hostilities intensified, and Georgia accused Russia of providing Abkhazia with military equipment. The Abkhazian forces succeeded in capturing Sukhumi in mid-September, and at the end of that month Georgian troops were expelled from the whole of Abkhazia.

A cease-fire was agreed on 1 December 1993, followed by Georgian proposals for extensive autonomy. The proposals were, however, rejected by the Abkhazian authorities.[64] In February 1994, talks took place between the two sides under the auspices of the United Nations (which had appointed a special envoy for the region in May 1993), with the Russian Federation playing the role of facilitator and the OSCE invited as a participant. During the talks, the two sides addressed the status of Abkhazia,[65] and the United Nations special envoy presented them with

[63] C. Dale, 'Turmoil in Abkhazia: Russian Responses', *Research Report* 2 *RFE/RL* (1993), p. 49.

[64] 'Georgians Propose Future for Abkhazia of Extensive Autonomy', *BBC Summary of World Broadcasts*, 23 Dec. 1993, p. 4.

[65] Another important issue considered at these talks was the return of the refugees and displaced persons. The return of refugees was not just a humanitarian but also a very important political problem, since the return of the almost 300,000 (mainly Georgian) refugees

a draft political declaration which contained a provision recognising the territorial integrity of Georgia. The proposal was immediately rejected by the Abkhazians and the negotiations failed.[66] The same issue led to the failure of a new round of talks in New York in March 1994. In November 1994, the Abkhazian parliament adopted a constitution which, in Article 1, declared Abkhazia to be a 'sovereign democratic state'. At the same time, the Abkhazian authorities issued a statement which called for the continuation of the talks with Georgia, with the objective of creating 'a union-state of two equal subjects'.[67] Ardzinba was sworn in as President of the Republic of Abkhazia in December 1994. These steps were interpreted by Georgia as impairing the territorial integrity of Georgia and it protested vigorously to the Security Council of the United Nations. In February 1995, Russia prepared a draft which provided for a federative arrangement. This was eventually accepted by the Georgian government but rejected by Abkhazia which interpreted the draft as an offer of autonomy, not equal membership in a union-state. This meant that the Abkhazian authorities had shifted their demand from territorial and political autonomy to a federal structure, and now to a confederal structure. These demands were rejected by Georgia which stated that a federation was as far as Georgia was prepared to go.

No solution was found in the following year. Instead, the parliamentary elections which were held in Abkhazia in 1996, without the participation of the refugees, seriously aggravated the situation and were condemned by the Security Council and the European Parliament as illegitimate.[68] In 1997, a large-scale spontaneous return of Georgian refugees and displaced persons destabilised the delicate politico-military balance in the area. The Abkhazians responded in the spring of 1998 with the forced expulsion of more than 30,000 returnees, which was condemned internationally as an act of (renewed) 'ethnic cleansing'.[69] On 3 October 1999, a referendum on

would have tilted the demographic and, correspondingly, the political balance in the republic. The Abkhazian authorities therefore did little to solve that problem. Khachikian, 'Multilateral Mediation in Intrastate Conflicts', p. 20.

66 *Ibid.* 67 *Ibid.*, p. 21.

68 SC Res. 1096 of 30 January 1997, para. 3; 'Resolution on the Situation in Abkhazia', (1996) European Parliament, Preamble, para. G and operative paras. 3 and 4.

69 OSCE Istanbul Summit Declaration, OSCE Doc. SUM.Doc/2/99 (1999), para. 17. In 1996 the European Parliament labelled the treatment of the refugees and displaced persons as 'ethnic cleansing'. See 'Resolution on the Situation in Abkhazia', (1990) Preamble, para. E. Although the Security Council did not use the term 'ethnic cleansing', it repeatedly condemned attempts to change the demographic composition of Abkhazia. See, e.g., SC Res. 896 of 31 January 1994, para. 12; SC Res. 1036 of 12 January 1996, para. 7

independence was held in Abkhazia which was declared to be illegitimate both by the Georgian government and by the international community.[70] On 12 October 1999 the Republic of Abkhazia issued the Act of State Independence of the Republic of Abkhazia, which, unlike previous declarations, was intended as a formal proclamation of independence of Abkhazia under international law. The republic has not been recognised by a single State.

The international (in particular the United Nations) stance towards the conflict is characterised by (a) consistent support for the preservation of the territorial integrity of Georgia, (b) a rejection of secession by Abkhazia, and (c) an insistence on the grant of extensive autonomy to the Abkhazians within the Republic of Georgia. For instance, in its Resolution 896 of 31 January 1994, the Security Council stressed

> that substantive progress must be made immediately on the political status of Abkhazia, respecting fully the sovereignty and territorial integrity of the Republic of Georgia, if the negotiations are to succeed and further conflict is to be avoided.[71]

The Security Council left no room for any misunderstandings about its point of view with respect to a possible Abkhazian secession when, in Resolution 1065 of 12 July 1996, it reaffirmed

> its commitment to the sovereignty and territorial integrity of Georgia, within its internationally recognised borders, and to the necessity of defining the status of Abkhazia in strict accordance with these principles, and *underline[d]* the unacceptability of any action by the Abkhaz leadership in contravention of these principles.[72]

This position has been endorsed by the European Union[73] and the Council of Europe.[74]

(condemning 'the ethnic killings and continuing human rights violations committed in Abkhazia, Georgia' and calling upon 'the Abkhaz side to ensure the safety of all persons in areas under its control'); SC Res. 1065 of 12 July 1996, para. 8; SC Res. 1187 of 30 July 1998, para. 4 (condemning 'the deliberate destruction of houses by Abkhaz forces, with the apparent motive of expelling people from their home areas').

70 See SC Res. 1287 of 31 January 2000, para. 5.

71 SC Res. 896 of 31 January 1994, para. 5. This formulation whereby the political status of Abkhazia is linked to the preservation of the territorial integrity of the Republic of Georgia has been repeated in numerous other resolutions on the conflict.

72 SC Res. 1065 of 12 July 1996, para. 3.

73 'Resolution on the Situation in Abkhazia' (1996), para. 2.

74 Council of Europe, Parliamentary Assembly Resolution of 22 April 1997 (referring to the need for an 'extensive autonomy status for Abkhazia').

The deadlock continues, with Georgia willing to consider a federal relationship, and Abkhazia, encouraged by its *de facto* independence, insistent on full independence. The Security Council, committed to the maintenance of the territorial integrity of Georgia, has condemned Abkhazia for its uncompromising stance.[75] On 31 January 2000, the Council called for the two parties to come to an agreement 'on the distribution of constitutional competences between Tbilisi and Sukhumi as part of a comprehensive settlement, with full respect for the sovereignty and territorial integrity of Georgia' and condemned as 'unacceptable and illegitimate the holding of . . . [the] referendum in Abkhazia, Georgia'.[76]

The question that now arises, in the context of the qualified right of secession, is whether Abkhazia enjoys a right to unilateral secession and, if so, why it has not been recognised by the international community.

There is no doubt that the Abkhazians qualify as a people for the purpose of self-determination. This was acknowledged by the Soviet Union when it conferred a special status on Abkhazia. On the other hand, it may be argued that the Abkhazian people did not meet the requirements of the qualified right to secession because they did not, prior to the outbreak of hostilities, constitute a clear majority within Abkhazia itself. This does not, however, seem to be the main obstacle in the way of recognition of Abkhazia's bid for independence. Instead the answer is to be found in Abkhazia's intransigence at the negotiating table and the absence of serious violations of the Abkhazian people's human rights by Georgia.

The Abkhazians have become more and more unwilling to enter into good faith negotiations on the future political status of Abkhazia within Georgia, whereas the Georgian government has been willing to grant a substantial amount of political autonomy since the end of 1993. The consistent rejection by the Abkhazians of Georgia's proposals for political and territorial autonomy within a federal arrangement, and of the appeals of the international community for such a settlement, suggests that the Abkhazians are not prepared to exhaust effective and peaceful remedies before claiming secession. Moreover, there is no evidence of widespread and serious violations of the fundamental rights of the Abkhazians by Georgia. On the contrary, the Abkhazians are themselves accused of violating the fundamental rights of Georgians resident in, or previously resident in, Abkhazia. Therefore, the conclusion must be that the Abkhazians do not, under the prevailing circumstances, possess a right

[75] See SC Res. 1096 of 30 January 1997; SC Res. 1339 of 31 January 2001, para. 5.
[76] SC Res. 1287 of 31 January 2000, paras. 4 and 5.

of unilateral secession and, consequently, that the proclamation of independence is in violation of the law of self-determination.[77]

This position is supported by the international community's consistent confirmation of the territorial integrity of the Republic of Georgia, its insistence on the implementation of self-determination within Georgia, and the Security Council's condemnation of the holding of a referendum on independence, which cannot mean anything other than the rejection of a right of unilateral secession for the Abkhazians.[78]

The experience of Abkhazia therefore tends to confirm the view that recognition will not be granted to an entity that fails to meet the criteria of the qualified right of secession.

B. *Successful secessions*

There are few examples of unilateral secessions since 1960 which have been universally recognised. This study will focus on two of the principal cases of successful secession of this period, namely the case of the unilateral secession of Bangladesh from Pakistan and that of Croatia from the Socialist Federal Republic of Yugoslavia (SFRY). The creation of Slovenia, the Former Yugoslav Republic of Macedonia (FYROM) and Bosnia-Herzegovina will also be considered within the context of the dissolution of Yugoslavia. The creation of Slovenia and FYROM are not, however, clear examples of *unilateral* secession, as the central Yugoslav government implicitly accepted their separation from Yugoslavia. Bosnia-Herzegovina presents different problems and will therefore be examined separately. The separation of Eritrea from Ethiopia will not be considered because, in this case, the eventual creation of Eritrea took place with the explicit prior consent of the central government of Ethiopia.[79]

[77] See Raič, *Statehood and the Law of Self-Determination*, pp. 384–86.

[78] In this respect *cf.* Judge Wildhaber and Judge Ryssdal who state: 'when the international community in 1983 refused to recognise the [Turkish Republic of Northern Cyprus] as a new state under international law it by the same token implicitly rejected the claim of the "TRNC" to self-determination in the form of secession'. Concurring Opinion of Judge Wildhaber joined by Judge Ryssdal, *Loizidou* v. *Turkey (Merits), Judgment, 18 Dec. 1996, 1996 VI Reports of Judgments and Decisions of the European Court of Human Rights*, p. 2216, at p. 2241.

[79] Eritrean separatism had its roots in World War II. With Italy's defeat in that war, Italy's colonies of Eritrea, Italian Somaliland and most of 'Libya' were placed under temporary British administration. In the Treaty of Peace with Italy of 1947, Italy renounced all claims to the three territories. It was furthermore stated that the final disposition of the territories was to be determined by France, the United Kingdom, the United States and

In all the above cases, the right of self-determination of peoples and recognition were of fundamental importance for either the creation of the entities as States or their (continued) survival as States.

1. Bangladesh[80]

The unilateral secession of Bangladesh is probably the most widely accepted example of lawful secession. The unitary State of Pakistan, established in 1947, consisted of two territorial units separated by 1200 miles of Indian territory. West Pakistan was, in geographical terms, much larger than East Pakistan (East Bengal) but had a substantially lower population density than its smaller counterpart.[81] The two units did not possess a common language, culture, economy or history, but were united by a common religion, Islam. From the inception of Pakistan, there were serious political and economic disparities between West and East Pakistan. In 1962 the Awami League, the dominant political party of the Bengali community under the leadership of Sheikh Mujibur Rahman, demanded full autonomy for East Bengal as the only way of resolving the disparity

the Soviet Union before 15 September 1948. If no agreement was reached by that time the Treaty provided for the question to be taken up by the UN. Because no agreement was reached, the question was referred to the UN. In 1952 the UN sought to satisfy the Eritrean demand for self-determination by creating an Ethiopian/Eritrean federation (see General Assembly Resolution 390 (V) of 2 December 1950). The federation was however unilaterally dissolved by Haile Selassie in 1962. This fact and Selassie's imperial rule over Eritrea resulted in the formation of the Eritrean Liberation Movement in 1958 and the Eritrean Liberation Front from which the Eritrean People's Liberation Front (EPLF) was formed in 1961. The rejection of Eritrea's demand for self-determination continued under president Mengistu Haile Miriam. In 1991, as a direct result of the withdrawal of Soviet support and military supplies to the Ethiopian central government, the EPLF troops eventually succeeded in defeating the central government's forces in Eritrea. After the fall of Mengistu's regime and with the agreement of the Ethiopian transitional government, a UN monitored referendum on independence was held in Eritrea in April 1993 in which an overwhelming majority of the Eritrean population voted in favour of independence. As a result the Eritrean authorities declared Eritrea an independent State on 27 April 1993. The new State was admitted to the UN on 28 May 1993 (see GA Res. 47/230 of 28 May 1993). See, generally, *The United Nations and the Independence of Eritrea*, The United Nations Blue Book Series, XII, 1996; G. H. Tesfagiorgis, 'Self-Determination: Its Evolution and Practice by the United Nations and its Application to the Case of Eritrea', *WILR* 6 (1987), p. 75; R. Iyob, *The Eritrean Struggle for Independence: Domination, Resistance, Nationalism, 1941–1993* (Cambridge: Cambridge University Press, 1995); M. Haile, 'Legality of Secessions: the Case of Eritrea', *Emory I. L. R* 8 (1994), p. 479.

80 See also Raič, *Statehood and the Law of Self-Determination*, pp. 335–42.

81 In a 1970 census the population of East Pakistan was 77 million and that of West Pakistan 50 million.

between Pakistan's two parts.[82] In 1969 Yayha Khan became Pakistan's new president. He promised the holding of general elections to a National Assembly of Pakistan which would be entrusted with the task of drafting a new constitution. The elections held in December 1971 led to an overwhelming victory for the Awami League in East Bengal, which would have given it a majority in the National Parliament and most probably would have led to the federalisation of Pakistan. In West Pakistan, the Pakistan People's Party under the leadership of Zulfikar Ali Bhutto won a majority of the seats allotted to West Pakistan. Bhutto's demand that his party be given a major part in the government of Pakistan lead to a political crisis. Against this background Yayha Khan indefinitely postponed the inaugural session of the National Assembly planned for 13 February 1971, which led Rahman to call for civil disobedience in East Bengal. In reaction to the peaceful actions by the people of East Bengal, a large-scale military operation was launched in the night of 25–26 March 1971. In response, Rahman proclaimed the independence of Bangladesh on 26 March. On the same day, Rahman and other Awami League leaders were taken into custody. On 10 April 1971, the leaders of the Awami League that were not imprisoned adopted the Proclamation of Independence Order which was declared to be operative retrospectively from 26 March 1971. The atrocities committed during the military operation by the Pakistani Army are a matter of common knowledge and have been documented elsewhere.[83] Over one million Bengalis were killed and some 10 million driven into exile in India.

India became directly involved in the conflict through a pre-emptive attack by (West) Pakistani warplanes on airfields in India on 3 December 1971. Not only did India respond with armed force to the military action, but it also recognised the independence of Bangladesh on 6 December. The Indo-Pakistan war lasted less than two weeks and the Pakistani Army capitulated on 16 December 1971. Although India's assistance did not therefore play a significant role in the decision to secede, it proved essential for the subsequent success of the secession of Bangladesh. Between January and May 1972, Bangladesh was recognised by some 70 States,[84] and by

[82] S. R. Chowdhury, *The Genesis of Bangladesh, A Study in International Legal Norms and Permissive Conscience* (Bombay: Asia Publishing House, 1972), p. 42.

[83] See, e.g., 'East Pakistan Staff Study', International Commission of Jurists, *The Review* 8 (1972), p. 23, at pp. 26–41.

[84] In addition to India, only Bhutan recognised Bangladesh prior to January 1972, namely on 7 December 1971. Numerous States granted recognition in the period January–May 1972, that is, after the surrender of the Pakistani Army on 16 December 1971. See J. J.

September 1973, she had been recognised by over 100 States and admitted to the Commonwealth.

Initially, Pakistan adopted a position similar to the Hallstein doctrine adopted by West Germany, under which West Germany declared that it would break off diplomatic relations with any State which recognised East Germany. Pakistan announced in early 1972 that it would break off diplomatic relations with States which recognised Bangladesh. It did in fact break diplomatic relations with Bulgaria, Yugoslavia, Poland and some other States and recalled ambassadors from Burma and Nepal for granting recognition to Bangladesh. But when the major powers, the Soviet Union and the United States, and the EC countries granted recognition in the first half of 1972, Pakistan was quick to abandon its Hallstein doctrine. Pakistan had sought to block Bangladesh's admission to the Commonwealth by threatening to quit, itself, if Bangladesh were admitted. Bangladesh was admitted as a full member of the Commonwealth on 18 April 1972. Pakistan, being forced to live up to its threat, withdrew from the Commonwealth. The only cases where a measure of success in 'delaying' recognition was achieved was with the Chinese and with some States of the Middle East. Bangladesh was admitted to the United Nations on 17 September 1974.[85]

The postponement of the admission, however, had nothing to do with the statehood of Bangladesh, which was generally accepted, or the mode of its creation, but was a result of opposition from China, a friend of West Pakistan. China insisted that Bangladesh did not comply with Security Council resolutions concerning the withdrawal of troops and the release of prisoners of war. Since a State should accept the obligations of the United Nations Charter, Bangladesh was, according to China, not qualified to be admitted to the United Nations. Accordingly, a draft resolution on the admission of Bangladesh, of 20 August 1972, was not adopted as a result of a Chinese veto.[86]

Supporters of the qualified right of secession agree that Bangladesh met all the suggested criteria for the exercise of a unilateral right to secede.[87] There is no doubt that the Bengalis constituted a people, in an ethnic

A. Salmon, 'Naissance et Reconnaissance du Bangladesh' in: *Multitudo legum, ius unum. Mélanges en honneur de Wilhelm Wengler* (Berlin: Interrecht, 1973), p. 467 at pp. 478–9.

[85] GA Res. 3203 of 17 September 1974.

[86] See *UN Yearbook* 26 (1972), pp. 215–20. Cf. also the position taken by Pakistan which maintained that Bangladesh 'failed to show that it was a peace-loving *State*'. *Ibid.*, p. 216 (emphasis added).

[87] See, e.g., 'East Pakistan Staff Study', pp. 49–52.

sense, which formed a majority within East Pakistan. It is also clear that the people of East Pakistan were exposed to serious harm in the form of a denial of internal self-determination and widespread violations of fundamental human rights. Moreover, all realistic options for the realisation of internal self-determination were exhausted.

The statehood of Bangladesh was recognised by many States at a time when there was no effective government, because it was not until the end of March 1972 that Indian troops left the country.[88] The Bangladesh government had, however, explicitly requested these troops to remain in the country for the purpose of helping the government in restoring and securing law and order. This was implicitly approved by the Security Council,[89] because it feared that reprisals would be taken against West Pakistanis in East Pakistan while the Bangladesh government was still unable to secure a safe environment. According to traditional international law, recognition would have been unlawful until all Indian troops had left the country and until the control of the territory was in the hands of the Bangladesh government itself.[90] Despite this, Bangladesh was recognised by more than fifty States before the end of March 1972. No State (except for Pakistan) raised objections.

2. Croatia[91]

The formation of the Republic of Croatia in 1991 is generally viewed as a case of State-creation following the dissolution of a federation. A closer examination, however, leads to the conclusion that it is better categorised as an example of unilateral secession.

This is not the place for a detailed examination of the dissolution of the Socialist Federal Republic of Yugoslavia (SFRY). Suffice it to recall that in the late 1980s the effective annulment of the constitutional autonomy of Kosovo and Vojvodina by Serbia, and the establishment of a pro-Serb government in Montenegro, gave Serbia more power in the federal government, enabling it to outvote Croatia, Slovenia and Macedonia in the federal decision-making process. This, together with the over-representation

[88] Salmon, 'Naissance et Reconnaissance du Bangladesh', pp. 477, 490.

[89] See SC Res. 307 of 21 December 1971.

[90] Cf. the opinion of the International Committee of Jurists with respect to the statehood of Finland in 1917–18. 'The Aaland Islands Question, Report of the Committee of Jurists' L.N.O.J. Spec. Supp. No. 3 (1920), p. 3, at pp. 8–9.

[91] For a detailed discussion of this case, see Raič, *Statehood and the Law of Self-Determination*, pp. 342–66.

of Serbs in the federal civil service and army,[92] and the exploitation of the more wealthy republics of Croatia and Slovenia for the purpose of providing welfare benefits for Serbia and the other republics, led to demands for greater autonomy on the part of Croatia and Slovenia. Multi-party elections in Slovenia and Croatia in 1990 resulted in new governments in these republics which favoured a decentralisation of power, in contrast to Serbia, whose communist government insisted on a greater centralisation of power.

The demand for more autonomy and possibly independence by Croatia and Slovenia triggered separatist demands by the Serbian minority in Croatia. The situation was aggravated when Serbia and its allies in the collective Presidency blocked the installation of the Croatian candidate, Stipe Mesić, for the post of federal President on 15 May 1991. As a result, both Croatia and Slovenia proclaimed independence on 25 June 1991. In response, the Yugoslav National Army (YNA) intervened in Slovenia but withdrew after a few days. In Croatia, however, the situation was different because of more active involvement of the YNA in Croatia in support of Serb irregulars. At this time the European Community offered its good offices to the parties, which resulted in the conclusion of the Brioni-Accord of 7 July 1991. This provided for a moratorium on the proclamations of independence on the part of Slovenia and Croatia for three months, during which period negotiations were to be conducted on the future constitutional structure of Yugoslavia.[93] Despite the Accord the conflict escalated. In August, the situation in Croatia erupted into a total war with the YNA fighting alongside the Serb irregulars. This was accompanied by widespread violations of human rights, including denial of the right to life, the destruction of towns and villages as well as of cultural and religious objects,[94]

[92] See, e.g., S. L. Burg, *Conflict and Cohesion in Socialist Yugoslavia, Political Decision Making Since 1966* (Princeton NJ: Princeton University Press, 1983), p. 113. For instance, in 1969, while Serbs constituted some 40 per cent of the total population of Yugoslavia, 72 per cent of the professional staff in the state administration and 83 per cent of the professional staff in governmental commissions and institutes was made up of Serbs. With respect to the judicial and prosecutory sector 64 per cent of the leading officers were Serbs. No significant changes occurred with regard to these ratios in subsequent years.

[93] Europe Documents, No. 1725, 16 July 1991, pp. 16–19.

[94] See, e.g., M. Cherif Bassiouni and P. M. Manikas, Final Report of the United Nations Commission of Experts established pursuant to SC Res. 780 of 6 October 1992, Annex IV, The Policy of Ethnic Cleansing, Part II, Paragraph III. Three confidential reports were written in January 1992 by an independent international research team and were concerned with the last four months of 1991. They describe a systematic campaign

and the 'ethnic cleansing'[95] of Croats and other nationalities inhabiting the areas of Croatia in which Serbs constituted a majority or a substantial minority. By November 1991, there were 600,000 refugees in Croatia (approximately twelve per cent of the total population of Croatia), of which the majority were Croats from the Serbian occupied territories,[96] constituting about one third of Croatian territory. On 1 October 1991, the YNA invaded the district of Dubrovnik and laid siege to the town. Dubrovnik was a city with virtually no defence against the Yugoslav forces and, it should be noted, without a substantial Serbian minority. Thus, the attack and destruction of the town could not be justified on grounds of military necessity,[97] or as necessary for the protection of a Serb minority against the Croats. Two days later, on 3 October, a bloodless *coup d'état* was conducted by the representatives of Serbia, Montenegro, Vojvodina and Kosovo in the collective Presidency, under the pretext of 'an immediate danger of war'. It was announced that the collective Presidency would henceforth take decisions on the basis solely of the votes of these four members and that the collective Presidency would take over certain tasks which constitutionally fell within the competence of the Federal Parliament.[98] In effect, this meant that decision-making in both the collective Presidency and the federal Parliament was taken over by Serbia and Montenegro. While the international community had already moved away from its initial neutral stance as a result of increasing evidence of partiality on the part of the YNA,[99] these events pressed the international

of violence, wholesale massacres and looting by the YNA and the Serbian irregulars with the purpose of driving-out the Croats from their places of residence. Mention is made of widespread violation of human rights, including 'barbarian' violations of international humanitarian law such as the widespread practice of mutilation of Croatian corpses, as well as the malicious destruction of churches and hospitals. See *The Washington Post*, 17 January 1992.

95 See, e.g., SC Res. 943 of 23 September 1994. See also Final Report of the United Nations Commission of Experts established pursuant to SC Res. 780 of 6 October 1992.

96 Report on the Situation of Human Rights in the Territory of the Former Yugoslavia, submitted by T. Mazowiecki, Special Rapporteur of the Commission on Human Rights, UN Doc. E/CN.4/1992/S-1/10, 27 October 1992, para. 13. And see the Vance Report of 25 October 1991 issued through the Report of the Secretary-General Pursuant to paragraph 3 of SC Res. 713 of 25 September 1991, UN Doc. S/23169 (1991), paras. 15–18, and Annex IV.

97 Final Report of the Commission of Experts Established Pursuant to Security Council Resolution 780 (1992), UN Doc. S/1994/674 (1994), Part IV, Section J ('Destruction of Cultural Property').

98 Declaration on Yugoslavia, Informal Meeting of Ministers of Foreign Affairs, Haarzuilens, 5 October 1991, reprinted in: Trifunovska, *Yugoslavia Through Documents*, p. 351.

99 Cf. EC Bulletin 7/8–1991, at p. 107.

community to take a position in the conflict. Accordingly, the usurpation of power by Serbia and Montenegro (leading to the so-called 'rump Presidency') was forcefully condemned by the EC[100] and the Conference on Security and Cooperation in Europe (CSCE).[101] It was furthermore declared that the YNA had 'resorted to a disproportionate and indiscriminate use of force' and that it had 'shown itself to be no longer a neutral and disciplined institution'.[102]

Because of these events Croatia reasserted its proclamation of independence on 8 October, the day after the lapse of the Brioni moratorium. However, international recognition of Croatia as a State under international law was withheld until the beginning of 1992. An important reason for the delay in recognising Croatia and Slovenia was concern about the internal political situation in the former Soviet Union in the final months of 1991. This situation changed dramatically, however, with the Soviet Union's recognition of the independence of the Baltic States on 6 September 1991 and the declaration at the tripartite meeting of Russia, Ukraine and Belarus at Minsk on 8 December 1991 that the Soviet Union had ceased to exist, a declaration later affirmed by the other republics at the Alma-Ata meeting. Freed from the danger of creating a precedent for the Soviet Union, the EC took a more favourable stance towards the issue of recognition of Croatia and Slovenia, although there was considerable disagreement with respect to the timing of recognition. Germany, in particular, favoured immediate recognition, but other EC members remained hesitant. There was, however, majority support for the position that an uncoordinated process of recognition should be prevented. On 16 and 17 December, the EC published two Declarations to reflect a common position on recognition on the part of the EC member States: a 'Declaration on the Guidelines for the Recognition of New States in Eastern Europe and in the Soviet Union', and a 'Declaration on Yugoslavia'.[103] The first Declaration detailed a number of requirements which were to be satisfied before recognition would be granted. After confirming their attachment 'in particular [to] the principle of self-determination', the EC member States expressed their readiness to recognise 'those new States which . . . have

[100] *Ibid.*

[101] Resolution adopted by the Committee of Senior Officials of the CSCE on the Situation in Yugoslavia, Prague, 10 October 1991.

[102] Declaration on Yugoslavia, Informal Meeting of Ministers of Foreign Affairs, Haarzuilens, 6 October 1991, reprinted in: Trifunovska, *Yugoslavia Through Documents*, pp. 351–2. See also Declaration of the European Community and its Member States on Dubrovnik, 27 October 1991.

[103] Both documents are reprinted in *ILM* 11 (1992), pp. 1485–7.

constituted themselves on a democratic basis . . .'. They continued by stating that recognition of these States was conditional on their demonstrating 'respect for the rule of law, democracy and human rights' and providing evidence that they guaranteed 'the rights of ethnic and national groups and minorities in accordance with the commitments subscribed to in the framework of the CSCE'. In the second Declaration, the member States of the EC agreed to recognise all Yugoslav republics which had declared before 23 December that they wished to be recognised as independent States, that they accepted the commitments in the Guidelines and that they accepted as well the so-called Draft Convention or Carrington Convention prepared during the peace conference on Yugoslavia.[104] The date set for possible recognition was 15 January 1992. It was also decided that the requests for recognition would be submitted to the Badinter Arbitration Commission, established within the framework of the Yugoslav Peace Conference, for approval before the implementation date. However, after the publication of the Guidelines, Germany made it clear that it had already decided to recognise Croatia and Slovenia, even before the Badinter Commission had delivered its opinions. At the same time, it stated that it would delay the implementation of that decision until 15 January 1992.[105] The Badinter Arbitration Commission found that Croatia did not satisfy all the conditions set down by the EC for recognition. The Commission did not find that Croatia's national legal system failed to meet the requirements for minority protection under general international law but rather that Croatia had not yet fully incorporated all the provisions of the Draft Convention, in particular those regarding autonomy for the Serb minority, into domestic law.[106] After President Tudjman made a formal written statement addressed to the President of the Arbitration Commission assuring it that Croatia would implement the relevant provisions contained in the Draft Convention, the EC

[104] UN Doc. S/23169 (1991) Annex VII. The Draft Convention which was prepared in November 1991 contained provisions guaranteeing, among other things, human rights and the rights of national or ethnic groups, including territorial autonomy (which provisions were, in particular, included with respect to the status of the Serb minority in Croatia).

[105] S. Terrett, *The Dissolution of Yugoslavia and the Badinter Commission* (Aldershot, Hants, England; Burlington, Vt.: Ashgate/Dartmouth, 2000), p. 82. In the meantime, other, non-Member States of the EC, had already decided to grant recognition: Estonia (31 December 1991), Iceland (19 December 1991), Latvia (14 December 1991) and Ukraine (11 December 1991). See Croatian Ministry of Foreign Affairs, *Povratak na vanjske poslove*, 1997–98. The recognition of Croatia by Lithuania on 30 July 1991 was without doubt premature and an unlawful intervention.

[106] Opinion 5, *ILM* 31(1992), pp. 1503–5.

announced on 15 January 1992 that the Community and its member States had decided to proceed with the recognition of Slovenia and Croatia.[107] Croatia was subsequently recognised by 76 States[108] before its admission to the United Nations on 22 May 1992.[109]

Returning to the question of secession, it should be emphasised that the break-up of Yugoslavia took place against the background of an applicable right of self-determination under international law. This was not only the view of academics[110] and of the Badinter Arbitration Commission,[111] but also of the international community.[112] Moreover, the importance of self-determination as the legal basis for the independence of Croatia, Slovenia, Bosnia-Herzegovina and Macedonia is implicit in the first paragraph of the EC Guidelines for the Recognition of New States in Eastern Europe and the Soviet Union, which states that recognition is based on the EC's 'attachment to the principles of the Helsinki Final Act and the Charter of Paris, in particular the principle of self-determination'.[113]

It was the secession of several federal republics that led to the dissolution of the SFRY. This shows that secession and dissolution are not mutually exclusive, as has often been argued. This view is supported by both

[107] Statement by the Presidency on the Recognition of Yugoslav Republics, reprinted in: Trifunovska, *Yugoslavia Through Documents*, p. 501.

[108] Department for Foreign Affairs of the Republic of Croatia, *Povratak na Vanjske Poslove*, 1998.

[109] GA Res. 46/238 of 22 May 1992.

[110] See, e.g., Terret, *The Dissolution of Yugoslavia and the Badinter Commission*, pp. 268–273; M. Weller, 'The International Response to the Dissolution of the Socialist Federal Republic of Yugoslavia', *AJIL* 86 (1992), p. 569, at p. 606; R. McCorquodale, 'Self-Determination: A Human Rights Approach', *ICLQ* 43 (1994), p. 857, at p. 861.

[111] Opinion 2, *ILM* 31 (1992), pp. 1497–99.

[112] See, e.g., EC Declaration on the Situation in Yugoslavia of 5 July 1991, which states that 'it is only for the peoples of Yugoslavia themselves to decide on the country's future' and calls for negotiations between these peoples which 'should be based on . . . respect for . . . the right of peoples to self-determination'. Reprinted in: Trifunovska, *Yugoslavia Through Documents*, p. 310. Later, on 6 October 1991, the EC and its member States again stressed the applicability of the right of self-determination when it was stated that '[t]he right of self-determination of all peoples of Yugoslavia cannot be exercised in isolation from the interests and rights of ethnic minorities within the individual republics'. Declaration on Yugoslavia, Informal Meeting of Ministers of Foreign Affairs, Haarzuilens, 6 October 1991, reprinted in: Trifunovska, *Yugoslavia Through Documents*, p. 501.

[113] The EC Guidelines were essentially followed by the United States. See US Dept. of State, *Dispatch* 3/13 (1992), p. 287. In addition, the Secretary-General of the United Nations, in responding to a letter from the German Minister of Foreign Affairs, stated: 'Let me recall that at no point did my letter state that recognition of the independence of particular Yugoslav Republics should be denied, or withheld indefinitely. Rather, I observe that the principle of self-determination is enshrined in the Charter of the United Nations itself.' Reuter, 14 December 1991.

the advisory opinions of the Badinter Arbitration Commission as well as the proclamations of independence by Croatia, Slovenia and Macedonia.[114] On 29 November 1991, the Commission, after analysing the factual circumstances of the Yugoslav case, came to the conclusion that 'the Socialist Federal Republic of Yugoslavia is *in the process* of dissolution'.[115] Later, in its opinion of 4 July 1992, the Commission observed that, since its opinion of 29 November, the federal authority could no longer be effectively exercised because the majority of the Yugoslav republics had constituted themselves as independent States which had been recognised by the international community. In addition, the Commission continued, Serbia and Montenegro had established a new State (the Federal Republic of Yugoslavia) and had adopted a new constitution on 27 April 1992. The Commission moreover recalled the Security Council's statement in its Resolution 757 that 'the claim by the Federal Republic of Yugoslavia . . . to continue automatically the membership of the former Socialist Federal Republic of Yugoslavia in the United Nations has not been generally accepted'.[116] On the basis of these facts, the Commission concluded that 'the process of dissolution of the SFRY referred to in Opinion No. 1 of 29 November 1991 is now complete and that the SFRY no longer exists'.[117]

These opinions leave no doubt that, according to the Commission, the SFRY was still in existence on the date of the (reaffirmed) proclamations of independence by Croatia and Slovenia on 8 October 1991. Therefore, the acts by Croatia and Slovenia, first in June 1991 and later in October 1991, set in motion the process of dismemberment of the SFRY, which eventually culminated in the latter's extinction. Accordingly, the proclamations of independence of these two republics – and also that of Macedonia on 17 September 1991, which was, as in the case of Slovenia, subsequently acquiesced in by the SFRY – must be seen as acts of secession which, in combination with other factors, *led to the dissolution* of the SFRY.[118] This view has support in doctrine,[119] and is furthermore supported by the

[114] Macedonia proclaimed independence on 17 September 1991.

[115] Opinion 1, *ILM* 31 (1992), pp. 1494–7, at p. 1497, para. 3 (emphasis added).

[116] SC Res. 757 of 30 May 1992.

[117] Opinion No. 8, *ILM* 31 (1992), pp. 1521–3, at p. 1523, para. 4. See also SC Res. 777 of 19 September 1992, preamble; and GA Res. 47/135 of 18 December 1992.

[118] See also Raič, *Statehood and the Law of Self-Determination*, pp. 356–361.

[119] See, e.g., Weller, 'The International Response', p. 606; Murswiek, 'The Issue of a Right of Secession – Reconsidered', pp. 30–32; Franck, 'Opinion Directed at Question 2 of the Reference', p. 11, paras. 2.14–2.15; I. Brownlie, 'International Law at the Fiftieth Anniversary of the United Nations', *Recueil des Cours* (1995), p. 9, at p. 68; A. Whelan, 'Wilsonian Self-Determination and the Versailles Settlement', *ICLQ* 43 (1994), p. 99, at p. 114.

positions of Croatia and Slovenia, as reflected in their proclamations of independence and through their acceptance of the Brioni Accord. It may therefore be concluded that the right of self-determination was applicable to the crisis in the former Yugoslavia and that the formation of the Croatian State was a result of unilateral secession.

The question of whether there existed a right of unilateral secession for the Croats at 8 October 1991 must be answered in the affirmative, as the situation met all the requirements for the exercise of such a right contained in the qualified secession doctrine.

3. Bosnia-Herzegovina

The creation of the State of Bosnia-Herzegovina may also be seen as an example of unilateral secession, as the independence of the State was established by recognition, without the consent of the Yugoslav Federation, before the Federation was dissolved.

The parliament of Bosnia-Herzegovina declared the republic's independence on 14 October 1991, but this was rejected by the Serb and Croat minorities who, together with the Bosnian Muslims or Bosniaks, made up the population of the republic.[120] The Bosnian Serbs expressed their desire to stay within the Yugoslav Federation and, on 9 January 1992, the Assembly representing the Serbian population in Bosnia-Herzegovina announced the formation of an autonomous (but not yet independent) Republic of the Serbian People of Bosnia-Herzegovina. The Bosnian Croats sought to secede from the Republic and to join Croatia but in the meantime they established the Republic of Herceg-Bosna on 3 July 1992. Alongside Croatia, Slovenia and Macedonia, Bosnia-Herzegovina requested recognition from the European Community and its member States on 24 December 1991. However, in Opinion No. 4, the Badinter Arbitration Commission held that the absence of a referendum in Bosnia-Herzegovina meant that 'the will of the peoples of Bosnia-Herzegovina to constitute [the Republic] as a sovereign and independent State cannot be held to have been fully established',[121] and that, consequently, recognition should not be granted. The Commission observed however that its assessment could be reviewed 'if appropriate guarantees were provided by the Republic . . . possibly by means of a referendum of all the citizens of the SRBH without distinction, carried out under international

[120] Before the war in the former Yugoslavia, the population of Bosnia-Herzegovina was 44 per cent Bosniak, 31 per cent Serb and 17 per cent Croat.

[121] *ILM* 31 (1992), p. 1501, at p. 1503.

supervision'.[122] On 29 February and 1 March 1992, a referendum was held, but this was boycotted by the Serb minority. Out of a 63 per cent turnout, a reported 99.4 per cent voted for complete independence.[123] Fighting erupted almost immediately between Bosniaks and both Serb irregulars and the YNA and Croatian irregulars. Five days later, on 6 March 1992 the Republic of Bosnia-Herzegovina was declared to be an independent State by President Izetbegovic. The EC countries and the United States recognised Bosnia-Herzegovina on 7 April 1992, which led to an intensification of fighting between the different ethnic groups in the country. Before the EC/US recognition, Bosnia-Herzegovina had been recognised by Bulgaria and Turkey, but the EC/US lead was quickly followed by many other countries in the following few weeks.[124] The Bosnian government applied for admission to the United Nations on 8 May[125] and was admitted to UN membership on 22 May 1992.[126]

It is highly questionable whether Bosnia-Herzegovina met the conditions for the existence of a right of unilateral secession *at the time* of its declaration of independence – and even possibly at the time of its recognition and admission to the United Nations.[127] At this stage, it was not clear which people (Bosniaks alone, or Bosniaks and Bosnian Croats) were exercising the right of self-determination; whether attempts at internal self-determination had been exhausted; and whether the human rights of the people had been seriously violated. Subsequent events in Bosnia-Herzegovina, particularly the massive 'ethnic cleansing' of Bosniaks by Serbian forces, show that the Bosniaks had good reason to fear that they would be subjected to the most vicious violation of human rights and denial of self-determination. Perhaps the secession of Bosnia-Herzegovina may be seen as a case in which the conditions for the existence of a right of unilateral secession were anticipated rather than fulfilled at the time of the proclamation of independence. Whatever the position, Bosnia-Herzegovina does not provide a good example of the exercise of the qualified right of secession in accordance with the principles expounded in this study. The secession of Bosnia-Herzegovina is further complicated by the fact that at the time of its recognition and admission to the United

[122] *Ibid.* [123] *Keesings Record of World Events*, 38/3 (1992), p. 38832.

[124] Within the period of April–May, recognition was granted by, for instance, Croatia, Canada, New Zealand, Czechoslovakia, Hungary, Poland, Egypt, Saudi Arabia and Australia. See R. Rich, 'Recognition of States: The Collapse of Yugoslavia and the Soviet Union', *EJIL* 4 (1993), p. 36, at pp. 50–1.

[125] UN Doc. A/46/921-S23971 (1992). [126] GA Res. 46/237 of 22 May 1992.

[127] See also Raič, *Statehood and the Law of Self-Determination*, pp. 414–18.

Nations it also failed to meet the requirements of statehood, particularly in that it lacked an effective government. This aspect is considered below.

VI. Non-recognition

The United Nations has resorted to non-recognition of claimant States in a number of cases that have a secessionist character. However, in all but one of these instances – that of Katanga – the United Nations has based its non-recognition largely on principles other than that of respect for territorial integrity.

The unilateral declaration of independence by Rhodesia in 1965 was a clear act of unilateral secession from the United Kingdom.[128] Rhodesia failed, however, to meet the criteria for the qualified right of secession as here a white minority regime that was itself suppressing the human rights of the majority in its territory attempted to secede from a parent State that could hardly be accused of violating the human rights of the white minority. The Security Council adopted several resolutions calling upon States not to recognise Rhodesia as an independent State.[129] These resolutions focused on the 'illegality' of the regime under British law and not on the illegality of secession from the United Kingdom under international law.[130] That Rhodesian independence failed to qualify as a genuine exercise in self-determination under Resolution 1514 (XV) was, however, stressed by the General Assembly.[131] While it may be possible to interpret resolutions of the United Nations on Rhodesia as a denial that the conditions for the exercise of the right of secession had been met, this was clearly not their main intent.

South Africa's four Bantustans – Transkei, Bophuthatswana, Venda and Ciskei – were also subjected to non-recognition by the United Nations.[132] In each Bantustan there was a people, constituting a majority in its own territory, which had been subjected to human rights abuses by the South African regime. But in this case, separation from South Africa was

[128] See, generally, Dugard, *Recognitions and the United Nations*, pp. 90–8; V. Gowlland-Debbas, *Collective Responses to Illegal Acts in International Law. United Nations Action in the Question of Southern Rhodesia* (Martinus Nijhoff, 1990); Raič, *Statehood and the Law of Self-Determination*, pp. 128–40.

[129] SC Res. 216 of 12 November 1965, 217 of 20 November 1965, 277 of 15 March 1970 and 288 of 17 November 1970.

[130] SC Res. 217 (1965) and 277 (1970).

[131] Resolutions 2151 (XXI) of 17 November 1966, 2383 (XXIII) of 7 November 1968, 2508 (XXIV) of 21 November 1969 and 2652 (XXV) of 3 December 1970.

[132] See Dugard, *Recognition and the United Nations*, pp. 90–108; Dugard, *International Law*, pp. 445–61.

imposed on the people by the South African regime itself in an attempt to rid South Africa of a large portion of its black population and to gain international credibility by the apparent promotion of self-determination in the Bantustans. Resolutions of the United Nations rightly refused to accept this 'decolonisation' of the Bantustans as a true exercise in self-determination.[133] Calls for non-recognition were based on the fact that the creation of the Bantustan States was designed to further the policy of apartheid. However, several of the General Assembly resolutions did condemn the Bantustans on the ground that their actions were designed 'to destroy the territorial integrity of the country'.[134]

The establishment of the Turkish Republic of Northern Cyprus (TRNC) in 1983 may be characterised as a forcible secession from Cyprus, following Turkey's invasion of the island in 1974. Indeed resolutions of the Security Council condemning the proclamation of the TRNC and calling on States to withhold recognition labelled the creation of the TRNC an exercise in secession. In Resolution 541 (1983), the Security Council deplored 'the declaration of the Turkish Cypriot authorities of the purported secession of part of the Republic of Cyprus' and requested States to respect the territorial integrity of Cyprus. Later, in Resolution 550 (1984), it reiterated its call to States 'not to recognise the purported State of the 'Turkish Republic of Northern Cyprus set up by secessionist acts'. The main reasons for the non-recognition of the TRNC, however, are that it is founded on Turkey's illegal use of force against Cyprus in 1974 and that it violates the 1960 Treaty of Guarantee between Cyprus, Greece, Turkey and the United Kingdom, which guarantees the territorial integrity of Cyprus and prohibits partition of the island.[135]

Katanga's attempted secession from the Congo in 1960 is the best example of United Nations' rejection of an unlawful secession.[136] Eleven days after Congo itself became independent, Katanga declared its independence. Although Belgium gave Katanga military assistance, neither it nor any other State accorded recognition to Katanga. In 1963, Katanga abandoned its claim to independence. In 1961, the Security Council, in

133 SC Res. 402 of 22 December 1976 and 407 of 25 May 1977; GA Res. 31/6A of 26 October 1976, GA Res. 32/105 N of 14 December 1977 and GA Res. 34/93 of 12 December 1979.

134 GA Res. 31/6 A of 26 October 1976, GA Res. 32/105 N of 14 December 1977 and GA Res. 34/93 of 12 December 1979.

135 See the statements by Cyprus in the Security Council debates preceding the adoption of Resolution 541 of 18 November 1983, *UN Chronicle* 21/1 (1984), pp. 76, 550, and SC Res. 550 of 11 May 1984, in *ibid.*, 21/4, p. 18.

136 See C. C. O'Brien, *To Katanga and Back: A UN Case History* (New York: Simon & Schuster, 1962); R. Higgins, *United Nations Peace Keeping* 1946 – 1967, vol 3: Africa (Oxford: Oxford University Press, 1980).

Resolution 169, rejected the claim that Katanga is a 'sovereign independent nation', deprecated 'the secessionist' activities illegally carried out by the provincial administration of Katanga, declared that 'all secessionist activities against the Republic of Congo are contrary to the *Loi fondamentale* and Security Council decisions', and demanded that such activities 'shall cease forthwith'.[137]

VII. Evaluation of the case studies in the context of the qualified right of secession

A qualified right of secession comes into being, it has been suggested, when a people forming a numerical minority in a State, but a majority within a particular part of the State, are denied the right of internal self-determination or subjected to serious and systematic suppression of human rights, and there are no reasonable and effective remedies for the peaceful settlement of the dispute with the parent State. In such a case, and if the criteria for statehood have been met, third States are permitted (but not obliged) to acknowledge the seceding entity's exercise of the right of external self-determination by recognising it as a State. As secession in today's world is discouraged on account of the tendency to place territorial integrity above external self-determination in the hierarchy of values, recognition is increasingly accorded in a collective manner. That is, when a regional arrangement such as the European Community decides, after careful collective deliberation, that the criteria for the exercise of the qualified right of secession have been met, despite the preference for the maintenance of the territorial integrity of a State, it will grant recognition collectively to the seceding entity. The subsequent admission of the entity to the United Nations constitutes a further act of collective recognition on a larger, more universal scale. In this way isolated, individual acts of recognition constituting an unlawful intervention in the domestic affairs of the parent State are discouraged, eliminated, or reduced to a minimum. If the international community decides that the criteria for secession have not been met, recognition will either be withheld or denounced by means of a call for non-recognition.

The cases examined in this study lend broad support to the above scheme. Bangladesh falls squarely into this scheme, as here an ethnic group constituting a majority within a part of Pakistan, that was denied internal self-determination and subjected to serious human rights violations, had exhausted all peaceful avenues before it resorted to secession. Although

[137] See too, GA Res. 1474 (ES-IV) of 20 September 1960.

its bid for statehood was assisted by individual acts of recognition, there is no doubt that Bangladesh's admission to the Commonwealth set the seal on its statehood, despite the delay in its admission to the United Nations. Although some may persist in suggesting that Croatia's independence was the result of the dissolution of the Yugoslav Federation, the more accepted perception, as has been shown above, is that it was a case of unilateral secession. Again, the criteria for the exercise of the qualified right of secession were met, and the final endorsement of this assessment was given in the form of collective recognition by the European Community and the United Nations (by means of admission to the Organization).

Bosnia-Herzegovina presents a special problem because of its complex ethnic composition of Bosniaks (Muslims), Croats and Serbs. The question may seriously be posed whether it met the first criterion for the exercise of the qualified right of secession – that is, a people constituting a majority in a particular part of the territory of the parent State. This issue clearly troubled the Badinter Arbitration Commission and the European Community which were only satisfied that the conditions for the exercise of self-determination had been met after the holding of a referendum (despite the fact that it was boycotted by the Serb community). Once the criterion of a 'people' was met, as evidenced by the referendum result, Bosnia-Herzegovina was seen to meet the requirements for the exercise of the qualified right of secession, although, as in the case of Croatia, some prefer to portray this as a case of dissolution rather than secession. As suggested above, it is also doubtful whether other conditions for the exercise of the qualified right of secession were properly met. However, recognition by the member States of the European Community and admission to the United Nations secured the independence of Bosnia-Herzegovina.

The creation of Slovenia and Macedonia are not examples of unilateral secession, as in these cases the parent State, the Yugoslav Federation, albeit reluctantly, acquiesced in or consented to their independence.

It must be noted, however, that in all the cases examined in this study, recognition was granted at a time when the entities in question did not exercise complete control over their territories or meet the traditional requirement for statehood of effective government. Recognition, therefore, had a consolidating effect, as it served to secure the independence of the State and to bolster the effectiveness of its government by lending international legitimacy.

It should not be assumed that the criterion of government was overlooked in these cases. In approaching the criterion of 'government', one must make a distinction between the existence of an exclusive right or title to exercise authority over a certain territory and its inhabitants, and the actual exercise of that authority.[138] In both situations, the statehood criterion of 'government' is met. An exclusive right to exercise authority *without* necessarily an actual exercise of authority may occur where there has been a transfer of sovereignty (as in many cases of decolonisation) or in cases of the exercise of an applicable right to external self-determination. For it is inherent in the right to establish an independent State that once such a right is exercised there is an exclusive right to exercise authority over the territory concerned by the relevant people or its legitimate representatives. Such a title may compensate for a lack of effective governmental power during the process of the State's empirical establishment, especially when the lack of effective governmental control is a result of unlawful conduct by the central authorities of the parent State.[139]

State practice since 1960 provides few examples of successful unilateral secession. Moreover, there is a tendency to portray successful secessions such as those of Croatia and Bosnia-Herzegovina as instances of dissolution of States rather than of unilateral secession, in order, no doubt, to discourage secessionist movements. In most instances, assertions of secession have simply fallen on deaf ears: States have failed to respond to appeals for recognition of statehood from peoples, often peoples whose right to internal self-determination has been denied and whose human rights have been seriously violated, because respect for territorial integrity is seen to occupy a higher place in the hierarchy of values upon which the contemporary legal order is founded. The non-recognition of Biafra is a glaring example of this; but, as shown above, there are other cases in which territorial integrity has been placed above humanitarian considerations.

Collective recognition is a useful instrument for the creation of States, but the other side of this instrument is collective non-recognition, and this has not been infrequently used to obstruct secession. Here one must have regard not only to those cases in which the Security Council or General Assembly has clearly and expressly called on States to deny recognition – as with Katanga and the Turkish Republic of Northern Cyprus – but also to cases such as Abkhazia, in which the Security Council and the European Union have in effect blocked secession by their disapproval.

The contemporary rules of secession have had a major impact on the rules of recognition. Whereas before 1960, States were free to confer recognition upon a secessionist entity claiming statehood that complied with

[138] Crawford, *The Creation of States in International Law*, p. 44.

[139] For a detailed discussion of this point see Raič, *Statehood and the Law of Self-Determination*, pp. 95–105, 402–413.

the requirements of statehood, subject only to the prohibition on premature recognition, States today may not recognise a secessionist entity as a state unless the entity in question can demonstrate that it comprises a people entitled to exercise the right of secession which has been oppressed within the meaning of 'qualification' contained in the 1970 Declaration on Friendly Relations. The unilateral recognition of seceding entities can no longer be expected other than in exceptional circumstances. The precedent of Panama is now relegated to the past. Individual States will simply not exercise their discretionary power of recognition in the absence of a clear indication from the United Nations or the relevant regional organisation. Consequently, the recognition of secessionist entities appears to have become mainly a matter for collective decision-making – either by way of a public declaration of recognition or by way of admission to the international organisation in question.

5

The State as a 'primary fact': some thoughts on the principle of effectiveness

THÉODORE CHRISTAKIS

The creation of States has often been compared to a meta-judicial fact which cannot be explained by legal rules. International law does not permit secession, but does not prohibit it either. Thus, the only criterion for the emergence of a new State, outside the colonial context, is the principle of effectiveness: if a secessionist entity succeeds in fulfilling the conditions of statehood, a new State is born. Secession is not a question of law, but a question of fact.

The goal of this chapter is to examine this traditional view and to discover the exact interactions between the law and the facts in the process of the creation of States.

Part I of the chapter confirms the actuality of the principle of effectiveness. Of course, no real 'automatism' exists in this field. As the study shows, in some cases the effectiveness of the secession did not permit the creation of a new State. In other cases, a State has been created without fulfilling the conditions for statehood. In a third type of case, the principle of *uti possidetis juris* clashed with the principle of effectiveness. Nonetheless, it remains the case that appeal to the principle of effectiveness is the only available solution in a society marked by a great paradox: States, which in the great majority prohibit unilateral secession in their internal legal orders, do not wish (or do not think it feasible) to create a prohibitive rule in the international legal order. They prefer to let the 'facts' decide, while trying to shape them according to their interests. The principle of effectiveness seems then compatible with the maxim *'ex factis ius oritur'*; but it is also very dangerous. If the theory of 'ultimate success' is the only path to independence, then only the 'law of the strongest' applies here, and the theory is an invitation to violence.

Part II of this chapter tries to define in what precise manner international law tries to 'discipline' the principle of effectiveness, in order to contain the dangers to international peace and security. It finds that in some salient cases (and especially in the case of external aggression), international law denies the quality of 'State' to a secessionist entity, notwithstanding its 'ultimate success'. Thus, secession is not only a question of 'fact', but also a question of 'law', and the traditional factual criteria for statehood need to be complemented by some legal ones. The maxim *'ex iniuria ius non oritur'* defines the external limits of acceptance of the principle of effectiveness.

L'ETAT EN TANT QUE 'FAIT PRIMAIRE': RÉFLEXIONS SUR LA PORTÉE DU PRINCIPE D'EFFECTIVITÉ

L'étude de l'existence d'une réglementation de la sécession par le droit international semble se heurter à une difficulté théorique fondamentale. Pour une très grande majorité de juristes, la sécession, ainsi que le processus de formation d'un nouvel Etat, relèvent du 'simple fait' et échappent par définition à toute emprise du droit. 'La naissance et la fin de l'Etat sont des faits métajuridiques'[1] et 'ne s'expliquent point par des règles juridiques'.[2] Seul le principe de l'effectivité est ici pertinent, qui permet au droit international d'ériger certaines circonstances en 'faits-conditions' et d'attribuer ainsi des conséquences juridiques à certaines situations réelles. En d'autres termes, toute entité infra-étatique peut essayer de faire sécession. Si elle échoue, tant pis; mais si en revanche elle réussit à instaurer une nouvelle effectivité, c'est-à-dire à réunir les 'éléments constitutifs' de l'Etat, un nouvel Etat est alors né. Le droit international se désengage donc et se borne à entériner le fait accompli, à délivrer, pour ainsi dire, un acte de naissance, 'sans mettre en question les facteurs qui ont amené sa formation'.[3] La naissance de l'Etat étant considérée comme un 'fait primaire',[4] un fait qui précède le droit, toute interrogation sur l'intervention du droit dans le processus de formation d'un nouvel Etat est inutile et vaine.

[1] H. Kelsen, 'Théorie générale du droit international public', *Recueil des cours* 42 (1932-IV), p. 261.

[2] Phrase de Jellinek citée par F. Münch, 'La force normative des faits', in: *Estudios de Derecho Internacional, Homenaje al profesor Miaja de la Muela* (Madrid: Ed. Tecnos, 1979), vol. I, p. 251.

[3] Ch. De Visscher, *Les effectivités du droit international public* (Paris: Pedone, 1967), p. 36.

[4] G. Abi-Saab, 'Cours général de droit international public', *Recueil des cours* 207 (1987-VII), p. 68. V. aussi sa conclusion dans ce volume.

Le renvoi au principe d'effectivité, et exclusivement à ce principe, a donc pour effet non seulement de neutraliser la règle de droit, mais aussi de transformer de façon quasi-ovidéenne la nature juridique de l'Etat: personne morale incontestable, et être corporatif par excellence, sa naissance se trouve le plus souvent comparée à celle d'une personne physique 'en ce sens que le droit peut encourager ou décourager la natalité, mais il ne peut pas 'causer' la naissance d'un être humain; il prend acte de son existence une fois qu'il est né'.[5] L'Etat aurait donc lui aussi une 'existence objective' dès la réunion des conditions nécessaires à son émergence. Et, par conséquent, le problème de la sécession ne pourrait se poser nullement en termes d''autorisation' ou de 'prohibition' par le droit positif, mais seulement en termes de 'succès' ou d''échec'.

Le principe d'effectivité aurait donc deux dimensions. Dans sa dimension positive, il pourrait être défini[6] comme le principe selon lequel une entité qui réussit à réunir les trois éléments constitutifs de l'Etat et à mettre en place des autorités effectives et stables accède au statut d'Etat et a donc droit à la protection que le droit international accorde à ce statut. Inversement, dans sa dimension négative, le principe dénie le statut d'Etat aux entités qui ne remplissent pas la condition de l'effectivité.

La présente étude essaiera de définir quelle est la portée précise du principe d'effectivité dans ce domaine et quelles sont – ou doivent être – les interactions entre le fait et le droit en matière de création d'Etat. Elle montrera ainsi que le principe d'effectivité joue incontestablement un rôle très important: il épargne le droit international du problème extrêmement délicat de la sécession, tout en le gardant au contact de la réalité et en lui permettant d''intégrer' les faits dans l'ordonnancement juridique. Le recours au principe de l'effectivité permet donc de pallier aux faiblesses d'un droit international volontairement lacunaire, donnant toute sa signification à la maxime *ex factis jus oritur* (I). Toutefois, à mesure que le droit international se développe, le recours à la seule théorie de l'effectivité s'avère nuisible. Cette étude va alors examiner le principe fondamental *ex iniuria ius non oritur*, pour montrer que le droit international *peut* intervenir dans ce qui a été qualifié de 'royaume des effectivités' et qu'en matière de formation d'Etat, comme d'ailleurs aussi dans d'autres domaines, une effectivité illicite – surtout résultant d'une agression – ne doit pas produire des effets de droit (II).

[5] *Ibid.*

[6] Le terme 'effectivité' pourrait être défini de manière brute comme le 'caractère d'une situation qui existe en fait, réellement', G. Cornu (dir.), *Vocabulaire juridique* (Paris: Quadrige/PUF, 2001), p. 323.

I. L'effectivité en lieu et place du droit: la naissance de l'Etat dans le monde des faits

Le recours au principe de l'effectivité en matière de création d'Etat se présente dans une large mesure comme inévitable. Contrairement aux personnes morales de droit interne (y compris les collectivités territoriales) dont la création fait appel à la technique de l'acte juridique, l'Etat naît, avant tout, dans l'univers des faits, c'est-à-dire par la réunion de certaines conditions matérielles que le droit prend en compte, en leur attribuant des conséquences juridiques. Il est donc incontestable que, sous réserve des remarques que nous formulerons dans la deuxième partie, la sécession est 'une question de fait' (A). Ce renvoi à l'univers des faits présente sans doute plusieurs mérites: le droit international sort sauf d'une épreuve difficile, tout en tirant les conséquences de la 'réalité triomphante', de l'interminable va-et-vient entre le fait et le droit, entre le *Sein* et le *Sollen*, pour emprunter la fameuse terminologie de Kelsen. Le problème toutefois est que le recours au principe de l'effectivité paraît aussi, à bien des égards, insatisfaisant et dangereux, car il signifie la mise à l'écart, le 'désengagement' du droit au profit de la loi du plus fort (B).

A) Le caractère incontournable du recours à l'effectivité

Affirmer que la formation de l'Etat est un 'fait juridique' revient à dire que 'l'Etat existe en droit dès lors que le pays existe en fait'.[7] Le principe de l'effectivité implique donc une concordance quasi-parfaite entre l'existence de certains 'faits-conditions' et la naissance de l'Etat (1). Pourtant, un examen plus attentif de la pratique révèle une inadéquation fréquente entre l'existence de l'Etat et l'existence des faits. Ce décalage ne remet pas en cause la nécessité du recours au principe d'effectivité. Elle montre néanmoins de manière éloquente le caractère illusoire des comparaisons avec la naissance des personnes physiques, et prouve que le principe d'effectivité ne suffit pas à expliquer à lui seul le phénomène de la formation de l'Etat (2).

(1) 'L'Etat existe en droit dès qu'il existe en fait'

Se nourrissant de la faiblesse du droit en matière de sécession, le principe d'effectivité met l'accent sur la force des faits et sur la réunion cumulative des 'éléments constitutifs' de l'Etat.

[7] J. Combacau et S. Sur, *Droit international public*, 5ème édn. (Paris: Montchrestien, 2001), p. 279.

a. La faiblesse du droit: l'existence de lacunes Le principe de l'effectivité intervient, dans une large mesure, dans une zone de 'non-droit', en tant que substitut au droit. Dans le monde post-colonial, le droit international n'autorise pas la sécession, mais il ne la prohibe pas non plus. Une lacune consciente existe dans ce domaine, faisant de la sécession beaucoup plus une question de fait et de force que de droit.

Nous avons déjà eu l'occasion de repousser[8] certaines affirmations doctrinales selon lesquelles la pratique récente témoignerait de l'existence d'un droit de sécession en dehors des situations de décolonisation et d'occupation militaire. Un tel droit n'est en effet nullement conféré par les textes interétatiques, conventionnels ou autres, concernant les droits des peuples, des minorités ou des populations autochtones. Au contraire, ces textes comportent, le plus souvent, des clauses de sauvegarde excluant de manière explicite toute idée d'un droit de sécession en dehors du contexte colonial. Parallèlement, la pratique étatique, individuelle ou collective (au sein des organisations internationales), ne va guère dans le sens de la reconnaissance d'un tel droit.[9] Le droit à l'autodétermination ne comporte donc pas de volet 'externe' en dehors des situations classiques de décolonisation et d'occupation étrangère. Ceci d'ailleurs n'a rien d'étonnant, le droit international est un droit créé par les Etats et il serait pour le moins paradoxal de voir ces Etats reconnaître à leurs composantes la capacité, en droit, de les mutiler.

Ce qui paraît, par contre, beaucoup plus étonnant est que, réserve faite de deux situations graves qui nous occuperont dans la deuxième partie de notre étude, ces Etats-'législateurs' n'ont pas voulu *interdire* la sécession, alors pourtant qu'une analyse comparative des constitutions des Etats montre que la majorité écrasante de celles-ci interdit la sécession unilatérale.[10] En réalité, il existe souvent un important contraste entre l'attitude des Etats face à une crise sécessionniste qui menace leur propre

[8] Th. Christakis, *Le droit à l'autodétermination en dehors des situations de décolonisation* (Paris: La documentation française, 1999), p. 141.

[9] La seule hypothèse d'émergence progressive d'un droit à l'autodétermination externe pourrait être celle de la 'sécession remède', qui ne concernerait que des cas particulièrement graves et irrémédiables de violation des droits de l'homme. Toutefois, comme nous l'avons souligné (*ibid.*, p. 295), l'*opinio juris* est ici ambiguë et ne pourrait, à la limite, concerner que certaines situations absolument extrêmes (telles que le génocide). La pratique est d'ailleurs quasi inexistante et l'ensemble de la théorie frappé d'un grand nombre d'ambiguïtés, surtout compte tenu de la nécessité d'une évaluation objective et centralisée des réclamations afin d'éviter les dangers d'une invocation abusive.

[10] Sur un ensemble de cent huit constitutions que nous avons examinées, provenant des pays de toutes les régions du monde, deux seulement reconnaissent un tel droit de sécession unilatérale, à savoir la Constitution de Saint Christopher et Nevis de 1983 et celle de l'Ethiopie

territoire, et celle qu'ils adoptent lorsqu'une crise menace l'intégrité territoriale d'un autre Etat. Les contradictions des Etats dans ce dernier cas, reflet de leurs intérêts et de leurs préférences politiques, expliquent sans doute en partie l'absence d'une interdiction de la sécession en droit international (le reste de l'explication étant fourni par le réalisme des Etats et le caractère techniquement quasi-impossible d'une règle prohibitive générale). Les Etats ne veulent pas et ne peuvent pas fermer définitivement la porte à la sécession. Certes, ils souhaitent ériger contre elle de sérieux obstacles susceptibles de protéger à la fois leur intégrité territoriale et la paix et la sécurité internationales, mais des obstacles tout de même surmontables. Les Etats résistent à la création d'une règle interdisant de manière générale et ferme la sécession. Ils préfèrent laisser le dernier mot à la politique, à la 'réalité', aux rapports de force: sans être entravés par des règles juridiques inflexibles, ils pourront ainsi agir sur les effectivités en essayant de les pétrir selon leur volonté.

b. La force des faits: le test de l'effectivité La question est alors de savoir à partir de quel moment précis il est possible juridiquement de constater que l'on est en présence d'un nouvel Etat. C'est le principe d'effectivité qui reconnaît en l'existence de certains faits bruts la réalisation des conditions nécessaires à l'émergence d'un Etat. Cette entité passera donc avec succès le 'test de l'effectivité' dès qu'elle aura réussi à réunir les fameux 'éléments constitutifs' de l'Etat,[11] c'est-à-dire à convaincre de l'existence d'une 'population', sise sur un 'territoire déterminé' et dotée d'un 'gouvernement souverain'.

Il y a peu de choses à redire en ce qui concerne les deux premières conditions. L'Etat est avant tout une collectivité territoriale, un 'être corporatif personnalisé', la 'représentation dans l'univers du droit d'[une] réalité sociale et spatiale'.[12] Ni l'importance de la population, ni son homogénéité,

de 1994. Plus de quatre-vingt contiennent en revanche des formulations qui montrent qu'une tentative de sécession unilatérale devrait être considérée comme anticonstitutionnelle, certaines d'entre elles prévoyant même que l'Etat doit adopter des mesures concrètes pour combattre les activités sécessionnistes. Le silence de la Constitution de certains pays en ce qui concerne la possibilité d'une sécession unilatérale a, d'ailleurs, été interprété le plus souvent par les juridictions suprêmes ou les organes politiques de ces Etats comme excluant tout droit de sécession, comme le montre le célèbre arrêt *Texas v. White* de 1868 de la Cour Suprême des Etats-Unis d'Amérique, l'avis de la Cour suprême du Canada rendu le 20 août 1998, ou encore la position de la Suisse devant le Comité des droits de l'homme des Nations Unies. Pour une analyse détaillée voir *ibid.*, pp. 237–46 et 286–94.

11 Appelés, plus prudemment et sans doute plus correctement, 'conditions d'émergence' par Combacau, *Droit international*, p. 272.

12 *Ibid.*

ni l'étendue du territoire, ni sa continuité ne sont des critères pertinents, le droit international exigeant seulement une population et un territoire 'déterminés'. Le terme 'déterminés' ne signifie pas d'ailleurs totalement et absolument définis; on sait, par exemple, qu'un Etat peut naître avant que ses frontières ne soient définitivement fixées et alors que certaines parties du territoire revendiqué font l'objet de contestations de la part d'autres Etats.[13] Encore faut-il que la population et l'assise spatiale du nouvel Etat soient globalement identifiables.

Il y a, par contre, beaucoup plus à dire en ce qui concerne la troisième condition, de loin la plus importante, à savoir le 'gouvernement souverain', qui pourrait être aussi analysée comme deux conditions distinctes, à savoir l'existence d'un 'appareil gouvernemental' d'une part, et 'souverain' (indépendant) d'autre part.

Comme le souligne Jean Combacau, l'exigence d'un appareil gouvernemental est liée à la qualité de personne morale de l'Etat: ce dernier est 'une collectivité considérée à l'extérieur comme un tout, et qui n'y est connue que par des organes réputés agir en son nom et des agents agissant pour le compte des premiers. Son apparition est donc proprement inconcevable si la collectivité ne se donne pas des organes par l'intermédiaire desquels les agissements de fait du corps social qu'elle constitue déjà pourront être imputés au corps de droit qu'elle prétend devenir.'[14] En érigeant cette exigence en 'condition d'émergence' le club des Etats préexistants assure la pérennité du modèle étatique classique. Chaque Etat souhaite s'assurer que le nouveau venu 'jouera le jeu' et respectera les droits de ses pairs. L'existence d'une autorité politique effective (faute d'être nécessairement représentative[15]), capable de maintenir un certain degré d'ordre et de prémunir le nouvel Etat de l'anarchie, offre une garantie de respect des règles fondamentales du droit international ou au moins, en cas de violation de ces règles, un destinataire pour la présentation des réclamations. Il s'agit, ici, d'une première dimension 'interne' du principe de l'effectivité qui est, néanmoins, d'une application plutôt souple, l'existence d'un gouvernement effectif étant généralement présumée.

[13] Voir, par exemple, l'avis rendu par la CPJI le 4 septembre 1924 dans l'*Affaire du Monastère de Saint-Naoum* concernant la frontière albanaise (Série B, n° 9), ou la décision rendue par le Tribunal arbitral mixte germano-polonais le 1er août 1929 dans l'affaire *Deutsche Continental Gas Gesellschaft c. Etat polonais* (*Rec. TAM*, 9, pp. 336–48).

[14] Combacau et Sur, *Droit international*, p. 274.

[15] Pour une analyse détaillée du problème de l'existence, en droit international, d'un 'principe de légitimité démocratique' voir Christakis, *Le droit à l'autodétermination*, pp. 328–506.

La seconde dimension du principe d'effectivité est, en revanche, beaucoup plus importante, et c'est, d'ailleurs, par excellence elle qui distingue le nouvel Etat de certaines collectivités territoriales organisées de l'ordre juridique interne. Il s'agit de la souveraineté qui, comme l'avait souligné Max Huber, signifie 'dans les relations entre Etats . . . l'indépendance'.[16] L'Etat n'a 'au-dessus de lui aucune autre autorité, si ce n'est celle du droit international'.[17] Un nouvel Etat ne peut donc naître à la suite d'une sécession que s'il parvient à se soustraire à l'ordre juridique de l'Etat prédécesseur, réussissant à imposer et à maintenir, à titre exclusif, sa propre autorité sur son territoire. Comme l'a souligné une étude concernant l'accession éventuelle du Québec à l'indépendance, cette 'sécession serait considérée comme réussie si, durant un temps suffisamment long, les autorités québécoises parvenaient à exclure l'application du droit canadien sur leur territoire et réussissaient à y faire régner l'ordre juridique découlant de leurs propres lois et décisions'.[18]

La naissance de l'Etat sur la base du seul principe de l'effectivité explique donc aisément pourquoi une déclaration d'indépendance par une entité sécessionniste, qui constitue la manifestation on ne peut plus claire du rejet de toute soumission à l'ordre juridique de l'Etat prédécesseur, ne produit, en elle-même, aucun effet juridique. Le principe d'effectivité exige que cette déclaration soit confortée par l'exercice d'un contrôle général du gouvernement sur la population et le territoire du pays. La conjonction des trois 'éléments constitutifs' suffit donc théoriquement à la prise en compte par le droit du 'pur fait' de la création d'un nouvel Etat.

(2) L'inadéquation entre l'existence de l'Etat et l'existence des faits

La concordance entre les faits (la réunion des conditions d'émergence de l'Etat) et la naissance d'un nouvel Etat n'est pas aussi parfaite que le principe d'effectivité pourrait le laisser croire. Les trois hypothèses que nous examinerons ci-après ne remettent pas vraiment en cause ce principe, mais démontrent qu'aucun automatisme n'existe dans ce

[16] Voir l'arbitrage dans l'affaire de l'*Ile de Palmas*, Cour permanente d'arbitrage, 4 avril 1928, *RSA*, vol. II, p. 838.

[17] Selon la description de la souveraineté par D. Anzilotti dans son opinion individuelle jointe à l'avis consultatif rendu par la CPJI le 5 septembre 1931 dans l'affaire du *Régime douanier entre l'Allemagne et l'Autriche*, Série A/B, n° 41, p. 57.

[18] Th. Frank, R. Higgins, A. Pellet, M. Shaw, Ch. Tomuschat, *L'intégrité territoriale du Québec dans l'hypothèse de l'accession à la souveraineté*, Etude commandée par la Commission d'étude des questions afférentes à l'accession du Québec à la souveraineté, in: *Les Attributs d'un Québec souverain* (Québec: Bibliothèque nationale, 1992), Exposés et études, vol. 1, p. 410, par. 2.41.

domaine et qu'aucun parallélisme n'est permis avec la naissance des personnes physiques. La naissance de cette personne morale *sui generis* qu'est l'Etat soulève, en effet, des questions très délicates de fait et de droit, et l'affirmation de l'existence 'objective' de l'Etat doit inévitablement être nuancée face à la subjectivité avec laquelle les Etats reconnaissent ou non la réunion, au bénéfice de l'entité sécessionniste, des éléments constitutifs d'un nouvel Etat.

a. L'effectivité sans l'Etat (la présomption contre la sécession) La première hypothèse est celle du mouvement sécessionniste qui réussit à établir une effectivité claire sur son territoire, mais qui n'est pourtant pas traité comme un Etat par les membres de la communauté internationale. Cette hypothèse ne se présente, évidemment, que lorsque l'Etat d'origine s'oppose (mais sans succès) aux prétentions de l'entité sécessionniste. Elle est assez courante dans la pratique. Pour ne mentionner que certains conflits sécessionnistes récents, on peut rappeler que les déclarations d'indépendance de la Republika Srpska (Bosnie-Herzégovine), de la République de Krajina (Croatie), de l'Abkhazie (Géorgie), de la Transnistrie (République de Moldova) et d'Anjouan et Moheli (Comores) étaient accompagnées d'une 'grande dose' d'effectivité, le gouvernement central des Etats englobant n'ayant dans certains cas pratiquement plus aucune prise sur les territoires en question. Ces entités n'ont pas, pour autant, été considérées par la communauté internationale comme ayant accédé au statut d'Etat.

L'exemple de la Tchétchénie est tout aussi parlant. La Tchétchénie a déclaré son indépendance en novembre 1991 et son gouvernement a eu, trois ans durant, un contrôle effectif de son territoire, à l'exclusion de tout contrôle de la Fédération russe.[19] Toutefois, et bien que la Tchétchénie ait réuni les trois 'éléments constitutifs', la communauté interétatique ne l'a non seulement jamais 'reconnue', mais ne l'a même pas traitée comme un Etat. Le conflit qui a suivi l'intervention de l'armée russe en décembre 1994 n'a jamais été considéré comme un conflit 'international'. Bien au contraire, les Etats et les organisations internationales ont, tout en exprimant leur préoccupation concernant la situation humanitaire, affirmé

[19] Comme le note D. Hollis: 'From its declaration of independence in December 1991, until Russian troops invaded on December 11, 1994, Chechnya possessed a permanent population, living within defined borders, governed by President Dudayev and his administration . . . Although Dudayev's authority did not go uncontested inside Chechnya, none of the opposition groups ever posed a serious threat to his government's effective control over the republic or its population.' D. Hollis, 'Accountability in Chechnya – Addressing Internal Matters with Legal and Political International Norms', *Boston College Law Review*, 36/4 (1995), 815–16 (*cf.* aussi 799–800).

que la Tchétchénie faisait partie intégrante de la Fédération russe.[20] Même après la défaite humiliante de la Russie et la mise en place d'une effectivité étatique solide et incontestable par la Tchétchénie à partir du mois d'août 1996, les Etats n'ont pas voulu reconnaître l'indépendance de la Tchétchénie, la nouvelle intervention de l'armée russe sur ce territoire, trois années plus tard, étant à nouveau considérée comme s'inscrivant dans le cadre d'un conflit interne.

Ces exemples montrent qu'il n'existe aucune automaticité en ce qui concerne la création 'objective' de l'Etat. La prise en compte par la communauté internationale d'une effectivité étatique, même d'une effectivité incontestable, peut être une affaire délicate et complexe et exiger beaucoup de temps. L'idée d'une effectivité 'durable' se substitue donc à l'idée d'une effectivité 'instantanée' qui, comme par un coup de baguette magique, transformerait en Etat l'entité sécessionniste ayant réussi à réunir les 'éléments constitutifs'. En d'autres termes, ce n'est pas vraiment le 'succès' de la sécession qui est pris en compte par le droit, mais plutôt son 'succès ultime', sa capacité à s'imposer et à créer une situation apparemment irréversible.

C'est précisément cette théorie de l''*ultimate success*', qui a été mise en avant par les rares juridictions internes (toutes anglo-saxonnes) ayant eu à se prononcer sur le problème de la sécession. Influencé par les décisions de la Cour Suprême des Etats-Unis après la guerre de sécession,[21] le *Privy Council* britannique a refusé en 1968, dans l'affaire *Madzimbamuto v. Lardner-Burke & Phillip George*, de reconnaître toute valeur juridique aux décisions adoptées par le gouvernement rhodésien, parce que, selon lui, l''*ultimate success*' de la sécession n'était pas établi. La Cour a certes reconnu que le gouvernement de Ian Smith avait clairement le contrôle effectif de tout le territoire du pays à l'époque, elle a cependant considéré que: 'the British Government acting for the lawful Sovereign is taking steps to regain control and it is impossible to predict with certainty whether or not it will succeed'.[22]

Selon la théorie de l''*ultimate success*' donc, la mise en place d'une simple effectivité étatique ne suffit pas. Une sécession ne doit être considérée comme aboutie qu'à condition que l'ancien régime n'adopte plus de mesures pour contester la validité de la sécession ou, au moins, s'il est

[20] Pour un résumé des réactions internationales face au conflit en Tchétchénie, voir D. Hollis, 'Accountability in Chechnya', 805–9. Le Secrétaire général des Nations Unies, B. Boutros-Ghali, déclarait aussi en décembre 1994 que 'it is purely an internal affair' (*ibid.*, pp. 793–4). Pour la position de la France dans ce sens, voir *AFDI* 41 (1995), 911.

[21] *Cf.*, par exemple, *Williams v. Bruffy*, 6 Otto 176, 96 U.S. (1877), p. 186.

[22] Publiée in: 1 A.C. 645, 1969, p. 725.

établi avec certitude qu'il ne peut plus réussir à restaurer son autorité. C'est ce que Hersch Lauterpacht soulignait déjà en 1947 quand il écrivait que l'effectivité doit être établie 'beyond all reasonable doubt' et que 'the parent State must in fact have ceased to make efforts, promising success, to reassert its authority'.[23] De la même manière, plus récemment, J. Crawford soutenait que le consentement de l'Etat prédécesseur à la sécession 'est nécessaire, au moins jusqu'à ce que l'entité sécessionniste ait fermement établi son contrôle *au-delà de tout espoir de retour*'.[24]

Le problème, bien sûr, est que le caractère 'irréversible' ou non de la sécession peut faire l'objet d'interprétations bien diverses et d'appréciations tout aussi subjectives. On se souvient, par exemple, que la Haute Cour de Rhodésie a répondu presque en écho à l'arrêt *Madzimbamuto*, mais dans le but inverse, afin de convaincre du 'succès ultime' de la sécession.[25] Le plus souvent ce sera par le biais de l'acte unilatéral de la reconnaissance que les Etats essaieront de consolider une effectivité nouvelle favorable (ou au moins qui ne nuit pas) à leurs intérêts. Et si les reconnaissances de collectivités qui ne réunissent pas encore complètement les 'éléments constitutifs' de l'Etat doivent sans doute, comme nous le verrons, être considérées comme 'prématurées' et illicites, rien n'empêche en principe un Etat d'essayer d'apporter son soutien, par le biais de la reconnaissance, à une effectivité incontestable considérant, au grand dam de l'Etat d'origine qui refuse toujours la sécession mais qui est incapable de rétablir son autorité sur le sol sécessionniste, que le point de 'non-retour' a déjà été franchi.

En définitive, il faut souligner que si le droit international 'n'interdit pas' la sécession, ceci ne signifie pas qu'il renvoie dos à dos l'Etat et le groupe sécessionniste. Le droit demeure *hostile* à la sécession, il la réprouve, faute de l'interdire, et érige contre elle des obstacles importants que l'effectivité peut sans doute surmonter, mais cela ne sera pas

[23] H. Lauterpacht, *Recognition in International Law* (Cambridge: Cambridge University Press, 1947), p. 8.

[24] Voir son avis sollicité par le Procureur général du Canada dans l'affaire du *Renvoi par le Gouverneur en conseil au sujet de certaines questions ayant trait à la sécession du Québec du reste du Canada*, intitulé 'La pratique des Etats et le droit international relativement à la sécession unilatérale', Cour suprême du Canada, n° 25506, février 1997, par. 28. C'est nous qui soulignons.

[25] L'*Appellate Division of the High Court of Rhodesia* a considéré, dans sa décision *R. v. Ndhlovu (1968)*, qu'il était désormais possible '[to] predict with certainty that sanctions will not succeed in their objective of overthrowing the present government and of restoring the British government to the control of the government of Rhodesia' (*R. v. Ndhlovu*, 1968, 4 *SALR* 515 (1968), 532).

automatique et ne se fera pas sans peine. Parmi ces obstacles, l'un des plus importants est celui de l'établissement d'une présomption contre l'effectivité de la sécession et en faveur de l'intégrité territoriale de l'Etat préexistant. Les effectivités ont ainsi souvent davantage un rôle à jouer sur le plan de l'acquiescement, ou plutôt de la résignation de l'Etat préexistant (qui, contraint par la force des faits, réalise qu'il n'a plus vraiment le choix et abandonne ses tentatives de récupération), que sur celui de la naissance 'automatique' d'un nouvel Etat. En tout état de cause, la reconnaissance des tiers, faute de celle de l'Etat prédécesseur, jouera ici un rôle déterminant pour la constatation de l'effectivité.

b. L'Etat sans l'effectivité (le rôle de la reconnaissance) L'hypothèse ici examinée est exactement l'inverse de celle précédemment invoquée. Dans un certain nombre de cas, les Etats ont procédé à des reconnaissances massives du statut étatique à des entités qui, pourtant, ne réunissaient manifestement pas les conditions exigées par le principe d'effectivité.

Ceci s'est produit, par exemple, dans le cadre du processus de décolonisation. L'opposition particulièrement ferme de certaines puissances coloniales (comme le Portugal) à l'accession à l'indépendance de certains de leurs 'territoires non autonomes', si elle a privé d'effectivité leurs différents gouvernements de fait, n'a pas empêché la reconnaissance massive ni l''indépendance prématurée' de ces Etats.[26] De la même manière, l'accession à l'indépendance avec l'accord de la Métropole, mais dans des conditions qui ne permettaient pas au gouvernement central du nouveau pays d'exercer un contrôle effectif sur le territoire (comme ce fut, par exemple, le cas du Congo ex-belge entre 1960 et 1962 ou de l'Angola en 1975), n'a pas empêché l'attribution prématurée de la qualité étatique à l'ex-colonie. Dans tous ces cas, c'est précisément l'existence d'un *droit à l'indépendance* pour les entités en question qui a milité en faveur d'une interprétation extrêmement souple et libérale des conditions traditionnelles d'émergence d'un nouvel Etat.

[26] Le meilleur exemple est, sans doute, celui de la Guinée-Bissau. Le Parti africain pour l'indépendance de la Guinée et du Cap-Vert a en effet proclamé l'indépendance de ce pays en septembre 1973. Malgré l'opposition ferme (et armée) du Portugal et le manque d'effectivité, quarante pays ont immédiatement reconnu le nouvel Etat, dont 'l'accession à l'indépendance' a aussi été saluée (avec une série de conséquences) par l'Assemblée générale des Nations Unies dans sa résolution 3061 (XXVIII) du 2 novembre 1973. Il faut d'ailleurs rappeler que la fameuse résolution 2625 de l'Assemblée générale des Nations Unies avait esquivé, en quelque sorte, le problème de l'effectivité, en soulignant que ces territoires non autonomes avaient 'un statut séparé et distinct de celui du territoire de l'Etat qui [les] administre' (5ème principe, al. 6).

En dehors des situations de décolonisation (et d'occupation militaire), un tel assouplissement ne devrait pas être possible. Pourtant, la pratique récente offre un exemple qui va dans le sens inverse, celui de la Bosnie-Herzégovine. Cette ex-république fédérée yougoslave ne réunissait manifestement pas les traditionnels éléments constitutifs de l'Etat et ne pouvait nullement prétendre passer le 'test de l'effectivité', son gouvernement central ne contrôlant même pas un cinquième du territoire du pays entre 1992 et 1995. Toutefois, les Etats ont, dès le mois de mars 1992, reconnu et accepté comme Etat indépendant la Bosnie-Herzégovine, et ils l'ont par la suite soutenue de plusieurs façons en affirmant sans cesse son intégrité territoriale. Dans ce cas donc, la création de l'Etat n'était pas une simple 'question de fait'. Ces reconnaissances allaient plutôt contre les effectivités sur le terrain (contrôle de la plus grande partie du territoire par les Serbes, mais aussi par les Croates bosniaques) et ont anticipé, ou plutôt *provoqué*, l'effectivité étatique. Comme l'a remarqué J. Verhoeven, dans le cas des conflits yougoslaves, la reconnaissance a permis 'tant de faire vivre' la Bosnie-Herzégovine 'que de tuer la Yougoslavie'.[27]

Bien que le cas de la Bosnie puisse aussi recevoir d'autres explications,[28] certains juristes se sont appuyés sur ce précédent ambigu pour avancer que la reconnaissance par des pays tiers, tout en étant simplement 'déclarative', peut suppléer au défaut d'effectivité. Ainsi, dans un avis rendu sur la question d'une sécession éventuelle du Québec, M. Shaw a soutenu que:

> the less effective is the overall control exercised by the government of the new State, the more important will be recognition by third States in the process of establishing without doubt statehood at international law . . . Thus were Quebec to secede and be recognised as an independent State by third States, this would in effect be determinative of its statehood at international law. Such recognition would also cure any weaknesses that there may be with regard to full and effective control over all of its territory at that time and would act to cancel out the effects of any Canadian objection, should that indeed be the case.[29]

[27] J. Verhoeven, 'La reconnaissance internationale: déclin ou renouveau?', *AFDI* (1993), pp. 30–1.

[28] Dans le cas de la Bosnie, c'était plutôt la disparition de la Yougoslavie qui a été présentée comme une simple 'question de fait'. Ce cas a été considéré comme un cas de *dissolution* d'Etat (et non de sécession) qui, avec l'effet combiné de l'*uti possidetis*, 'devait' conduire à l'indépendance toutes les ex-Républiques yougoslaves le souhaitant. En d'autres termes, dans ce cas les Etats de la communauté internationale ont considéré que la Bosnie-Herzégovine avait un droit d'exister en tant qu'Etat après la dissolution de la Yougoslavie et lui ont donc accordé leur reconnaissance et leur soutien malgré l'absence, pendant trois ans, de toute effectivité de cet Etat.

[29] Voir le rapport du professeur M. Shaw in: *Rapports d'experts de l'amicus curiae*, Cour suprême du Canada, n° 25506, décembre 1997 (précité), par. 65 et 69.

Ainsi, à l'approche exclusivement factuelle selon laquelle l'Etat naît grâce à la seule conjugaison de ces trois éléments constitutifs, on tente d'y substituer une approche beaucoup plus souple et politisée selon laquelle l'Etat existe même *sans* ses éléments constitutifs, à condition qu'il y ait un certain nombre de reconnaissances. Toutefois, s'il est vrai que la reconnaissance peut permettre de consolider une effectivité précaire, la question de la reconnaissance d'une situation fictive qui ne serait pas fondée sur une effectivité est beaucoup plus complexe, car cette reconnaissance pourrait être considérée comme une *ingérence* prohibée dans les affaires intérieures d'un Etat souverain. La proposition selon laquelle la reconnaissance peut venir suppléer au défaut d'effectivité s'éloigne même de l'approche traditionnelle de la 'théorie constitutive' de la reconnaissance elle-même, qui considère que la reconnaissance *s'ajoute* mais ne remplace pas les trois éléments constitutifs de l'Etat. Une reconnaissance prématurée faite sur une base complètement *fictive*, avant la mise en place d'une effectivité étatique par l'entité sécessionniste et qui vise précisément à aider la création de cette effectivité, constitue ainsi une violation de la souveraineté de l'Etat qui résiste à la sécession et une immixtion dans la sphère de sa compétence nationale.[30]

c. L'effectivité partagée (le problème de l'*uti possidetis*) La dernière hypothèse est celle d'une effectivité partagée entre l'Etat d'origine et le mouvement sécessionniste. Que se passe-t-il en effet si, à la suite d'hostilités, le gouvernement central maintient par la force son contrôle sur une partie du territoire, le gouvernement sécessionniste réussissant, quant à lui, à conserver le contrôle du reste du territoire? Les opinions doctrinales divergent sur ce point car trois solutions sont envisageables.

Tout d'abord, certains auteurs considèrent que dans un tel cas 'le territoire devrait être partagé à la fin des hostilités entre l'ancien Etat englobant et le nouvel Etat né de la sécession'.[31] Il s'agit d'une solution qui pourrait sembler conforme à l'esprit de l'effectivité: après la bataille on repart avec ce que l'on a pu effectivement gagner.

[30] Cette idée a été acceptée par la majorité écrasante de la doctrine. Hersch Lauterpacht écrivait par exemple: 'It is generally agreed that premature recognition is more than an unfriendly act; it is an act of intervention and an international delinquency ... [T]he parent State must in fact have ceased to make efforts, promising success, to reassert its authority. Recognition is unlawful if granted *durante bello*, when the outcome of the struggle is altogether uncertain. Such recognition is a denial of the sovereignty of the parent State.' (Lauterpacht, *Recognition in International Law*, p. 8).

[31] J. Woerling, 'Éléments d'analyse institutionnelle, juridique et démolinguistique pertinents à la révision du statut politique et constitutionnel du Québec', *Commission sur l'avenir politique et constitutionnel du Québec*, document de travail n° 2, p. 102.

Une deuxième solution, fondée sur une application rigoureuse du principe d'effectivité, nie la qualité étatique à un mouvement sécessionniste qui n'a pu étendre son contrôle effectif qu'à une partie seulement du territoire revendiqué. Jean Combacau, par exemple, souligne que même si les insurgés maîtrisent pleinement une fraction du territoire de la collectivité, celle-ci 'ne peut constituer la base d'un Etat sécessionniste puisqu'ils veulent se substituer globalement au gouvernement en place dans l'ensemble du pays et ne peuvent se tenir pour satisfaits d'une effectivité seulement partielle'. Il faut donc, selon lui, 'attendre l'issue des opérations militaires pour déterminer si le pays est ou non devenu indépendant'.[32] C'est seulement si l'entité sécessionniste possède un droit d'accession à l'indépendance (comme c'était le cas avec le droit à la décolonisation) que l'on peut se contenter d'une effectivité partielle. Dans ce cas, en vertu du principe de l'*uti possidetis juris*, la colonie accède à l'indépendance dans ses anciennes limites administratives, aucun morcellement de son territoire n'étant considéré comme compatible 'avec les buts et les principes de la Charte des Nations Unies'.[33]

La troisième solution, très en vogue ces dernières années chez une partie de la doctrine, tend précisément à étendre l'application du principe de l'*uti possidetis* en dehors des situations de décolonisation. Selon cette approche, si l'effectivité est établie sur une partie du territoire, la collectivité peut accéder à l'indépendance qui concernera alors l'ensemble du territoire, y compris la partie occupée par les autorités de l'Etat préexistant. Le territoire doit donc être dévolu à l'Etat nouveau sur la base des frontières administratives préexistantes.

La transposition du principe de l'*uti possidetis* en dehors du cadre de la décolonisation continue à faire l'objet de vives controverses. Si la majorité de la doctrine considère que la positivité de l'*uti possidetis* dans ce cadre ne fait pas de doute, d'autres auteurs soulignent néanmoins que la démonstration n'est pas convaincante, car la transposition de l'*uti possidetis* n'est pas 'admise par tous les Etats intéressés, et sa valeur de règle de droit international général reste encore mal assurée'.[34] Sans entrer dans ce débat,[35] nous nous limiterons à remarquer que l'affirmation selon

[32] J. Combacau et S. Sur, *Droit international*, p. 278.

[33] *Cf.* le par. 6 de la résolution 1514 (XV) du 14 décembre 1960 de l'Assemblée générale.

[34] J. Combacau et S. Sur, *Droit international*, p. 435.

[35] Pour un traitement global de la question, avec des contributions très argumentées pour et contre la transposition du principe dans le contexte post-colonial, voir O. Corten, B. Delcourt, P. Klein, N. Levrat (eds.), *Démembrements d'Etats et délimitations territoriales: l'uti possidetis en question(s)* (Bruxelles: ULB, Bruylant, 1999), 455 p.

laquelle l'entité sécessionniste doit bénéficier de l'ensemble du territoire préexistant apparaît comme une sorte de 'canalisation juridique' des trois 'éléments constitutifs', qui, pourtant, selon les prémisses même de la théorie de l'effectivité, sont des faits extra-juridiques. A la proposition neutre et abstraite selon laquelle un Etat doit tout simplement disposer d'une assiette spatiale 'identifiable', vient s'ajouter l'exigence selon laquelle un Etat, en absence d'accord avec l'Etat préexistant, doit nécessairement accéder à l'indépendance dans ses limites administratives antérieures. En dehors des situations de décolonisation, le principe de l'*uti possidetis* peut alors se trouver en tension, voire même en conflit direct, avec le principe de l'effectivité, qui constitue, comme nous l'avons noté, la seule base juridique possible d'accueil d'une entité sécessionniste dans la société interétatique. Que se passe-t-il, par exemple, si l'entité sécessionniste ne réussit, en définitive, qu'à avoir un contrôle exclusif sur seulement 40, 50 ou 60 pour cent du territoire administratif antérieur, l'Etat englobant gardant le contrôle du reste? Faut-il considérer que cette entité n'accède pas à l'indépendance même si elle le souhaite? Ou faut-il plutôt penser qu'elle peut accéder à l'indépendance, mais l'Etat englobant doit lui restituer le reste du territoire, pour lequel il possède pourtant toujours à la fois le titre juridique et la possession effective? Et si c'est le cas, quel est le pourcentage de territoire que l'entité sécessionniste doit contrôler effectivement pour accéder à l'indépendance et demander restitution du reste? 20 pour cent suffisent-t-ils? Comment définir ce pourcentage? Toutes ces questions ne se posaient évidemment pas dans le cadre de la décolonisation, car dans ce cadre, comme nous l'avons dit, l'application de l'*uti possidetis* était inextricablement liée à l'existence d'un droit à la création d'un Etat et d'un droit corrélatif à bénéficier d'un territoire et de frontières prédéfinies.

Certes, rien n'interdit qu'un principe juridique puisse régir les modalités de l'accession d'une entité à l'indépendance. Encore faut-il appeler les choses par leur nom, car de deux choses l'une: ou bien la sécession est une question de 'pur fait', et seul le principe de l'effectivité est pertinent pour la naissance du nouvel Etat; ou bien certains principes juridiques sont capables de reléguer les effectivités au second rang, attribuant, par exemple, à un nouvel Etat des fractions entières d'un territoire sur lequel son gouvernement n'exerce aucun contrôle. Si les partisans de la transposition de l'*uti possidetis* dans le contexte post-colonial essayent de 'neutraliser' le principe en mettant l'accent uniquement sur ses présumées 'vertus sécurisantes', il n'existe aucun doute sur le fait que le principe n'est nullement neutre: il favorise clairement l'entité sécessionniste, lui permettant d'accéder à l'indépendance avec une effectivité seulement partielle, et lui confère un 'droit' sur un territoire prédéterminé. Ceci est assez paradoxal, eu égard à la protection que le droit international souhaite toujours accorder à l'intégrité territoriale des Etats existants. Au-delà de toutes autres objections, c'est donc le fondement 'logique' de la transposition de l'*uti possidetis* qui fait aujourd'hui l'objet d'une sérieuse remise en cause,[36] tandis que le constat de l'inadaptabilité du principe à un grand nombre de situations post-coloniales appelle inévitablement les juristes à envisager des solutions plus satisfaisantes.

B) *Une appréciation critique du recours à l'effectivité*

Le recours au principe de l'effectivité semble méritoire dans la mesure où il épargne le droit international du problème extrêmement délicat de la sécession, tout en le gardant en contact avec la réalité et en lui permettant ainsi d''intégrer' les faits dans l'ordonnancement juridique (1). Le recours à ce principe apparaît toutefois à bien des égards insatisfaisant et dangereux, car il signifie la mise à l'écart, le 'désengagement' du droit, au profit de la loi du plus fort (2).

(1) Un principe méritoire: *ex factis ius oritur*

Le premier mérite de l'effectivité est qu'elle est susceptible de protéger le droit international. En renvoyant l'épineuse question de la sécession à la simple force des faits, elle semble offrir un grand service au droit des gens. Celui-ci ne doit pas entrer dans les labyrinthes obscurs et tortueux de la sécession pour mener une quelconque bataille. Il reste en dehors, en pleine sécurité. Le droit ne doit pas rendre de jugements; il doit seulement constater les effectivités et 'entériner le fait accompli'.

Le juriste, en fait, ne peut être scientifiquement crédible 'que s'il tient compte de la réalité et ne se réfugie pas dans un idéalisme dont se gaussent les faits'.[37] Il faut se rendre à l'évidence: le droit international ne peut pas tout appréhender. 'Tous les problèmes ne sont pas susceptibles

[36] Voir surtout la réfutation méthodique de ce lien 'logique' opérée par O. Corten, 'Droit des peuples à disposer d'eux-mêmes et *uti possidetis*: deux faces d'une même médaille ?', in: *ibid.*, p. 403. Pour une opinion contraire voir, par exemple, M. Kohen, 'Le problème des frontières en cas de dissolution et de séparation d'Etats: quelles alternatives?', in: *ibid.*, p. 365.

[37] J. Salmon, 'Les contradictions entre fait et droit en droit international', in: *Estudios de Derecho Internacional*, p. 337.

d'être résolus par le droit'.[38] La sécession est précisément l'une de ces questions épineuses qui dépassent le droit, qui se situent au-dessus, qui échappent à l'appréciation juridique. Et ceci, parce que toute tentative de réglementation globale de la sécession semble se heurter non seulement à des objections politiques et morales fondamentales, mais aussi à des obstacles techniques quasiment insurmontables, comme en témoignent les innombrables difficultés de mise en oeuvre de la prohibition d'une forme précise de sécession (celle résultant d'une agression) que nous analyserons dans la deuxième partie. Il vaut donc mieux épargner le droit de cette épreuve difficile. Il vaut mieux le mettre à l'abri, laissant la force des faits, l'effectivité, trancher. La sécession ne fait partie que de l'un de ces 'morceaux de la vie sociale qu'il est prématuré ou peu souhaitable de normativiser'.[39] Il vaut mieux laisser le soin de sa réglementation aux générations futures, qui auront sans doute plus de sagesse pour dégager les bonnes solutions.

Ceci est d'autant plus justifié qu'il n'y a rien de frappant à ce que le droit fasse appel à la force des faits. Le droit international doit laisser sa porte ouverte sur la réalité. Il existe un incessant va-et-vient entre le fait et le droit, une relation dialectique qui, jusqu'à ce jour, a beaucoup profité à l'ordonnancement juridique. En effet, l'effectivité essaye précisément de compenser les déficiences de cet ordre international, 'à parer à ses étroitesses formelles, à ses faiblesses les plus notoires'.[40]

Il serait superflu d'entrer ici dans une analyse théorique du droit pour montrer quels sont ses rapports mutuels avec les faits, comment ceux-ci influencent le processus de création et d'évolution de la règle juridique, et comment finalement l'effectivité profite au droit. Il est évident que le droit ne peut se détacher de la vie; il est né, dans une large mesure, des faits; il se réalise dans les faits et il a pour vocation de régir ces faits. Ce qui est effectif – ce qui existe réellement, positivement – influence d'une manière ou d'une autre le droit; il l'informe et parfois le transforme. L'effectivité joue donc un rôle important dans plusieurs domaines du droit international, à tel point qu'il a été dit que, bien qu'elle soit une 'notion a-juridique', elle 'a envahi le champ du droit international jusqu'à en devenir une notion centrale'.[41] Au-delà de sa pertinence dans la formation ou la transformation du droit (surtout dans le processus coutumier, présenté

[38] P. Weil, 'Le droit international en quête de son identité. Cours général de droit international public', *Recueil des cours* 237 (1992-VI), p. 65.

[39] *Ibid.* [40] De Visscher, *Les effectivités du droit international*, p. 11.

[41] M. Chemillier-Gendreau, 'A propos de l'effectivité en droit international', *RBDI* (1975), 38.

comme un processus de 'normativisation' des faits), elle joue aussi un rôle-clé dans une série d'autres hypothèses où elle comble les lacunes du droit.[42] Dans l'hypothèse d'un *vacuum juris*, donc, il est clair que l'effectivité joue un rôle important et que finalement *ex factis ius oritur*.[43]

Cette conclusion est évidemment particulièrement pertinente en matière de sécession. Dans la mesure où celle-ci n'est pas réglementée par le droit, la prise en compte de ce qui est effectif, de ce qui existe, ne signifie en fin de compte que la part du réalisme du droit. Ce dernier reste en contact avec le 'fait', constate son existence et procède par la suite à sa 'captation' juridique afin de le soumettre à la réglementation existante des rapports sociaux. Une fois né dans les faits, l'Etat est donc pris en compte par le droit qui lui confère un statut, une personnalité juridique internationale et, par conséquent, une série de droits et d'obligations. Dans la mesure où la sécession n'est ni autorisée, ni prohibée par le droit international, le recours à la force des faits est inévitable.

(2) Un principe dangereux: l'appel à la loi du plus fort

Le fait que le droit international cède la place au jeu libre des forces, ne faisant qu'attendre le vainqueur pour le récompenser, est sans aucun doute dangereux. Chaque minorité, chaque groupe ethnique, chaque groupe de personnes unies par un objectif commun peut tenter de faire sécession et mettre en œuvre pour ce faire tous les moyens nécessaires (sous réserve, néanmoins, de l'obligation de respecter certaines règles telles que celles du droit humanitaire). La théorie de l'effectivité donne ainsi 'carte blanche' aux mouvements sécessionnistes qui penseront, probablement à raison, que plus leurs actions seront vigoureuses, plus ils augmenteront leurs chances de mettre en place une autorité étatique effective. Inversement, cette même théorie donne aussi toute latitude aux gouvernements pour réprimer ces mouvements sécessionnistes, afin d'empêcher le jeu de l'effectivité. L'appel à l'effectivité est donc inévitablement un

[42] On sait, par exemple, que l'occupation effective permet l'acquisition de la souveraineté sur un territoire sans maître ou sur lequel aucun titre ne peut être prouvé et on peut aussi se rappeler le rôle de l'effectivité en matière d'opposabilité de la nationalité d'une personne physique dans le cadre de l'exercice de la protection diplomatique (*Affaire Nottebohm (Liechtenstein c. Guatemala), Deuxième phase, arrêt du 6 avril 1955*, *CIJ, Recueil 1955*, v. not. p. 23).

[43] Sans entrer dans une analyse des différentes théories concernant une éventuelle 'plénitude' de l'ordre juridique international, on pourrait noter que, dans la mesure où le principe d'effectivité comble les lacunes du droit, il n'y aurait tout simplement pas de lacunes! En d'autres termes, c'est le droit lui-même qui attribue à l'effectivité, de manière certes résiduelle, le rôle de créateur d'un titre ou d'un lien.

appel aux rapports de force : la force diplomatique, qui vise à convaincre adroitement les Etats tiers de reconnaître ou de ne pas reconnaître l'entité sécessionniste; la force médiatique, qui vise à gagner la sympathie de la communauté internationale; et, surtout, sinon exclusivement, la force armée. Cette dernière est le véritable pôle magnétique de l'effectivité.[44] Comme il a été remarqué: 'military success is not just the only path to independence but it may also be the only way for a parent state to maintain its territorial integrity'.[45]

Il ne faut donc pas s'étonner que les conflits sécessionnistes soient parmi les plus meurtriers. C'est après tout une logique de laissez-faire – laissez-passer que le principe de l'effectivité introduit. Cet appel à la loi du plus fort n'est pas seulement peu satisfaisant pour tout ordre juridique; il est aussi certainement peu sécurisant et remet en cause les objectifs de la Charte des Nations Unies, dont le principe premier est de 'préserver les générations futures du fléau de la guerre' et de 'maintenir la paix et la sécurité internationales' (préambule et art. 1, par. 1). Plusieurs conflits sécessionnistes ont ainsi été qualifiés de 'menaces contre la paix' par le Conseil de sécurité ces dernières années.[46]

Certes, on pourrait penser que ces conflits sont, de toute façon et quel que soit l'état du droit, inévitables. Toutefois, l'attachement à l'effectivité, la glorification du 'fait accompli' par le droit, constituent une invitation ouverte à la révolte et à la violence. Le droit international est pourtant soucieux d'ordre et de sécurité. Pour aussi longtemps qu'il demeure lacunaire en la matière, le recours au principe de l'effectivité apparaît inévitable, et l''accouchement' sans douleur restera rare.[47] Rien n'empêche néanmoins le droit international de développer des règles moins primitives et grossières que celle de l'effectivité pour aborder le problème de la sécession et limiter surtout les dangers pour la sécurité internationale. Comme nous le verrons, c'est précisément afin de réglementer certaines situations particulièrement graves et dangereuses que de telles règles se sont déjà développées.

[44] Les différentes tentatives doctrinales d'étendre le principe de prohibition du recours à la force aux conflits internes ne peuvent trouver aucun fondement sérieux en droit positif. Voir à cet égard notre analyse in: Th. Christakis, *Le droit à l'autodétermination*, pp. 252–6.

[45] L. Frankel, 'International Law of Secession: New Rules for A New Era', *Houston J.I.L.* 14 (1992), p. 539.

[46] Voir par exemple *infra*, pp. 167–8.

[47] M. Mouskhély, 'La naissance des Etats en droit international public', *RGDIP* (1962), p. 474.

II. La soumission de l'effectivité au droit: le respect des conditions de licéité

Que se passe-t-il donc si le droit *intervient* dans certains cas pour réglementer le problème de la sécession? Que se passe-t-il si le droit, soucieux du caractère insatisfaisant de l'appel à la loi du plus fort, octroie dans certaines circonstances un droit de sécession ou, inversement, interdit certains types de sécession? Le droit l'emporte-t-il sur une effectivité contraire? Ou faut-il plutôt admettre que les effectivités jouent ici un rôle tellement important que le droit se soumet ultimement à celles-ci, acceptant le 'fait accompli' d'une sécession autorisée mais étouffée ou, inversement (hypothèse qui nous occupera particulièrement ici) d'une sécession interdite qui a pourtant réussi? Plusieurs auteurs considèrent que, pour des raisons diverses, l'effectivité d'une situation peut l'emporter sur l'illégalité dont elle est issue (A). Bien que réaliste, cette thèse va toutefois à l'encontre du principe fondamental *ex iniuria ius non oritur* selon lequel une action illégale ne doit pas créer de droits en faveur de son auteur (B).

(A) La thèse selon laquelle l'effectivité l'emporte sur la légalité

Cette thèse s'appuie principalement sur la nécessité de préserver la stabilité et la sécurité des relations internationales. Selon le vieux principe *ut sit finis litium* tout litige doit avoir un terme. Une effectivité qui se prolonge doit donc être accueillie par le droit (1). L'explication serait encore plus aisée en matière de naissance d'Etat: compte tenu des circonstances dans lesquelles se réalise l'Etat (un simple 'fait juridique' obéissant simplement à des conditions matérielles), aucun laps de temps n'est ici nécessaire: l'effectivité 'instantanée' de la naissance d'un nouvel Etat s'impose, quelles que soient les circonstances qui ont amené à sa création (2).

(1) Le triomphe de l'effectivité prolongée

Jean Touscoz remarquait en 1964, dans sa thèse sur le principe de l'effectivité, que le juriste ne doit pas se contenter d'une étude purement formelle et déductive du droit international et que cette étude 'ne peut être entreprise du seul point de vue de la légalité'. Il soulignait, que 'le droit des gens, qui est un droit primitif, ne dispose pas d'une technique assez évoluée pour pouvoir contester toute validité juridique à un pouvoir politique créé en violation du droit, mais durable et effectif'. Certes, expliquait Jean Touscoz, la légalité devrait être préférée à l'effectivité; mais la stabilité et la sécurité des relations internationales exigent que la tension entre la loi et la réalité soit résolue. Il faut donc se rendre à l'évidence: 'le temps efface l'illégalité et valide l'effectivité'.[48]

Par ces réflexions, Jean Touscoz n'a fait qu'exprimer la thèse, acceptée par de nombreux autres juristes, selon laquelle la violation du droit international peut être avalisée si la situation qui résulte de l'acte illicite parvient à s'imposer. Cette situation n'est pas propre au droit international: 'dans les droits internes aussi, il y a des faits qui, encore que punissables, ont un caractère créateur de droit'.[49] Mais le problème est plus grave en droit international du fait de la 'primitivité' de ce dernier. L'ordre juridique international ne possède pas de sanctions – ou un système cohérent de nullités – susceptibles de faire respecter la légalité internationale. L'ordre international ne dispose pas, à l'inverse des ordres internes, d'un juge automatiquement compétent pour déclarer les nullités et sanctionner les illicéités. Ce sont donc les Etats, individuellement par leur pouvoir d'auto-appréciation ou par leur action commune au sein des organisations internationales, qui peuvent constater les nullités et s'y opposer. Mais dès que l'acte illicite cesse d'être effectivement contesté par les Etats, une nouvelle situation légale peut naître. Comme le disait Charles de Visscher, 'le refus de reconnaître une situation issue d'agissements illicites, ne conserve pas indéfiniment sa signification juridique. Une tension trop prolongée entre le fait et le droit doit fatalement se dénouer, au cours du temps, au bénéfice de l'effectivité.'[50] Selon cet auteur, il ne s'agissait pas là d'une solution arbitraire, et il soulignait d'ailleurs qu''en principe, l'effectivité ne confère pas de titre valable à un acte illicite'.[51] Mais il rappelait aussi que l'exigence fondamentale de la stabilité et de la sécurité des rapports internationaux veulent que toute réclamation, tout litige aient un terme. Ainsi Charles De Visscher, comme Hans Kelsen ou Paul Guggenheim, considérait que même la *debellatio* peut créer des effets juridiques. L'effectivité de la conquête allait lutter contre l'effectivité de la résistance qu'elle rencontrerait chez les Etats tiers: le jour où les tentatives de restauration cesseraient de trouver une assistance effective, la *debellatio* serait juridiquement acquise. La bataille

48 J. Touscoz, *Le principe d'effectivité dans l'ordre international* (Paris: LGDJ, 1964), pp. 6–7 et 229–32.

49 H. Kelsen, 'Théorie générale du droit international public', *Recueil des cours* 42 (1932-IV), p. 209.

50 De Visscher, *Les effectivités du droit international*, p. 25.

51 Ch. De Visscher, *Théories et réalités en droit international public*, 4ème édn (Paris: Pedone, 1970), p. 319.

entre légalité et illégalité se présente ainsi comme une bataille entre deux effectivités contraires. Quand les gouvernements n'appuient pas leurs déclarations, même collectives, de non-reconnaissance, de moyens capables de rétablir le droit, nous sommes en présence, selon la phrase de Charles De Visscher, d'une 'transition honorable vers l'acceptation du fait accompli'.[52]

(2) Le triomphe de l'effectivité instantanée

Ces réflexions seraient évidemment particulièrement pertinentes en matière de sécession et de formation de nouveaux Etats, dans la mesure où ces phénomènes sont régis par le droit. Dans ce domaine, 'les sanctions internationales ne vont jamais jusqu'à effacer l'illégalité en rétablissant le *statu quo ante*... Ici, le fait triomphe du droit'.[53] Ici, la 'structuration rudimentaire' de l'ordre international est tellement apparente qu'elle conduit 'tant à privilégier l'effectivité au détriment de la légalité pour assurer la sécurité des rapports juridiques qu'à restreindre les effets des illégalités, eu égard à la difficulté, et de les faire constater et de faire respecter leurs conséquences logiques'.[54] Point n'est besoin d'attendre ici un long écoulement de temps: la simple réalisation des conditions nécessaires à la formation de l'Etat, c'est-à-dire la simple réunion effective de ses 'éléments constitutifs', a pour effet légal l'institution de l'Etat et l'opposabilité de son statut aux autres membres de la communauté internationale. La naissance de l'Etat est un 'instantané' (même s'il est difficile souvent d'établir avec précision le moment précis de sa survenance) qui s'impose 'objectivement' et est insusceptible de contestations. La naissance de l'Etat est un fait aussi primaire que la naissance de l'homme: '[L]'existence de l'Etat repose en principe exclusivement sur une effectivité, quelles que puissent être les circonstances – de droit ou de fait – qui ont permis qu'elle se réalise. De la même manière qu'un enfant naît de l'accouplement de ses auteurs . . . sans avoir égard aux circonstances, même monstrueuses, de son engendrement. Il convient peut-être de punir l'un ou l'autre de ses parents de la violation du droit dont il est issu . . . Cela n'empêche que l'enfant soit, dès l'instant où il est sorti vivant (viable) du ventre de sa mère . . .'[55]

[52] De Visscher, *Les effectivités du droit international*, p. 25; voir aussi pp. 37–8.

[53] Mouskhély, 'La naissance des Etats en droit international', p. 482.

[54] J. Verhoeven, *La reconnaissance internationale dans la pratique contemporaine. Les relations publiques internationales* (Paris: Pedone, 1975), p. 751.

[55] Verhoeven, 'La reconnaissance internationale', p. 38.

(B) La réfutation de cette thèse: ex iniuria ius non oritur

Cette thèse va manifestement à l'encontre du principe *ex iniuria ius non oritur*, principe fondamental du droit constituant une sorte de clef de voûte de tout système juridique.[56] Une action illégale ne doit pas, en principe, créer de droits subjectifs en faveur de son auteur, elle ne doit pas être avalisée par le droit. Accepter qu'un acte illicite puisse *suo vigore* être accueilli par le droit équivaut, comme le soulignait Hersch Lauterpacht, à introduire 'into the legal system a contradiction which cannot be solved except by a denial of its legal character'.[57] Examinons donc, tout d'abord, la pertinence du principe *ex iniuria ius non oritur* pour le droit international en général (1), avant d'examiner plus particulièrement sa pertinence dans le domaine extrêmement délicat de la formation ou de la disparition d'Etat (2).

(1) Effectivité contre licéité en droit international en général

Aucun des arguments avancés pour justifier la position selon laquelle l'effectivité l'emporte ultimement sur la légalité ne semble convaincant. On a ainsi essayé, par exemple, de faire un parallèle avec l'institution de la prescription acquisitive en droit interne qui permet à un possesseur effectif, fut-il de mauvaise foi, de devenir propriétaire d'un bien après l'écoulement d'un certain laps de temps. Dans ce cas, il est clair qu'une situation contraire au droit mais prolongée se trouve après un certain délai 'régularisée' par ce dernier. Toutefois, l'institution de la prescription acquisitive en droit civil ne constitue pas une récompense pour le possesseur de mauvaise foi. La raison d'être de cette institution est toute autre: elle vise à protéger les tiers qui, ignorant la véritable situation juridique, ont engagé de bonne foi des transactions avec le possesseur. La prescription acquisitive vise à préserver la croyance légitime des tiers, c'est-à-dire à éviter de ruiner 'les légitimes prévisions . . . de tous ceux qui, constatant que le titulaire de la situation apparente n'était pas dérangé dans l'exercice de son droit, ont pu valablement croire que cette situation était juridiquement fondée'.[58] Il ne s'agit donc pas vraiment ici d'une acceptation de la maxime '*ex iniuria ius oritur*', mais plutôt d'une atténuation du principe

[56] Reconnu comme un 'principe général de droit' de manière explicite par la CDI dans un tout autre contexte. Voir O. Corten, 'Commentaire de l'article 52', in: O. Corten, P. Klein (eds), *Les Conventions de Vienne sur le droit des traités, Commentaire article par article* (Bruxelles, à paraître).

[57] Lauterpacht, *Recognition in International Law*, p. 421.

[58] A. Weill, F. Terré, *Droit civil – Introduction générale*, 4ème édn (Paris: Précis Dalloz, 1979), p. 308.

'*ex iniuria ius non oritur*' par la reconnaissance que '*error communis facit ius*'.[59] En droit interne, la protection du tiers qui a agi de bonne foi se trouve en réalité derrière la plupart des hypothèses de création de droits par un fait illicite.[60]

Mais une telle hypothèse de protection de la croyance légitime des tiers est beaucoup plus improbable en droit international public. Dans l'ordre interne en effet, les sujets de droit sont innombrables. En droit international, en revanche, le nombre de sujets directs susceptibles d'être concernés par le principe de l'effectivité est loin d'être infini. Tout sujet de droit sait si le Koweït avait été annexé par l'Irak ou si l'Indonésie occupait le Timor oriental. L'argument de la protection des tiers agissant de bonne foi n'est donc pas pertinent en ce qui concerne les relations de droit public entre les Etats.

La justification fondée sur la 'primitivité' du droit des gens n'est pas non plus convaincante. Tout d'abord, il faut rappeler que de nombreux juristes ont essayé de repousser les reproches de primitivité du droit international, en soulignant qu'il s'agit d'"un droit *différent* beaucoup plus que d'un droit *primitif*'.[61] Mais, surtout, il faut souligner qu'il est quelque peu paradoxal et trompeur de prétendre que l'on peut rendre le droit international plus efficace en 'normalisant' précisément ces situations qui portent atteinte à son autorité. Si la sanction internationale n'est pas suffisamment développée à l'heure actuelle, on ne la renforcera certainement pas en acceptant que tout acte illicite qui lui échappe crée automatiquement des droits pour son auteur. Une telle approche signifie la négation, la fin même du droit. Or, 'tout ordre juridique doit résoudre un problème essentiel, qui est de soumettre la force au droit'.[62] Quelle serait finalement l'utilité de la règle juridique si l'on acceptait qu'elle n'est plus applicable à celui qui parvient à la violer effectivement ?

S'attacher au principe *ex iniuria ius non oritur* ne signifie pas adhérer à une approche utopique du droit international. Ce droit, comme tout droit, est le résultat de rapports de force. Jean-Jacques Rousseau écrivait déjà que 'le plus fort n'est jamais assez fort pour être toujours le maître s'il

[59] *Ibid.*, p. 324.

[60] Il en va de même, par exemple, des conséquences légales restreintes que peut produire le mariage nul. En droit pénal, il est vrai, la prescription ne vise pas la protection des tiers, mais plutôt la protection de l'ordre public. Toutefois, la prescription du droit pénal n'aboutit pas à la création de droits subjectifs pour l'auteur d'un délit ou d'un crime, mais plutôt à la prescription soit de l'action publique soit de la peine.

[61] M. Virally, 'Sur la prétendue "primitivité" du droit international', in: M. Virally, *Le droit international en devenir. Essais écrits au fil des ans* (Paris: PUF, 1990), p. 92.

[62] *Ibid.*, p. 95.

ne transforme sa force en droit'.[63] L'histoire du droit international montre comment 'le *sein* était transformé en *sollen*' par la puissance, comment le droit prenait le relais de la force car 'ce qui avait été obtenu par la force se maintiendrait à l'avenir par cette autre forme de force qu'est le droit'.[64] Le droit change, au fur et à mesure qu'évoluent les rapports de forces entre les composantes de la société internationale. Mais pour pénétrer le droit, les faits doivent être 'conceptualisés', doivent suivre le processus de formation du droit, processus 'sage' ou processus 'sauvage', mais 'processus' quand même. Et il est vrai que l'illicéité peut non seulement produire des effets de droit, mais aussi parfois devenir elle-même le droit, si elle suit ce processus de formation, comme le montre ce passage mystérieux entre la violation d'une règle préexistante et la naissance d'une règle coutumière nouvelle. Mais la formation d'une règle coutumière qui remplace le droit existant sur la base des nouveaux rapports de force est un phénomène très différent de l'accueil par le droit d'une situation illicite sur la seule base de son 'effectivité'.

On pourrait donc considérer que, sans l'accord de la personne protégée par la règle violée, et mises à part, peut-être, certaines hypothèses extraordinaires où les comportements concordants des membres de la communauté internationale pourraient avoir un effet quasi-législatif, les effectivités ne peuvent pas tenir lieu et place de droit. La stabilité et la sécurité internationales ne sont guère protégées par le message selon lequel une agression armée, suivie d'une occupation effective et d'une installation de colons, pourrait donner un titre de souveraineté. Tout au contraire, le droit international risque le pire si, précisément, il ne combat pas ces situations illicites, combat dont, contrairement à l'idée communément répandue, il peut sortir vainqueur. Dans les domaines autres que la création et la disparition d'Etats, les effectivités jouent incontestablement un rôle de plus en plus limité au fur et à mesure que le droit international se développe.[65] Cette conclusion doit-elle être modifiée dès que l'on entre dans un domaine aussi délicat que la création ou la disparition d'Etat?

(2) Effectivité contre licéité en matière de formation d'Etat

Cette idée ne résiste ni à une analyse théorique, ni à un examen de la pratique qui témoigne du fait que la communauté internationale refuse

[63] Dans le chapitre III du *Contrat social.*

[64] Salmon, 'Les contradictions entre fait et droit', p. 338.

[65] Marcelo Kohen a montré par exemple que, quoi qu'on ait pu dire, les titres juridiques de souveraineté territoriale l'emportent toujours sur une effectivité contraire (*Possession contestée et souveraineté territoriale* (Paris: PUF, 1997)), p. 485.

de traiter comme 'Etats' certaines entités nées en violation de certaines règles capitales du droit international. La résistance du droit aux effectivités illicites pose toutefois des difficultés techniques qui doivent attirer davantage l'attention des juristes.

a. Analyse théorique Nous avons vu que, selon la position traditionnelle de la doctrine, la naissance de l'Etat n'obéit qu'au principe de l'effectivité. Même si un Etat est né en violation flagrante du droit international, il ne constitue pas moins un 'Etat' car, comme le disait Anzilotti, 'il n'y a pas (et il n'y aura jamais) d'Etats légitimes et d'Etats illégitimes: la légitimation de l'Etat réside dans son existence même'.[66] À la limite, si la communauté internationale souhaite réagir à l'illicéité, la seule sanction sera de réduire cet Etat 'au statut peu envié d'Etats que personne ou presque ne reconnaît'.[67] Mais l'Etat non reconnu est toujours un Etat existant. Et dire que l'Etat existe, 'c'est donc déclarer que son statut s'impose'. Les autres Etats, même l'Etat victime d'une agression qui a conduit à la sécession, sont légalement tenus 'de lui accorder le statut auquel ce nouveau sujet a droit' et les droits attachés à ce statut, faute de quoi ils engageront leur responsabilité internationale.[68]

Selon cette conception traditionnelle, donc, en matière de formation d'Etats *ex iniuria ius oritur*, les effectivités jouent un rôle omnipotent et immédiat et excluent toute prise en considération du droit. Les résultats qui en découlent sont assez impressionnants. Ainsi, si un Etat agressait son voisin et annexait une partie de son territoire, cette effectivité, comme nous l'avons vu, ne pourrait jamais produire d'effets juridiques (ou ne les produirait, à la limite, si l'on acceptait la thèse de l'effectivité triomphante, qu'à long terme). Si, en revanche, l'Etat agresseur avait l'intelligence d'installer sur le territoire occupé un gouvernement 'indépendant' (issu, sans doute, de la minorité nationale au nom de laquelle cet Etat est intervenu), l'effectivité doterait immédiatement l'entité en question d'un statut étatique protégé par le droit international et serait donc désormais incontestable et à l'abri de toute tentative de récupération. Si, pour utiliser un exemple, Chypre avait la possibilité de reconquérir les territoires occupés, une telle tentative pourrait être considérée comme une violation de l'article 2, paragraphe 4 de la Charte, car la 'République turque de Chypre du nord' devrait être considérée comme un 'Etat'! Certes, devant cette grande anomalie qui fait du droit un instrument de protection du malfaiteur contre sa propre victime, on a essayé de répondre par l'argument

[66] D. Anzilotti, *Cours de droit international* (1929) (Paris: Ed. Panthéon Assas, 1999), p. 169.
[67] Combacau et Sur, *Droit international*, p. 280. [68] *Ibid.*, pp. 282–3.

selon lequel 'la politique revient' pour nuancer cette anomalie juridique. On a ainsi essayé d'expliquer que 'les droits dont jouit l'Etat hors de toute reconnaissance, il ne peut les faire valoir par les moyens que lui attribue le droit international qu'une fois reconnu par un nombre suffisant d'Etats'.[69] En d'autres termes, la 'République turque de Chypre du nord' aurait toujours un droit de protection qu'elle ne pourrait toutefois pas faire valoir pour des raisons politiques. Ceci nous conduit alors à une réglementation des relations internationales en dehors de toute intervention du droit international.

La nécessité de soumettre des effectivités au droit est donc évidente car aucune solution alternative ne peut aboutir à des résultats satisfaisants. Nous avons vu que la non-reconnaissance n'est pas une panacée (car la reconnaissance n'a pas d'effet constitutif et le statut d'Etat s'oppose objectivement en dehors d'elle); il en va de même avec la théorie de l''Etat fantoche', qui n'est qu'une tentative académique (d'une efficacité malheureusement limitée) pour donner des solutions moralement satisfaisantes à certaines situations issues d'actes illicites, sans aborder de front le problème délicat de l'existence ou non d'une condition de légalité pour l'attribution de la qualité étatique.[70]

La seule véritable solution est d'accepter que la naissance de l'Etat n'est pas seulement une 'question de fait' mais aussi une 'question de droit' et que les entités sécessionnistes constituées à la suite d'une violation des règles fondamentales du droit international (plus précisément, de celle concernant l'interdiction du recours à la force et de celle concernant le droit à l'autodétermination) ne doivent pas être traités comme des Etats, quelle que soit leur effectivité.[71] Certes, le problème qui se pose immédiatement est de savoir qui procédera à cette qualification. Confier cette tâche aux Etats existants est très dangereux car il peut conduire à des abus considérables, en ouvrant, comme le soulignait Hersch Lauterpacht, grande la porte 'to arbitrarness, to attempts at extortion, and to intervention at the very threshold of statehood'.[72] On peut en tout cas 'douter de la sagesse qui conduit à laisser entre les mains de vieillards le contrôle des naissances'.[73]C'est pour cela qu'il 'vaut mieux dès lors', 'au moins dans l'Etat actuel des choses, laisser l'effectivité décider seule de la naissance

[69] *Ibid.*, p. 287. [70] *Cf.* Christakis, *Le droit à l'autodétermination*, pp. 280–3.

[71] Inversement, nous avons vu que quand un droit à l'indépendance existe (comme c'était le cas dans le cadre de la décolonisation) la nécessité de soumission des effectivités au droit amène à une application très souple de la théorie des 'éléments constitutifs' et à des indépendances 'prématurées' avant la réunion effective de ces éléments.

[72] Lauterpacht, *Recognition in International Law*, p. 31.

[73] Selon l'image donnée par Verhoeven dans 'La reconnaissance internationale', p. 39.

ou de la mort de l'Etat. C'est probablement plus réaliste et peut-être plus prudent.'[74]

Ces arguments sont forts. Toutefois, au-delà des remarques que nous formulerons sur le rôle des organisations internationales dans ce domaine, force est de constater que l'appréciation subjective des Etats sur la réalisation des 'conditions de droit' par une entité sécessionniste ajoute peu de choses au subjectivisme déjà existant en ce qui concerne la réalisation des 'conditions de fait'. Nous avons vu que l''existence objective' de l'Etat constitue en grande partie une illusion, car aucun véritable automatisme n'existe dans ce domaine. Le 'contrôle des naissances' est donc de toute façon laissé en partie entre les mains de 'vieillards', et leur demander de décider en tenant aussi compte de certaines règles fondamentales pour l'ordre juridique international n'a, finalement, rien de très choquant.

b. Vérification pratique Une première confirmation de cette analyse nous vient de la 'clause de légalité' insérée dans les deux conventions internationales de l'ONU (aujourd'hui en vigueur) sur la succession d'Etats. Tant l'article 3 de la *Convention de Vienne sur la succession d'Etats en matière de traités* de 1978 que l'article 6 de la *Convention sur la succession d'Etats en matière de biens, archives et dettes d'Etat* de 1983 prévoient que chacune de ces conventions 's'applique uniquement aux effets d'une succession d'Etats se produisant conformément au droit international et, plus particulièrement, aux principes du droit international incorporés dans la Charte des Nations Unies'. Cette clause s'inspire du principe *ex iniuria ius non oritur* et souhaite mettre l'accent sur le fait qu'une succession illicite (y compris une sécession) ne peut provoquer des droits en faveur de son auteur, quelle que soit son effectivité. Comme l'a expliqué un membre de la CDI lors de l'élaboration de cette clause, l'Etat qui a violé le droit est tout simplement un Etat 'non successeur', et finalement 'il n'y a pas lieu de mentionner les droits que l'Etat non successeur pourrait avoir, puisqu'il ne peut en avoir aucun'.[75] Cette 'condamnation du fait accompli', 'fruit d'une longue réflexion de la part de la CDI',[76] a été reprise mot pour mot dans le projet récent de la Commission sur la nationalité en relation avec la succession d'Etats.[77]

[74] *Ibid.* [75] Selon M. Bedjaoui, *Annuaire de la CDI*, 1974, vol. I, p. 81.

[76] Selon le représentant de la Grèce lors de la *Conférence des Nations Unies sur la succession d'Etats en matière de traités*, Vienne, 1977–8, Documents de la Conférence, (vol. III), A/CONF.80/16 (vol. I), CR.9, par. 7.

[77] Voir l'art. 3 du projet adopté en 1999, in: A/54/10, p. 30.

De manière plus concrète maintenant, la pratique montre que c'est la violation de deux normes impératives du droit international qui a amené la communauté internationale à refuser de traiter comme 'Etats' les entités créées après cette violation. Et tout d'abord, la violation du droit à l'autodétermination. Ainsi, la Rhodésie du Sud n'a jamais été considérée comme un Etat ni par les Nations Unies ni par la communauté internationale, et ceci malgré son effectivité incontestable.[78] L'examen de quinze années de résolutions et décisions des organes des Nations Unies montre clairement que ceux-ci ne considéraient pas la Rhodésie du Sud comme un Etat mais, toujours, comme un territoire non-autonome du Royaume-Uni. En soulignant que 'la déclaration d'indépendance proclamée par [la minorité raciste] n'a aucune *validité légale*' (S/RES 217), en écartant tout argument fondé sur l'effectivité, en rejetant la demande rhodésienne de participer aux débats au sein du Conseil de sécurité sur la base de l'argument que la Rhodésie n'était pas un 'Etat' au sens de l'article 32 de la Charte mais un territoire non autonome, les organes des Nations Unies ont placé le débat sur le plan de l'illicéité, de la non-validité et de la nullité plutôt que sur celui de la simple non reconnaissance d'une situation 'objectivement' opposable. De manière similaire, les bantoustans, bien que dotés des attributs étatiques formels, n'étaient pas considérés comme des Etats car leur création était, entre autres choses, contraire au droit à l'autodétermination des peuples les constituant.[79]

La deuxième règle impérative à laquelle les effectivités doivent se soumettre est celle de la prohibition de l'agression. Ainsi, la tentative de la 'République turque de Chypre du nord' ('RTCN') de s'ériger en Etat en 1983, soit neuf ans après l'invasion de Chypre par l'armée turque, s'est heurtée à la vive opposition du Conseil de sécurité qui a immédiatement dénoncé cette tentative de sécession, en considérant la proclamation de l'indépendance comme 'juridiquement nulle'.[80] Quelques mois plus tard, en réponse à l'échange d''ambassadeurs' entre la 'RTCN' et la Turquie (le seul Etat au niveau mondial qui ait reconnu la sécession), le Conseil de sécurité a condamné par sa résolution 550 (1984) 'toutes les mesures sécessionnistes, y compris le prétendu échange d'ambassadeurs entre la

[78] Le gouvernement minoritaire de Ian Smith a, sans aucun doute, exercé un contrôle effectif sur l'ensemble du territoire de la Rhodésie du Sud. Comme l'a souligné James Crawford (*The Creation of States in International Law* (Oxford: Clarendon Press, 1979), p. 103): 'there can be no doubt that, if the traditional tests for independence of a seceding colony were applied, Rhodesia would be an independent State'.

[79] *Cf.* Christakis, *Le droit à l'autodétermination*, pp. 266–7.

[80] Par. 2 du dispositif de la rés. 541 (1983) du CS du 18 novembre 1983.

Turquie et les dirigeants chypriotes turcs' et a déclaré 'ces mesures illégales et invalides'.[81] Plusieurs autres organes et organisations internationales ont réagi de façon toute aussi déterminée en soulignant l'"illégalité' ou la 'nullité' de la proclamation d'indépendance et en appuyant les résolutions du Conseil de sécurité. Si ces décisions ont été accompagnées d'une 'demande à tous les Etats de ne pas reconnaître d'autre Etat chypriote que la République de Chypre' (par. 7 de la S/RES/541), elles sont en fait allées bien au-delà de la simple question de la 'non-reconaissance'. Pour la communauté internationale en effet, la 'RTCN' n'est pas un 'Etat non reconnu' mais une 'entité sécessionniste' (par. 3 de la S/RES/550) qui, bien que dotée d'un 'territoire', d'une 'population' et d'un 'gouvernement', ne peut accéder au statut d'Etat parce qu'elle est le produit d'une violation du droit international.[82] Les juridictions internationales ont d'ailleurs confirmé cette position comme le montre, entre autres, l'arrêt *Loizidou c. Turquie (Fond)*, que la Cour européenne des droits de l'homme (CEDH) a rendu le 18 décembre 1996. Refusant l'argumentation du défendeur selon laquelle la 'RTCN' était un Etat indépendant, la Cour a souligné que 'la communauté internationale ne tient pas la "RTCN" pour un Etat au regard du droit international' et que donc 'la République de Chypre demeure l'unique gouvernement légitime de Chypre'.

c. Problèmes de mise en oeuvre On peut donc conclure que les Etats exigent aujourd'hui de leurs futurs pairs la réalisation de certaines conditions de droit (au-delà des conditions de fait) qu'eux-mêmes n'avaient pas satisfaites lors de leur formation, car ni ces conditions, ni même, le plus souvent, les règles impératives qui se trouvent à leur origine, n'existaient encore. Mais la mise en oeuvre de ces conditions ne va pas sans difficultés.

Une première difficulté a déjà été évoquée, c'est celle de l'organe chargée de constater les illicéités et les nullités qui en découlent. Une qualification centralisée est ici nécessaire, non seulement pour limiter les risques de l'arbitraire, mais aussi pour éviter des complications bien sérieuses pour les relations internationales du fait inévitable que toute 'illégalité nationalement déclarée n'aura jamais qu'une autorité "relative" dans l'ordre international'.[83] Dans ce cadre, le rôle joué par les organes des

[81] Par. 2 du dispositif de la rés. 550 (1984) du CS du 11 mai 1984.

[82] Pour le Conseil de sécurité et l'Assemblée générale donc, toute solution au problème chypriote doit respecter les 'principes fondamentaux' de la souveraineté, de l'indépendance, et de l'intégrité territoriale de la République de Chypre.

[83] J. Verhoeven, *Les nullités du droit des gens* (Paris: Pedone, 1981), coll. 'Droit international', n° 1, p. 28.

Nations Unies, et plus précisément par le Conseil de sécurité et l'Assemblée générale, est sans doute d'une importance fondamentale. Mais l'absence, regrettable, d'une réaction centralisée ne doit pas avoir pour effet le triomphe des effectivités illicites.

La deuxième difficulté est de taille: il s'agit de déterminer le régime de validité des actes d'une entité créée à la suite de la violation d'une règle impérative. Cette entité *de facto* va en effet produire, grâce à son effectivité, une série d'actes. Et, s'il est logique de considérer que les actes internationaux d'une telle entité doivent être considérés comme inexistants, voire comme 'nuls' ou 'sans validité' (pour reprendre la terminologie utilisée par le Conseil de sécurité, v. *supra*),[84] le problème est beaucoup plus sérieux en ce qui concerne les actes internes. Ainsi, dans l'affaire *Loizidou*, la CEDH a refusé d'attribuer 'toute validité juridique . . . à des dispositions comme l'article 159 de la loi fondamentale' de la 'RTCN' qui prévoyait l'expropriation des biens des grecs chypriotes situés dans les territoires occupés. Elle a toutefois noté, avec prudence, qu'en refusant d'attribuer toute valeur juridique à la constitution de la 'RTCN' elle ne souhaitait pas 'énoncer une théorie générale sur la légalité des actes législatifs et administratifs de la "RTCN"'. Renvoyant à l'avis consultatif de la CIJ sur le *Sud-Ouest africain* du 21 juin 1971, la CEDH a souligné que 'le droit international reconnaît en pareil cas la légitimité de certains arrangements et transactions juridiques, par exemple en ce qui concerne l'inscription à l'Etat civil des naissances, mariages ou décès, "dont on ne pourrait méconnaître les effets qu'au détriment des habitants du territoire"'.[85] Paradoxalement, la CEDH a abandonné cette prudence dans son arrêt rendu le 10 mai 2001 dans l'affaire *Chypre c. Turquie* où, tout en réaffirmant sa position sur le fait que la 'RTCN' ne constitue pas un Etat, elle a pu déduire du passage précité de l'avis de la CIJ que 'dans des situations analogues à celle de l'espèce, l'obligation de ne pas tenir compte des actes des entités de fait est loin d'être absolue'. Elle a ainsi conclu qu'elle ne pouvait pas faire abstraction des organes judiciaires de la 'RTCN' et que par conséquent ses voies de recours internes (assimilées, bien sûr, aux

[84] *Cf.* aussi l'obligation de non reconnaissance codifiée par la CDI dans l'article 41 de son projet d'articles sur la responsabilité internationale des Etats in *Rapport de la Commission du droit international, 53ème session*, A/56/10, 2001, p. 308.

[85] Par. 45 de l'arrêt. La citation renvoie au par. 125 de l'avis consultatif de la CIJ (*Conséquences juridiques pour les Etats de la présence continue de l'Afrique du Sud en Namibie (Sud-ouest africain) nonobstant la résolution 276 (1970) du Conseil de sécurité*, avis consultatif du 21 juin 1971, CIJ, *Recueil 1971*, p. 56).

voies de recours internes de l'Etat occupant, la Turquie) devaient être, en principe, épuisées.[86]

Une troisième difficulté est liée à la précédente: elle concerne la mise en oeuvre de la responsabilité internationale du fait des actes ou des comportements de ces entités. L'exemple de la 'RTCN' montre que le problème peut être résolu assez facilement en cas d'agression: les comportements illicites sont attribués à l'Etat qui contrôle le territoire ou sous les instructions ou les directives duquel agissent les personnes concernées.[87] La CEDH n'a ainsi eu aucune difficulté à condamner à plusieurs reprises la Turquie pour les violations de la convention commises sur le sol de la 'RTCN'. Le problème peut devenir plus délicat néanmoins en cas de retrait complet de l'Etat agresseur ou (et surtout) dans l'hypothèse de la violation du droit à l'autodétermination (comme avec la Rhodésie du Sud) où aucun Etat tiers ne peut se voir endosser la responsabilité de l'entité sécessionniste.

D'autres difficultés encore (relatives, par exemple, à des problèmes de droit intertemporel ou à celui de la 'couverture' des illicéités et des nullités par le biais de la renonciation ou de l'acquiescement de l'Etat lésé) montrent que la mise en oeuvre des 'conditions de droit' pour l'émergence de nouveaux Etats par la voie de la sécession peut s'avérer extrêmement délicate. On comprend donc aisément les hésitations de la doctrine traditionnelle qui, de manière pragmatique, a toujours préféré mettre l'accent sur le seul principe de l'effectivité. Toutefois, ces difficultés sont surmontables. Elles ne peuvent pas et ne doivent pas mettre en cause la primauté de certaines règles fondamentales du droit international. Ici, comme ailleurs, l'excès de réalisme peut s'avérer beaucoup plus dangereux pour le développement de l'ordre juridique international que l'attachement à une vision quelque peu idéale des fonctions du droit international.

[86] *Cf.* par. 82 et point I par. 5 du dispositif. Cette position, adoptée par dix voix contre sept, a été très critiquée par les juges de la minorité qui ont souligné, entre autres, dans leur opinion dissidente, que l'obligation d'épuiser les voies de recours de la 'RTCN' ne peut exister qu'au détriment des grecs chypriotes, chassés de leurs propriétés après l'invasion, et va ainsi à l'encontre du raisonnement opéré dans le passage mentionné de l'avis de la CIJ de 1971.

[87] *Cf.* l'art. 8 du projet de la CDI sur la responsabilité des Etats et son commentaire in: *Rapport de la Commission du droit international, 53ème session*, A/56/10, 2001, p. 109.

6

A normative 'due process' in the creation of States through secession

ANTONELLO TANCREDI

I. Description of a paradigm: the factual nature of the creation of States

Traditionally, from Jellinek onwards, it has always been affirmed that the formation or disappearance of a State is a pure fact, a political matter,[1]

[1] As is well-known, this theory may be traced back to the idea by Jellinek of the 'Drei-Elemente-Lehre' at the beginning of the 20th century. See G. Jellinek, *Allgemeine Staatslehre*, 3rd edn. (Berlin: Springer, 1922), p. 332. The same theory was later codified in several international instruments. In this regard, the most traditional reference is the Montevideo Convention on the Rights and Duties of States, 1933, *League of Nations Treaty Series*, vol. 165, at p. 19. Article 1 stipulates that: 'the State as a person of International Law should possess the following qualifications: a) a permanent population; b) a defined territory; c) a government; and d) capacity to enter into relations with other States'. Although the Convention refers to 'the capacity to enter into relations with other states', this has generally been treated as meaning 'independence'. See J. Crawford, *The Creation of States in International Law* (Oxford: Oxford University Press, 1979), pp. 47–8. The theory of the 'three elements' has been routinely adopted even by national courts. See, for example, the Supreme Court of the United States in *Texas v. White* (1868), 74 US (7 Wallace), p. 700, at pp. 720–1. More recently, see the decision delivered on 7 July 1969 by the Cour d'Appel de Paris in *Paul Clerget c. Banque commerciale pour l'Europe du nord et Banque du commerce extérieur du Vietnam*, 7 June 1969 (reprinted in *Revue générale de droit international public* (1970), p. 522); the decision of 25 June 1985 by the Italian Corte di Cassazione in the *Arafat and Salah* case (reprinted in *Rivista di diritto internazionale* (1986), p. 884); the decision adopted on 21 February 1980 by the District Court of The Hague in *Frente Revolucionária de Timor Leste Independente v. The Netherlands* (reprinted in the *Netherlands Yearbook of International Law* (1981), at pp. 302–4). For the jurisprudence of British courts see I. Brownlie, *Principles of Public International Law* (Oxford: Oxford University Press, 2003), p. 15. Worthy of note is the definition of 'effective control' given by Lord Atkin in *The Arantzazu Mendi Case* (see All England Law Reports, 1939, vol. I, p. 719, at p. 722). This definition has been recently summarised by the Commercial Court (Queen's Bench Division) in *Republic of Somalia v. Woodhouse Drake & Carey (Suisse) SA and Others the Mary* (in All England Law Reports, 1993, vol. I, p. 371).

remaining outside the realm of law (which does not create States but presupposes their existence as *de facto* sovereign entities.)[2]

Consequently, it has long been a widely held assumption that international law neither prohibits nor authorizes secession,[3] but simply acknowledges the result of *de facto* processes which may lead to the birth of new States. These phenomena represent factual rearrangements of power and do not amount to the successful exercise of a legal right, existing *a priori*, or *ante rem* (before the fact). This implies the absence of norms giving rise to the right to independence to any ethnic, religious or linguistic group whatsoever.

In cases of secession, the normal requirements for statehood – a permanent population, a territory and an independent government[4] – would only be applied more strictly than would be required in cases of dissolution

[2] G. Arangio-Ruiz, *Gli enti soggetto dell'ordinamento internazionale*, (Milan: Giuffrè, 1951), p. 20.

[3] See the contribution of Corten to this volume. More generally, in doctrine, see Crawford, *The Creation of States*, p. 267; H. Ruiz Fabri, 'Genèse et disparition de l'Etat à l'époque contemporaine', *AFDI* 38 (1992), p. 153, at p. 154 and 157; C. Carpentier, 'Le principe mythique des nationalités: tentative de dénonciation d'un prétendu principe', *RBDI* 25 (1992), p. 351, at p. 355; S. Blay, 'Self-Determination: A Reassessment in the Post-Communist Era', *Denver J.I.L.P.* 22 (1993), p. 275, at p. 281; T. Franck, 'Fairness in the International Legal and Institutional System', *Recueil des Cours*, 1993, vol. III, p. 125; R. Higgins, 'International Law and The Avoidance, Containment and Resolution of Disputes', *Recueil des Cours*, 1991, vol. V, p. 154, at pp. 170–1; R. Higgins, *Problems and Process. International Law and How We Use It* (Oxford: Oxford University Press, 1994), p. 125; A. Binette, 'Le droit des peuples: l'autodétermination dans le contexte canadien', *CYIL* (1996), p. 215, at p. 221; T. D. Musgrave, *Self-Determination and National Minorities* (Oxford: Oxford University Press, 1997), pp. 235–6; P. Malanczuk, *Akehurst's Modern Introduction to International Law* (London, New York: Routledge, 1997), p. 78; A. Sáenz de Santa Maria, 'La libre determinacíon de los pueblos en la nueva sociedad internacional', *Cursos Euromediterráneos Bancaja de Derecho Internacional*, vol. I, 1997, p. 119, at pp. 188–9; P. Hilpold, 'Sezession und humanitäre Intervention – völkerrechtliche Instrumente zur Bewältigung innerstaatlicher Konflikte?', *ZaöRV* 54 (1999), p. 529, at p. 564; O. Corten, 'À propos d'un désormais "classique": Le droit à l'autodétermination en dehors des situations de décolonisation, de Théodore Christakis', *RBDI* 32 (1999), p. 329.

[4] After Jellinek (*Allgemeine Staatslehre*), see for example, among many others, R. Erich, 'La naissance et la reconnaissance des Etats', *Recueil des Cours*, 1926, vol. III, p. 427 at p. 442; K. Strupp, *Elements du droit international public universel, européen et américain* (Paris: Les Éditions Internationales, 1930), p. 80; G. Morelli, 'Cours général de droit international public', *Recueil des Cours*, 1956, vol. I, p. 437 at p. 517; C. De Visscher, *Théories et réalités en droit international public* (Paris: Pedone, 1970), pp. 184 ff.; M. Virally, 'Panorama du droit international contemporain', *Recueil des Cours*, 1983, vol. V, p. 9 at p. 50; R. Quadri, 'Stato (Diritto Internazionale)', in *Scritti giuridici* (Milan: Giuffrè, 1988), vol. I, at p. 191; Crawford, *The Creation of States*, p. 267; G. Abi-Saab, 'Cours général de droit international public', *Recueil des Cours*, 1987, vol. VII, p. 67; M. Giuliano, T. Scovazzi & T. Treves, *Diritto internazionale, Parte generale* (Milan: Giuffrè, 1991), p. 84.

(where the parent State ceases to exist) or devolution (which happens with the consent of the parent State).[5] With secession being a unilateral act which occurs *without* the consent of the parent State, the seceding entity has to struggle to establish effective control in the face of a presumption in favour of the integrity and effectiveness of the territorial State.[6]

Notwithstanding this, the principle of territorial integrity maintains an exclusive intergovernmental character which prohibits States from using force or intervening in the affairs of other States. Consequently, minorities are *not prohibited* from seceding under international law.[7] As has been said: 'Le droit, sur ce point, s'en remet au fait. Le peuple s'est constitué en État, non parce qu'il avait "le droit" (subjectif), mais parce qu'il avait la volonté et la force.'[8] Under this reconstruction, the

[5] In cases of secession, according to the jurisprudence of some national courts, one may refer to the so-called 'ultimate success' doctrine. This contends that the effectiveness required to assess the birth of a new State through secession must be established beyond any reasonable doubt. For applications of this doctrine in the case of Southern Rhodesia, see the Privy Council in *Madzimbamuto v. Lardner Burke*, Appeal Cases, 1969, p. 645; in the case of the Turkish Republic of Northern Cyprus, see the US Court of Appeals in *Autocephalous Greek-Orthodox Church of Cyprus and the Republic of Cyprus v. Goldberg and Feldman Fine Arts, Inc.* (1990), 917 F.2d (7th Circuit 1990), p. 278. The 'ultimate success' doctrine can be traced back to the jurisprudence of the US Supreme Court in the post-war-of-secession period (the leading decision being *Williams v. Bruffy* (1877), 96 US (23 Wallace), p. 176). An *a contrario* application of this doctrine has been made in the cases of Katanga and Biafra and, more recently, in those of Chechnya, Srpska Republic, Nagorno-Karabakh, South Ossetia, Abkhazia, Anjouan, Somaliland, where, even though the secessionist groups exercised significant control over the disputed territory, the majority of States refused to accord them recognition out of respect for the sovereignty of the parent States – respectively Congo, Nigeria, Russia, Bosnia and Herzegovina, Azerbaijan, Georgia, Islamic Republic of the Comoros. (For a discussion of this practice see A. Tancredi, *La secessione nel diritto internazionale* (Padova: Cedam, 2001), p. 377).

[6] See M. N. Shaw, *Title to Territory in Africa* (Oxford: Clarendon Press, 1986), at pp. 214–16. Indeed, as H. Lauterpacht noted (*Recognition in International Law* (Cambridge: Cambridge University Press, 1947), p. 45), in cases of secession, recognition is legitimate only once it is clear that the parent State has ceased (giving *de facto* its acquiescence) or is unlikely to be able to reassert control.

[7] See, in this sense, the report of T. Franck, R. Higgins, A. Pellet, M. N. Shaw, and C. Tomuschat, 'L'integrité territoriale du Québec dans l'hypothèse de l'accession à la souveraineté, Assemblée nationale du Québec, Commission d'étude des questions afférentes à l'accession du Québec à la souveraineté', *Exposés et études, Les attributs d'un Québec souverain*, vol. I, 1992, pp. 429–30 (English text reproduced in A. F. Bayefsky (ed.), *Self-Determination in International Law: Quebec and Lessons Learned* (The Hague, London, Boston: Kluwer Law International, 2000), p. 241).

[8] A. Pellet, 'Quel avenir pour le droit des peuples à disposer d'eux-mêmes?', in M. Rama Montaldo (ed.), *El derecho internacional en un Mundo en Trasformación. Liber Amicorum – Homenaje al Profesor Eduardo Jiménez de Aréchaga* (Montevideo: Fundación de Cultura Universitaria, 1994), p. 264.

conflict between secessionists and governmental authorities would still be regulated by the traditional law of *internal* armed conflicts, and generally treated as a 'domestic affair', in light of fundamental human rights prescriptions.

As to the 'neutralist' approach here briefly described, it must be emphasised that the absence of international law from processes of States' creation (but with the exception of decolonisation) has never been seriously contradicted. Even the doctrinal dispute between dualist proponents of the '*bloßes Faktum*' (pure fact) theory and monist supporters of the Kelsenian theory of the 'legal fact'[9] dating back to the first decades of the last century, concerned a question posed subsequent to the creation of States, namely the capacity of the birth of a State (regarded as an already existing fact) to produce legal effects in and of itself. For both groups of scholars, however, international law is not regarded as creating States through its norms, but rather, it remains outside the substance of the dynamic process which results in statehood.

As a corollary of the passive role attributed to international rules in this field, the process through which a new social entity comes into being would have no influence on its statehood and legal personality. In other words, international law governs neither the *substance* of this phenomenon ('if' there is a normative title to produce it), nor its *procedural* aspect ('how' it takes place). Neither profile could be subject to a judgment of legality or illegality founded on international norms. Once the effectiveness test is satisfied, it would not matter how a new government gained control over a territory and its permanent population. If the birth of the new State is due to foreign intervention, if it corresponds to the will of the population concerned, and if it respects territorially defined boundaries, these are aspects totally absorbed into the effectiveness of title.[10]

[9] See generally A. Verdross, 'Entstehung von Neustaaten', in K. Strupp (ed.), *Wörterbuch des Völkerrechts und der Diplomatie* (Leipzig: Berlin, de Gruyter, 1924–5), p. 283: '. . . der sog. "de facto" Staat kein bloßes "Faktum", sondern ein Tatbestand des Völkerrechts ist, an den bestimmte Rechtswirkungen geknüpft werden. Auch der "de facto"-Staat ist daher, wie jede Rechtserscheinung de jure'; *Verdross, Die Verfassung der Völkerrechtsgemeinschaft*, (Wien, Berlin: Springer, 1926), p. 129.

[10] Very significant in this regard are Kelsen's words: '. . . lors de la naissance d'un Etat, peu importe que l'efficacité de l'ordre nouveau, et par conséquent la sécession de l'Etat, reposent sur la volonté exprimée par la population dans une forme constitutionelle . . . , que la naissance de l'Etat s'effectue avec ou sans l'aide militaire d'un tiers Etat en guerre avec l'ancien Etat. Peu importe surtout que le territoire sur lequel s'établit l'Etat nouveau "se détache" de la mère-patrie, ou que soit un tiers-Etat qui, par une guerre, le détache

II. Doctrinal attempts to refute the paradigm. The incidence of principles of legality on the creation of States: from anti-colonial self-determination to remedial secession

The principle described above (namely the absence of international norms to regulate processes of State creation) has always remained valid but for one case, namely the *possible* exercise of self-determination by colonised peoples as a title for independence. During decolonisation (a period which saw the birth of nearly one hundred new sovereign countries), the creation of States was for the first time transformed into a legal matter through an international norm, the principle of self-determination, directly pertaining to the *substance* of these processes, leaving out any effectiveness rule. Peoples who were in a condition of foreign subjugation could claim to constitute themselves as independent States, relying on a norm directly constitutive of statehood.[11] International law did not take notice of the '*fait accompli*', but aimed at producing a new effectiveness, in order to promote values commonly perceived as fundamental (e.g. the right of all peoples to equality).

This novel rule remained confined to the specific case of decolonisation and to this specific historical period. The *vexata quaestio* regarding the broadening of the normative content of the principle of self-determination has, therefore, merely represented another way of determining whether this principle could express the same *constitutive* function (in terms of statehood) outside decolonisation, in extreme situations of denial of fundamental minorities' or peoples' rights.

The proponents of the 'secessionist self-determination' model affirm that contemporary international law also recognises this function in cases of 'extreme persecution', as an *ultima ratio*:[12] hence the idea of a *remedial*

de l'Etat ancien. Ce qui est décisif, et seul décisif, c'est l'effectivité de l'autorité nouvelle, c'est l'efficacité de l'ordre nouveau' (see H. Kelsen, 'La naissance de l'Etat et la formation de sa nationalité. Les principes, leur application au cas de la Tchécoslovaquie', *RDI* 3 (1929), p. 620). In the same vein see also Arangio-Ruiz, *Gli enti soggetto dell'ordinamento internazionale*, pp. 178–9; Morelli, 'Cours général', at p. 518. More recently, in this sense, see G. Dahm, J. Delbrück, and R. Wolfrum, *Völkerrecht* (Berlin, New York: de Gruyter, 1989), pp. 132–3; V. Đ. Degan, 'Création et disparition de l'État (à la lumière du démembrement de trois fédérations multiethniques en Europe)', *Recueil des Cours*, 1999, vol. 279, pp. 199, 227 and 232.

[11] On this issue, see M. Kohen, *Possession contestée et souveraineté territoriale* (Paris: Presse Universitaire de France, 1997), pp. 422–3 and 467–8.

[12] See D. Murswiek, 'The Issue of a Right to Secession – Reconsidered', in C. Tomuschat (ed.), *Modern Law of Self-Determination* (Dordrecht, Boston, London: M. Nijhoff, 1993), p. 21, at pp. 38–9.

secession. This idea is today supported by a vast number of writers,[13] who maintain that the traditional conflict between self-determination of peoples and the territorial integrity of States continues to be resolved in favour of State sovereignty, with one possible exception: the case in which infra-State groups with a particular identity (minorities, indigenous peoples) are victims of serious breaches of their fundamental civil and human rights. This extreme situation, giving rise to a claim of abuse of sovereign power, would entitle the victim group to exercise an internationally recognised and protected right to secession. Such a right would, as

[13] Among many others, often with different emphases, see U. O. Umozurike, *Self-Determination in International Law* (Hamden: Archon Books, 1972), p. 196; K. Doehring, 'Das Selbstbestimmungsrecht der Völker als Grundsatz des Völkerrechts', *Berichte der deutschen Gesellschaft für Völkerrecht* 14 (1974), p. 30; *ibid.*, 'Self-Determination', in B. Simma (ed.), *The Charter of the United Nations: A Commentary* (Oxford: Oxford University Press, 2nd ed., 2002), p. 97, at p. 58; Y. Dinstein, 'Collective Human Rights of Peoples and Minorities', *ICLQ* 25 (1976), p. 102, at p. 108; Y. Dinstein, 'Self-Determination Revisited', in M. Rama Montaldo (ed.), *El Derecho Internacional en un Mundo en Transformación. Liber amicorum – Homenaje al Profesor Eduardo Jiménez de Aréchaga* (Montevideo: Fundación de cultura Universitaria, 1994), p. 241; Y. Dinstein, 'Is There a Right to Secede?', *ASIL Proceedings* (1996), pp. 297, 299; L. C. Buchheit, *Secession, The Legitimacy of Self-Determination* (New Haven, London: Yale University Press, 1978), pp. 220–3; A. Cristescu, 'The Right to Self-Determination, Historical and Current Development on the Basis of United Nations Instruments', UN Doc. E/CN.4/Sub.2/ 404/Rev.1, New York, 1981, p. 26; D. Turp, 'Le droit de sécession en droit international public', *CYIL* 20 (1982), p. 24; G. Arangio-Ruiz, 'Autodeterminazione (diritto dei popoli alla)', *Enciclopedia giuridica*, vol. IV (Rome, 1988), p. 1, at p. 6; D. Thürer, 'Das Selbstbestimmungsrecht der Völker', *Archiv des Völkerrechts* 22 (1984), p. 113, at p. 127; D. Thürer, 'Self-Determination', in R. Bernhardt (ed.), *Encyclopedia of Public International Law*, vol. IV (Amsterdam, North-Holland, 2000), p. 364, at p. 367; M. Koteswara Rao, 'Right of Self-Determination in the Post-Colonial Era: A Survey of Juristic Opinion and State Practice', *IJIL* 27 (1988), p. 59; H. Hannum, *Autonomy, Sovereignty and Self-Determination: The Accommodation of Conflicting Rights* (Philadelphia: University of Pennsylvania Press, 1990), p. 471; A. Heraclides, 'Secession, Self-Determination and Non-Intervention: in Quest of a Normative Symbiosis', *JIA* 46 (1992), p. 399, at p. 407; M. Weller, 'The International Response to the Dissolution of the Socialist Federal Republic of Yugoslavia', *AJIL* 86 (1992), p. 569, at p. 606; C. Tomuschat, 'Self-Determination in a Post-Colonial World', in C. Tomuschat (ed.), *Modern Law of Self-Determination* (Boston, London: M. Nijhoff, 1993), p. 8; Murswiek, 'The Issue of a Right to Secession', pp. 38–9; R. McCorquodale, 'Self-Determination: A Human Rights Approach', *ICLQ* 43 (1994), p. 241; H.-J. Heintze, *Selbstbestimmungsrecht und Minderheitenrechte im Völkerrecht* (Baden-Baden: Nomos, 1994), at p. 88; L. Wildhaber, 'Territorial Modifications and Breakups in Federal States', *CYIL* (1995), p. 41, at p. 71; J. Duursma, *Fragmentation and the International Relations of Micro-States: Self-Determination and Statehood* (Cambridge: Cambridge University Press, 1996), at p. 89; P. H. Kooijmans, 'Tolerance, Sovereignty and Self-Determination', *NYIL* 43 (1996), p. 211, at pp. 215–16; R. Lefeber and D. Raic, 'Frontiers of International Law, Part One: The Chechen People', *LJIL* 9 (1996), p. 1; T. Christakis, *Le droit à l'autodétermination en dehors des situations de decolonisation* (Paris: La documentation française, 1999), p. 296, at pp. 314–15.

a remedial *extrema ratio* ('*Abwehrrecht im Sinne eines Notwehrrechts*'[14]), be consequent on the material concurrence of two unlawful acts, namely the violation of the group's right to internal self-determination (denial of the right to take part in the decision-making processes or to enjoy autonomy through forms of self-organization) and the commission of gross violations of human rights to its detriment.[15] Other writers, however, assert that the alternative recurrence of one of the two violations would be sufficient to give title to secede.[16]

In any case, the State responsible would find itself in a position very similar to that of the former colonial powers. It could not legally resort to the use of force to put down the secessionist attempt; it could not ask for or receive military support from third States; the secessionist group would be fully entitled to seek and receive external aid; and third-party actors would have no duty to refrain from interference.[17] In a word, the whole regime of guarantees which accompanied the 'classical' right of self-determination would find under these circumstances a new field of implementation. International law, therefore, would recognise 'a continuum of remedies ranging from the protection of individual rights to minority rights, and ending with secession as the ultimate remedy'.[18]

The approach briefly summarised above takes its origin from the advisory opinion given by the second Commission of Rapporteurs in the

[14] T. Marauhn, 'Anspruch auf Sezession?', in H.-J. Heintze (ed.), *Selbstbestimmungsrecht der Völker – Herausforderung der Staatenwelt* (Bonn: Dietz, 1997), p. 112.

[15] In this sense see, for instance, A. Cassese, *Self-Determination of Peoples: A Legal Reappraisal* (Cambridge: Cambridge University Press, 1995), pp. 119–20: '. . . denial of the basic right to representation does not give rise per se to the right of secession. In addition, there must be gross breaches of fundamental human rights, and, what is more, the exclusion of any likelihood for a possible peaceful solution within the existing State structure . . .'

[16] See T. Marauhn, 'Der aktuelle Fall: Die Auseinandersetzungen um die Unabhängigkeitsbestrebungen der jugoslawischen Teilrepublik Slowenien – Das Selbstbestimmungsrecht der Völker im Wandel', *Humanitäres Völkerrecht – Informationsschriften* 4 (1991), p. 107, at p. 111; Marauhn, 'Anspruch auf Sezession?', pp. 119–20 (with reference to the breach of internal self-determination).

[17] In this sense see S. Oeter, 'Selbstbestimmungsrecht im Wandel, Überlegungen zur Debatte um Selbstbestimmung, Sezessionsrecht und "vorzeitige" Anerkennung', *ZaöRV* 52 (1992), p. 741, at p. 765; Weller, 'The International Response', p. 607; Marauhn, 'Anspruch auf Sezession?', at pp. 114 ff.; D. Frey, 'Selbstbestimmungsrecht, Sezession und Gewaltverbot', in I. Seidl-Hohenveldern and H. J. Schrötter (eds.), *Vereinte Nationen, Menschenrechte und Sicherheitpolitik – Völkerrechtliche Fragen zu internationalen Konfliktbegrenzungen* (Köln: Heymann, 1994), p. 71; V. Grado, *Guerre civili e Stati terzi* (Padova: Cedam, 1998), pp. 350–4.

[18] Buchheit, *Secession, The Legitimacy of Self-Determination*, p. 222.

Aaland Islands case (1921). After excluding the existence of a general right to secede, this Commission observed in fact that '[t]he separation of a minority from the State of which it forms part and its incorporation into another State may only be considered as an altogether *exceptional* solution, *a last resort* when the State lacks either the will or the power to enact and apply just and effective guarantees'.[19] The reference here was intended for the guarantees provided for in the system of protection of minorities brought under the supervision of the League of Nations.

More recently, this 'remedial' approach has been acknowledged in the famous 'safeguard clause' embodied in the chapter of the 'Declaration on Friendly Relations among States' (GA Res. 2625 (XXV)) dedicated to the principle of self-determination. The importance of this clause lies in the fact that apparently, for the first time in a UN instrument, the protection of the territorial integrity of States became subject to the respect by its authorities for the right to internal self-determination of entire populations. The corresponding obligation incumbent on the State was, then, to ensure the adequate representation of the whole people without distinctions as to race, creed or colour. Reasoning *a contrario*, the exclusion of a group from the decision-making process, amounting to a violation of its right to be represented being formulated as the normative content of the right to internal self-determination, would suffice to confer on the victim group title to secede. This title would have prevailed on the competing right of the responsible State to protect its territorial integrity.

The same provision contained in paragraph 7 of GA Resolution 2625 (XXV) was reformulated in the Vienna Declaration and Programme of Action adopted by the UN World Conference on Human Rights in 1993, with one meaningful change: the right to preserve its own territorial integrity was recognised as applicable only to a 'Government representing the whole people belonging to the territory without distinction *of any kind*',[20] thus eliminating the limitation contained in GA Resolution 2625 (XXV) which confined the right to instances of discrimination founded on race, creed or colour. This amendment was confirmed in the text of the UN General Assembly's Declaration on the Occasion of the Fiftieth Anniversary of the United Nations, adopted in 1995.[21]

[19] Report submitted to the Council of the League of Nations by the Commission of Rapporteurs, League of Nations Document B7.21/68/106, 16 April 1921, at pp. 21, 28.

[20] UN Doc. A/Conf.157/24.

[21] GA Res. 50/6 of 24 October 1995.

Further references by UN bodies to the 'remedial secession' theory may be found, for instance, in the 'General Recommendation XXI' adopted on 8 March 1996 by the Committee on the Elimination of Racial Discrimination[22] and in the Report on *Possible Ways and Means of Facilitating the Peaceful and Constructive Solution of Problems Involving Minorities*, presented on 10 August 1993 by the Rapporteur Asbjorn Eide to the UN Sub-Commission against the discrimination and the protection of minorities.[23]

As for State practice, the existence of a right to remedial secession is commonly supported by making reference to the 1971 secession of Bangladesh from Pakistan, and more recently, to the process of 'chain-secession', which has ultimately resulted in the dissolution of the Socialist Federal Republic of Yugoslavia (SFRY).

In the first case, the recognition given by the international community to the independence of Bangladesh, notwithstanding the decisive role played by the Indian armed intervention against Pakistan, seemed justifiable on the ground that the Bengali population had been the victim of massive economic and political discrimination and that the general elections, which ended with the victory of the Bengali party, had been annulled by the central authorities. This annulment had been the premise of a successive period of violence and repression unleashed against the political leaders of East Pakistan. Nonetheless, it should be recalled that Bangladesh was admitted to the United Nations only in 1974, after recognition was given by Pakistan.[24]

As regards the breaking-up of the SFRY, the premature recognition given by third States to some components of the Federation (first Slovenia, then Croatia and Bosnia and Herzegovina), would have expressed the will of the international community to support the secessionist claims of those federative units against the territorial integrity of Yugoslavia. In that

[22] See Report of the Committee on the Elimination of Racial Discrimination, in General Assembly Official Record, 51st Session, Supplement no. 18, A/51/18, at pp. 125–6, para. 11.

[23] A. Eide, 'Protection of Minorities: Possible Ways and Means of Facilitating the Peaceful and Constructive Solution of Problems Involving Minorities', in UN Doc. E/CN.4/Sub.2/1993/34, para. 84. According to Eide: 'Only if the representative of the group [living compactly in an administrative unit of the State or dispersed within the territory of a sovereign State] can prove, beyond reasonable doubt, that there is no prospect within the foreseeable future that the Government will become representative of the whole people, can it be entitled to demand and to receive support for a quest for independence. If it can be shown that the majority is pursuing a policy of genocide against the group, this must be seen as very strong support for the claim of independence.'

[24] GA Res. 3203 (XXIX) of 17 September 1974.

context, international recognition would have assumed a 'regulatory function . . . aiming at implementing the right of self-determination against colliding claims to sovereignty', in such a way that 'a right of secession exists in this case based on the right of self-determination'.[25]

Even the national courts of some States directly involved in problems of secession, such as Canada and Russia, have made reference to the 'remedial approach'. Thus, the Canadian Supreme Court, in the consultative judgment delivered on 20 August 1998 in the *Reference re Secession of Quebec from Canada*,[26] having to decide whether a right existed to secede for the province of Quebec (both on the basis of the Canadian Constitution and of international law), expressly cited the 'safeguard clause'. In fact, the Court excluded that Quebec had title to secede because the Canadian government had constantly guaranteed a fair and adequate institutional representation and a wide autonomy in favour of this province. For both reasons, applying the typical reasoning *a contrario* of the GA Resolution 2625 (XXV), the Court concluded that Canada had always respected the internal self-determination of the *Québécois* and, therefore, was in the position to demand respect for its territorial integrity.

Before performing such a test of adequate representation however, while generally observing that the state of international law with respect to the right to self-determination 'is that the right operates within the overriding protection granted to the territorial integrity of parent states', the Court pointed out that the right to external self-determination undoubtedly finds application in two situations, that of colonial or alien subjugation, domination or exploitation, noting, furthermore, that:

> A number of commentators have further asserted that the right to self-determination may ground a right to unilateral secession in a *third circumstance*... when a people is blocked from the meaningful exercise of its right to self-determination internally, it is entitled, as a last resort, to exercise it by secession.

Nonetheless the Court specified that: 'it remains unclear whether this third proposition actually reflects an established international law standard'.[27]

[25] Oeter, 'Selbstbestimmungsrecht im Wandel', p. 741. See also P. Radan, *The Break-up of Yugoslavia and International Law* (London, New York: Routledge, 2002), pp. 202–3.

[26] *Reference by the Governor in Council, pursuant to Art. 53 of the Supreme Court Act, concerning the secession of Quebec from Canada*, [1998] 2 S.C.R. 217; *ILM* 37 (1998), at p. 1342.

[27] See *ILM* 37 (1998), pp. 1372–3.

The same test had been previously applied, with the same final result, by the Russian Constitutional Court in a sentence delivered on 31 July 1995 with reference to the conflict in Chechnya.[28]

III. The incidence of principles of legality on the creation of States: *de facto* entities created in violation of peremptory norms

The second direction along which the doctrine, particularly in the 1970s, has confuted the idea of the pre-juridical nature of the birth of States has been mainly inspired by the practice regarding as *de facto* regimes whose statehood and legal personality have been questioned owing to their unlawful origin. In particular, the reference is here made to the cases of Southern Rhodesia, South-African Bantustans and Northern Cyprus (the latter two clearly being hypotheses of secession). The stand taken by the international community through the non-recognition of these entities, according to some writers, would show that whether an event of secession occurs in breach of the ban on the use of force against a State's territorial integrity and/or of the principle of self-determination, the resulting illegitimacy would prevent an otherwise effective entity from being regarded as a State or as a subject of international law endowed with full legal capacity.[29]

[28] The original text of the decision is published in *Sobranie Zakonodatel'stva Rossijskoj Federacii*, 1995, n. 33, p. 6293 and n. 35, p. 6589. For the German translation see T. B. Beknazar, 'Übergesetzliches Staatsnotrecht in Rußland: Staatsnotstand und Notstandbefugnisse der Executive. Zum Tschetschenien-Urteil des russischen Verfassungsgerichts vom 31. Juli 1995', *ZaöRV* 57 (1997), p. 161, at p. 180.

[29] Such a current of doctrine finds its origin mainly in the works of Lauterpacht, *Recognition in International Law*, p. 409, according to whom, in very general terms, '. . . facts, however undisputed, which are the result of conduct violative of international law cannot claim the same right to be incorporated automatically as part of the law of nations' (at p. 410); in the same sense, see Lauterpacht (ed.), *Oppenheim's International Law: A Treatise*, vol. I, (London, New York, Toronto: Longmans, 1948), p. 137. The idea put forward in these works is that every unlawful situation or act is *ipso iure* null and void; therefore, the emphasis is always placed on the legal consequences arising from the violation. Only subsequently did the doctrine start to investigate the problem of statehood directly. Thus, analysing the international community's reaction towards Southern Rhodesia, J. E. Fawcett, in *The Law of Nations: An Introduction to International Law* (London: Penguin Press, 1968), pp. 38–9, argued that the respect for self-determination was an indispensable criterion for statehood, and that where 'there is a systematic denial to a substantial minority, and still more to a majority of the people, of a place and a say in the government, the criterion of organized government is not met'; in this same sense see also, by the same author, 'Security Council Resolutions on Rhodesia', *BYIL* 41 (1965–66), p. 103, at pp. 112–13 and 'Note in Reply to Devine', *MLR* 33 (1971), p. 417.

Thus, whereas in the framework of decolonisation the principle of self-determination served as a legal basis for statehood, it stems from this second body of practice that peremptory norms could also play a negative role, since their violation would obviate statehood by *prohibiting* secession.

The question here at issue is closely linked to the general debate regarding the criteria for statehood. With reference to this, indeed, the doctrine examined above affirms the existence, in addition to the traditional triad (population, territory and an independent government), of a fourth element, namely the *lawfulness* of the process of State creation. If this process is the product of a breach of cogent norms, then the *de facto* entity would be prohibited from claiming statehood.[30]

The question regarding the existence of a 'legal regulation of statehood on a basis other than that of effectiveness' was positively answered by Crawford, albeit only with reference to 'self-determination units' (the dependent territories falling under Chapter XI of the UN Charter), and therefore excluding States already formed, in *The Creation of States*, at pp. 77–8, 83–4 and 103–6 (where, dealing with the status of Southern Rhodesia, he argues that 'the principle of self-determination in this situation prevents an otherwise effective entity from being regarded as a State', so that '[i]t appears then a new rule has come into existence, prohibiting entities from claiming statehood if their creation is in violation of an applicable right to self-determination'). An analogous position has more recently been upheld by Shaw, *Title to Territory in Africa*, p. 159, and by the same author, *International Law* (Cambridge: Cambridge University Press, 2003), p. 177, at p. 185 ('The best approach is to accept the development of self-determination as an additional criterion of statehood, denial of which would obviate statehood'; V. Epping, 'Völkerrechtssubjekte', in K. Ipsen (ed.), *Völkerrecht* (München: Beck, 1999), p. 51, at p. 58; Christakis, *Le droit à l'autodétermination*, at p. 262 ('... il n'y a aucune raison pour ne pas considérer qu'un quatrième élément, celui de la légalité de la création d'un État, est nécessaire pour l'attribution de la qualité étatique à une entité sécessioniste. Tout au contraire, l'acceptation d'un tel critère est indispensable pour la préservation de la légalité internationale et la sanction de sa violation'), and at p. 317; M. G. Kohen, *La creation d'Etats en droit international contemporain*, in *Cursos Euromediterráneos Bancaja de Derecho Internacional*, vol. VI, 2002, p. 629.

30 For a systematic analysis, see E. Stabreit, *Der völkerrechtliche Status der Transkei, Ciskei, Bophuthatswanas und Vendas während der Zeit ihrer formellen Unhabhängigkeit von der Republik Südafrika* (Frankfurt am Main: Lang, 1997), p. 97; H. Krieger, *Das Effektivitätsprinzip im Völkerrecht* (Berlin: Duncker und Humblot, 2000), p. 102, at p. 176; T. D. Grant, *The Recognition of States: Law and Practice in Debate and Evolution* (Westport: Praeger, 1999), p. 83. This latter work analyses the existence of 'what might be called addenda to the Montevideo criteria – additional elements in what makes a state', taking into consideration as 'new criteria for statehood' the respect for the principles of self-determination and democracy, the rights of minorities and the principle of constitutional legitimacy. Only in the case of self-determination does the author deem it acceptable to affirm the emergence of a new criterion for statehood (particularly on the basis of the practice regarding Southern Rhodesia and South-African Bantustans). As to the other rules (democracy, rights of minorities, constitutional legitimacy), they are evidence of the existence of mere trends.

The argument that an unlawful process of State creation results in a denial of statehood is also maintained by other writers, who base this result on different reasoning. Distinguishing between acts or situations *non-existent* due to the lack of the essential constitutive requirements and acts or situations *null and void* by reason of contrast with legal norms, these writers criticise the assumption of lawfulness as a fourth requirement for statehood (so that the unlawful regime would not be inexistent because of the lack of a constitutive element), affirming that the birth of a *de facto* entity, even in the presence of the traditional elements of statehood, would be null owing to the breach of peremptory norms.[31]

From the violation of the norms pointed out above, there could even derive consequences different from the denial of statehood. According to this third position, indeed, the birth of a State remains a fact, even if it is attained unlawfully. On this premise, the violation of principles of *jus cogens* would play a role 'dans l'évaluation de l'effectivité de son existence *juridique*', that is to say, with reference not to statehood but to the legal personality of the *de facto* entity.[32]

However, under each of these reconstructions, unlike the traditional doctrine, the process of the birth of new sovereign entities would fall

[31] In substance: 'the criteria for statehood remain unchanged but . . . a State will not come into existence if its act of creation violates a norm having the character of *jus cogens*', see J. Dugard, *Recognition and the United Nations* (Cambridge: Cambridge University Press, 1987), p. 127, at p. 147 and, by the same author, 'Collective Non-Recognition: The Failure of South Africa's Bantustan States', in *Boutros Boutros-Ghali Amicorum Discipulorumque Liber*, vol. I (Brussels: Bruylant, 1998), p. 383, at p. 400. A similar view is held by V. Gowlland-Debbas, *Collective Responses to Illegal Acts in International Law – United Nations Action in the Question of Southern Rhodesia* (Dordrecht, Boston, London: M. Nijhoff, 1990), p. 237.

[32] See in this sense Georges Abi-Saab's report in the *Reference Re Secession of Québec, Re: Order in Council P. C.* 1996–1497 of 30 September 1996, 'L'effectivité requise d'une entité qui déclare son indépendance pour être considérée comme un État en droit international', in *Supplément au dossier, Rapport d'experts de l'amicus curiae, numéro 25506*, at p. 4, para. 2(b) (English text reproduced in Bayefsky (ed.), *Self-Determination in International Law*, pp. 69 ff.). See also C. Hillgruber, *Die Aufnahme neuer Staaten in die Völkergemeinschaft*, (Frankfurt am Main, etc.: Lang, 1998), p. 746. ('Die Nichtanerkennung eines sich tatsächlich etablierenden Neustaates . . . die unerwünschte Konsequenz hat, daß es nicht in die völkerrechtliche Pflicht und Verantwortung genommen werden kann'), and Krieger, *Das Effektivitätsprinzip im Völkerrecht*, pp. 176 and 473. Previously, a similar opinion had been maintained with regard to Southern Rhodesia and South-African Bantustans by I. Dore, 'Recognition of Rhodesia and Traditional International Law: Some Conceptual Problems', *Vanderbilt J. T. L.* 13 (1980), p. 25, at p. 31 ('This policy of non-recognition in turn resulted in the denial of international personality'), and by E. Klein, 'Die Nichtanerkennungspolitik der Vereinten Nationen gegenüber den in die Unabhängigkeit entlassenen südafrikanischen homelands', *ZaöRV* 39 (1979), p. 469, at p. 490.

under the discipline of international law: any violation of the principles of self-determination or of the prohibition of the use of force would result in the denial of statehood or personality of the unlawful entity.

IV. A different way to challenge the paradigm. The existence of 'due process' in the birth of States through secession: the normative content

In the first part of our analysis, it has been pointed out that, according to traditional theory, international law neither creates States nor guides processes of State creation. In the second part, it has been described how this paradigm has indisputably been derogated from in the framework of decolonisation. Beyond that, it is today open to discussion whether this exception has widened, including, under the profile of the existence of a right to secessionist self-determination, the above-described hypothesis of 'remedial secession', and, on the other hand, providing for a prohibition of secession. Both suggestions deal with the *substance* (the 'if') of State-creating processes.

An attempt to respond to these questions may be based on the practice of the last decade, a period which hosted a large number of processes of State creation. We shall proceed with analysing firstly the debated existence of a right to remedial secession, leaving aside momentarily the problem related to the emergence of a prohibition to secede in cases of breach of cogent norms. We will revert later to the latter point, dealing with the consequences of the 'procedural approach' here proposed.

Focusing, then, on the first issue, it is to be stressed that the *remedial secession* thesis has generated considerable literature during the last twenty years. It may be correctly affirmed that today most writers uphold this theory, at least from a *de lege ferenda* perspective. Notwithstanding its popularity among legal scholars, its correspondence to positive international law can still be doubted with good reason.

The theory's main flaw is the lack of a sufficient basis in State practice. Putting aside the Bangladesh case, whose exceptional character has been widely underscored, one can barely cite a case in which the scheme of remedial secession has been concretely applied.

As for the 'saving clause' enhanced in GA Resolution 2625 (XXV), its application has remained confined to the political situation that prompted its inclusion in the Declaration on the Friendly Relations among States: apartheid in South Africa, which has been dead for over a decade. Consequently, according to practice, that disposition has proven to be consistent with customary law only insofar as incidents of racially grounded discrimination in the access to the decision-making process take place.[33]

Even in the case of the SFRY, one gets the general impression that what the EC member States recognised was not the right to create new States exercising secessionist self-determination, but simply the inevitability of a *de facto* process which was already under way and which would have produced the dissolution of the SFRY in any case. Such an assertion was already contained in Opinion No. 1, given by the Arbitration Commission at the end of November 1991, before any declaration of recognition. It must be underlined that this Opinion followed the entry into force of the two declarations of independence issued by the Parliaments of Slovenia and Croatia on 25 June 1991, suspended for three months after the Brioni cease-fire agreement reached in July 1991, and finally implemented on 8 October 1991 as a consequence of the failure of the peace talks among the SFRY Republics. Never until that moment – which has been considered by the Arbitration Commission in its Opinion No. 11 (delivered on 16 July 1993) as the 'critical date' to which Slovenia and Croatia can point as their birth as independent States – had the international community recognised the existence of a right to secede from the SFRY. To the contrary, the European Community,[34] its member States,[35] the

[33] See in this sense P. Thornberry, 'Self-Determination, Minorities, Human Rights: A Review of International Instruments', *ICLQ* 38 (1980), p. 867, at p. 876; Cassese, *Self-Determination of Peoples*, p. 122; G. H. Fox, 'Self-Determination in the Post-Cold War Era: A New Internal Focus?', *Michigan J. I. L.* 16 (1995), p. 733, at p. 740.

[34] See the common declarations adopted on 26 March 1991 (in EC Bull., 1991, n. 3, at p. 70), 5 July (in EC Bull., 1991, n. 7/8, at p. 105), and the Joint Declaration of the EC Trojka and the parties directly concerned with the Yugoslav crisis, the so-called 'Brioni Accord', adopted on 7 July, text in S. Trifunovska (ed.), *Yugoslavia Through Documents: From Its Creation to Its Dissolution* (Dordrecht, Boston, London: M. Nijhoff, 1994), p. 311.

[35] See, for instance, the declaration made by the French Minister of Foreign Affairs on 27 June 1991, following the declarations of independence of Slovenia and Croatia: 'Nous pensons que tout démembrement de l'Etat yougoslave risque de conduire à une période d'instabilité, d'affrontements, qui vont voir resurgir les anciennes querelles, les rivalités locales, et pour l'instant, dans tout l'Occident, et partout dans le monde, les points de vue qui s'expriment sont en faveur du maintien de l'Etat fédéral' (in J. Charpentier, 'Pratique française de droit international', *AFDI* 37 (1991), p. 986). The same opinion was expressed by German Minister of Foreign Affairs and by German Prime Minister Kohl (see D. Caccamo, 'La questione jugoslava (1989 – gennaio 1992)', *Rivista di studi politici internazionali* 59 (1992), p. 51, at p. 58). As for the British Government, see the declaration made by its representative in the House of Commons on 13 February 1991: 'The United Kingdom is obliged under the CSCE Final Act to continue to support the unity and integrity of Yugoslavia and also the right of individual peoples to national self-determination' (quoted in G. Marston, 'United Kingdom Materials on International Law', *BYIL* 62 (1991), at pp. 573–4).

Conference on Security and Co-operation in Europe (CSCE),[36] the United States[37] and the Soviet Union[38] supported the indivisibility of the SFRY. Only on 5 July 1991, in a common declaration, did the European Community and its member States establish that in the former Yugoslavia all the parties to the conflict had accepted the *fact* that a new situation had been created.[39]

In addition, the secessionist claims advanced by the Serbian populations living in the Republics of Croatia and Bosnia and Herzegovina have always been rejected by the international community, which has constantly called for the respect of the pre-existing federal boundaries. In fact, put before the intention manifested by the two Serbian Parliaments of Knin (capital of the Serbian populated region of Kraijna, located in Croatia) and Pale (in Bosnia and Herzegovina) to merge into a self-proclaimed Serbian Republic of Krajina and Bosnia and Herzegovina, on 2 June 1995 the European Union reaffirmed its commitment for the respect of the territorial integrity of the former SFRY Republics within the internationally recognised frontiers. Consequently, it was said that the effects of the announced fusion, if carried out, would have been 'null and void'.[40] As a result, the 1995 Dayton-Paris Agreement created one State, the Republic of Bosnia and Herzegovina, composed of two autonomous units: the Federation of Bosnia and Herzegovina and the Srpska Republic.[41]

[36] With the declaration adopted on 19 June 1991, the participating States affirmed their support 'for democratic development, unity, and territorial integrity of Yugoslavia' (quoted in *Yugoslav Survey* 32 (1991), at pp. 75–6). In the same sense, see the declaration of the Ministers of Foreign Affairs participating in the Council meeting held in Berlin on 19–20 June 1991 (in P. Trichilo, 'L'azione della CSCE per i diritti umani nella ex Jugoslavia', *Rivista internazionale dei diritti dell'uomo* 6 (1993), p. 123, at p. 127).

[37] On 28 March 1991, President Bush, in a letter addressed to the Yugoslav Prime Minister, wrote: 'the United States . . . will not encourage those who would break the country apart'. The same position was reaffirmed by the State Department in May 1991, in a declaration that read: 'the United States will not encourage or reward secession', and expressed the support of the United States 'for the territorial integrity of Yugoslavia within its present borders' (see P. Radan, 'Secessionist Self-Determination: The Cases of Slovenia and Croatia', *Australian J.I.A.* 48 (1994), p. 183, at p. 187 and M. H. Halperin, D. J. Scheffer & P. L. Small, *Self-Determination in the New World Order* (Washington DC: Carnegie Endowment for International Peace, 1992), at p. 33).

[38] In April 1991, the Russian Minister of Foreign Affairs affirmed that the protection of the Yugoslavian territorial integrity was 'one of the essential preconditions for the stability of Europe' (see Radan, 'Secessionist Self-Determination', p. 187).

[39] In EC Bull., 1991, n. 7/8, p. 105.

[40] The text of the declaration is reproduced in Marston, UKMIL, *BYIL* 66 (1995), p. 614.

[41] See Article 3 of the new Constitution of Bosnia and Herzegovina, which represents the fourth Annex to the General Framework Agreement for Peace in Bosnia and Herzegovina,

Moreover, it does not seem, in the case of the former SFRY, that a persistent and irremediable denial of the right of the constituent Republics to participate in the essential organs of Yugoslavia had occurred. The problem concerned mainly the failure of the constituent units to reach an agreement on the institutional reforms in the post-Tito era.[42] If this is correct, one of the unlawful acts required to legitimate a claim to secede (the breach of internal self-determination) did not recur.

Accordingly, many scholars have pointed out that the whole process of Yugoslavia's dismemberment should be considered as a factual redistribution of sovereign powers,[43] not sustained by any legal title. In this sense, acts of premature recognition 'internationalized an internal conflict, extending to all entities the ban on the use of force and the duty to respect established borders'.[44]

Finally, the conflict in Kosovo has proved to be an ideal test-case for the current validity of the remedial secession theory. Legally speaking, it has failed. The international community, through the UN,[45] the European

reprinted in *ILM* 35 (1996), at p. 89. Article 1 affirms that the Republic of Bosnia and Herzegovina 'shall continue its legal existence under international law as a state, with its internal structure modified as provided herein and with its present internationally recognized borders'.

42 This interpretation has been upheld in the initial report presented by Croatia to the Human Rights Committee. In fact, in the part dedicated to the means adopted to implement the principle of self-determination embodied in Article 1 of the Covenant on Civil and Political Rights, it is affirmed that following the first multi-party elections held in Croatia on 22 April 1990, local authorities '. . . requested from the federal bodies the establishment of more equal relations within the federation at the time. After the unsuccessful termination of negotiations between the presidents of the former Yugoslav republics on the future organization of the federation or a confederation at the meeting in Ohrid held on April 1991, it was decided that a referendum on remaining within the federation was to be held in each of the republics.' The final step of the whole process was reached on 8 October 1991, when, once the moratorium of three months provided for by the Brioni Agreement had expired, it became clear that '[t]he mentioned negotiations were unsuccessful' (see UN Doc. CCPR/C/HRV/99/1, 7 March 2000, paras. 3–6).

43 Thürer, 'Self-Determination', at p. 371. See also Pellet, 'Quel avenir pour le droit des peuples à disposer d'eux-mêmes?', at p. 263; J. Crawford, 'State Practice and International Law in Relation to Secession', *BYIL* 69 (1998), p. 85, at pp. 105–6; Corten, 'À propos d'un désormais "classique"', at pp. 179–80; Fox, 'Self-Determination in the Post-Cold War Era', at p. 746; C. Simmler, *Selbstbestimmungsrecht der Völker contra uti possidetis?*, *VRU* 32 (1999), p. 210, at p. 230.

44 See C. Hillgruber, 'The Admission of New States to the International Community', *EJIL* 9 (1998), p. 491, at p. 493.

45 See for instance Res. 1244 (1999) adopted by the UN Security Council on 10 June 1999 and, subsequently, Res. 1345 (2001), adopted unanimously on 21 March 2001; see also UN GA Res. 54/183, adopted on 29 February 2000.

Union[46] and NATO,[47] has never recognised the existence of a legally enforceable title to secede in favour of the Kosovars, notwithstanding the fact that Kosovo had been deprived of its status of autonomy and of any kind of substantial representation in the central bodies of the Yugoslav Federation. All that had been sought from the government of Belgrade is to stop the wrongful conduct and to restore the *status quo ante*, through the reintroduction of an autonomous regime. In summary, international law, as it now stands, recognises neither a general nor a remedial right to secede in oppressive contexts. According to practice, the consequence arising from the type of unlawful acts contemplated by the 'remedial' theory remains the duty to cease the wrongful conduct and, where possible, to restore the *status quo ante* (which normally is tantamount to creating *ad hoc* mechanisms or institutions to guarantee an indiscriminate representation to the different components of a people).

But recent practice has seemed to display something more than a negative answer. Indeed, even though no conclusive evidence of the existence of a right to secession has been reached, it has nevertheless been proved that the international community is increasingly concerned with conflicts which seriously threaten common values, such as international peace and stability. These social goods can be safeguarded only by channelling factual processes of redistribution of sovereignty through international norms. If, then, international law abstains from dictating conditions *ante rem* for statehood, it assumes a novel role by pointing out that the necessary conditions in fact exist. However, international norms do not address the *substance* of these processes (which remains factual), but rather their *procedure*.[48]

In other words, once a process of State secession begins, the whole question remains, from a substantive point of view, an internal matter. This means that all other consociates (i.e. third States) are bound to respect

[46] See for instance the declarations adopted by the European Union and its member States on 14 and 17 April 1999 (reproduced in UN Doc. S/1999/429 and UN Doc. S/1999/589, respectively).

[47] See the 'Statement on Kosovo' adopted by the Atlantic Council at the end of the summit held at Washington on 23–24 April 1999, NATO Press Release S-1(99)62, 23 April 1999.

[48] A first brief enunciation of this 'procedural model' can be found in T. Franck, 'Communities in Transition: Autonomy, Self-Governance and Independence', *Proceedings of the American Society of International Law* (1993), p. 261. For a more articulated elaboration of this approach, albeit with some differences on employed criteria, see A. Tancredi, 'Secessione e diritto internazionale', *Rivista* (1998), p. 758, and the monograph *La secessione nel diritto internazionale*, p. 669. See also Kohen, *La creation d'Etats*, at p. 601. For an evaluation, see Hilpold, 'Sezession und humanitäre Intervention', p. 561.

the 'radical title' of sovereignty, except in cases in which secessionists gain control of part of the territory. The international community has no interest in favouring or opposing secession; its legal system does not contain any norm which prohibits or authorises it.

However, this *substantive* profile does not exhaust all possible interrelations between secession and international law. The dynamics of secession represent a process which potentially collides with international rules at a higher level, designed to protect the common interests of the intergovernmental community. These rules, considered together, constitute a sort of 'normative course' through which secessionist processes are channelled. These rules neither provoke nor prevent the birth of new States; they simply 'guide' these processes.

Consequently, it is still legally founded to assert that international law intervenes once secession is a *fact*, regulating its consequences under different profiles: recognition or non-recognition, State succession, international personality. Nonetheless, it is here submitted that international law intervenes even earlier, setting out a normative 'due process' through which a secessionist act must happen. Accordingly, whereas it is still true that international law does not deal with the *substance* of State creation (the 'if'), it is possible to isolate a different normative profile which attains to the *procedure*, i.e. the 'how' with regard to the occurrence of these phenomena.[49]

The 'due process' discussed here is structured on the joint application of three rules, legally addressed to secessionist groups' responsible authorities.

First of all, to produce this effect of 'procedural' legitimacy, it is required that the process of secession take place without the direct or

[49] As affirmed by Franck, 'Communities in Transition', at p. 261, recalling the conclusions drawn by the 'five experts' in the 1992 Opinion on the consequences of a secession of Quebec from Canada: 'Is there a right of secession? We don't know. There is no right to secession, and there is no right to put down a secession. International law does not have an answer . . . We don't know whether there is a right to secession, but we do know something about ways of seceding that are unacceptable to the rest of the international community. So we were able to say to the Quebec government, international law does not tell you whether you have a right to secede or not, but it does tell you that unless you do it according to the following three rules you are likely to run into a lot of flak from the international community.' The three rules, expounded on the basis of the Opinions given by the Arbitration Commission, are the following: 'no change of boundaries through military force . . . no secession without some kind of due process within the seceding State . . . no secession without the seceding government guaranteeing the rights of its own minorities'.

indirect military support of foreign States.[50] In a wider perspective (with regard to whatever kind of external support, even if not of a military nature), then, secessionist rebels are not entitled to seek and receive external aid, a prerogative which is attributed only to liberation movements (see GA Res. 2625 (XXV), adopted on 24 October 1970 and paragraph 7 of GA Res. 3314 (XXIX) on the definition of aggression, adopted on 14 December 1974). From the point of view of third States, the prohibition to intervene in civil wars is one of the traditional rules of non-international conflicts, which conjointly results from the ban on the use of force, the principle of non-interference and the principle of territorial integrity. Consequently, it may be affirmed that the regime observed in the framework of decolonisation to assist the exercise of self-determination by colonial peoples is *not* transposable to secessionist conflicts, which are still regulated by the law of civil wars.[51] This is mainly due to the fact that secessionist struggles remain, in the view of international law, an internal matter falling within the domestic jurisdiction of the State in question.[52] Consequently, international law would apply to this situation only through the rules of international protection of human rights or the principles of international humanitarian law, if applicable to armed conflicts not of an international character.

Secondly, the secessionist attempt must be founded on the consent of a majority of the local population, democratically expressed through plebiscites or referenda. In this sense, recent secessionist practice (in the Soviet Union, Yugoslavia, Eritrea, and Kosovo) demonstrates how secessionist movements tend to legitimate their claim to independence

[50] In this sense, see, for instance, the stand taken by Franck, 'Opinion Directed at Question 2 of the reference', para. 2.18 (reproduced in Bayefsky (ed.), *Self-Determination in International Law*, p. 81), Pellet, 'Avis juridique sur certaines questions de droit international soulevées par le Renvoi', para. 19 (English text in Bayefsky (ed.), *Self-Determination in International Law*, p. 85, at p. 99) and Crawford, 'Response to Experts Reports of the Amicus Curiae', para. 4 and para. 13 (Bayefsky (ed.), *Self-Determination in International Law*, p. 153, at pp. 155–6) in the framework of the *Reference Re Secession of Québec, Re: Order in Council P.C.* 1996–1497 of 30 September 1996.

[51] As pointed out by Abi-Saab, 'L'effectivité requise d'une entité qui déclare son indépendance', para. III (reproduced in Bayefsky (ed.), *Self-Determination in International Law*, p. 72): '. . . all the essentially interventionist rules and advanced protections, that come along with the right of peoples to self-determination once it is considered applicable, remain out of reach in this situation'.

[52] Therefore, as Crawford points out: '. . . if the metropolitan state wishes to oppose the secession by whatever lawful means, other states will stand aside and allow it to do so (as for a long time in the case of Eritrea and most recently in Chechnya)', 'Response to Experts Reports', Bayefsky (ed.), *Self-Determination in International Law*, pp. 160–1, para. 13.

by resorting to public consultations.[53] The growing importance of this requirement is confirmed by the fact that, in the absence of a referendum, the international community has requested that one be held (for example in Bosnia-Herzegovina after Opinion No. 4 of the Badinter Commission),[54] on the other hand manifesting its satisfaction when such will has been democratically expressed (beginning with the Baltic States).[55] In any case, popular consent does not give rise to a legal right to secession. The birth of a new State is substantively legitimated only by its eventual success.

Thirdly, secession must respect the *uti possidetis juris* principle ('*uti possidetis, ita possideatis*', i.e. 'as you have possessed, so you shall continue to possess').[56] The creation of a new entity must occur within previous (administrative) boundaries, as happened in Bangladesh, the Baltic States, Yugoslavia and Eritrea. This rule, though initially applied in the context of the decolonisation process in Latin America, and then in Africa (see for instance Resolution 16(1) of the Organization of African Unity 1964, the so-called 'Cairo Declaration')[57] 'is today recognized as a general principle' (i.e. generally applicable in every process of a State's creation), as stated by the International Court of Justice in its Judgment of 22 December 1986 in the dispute between Burkina Faso and Mali.[58] The *uti possidetis* principle provides for a transitional mechanism which regulates the transmission of territorial sovereignty from the previous sovereign to the new State.[59] Its effect, then, is to 'freeze the territorial title', converting internal administrative lines into the international frontiers of the newly emerged State. The implementation of this norm favours the rapid stabilisation

[53] For this practice, see Tancredi, *La secessione nel diritto internazionale*, p. 378.

[54] For the text, see *ILM* 31 (1992), at p. 1501.

[55] See EC Bull., 1991, nn.1–2, point 1.4.21 and n. 3, point 1.4.2.

[56] On the role of the *uti possidetis* rule in secessionist conflicts, see M. G. Kohen, 'Le problème des frontières en cas de dissolution et de séparation d'États: quelles alternatives?', *RBDI* 31 (1998), p. 129, at p. 135, and G. Nesi, 'L'uti possidetis hors du contexte de la décolonisation: le cas de l'Europe', *AFDI* 44 (1998), p. 1.

[57] Text reproduced in I. Brownlie, *Basic Documents on African Affairs* (Oxford: Oxford University Press, 1971), p. 360.

[58] *Frontier Dispute (Burkina Faso / Mali), Judgment of 22 December 1986, ICJ Reports* 1986, pp. 554 and 565. The Arbitration Commission quoted the following passage of the ICJ decision: 'Nevertheless the principle is not a special rule which pertains solely to one specific system of international law. It is a general principle, which is logically connected with the phenomenon of the obtaining of independence, wherever it occurs. Its obvious purpose is to prevent the independence and stability of new States being endangered by fratricidal struggles.'

[59] See Shaw's report in the *Reference Re Secession of Québec, Re: Order in Council P.C.* 1996–1497 of 30 September 1996, text in Bayefsky (ed.), *Self-Determination in International Law*, p. 125, at p. 146, para. 79.

of new international frontiers, protecting stability and peace. As already happened during the decolonisation period, the resort to *uti possidetis* represents a '*solution de sagesse*',[60] which facilitates the channelling of these processes defending collective security.

An important distinction must be drawn between *uti possidetis* and territorial integrity. *Uti possidetis juris* does not operate *after* the formation of a new State, but *during* this process of creation. After the birth of a new subject, once a new *stasis* has emerged, the principle to respect is that of States' territorial integrity. Even the function displayed is different: while the *uti possidetis* rule *establishes* the border, the territorial integrity principle protects it *vis-à-vis* third parties once the State is created.[61] That is precisely why it must operate already within the dynamics of State creation, i.e. to transmit existing administrative borders without changes which have not been mutually agreed upon.[62] It must also be stressed that the binding effects of the *uti possidetis* rule are bilaterally directed towards the secessionist entity and the parent State. Both are compelled to respect pre-existing boundaries, and thus prohibited from resorting to force to alter them.[63] In this regard, the international response to the Yugoslav crisis has demonstrated the pre-eminence of the interest in avoiding

[60] See *Frontier Dispute*, p. 567.

[61] M. N. Shaw, 'The Heritage of States: The Principle of *Uti Possidetis Juris* Today', *BYIL* 67 (1996), at pp. 93 and 124–5. See also, by the same author, 'Peoples, Territorialism and Boundaries', *EJIL* 8 (1997), p. 478. See also the works of Kohen, 'Le problème des frontières' and Nesi, 'L'uti possidetis hors du contexte de la décolonisation'.

[62] This distinction also has a direct bearing on the notion of 'critical date'. If it is correct to assert that *uti possidetis* already operates during the process of State creation (as part of this normative 'due process' we are dealing with), the consequence would be that it deploys its protective effects all through the *de facto* course of secession, which consists of a process and not of a moment. Obviously, there may be a chronological gap between the beginning of the process (normally marked by a declaration of independence opposed by force or declared illegitimate and invalid by the parent State) and its final outcome. Notwithstanding this, internal administrative borders will be put under the protection of the *uti possidetis* rule during the whole length of that process, and not only in its final moment. Otherwise, the *uti possidetis* rule would only register the factual result of the conflict, losing any autonomous normative function. (This kind of criticism has been developed in several works by L. I. Sánchez Rodríguez; see for instance 'L'uti possidetis et les effectivités dans les contentieux territoriaux et frontaliers', *Recueil des Cours*, vol. 263, 1997, pp. 199 (n. 129), 228 and 285–7).

[63] See in this regard, SC Res. 947 of 30 September 1994, by which the UN Security Council called for the Serb forces in Bosnia to abstain from violating the frontier with Croatia. See also the statements issued by the President of the UN Security Council on 13, 18 and 26 November 1994 (UN Doc. S/PRST/1994/66, UN Doc. S/PRST/1994/69 and UN Doc. S/PRST/1994/71, respectively), together with SC Res. 959 of 19 November 1994 by the UN Security Council, in which the Security Council demanded that all parties to the conflict 'and in particular the so-called Krajina Serb forces' respect the border between Croatia and Bosnia-Herzegovina.

non-consensual modifications of borders, often imposed by resorting to the use of force.[64] International law begins to regulate phenomena of sovereignty redistribution, which often provoke widespread illegalities, starting with the guarantee of borders (seen, from the Schmittian perspective, as the 'token' of law)[65] in this way reaffirming its imperativeness. When internal borders become international, they are automatically protected by the rule of inviolability. Furthermore, this introduces into conflicts the duty to respect the prohibitions against the use of force, against interference with other States' internal affairs, etc. (as happened in the case of Bosnia-Herzegovina through the resolutions of the UN Security Council).[66]

A final remark concerns the relationship between *uti possidetis* and self-determination. Self-determination pertains to the *substance* of State creation, providing, in certain situations, for a right to independence. In contrast, *uti possidetis* does not give any title to secede; it simply fixes the boundaries which the new entity will eventually inherit. The rule acts as a part of a normative 'due process' through which these phenomena are channelled. In any case, the birth of a new State will occur only if the effectiveness test is satisfied, not as the exercise of a right to the territory.[67]

V. A 'due process' in the birth of States through secession: the consequences

Let us now turn to analysing the consequences resulting from the procedural approach. In this regard, we will revert to examining the thesis according to which the unlawful formation of a *de facto* sovereign entity would prevent it from claiming statehood or legal personality. Indeed, the peremptory norms (non-use of force and self-determination) recalled by the proponents of this position are somewhat similar to the 'procedural'

64 This will has been expressed in several documents and declarations throughout the Yugoslav crisis. See, for all, Opinion No. 3, Conference on Yugoslavia, Arbitration Commission, 11 January 1992, 92 *ILR* 1992, p. 170.

65 C. Schmitt, *Der Nomos der Erde im Völkerrecht des Jus Publicum Europaeum* (Köln: Greven, 1950), at p. 3.

66 See Security Council Resolutions on Bosnia: 752 (1992), 757 (1992), 770 (1992), 787 (1992), 819 (1993), 820 (1993), 824 (1993), 836 (1993), 838 (1993), 847 (1993), 859 (1993), 871 (1993), 913 (1994), 941 (1994), 959 (1994).

67 See G. Nesi, *L'uti possidetis iuris nel diritto internazionale* (Padova: Cedam, 1996), p. 230; Kohen, *Possession contestée et souveraineté territoriale*, at p. 158. For an example of the view criticised here, see, for instance, M. Craven, 'The European Community Arbitration Commission on Yugoslavia', *BYIL* 66 (1995), pp. 389–90.

rules previously described, with the exception of the *uti possidetis* principle.

It is submitted that when the process of secession respects the 'due process' at issue, and *only* if the secessionist attempt ends successfully, can it be considered to have occurred 'lawfully', with the consequent birth of a new sovereign subject, endowed with the full international legal personality accompanying statehood. When such is not the case, the reaction of the international community, through its various articulations, is normally twofold: on the one hand, international and regional organisations declare the formation of the new entity invalid and all the acts, orders and laws enacted by its authorities null and void; on the other hand, there is a consistent practice of resolutions or decisions taken by States or international organisations calling for the non-recognition of *de facto* entities created in breach of the non-use of force or of the principle of self-determination.

Such a stand was adopted, for instance, by the Assembly of the League of Nations (thus applying the famous *Stimson doctrine* expounded on that occasion by the U.S. Secretary of State)[68] in the case of Manchukuo[69] and by the General Assembly and the Security Council of the United Nations in the cases of Southern Rhodesia,[70] South-West

[68] See the text in *AJIL* 36 (1932), p. 342.

[69] On 23 February 1933, the Assembly of the League of Nations recommended to all member States not to recognise 'the existing regime in Manchuria', formed in violation of Article 10 of the Covenant (which prohibited member States to use force against other States' territorial integrity) (see *League of Nations Official Journal*, Special Supplement no.112, 1933, p. 76). Already previously, in the resolution adopted on 11 March 1932, the same Assembly declared incumbent upon the members of the League of Nations the obligation not to recognise any situation, treaty or agreement which may be brought about by means contrary to the Covenant of the League of Nations or to the 1928 Pact of Paris (see *League of Nations Official Journal*, Special Supplement no. 101, 1932, p. 87).

[70] See SC Res. 216 of 12 November 1965, followed by SC Res. 217 of 20 November 1965. With the former, all the member States were asked 'not to recognize the illegal racist minority regime in Southern Rhodesia'. With SC Res. 277, adopted on 18 March 1970, the Security Council condemned the illegal proclamation of the Republic by the racist Rhodesian regime, demanding that all member States not recognise this regime, and asking them 'to take appropriate measures, at the national level, to ensure that any act performed by officials and institutions of the illegal regime in Southern Rhodesia shall not be accorded any recognition, official or otherwise, including judicial notice, by the competent organs of their State'. The measure of non-recognition was then reaffirmed in the following resolutions: Res. 288 (1970) of 17 November 1970; 328 (1973) of 10 March 1973; 423 (1978) of 14 March 1978; 445 (1979) of 8 March 1979; and 448 (1979) of 30 April 1979. Even the UN General Assembly, despite the imminence of the unilateral declaration of independence proclaimed on 11 November 1965, recommended in Res. 2012 (XX) of 12 October 1965, and Res. 2022 (XX) of 5 November 1965, that member States not

Africa,[71] South African Bantustans[72] and the Turkish Republic of Northern Cyprus.[73] In the latter case, the same measure was adopted by the European Community,[74] the Heads of Government of the Commonwealth[75] and the Council of Europe,[76] whereas in the case of Bantustans it was

recognise the Rhodesian authorities. See in this sense also the following GA Res. 2379 (XXIII) of 25 October 1968, and GA Res. 33/38 of 13 December 1978.

71 See SC Res. 276 of 18 March 1970. See also the advisory opinion given on the *Namibia* case by the International Court of Justice, *Legal Consequences for States of the Continued Presence of South Africa in Namibia (South West Africa) notwithstanding Security Council Resolution 276 (1970), Advisory Opinion of 21 June 1971, ICJ Reports* 1971, p. 56.

72 For the position of the General Assembly, see Res. 2775E (XXVI) of 29 November 1971, in which the GA condemned 'the establishment by the Government of South Africa of Bantu Homelands (Bantustans) and the forcible removal of the African People of South Africa and Namibia to those areas as a violation of their inalienable rights, contrary to the principle of self-determination and prejudicial to the territorial integrity of the countries and the unity of their peoples'. See also GA Res. 2923E (XXVII) of 15 November 1972; GA Res. 3151G (XXVIII) of 14 December 1973; and GA Res. 3324E (XXIX) of 16 December 1974. By GA Res. 3411D (XXX) of 28 November 1975, the Assembly reaffirmed its position, calling for all member States 'not to deal with any institutions or authorities of the Bantustans or to accord any form of recognition to them'. On 27 October 1976, by GA Res. 31/6A, the Assembly condemned again the policy of 'bantustanization', qualifying as invalid the independence of Transkei (one of the four Bantu Homelands). See also SC Res. 31/34 of 30 November 1976 and SC Res. 402 of 22 December 1976. Thus after the proclaimed independence of Bophuthatswana, the UN General Assembly adopted Res. 32/105 on 14 December 1975, calling again for non-recognition. A similar position was taken in GA Res. 34/93G of 12 December 1979, following the declaration of independence of Venda. See also the declaration made by the President of the Security Council after the independence proclaimed by the fourth Homeland, the Ciskei (see UN Doc. S/14794, 15 December 1981).

73 See UN GA Res. 37/253 of 13 May 1983. For the position of the Security Council see Res. 541 (1983) of 18 November 1983. In this resolution the Security Council: '1. Deplores the declaration of the Turkish Cypriot authorities of the purported secession of part of the Republic of Cyprus; 2. Considers the declaration referred to above as legally invalid and calls for its withdrawal . . . 6. Calls upon all States to respect the sovereignty, independence, territorial integrity and non-alignment of the Republic of Cyprus; 7. Calls upon all States not to recognize any Cypriot State other than the Republic of Cyprus'. In this sense, see also SC Res. 550 (1984) of 11 May 1984, in response to the exchange of ambassadors between Turkey and the Turkish Republic of Northern Cyprus. By this resolution the Security Council reiterated: 'the call upon all States not to recognize the purported State of the "Turkish Republic of Northern Cyprus" set up by secessionist acts and calls upon them not to facilitate or in any way assist the aforesaid secessionist entity'.

74 See EC Bull., 1983, n. 11, points 2.4.1 and 2.4.2.

75 On the occasion of the meeting held in New Delhi from 23 to 29 November 1983, see UN Doc. A/38/707-S/16206, 8 December 1983.

76 See Recommendation 974 adopted by the Assembly of the Council of Europe on 23 October 1983 and Res. 816 adopted by the same Assembly on 21 March 1984.

the Organization of African Unity which asked its member States not to recognise any of these entities.[77]

The principle of non-recognition of territorial acquisitions brought about by force or aggression has also been included in many regional conventions (see for instance Article 11 of the 1933 Montevideo Convention on the Rights and Duties of States[78] and Article 17 of the Bogotá Charter founding the Organization of American States[79]) and in declarations of principles by the UN General Assembly (see in particular GA Res. 2625 (XXV)[80] and GA Res. 3314 (XXIX) on the definition of aggression).[81] Furthermore, the same rule is spelled out in Principle IV of the CSCE Helsinki Final Act. On a national level, this is provided for by paragraph 202(2) of the US *Restatement of the Law (Third)*.[82]

Finally, Article 53 of the Draft on international responsibility approved on its first reading by the International Law Commission in 1996 spelled out the existence of a duty of third States not to recognise as legitimate the situation created by an international crime and provided for the obligation not to render any aid or assistance to the responsible State in maintaining the situation so created. These same obligations have been reaffirmed in the draft definitively adopted on second reading by the International Law Commission in its session of 2001 (see Article 41(2)[83]), whereas the notion of State crime has been deleted from the text.

[77] On the occasion of its 27th extraordinary session, the Council of Ministers of the O.A.U., in July 1976, invited all the member States '. . . not to accord recognition to any Bantustan, in particular, the Transkei whose so-called independence is scheduled for the 26 October 1976' (Res. 493 (XXVII), reprinted in *ILM* 15 (1976), at p. 1221).

[78] See League of Nations Treaty Series, vol. 165, 1936, p. 19.

[79] 'No territorial acquisitions or special advantages obtained either by force or by other means of coercion shall be recognised' (United Nations Treaty Series, vol. 119, p. 50, at p. 57).

[80] Among the consequences arising from the breach of the ban on the use of force, it is provided that: 'no territorial acquisition resulting from the threat or use of force shall be recognized as legal'.

[81] According to Article 5(3): 'No territorial acquisition or special advantage resulting from aggression is or shall be recognized as lawful'.

[82] 'A state has an obligation not to recognize or treat as a state an entity that has attained the qualifications for statehood as a result of a threat or use of armed force in violation of the United Nations Charter.'

[83] Article 41(2) provides that: 'No State shall recognize as lawful a situation created by a serious breach within the meaning of article 40, nor render aid or assistance in maintaining that situation.' According to Article 40(2), a breach by a State of an obligation arising under a peremptory norm of general international law '. . . is serious if it involves a gross or systematic failure by the responsible State to fulfil the obligation'. The final text of the Draft Articles is appended to GA Resolution 56/83 of 12 December 2001.

In order to understand what impact the declaration of invalidity and the demand for collective non-recognition produce on the existence (both factual and legal) of the illegitimate entity, important value must be attached to the relationship between these two measures. As to this issue, it is to be observed that in public international law, due to the lack of compulsory jurisdiction, the function of protecting values of public policy, which motivates the existence in every juridical order of the sanction of nullity, can only be absolved by resorting to 'original' techniques.[84] More precisely, the absence of an obligatory (or 'natural') judge – competent to annul a voidable act or to ascertain the recurrence of the conditions required by law for nullity – means that this role may be replaced with the duty of third-party subjects to consider, diffusely, an unlawful act or situation deprived of its legal effects. Therefore, in these cases, absolute nullity does not work 'by operation of law (*de plein droit*)',[85] and it is not automatic. The denial of effectiveness is, instead, the result of the concurrence of material conduct carried out by those subjects who do not recognise the effects of the wrongful act or event. Therefore, the *erga omnes* void character of an unlawful act does not precede collective non-recognition; on the contrary, it represents its consequence. In the logical order, the ascertainment of illegitimacy (normally performed by organs of the United Nations) is followed by the rise of a duty of non-recognition under

[84] On this point see, for instance, R. P. Dhokalia, 'Nullity or Invalidity of Treaties', *IJIL* 9 (1969), p. 177, at p. 191 and P. Cahier, 'Les caractéristiques de la nullité en droit international et tout particulièrement dans la Convention de Vienne de 1969 sur le droit des traités', *RGDIP* 76 (1972), p. 645, at p. 647. Previously see J. L. Brierly, 'The Hague Convention and the Nullity of Arbitral Awards', *BYIL* 9 (1928), at p. 114 and H. W. Baade, 'Nullity and Avoidance in Public International Law: A Preliminary Survey and a Theoretical Orientation', *Indiana Law Journal* 39 (1964), p. 497.

[85] R. Y. Jennings, 'Nullity and Effectiveness in International Law', in D. Bowett (ed.), *Cambridge Essays in International Law: Essays in Honour of Lord McNair* (Dobbs Ferry: Oceana, 1965), p. 64, at p. 66. In doctrine, on the automatic operation of nullity even in the absence of Courts endowed with compulsory jurisdiction, see also A. Verdross, 'L'excès de pouvoir dans le droit international public', *Revue de droit international et de législation comparé* 9 (1928), p. 241; G. Morelli, 'La théorie générale du procès international', *Recueil des Cours*, 1937, vol. III, p. 327; E. Borel, 'Les voies de recours contre les sentences arbitrales', *Recueil des Cours*, 1935, vol. II, at p. 36; A. Balasko, *Causes de nullité de la sentence arbitrale en droit international public* (Paris: Pedone, 1938), at p. 321. In a similar vein, see also the separate opinion attached by Judge Winiarski to the Advisory Opinion given by the International Court of Justice in the *Effect of Awards of Compensation Made by the United Nations Administrative Tribunal, ICJ Reports* 1954, p. 65. *Contra* see P. Guggenheim, 'La validité et la nullité des actes juridiques internationaux', *Recueil des Cours*, 1949, vol. I, at pp. 208 and 214.

general international law, whose implementation deprives the wrongful act or situation of its legal effects. For this reason, it may be correctly affirmed that the declaration of invalidity operates *through* the collective conduct of non-recognition, only whether and to the extent that such policy-line is respected by third-party subjects.

This said, let us now examine in sequence the solutions proposed by the authors who maintain that an illegitimate birth hinders: a) statehood; and b) the legal personality of a *de facto* entity.

a) As to the first possibility, according to which the entity formed in breach of the norm prohibiting the use of force or of the principle of self-determination should not be considered as a State for the purposes of international law, it must be kept in mind that, if the State is a mere fact – a real (and not a juridical) person – the law cannot cancel its very existence. It might determine the legal consequences arising from that event, and therefore its legal personality, but it cannot do away with a fact. International law, like every other juridical order, cannot create or suppress the facts of social life.[86] Only another fact (such as the dissolution of the illegitimate entity) could achieve this result. This leads to the rejection of the argument that the lawfulness of State creation could be considered as the fourth requirement of *statehood.* Neither the UN General Assembly nor the UN Security Council is vested with the power to eliminate the factual existence of an entity (albeit unlawfully created) by a resolution. Accordingly, it is not possible to share the opinion of those who argue for the existence of a prohibition to secede, so that a secession carried out in breach of self-determination or of the prohibition of the use of force would prevent the thereby illegitimate entity from becoming a new State.[87] To affirm the existence of a prohibition to secede is tantamount to saying that international law creates States or suppresses State-creation, and not that it presupposes the State as a (legal) fact, an idea which clashes with the principle that the State is a social, and not a juridical, person.
b) As to the second solution under scrutiny regarding the effects of collective non-recognition on the (juridical) existence of the unlawful entity, it might be questioned whether non-recognition: i) affects the legal

[86] In this regard, see Abi-Saab, 'Cours général de droit international public', at p. 68, who notes that international law takes cognisance of the '*fait primaire*' represented from the birth of a new State, but nonetheless '. . . il ne peut pas créer ni détruire le fait primaire directement (le droit n'étant pas dans ce contexte une "cause efficiente" au sens aristotélien du terme)' (emphasis added).

[87] See, however, the contributions of Christakis and Corten to this volume.

capacity of the illegitimate entity (i.e. its abstract ability to be the addressee of international norms); ii) denies the entity's capacity to perform valid acts or iii) affects only its *material* possibility to act.

i) In regards to the first proposition, practice shows that the entity unlawfully created, and therefore not recognised by the international community as a whole, is not deemed *legibus solutus*, that is to say, is not exempted from the duty to comply with generally binding norms. Even that regime shall abstain from using force against other States and will be obliged to respect human rights prescriptions and the self-determination of its people. No territorial *vacuum* in the validity of fundamental norms of international coexistence can be tolerated (otherwise genocide, mass murders, torture or apartheid to the detriment of the local population should be considered not prohibited by law). In support of this solution, it should be recalled that the racist regime of Southern Rhodesia in 1979 was condemned by the UN Security Council for having used force against neighbouring States. This implies that if this entity were capable of violating the principle of non-use of force, it was logically the addressee of the relative duty.[88] Secondly, the United Nations never considered resorting to the use of force to bring down the Smith regime (sometimes explicitly recalling the ban on the use of force imposed by Article 2(4) of the UN Charter and by customary law).[89] Thirdly, even collective non-recognition towards Southern Rhodesia was motivated by the breach of cogent norms (particularly the principle of self-determination), which the illegal regime

[88] See SC Res. 445 of 8 March 1979. In this Resolution the UN Security Council directly condemned the cross-border raids carried out by Rhodesian armed forces against the territories of Angola, Mozambique and Zambia, characterising these acts as 'a flagrant violation of the sovereignty and territorial integrity of these countries'.

[89] See General Assembly Official Record, 20th year, Plen., 1367th meeting, for the intervention of Costa Rica, para. 70; Mexico, para. 149–51; the United States of America, para. 171. See also *ibid.*, 4th Committee, 1540th meeting, for the intervention of Ireland, para. 17; Chile, para. 22 ('Force could only be used in accordance with the provisions of the United Nations Charter and by the competent organ, which was the Security Council'); Colombia, *ibid.*, 1541st meeting, para. 14 ('. . . the use of force for the settlement of disputes was contrary to the principles of the Charter and infringed the sovereignty of countries'); Greece, para. 27; Australia, para. 35; Argentina, para. 45; the Netherlands, para. 52; Venezuela, para. 68; the United Kingdom, *ibid.*, 1544th meeting, para. 4; Canada, para. 20; Uruguay, para. 22; Italy, para. 34; South Africa, para. 36; Belgium, para. 44; Norway, para. 46; Denmark, *ibid.*, 1545th meeting, para. 3; France, para. 5; Costa Rica, para. 11 ('the request to the United Kingdom . . . was a dangerous precedent in that the General Assembly would be leaving it to the discretion of a Member State to take coercive action outside the provisions of Chapter VII of the Charter').

was evidently deemed bound to respect. Moreover, in cases of illegal *de facto* entities, one can apply by analogy the general principle expounded by the International Court of Justice in its Advisory Opinion on *Namibia* (1971), that: '*[p]hysical control* of a territory, and *not sovereignty* or *legitimacy of title*, is the basis of State *liability* for acts affecting other States'.[90] This strongly indicates that the *de facto* authority, albeit unlawfully formed, remains responsible for the breach of general international norms in the territory factually under its control.

ii) For what concerns the ability to perform valid acts, there is no doubt that the call for international non-recognition aims to deprive the illegitimate entity of this capacity. Therefore, every conduct carried out by its authorities should be deemed automatically void.

Although this is the intention expressed by the resolutions adopted by international organs, it must nonetheless be recalled that the sanction of invalidity may operate only through the material non-recognition by third-party subjects, complying with the correspondent duty imposed by customary law. In other words, a void character does not represent the automatic effect of the resolution which contains the declaration of invalidity and the demand for non-recognition, since there is no organ having compulsory jurisdiction, endowed with the power to annul wrongful acts or situations (and certainly the UN organs are not empowered to do so).[91] Again, the act, order or law enacted by the unlawful authority will be deprived of legal effect only if and to the extent that other international subjects do not recognise such effect through their concrete behaviour. And sometimes – as we shall see – third States fail to comply with the policy of non-recognition, breaking down the veil of factual and legal inexistence that the international community had tried to erect against the unlawful entity. Even when one State decides to disregard the call for non-recognition by, for example, concluding a treaty, exchanging diplomatic representatives or, simply, recognising in a single case the effect of an act adopted by the authorities of the illegitimate regime, then the acts performed by the latter will have some legal effect, obviously with a sphere of validity limited to the transgressor State. (However, treaties,

[90] In *ICJ Reports* 1971, p. 54 (emphasis added).

[91] Different, in this regard, is the opinion of V. Gowlland-Debbas, 'Legal Significance of the Legitimizing Function of the United Nations: The Cases of Southern Rhodesia and Palestine', in *Le droit international au service de la paix, de la justice et du développement, Mélanges Virally* (Paris: Pedone, 1991), p. 323, at p. 327, who considers these resolutions as 'quasi-judicial pronouncements'. Similar is the position of Krieger, *Das Effektivitätsprinzip im Völkerrecht*, at p. 210, who speaks of '*Nichtigkeitsurteil*' (judgment of nullity).

for instance, are not presumed to produce effects even for third parties). Besides this, all that can be said is that the effect of the acts concluded in breach of collective non-recognition will not be opposable to third-party subjects.

Under what circumstances, then, do third States tend to recognise the existence of the unlawful regime and the effectiveness of its acts? According to practice, recognition occurs in three circumstances: 1) for humanitarian reasons; 2) with regard to arrangements and transactions of a private or domestic nature and 3) with regard to matters of routine administration (such as registrations of births, deaths and marriages).[92] As reckoned by the International Court of Justice in the *Namibia* Opinion: 'international law recognises the legitimacy of certain legal arrangements and transactions . . . the effects of which can be ignored only to the detriment of the inhabitants of the territory'.[93] Since non-recognition is a measure adopted *vis-à-vis* the unlawful regime, its implementation, where possible, should not affect the interests and rights of the people living under the control of that authority.[94] Therefore, the isolation to which the regime is condemned must not endanger the day-to-day affairs of the people. This idea is the essence of the so-called 'doctrine of necessity', which finds its origin in the jurisprudence of the Supreme Court of the United States in the period subsequent to the end of the war of secession (the leading decision being *Texas v. White* (1868)[95]). Having to decide whether the acts enacted by the rebellious authorities of the South during the secessionist

[92] For practice relevant on this point see Tancredi, *La secessione nel diritto internazionale*, at p. 764.

[93] *ICJ Reports* 1971, p. 56, para. 125. The whole passage reads as follows: 'In general, the non-recognition of South Africa's administration of the Territory should not result in depriving the people of Namibia of any advantages derived from international co-operation. In particular, while official acts performed by the Government of South Africa on behalf of or concerning Namibia after the termination of the Mandate are illegal and invalid, this invalidity cannot be extended to those acts, such as, for instance, the registration of births, deaths and marriages, the effects of which can be ignored only to the detriment of the inhabitants of the Territory.'

[94] As reckoned, with reference to the case of Southern Rhodesia, by two components of the Privy Council (Lord Read and Lord Morris of Borth-Y-Gest), it is necessary to avoid 'the hardship and inequity which would have resulted to millions of people, who had for four years been living under the laws of the rebel governments, if no recognition had been accorded to those acts and laws necessary for maintaining the bonds of society': *Madzimbamuto v. Lardner-Burke*, in Appeal Cases, 1969, respectively at pp. 706 and 708.

[95] *Texas v. White* (1868), 74 US (7 Wallace), p. 700, at p. 733 ('It may be said, perhaps, with sufficient accuracy, that acts necessary to peace and good order among citizens, such for example, as acts sanctioning and protecting marriage and the domestic relations, governing the course of descents, regulating the conveyance and transfer of property, real and personal, and providing remedies for injuries to person and estate, and other similar acts, which would be valid if emanating from a lawful government, must be regarded in

war were valid, in fact, the US Supreme Court elaborated upon this sort of general principle of equity,[96] which was later adopted by other national courts[97] (especially by British tribunals, concerning the problems arising from the controversial *status* of Southern Rhodesia,[98] South-African Bantustans[99] and Northern Cyprus[100]). The same principle has been evoked

general as valid when proceeding from an actual though unlawful government.'). The US Supreme Court applied the same doctrine in many subsequent judgments: see, among others, *Thorington v. Smith* (1869), 75 US (8 Wallace), p. 1; *Thomas v. City of Richmond* (1871), 79 US (12 Wallace), p. 349; *Delmas v. Merchants' Mutual Ins. Co.* (1871), 81 US (14 Wallace), p. 661; *Hanauer v. Woodruff* (1872), 82 US (15 Wallace), p. 439; *Planters' Bank v. Union Bank* (1873), 83 US (16 Wallace), p. 483; *Horn v. Lockhart* (1873), 84 US (17 Wallace), p. 570; *The First National Bank of Washington v. Texas* (1873), 87 US (20 Wallace), p. 72; *Baldy v. Hunter* (1898), 171 US, p. 388.

96 Explicit references to equity are contained in a number of decisions: see *The Confederate Note Case* (*The Atlantic, Tennessee and Ohio Railroad Company v. The Carolina National Bank of Columbia*) (1873), 86 US (19 Wallace), p. 548, at pp. 556–7; *United States v. Insurance Companies* (1874), 89 US (22 Wallace), p. 99, at pp. 99–103; *Sprott v. United States* (1874), 87 US (20 Wallace), at p. 459; *Williams v. Bruffy* (1877), 96 US (23 Wallace), at pp. 176, 187 and 189; *Keith v. Clark* (1878), 97 US (23 Wallace), at pp. 454 and 476; *Ketchum v. Buckley* (1878), 99 US, at p. 188; *Lamar v. Micou* (1884), 112 US (5 Davis), at p. 452. Considerations of commonsense and fairness were, instead, deployed by Judge Cardozo in *Sokoloff v. National City Bank of New York* (1924), 239 NY, p. 158, 145 N. E., p. 917. These considerations recur in more recent judgments: see, among others, *M. Salimoff and Co. v. Standard Oil Co. Of New York* (1933), 262 NY, p. 220, 186 N. E., p. 679; *Upright v. Mercury Business Machines Co. Inc.* (1961), 213 NY S.2d, p. 417.

97 See, for instance, the Supreme Court of New Zealand, in *Bilang v. Rigg* [1972] N.Z.L.R. 954 at p. 961 (per Henry J.), also reproduced in 48 *ILR* 1975, p. 30; the Supreme Court of Pakistan, in *Special Reference No. 1* of 1955, in Federal Court Reports (India), vol. I, 1955, p. 439; the Supreme Court of Cyprus in *Attorney General of the Republic v. Mustafa Ibrahim* (1964), reprinted in 48 *ILR* 1975, p. 6.

98 See again *Madzimbamuto v. Lardner-Burke*, in Appeal Cases, 1969, at p. 732. Subsequently, see *In Re James (An Insolvent) (Attorney General intervening)* [1977], The Weekly Law Reports, 1977, vol. 2, p. 1, at pp. 15–16 (per Lord Denning). In this judgment, it was recalled what Lord Wilberforce had observed in *Carl Zeiss Stiftung v. Rayner & Keeler Ltd. (No. 2)*, All England Law Reports, 1966, vol. II, p. 536, at p. 577, namely that: '. . . where private rights, or acts of everyday occurrence, or perfunctory acts of administration are concerned . . . the courts may, in the interests of justice and common sense, where no consideration of public policy to the contrary has to prevail, give recognition to the actual facts or realities found to exist in the territory in question'.

99 See the Court of Appeal of London in *GUR Corporation v. Trust Bank of Africa Ltd. (Government of the Republic of Ciskei, Third Party)*, All England Law Reports, 1986, vol. III, p. 449, at p. 463 (per Sir Donaldson MR: '. . . it is one thing to treat a state or government as being "without the law", but quite another to treat the inhabitants of its territory as "outlaws" who cannot effectively marry, beget legitimate children, purchase goods on credit or undertake countless day-to-day activities having legal consequences').

100 See the two decisions given by the Court of Appeal of London in *Hesperides Hotels Ltd. and Another v. Aegean Turkish Holidays Ltd. and Another*, The Weekly Law Reports, 1977, vol. 3, p. 656 and *Polly Peck International plc. v. Nadir and Others*, All England Law Reports,

by international tribunals, such as the International Court of Justice in its Advisory Opinion on *Namibia*,[101] and more recently, by the European Court of Human Rights in the *Loizidou* case (1996)[102] and in the fourth inter-State application *Cyprus v. Turkey*.[103] In the latter judgment, on 10 May 2001, the Strasbourg Court openly recognised the exercise of a *de facto* authority by the organs of the Turkish Republic of Northern Cyprus (which to date remains an entity not recognised by the international community, with the exception of Turkey),[104] underlining the need 'to avoid in the territory of northern Cyprus the existence of a *vacuum* in the protection of the human rights guaranteed by the Convention'.[105] Concerning the *Namibia* jurisprudence, the Court recalled that in this Opinion the International Court of Justice 'resolutely rejected the approach refusing any effect to unlawful de facto regimes'.[106] This is tantamount to affirming that the duty not to recognise the validity of acts adopted by the unlawful entity is far from absolute. Life goes on in the territory concerned for its inhabitants. That life must be made tolerable and be protected by the de facto authorities, including their courts. For this reason, such an entity 'cannot be simply ignored by third states or by international institutions,

1992, vol. IV, p. 769. On the status of Northern Cyprus, see also *In re Busytoday Ltd.*, The Weekly Law Reports, 1992, vol. 1, p. 683 and *Muduroglu Ltd. v. T. C. Ziraat Bankasi*, in Law Reports, Queen's Bench Division, 1986, vol. 1, p. 1225. Reference to the doctrine of necessity with regard to Northern Cyprus has been made also in *Caglar and Others v. Billingham (Inspector of Taxes)* [1996] STC (SCD) 150, [1996] 1 LRC 526; 108 *ILR* 1996, p. 510 at p. 534.

[101] See note 93.

[102] *V. Loizidou v. Turkey*, Judgement (Merits), in Reports of Judgements and Decisions, No. 26, 1996-VI, at p. 2231, paragraph 45. While the Court refused to attribute legal validity to such provisions as article 159 of the TRNC Constitution (*ibid.*, paragraph 44), a different view was maintained in two dissenting opinions. Indeed, according to Judge Jambrek: '. . . it would be going too far to say that no purportedly legal acts of the "TRNC" administration are valid. For example, a marriage conducted by a "TRNC" official, and registered in the "TRNC", would have legal effect outside that "jurisdiction". Similarly, a transfer of property between private individuals in northern Cyprus, registered by an official of the "TRNC", would have legal effect elsewhere in the world' (*ibid.*, p. 2248). See also the dissenting opinion appended by Judge Pettiti, *ibid.*, at pp. 2252–3.

[103] *Cyprus v. Turkey*, Application No. 25781/94. The text of the decision can be read on the website of the European Court of Human Rights: http://www.echr.coe.int.

[104] The same opinion had been upheld by the European Commission on Human Rights in its report on the case, issued on 4 June 1999 ('it cannot be denied that the TRNC regime *de facto* exists and that it exercises *de facto* authority in the northern part of Cyprus', para. 123).

[105] *Cyprus v. Turkey*, Application No. 25781/94, Judgement, para. 91.

[106] *Ibid.*, para. 94.

especially courts';[107] otherwise local inhabitants would be deprived of the minimum standard of protection of the rights guaranteed by the Convention of Rome. As a practical consequence, the duty to exhaust *local* remedies (i.e. the remedies existing before the Courts of Northern Cyprus) had to be fulfilled.

Such argumentation strengthens the contention that non-recognition *per se* neither automatically determines the inexistence (factual or legal) of the unlawful regime nor the absolute nullity of all its acts; it simply obliges third subjects to deny the effect of these acts through their conduct, in compliance with a collective (and political) decision of behaviour.[108] Therefore, the acts adopted by the unlawful regime will not be null and void, but only deprived of the *possibility* to display their effect in single cases, remaining effective in different contexts before different authorities. In other words, the act will not be effective *vis-à-vis* the State which complies with the duty of non-recognition. However, the act will remain potentially effective (and therefore abstractly valid), where a national or international court upholds the doctrine of *necessity*, or where a government considers the protection of its national interests (for instance, where it has political, administrative or economic contacts with the unrecognised regime) as prevailing over its duty of non-recognition.[109]

Therefore, in the light of the preceding discussion, the 'constitutive' view upheld by the United Nations and by many authors cannot be shared.[110] According to this opinion, by virtue of the general principle

[107] *Ibid.*, para. 96. See also para. 97 for an explicit reference to the jurisprudence of national courts on the doctrine of necessity.

[108] In this sense, see G. Ziccardi Capaldo, *Le situazioni territoriali illegittime nel diritto internazionale* (Napoli: Editoriale Scientifica, 1977), p. 102.

[109] In this regard, see S. Talmon, 'The Cyprus Question Before the European Court of Justice', *EJIL* 12 (2001), p. 727, who notes that, according to State practice (including cases of non-recognition of unlawful entities such as Manchukuo or Northern Cyprus), informal or administrative cooperation (i.e. not of an intergovernmental or diplomatic character) with the authorities of an unrecognised entity is not excluded. For this reason, the author criticises the stand taken by the European Court of Justice ruling that EU members must not accept phytosanitary certificates issued by the administrative authorities of the Turkish Republic of Northern Cyprus, because cooperation required under the certificate system is excluded from the TRNC as it is not recognised either by the EU or its members (see Case C-432/92, *Anastasiou I* [1994], in ECR-I, vol. 7, p. 3087, and Case C-219/98, *Anastasiou II* [2000], in CMLR, 2000, p. 339).

[110] This criticism finds support, for instance, in the US Restatement of the Law (Third), *The Foreign Relations Law of the United States*, vol. 1 (Minnesota: St. Paul, 1987), para. 205, according to which, non-recognition does not affect the validity of acts 'dealing solely with private, local and domestic matters'. Consequently '[a] regime representing a non-state or an unrecognized regime is not an absolute nullity'. Similarly, see W. Wengler, *Völkerrecht*, vol. I (Berlin: Springer, 1964), at pp. 570–2.

ex iniuria ius non oritur, 'an illegality cannot, as a rule, become a source of legal right to the wrongdoer',[111] so that 'both the unrecognised government and its acts are a nullity',[112] while every act performed by the transgressor 'is in itself devoid of legal force'.[113]

Nor can we concur with the argument that the non-recognised unlawful entity would be endowed with a *partial* legal capacity as a *de facto* regime, by virtue of the fact that some general norms (such as the prohibition of the use of force or the respect for fundamental human rights) would be addressed to that entity, whereas other principles, especially those regulating the law of treaties or diplomatic relations, could not be applicable.[114] Again, it is true that some international norms will not be addressed to the *de facto* entity, but this is not as a result of its legal incapacity (partial or total), but is rather due to the fact that collective non-recognition will impede the material occurrence of the situation regulated through that norm. The illegitimate entity is *qualitatively* a subject equal to every State; its legal capacity will be only *factually* limited due to non-recognition. International personality remains a unitary *status*, not susceptible of special qualifications. One needs only to determine which relations, acts or transactions the entity has entered into in order to establish the legal character thereof.[115]

In conclusion, the 'illegitimately born' State (namely the entity formed in breach of the 'due process' proposed in this chapter) is not inexistent, from a factual or a legal point of view.[116] As has been said, international

[111] Lauterpacht, *Recognition in International Law*, at p. 420.

[112] *Ibid.*, at p. 145. This position is shared by, among others, F. A. Mann, 'The Judicial Recognition of an Unrecognised State', *ICLQ* 36 (1987), at p. 348 ('In law, therefore, the non-recognised State does not exist. It is, if one prefers so to put it, a nullity'); Dugard, *Recognition and the United Nations*, at p. 131; Gowlland-Debbas, *Collective Responses to Illegal Acts in International Law*, at p. 240; C. Antonopoulos, 'Effectiveness v. the Rule of Law Following the East Timor Case', *NYIL* 27 (1996), p. 75, at p. 102; Christakis, *Le droit à l'autodétermination*, at p. 317 ('Toute sécession qui serait le produit d'une aggression doit être considérée comme nulle et sans effet').

[113] Lauterpacht, *Recognition in International Law*, at p. 420 (emphasis added).

[114] This opinion has been particularly maintained by German authors sharing the view of J. A. Frowein, *Das de facto-Regime im Völkerrecht* (Köln: Carl Heymanns Verlags, 1968), at p. 224. See, for instance, Klein, 'Die Nichtanerkennungspolitik der Vereinten Nationen', p. 482; Krieger, *Das Effektivitätsprinzip im Völkerrecht*, at pp. 202–3.

[115] We share here the authoritative view of G. Arangio-Ruiz, 'Stati e altri enti (soggettività internazionale)', *Novissimo Digesto Italiano*, vol. XVIII, Turin, 1971, at p. 157.

[116] See in this sense R. H. Sharp, *Non-recognition as a Legal Obligation 1775–1934* (Geneva: Thone, 1934), at p. 152; Guggenheim, 'La validité et la nullité des actes juridiques internationaux', at p. 229 (with specific reference to Manchukuo); H. Mosler, 'The International Society as a Legal Community', *Recueil des Cours*, 1973, vol. III, at p. 62; A. Cassese, *International Law* (Oxford: Oxford University Press, 2001), at p. 51.

law does not discriminate between 'good and bad' entities, by conferring legal status on the former and not on the latter.[117] Non-recognition of unlawfully created States is a measure which is certainly the object of a customary duty – and this is the *properly juridical* aspect[118] – whose implementation does not determine either the inexistence, or the absolute or partial loss of personality to the detriment of the unlawful entity, but a condition of social isolation which results in the *material impossibility* of acting.[119] Such a measure, then, does not exclude the legal capacity of the new entity, but simply represents a cause of *factual* limitation of its legal sphere and of the effects deriving from the acts performed by its organs. Consequently, this entity will be the addressee of a lesser number of norms (being part of a lesser number of relations, transactions or acts), having especially a conventional origin, nevertheless remaining the addressee of (and therefore both protected by and bound to comply with) the fundamental norms which regulate the life of the international community.

Obviously, this is valid only if the new regime, albeit unlawfully formed, satisfies the test for statehood, displaying a stable, peaceful and independent control over a territory and a permanent population. If such is not

[117] Arangio-Ruiz, 'Stati e altri enti (soggettività internazionale)', at p. 175.

[118] For the view that an obligation not to recognise a situation created by the unlawful use of force is 'self-executory', see Legal Consequences of the Construction of a Wall in the Occupied Palestinian Territory, ICJ Reports 2004, p. 200, para 159; Judge Skubiszewski (dissenting opinion), *East Timor (Portugal v. Australia), ICJ Reports* 1995, p. 264, and, previously, the dissenting opinion attached by Judge Dillard in the *Legal Consequences for States of the Continued Presence of South Africa in Namibia (South-West Africa) Notwithstanding Security Council Resolution 276 (1970), ICJ Reports* 1971, at p. 165). See also *US Restatement of the Law (Third)*, para. 202. In doctrine, the existence of a general obligation not to recognise any situation brought about by the use of force or in breach of the self-determination's principle is maintained by Lauterpacht, *Recognition in International Law*, at p. 420; Dugard, *Recognition and the United Nations*, at p. 135; Brownlie, *Principles of Public International Law*, at p. 94; T. Franck, *Fairness in International Law and Institutions* (Oxford: Oxford University Press, 1995), at p. 158; Gowlland-Debbas, *Collective Responses to Illegal Acts in International Law*, at p. 294; J. A. Frowein, 'Nullity in International Law', in R. Bernhardt (ed.), *Encyclopedia of Public International Law*, vol. III (Amsterdam, North Holland, 1997), p. 743, at p. 746; Christakis, *Le droit à l'autodétermination*, at pp. 283–5; Krieger, *Das Effektivitätsprinzip im Völkerrecht*, at p. 194. Finally, see the view taken by the ILC Special Rapporteur on State responsibility, J. Crawford, 'First Report on State Responsibility', UN Doc. A/CN.4/490/Add.1, para. 51 and 'Third Report on State Responsibility', UN Doc. A/CN.4/507/Add.4, para. 410.

[119] On the distinction between legal incapacity and material impossibility of acting see R. Quadri, 'Cours général de droit international public', *Recueil des Cours*, 1964, vol. III, at p. 373, and, by the same author, *Diritto internazionale pubblico* (Napoli: Liguori, 1968), at pp. 460–1.

the case, it should be held that the State – as a fact – is not fully formed (and therefore still not existent), and not that it constitutes a nullity because it is illegitimately created (as was probably the situation of Manchukuo and of the Bantustans, due to their lack of independence towards Japan and South Africa respectively).[120]

[120] See Lauterpacht, *Recognition in International Law*, at p. 420 (with regard to Manchukuo); Crawford, *The Creation of States*, at p. 222 and Dugard, *Recognition and the United Nations*, at p. 393 (on the lack of statehood of Bantustans).

7

Secession and the law of State succession

ANDREAS ZIMMERMANN

I. Introduction

Instances of secession[1] have in the past constituted the most important cases of State succession, ranging from the secession of the United States of America to the secession of Eritrea from Ethiopia in 1994.[2] Still it remains doubtful whether and, if so, to what extent *specific* rules of State succession have developed with regard to cases of secession, and further, whether and, if so, how, situations of secession can be distinguished from other cases of separation or dismemberment.

Finally, one might wonder whether it is relevant *for the purposes of State succession* whether or not the secession took place in conformity with international law. It is against this background that this chapter will try to analyse what rules of State succession do indeed apply in situations of secession with regard to treaties, debts and property and finally the nationality of natural persons. Before doing so, however, one has first briefly to define the notion of State succession itself.

II. General issues

A. *Defining State succession with regard to situations of secession*

It seems that in recent times a consensus has emerged as to what the term 'State succession' encompasses, i.e., 'the replacement of one State by another in the responsibility for the international relations of territory'.

[1] For a discussion of the notion and meaning of the term 'secession' under international law, see generally the Introduction to this volume, as well as the contribution of Corten, chapter 8.

[2] For the development until the 1960s, see generally D.P. O'Connell, *State Succession in Municipal Law and International Law*, Vol. II (Oxford: Oxford Univ. Press, 1967), p. 90; and with regard to later developments, see A. Zimmermann, *Staatennachfolge in Verträge – zugleich ein Beitrag zu Möglichkeiten und Grenzen völkerrechtlicher Kodifikation* (Berlin: Springer, 2000), pp. 20, 138, 143, 166 and 369.

This is mainly due to the fact that this definition was not only used in Article 2(1)(b) of the 1978 Vienna Convention on Succession of States in Respect of Treaties, Article 2(1)(a) of the 1983 Vienna Convention on Succession of States in Respect of State Property, Archives and Debts and in Article 2(a) of the International Law Commission's Draft Articles on Nationality in Relation to the Succession of States,[3] but was also referred to by both the arbitral tribunal in the case between Guinea-Bissau and Senegal[4] and by the Badinter Arbitration Commission for the former Yugoslavia.[5]

Against the background of this definition, instances of secession will indeed constitute cases of State succession, provided the secessionist movement is effectively in a position to create a new State, thereby replacing the former territorial State with regard to responsibility for the international relations of the territory which formed the subject of the detachment from the former State.

Still, even if cases of secession accordingly give rise to questions of State succession, one might still wonder whether they form a *separate* category of State succession of their own, or whether, instead, instances of secession might simply form part of one or more categories of State succession.

B. *Secession as a separate category of State succession*

1. Definition of secession with regard to the law of State succession

Unlike State succession, the term 'secession' is still an amorphous one which has no clear-cut legal connotation. Indeed, with regard to the law of State succession, the term 'secession' is only infrequently used.[6] Instead, more technical terms such as 'separation of parts of a State', 'dismemberment' or the creation of 'newly independent States' have been used in the past. All these terms describe situations, however, which at the same time might at least partially be also described as instances of secession. Therefore one has to consider whether and to what extent the different

[3] See Report of the International Law Commission (1999), available at http://www.un.org/law/ilc/reports/1999/English/chap4.html (hereinafter 'ILC Report').

[4] Decision of 31 July 1989, *ILR* 83, p. 1.

[5] Opinion No. 1 of 29 November 1991, *ILM* 1992, p. 1494. See also the explanatory report to the 1997 European Convention on Nationality, which also refers to said definition: Council of Europe Doc. DIR/JUR (97) 6, Explanatory Report, para. 104.

[6] But see, e.g., Z. Mériboute, *La codification de la succession d'Etats aux traités: décolonisation, sécession, unification* (Paris: Press Univ. de France, 1984), p. 141.

categories of State succession would at the same time also cover cases of secession.

2. Secession and newly independent States

Under the terms of both the 1978 Vienna Convention on Succession of States in Respect of Treaties and the 1983 Vienna Convention on Succession of States in Respect of State Property, Archives and Debts, the term 'newly independent State' means a successor State, the territory of which immediately before the date of the succession of States was a dependent territory, the international relations for which the predecessor State was responsible.[7] The notion 'newly independent State' thereby seeks to cover the situation of former colonies and other territories such as non-self-governing territories, trust territories or former mandates, which were in a similar situation vis-à-vis the State they were considered part of, or which was otherwise responsible for their external relations.

It has to be noted that an important number of these 'newly independent States' gained independence regardless of the wish of their predecessor State in their exercise of the right of their peoples to self-determination. Accordingly one might consider – at least at first glance – that these situations also constitute cases of secession. On the other hand, it also has to be noted that under the Friendly Relations Declaration of the General Assembly, those territories did possess a legal status separate and distinct from the territory administering it. Accordingly, even if specific rules of State succession governing the legal situation of 'newly independent States' have developed, those instances will not be considered here, given their specificities. Moreover, it should be noted that, with the end of the historic process of decolonisation, the relevance of that specific group of cases of State succession has lost most, if not all, of its practical relevance.

3. Secession, separation and dismemberment

The question arises whether other instances of secession might – from the perspective of the law of State succession – eventually be considered as separations or whether, instead, they could also form part of a process of dismemberment, the distinction between these two categories of State succession being based on whether or not the respective predecessor continues to exist.[8]

[7] See Art. 2(f) of the 1978 Vienna Convention on Succession of States in Respect of Treaties and Art. 2(e) of the 1983 Vienna Convention on Succession of States in Respect of State Property, Archives and Debts.

[8] See Zimmermann, *Staatennachfolge in Verträge*, p. 66.

This problem becomes manifest when one analyses the historical process of the dissolution of the former Socialist Federal Republic of Yugoslavia, which – at least during its initial stages – may by and large be described as a process of secession first by Slovenia, then by Croatia and later by Bosnia and Herzegovina and the Former Yugoslav Republic of Macedonia. However, the admission of the Federal Republic of Yugoslavia to the United Nations on 1 November 2000 as a new member confirmed – if indeed there was a need for any further proof – that the claim by the Federal Republic of Yugoslavia (which in the meantime has changed its constitutional name to Serbia and Montenegro) to continue the legal personality of the former Socialist Federal Republic of Yugoslavia could not be upheld, since otherwise there would have been no need to admit the Federal Republic of Yugoslavia to the organisation. Indeed, such claim of identity is no longer entertained by the Federal Republic of Yugoslavia / Serbia and Montenegro itself, as demonstrated by the fact that the Federal Republic of Yugoslavia / Serbia and Montenegro has by now made numerous declarations of *succession* with regard to treaties to which previously the Socialist Federal Republic of Yugoslavia had been a party. Thus, at least by now, the break-up of the former Yugoslavia can no longer be considered as a chain of separations, but rather as a continuous process leading to a complete dismemberment of the Socialist Federal Republic of Yugoslavia. It is still true however, that even this process of dismemberment did include initial instances of secession by at least Slovenia, Croatia and Bosnia and Herzegovina, which by their cumulative effect later turned into a complete dissolution of the former Yugoslavia.

On the other hand, where the predecessor continues to exist as is, *inter alia*, the case with regard to Ethiopia vis-à-vis Eritrea, such a process of secession does not constitute a complete dismemberment, but solely a separation. Accordingly, different cases of secession can either be characterised as instances of *dismemberment* or as cases of *separation*.

C. *The law of State succession with regard to secessions taking place in violation of applicable rules of international law*

Both Article 6 of the 1978 Vienna Convention on Succession of States in Respect of Treaties and Article 3 of the 1983 Vienna Convention on Succession of States in Respect of State Property, Archives and Debts, as well as Article 3 of the 1999 International Law Commission Draft Articles on Nationality of Natural Persons in Relation to the Succession of States[9] limit the applicability of the respective texts to succession of States occurring in conformity with international law and, in particular, the principles of international law embodied in the Charter of the United Nations. The question arises, however, whether this is indeed solely to be seen as a limitation on the scope of application of the respective treaties or draft articles, or whether it can instead be argued that situations that do not take place in accordance with international law cannot *per se* be considered as instances of State succession, as is indeed argued by some legal commentators.[10]

In particular, the question might arise whether cases of secession, not justified under international law, would accordingly *ipso facto* not be governed by the otherwise applicable rules of State succession. Such an approach was indeed argued in the *Case Concerning Application of the Convention on the Prevention and Punishment of the Crime of Genocide (Bosnia and Herzegovina / Yugoslavia)*, in which the Federal Republic of Yugoslavia claimed that: 'Since Bosnia and Herzegovina has not obtained its independence in conformity with the principle of equality and self-determination of peoples, *it cannot succeed* to the multilateral treaties of the predecessor State.'[11]

On the other hand, both the drafting history of the 1978 Vienna Convention on Succession of States in Respect of Treaties,[12] as well as the last paragraph of the preamble of the Convention,[13] demonstrate that even situations which have come about in violation of international law might produce legal effects in the field of State succession. Indeed, the International Court of Justice itself found that Bosnia and Herzegovina – once admitted as a member State of the United Nations – is to be considered

[9] ILC Report.

[10] See e.g., I. Brownlie, *Principles of Public International Law*, 6th edn (Oxford: Oxford Univ. Press, 2003), p. 654, as well as H.-J. Heintze, *Der Übergang des Staatsvermögens vom Vorgängerstaat auf den Nachfolgestaat im Fall der Staatennachfolge: eine Untersuchung unter besonderer Berücksichtigung der Kodifikation der Staatennachfolge durch die Völkerrechtskommission der UNO* (Leipzig: Univ., Diss., 1977), p. 10; W. Poeggel and R. Meißner, *Staatennachfolge im Völkerrecht* (Berlin (Ost): Staatsverlag der DDR, 1986), p. 76, and S. Kadelbach, *Zwingendes Völkerrecht* (Berlin: Duncker&Humboldt, 1992), p. 246, n. 228.

[11] Emphasis added. See also *Case Concerning Application of the Convention on the Prevention and Punishment of the Crime of Genocide (Bosnia and Herzegovina v. Yugoslavia), Preliminary Objections, ICJ Reports* 1996, p. 595, (hereinafter '*Genocide Case*'), Dissenting Opinion Kreca, para. 83.

[12] For further details see Zimmermann, *Staatennachfolge in Verträge*, p. 34.

[13] This part of the preamble confirms, 'that the rules of customary international law will continue to govern questions not regulated by the provisions of the present Convention'.

a successor State of the former Socialist Federal Republic of Yugoslavia, regardless of the circumstances of its accession to independence.[14]

Accordingly, cases of secession are indeed covered by the regular rules governing State succession, regardless of the question of whether or not the secession did take place in conformity with international law. On the other hand, Article 6 of the 1978 Vienna Convention on Succession of States in Respect of Treaties, Article 3 of the 1983 Vienna Convention on Succession of States in Respect of State Property, Archives and Debts, as well as Article 3 of the 1999 International Law Commission Draft Articles on Nationality of Natural Persons in Relation to the Succession of States simply describe the scope of application of the two conventions and the draft articles as being *mutatis mutandis* identical in their effect to Article 3 of the 1969 Vienna Convention on the Law of Treaties.

Having thus defined the scope of application of the law of State succession *vis-à-vis* cases of secession, one must now focus on the different areas of State succession, starting with succession concerning treaties.

III. Succession with regard to treaties

A. General issues

Seceding States have traditionally – at least as a matter of principle – claimed not to be automatically bound by treaties concluded by their respective predecessor States.[15] On the other hand, the 1978 Vienna Convention on Succession of States in Respect of Treaties does not follow such a uniform approach for all situations of secession. Instead – as previously mentioned – it distinguishes between the abovementioned group of 'newly independent States' on the one hand, and other successor States arising from a process of separation or dismemberment *not* connected with the historic process of decolonisation on the other.

Under the regime provided for in the Convention, the first group is considered not to be automatically bound by the treaties of their respective predecessor States.[16] In contrast thereto, Article 34 of the Convention provides for the remaining cases, that – at least in principle – any treaty in force at the date of the succession of States in respect of the entire territory

[14] *Genocide Case*, para. 19.
[15] See Zimmermann, *Staatennachfolge in Verträge*, pp. 138, 143 and 166.
[16] See in particular Art. 16 of the Convention.

of the predecessor State continues in force in respect of a successor State so formed.

State practice with regard to *former colonies*, covering both the period before 1978 and that after 1978, indeed confirms that 'newly independent States' were not obliged to take over the treaty obligations of their respective predecessor States.[17] Thus, one might conclude that in most instances of separation occurring after 1945, during the process of decolonisation, such successor States did not automatically inherit the contractual obligations of the former colonial power, but were generally free to decide whether or not to become a contracting party by notifying their succession, acceding to the respective treaty, or by not becoming a contracting party at all.

With regard to cases of secession arising *outside the context of decolonisation*, State practice, in particular that of the last fifteen years, is significantly less uniform. Still, when analysing relevant State practice, at least certain trends may be described, albeit with some nuances. Thus one might argue that where the process of secession finally leads to a complete dismemberment of the predecessor State, as was the case with regard to the former Socialist Federal Republic of Yugoslavia, a tendency may be discerned that – at least as a matter of principle – *all* treaties automatically devolve upon the seceding State. On the other hand, State practice is not completely uniform and even States which have normally taken the view that the content of Article 34 of the 1978 Vienna Convention has, at least with regard to complete dismemberments, become part of customary international law, have from time to time still *acceded* to treaties which beforehand had been ratified by their predecessor State. Given this ambiguity, one must question whether it is safe enough to state that the rule contained in Article 34 of the 1978 Vienna Convention – which at least at the time it was drafted may be considered more of a progressive development than a codification of international law – has really crystallised into a rule of positive customary international law, given the requirements identified by the International Court of Justice in the *North Sea Continental Shelf* case for the formation of a new rule of customary international law.[18]

Still, one cannot but acknowledge the fact that State practice is somewhat inclined towards applying the model of automatic succession in

[17] Zimmermann, *Staatennachfolge in Verträge*, pp. 146 and 225.

[18] *North Sea Continental Shelf Cases (Germany/Denmark; Germany/Netherlands), ICJ Reports* 1969, p. 43.

particular in cases where the secessionist development finally leads to a complete dissolution of the predecessor State.

Such a tendency is, however, less clear with regard to instances of a pure separation, i.e. where the predecessor State continues to exist regardless of certain territories seceding or otherwise separating, as was the case with regard to Eritrea or the former USSR. Indeed, at least certain – if not all – of the successor States of the former USSR, as well as those of Eritrea, have at least to some extent become parties to treaties previously concluded by the USSR or Ethiopia by way of *accession*,[19] thus demonstrating the fact that they did not consider themselves bound by virtue of State succession. Accordingly, one is advised to be even more cautious when claiming a possible automatic succession of a seceding State with regard to treaties of the still-existing predecessor State, notwithstanding the fact that a considerable number of third States seem to favour applying a general principle of automatic succession.

In such an ambiguous normative situation, notifications of succession by the seceding State to the depositary of a multilateral treaty, or bilateral exchanges of notes between a seceding State and third parties, both confirm the extent to which treaties have indeed devolved upon a seceding State, and at the same time clarify which treaties are *not* subject to succession.

Notwithstanding this ambiguity, it has to be seen whether not at least certain categories of treaties always devolve automatically upon a seceding State.

B. *Succession of seceding States with regard to specific categories of treaties*

1. Secession and boundary treaties

Traditionally, boundary treaties have always been considered as automatically devolving upon a seceding State. Such a rule can also be found in Article 11 of the 1978 Vienna Convention with Respect to Treaties.[20] Furthermore, both State practice[21] as well as the jurisprudence of the Badinter

[19] As to the practice of the successor States of the USSR, see Zimmermann, *Staatennachfolge in Verträge*, p. 390, and as to the practice of Eritrea, see *ibid*, p. 423.

[20] Art. 11 of the Convention states: 'A succession of States does not as such affect: (a) a boundary established by a treaty; or (b) obligations and rights established by a treaty and relating to the regime of a boundary.'

[21] For a survey of relevant State practice and decisions of international tribunals see Zimmermann, *Staatennachfolge in Verträge*, p. 451.

Arbitration Commission for the former Yugoslavia confirm that boundary treaties must be respected by a seceding State. In particular, the Badinter Commission correctly stated that '. . . whatever the circumstances, the right to self-determination must not involve changes to existing frontiers at the time of independence'.[22]

Accordingly, a successor State which comes into existence through a process of secession is bound to continue to apply boundary treaties previously entered into by its predecessor State and which relate to the territory which formed the subject of the successful secession process. By establishing this rule, the international community thus demonstrates its clear concern that boundaries not be put into question by secession.[23]

Similar considerations also apply to other forms of localised treaties.

2. Secession and other forms of localised treaties

Already before the attempted codification of the law of State succession with regard to treaties, State practice as well as decisions of national and international courts were lending support to the general proposition covering all different forms of State succession – and thereby also covering cases of secession – that the successor State inherits localised treaties which had been applied to the seceding territory.[24] This principle is now also codified in Article 12 of the 1978 Vienna Convention on Succession of States in Respect of Treaties. According to that provision, a succession of States does not, as such, affect obligations relating to the use of any territory established by a treaty which is considered as attaching to the territory in question.

State practice after 1990 similarly confirms the customary law nature of the principle that such treaties, also referred to as treaties *in rem*, treaties attaching to the territory, treaties running with the land, or dispositive treaties, automatically devolve upon the successor State. Indeed, even those States such as Austria, which had – at least initially – taken the position that Article 34 of the 1978 Vienna Convention on Succession of States in Respect of Treaties may *not* be considered an expression of customary international law, have never denied the fact that such localised treaties continue to apply even with regard to States such as Slovenia

[22] Opinion No. 2, *ILM* 1992, p. 1497. See also Opinion No. 3 (*ibid*, p. 1499), where the Commission specifically refers to Art. 11 of the 1978 Vienna Convention on Succession of States in Respect of Treaties.

[23] See also the contribution by Tancredi, in this volume.

[24] See O'Connell, *State Succession in Municipal Law and International Law*, p. 232.

or Croatia, which had seceded from the Socialist Federal Republic of Yugoslavia.[25]

In 1997, the International Court of Justice expressly confirmed this rule and found that a 1977 treaty between Hungary and Czechoslovakia dealing with the Danube would fall in that category, stating:

> *The Court considers that Article 12 reflects a rule of customary international law; it notes that neither of the Parties disputed this.* Moreover, the [International Law] Commission indicated that 'treaties concerning water rights or navigation on rivers are commonly regarded as candidates for inclusion in the category of territorial treaties' . . . The Court observes that Article 12, in providing only, without reference to the treaty itself, that rights and obligations of a territorial character established by a treaty are unaffected by a succession of States, appears to lend support to the position of Hungary rather than of Slovakia. . . . Taking all these factors into account, the Court finds that the content of the 1977 Treaty indicates that it must be regarded as establishing a territorial regime within the meaning of Article 12 of 1978 Vienna Convention. *It created rights and obligations 'attaching to' the parts of the Danube to which it relates; thus the Treaty itself cannot be affected by a succession of States.*[26]

Accordingly, one can no longer seriously doubt the rule that seceding States remain bound by territorial regimes enshrined in localised treaties concluded by their respective predecessor States.

In contrast, it remains doubtful whether that principle would by now also extend to human rights treaties, such automatic succession being based on the idea that such treaties might have created individual rights which might remain unaffected by a secession of part of a State.

3. Secession and the possible continued automatic applicability of human rights treaties

In situations of State succession in general, but even more so in cases of secession, individuals are frequently subject to violations of their human rights, previously guaranteed under human rights treaties entered into by the predecessor State. Thus, the question of whether seceding States remain automatically bound by such treaties regardless of a notification of succession or a possible accession is of particular importance.

[25] Zimmermann, *Staatennachfolge in Verträge*, p. 505.

[26] Judgment of 25 September 1997, *Case Concerning the Gabcikovo-Nagymaros-Project (Hungary/Slovakia), ICJ Reports* 1997, p. 7 and para. 123 (emphasis added).

This question has, so far, been expressly left open by the International Court of Justice in the *Case Concerning Application of the Convention on the Prevention and Punishment of the Crime of Genocide (Bosnia and Herzegovina / Yugoslavia)* with regard to the Genocide Convention, where the Court stated:

> Without prejudice as to whether or not the principle of 'automatic succession' applies in the case of certain types of international treaties or conventions, the Court does not consider it necessary . . . to make a determination on the legal issues concerning State succession in respect of treaties which have been raised by the Parties.[27]

It has to be noted, however, that the question of automatic succession with regard to human rights treaties generally, and more particularly with regard to the Genocide Convention, will eventually have to be decided by the Court. This is due to the fact that the outcome in the *Genocide Case* between Croatia and the Federal Republic of Yugoslavia / Serbia and Montenegro[28] might depend on the question of whether the Federal Republic of Yugoslavia / Serbia and Montenegro – which has in the meantime abandoned its claim to be identical to the former Socialist Federal Republic of Yugoslavia – did automatically succeed to the Genocide Convention. The Federal Republic of Yugoslavia / Serbia and Montenegro decided not to notify its succession with regard to the Genocide Convention, but, instead, acceded to it, at the same time entering a reservation with regard to Article IX of the Genocide Convention, which could have otherwise eventually provided for the jurisdiction of the Court in the said case.[29]

The question of whether or not human rights treaties automatically devolve upon a successor State and thus also continue to be binding upon seceding States has been frequently addressed in the practice of the

[27] *Genocide Case*, p. 595, para. 23; see also *Case Concerning Application of the Convention on the Prevention and Punishment of the Crime of Genocide (Bosnia and Herzegovina/Yugoslavia) (Request for the Indication of Provisional Measures)*, *ICJ Reports* 1993, p. 1 and *Case Concerning Application of the Convention on the Prevention and Punishment of the Crime of Genocide (Bosnia and Herzegovina/Yugoslavia) (Further Request for the Indication of Provisional Measures)*, *ICJ Reports* 1993, p. 316, where the question also remained unsettled.

[28] *Case Concerning Application of the Convention on the Prevention and Punishment of the Crime of Genocide (Croatia v. Yugoslavia)*, still pending, see http://www.icj-cij.org/icjwww/idocket/icry/icryframe.htm.

[29] In the *Application for Revision of the Judgment of 11 July 1996 in the Case Concerning Application of the Convention on the Prevention and Punishment of the Crime of Genocide (Bosnia and Herzegovina v. Yugoslavia – Preliminary Objections)* case, the question was not touched upon by the Court. See its decision of 3 February 2003, available at: http://www.icj-cij.org/icjwww/idocket/iybh/ iybhjudgment/iybh ijudgment 20030203.PDF.

different treaty bodies set up under the various human rights treaties. Those treaty bodies have unanimously taken the position that the protection granted under such treaties automatically extends to the population of successor States, thus also to the population of seceding States, provided the predecessor State had been a contracting party thereof.[30] That approach was confirmed in General Comment No. 26 adopted by the Human Rights Committee on issues relating to the continuity of obligations to the International Covenant on Civil and Political Rights and a joint statement of the chairpersons of all concerned United Nations human rights bodies, which explicitly stated:

> . . . that successor States were automatically bound by obligations under international human rights instruments from the respective date of independence and that observance of the obligations should not depend on a declaration of confirmation made by the Government of the successor State.[31]

Still, here once again State practice is less than homogeneous. While most of the successor States of the former Yugoslavia and the two successor States of the CSFR have notified their succession to almost all of the respective human rights treaties, the practice of the successor States of the former Soviet Union is considerably less uniform. Indeed, a very significant number of these successor States have either *acceded* to such treaties or have so far *taken no treaty action whatsoever* with regard to the International Covenant of Civil and Political Rights, the International Covenant of Economic, Social and Cultural Rights, the Convention on the Elimination of all Forms of Discrimination against Women, the Convention Against Torture and other Cruel, Inhuman or Degrading Treatment or Punishment, the Convention on the Rights of the Child, the Convention on the Elimination of all Forms of Racial Discrimination, the Convention on the Non-applicability of Statutory Limitations to War Crimes and the International Convention on the Suppression and Punishment of the Crime of Apartheid.

Given this lack of uniformity, and taking into account the above-mentioned holding of the International Court of Justice in the *North Sea Continental Shelf Case*,[32] the outcome of the above-mentioned case

[30] See generally Zimmermann, *Staatennachfolge in Verträge*, p. 543, for further detailed references.

[31] UN Doc. E/CN.4/1995/80, Report by the Secretary General, 'Succession of States in respect of International Human Rights Treaties', 28 November 1994, p. 3.

[32] See note 18.

between Croatia and the Federal Republic of Yugoslavia / Serbia and Montenegro currently pending before the ICJ might be particularly illuminating. In this case, the Court must eventually determine whether the principle of automatic succession applies with regard to the Genocide Convention generally and whether, contrary to its findings in the case brought by Serbia and Montenegro against various NATO member States, Serbia and Montenegro could be a party to proceedings before the Court. Should it so find, the Court will eventually also have to deal with the issue of whether or not such automatic succession would then also extend to treaty clauses such as Article IX of the Genocide Convention, providing for the jurisdiction of the ICJ.

4. Secession and possible continued membership in international organisations

By now, it seems to be commonly accepted that in cases of secession, membership in international organisations cannot be acquired by way of succession[33] – some exceptions with regard to financial organisations such as the IMF, the World Bank or comparable regional organisations notwithstanding, where the practice of the respective organisations lends support for such possibility.[34] Accordingly, a seceding State *must apply for membership* in those organisations, even if its respective predecessor State has been, or continues to be, a member. This is confirmed by the practice of the successor States of the former Yugoslavia, which have *all* been admitted as *new* members of the United Nations, as well as by the fact that all successor States of the Soviet Union, which – unlike Belarus and Ukraine – had not themselves been members of the organisation in their own right, have similarly been admitted in the regular procedure provided for in Article 4 of the Charter.

The predecessor State, part of whose territory secedes, may, on the other hand, only retain its membership in international organisations provided it can successfully claim to continue the international legal personality of said State, as was the case with regard to the Russian Federation *vis-à-vis* the USSR.[35] In contrast, such claim was never –

[33] *Ibid.*, p. 589.

[34] For a detailed analysis of the practice of these organisations, see Zimmermann, *Staatennachfolge in Verträge*, p. 629. See also generally, K. Buehler, *State Succession and Membership in International Organizations: Legal Theories versus Political Pragmatism* (The Hague: Kluwer Law International, 2001), *passim*.

[35] *Ibid.*, p. 85. With regard to the continuance of Soviet UN membership by the Russian Federation, see *ibid.*, at p. 594.

some legal uncertainties notwithstanding – recognised as far as the relationship of the Federal Republic of Yugoslavia/Serbia and Montenegro *vis-à-vis* the former Socialist Federal Republic of Yugoslavia is concerned.[36]

IV. Succession with regard to debts and property

A. General principles

The current status of customary law in the field of succession with regard to debts and property is at least as vague, if not more so, than the field of succession of States to treaties. This is due, *inter alia*, to the fact that the 1983 Vienna Convention on State Succession in Respect of State Property, Archives and Debts has so far only received five ratifications and has thus, unlike the 1978 Vienna Convention on Succession of States in Respect of Treaties, not yet entered into force. Moreover, relevant State practice is rather scarce, in particular where – as in cases of secession – the States concerned are normally not willing to enter into a negotiated settlement on succession issues.

Nonetheless, a number of general principles may be recalled. First, it might be said, as stated by the Badinter Arbitration Commission for the former Yugoslavia in its Opinion No. 9,[37] that States involved must settle outstanding succession issues – and particularly those concerning debts and property – by agreement, thereby trying to achieve an equitable solution.[38] Indeed, such agreed settlements have, by and large, by now been reached with regard to all major cases of State succession of the last

[36] See in this regard the judgment of the ICJ of 3 February 2003 in the *Case concerning Application for Revision of the Judgment of 11 July 1996 in the Case Concerning Application of the Convention on the Prevention and Punishment of the Crime of Genocide (Bosnia and Herzegovina v. Yugoslavia – Preliminary Objections)*, where the Court stated that the FRY had found itself – until its admission as a new member – in a *sui generis* position *vis-à-vis* the United Nations, *ibid.* para. 71. In its most recent judgments in the various cases brought by Serbia and Montenegro against several NATO member States, the Court clearly stated, however, that Serbia and Montenegro was not a member of the United Nations, and therefore not a State party to the Statute of the International Court of Justice, before it was admitted to the United Nations on 1 November 2000, *Cases concerning Legality of Use of Force (Serbia and Montenegro v. Belgium et al.), Preliminary Objections, Judgments of 15 December 2004*, texts available at: http://www.icj-cij.org/icjwww/idocket/iybe/iybeframe.htm, para. 79.

[37] *ILM* 1992, p. 1525.

[38] See also Opinion No. 14 (*ILM* 1992, p. 1591), which stipulates specifically in relation to State succession with regard to debts and property that 'the successor States should consult with each other and agree to a settlement of all questions relating to the succession'.

years, i.e. the break-up of the USSR,[39] the Socialist Federal Republic of Yugoslavia[40] and the CSFR.[41]

Failing such agreement, the fundamental rule is that the States concerned must reach an equitable result. This rule does not, however, presuppose that each category of assets or liabilities be divided in equitable proportions, but that only the overall outcome should lead to such an equitable division.[42] Any such division between the seceding State on the one hand and the remaining rump State on the other does, however, only relate to State property of the predecessor State, the domestic law of which, in turn, defines the notion and extent of such State property.[43] On the other hand, property of third States, as well as private property located on the territory concerned, is not affected as such by the secession.[44]

B. *Distribution of immovable property located on the territory of the seceding State*

According to a well-established rule of the law of State succession,[45] immovable property situated on the territory of a seceding State passes exclusively to that State without compensation,[46] subject to the general rule that an overall equitable result should be reached. This has recently

[39] For a detailed analysis, see T. Schweisfurth, 'Das Recht der Staatensukzession – Die Staatenpraxis der Nachfolge in völkerrechtliche Verträge, Staatsvermögen, Staatsschulden und Archive in den Teilungsfällen Sowjetunion, Tschechoslowakei und Jugoslawien', *Berichte der Deutschen Gesellschaft für Völkerrecht*, 35 (1998), pp. 49 and 146.

[40] Agreement on Succession Issues of 29 June 2001 and its Annexes A to G, available at http://www.ohr.int/succession.html. For a more detailed analysis of this agreement, see C. Stahn, 'The Agreement on Succession Issues of the Former Socialist Federal Republic of Yugoslavia', *AJIL* 96 (2002), p. 379, as well as G. Acquaviva, 'The Dissolution of Yugoslavia and the Fate of its Financial Obligations', *Denver J.I.L.P.* 30 (2002), pp. 173 and 211.

[41] See Schweisfurth, 'Das Recht der Staatensukzession', p. 162.

[42] See in that regard already Opinion No. 13 of the Badinter Arbitration Commission for the former Yugoslavia, para. 2, *ILM* 1992, p. 1591.

[43] See Opinion No. 14 of the Badinter Arbitration Commission for the former Yugoslavia, para. 5, *ILM* 1992, p. 1593.

[44] See articles 6 and 12 of the 1983 Vienna Convention on Succession of States in Respect of State Property, Archives and Debts.

[45] For such a proposition, see Opinion No. 14 of the Badinter Arbitration Commission for the former Yugoslavia, and see also Art. 17(1)(a) of the 1983 Vienna Convention on Succession of States in Respect of State Property, Archives and Debts.

[46] See Opinion No. 14 of the Badinter Arbitration Commission for the former Yugoslavia, as well as articles 17(1)(a) and 18(1)(a) of the 1983 Vienna Convention on Succession of States in Respect of State Property, Archives and Debts.

been confirmed by the agreement reached by the respective Yugoslav successor States.[47]

C. *Distribution of movable property located on the territory of the seceding State*

The situation with regard to movable property located on the territory of the seceding State is less clear. Article 17(1)(c) of the 1983 Vienna Convention provides that, in such a situation, only such movable property of the predecessor which is connected with the activity of the predecessor State in respect of the seceding territory shall pass to the successor State. This principle was by and large followed in the case of the dissolution of the CSFR.[48] In contrast, the Badinter Arbitration Commission for the former Yugoslavia stated in its Opinion No. 14 that, 'public property passes to the successor State on whose territory it is situated', a position that has now also been formulated in the agreement concluded by the Yugoslav successor States.[49]

Given this ambiguity in the law and the lack of uniform State practice, it is largely up to the States concerned to come up with an *ad hoc* agreed solution.

D. *Distribution of immovable property located abroad*

In the case of a complete dismemberment of the respective predecessor State, Article 18(1)(b) of the 1983 Vienna Convention provides that immovable State property shall pass to the successor States in equitable shares, a solution that was retained by both the successor States of the CSFR[50] and, more recently, by the successor States of the Socialist Federal Republic of Yugoslavia.[51]

Where the secession does not, however, lead to complete dismemberment, the 1983 Convention is silent. It thus leaves it open whether – as had been claimed by the Federal Republic of Yugoslavia / Serbia and Montenegro before it gave up its claim to be identical with the former Socialist Federal Republic of Yugoslavia – such property should remain

[47] Art. 8(1) of Annex A of the Agreement on Succession Issues of the former Socialist Federal Republic of Yugoslavia of 29 June 2001.
[48] Schweisfurth, 'Das Recht der Staatensukzession', p. 163.
[49] See Art. 3(1) of Annex A of said agreement.
[50] Schweisfurth, 'Das Recht der Staatensukzession', p. 163.
[51] See Art. 2 of Annex B of the above-mentioned agreement.

with the predecessor State[52] or whether it should be similarly apportioned in equitable shares among the seceding State and the predecessor State.[53] In view of the fact that the law of State succession is governed by the general principle of equity,[54] there is stronger support for the view that such property should be equally divided, regardless of whether the secession has finally led to a complete dismemberment of the predecessor State or not. This is even more true since, as demonstrated by the Yugoslav case, it may take years before it is finally determined whether or not the respective instance of secession is to be considered as having solely constituted a separation, or whether instead, it has led to a complete dismemberment of the predecessor State.

E. Distribution of State debts and movable financial assets located abroad

In recent years, State practice with regard to the distribution of external debts and financial assets located abroad has largely been influenced by the practice of the different international financial institutions such as the IMF or the World Bank.[55] This is once more demonstrated by the recent agreement concluded by the Yugoslav successor States. This agreement is in line with the key previously used by the IMF based on a bundle of factors, including the share of the seceding State in the GNP of the predecessor State and its part in export earnings. An exception exists where the States concerned, like the two successor States of the CSFR, had by themselves been able to reach a mutually agreeable solution.[56]

[52] See *inter alia* M. N. Shaw, *International Law*, 5th edn (Cambridge: Cambridge University Press, 2003), p. 702.

[53] P. K. Menon, *The Succession of States in respect to Treaties, State Property, Archives, and Debts* (New York: The Edwin Mellen Press, 1991), p. 111.

[54] See generally W. Czaplinski, 'Equity and Equity Principles in the Law of State Succession', in M. Mrak (ed.), *Succession of States* (The Hague: Kluwer Law International, 1999), p. 61, as well as S. Maljean-Dubois, 'Le role de l'équité dans le droit de la succession d'Etats', in P. Eisemann and M. Koskennienmi (eds.), *State Succession – Codification tested against the Facts* (The Hague: Kluwer Law International, 2000), p. 137.

[55] As to the practice of the IMF and the World Bank, see A. Gioia, 'State Succession and International Financial Organizations', in P. Eisemann and M. Koskennienmi (eds.), *State Succession – Codification tested against the Facts* (The Hague: Kluwer Law International, 2000), p. 327.

[56] In the case of the former CSFR, the distribution was simply based on the size of the population, i.e. on a 2:1 basis, see J. Malenovsky, 'Problèmes juridiques liés à la partition de la Tchécoslovaquie', *AFDI* 39 (1993), pp. 305 and 331; see also, generally, M. Hoskova, 'Die Selbstauflösung der CSFR. Ausgewählte rechtliche Aspekte', *ZaöRV* 53 (1993), p. 689.

As to the distribution of the external debt, it is similarly subject to the principle of equity, based on the aforementioned criteria. It has to be noted, however, that recent State practice tends toward applying a rule under which both local debts *stricto sensu*, i.e. debts contracted by sub-entities located on the territory of the seceding State, as well as other localised debts, i.e. debts concluded by the predecessor State but for the benefit of the seceding part, are inherited by the seceding State concerned.

V. Succession with regard to the nationality of natural persons[57]

A. General questions

A last issue of vital importance for the population living on the seceding territory concerns their nationality status. In particular, the two related questions that arise are, firstly, what are the criteria for the seceding State to grant its nationality to persons living on the territory? Secondly, who may be considered to have retained the nationality of the predecessor State, where indeed such predecessor continues to exist regardless of a successful secession?

Unlike issues of State succession with regard to treaties, and the problems of State succession with regard to debts and property, the impact of State succession – and thus also of secession – on the nationality of natural persons has not yet been codified in the form of a treaty. Those questions have, however, formed the basis of a project of the International Law Commission which, in 1999, adopted the above-mentioned Draft Articles on Nationality in Relation to the Succession of States.[58] In addition, the European Convention on Nationality, opened for signature on 7 November 1997, which has so far entered into force for twelve States, contains in its Article 18 provisions dealing with cases of the emergence of a new State.[59]

[57] As to the effect of State succession on the nationality of natural persons, see generally A. Zimmermann, 'State Succession and the Nationality of Natural Persons – Facts and Possible Codification', in P. Eisemann and M. Koskennienmi (eds.), *State Succession – Codification Tested Against the Facts* (The Hague: Kluwer Law International, 2000), p. 611.

[58] See note 3.

[59] Article 18 of the said Convention stipulates, *inter alia*:

'(1) In matters of nationality in cases of State succession, each State Party concerned shall respect the principles of the rule of law, the rules concerning human rights and the principles contained in Articles 4 and 5 [dealing with the prohibition of an arbitrary deprivation of nationality and the prohibition of discrimination in matters of

When analysing the impact of a secession on the nationality of natural persons, the above-mentioned distinction is even more imperative, whether or not the secession finally leads to a complete dismemberment of the predecessor State. In the latter case, the question is also one of *denationalisation*, relating to the individuals who previously were nationals of the undivided predecessor State, but who may no longer be considered nationals of the remaining rump predecessor State.

On the other hand, in the case of a process of secession leading to the complete dissolution of a State, the question solely addresses the extent to which the different successor States may *positively grant* their newly established nationality.

B. *Cases of secession where the predecessor State continues to exist*

In such cases, State practice seems to confirm that in order to be able to grant their nationality, the seceding State must consider whether the individuals concerned have a genuine link to the respective territory. To determine such a link, however, States have chosen different sorts of criteria, such as residence, domicile or ethnic origin. The leeway that seceding States have in choosing factors which determine the initial group of their nationals is also confirmed by Article 18 of the European Convention on Nationality, which provides that the States deciding on the granting or the retention of nationality shall consider, in particular, the habitual residence, the territorial origin and the will of the person concerned.

Where the predecessor State possessed a federal structure, successor States, such as those of both the CSFR and the USSR, have shown a tendency to choose as their main criterion the legal link of the individual to the sub-entity from which the successor State has derived its existence. In other words, the granting of the nationality of the successor State was made dependent on whether the individual had possessed the secondary citizenship of the State entity in question. Indeed, under Article 24 of the

nationality] of the present Convention and in paragraph 2 of this Article, in particular in order to avoid statelessness;

(2) In deciding on the granting or the retention of nationality in cases of State succession, each State party concerned shall take in particular account of:
   a) the genuine and effective link of the person concerned with the State;
   b) the habitual residence of the person concerned at the time of State succession;
   c) the will of the person concerned;
   d) the territorial origin of the person concerned . . .'

International Law Commission's Draft Articles on Nationality in Relation to the Succession of States,[60] the successor State would, subject to the right of option, be under an obligation to grant its nationality not only to the persons habitually residing within the succeeding territory but also to the persons who had an appropriate legal connection to the constituent unit that has become part of the successor State. It remains doubtful, however, whether such a rule forms part of customary international law, given the lack of uniform State practice in this regard.

On the other hand, the remaining rump State, the legal existence of which has not been put into question by the process of secession, seems to be in a position to claim as its own citizens not only those persons residing on its territory but also all those nationals living in a seceding State or in a third State who had not acquired the nationality of the said seceding State.

C. *Cases of secession where the predecessor State ceases to exist*

In recent history, there are only a few cases of secession where none of the successor States carries on the legal personality of the predecessor State, the case of the former Yugoslavia being the most important example of this.

State practice demonstrates that in the case of a secessionist development leading to the complete dismemberment of the predecessor State, the granting of citizenship by the different seceding States is similarly based on some form of connection with the given territory, which normally takes the form of their prior habitual residence. In the more recent cases of the complete break-up of federal States, where the constituent entities already *ex ante* possessed a 'secondary citizenship' of their own, there has also been a clear tendency to no longer primarily rely on either domicile or residence to determine the nationality of the successor State. Instead, successor States have taken the previous 'secondary citizenship' as the starting point in determining their nationals. This tendency is again reflected in Article 22(b)(i) of the above-mentioned International Law Commission's draft articles, according to which successor States that are the result of the complete dissolution of their predecessor State are to attribute their nationality, subject to the exercise of the right of option, to persons who have an appropriate legal connection with a constituent unit of the predecessor State that has become part of the successor State.

[60] See note 3.

D. Secession and the obligation to avoid statelessness

Traditionally, it has been argued that 'undesirable as it may be that any persons become stateless as a result of a change of sovereignty, it cannot be asserted with any measure of confidence that international law, at least in its present stage of development, imposes any duty on the successor State to positively grant its nationality'.[61] On the other hand, it may well be argued that emerging standards of human rights have come to oblige predecessor and successor States 'to avoid creating cases of statelessness'.[62]

However, no human rights treaty specifically deals with issues of State succession, let alone with the particular issue of whether a seceding State should confer its nationality upon a person. Even the recent International Law Commission draft articles[63] solely provide that the States concerned are to take all appropriate measures to prevent persons from becoming stateless as a result of succession and leave aside the crucial question of which one of several seceding States should eventually have the primary responsibility to grant nationality in order to avoid statelessness of persons affected.

Similar considerations apply with regard to the United Nations Convention on the Reduction of Statelessness, since it only contains provisions as to the *deprivation* of nationality and is therefore not applicable to a seceding State which can only *withhold* its nationality from individuals.

Accordingly, it is submitted that under current customary law, States are under no general obligation to avoid statelessness, a position which is confirmed by the fact that Article 15 of the Universal Declaration of Human Rights, the customary nature of which is not beyond doubt,[64] only contains the obligation not to arbitrarily *deprive* a person of his or her citizenship, and does not refer to obligations of seceding States to positively *grant* nationality.

The only standard that may be deduced from State practice is that concerned States are under a *joint* obligation to avoid statelessness. Thus, in practice, the seceding State or States and the remaining predecessor State

[61] O'Connell, *State Succession in Municipal Law and International Law*, p. 503; see also J. Crawford, *The Creation of States in International Law* (Oxford: Clarendon Press, 1979), p. 41.

[62] See e.g., No. 6 of the 'Declaration on the Consequences of State Succession for the Nationality of Natural Persons' adopted on 13–14 September 1996 by the Commission for Democracy through Law established by the Council of Europe, 7 CDL-NAT (1996).

[63] Art. 3 of the ILC Draft Articles on Nationality in Relation to the Succession of States.

[64] See e.g., J. Chan, 'The Right to a Nationality as a Human Right: The Current Trend Towards Recognition', *HRLJ* 12 (1991), pp. 1–3.

would seem to be under an obligation to harmonise their respective rules and procedures and to negotiate in good faith on questions of nationality as part of their general obligation to regulate succession issues through negotiations.[65] In so doing, one would assume a similar obligation to take into account, in particular, the obligation not to discriminate against certain groups.

It remains doubtful, however, whether such an obligation will effectively be fulfilled in a situation of secession which takes place against the clearly articulated will of the remaining part. Indeed, the most promising solution would be to grant the nationals concerned the possibility to opt for one of the respective nationalities, but again, it remains doubtful whether the States concerned by the secession are indeed under an obligation to grant such option.[66]

E. Conclusions

As is evident from the above, the impact of State succession on nationality is quite similar to its impact on treaties or on debts and assets. Legal uncertainty still prevails and only a few fixed rules of customary international law have developed. Indeed, as regards instances of secession in particular, one may say that although seceding States enjoy some discretion as to the factors that they can take into account in determining their national base, they have regularly taken as their starting point either the place of permanent residence or, more recently, the 'secondary nationality' of the individual and have looked for a genuine link with the successor State. Where – as normally in cases of secession – one State continues to exist as the predecessor State, this State tends to look at nationality issues from a viewpoint that is quite different from the one adopted by the successor States. Such a predecessor State would normally continue to consider those nationals of the dissolved State who reside abroad and those who had a close connection to that State as its own nationals.

In any event, the avoidance of statelessness and the establishment of a possible right of the individual to exercise an option are of paramount

[65] See the divergent views expressed in the Sixth Committee on the question of whether there is an obligation to negotiate in order to avoid statelessness and what the exact scope of such negotiations would be, A/CN.4/472/Add.1, para. 16. The ILC Draft Articles on Nationality in Relation to the Succession of States, provide in Art. 18(2) that: 'States concerned shall, when necessary, seek a solution to eliminate or mitigate such detrimental effects by negotiation and, as appropriate, through agreement.'

[66] In regard to the right of option under international law, see generally, K. Meessen, *Die Option der Staatsangehörigkeit* (Berlin: Duncker&Humboldt, 1966), *passim.*

importance in cases of secession. Furthermore, attempts should be made *de lege ferenda* to avoid, as far as possible, situations of multiple nationalities arising from situations of secession, since otherwise such situations could give rise to long-term bitter conflict. Notwithstanding the fact that recent State practice has demonstrated that the 'secondary citizenship' of a person constitutes a valid genuine link in granting the nationality of the successor State, it still seems to hold true that the most satisfactory and the most natural criterion for determining the initial set of nationals of a seceding State is habitual residence.[67] Therefore, habitual residence should be taken as the decisive criterion in determining who can validly acquire *ex lege* the nationality of a seceding State.

VI. Overall conclusions

As demonstrated, the law of State succession is – certain clear exceptions notwithstanding – still characterised by a certain lack of undisputed rules of customary law. Nonetheless, certain tendencies and general principles should serve as guidelines for States which come into existence as a result of secession.

Given the circumstances normally surrounding instances of State secession, and the lack of legal clarity with regard to applicable rules, it is of utmost importance that the States concerned make *bona fide* efforts to come up with agreed solutions or otherwise agree to third party settlement of outstanding succession issues. The succession agreement among the five Yugoslav successor States could in that regard serve as a useful model. It also demonstrates, however, that sometimes it might take not only years but also very bitter experiences before any such settlement can be reached.

[67] For early practice in this regard, see O'Connell, *State Succession in Municipal Law and International Law*, p. 518.

8

Are there gaps in the international law of secession?

OLIVIER CORTEN

Developments in current international law have raised the perception of gaps in the field of secession. It seems that States constantly oscillate between two tendencies. The first is characterised by the refusal to extend international legal regulation (apart from that applicable to protecting human rights) to what is *a priori* a matter of State sovereignty and 'internal affairs'. It does not appear therefore to be a question of a *lacuna*, this term implying that the law does not give an answer to a question that arises in its field of application, this last condition not having been filled.

The second tendency consists of opposing to secessionist groups and their sources of external support the obligation to respect the territorial integrity of the threatened State and, in parallel, legalising the principle of military response of the latter. Then, far from being neutral or silent on the matter, international law seems to rule very clearly in favour of the State.

LE DROIT INTERNATIONAL EST-IL LACUNAIRE SUR LA QUESTION DE LA SÉCESSION?**

On a généralement défini la sécession comme 'la démarche par laquelle un groupe ou une partie d'un Etat cherche à se détacher de l'autorité politique et constitutionnelle de cet Etat, en vue de former un nouvel Etat doté d'une assise territoriale et reconnu au niveau international'.[1] Pour notre part, nous envisagerons plus spécifiquement la sécession comme la

** Cette étude est dédiée à Jean Salmon, qui a nourri ma réflexion sur ce sujet depuis de nombreuses années.

[1] Cour suprême du Canada, Affaire de l'*Article 53 de la loi sur la Cour suprême. L.R.C. (1985), ch. S-26* et dans l'affaire d'un *Renvoi par le gouverneur en conseil au sujet de certaines questions ayant trait à la sécession du Québec du reste du Canada formulées dans le décret C.P.1996–1497 du 30 septembre 1996*, N° 25506, décision du 20 août 1998, par. 83.

tentative de créer un Etat par la force ou la violence, en ne retenant pas les hypothèses de création d'Etat opérées par la voie pacifique que l'on qualifiera de séparation voire, si l'Etat prédécesseur a cessé d'exister, de dissolution.[2] Les débats sur la légitimité de la sécession ne sont sans doute pas prêts de s'apaiser. Réactivés aux débuts des années 1990 avec l'éclatement de la République socialiste fédérative de Yougoslavie, ils ont été relancés ensuite tant en Europe (Abkhazie, Nagorno-Karabach, Tchétchénie, Kosovo, . . .) qu'en Afrique (Somaliland, Puntland, Comores, . . .), en Amérique (Québec) ou en Asie (en particulier dans plusieurs parties de l'Indonésie et des Philippines). Sur le plan du droit international, la discussion s'articule essentiellement autour de deux pôles. D'un côté, certains auteurs estiment que le droit des peuples à disposer d'eux-mêmes, traditionnellement limité dans sa dimension externe aux situations de décolonisation ou d'occupation étrangère, peut désormais être invoqué par certaines minorités, en particulier celles qui subissent une discrimination et une répression féroces de la part des autorités étatiques.[3] Le succès de certaines accessions récentes à l'indépendance (comme en Croatie) aurait marqué une évolution radicale des règles juridiques depuis le début des années 1990.[4] D'un autre côté, une partie importante de la doctrine estime que le droit international se caractérise sur ce point par ce qui est désigné comme une véritable 'neutralité juridique': la sécession ne serait ni autorisée ni interdite.[5] C'est dans ce contexte qu'on a pu évoquer le caractère lacunaire du droit international, qui se contenterait de prendre acte des effectivités observables sur le terrain (la réussite ou l'échec de

[2] On peut, dans le premier cas de figure, ranger des précédents comme ceux de l'Erythrée et, dans le second, un précédent comme celui de la République tchèque et de la Slovaquie.

[3] V. p. ex. L. Buchheit, *Secession – The Legitimacy of Self-Determination* (New Haven and London: Yale University Press, 1978); A. D. Murswiek, 'The Issue of a Right of Secession – Reconsidered', *in:* Ch. Tomuschat (ed.), *Modern Law of Self-Determination* (Dordrecht: Martinus Nijhoff, 1993), pp. 21–40.

[4] Nous n'entrerons pas ici dans le débat concernant la qualification de l'accession à l'indépendance de la Croatie: sécession, dans la mesure où, à la date de son indépendance, la Yougoslavie était encore un Etat existant, ou dissolution, dans la mesure où la Yougoslavie sera ultérieurement considérée comme ayant cessé d'exister (v. B. Stern, *Le Statut des Etats issus de l'Ex-Yougoslavie à l'ONU* (Paris: Montchrestien, 1996)).

[5] V. p. ex. 'Sécession', *in:* J. Salmon (dir.), *Dictionnaire de droit international public* (Bruxelles: Bruylant-AUPELF, 2001), p. 1022; J. Salmon, 'Le droit des peuples à disposer d'eux-mêmes. Aspects juridiques et politiques', *in: Le nationalisme, facteur belligène. Etudes de sociologie de la guerre* (Bruxelles: Bruylant, 1972), p. 364; R. Higgins, *Problems & Process. International Law and How We Use It* (Oxford: Clarendon Press, 1993), p. 125; J. Crawford, *The Creation of States in International Law* (Oxford: Clarendon Press, 1979), pp. 266–8.

la sécession), sans conférer sa légitimité à l'une (les sécessionnistes) ou à l'autre (les autorités étatiques) des parties en conflit. Dans cette perspective, la création de nouveaux Etats ne témoignerait nullement d'une évolution du régime juridique existant: la reconnaissance ces dernières années de certains Etats issus d'une sécession n'implique pas en tant que telle la reconnaissance d'un *droit* à la sécession, mais seulement la prise d'acte d'un *fait* sécessionniste.[6] Pour reprendre les termes du professeur Salmon, dans de tels cas, 'on se trouve dans le domaine de la neutralité juridique ou, autrement dit, d'une lacune du droit'.[7] Théodore Christakis évoquait en ce sens 'l'idée de l'existence d'une lacune du droit international public en matière de sécession'.[8]

L'objet du présent chapitre est de tester l'hypothèse de la lacune, ainsi que celle de la neutralité juridique qui y est souvent associée.

Encore faut-il, avant d'entamer la démonstration, préciser ce qu'on entend par une 'lacune'. Le concept sera défini comme l'absence de règle de droit pour régir un rapport donné que le système juridique a vocation à régir.[9] Le premier élément, 'l'absence de règle de droit', ne pose pas de problème dans son principe même si, comme on le verra, son application prête tout particulièrement à interprétation.[10] Le second, 'que le système a vocation à régir', mérite une explication. Comme l'a montré le professeur Salmon, la détermination de l'existence d'une lacune suppose de

[6] J. Crawford, 'State Practice and International Law in Relation to Secession', *BYBIL* LXX (1999), p. 87. V. aussi H. Quane, 'The United Nations and the Evolving Right to Self-Determination', *ICLQ* 47 (1998), p. 563; M. Shaw, 'Peoples, Territorialism and Boundaries', *EJIL* 8 (1997), pp. 482–3.

[7] J. Salmon, 'Vers l'adoption d'un principe de légitimité démocratique?', *in:* O. Corten, B. Declourt, P. Herman, P. Klein, O. Paye, E. Remacle, E. Robert et J. Salmon (eds.), *A la recherche du nouvel ordre mondial. Tome I. Le droit international à l'épreuve* (Bruxelles: edn. complexe, 1993), p. 63, et, du même auteur, 'Internal Aspects of the Right to Self-Determination: Towards a Democratic Legitimacy Principle', *in:* Ch. Tomuschat (ed.), *Modern-Law of Self-Determination*, p. 256. V. aussi C. Quaye, *Liberation Struggles in International Law* (Philadelphia: Temple University Press, 1991), pp. 212–13.

[8] Th. Christakis, *Le droit à l'autodétermination en dehors des situations de décolonisation* (Paris: La documentation française, 1999), p. 74. L'auteur reprend cette idée à son compte plus bas, en affirmant que 'le droit international [est] lacunaire en cette matière' (p. 118).

[9] On s'inspire ici de la définition de la lacune au sens strict, qui renvoie à l' 'état d'un système normatif qui n'est pas complet, c'est-à-dire qui ne contient pas de dispositions définissant le statut déontique d'un cas déterminé, alors que cette présence était attendue' (v° lacune, *in:* A. J. Arnaud (ed.), *Dictionnaire encyclopédique de théorie et de sociologie du droit* (Paris: L.G.D.J., Bruxelles: Story Sciencia, 1988), p. 219.

[10] O. Corten, *L'utilisation du 'raisonnable' par le juge international* (Bruxelles: Bruylant, 1997), pp. 213–20.

déterminer au préalable par rapport à quoi l'absence, ou le manque, doit être évalué.[11] Ainsi, si on choisit comme référence une série de nombres de 1 à 50, l'absence du nombre 25 peut être considérée comme une lacune, mais pas celle du nombre 60. Dans ce dernier cas, il n'y a pas à strictement parler de lacune, puisque le système n'a pas vocation à s'étendre à l'élément concerné.[12] Le terme 'lacune' est alors inapproprié, dans la mesure où il suggère une applicabilité de principe du système juridique à une situation qui lui est radicalement étrangère.[13] Enfin, précisons que la lacune se comprend dans ce contexte par rapport au droit tel qu'il est, et non par rapport au droit tel que l'on souhaiterait qu'il soit. On peut ainsi moralement estimer qu'une règle juridique est 'lacunaire' sans que, du point de vue du droit existant, une lacune ne puisse en toute rigueur être identifiée.[14]

Qu'en est-il dans le cas de la sécession ? Pour pouvoir démontrer que le droit international est lacunaire au sens que nous venons de préciser, trois éléments devraient être réunis. *Premièrement*, la lacune suppose que les rapports entre l'Etat et le mouvement sécessionniste aient vocation à être régis par le droit international public ou, en d'autres termes, que ce mouvement puisse être considéré comme un véritable sujet de l'ordre juridique international. Dans la négative, il ne saurait être question de lacune, la sécession n'étant même pas susceptible d'être appréhendée par le droit international. *Deuxièmement*, et à supposer que le droit international ait bien vocation à donner une solution à la question de la sécession, il faudrait démontrer que celle-ci n'est en tant que telle pas réglementée, la neutralité juridique se traduisant par un refus de se prononcer sur la licéité ou l'illicéité du phénomène sécessionniste.

A l'issue de notre réflexion, nous pensons pouvoir énoncer la thèse qui sous-tend l'ensemble des pages qui suivent de la manière suivante: les dernières évolutions du droit international semblent osciller entre

[11] J. Salmon, 'Quelques observation sur les lacunes en droit international public', *in:* Ch. Perelman (ed.), *Le problème des lacunes en droit* (Bruxelles: Bruylant, 1968), p. 320.

[12] G. I. Tunkin, 'Droit international et modèle généralement reconnu du système international', *in: Mélanges Chaumont, Le droit des peuples à disposer d'eux-mêmes. Méthode d'analyse du droit international* (Paris: Pedone, 1984), pp. 546–7.

[13] On peut encore comprendre cette condition à partir du constat selon lequel l'absence de règle juridique régissant l'heure de levée du soleil, ou les relations entre un chat et une souris, n'est nullement le signe d'une lacune du système juridique considéré. Plus près des problèmes concrets susceptibles de se poser aux juridictions internationales, M. G. Kohen donne l'exemple de négociations sur le niveau d'armements, dont le résultat échappe à l'emprise de la réglementation juridique; 'L'avis consultatif de la CIJ sur la *Licéité de la menace ou de l'emploi d'armes nucléaire* et la fonction judiciaire', *EJIL* 8 (1997), p. 343.

[14] H. Kelsen, *Théorie pure du droit*, trad. Ch. Eisenmann (Bruxelles: Bruylant, 1999), p. 246.

deux cas de figure qui rendent délicate la démonstration de l'existence d'une lacune. Le premier est celui où aucun statut de sujet juridique n'est reconnu aux entités sécessionnistes. Faute de pouvoir bénéficier de ce statut, l'entité n'est alors, par définition, pas susceptible de bénéficier de droits quelconques; il n'est alors pas question de lacune, la première étape envisagée ci-dessus ne pouvant même pas être franchie. Un deuxième cas de figure est celui où, le plus souvent à la suite du déclenchement d'un conflit armé non international, l'entité sécessionniste s'est vue reconnaître une certaine capacité juridique, et se voit par conséquent accorder certains droits et devoirs. Plutôt que de se révéler à strictement parler lacunaire ou neutre, le droit international a alors tendance à se prononcer à l'encontre de la sécession et en faveur du maintien de l'intégrité territoriale de l'Etat.

En tout cas, la 'neutralité juridique' est, dans l'un et l'autre de ces cas, une expression qui ne convient pas: dans le premier, elle laisse faussement entendre que l'Etat comme le mouvement sécessionniste sont placés sur le même pied (I) alors que, dans le second, elle suppose qu'aucune de ces deux parties ne bénéficie d'un statut préférentiel, ce qui ne semble pas être le cas (III).

I. Le refus d'accorder un statut de sujet de droit international à l'entité sécessionniste: le cas typique des 'troubles intérieurs'

Les tentatives de sécession ne se traduisent pas toujours, en tout cas dans l'immédiat, par le déclenchement de véritables conflits armés au cours desquels s'opposent des 'groupes armés organisés qui, sous la conduite d'un commandement responsable, exercent sur une partie du territoire un contrôle tel qu'il permette de mener des opérations militaires continues et concertées et d'appliquer le présent protocole'.[15] Dans certains cas, comme celui du Québec, ou du Kosovo de 1990 à 1997, les groupes favorables à l'accession à l'indépendance utilisent des moyens pacifiques, sans qu'il soit question de prendre les armes. Dans d'autres, comme au pays basque, on est véritablement devant une tentative de sécessions au sens défini par la présente étude, les indépendantistes utilisant la violence pour parvenir à leurs fins. On se trouve alors dans une situation de troubles intérieurs ou d' 'actes isolés et sporadiques de violence et d'autres actes analogues, qui ne sont pas considérés comme des conflits armés'.[16] Dans toutes ces

[15] Art. I, par. 1, du Deuxième Protocole de Genève de 1977, additionnel aux Conventions de Genève du 12 août 1949 relatif à la protection des victimes des conflits armés non internationaux.

[16] Art. I, par. 2, du Deuxième Protocole, précité.

hypothèses,[17] le droit international se caractérise par un refus d'accorder un statut juridique spécifique au mouvement sécessionniste (A). Il se contente de régir les relations juridiques liant l'Etat menacé aux autres sujets de l'ordre juridique international (B).

A. Le refus d'accorder un statut juridique spécifique au mouvement sécessionniste

Tant que l'on se trouve dans une simple situation de troubles intérieurs, le groupe sécessionniste n'a aucun statut juridique défini; il ne s'agit pas d'un 'mouvement insurrectionnel', au sens donné à cette notion dans le droit de la responsabilité internationale.[18] On ne peut non plus véritablement évoquer le concept de peuple, à moins d'étendre ce dernier à toutes les minorités culturelles ou nationales, ce qui semble loin de refléter l'état du droit international.[19] Le groupe sécessionniste est alors dans une situation ou, non seulement il ne bénéficie juridiquement d'aucun droit mais, bien plus, il n'est pas susceptible d'en bénéficier faute d'un statut de sujet de droit international. Aucune capacité, même limitée, ne lui est reconnue.

Etant donné son importance aux fins de notre raisonnement, on rappellera la définition du sujet de droit international comme désignant une 'entité susceptible d'être titulaire de droits et d'obligations trouvant leur source dans l'ordre international'.[20] En tant que 'non sujet', le groupe sécessionniste non seulement n'a pas de droit, mais encore n'est pas susceptible d'en avoir.

En pratique, ceci se traduit souvent par l'absence de toute prise de position officielle de la part des Etats tiers à la situation. Dans les cas du Québec ou du pays basque, la société internationale semble avoir considéré que les revendications sécessionnistes n'étaient en tant que telles

[17] J. Crawford cite encore des cas comme la Padanie, la Corse ou la Catalogne, *in*: 'State Practice', 108.

[18] V. l'art. 10 du projet adopté par la Commission du droit international en août 2001, A. G., Doc. off., 56ème sess., Supp. n° 10 (A/56/10).

[19] E. Gayim, *The Concept of Minority in International Law: A Critical Study of the Vital Elements* (Rovaniemi: University of Lapland Press, 2001), p. 122; R. Higgins, *Problems & Process*, p. 127; M. N. Shaw, 'Peoples', p. 484; H. Quane, 'The UN and the Evolving Right', p. 571; A. Pellet, 'Quel avenir pour le droit des peuples à disposer d'eux-mêmes?', *in: Mélanges Jiménez de Aréchaga* (Montevideo: Fundacion de Cultura Universitaria, 1994), p. 258; et P. Thornberry, 'Self-Determination, Minorities, Human Rights: A Review of International Instruments', *ICLQ* 38 (1989), not. 887–9; V. en ce sens les observations du Comité du Pacte sur les droits civils et politiques, commentaire de l'article 27, Commentaire général n° 23 (50), CCPR/C/21/Rev.1/Add.5 (1994), p. 1.

[20] Salmon (dir.), *Dictionnaire*, p. 1062.

susceptibles d'entraîner aucune conséquence sur le plan du droit international. Aucune résolution d'une organisation internationale ne semble mentionner le problème, qui reste considéré comme une affaire relevant essentiellement des affaires intérieures des Etats.

Le cas du Kosovo est lui aussi significatif, si on prend la période qui s'étend des premières revendications d'indépendance jusqu'aux débuts de l'année 1998.[21] L'une de ses particularités est sans doute une implication substantielle de plusieurs organisations internationales. Il résulte de la lecture des nombreux documents produits en cette occasion que, si les revendications des Albanophones sont entendues, c'est essentiellement dans le cadre juridique de la Fédération yougoslave.[22] Les revendications sécessionnistes sont quant à elles soit ignorées, soit écartées d'emblée comme irrecevables. Les dirigeants albanais sont ainsi considérés non comme les représentants d'un mouvement sécessionniste ou insurrectionnel mais comme ceux d'individus victimes de pratiques discriminatoires de la part de l'Etat souverain. Lorsque des textes officiels sont adoptés, ils visent dès lors les violations des droits de la personne,[23] ou encore les problèmes que la détérioration de la situation serait susceptible de causer sur le plan du maintien de la paix.[24] Aucun groupe sécessionniste ne se voit en tant que tel reconnaître une personnalité juridique propre. Si l'on peut occasionnellement relever certaines références à la nécessité de rétablir l'autonomie de la Province, on ne peut déduire de ces textes la reconnaissance comme sujet de droit international d'un mouvement sécessionniste quelconque. L'autonomie est perçue comme une solution politiquement souhaitable, pas comme une obligation juridique internationale à laquelle la Yougoslavie serait tenue au bénéfice d'un mouvement albanais. Ce n'est que dans le courant de l'année 1998 que l'Année de libération de Kosovo (UCK) sera désigné comme un titulaire de droits et d'obligations, comme on le verra dans la deuxième partie de cette étude.

Cette réticence des Etats à admettre que des mouvements sécessionnistes émergent comme de nouveaux sujets de droit international est

[21] V. la déclaration d'indépendance du 22 octobre 1991 reproduite dans H. Krieger (ed.), *The Kosovo Conflict and International Law. An Analytical Documentation 1974–1999* (Cambridge: Cambridge University Press, 2001), pp. 12–13.

[22] On se référera aux documents reproduits dans M. Weller (ed.), *The Crisis in Kosovo 1989–1999. From the Dissolution of Yugoslavia to Rambouillet and the Outbreak of Hostilities* (Cambridge: Documents & Analysis Pub. Ltd, 1999), not. p. 89.

[23] V. les résolutions adoptées chaque année par l'Assemblée générale de l'ONU sur ce sujet, *ibid.*, pp. 125–32 (il s'agit notamment des résolutions 47/147 du 18 décembre 1992, 48/153 du 20 décembre 1993, 49/196 du 23 décembre 1994).

[24] V. p. ex. la S/RES/855 adoptée par le Conseil de sécurité le 9 août 1993.

d'autant plus manifeste qu'elle semble bien souvent perdurer alors même qu'il est de moins en moins contestable que la tentative de sécession s'est traduite par l'émergence d'un véritable mouvement insurrectionnel, qui serait cette fois parvenu à contrôler durablement une partie du territoire national.[25] Dans le cas de la Tchétchénie, par exemple, les textes adoptés dès les débuts du soulèvement par les Etats européens ne mentionnent jamais les forces indépendantistes tchétchènes en tant que telles, alors même que celles-ci pouvaient certainement se prévaloir du statut de 'mouvement insurrectionnel'.[26] Ce n'est que rarement que le droit des conflits armés non internationaux est évoqué et, lorsqu'il l'est, c'est sans désigner le mouvement sécessionniste lui-même. Tout au plus ose-t-on évoquer la 'situation en Tchétchénie', une 'crise tchétchène' et plus rarement des 'attaques contre les Tchétchènes' encore que, pendant la majeure partie du conflit, on préfère tout simplement s'abstenir de toute prise de position.

La manière dont a été gérée le conflit en République de Macédoine en 2001 constitue une autre illustration de cette position. Alors même que des forces irrédentistes contrôlaient visiblement une partie du territoire, les résolutions adoptées par le Conseil de sécurité ne mentionnent pas le mouvement insurrectionnel concerné (l'U.C.K.), et préfèrent évoquer les 'extrémistes de souche albanaise', 'ceux qui mènent une action armée contre les autorités de l'Etat' ou, en une occasion 'toutes les parties'.[27] La même rhétorique peut être relevée dans des déclarations de l'OTAN, de l'UE ou du groupe de contact.[28]

On comprend bien au vu de ces précédents récents comment le droit international réagit à une tentative de sécession. Le premier réflexe est indéniablement de dénier tout statut juridique et toute identité politique au mouvement sécessionniste même si, dans certains cas, celui-ci pourrait valablement se prévaloir d'un statut de sujet au regard du droit de la

[25] V. E. David, *Droit des conflits armés*, 2ème édn (Bruxelles: Bruylant, 1999), pp. 105–7.

[26] V. p. ex. Communiqué de la Présidence au nom de l'U. E. sur la Tchétchénie (Bruxelles, 17 janvier 1995), *DAI* 5 (1er mars 1995), p. 160; Déclaration de l'U. E. (Bruxelles, 17 janvier 1995), *DAI* 6 (15 mars 1995), p. 177; Résolution du Parlement européen du 19 janvier 1995, *DAI* 6 (15 mars 1995), pp. 177–8; Déclaration de l'U. E. (Bruxelles, 1er avril 1995), *DAI* 11 (1er juin 1995), p. 318; Déclaration de l'U. E. sur la crise tchétchène du 18 janvier 1996, *DAI* 6 (15 mars 1996), p. 243.

[27] Résolution 1345 du 21 mars 2001; v. aussi la résolution 1371 du 26 septembre 2001.

[28] V. p. ex. Déclaration de l'OTAN/UE, Budapest, 30 mai 2001, *DAI* 14 (15 juillet 2001), p. 535; Déclaration du Groupe de contact, Paris, 11 avril 2001, *DAI* 11 (juin 2001), p. 415; Déclaration de la Présidence de l'U. E. du 6 mars 2001, Press Release, Press: 91-Nr: 6750/01; Déclaration de l'U. E. sur la situation dans l'ARYM, 3 mai 2001, Press Release, Press: 167-Nr: 8439/01.

responsabilité internationale et du droit des conflits armés non internationaux. Ceci peut se traduire soit par l'absence de toute prise de position, soit par l'utilisation de termes tout empreints de retenue diplomatique sur ce point particulier. Ce qui ne signifie pas que le droit international public soit pour autant totalement absent. Il se concentrera simplement sur des rapports juridiques entre les sujets classiques que sont les Etats, les individus et les organisations internationales.

B. La réglementation internationale des rapports juridiques liant l'Etat aux autres sujets de l'ordre juridique international

Les rapports juridiques envisagés seront plus précisément de deux ordres: il s'agit, d'une part, de ceux qui lient l'Etat aux individus sur lesquels il exerce sa juridiction et, d'autre part, de ceux qui lient ce même Etat à d'autres Etats ou organisations internationales qui pourraient être indirectement impliqués dans cette situation.

Le premier cas de figure renvoie au domaine des droits de la personne. L'Etat ne peut sous prétexte de lutte contre la sécession violer les engagements auxquels il a souscrits en ce domaine. Il est vrai que l'existence d'un mouvement sécessionniste peut dans son principe justifier la mise en œuvre de mesures restrictives justifiées par la protection de la sécurité nationale, comme l'a reconnu la Cour européenne des droits de l'homme.[29] Cependant, même si un Etat va jusqu'à utiliser les clauses dérogatoires prévues dans certains instruments conventionnels en cas de danger pour sa sécurité, il devra en tout état de cause respecter certains principes fondamentaux (comme le droit à la vie et à l'intégrité physique, ou l'interdiction de la torture ou des traitements inhumains et dégradants). Les suites des attentats du 11 septembre 2001 semblent renforcer les pouvoirs de répression des Etats, qui se prononcent en faveur de définitions larges du terrorisme en vue de justifier certaines pratiques normalement contraires aux règles protectrices des droits de la personne.[30] Ces définitions pourraient en effet parfaitement être appliquées à des mouvements sécessionnistes, comme le laissent penser

[29] CEDH, Affaire *Parti communiste unifié de Turquie et autres c. Turquie*, arrêt du 30 janvier 1998, (133/1996/752/951), par. 39 à 41. En l'espèce, les mesures adoptées (essentiellement la dissolution du parti) sont condamnées pour leur caractère disproportionné.

[30] Proposition de Décision-cadre du Conseil européen relative à la lutte contre le terrorisme (Bruxelles, 6 décembre 2001); v. doc. 14925/01, *JAI* 165 (7 décembre 2001), cité dans A. Weyembergh, 'L'impact du 11 septembre sur l'équilibrage sécurité/liberté dans l'espace pénal européen', *in:* E. Bribosia et A. Weyembergh (dir.), *Lutte contre le terrorisme et droits fondamentaux* (Bruxelles: Bruylant et Nemesis, 2002), p. 153, n. 1.

les discours tenus par certains Etats et organisations internationales au sujet des mouvements sécessionnistes au Kosovo, en Tchétchénie ou en Macédoine.[31]

En tout état de cause, la relation juridique concernée oppose l'Etat à des individus, et non à un groupe bénéficiant d'une sorte de statut politique et juridique intermédiaire entre l'Etat et le citoyen. Le statut de 'minorité', auquel pourrait éventuellement renvoyer les dirigeants séparatistes, n'est pas de nature à modifier ce schéma: comme on le sait, ce concept intervient non pour conférer un statut nouveau de sujet de droit international, mais comme catégorie pertinente aux fins d'évaluer le respect de droits individuels exercés dans un cadre collectif (droit, par example, à l'enseignement, à l'identité culturelle, à non-discrimination).[32] Par ailleurs, la question reste posée de déterminer à quel titre les mouvements séparatistes peuvent prétendre représenter les minorités concernées.

Les autres rapports juridiques susceptibles d'intervenir dans ces situations de sécession renvoient aux relations entre l'Etat concerné et d'autres Etats ou organisations internationales. Un Etat menacé par une tentative de sécession sera en effet en mesure d'invoquer le principe de non-intervention dans ses affaires intérieures pour s'opposer à toute ingérence exercée à partir de l'extérieur (appui militaire, logistique, économique ou autre).[33] Il se peut cependant qu'un Etat en accuse un autre de violer les droits de la personne, sans pour autant mettre en œuvre à son encontre une mesure de contrainte. On est alors devant le cas non d'une ingérence, mais d'un différend international, qui porte en l'occurrence sur la question du respect des droits de la personne. Le droit international régit alors la situation par le biais de l'obligation de régler pacifiquement les différends, qui trouve alors logiquement à s'appliquer. Théoriquement, tout ceci ne peut par ailleurs remettre en cause le pouvoir du Conseil de sécurité de prendre des mesures, le cas échéant coercitives, si la situation a dégénéré en 'menace contre la paix et la sécurité internationales'.[34] Le cas de figure reste toutefois largement hypothétique puisque, comme on l'a signalé,

[31] La qualification de 'terroriste' est en effet régulièrement employée pour désigner ces mouvements; v. les textes de l'ONU ou d'autres organisations internationales cités ci-dessus (v. aussi not. la S/RES/1160 adoptée par le Conseil de sécurité en mars 1998).

[32] Higgins, *Problems & Process*, pp. 126–7; Gayim, *The Concept of Minority*, p. 122 (cf. note 19).

[33] Pellet, 'Quel avenir pour le droit des peuples . . .?', p. 262.

[34] Christakis, *Le droit à l'autodétermination*, pp. 110–14.

on ne se trouve à ce stade tout au plus qu'en présence de troubles intérieurs.[35]

On constate que, quelle que soit la manière dont on appréhende la question, il ne saurait théoriquement être question de lacune. Le droit international opère une lecture particulière de la situation, en envisageant les droits et obligations respectifs, d'une part, de l'Etat et des individus qui sont sous sa juridiction et, d'autre part, de cet Etat et des autres Etats ou organisations internationales. Le rapport politique entre le groupe sécessionniste et l'Etat dont il cherche à se séparer n'est en revanche pas couvert par le système juridique, non pas en raison d'une quelconque lacune mais, plus simplement, parce que le droit international n'a aucune vocation à le régir, et nie dès lors la qualité même de sujet à l'entité sécessionniste. La légitimité de la sécession est alors une question hors droit; elle renvoie à une réalité sociologique qui est à la base du droit international, et qui est celle de l'Etat. En cas de sécession, celui-ci se prévaut de l'essence même de son pouvoir souverain, ce 'monopole de la violence légitime' qui est en l'occurrence mise en cause, en même temps que sa préservation.[36] La référence à ses affaires intérieures traduit alors un refus non seulement que l'on reconnaisse des droits quelconques au groupe séparatiste, mais aussi que l'on envisage la possibilité de lui reconnaître des droits, ce qui serait le cas s'il bénéficiait d'un statut de sujet.

Bien entendu, la plupart des hypothèses que l'on envisage généralement pour illustrer le mécanisme de la sécession renvoient à des situations de conflits armés, au cours desquelles chaque partie assure son autorité sur une partie du territoire national. Le droit international est alors, conformément aux engagements pris par l'Etat concerné, susceptible de régir les rapports entre les deux autorités politiques concurrentes, ce qu'il fait en premier lieu en rendant applicable l'ensemble du droit des conflits armés non internationaux. Les 'affaires intérieures' ne peuvent plus être valablement invoquées, l'Etat ayant accepté de soumettre le problème à la règle de droit. Cependant, même dans cette situation, la thèse de la lacune est selon nous sujette à caution. En effet, si le mouvement sécessionniste se voit occasionnellement accorder un statut de sujet à capacité limitée, c'est

[35] Ce qui n'empêche pas que, si la situation se détériore au point de pouvoir être qualifiée de conflit armé non international, le Conseil de sécurité puisse exercer plus activement ses responsabilités, comme on le constatera dans la deuxième partie du présent chapitre.

[36] V. les réflexions de M. Kohen, 'The Notion of "State Survival" in International Law', *in:* L. Boisson de Chazournes and Ph. Sands (eds.), *International Law, The International Court of Justice and Nuclear Weapons* (Cambridge: Cambridge University Press, 1999), not. pp. 311–12.

aussitôt pour se voir opposer des règles internationales comme le respect de l'intégrité territoriale ou de la souveraineté de l'Etat. On observe ainsi une tendance à une prohibition de la sécession et à une légalisation de la répression qui se révèle *a priori* incompatible avec l'existence d'une 'lacune'.

II. Les tendances naissantes à une prohibition de la sécession et à une légalisation de la répression: le cas typique des conflits armés non internationaux

Que ce soit dans les cas de la Croatie, à partir du mois de juin 1991, du Kosovo, dans le courant de l'année 1998 ou encore, pour se limiter à l'Europe, de l'Abkhazie dans les années 1990, les revendications séparatistes se sont traduites par la formation d'une armée dissidente qui a rapidement réussi à contrôler une partie du territoire d'un Etat internationalement reconnu. Un 'mouvement insurrectionnel' a alors été reconnu comme tel, de sorte qu'on se trouve à première vue dans un cas de figure différent de celui que nous avons envisagé dans la première partie. Comme nous l'indiquions en commençant, certains ont cru pouvoir déduire de ces précédents une forme d'extension du droit des peuples à disposer d'eux-mêmes en dehors des hypothèses classiques liées à la décolonisation et à ses suites (peuples des territoires non-autonomes, sous occupation étrangère ou sous régime raciste). A notre sens, une analyse attentive de la position juridique des Etats mène toutefois à une conclusion toute différente. Un seul précédent pourrait sans doute prêter à interprétation, et encore de manière limitée: dans le cas du démantèlement de la Yougoslavie en 1991–2, certains Etats européens ont semblé admettre un droit des minorités nationales à l'autodétermination, encore que cette reconnaissance ne puisse être déduite que de textes profondément ambigus.[37] Les autres Etats, en particulier au sein de l'ONU, se sont contentés de reconnaître les Etats issus de la sécession lorsque celle-ci avait réussi sur le terrain,[38] avec l'accord tacite mais certain en provenance de Belgrade, une nouvelle Yougoslavie ayant officiellement été créée avec

[37] V. les textes cités et commentés dans B. Delcourt et O. Corten, 'Les ambiguïtés de la position belge sur le droit à l'autodétermination des peuples en Croatie', *RBDI* XXX/1 (1997), pp. 357–79, et, des mêmes auteurs, *Ex-Yougoslavie. Droit international, politique et idéologies* (Bruxelles: Bruylant, 1998), pp. 22–6.

[38] Les résolutions adoptées de septembre 1991 à avril 1992 ne comprennent aucune reconnaissance des nouveaux Etats, ni *a fortiori* d'un quelconque droit à l'autodétermination (v. les résolutions 713 du 25 septembre 1991, 721 du 27 novembre 1991, 724 du 15 décembre 1991, 727 du 8 janvier 1992, 740 du 7 février 1992, 743 du 21 février 1992). La

pour seuls membres la Serbie et le Monténégro.[39] Il est donc bien délicat de considérer sur la seule base du précédent yougoslave qu'une extension du droit des peuples à disposer d'eux-mêmes ait été consacrée.[40] En tout état de cause, des précédents plus récents ont confirmé de manière particulièrement éclatante la profonde réticence des Etats à étendre le droit des peuples à disposer d'eux-mêmes à des groupes minoritaires, et ce même lorsque, selon ces mêmes Etats, les groupes concernés subissaient une répression particulièrement meurtrière. On a d'ailleurs déjà signalé que, dans le cas de la Tchétchénie, même le statut de sujet de l'ordre juridique international semblait avoir été dénié au mouvement indépendantiste, la reconnaissance d'un quelconque droit (et *a fortiori* celui de créer un nouvel Etat) n'ayant même pas été envisagée.[41] D'autres cas peuvent encore être cités en ce sens, comme le refus de reconnaître un droit à l'indépendance au profit de l'Abkhazie, l'Ossétie du sud,[42] la Transdniestrie,[43] ou le Haut-Karabach.[44] Quant au cas du Kosovo, il suffirait à lui seul à conclure en ce sens. Alors même qu'une intervention militaire a été menée officiellement en vue de faire cesser ce qui a été

Bosnie-Herzégovine est, pour la première fois, nommément mentionnée le 7 avril 1992 (S/RES/749, par. 6), alors que ce n'est que le 15 mai 1992 que le Conseil se réfère à l'‘ancienne république fédérative socialiste de Yougoslavie’ (S/RES/752, 3e cons.). Dans le même sens, on se rappellera que la résolution 713 a été adoptée à la suite d'une demande expresse des autorités yougoslaves, ce qui rend difficile une interprétation de cette résolution en termes de soutien aux sécessionnistes. On consultera à cet égard les discussions qui ont précédé cette résolution; Doc. ONU, S/PV.3009.

[39] En ce sens, Crawford, ‘State Practice’, p. 102.

[40] Ch. Tomuschat, ‘Self-Determination in a Post-Colonial World’, *in:* Ch. Tomuschat (ed.), *Modern Law of Self-Determination*, p. 19, ainsi que sa contribution au présent volume (*supra*, chap. I).

[41] V. les références citées dans Crawford, ‘State Practice, pp. 110–11, ainsi que dans Delcourt et Corten, ‘Les ambiguïtés de la position belge’, 368, note 62.

[42] V. les résolutions du Conseil de sécurité se prononçant en faveur de l'intégrité territoriale de la Géorgie (S/RES/876 (1993), 896 (1994), 906 (1994), 937 (1994), 977 (1995), 993 (1995), 1036 (1996) et 1077 (1996)). V. aussi la Déclaration de Rome du 1er décembre 1993, Fourth Meeting of the CSCE Council et les autres déclarations citées et commentées par O. Paye et E. Remacle, ‘UN and CSCE Policies in Transcaucasia’, *in:* B. Coppieters (ed.), *Contested Borders in the Caucasus* (Brussels: Vubpress, 1996), pp. 103–36. V. encore la Déclaration de Lisbonne de l'O.S.C.E. de 1996, par. 20, ou encore le Résumé du Président de l'O.S.C.E. sur le 6ème sommet ministériel de l'O.S.C.E. (Copenhague, 19 décembre 1997), *DAI* 4 (15 février 1998), p. 134.

[43] V. la position belge en faveur de l'unité de la Moldavie dans *RBDI* XXVIII/2 (1995), p. 641, n° 2330, et, par exemple, la Déclaration de Lisbonne de 1996 précitée, par. 21.

[44] V. les résolutions du Conseil de sécurité se prononçant en faveur de l'intégrité territoriale de l'Azebaïdjan (S/RES/822 (1993), 853 (1993), 874 (1994) et 884 (1993)); v. les déclarations citées et commentées par Paye et Remacle, ‘The Role of the UN and the CSCE’.

qualifié de politique criminelle et discriminatoire,[45] aucun Etat (en particulier en Europe) n'a accepté de reconnaître un droit à l'indépendance en faveur des autorités indépendantistes albanophones.[46] Bien au contraire, les Etats du Groupe de Contact ont explicitement affirmé qu'ils étaient 'fermement opposés à l'indépendance du Kosovo'.[47] C'est ce refus tranché de toute légitimité à la création d'un nouvel Etat qui a motivé une construction juridique et institutionnelle complexe assurant officiellement le maintien du Kosovo à l'intérieur de l'Etat yougoslave: visiblement, on préfère s'en tenir à ce type de fiction juridique plutôt que d'ouvrir la voie à une remise en cause de l'intégrité territoriale des Etats existants.[48]

Par ailleurs, il va de soi qu'un mouvement sécessionniste ne pourrait invoquer un quelconque principe de liberté en prétendant que, tout ce qui n'est pas interdit étant permis, la sécession serait implicitement autorisée par le droit international.[49]

Il est sans doute vrai que, à notre sens en tout cas, on peut considérer que ce principe découle directement de celui de la souveraineté des Etats: un Etat, n'étant lié que par ses engagements internationaux, reste par définition libre d'agir lorsque de tels engagements n'existent pas. Ce principe de liberté a certes été critiqué, y compris dans une jurisprudence récente.[50] Encore faut-il relever que, dans son avis sur la *Licéité*

[45] V. les déclarations exposées et commentées par L. Weerts, 'Le discours justificatif des institutions européennes et internationales', *in:* O. Corten et B. Delcourt (eds.), *Droit, légitimation et politique extérieure: la Belgique, l'Europe et la guerre du Kosovo* (Bruxelles: Bruylant et ed., U.L.B., 2001), pp. 85–121.

[46] V. les nombreuses prises de position des Etats reproduites dans les recueils de documents édités par M. Weller, *The Crisis in Kosovo*, et H. Krieger, *The Kosovo Conflict*.

[47] Déclaration du 29 avril 1998, *DAI* 13 (1er juillet 1998), p. 494; v. aussi la Déclaration du Groupe de Contact sur le Kosovo du 8 janvier 1998, *DAI* 6 (15 mars 1998), p. 206; la Déclaration de l'U. E. du 9 avril 1996, *BYBIL* LXVII (1996), p. 708, et *RGDIP* 100/3 (1996), p. 864; et la Décision n° 218 du Conseil permanent de l'O.S.C.E. du 11 mars 1998 (PC.DEC/218, 156ème séance plénière); v. aussi la lettre franco-allemande du 1er janvier 1998 adressée à la R.F.Y., *DAI* 1(1er janvier 1998), p. 36, et la lettre de la Grande-Bretagne à la R.F.Y. du 7 mai 1996, *BYIL* 67 (1996), p. 707.

[48] V. en particulier l'accord annexé à la résolution 1244 du 10 juin 1999, ainsi que le 10e cons. de cette résolution.

[49] Notre propos n'est pas de nous prononcer de manière détaillée sur ce point particulier dans le cadre du présent chapitre; v. H. Lauterpacht, 'Some Observations on the Prohibition of "Non Liquet" and the Completeness of the Law', *in: Symbolae Verzijl* (The Hague: Nijhoff, 1958), pp. 196–221; J. Stone, '*Non liquet* and the Function of Law in the International Community', *BYIL* 35 (1959), pp. 124–61.

[50] V. J. Salmon, 'Le problème des lacunes à la lumière de l'avis "Licéité de la menace ou de l'emploi d'armes nucléaires" rendu le 8 juillet 1996 par la Cour internationale de Justice', *in: Mélanges Valticos* (Paris: Pedone, 1999), pp. 197–214.

de la menace ou de l'emploi de l'arme nucléaire la Cour n'écarte pas formellement ce principe. Elle affirme simplement qu'elle n'est pas en mesure de donner une réponse à l'un des aspects de la question qui lui a été posée.[51] Mais elle ne prétend pas explicitement que cette réponse n'existe pas.[52] A supposer que l'on puisse y déceler un précédent de *non liquet*,[53] il n'est pas évident que le refus de trancher soit fondé sur l'existence d'une lacune.[54] L'ambiguïté de l'avis s'explique évidemment par le désaccord qui a visiblement opposé les juges sur ce point, les uns considérant que ce principe de liberté n'était plus applicable au droit international contemporain, les autres affirmant expressément le contraire.[55]

Quoiqu'il en soit, il ne nous semble pas que ce principe de liberté, à supposer qu'on admette son existence, puisse être revendiqué avec succès par une entité sécessionniste. En effet, et comme on vient de le rappeler, ce principe est logiquement lié à celui de la souveraineté, et donc au concept même d'Etat. On ne saurait donc l'appliquer qu'aux Etats souverains, et non à des sujets à capacité limitée, quels qu'ils soient.[56]

Enfin, et en tout état de cause, le recours au principe de liberté suppose que l'on ait d'abord pu démontrer que le droit international n'interdisait nullement le phénomène sécessionniste, ce qui nous semble loin d'aller de soi. Comme on le détaillera dans les lignes qui suivent, il semble en effet que certaines tendances récentes du droit international puissent être dégagées dans le sens à la fois d'une condamnation de la sécession et d'une autorisation de sa répression. On est ici en présence de deux questions qui sont logiquement liées puisque, dans l'hypothèse d'une neutralité

[51] Selon le texte du dispositif de l'avis, 'au vu de l'état actuel du droit international, ainsi que des éléments de fait dont elle dispose, la Cour ne peut cependant conclure de manière définitive que la menace ou l'emploi d'armes nucléaires serait licite ou illicite dans une circonstance extrême de légitime défense dans laquelle la survie même d'un Etat serait en cause' (*CIJ*, *Recueil 1996*, p. 266, par. 105, point 2).

[52] D. Bodansky, '*Non Liquet* and the Incompleteness of International Law', *in:* L. Boisson de Chazournes and Ph. Sands (eds.), *International Law, The International Court of Justice*, p. 153.

[53] M. Koskiennemi, 'The Silence of Law / The Voice of Justice', *in: ibid.*, p. 489; M. G. Kohen, 'L'avis consultatif de la CIJ sur la *Licéité*', pp. 346–9.

[54] 'Non liquet' *in:* J. Salmon (dir.), *Dictionnaire*, p. 747. Le *non liquet* renvoie seulement à l'impossibilité pour le juge de trancher au fond, cette impossibilité pouvant elle-même s'expliquer par plusieurs facteurs, l'existence d'une lacune ne constituant que l'un d'entre eux.

[55] Comp. p. ex. les positions des juges Bedjaoui (CIJ, *Recueil 1996*, pp. 270–1), Guillaume (*ibid.*, p. 290), et Higgins (*ibid.*, p. 589).

[56] Christakis, *Le droit à l'autodétermination*, p. 81.

juridique, il va de soi que le droit international devrait dans les deux cas rester lacunaire. En d'autres termes, et toujours dans l'hypothèse où l'on envisage un rapport juridique entre l'Etat et le groupe sécessionniste, le droit du premier à combattre le second semblerait indiquer que celui-ci aurait violé une obligation à charge de celui-là ou, au moins, aurait adopté un comportement condamnable.

A. Une tendance naissante à la prohibition de la sécession?

Si l'on repart de la logique même de l'ordre juridique international, aucun argument décisif n'est susceptible de trancher la question qui nous intéresse à ce stade. Par hypothèse, on est dans une situation où l'on a reconnu à une entité sécessionniste un statut de sujet, et ce dans la mesure où l'on est en présence d'un conflit armé non international. En même temps, nous venons de voir qu'aucun statut territorial séparé n'avait été reconnu à cette entité. Deux réponses peuvent alors être apportées à notre question.

- Il peut alors être logique de considérer que l'entité sécessionniste doit être soumis au respect de la souveraineté et de l'intégrité territoriale de l'Etat au sein duquel il se situe, ce qui semble bien impliquer l'illicéité d'une tentative de modifier ses frontières par la force. Pourrait-on en effet concevoir qu'un sujet de droit international échappe à l'obligation de respecter la souveraineté des Etats? Ce serait alors contredire la vocation même du concept de souveraineté, qui semble de pouvoir être opposé à tout sujet de l'ordre juridique, national comme international. On ne pourrait ainsi concevoir qu'un groupe séparatiste soit exonéré d'une obligation de respecter la souveraineté de l'Etat alors que d'autres sujets, qu'ils aient une capacité juridique limitée (comme les organisations internationales) ou pleine et entière (comme les autres Etats) y seraient quant à eux tenus.[57]
- Cette logique peut toutefois être écartée au profit d'une autre, qui insisterait sur les spécificités des règles du droit des conflits armés, qui ne conféreraient au groupe sécessionniste qu'une capacité limitée, ce groupe n'étant titulaire de droit et d'obligations *que* dans le cadre du droit des conflits armés. Cette deuxième option implique de considérer

[57] V. R. Monaco, 'Observations sur le droit des peuples dans la communauté internationale', *in: Mélanges Jiménez de Aréchaga*, pp. 221–2, et, semble-t-il, A. N'Kolombua, 'L'ambivalence des relations entre le droit des peuples à disposer d'eux-mêmes et l'intégrité territoriale des Etats en droit international contemporain', *in: Mélanges Charles Chaumont*, p. 461.

que la souveraineté de l'Etat n'a pas pour vocation de s'appliquer à tout sujet de l'ordre juridique international. A l'instar des individus, les mouvements sécessionnistes ne seraient pas en tant que tels visés par l'obligation de respecter la souveraineté et l'intégrité territoriale des Etats.

Il est bien délicat de départager ces deux options sans entrer dans des débats de type philosophique sur les fondements mêmes du droit international. Un examen de la pratique récente qui s'est développée à la suite de plusieurs tentatives de sécessions apporte cependant des arguments à ceux qui considèrent que la souveraineté – ainsi que l'intégrité territoriale – sont des concepts qui sont interprétés de manière très large, y compris dans les situations de sécession.

C'est en ce sens que l'on peut lire les nombreux textes officiels qui insistent très généralement sur la nécessité de concilier les grands principes sur les relations amicales avec le respect de l'intégrité territoriale et de l'unité politique d'un Etat souverain.[58] On connaît en particulier le paragraphe de la résolution sur les relations amicales qui, précisant la portée du droit des peuples à disposer d'eux-mêmes, précise que 'rien dans les paragraphes précédents ne sera interprété comme autorisant une action, quelle qu'elle soit, qui démembrerait ou menacerait, totalement ou partiellement, l'intégrité politique de tout Etat souverain et indépendant'.[59] Ce type de clause vise les tentatives de sécession, condamne en premier lieu les interventions étrangères qui seraient susceptibles de les appuyer. Il va de soi qu'un Etat étranger qui soutiendrait un groupe séparatiste violerait à la fois la souveraineté et l'intégrité territoriale de l'Etat menacé, mais aussi le droit de son peuple (compris ici comme la population dans son ensemble, et non une partie de celle-ci) à disposer librement de lui-même. Mais, comme Théodore Christakis l'a démontré après avoir consulté les débats ayant précédé l'adoption des textes pertinents en même temps que leur reproduction dans le cadre de plusieurs précédents, le

58 Le passage qui suit de la résolution 2625 (XXV) se retrouve notamment en 1993 dans le Programme d'action de Vienne et en 1995 dans la Déclaration des Chefs d'Etats faite à l'occasion du cinquantième anniversaire de l'ONU; v. les commentaires de Christakis, *Le droit à l'autodétermination*, p. 295.

59 Suit une formule qui a été utilisée pour affirmer l'existence d'un droit à la sécession en cas de violation du droit des peuples à disposer d'eux-mêmes envisagé dans son aspect interne, à tort selon nous; O. Corten, 'A propos d'un désormais classique: *Le droit à l'autodétermination en dehors des situations de décolonisation*, de Théodore Christakis', *RBDI* XXXI (1999), pp. 340–7; v. aussi H. Quane, 'The UN and the Evolving Right', p. 563; M. N. Shaw, 'Peoples', pp. 482–83, et M. G. Kohen, 'L'emploi de la force et la crise du Kosovo: vers un nouveau désordre juridique international', *RBDI* XXXII (1999), pp. 127–8.

respect de l'intégrité territoriale constitue un principe juridique qui est *aussi* opposé au mouvement sécessionniste lui-même.[60] Il est vrai que, dans leur sens littéral, les termes des déclarations concernées signalent seulement qu'aucun principe ne peut être utilisé pour remettre en cause l'intégrité territoriale, sans aller jusqu'à affirmer explicitement que cette remise en cause est interdite. Ainsi, on s'adresse (quoiqu'implicitement, puisqu'ils ne sont même pas nommés) aux mouvements sécessionnistes, pour les avertir que, s'ils décident de faire sécession, ils ne pourront pas se prévaloir du droit international.[61] En ce sens, les textes confirment qu'il n'existe aucun droit à la sécession, sans explicitement aller jusqu'à une interdiction formelle de celle-ci, mais tout en paraissant implicitement impliquer une interdiction.

C'est en tout cas en ce sens que l'on peut appréhender les précédents, non seulement anciens[62] mais surtout récents, où le Conseil de sécurité de même que certaines organisations régionales ont fermement condamné la remise en cause de l'intégrité territoriale de certains Etats existants, qu'il s'agisse de la Bosnie-Herzégovine, de la Géorgie, de la République Fédérale de la Yugoslavia (R.F.Y.) ou encore de l'Azerbaïdjan.[63] Pour revenir sur le précédent décisif du Kosovo, les résolutions pertinentes du Conseil de sécurité insistent toutes sur la nécessité de respecter la souveraineté et l'intégrité territoriale de la Yougoslavie, l'accession éventuelle à l'indépendance de la province serbe ne semblant possible que par le biais d'une acceptation des autorités de Belgrade qui se prononceraient au nom du peuple yougoslave dans son ensemble.[64] C'est encore dans le même sens qu'on peut comprendre que le préambule de la Convention-cadre du Conseil de l'Europe sur la protection des minorités insiste nommément sur le respect 'de l'intégrité territoriale et de la souveraineté nationale'.[65] Enfin, on se référera à la déclaration émise le 12 mars 2001 par le Président du Conseil de sécurité alors que des forces irrédentistes albanophones

[60] Christakis, *Le droit à l'autodétermination*, pp. 190–3.

[61] *Ibid.*, pp. 192–3; Th.D. Musgrave, *Self-Determination and National Minorities* (Oxford: Clarendon Press, 1997), pp. 181–3.

[62] On pourrait remonter au Katanga et au Biafra (v. les documents reproduits dans J. Salmon, *La reconnaissance d'Etat (Mandchoukouo, Katanga, Biafra, Rhodésie du sud)* (Paris: Armand Colin, 1971), not. pp. 126 et 180, mais on se concentre ici sur les évolutions récentes.

[63] V. les références citées *supra* (notes 42, 44 et 46).

[64] Outre les résolutions 1160 (1998), 1199 (1998) et 1203 (1998), on se reportera à la résolution 1244 (1999).

[65] Convention du 1er février 1995. Le rapport explicatif précise explicitement que la Convention ne peut être interprétée comme conférant des droits collectifs aux minorités (texte dans *RUDH* (1995), pp. 174–81, ainsi que sur http://www.coe.int).

menaçaient les autorités officielles, par laquelle 'le Conseil rappelle qu'il est impératif de respecter la souveraineté et l'intégrité territoriale de l'ex-République de Macédoine', pour affirmer ensuite que, 'à cet égard', l'accord de démarcation de frontières de Skopje du 23 février 2001 'doit être respecté par tous'.[66]

L'ensemble de ces éléments, et en particulier la pratique récente, y compris du Conseil de sécurité, nous permet de poser l'hypothèse que le droit international connaît une tendance naissante à condamner, voire à interdire, les mouvements sécessionnistes. Il est vrai que cette tendance n'est pas systématique, et ne se traduit pas par des textes ou de précédents limpides, en tout cas à l'échelle universelle.[67] Les mouvements sécessionnistes sont rarement désignés comme tels, et l'on préfère le plus souvent leur dénier la possibilité d'invoquer des droits plutôt que de confirmer leur statut de sujet en leur opposant des obligations juridiques. On pourrait donc théoriquement maintenir que la sécession, sans être permise, n'est pas formellement interdite. Evoquer dans cette perspective une 'neutralité juridique' nous semblerait exagéré. D'abord parce qu'il est incontestable que le droit international ne met pas les deux parties au conflit sécessionniste sur le même pied, puisqu'il insiste constamment sur le respect de la souveraineté et l'intégrité territoriale des Etats.[68] Ensuite parce que, comme on s'en rendra compte dans les lignes qui suivent, ces Etats semblent se voir reconnaître un droit à rétablir l'ordre sur leur territoire lorsqu'ils sont victimes d'une tentative de sécession. Dans cette perspective, la thèse de la lacune est sans doute de plus en plus difficile à soutenir.

B. Une tendance naissante à la légalisation des tentatives de l'Etat de rétablir son autorité?

Tous les textes et les précédents qui ont été cités ci-dessus peuvent aussi être interprétés dans le sens d'une reconnaissance à chaque Etat d'un droit à rétablir l'ordre sur son territoire. On sait que le deuxième Protocole de Genève évoque expressément la 'responsabilité du gouvernement de maintenir ou de rétablir l'ordre public dans l'Etat ou de défendre l'unité

[66] S/PRST/2001/7.

[67] Théodore Christakis cite un mémorandum de la C.E.I. du 10 février 1995 dans lequel les Etats s'engagent à une répression conjointe des mouvements sécessionnistes ou irrédentistes (*Le droit à l'autodétermination*, p. 234).

[68] Crawford, 'State Practice', pp. 86–7.

nationale et l'intégrité territoriale de l'Etat par tous les moyens légitimes',[69] alors que l'article 8(3) du Statut de la Cour pénale internationale précise qu'il n'affecte pas la 'responsabilité d'un gouvernement de maintenir ou rétablir l'ordre public dans l'Etat ou de défendre l'unité et l'intégrité territoriale de l'Etat par tous les moyens légitimes'. Ce principe se trouve assez clairement admis au sein de certains instruments élaborés au sein de la Conference on Security and Cooperation in Europe/Organization for Security and Co-operation in Europe (C.S.C./O.S.C.) qui en fixent d'ailleurs certaines limites. Ainsi, dans le document de Copenhague du 29 juin 1990, on peut lire que les Etats

> reconnaissent la responsabilité qui leur incombe de défendre et de protéger, conformément à leurs lois, à leurs obligations internationales en matière de droits de l'homme et à leurs engagements internationaux, l'ordre démocratique librement établi par la volonté du peuple *contre les activités des personnes, groupements ou organisations qui prennent part ou qui refusent de renoncer à des actes de terrorisme ou de violence visant à renverser cet ordre ou celui d'un autre Etat participant.*[70]

Ce texte ne vise pas explicitement la sécession, mais il s'y applique bel et bien, dans la mesure où le phénomène sécessionniste consiste par définition à remettre en cause l'ordre établi par la voie de la violence.[71] On citera dès lors également en ce sens le Code de conduite relatif aux aspects politico-militaires de la sécurité, annexé au document de Budapest du 6 décembre 1994, qui ouvre explicitement la voie au 'recours à la force' pour le réglementer.[72] L'obligation de respecter mais aussi de faire respecter les droits de l'homme impose une véritable obligation positive aux Etats de faire tout ce qui est en leur pouvoir pour éviter les situations de désordre et d'anarchie qui caractérisent le plus souvent les guerres de sécession.[73] C'est encore en ce sens que l'on citera la déclaration du Président du Conseil de sécurité du 12 mars 2001, en vertu de laquelle

[69] Article 3, par. 1.

[70] Document de la Réunion de Copenhague de la Conférence sur la dimension humaine de la CSCE, 29 juin 1990, point 6 (texte sur http://www.osce.org/docs/english/1990–1999/hd/cope90e.htm).

[71] V. la définition de la sécession retenue dans le cadre du présent chapitre, énoncée au début de son introduction.

[72] V. not. le par. 36.

[73] C'est en ce sens que le Secrétaire général de l'ONU a pu considérer que 'Les autorités de la RFY ont le droit inhérent, de même que le devoir, de maintenir l'ordre et la sécurité et de réagir face à des actes violents de provocation. Toutefois, ceci ne saurait en aucune façon justifier la terreur systématique infligée aux civils . . .' (Rapport SG ONU du 3 oct. 1998, par. 29, reproduit dans *DAI* 23 (1er décembre 1998), p. 887).

> Le Conseil souligne que le Gouvernement de l'ex-République yougoslave de Macédoine a la responsabilité de faire respecter la primauté du droit sur son territoire. Il approuve les mesures prises par ce gouvernement pour réprimer la violence tout en exerçant la retenue nécessaire.[74]

Quelle que soit la manière dont on procède pour l'établir, il est vrai que, dans son acception traditionnelle en tout cas, ce droit au maintien de l'ordre est conçu comme devant régir les relations entre l'Etats et les personnes, les mouvements séparatistes n'étant une fois encore que rarement désignés comme tels. Les incertitudes du droit international actuel subsistent donc, et on doit alors se pencher sur la pratique récente pour en préciser les contours.

Comment dans ce contexte interpréter certains extraits de résolutions du Conseil de sécurité[75] qui, dans des situations de sécession, renvoient au caractère 'inacceptable' de l'acquisition de territoires par la force? Selon certains, on devrait y voir le signe d'une extension de l'interdiction du recours à la force à l'intérieur des Etats, et non plus seulement 'dans les relations internationales', selon le texte de l'article 2, paragraph 4 de la Charte.[76] L'interdiction d'utiliser des moyens militaires serait alors également prohibée à l'intérieur de chaque territoire national. L'Etat ne pourrait donc pas empêcher par la force le mouvement sécessionniste de maintenir son autorité territoriale récemment acquise, tout comme le mouvement ne pourrait obtenir par la force une autorité sur une partie du territoire national, ni *a fortiori* accroître le territoire qu'il serait parvenu à contrôler. Dans cette perspective, la 'neutralité juridique' semblerait réapparaître, les deux parties au conflit interne étant apparemment logés à la même enseigne. Le raisonnement ne nous semble cependant guère convaincant, et ce pour deux raisons principales. *En premier lieu*, les textes cités peuvent difficilement être interprétés comme reflétant une volonté des Etats de modifier des règles juridiques existantes.[77] Il s'agit le plus souvent de considérants placés dans les préambules des résolutions, qui ne sont pas rédigés en des termes susceptibles de témoigner d'une *opinio juris* naissante. Le principe qu'ils proclament (le caractère 'inacceptable', et non pas 'illicite', d'acquisitions de territoires dans le cadre de conflits armés non internationaux) doit être mis en relation avec l'objectif

[74] S/PRST/2001/7.

[75] V. not. la résolution 713 (1991), précitée.

[76] V. le rapport rédigé par A. Pellet cité dans Christakis, *Le droit à l'autodétermination*, p. 253.

[77] Christakis, *ibid.*, p. 254, et, du même auteur, *L'ONU*, VII *le chapitre et la crise yougoslave* (Paris: Montchrestien, 1996), pp. 32–4.

du maintien de la paix et de la sécurité internationales, qui peut impliquer une action du Conseil tendant à geler la situation intérieure, le cas échéant par la proclamation d'un cessez-le-feu.[78] Le maintien ou le rétablissement de la paix peut cependant tout aussi bien dicter la consécration de conquêtes territoriales opérées dans le cadre de ces conflits, comme l'ont montré les résolutions du Conseil de sécurité donnant une suite aux plans de paix consacrant le partage territorial interne à la Bosnie-Herzégovine.[79] *En deuxième lieu*, les formules utilisées pourraient au contraire être interprétées comme interdisant la réalisation d'une sécession unilatérale, celle-ci consistant bien à réaliser des gains territoriaux par la force. Dans la même perspective, à supposer même que l'on soit en présence d'une extension de l'interdiction du recours à la force à l'intérieur des Etats (ce qui, répétons-le, ne nous semble nullement être le cas), la sécession renvoie par définition (dans la mesure où elle se traduit par l'utilisation de la force pour assurer son autorité sur le territoire qu'il revendique) à une violation de cette interdiction, ce qui ouvre la voie à une sorte de légitime défense de la part de l'Etat 'agressé'. Les deux parties ne sont donc nullement sur le même pied ou, pour l'écrire autrement, il n'existe pas de 'neutralité juridique' ni *a fortiori* de lacune.

Il est vrai que, dans des cas comme ceux du Kosovo ou de la Tchétchénie, les actions militaires menées par les autorités des Etats yougoslave et russe ont occasionnellement été critiquées.[80] Il faut toutefois relever que c'est l'usage 'excessif' ou 'disproportionné' de la force qui a été remis en cause, et non l'usage dans son principe. Il semble bien que ce soit la violation des règles relatives à la protection des droits de la personne, y compris en situation de conflit armé, qui a été dénoncée. Il va de soi que, comme on l'a déjà indiqué, le droit souverain d'un Etat d'utiliser ses troupes pour faire face à une tentative de sécession ne porte en rien atteinte aux obligations qui lui imposent de ne pas s'attaquer aux civils. Et c'est bien en ce sens que les autorités yougoslaves et russes ont été critiquées.

Enfin, on relèvera que, en pratique, ce droit souverain ne saurait faire de doute lorsqu'il s'exerce à l'encontre non seulement de groupes séparatistes qui ont bénéficié du statut de sujet en application du droit applicable aux conflits armés non internationaux, mais d'autres Etats qui leur ont donné leur appui. Ce cas de figure est de loin le plus fréquent, et on pourrait

[78] Christakis, *Le droit à l'autodétermination*, p. 253.

[79] V. les textes cités et commentés dans Delcourt et Corten, *Ex-Yougoslavie*, pp. 26–9.

[80] V. la position des Etats de l'U. E. exposée ci-dessus.

même considérer qu'il est le seul envisageable. Il nous serait en tout cas bien difficile de pouvoir citer un seul précédent dans lequel une entité sécessionniste a réussi à contrôler durablement une partie de territoire sans aucune forme d'appui extérieur.

Il est vrai que, à l'inverse, l'Etat central fait lui aussi appel à la coopération de ses alliés en pareille situation. Mais, précisément, et c'est là un autre signe du rejet de la thèse de la neutralité, une aide en faveur de l'Etat semble bien plus largement admise qu'un quelconque appui à des formes d'opposition, comme le laisse entendre tant la jurisprudence internationale[81] que certains précédents récents comme le Libéria ou la Sierra Léone, où le Conseil de sécurité a appuyé des interventions extérieures officiellement destinées à rétablir l'autorité de gouvernements menacés de l'intérieur. Ces deux derniers cas ne sont pas assimilables à des tentatives de sécession, mais le principe reste identique. Pour s'en convaincre, on peut dans le même sens citer le cas des combats qui ont eu lieu en République de Macédoine dans le courant de l'année 2001. Les Etats tiers, y compris au sein du Conseil de sécurité de l'ONU, semblent là aussi avoir défendu une position tendant à s'opposer à toute velléité sécessionniste et à soutenir résolument l'intégrité territoriale de l'Etat existant, tout en insistant pour que celui-ci respecte les droits de personnes relevant de sa juridiction (en particulier ceux qui s'exercent dans un cadre collectif).[82]

Ces derniers éléments sont certainement décisifs pour notre propos. S'il peut paraître difficile de démontrer que la sécession soit interdite de manière directe et explicite, la reconnaissance d'un droit aux autorités étatiques d'assurer le respect de sa souveraineté territoriale semble plus clairement pouvoir être établie.

III. Conclusion

Finalement, il semble que la pratique récente relative aux situations de sécession se caractérise par une certaine incohérence si l'on veut la confronter à la problématique de la lacune ou de la neutralité juridique.

[81] V. la formule ambiguë de la Cour internationale de Justice, selon laquelle on voit mal ce qui resterait du principe de non-intervention si l'intervention, 'qui *peut déjà être justifiée* par la demande d'un gouvernement, devait aussi être admise à la demande de l'opposition de celui-ci' (c'est nous qui soulignons; C.I.J., *Activités militaires et paramilitaires au Nicaragua et contre celui-ci, Recueil 1986*, par. 246, p. 126).

[82] V. les références reproduites ci-dessus.

Théoriquement, on pourrait se trouver face à l'alternative suivante:

- soit le mouvement sécessionniste n'est pas reconnu comme un sujet (même à capacité limitée) de droit international, et il ne saurait être question de lacune,
- soit ce mouvement est reconnu comme sujet, et la démonstration de l'existence d'une lacune suppose que le système juridique international s'abstienne de réglementer la question.

En pratique, des précédents comme ceux de la Tchétchénie ou du Kosovo montrent que l'on passe souvent d'une branche de l'alternative à l'autre sans logique apparente. Pour une même situation, tantôt on refuse de reconnaître le mouvement sécessionniste comme sujet, tantôt on le reconnaît comme tel, mais il semble que le droit international ait tendance à interdire la sécession ou à légaliser sa répression. Dans ce dernier cas, il reste cependant difficile de montrer que l'interdiction s'adresse *nommément* aux mouvements sécessionnistes comme tels, même si tel semble être implicitement le cas.

Quelle conclusion tirer de cette pratique quelque peu disparate? D'abord que, à l'évidence, les Etats semblent partagés entre deux tendances. La première reste marquée par le refus d'étendre (autrement que *via* l'application des règles protectrices des droits de la personne) la réglementation à une hypothèse qui renvoie *a priori* par excellence à ce qui reste de leur souveraineté, et ce alors même qu'un conflit armé a éclaté. Une seconde tendance consiste à opposer aux groupes sécessionnistes et à leurs soutiens extérieurs la nécessité de respecter l'intégrité territoriale de l'Etat menacé et, parallèlement, à légaliser, dans son principe, la réaction militaire de ce dernier. Par rapport au débat sur l'existence d'une 'lacune', il reste en tout cas largement ouvert même si, à notre sens, il devient de plus en plus formaliste de nier que le droit international connaisse une tendance à réglementer cette question. Dans ce contexte, l'expression de 'neutralité juridique' nous semble en tout cas fondamentalement inappropriée, le droit international favorisant visiblement l'Etat dans ses relations avec les mouvements sécessionnistes qui le menacent.

PART II

International and Domestic Practice

9

The question of secession in Africa

FATSAH OUGUERGOUZ AND

DJACOBA LIVA TEHINDRAZANARIVELO[*]

This chapter analyses the current state of the African legal order on the right of peoples to secession. It points out first the huge complexity of this question for African States which, given the arbitrary partition of Africa by colonial powers, are composed of numerous ethnic groups, and in which individuals belonging to a same ethnic group have different nationalities, generally those of neighbouring States. This particular situation has led the Organization of African Unity, and its successor the African Union, not to recognise, as a matter of principle, a right to secession to any African people. This aversion to secession seems to have been reinforced by the new right of the African Union to intervene within a member State to restore peace and stability in the case of a serious threat to the legitimate order of that State.

However, the potentialities offered by the African Charter on Peoples and Human Rights for a right to secession, as a last resort, can not be ignored. On the basis of the right of people to self-determination, the contemporary African legal order has been promoting the respect of internal self-determination, which could be seen as an alternative to secession. This promotion operates through the respect of democratic principles and good governance, and election monitoring and observing, culminating in the rejection and condemnation of unconstitutional changes of government. It is argued that the failure to respect this internal right to self-determination can legally justify secession which appears to be the sole means for peoples to enjoy their right to self-determination.

LA PROBLÉMATIQUE DE LA SÉCESSION EN AFRIQUE

Introduction

Les études de droit international ou de science politique qui abordent la question de l'Etat en Afrique échappent rarement à l'évocation du caractère arbitraire et artificiel des frontières dessinées sur ce continent. Les frontières africaines sont *arbitraires* car leur tracé géométrique[1] évoque le rôle ingrat d'échiquier jadis imposé au continent par les puissances coloniales; elles sont *artificielles* car elles respectent rarement la distribution géographique réelle de certains groupes sociaux, et brisent l'unité 'naturelle' de l'ethnie.[2] L'Etat africain est ainsi une construction fragile, creuset juridique de plusieurs entités sociologiques animées de puissants mouvements centrifuges.[3] L'Afrique est le théâtre de très nombreux conflits dont les racines sont à chercher dans la crise de l'Etat-nation;[4] la

[1] K. M. Barbour notait à ce propos que les proportions des différents types de frontières étaient approximativement les suivants: lignes astronomiques, 44 pour cent; lignes mathématiques, 30 pour cent; frontières naturelles, 26 pour cent, 'A Geographical Analysis of Boundaries in Inter-Tropical Africa', *in:* K. M. Barbour & R. M. Prothero (eds.), *Essays on African Population* (London: Routledge & Kegan Paul, 1961), p. 305. Sur l'inexistence de frontières fixes et l'incompatibilité de la notion de frontière stable et permanente avec la nature physique et les structures sociales de l'Afrique noire précoloniale, voir D. Bardonnet, 'Frontières et cultures', *in:* R.-J. Dupuy (ed.), *L'avenir du droit international dans un monde multiculturel*, Actes du Colloque des 17–19 novembre 1983, La Haye (The Hague: Nijhoff, 1984), p. 304.

[2] C'est notamment le cas des Haoussa du Nigeria et du Niger, des Yoruba du Nigeria et du Bénin (ex–Dahomey) et des Peuls qui ont essaimé du Nigeria au Sénégal; M. Glélé Ahanhanzo, 'La Déclaration d'Alger et l'Afrique', *in:* A. Cassese & E. Jouve (dir.), *Pour un droit des peuples* (Paris: Berger-Levrault, 1978), p. 204.

[3] 'In Africa, there were many "selves" within the colonial territory, and they have never had the time nor the opportunity to integrate into one "self" which should become the nation', Ch. C. Mojekwu, 'Self-Determination: The African Perspective', *in:* Y. Alexander and R. A. Friedlander (eds.), *Self-Determination: National, Regional, and Global Dimensions* (Westview Press: Boulder, Colorado, 1980), p. 234. Voir aussi L. M. Sachikonye, 'The Nation-State Project and Conflict in Zimbabwe', *in:* A. O. Olukoshi and L. Laakso (eds.), *Challenges to the Nation-State in Africa* (Nordiska Afrikainstituted: Uppsala, in cooperation with The Institute of Development Studies, University of Helsinki, 1996), p. 137.

[4] Voir par exemple L. Laakso et A. O. Olukoshi selon lesquels: 'It is perhaps in Africa, more than in other parts of the world, that the crisis of the nation-state project has been most obvious and overwhelming. The dramatic collapse of the nation-state in Somalia and Liberia, the state of paralysis in Zaire, Cameroon, and Togo, the genocidal violence in Rwanda and Burundi, the organized killings carried out by government forces and Muslim fundamentalists in Algeria and Egypt, the ethnic cleansing episodes in Kenya's Rift Valley, the gradual slide of Sierra Leone into a civil war and the worsening crisis in the Sudan, the continuing political tensions in Angola and Ethiopia, the uneasy state of affairs in Nigeria following the annulment of the 1993 presidential election by the ruling military junta,

stabilité politique et territoriale d'une grande partie des Etats africains est sans cesse menacée par des velléités sécessionnistes.

De telles revendications sécessionnistes, réussies ou avortées, furent par exemple observées – et le sont parfois encore – au Congo (avec le Katanga), au Nigeria (avec le Biafra), au Sénégal (avec la Casamance), en Somalie (avec la Somaliland), au Soudan (avec le conflit en cours dans la partie Sud de son territoire), en Ethiopie (avec l'Erythrée), aux Comores (avec les îles de Mayotte et d'Anjouan), et plus récemment, lors de la guerre civile aux aspects multiples en République démocratique de Congo, pour ne citer que quelques exemples de situations où la problématique de la sécession a été ou est encore fortement débattue.

Rappelons qu'on entend par sécession, une

> [a]ction d'une partie de la population d'un Etat, visant à dissocier un territoire de l'Etat de la souveraineté duquel il relève, en vue de l'ériger en un Etat nouveau ou de l'unir à un autre Etat, l'Etat affecté par cette réduction de son territoire conservant sa personnalité internationale et, donc, son identité,[5]

et que l'on en parle surtout et, partant, s'interroge sur sa licéité internationale lorsque cette séparation ou ce démembrement se font sans le consentement de l'Etat qui en est affecté.[6]

Notre propos sera justement de préciser l'état du droit international régional africain en matière de sécession. Celui-ci adopte-t-il une 'neutralité juridique' face à la sécession, comme c'est le cas pour le droit international général?[7] La condamne-t-il en toutes circonstances ou prévoit-il des cas où la sécession serait autorisée?

the numerous low-intensity, mostly ethnically-based confrontations in various parts of Africa as diverse as Ghana (Nanumbas vs. Konkonbas), Nigeria (Kuteb vs. Hausa, Jukun vs. Tiv, Ogoni vs. Andoni), South Africa (Zulu vs. Xhosa), Zimbabwe (Shona vs. Ndebele), and Niger and Mali (where sections of the local populations have been pitched against the Tuaregs), and the increasing salience of popular religious identities, often mixed with competing ethnicities, in the political processes of most countries have combined to create a sense of profound disorder on the continent.' 'The Crisis of the Post-Colonial Nation-State Project in Africa', *in:* A. O. Olukoshi and L. Laakso (eds.), *Challenges to the Nation-State*, p. 8.

5 J. Salmon (dir.), *Dictionnaire de droit international public* (Bruxelles: Bruylant, 2001), pp. 1021–2.

6 C'est ce qui explique l'absence de condamnation de la séparation du Sénégal de la Fédération du Mali en 1960, de la sortie de la Syrie de la République arabe unie en 1961 (l'unissant à l'Egypte), ou encore de la séparation du Singapour de la Fédération de Malaisie en 1965, toutes faites avec le consentement de l'Etat démembré dans l'exercice de sa souveraineté.

7 Voir sur cette question de 'neutralité juridique' l'Introduction de M. G. Kohen, dans le présent ouvrage.

Comme en droit international général, la réponse à ces questions dépend pour une large part du champ d'application réel du droit des peuples à disposer d'eux-mêmes, qui est lui-même tributaire de la détermination de la collectivité qui constitue un 'peuple'. Dans l'absolu, l'exercice de ce droit par le biais de la sécession n'est pas condamné dans l'ordre juridique africain, que ce soit en vertu de la Charte constitutive de l'Organisation de l'unité africaine (OUA), adoptée à Addis-Abeba (Ethiopie) le 25 mai 1963, ou de la Charte africaine des droits de l'homme et des peuples (ci-après Charte africaine), adoptée à Nairobi (Kenya) le 27 juin 1981; tout au plus celui-ci le confine-t-il dans certains contextes bien déterminés.

Alors que dans la Charte constitutive de l'OUA le droit des peuples à l'autodétermination n'est évoqué que dans son seul préambule, il est consacré de manière emphatique par la Charte africaine. Il est vrai que les deux textes ne possèdent pas la même vocation et ont été adoptés à vingt années d'intervalle. En 1963, les fondateurs de l'OUA étaient surtout soucieux de consolider la stabilité politique de leurs Etats et d'asseoir leurs pouvoirs sur l'ensemble des territoires nouvellement indépendants. C'est ainsi que les articles 5 et 6 de la Charte de l'OUA, consacrés aux droits et devoirs des Etats, n'aménagent aucune obligation de l'Etat vis-à-vis du peuple ou de l'individu. Par contre, les principes de souveraineté nationale et de non-interférence dans les affaires intérieures des Etats ont été consacrés avec force. Le souci à l'égard des peuples était alors limité à la lutte pour l'émancipation de ceux qui étaient encore colonisés ou sous domination d'une minorité raciste.[8]

Pour sa part, la Charte africaine des droits de l'homme et des peuples consacre six articles aux droits des peuples (art. 19 à 24), et affirme solennellement que 'tout peuple a un droit imprescriptible et inaliénable à l'autodétermination' (art. 20). Les Etats africains y reconnaissent également que 'la réalité et le respect des droits du peuple doivent nécessairement garantir les droits de l'homme' (al. 5 du préambule).

De cette différence de préoccupation des deux Chartes et de la place que chacune accorde au droit des peuples à disposer d'eux-mêmes dérive une différence de perception du phénomène sécessionniste. Si la Charte de l'OUA, et l'Acte constitutif de l'Union africaine qui l'a remplacé en 2000,

[8] Voir sur ces points, F. Ouguergouz, *La Charte africaine des droits de l'homme et des peuples. Une approche juridique des droits de l'homme entre tradition et modernité* (Paris: P. U. F., 1993), p. 36; F. Ouguergouz, *The African Charter on Human and Peoples' Rights – A Comprehensive Agenda for Human Dignity and Sustainable Democracy in Africa* (The Hague / London / New York: Martinus Nijhoff Publishers, 2003), p. 249.

mettent l'emphase sur l'intégrité territoriale des Etats, entraînant ainsi la négation d'un droit à la sécession (I), la Charte africaine des droits de l'homme et des peuples offre au contraire certaines potentialités à ce droit (II). On peut néanmoins relever que la promotion, au cours des dernières années, du respect du droit à l'autodétermination dans sa dimension interne[9] semble opérer un certain rapprochement entre ces deux positions. Encore faudra-t-il déterminer si la promotion de l'autodétermination interne est conçue comme une alternative à la sécession, laquelle deviendrait de fait sans objet, ou si la sécession ne serait pas, malgré tout, permise à titre ultime en cas de non respect du droit des peuples à l'autodétermination interne, jouant en quelque sorte le rôle d'une soupape de sureté (III).

I. La négation d'un droit à la sécession dans les textes constitutifs de l'OUA et de l'Union africaine

A. La Charte de l'OUA et la pratique subséquente

Cette négation résulte des principes sur lesquels l'OUA fonde ses actions pour atteindre les objectifs fixés dans la Charte d'Addis-Abeba (1). Et elle s'est vérifiée à travers les prises de position des organes de l'Organisation à l'égard de certaines tentatives de sécession sur le continent africain (2).

1. Les principes fondateurs de l'OUA ou la négation implicite d'un droit à la sécession

L'attachement des dirigeants africains au respect de l'intégrité territoriale se traduit par le refus de tout droit à la sécession à l'intérieur d'un Etat issu de la décolonisation. Peu avant la vague des indépendances du début des années soixante, l'attitude de ceux-ci à l'égard de l'intégrité territoriale des futurs Etats indépendants n'était pas toutefois dénuée d'ambiguïté. Le mécontentement à l'égard des découpages territoriaux d'alors trouve notamment une illustration dans une résolution de la Conférence de 'All Africa People's' adoptée en 1958 à Accra (Ghana),

[9] L'on sait en effet que ce droit a deux dimensions: une dimension externe dont l'exercice mène à l'indépendance, à l'intégration ou à l'association avec un autre Etat, voire à la sécession; une dimension interne qui comporte, entre autres, le droit des peuples à choisir le mode de gouvernement et l'orientation politique de leurs Etats, le choix de leurs dirigeants par des procédés assurant la participation de tous les composants du peuple. Voir. Th. Christakis, *Le droit à l'autodétermination en dehors des situations de décolonisation* (Paris: La Documentation française, 1999), qui consacre la première partie de son étude sur l'autodétermination externe et la deuxième sur l'autodétermination interne.

dénonçant les frontières artificielles découpant les ethnies et les peuples et appelant à l'abolition ou au réajustement des frontières coloniales 'dans un sens qui réponde au mieux aux désirs véritables des peuples concernés'.[10] Les leaders africains de l'époque n'excluaient pas que les frontières puissent être modifiées une fois l'indépendance acquise, tant les délimitations effectuées par le colonisateur leur semblaient artificielles sur le plan géographique, économique et ethnique.[11]

Cette position, qui pouvait préfigurer une attitude favorable à la sécession, a été cependant renversée lors de l'adoption de la Charte constitutive de l'OUA en 1963. Cette Charte fait une brève référence au droit des peuples à disposer d'eux-mêmes dans son préambule,[12] mais elle ne le mentionne pas au rang des principes directeurs de l'Organisation.[13] Dans le contexte général de la Charte de l'OUA, les peuples titulaires du droit à l'autodétermination sont définis par rapport au territoire, tel qu'hérité de la colonisation, et non pas sur la base de critères sociologiques. Ainsi limité, ce droit ne couvre dès lors pas les situations de sécession.

La Charte d'Addis Abeba circonscrit étroitement le principe d'autodétermination quand elle proclame le 'dévouement sans réserve [des dirigeants africains] à la cause de l'émancipation totale des territoires africains non encore indépendants'[14] et affirme en même temps leur attachement au principe d'intégrité territoriale.[15] Il est tout à fait remarquable, comme le souligne Théodore Christakis, que la Charte de l'OUA présente le principe du respect de l'intégrité territoriale de manière autonome, et non en association avec l'interdiction du recours à la force comme le fait l'article 2, paragraphe 4 de la Charte des Nations Unies.[16]

Les Etats africains adhèrent non seulement aux principes du respect de la souveraineté et de l'intégrité territoriale de chaque Etat ainsi qu'au droit inaliénable à une existence indépendante (art. 3, par. 3 de la Charte d'Addis Abeba), mais ils consacrent également comme objectif

[10] Voir le texte de la résolution dans B. Boutros-Ghali, *Les conflits de frontières en Afrique (Etude et documents)* (Paris: Ed. techniques et économiques, 1972), document n° 4, pp. 91–2. Voir aussi M. Shaw, *Title to Territory in Africa. International Legal Issues* (Oxford: Clarendon Press, 1986), p. 183.

[11] M. Shaw, *ibid.*, p. 183.

[12] '[Nous, chefs d'Etat, ...] Convaincus que les peuples ont le droit inaliénable de déterminer leur propre destin' (1er Considérant).

[13] Cf. l'article 3 de la Charte, qui énumère ces principes.

[14] Article 3, 6ème principe; voir également l'article 2, al. 1(d) consacré aux objectifs de l'Organisation.

[15] Article 3, al. 3; cf. également article 2, al. 1(c).

[16] Voir Christakis, *Le droit à l'autodétermination*, p. 179.

de l'OUA la nécessité de *défendre* leur souveraineté, leur intégrité territoriale et leur indépendance (art. 2, al. *c*). S'il y a là une volonté de se prémunir contre les menaces externes à l'intégrité territoriale, le principe est également et essentiellement conçu comme visant à prévenir les tentatives sécessionnistes qui pourraient survenir ici ou là et compromettre la stabilité des Etats.

Ainsi compris, le principe d'intégrité territoriale énoncé par la Charte de l'OUA peut être rapproché de celui de respect des frontières héritées de la colonisation[17] qui sera expressément consacré une année plus tard par les Etats membres de l'Organisation, à l'exception notable du Maroc et de la Somalie. Dans la résolution du Caire, adoptée le 21 juillet 1964, la Conférence des Chefs d'Etat africains réaffirme en effet sa totale adhésion au principe d'intégrité territoriale et déclare

> solennellement que tous les Etats membres s'engagent à respecter les frontières existant au moment où ils ont accédé à l'indépendance.[18]

En consacrant dans la foulée le principe du droit des peuples à disposer d'eux-mêmes et la règle du respect des frontières issues de la colonisation, l'OUA excluait d'avance toute application du principe aux situations

[17] Pour une différenciation des deux principes, cf. S. Regragui, *Le devoir d'assistance étrangère aux peuples en danger*, Thèse de Doctorat d'Etat en droit, Nancy II (octobre 1985), pp. 102–3.

[18] Résolution AHG/Rés. 16(I); voir également la déclaration du Secrétaire général de l'OUA, lors du débat sur la République démocratique du Congo, tenu au siège de l'ONU à New York le 24 janvier 2000, qui réaffirme l'attachement de l'OUA, entre autres, aux principes de l'unité et de l'intégrité territoriale de ses Etats membres et fait part de l'inquiétude de l'Organisation 'à propos des risques de violation de ces principes en République démocratique de Congo à cause des dimensions internes et externes de ce conflit', *DAI* 6 (15 mars 2000), 239. A propos de la même situation, l'Organe central de prévention et de gestion des conflits de l'OUA 'clearly articulated its support to the government of the Democratic Republic of the Congo and OAU's commitment to the unity, cohesion and respect of the sovereignty and territorial integrity of the DRC . . . The Ouagadougou Central Organ Summit reaffirmed its support to the Government of the DRC as well as the commitment of the OAU to the respect for the sovereignty, unity and territorial integrity of the DRC in accordance with the provision of the OAU Charter and, in particular, Resolution AHG/res 16(I) adopted in Cairo in 1964', *in:* Conseil des ministres, 70ème session ordinaire/5ème session ordinaire de la CEA, 6–10 juillet 1999, Alger (Algérie), *Rapport du Secrétaire général sur la situation en République démocratique de Congo*, CM/2099 (LXX-d), par. 4, 7 et 38. Citons encore une résolution de la Commission africaine des droits de l'homme et des peuples sur la situation en Somalie, adoptée lors de sa 27ème session ordinaire tenue à Alger du 27 avril au 11 mai 2000, qui lance un appel à l'ensemble de la société somalienne et aux chefs traditionnels et leaders politiques de la Somalie 'afin qu'ils participent au processus de règlement pacifique de leur différend et qu'ils accordent la priorité au maintien de l'unité nationale et de l'intégrité de la Somalie'.

autres que coloniales ou de domination raciale.[19] Pour les Etats africains membres de l'OUA, il existe donc bien une hiérarchie entre les deux règles, mais dans cette hiérarchie c'est le respect des frontières coloniales qui constitue la norme supérieure et le droit des peuples à disposer d'eux-mêmes la règle inférieure, du moins en ce qui concerne les pays africains indépendants du continent. L'application du droit des peuples à l'autodétermination trouve son cadre et ses limites dans le respect absolu de l'intégrité territoriale.[20]

L'acceptation par les Etats africains d'un régime territorial basé sur la validité des frontières coloniales des Etats indépendants était motivée par la crainte de l'instabilité territoriale qui ne manquerait pas de s'installer si la carte du continent africain devait être redessinée sur des bases ethniques, mais aussi par le besoin de fournir une source de légitimation aux Etats nouvellement indépendants. Comme le souligne à juste titre Malcolm Shaw:

> The vast majority of African countries does not consist of a defined 'nation' as such in the Western sense, and accordingly have sought the root of their legitimacy in the territorial unit rather than in the ethnic characteristics of the State.[21]

On mentionnera encore que, dans le cadre des travaux de révision de la Charte constitutive de l'OUA,[22] une proposition somalienne visant à consacrer le 'Respect du principe de l'égalité entre les peuples et de leur droit à l'autodétermination' dans l'article III (Principes) de la Charte avait été rejetée, bien qu'il ait été précisé par le Secrétaire général de l'OUA, qui la présentait, qu'en parlant de l'autodétermination des peuples, il s'agissait d'une référence aux peuples sous domination coloniale.[23]

[19] Voir également dans ce sens, I. Fall, *Contribution à l'étude du droit des peuples à disposer d'eux-mêmes en Afrique*, Thèse de Doctorat d'Etat en droit, Paris I (octobre 1972), p. 355.

[20] *Ibid.*, p. 357; voir, dans ce sens, l'arrêt rendu le 22 décembre 1986 par la Cour internationale de Justice dans le différend frontalier Mali/Burkina Faso, CIJ, *Recueil 1986*, p. 17 (par. 25).

[21] Voir Shaw, *Title to Territory*, p. 186; voir en ce sens S. Ratner, 'Drawing a Better Line: Uti Possidetis and the Borders of New States', *AJIL* 90 (1996), 595. Voir également les développements de A. N'Kolombua, 'L'ambivalence des relations entre le droit des peuples à disposer d'eux-mêmes et l'intégrité territoriale des Etats en droit international contemporain', *in: Mélanges Charles Chaumont*, p. 447.

[22] Ces travaux d'actualisation de la Charte d'Addis Abeba furent décidés à la 16ème session ordinaire de la Conférence des chefs d'Etat et de gouvernement africains, Monrovia, 17–20 juillet 1979, Rés. AHG/Déc. 111 (XVI) Rev.1; voir aussi sur ce point, M. O. Abie, 'Droit des peuples dans la Charte africaine des droits de l'homme et des peuples: quelle réalité dans le contexte africain?', *ASICL Proceedings* 10 (1998), pp. 230–1.

[23] *Projet de rapport du rapporteur du comité de révision de la Charte de l'OUA*, Doc. OUA, CAB/LEG/97/DRAFT/RAPT.RPT (III) Rev. 2, (# 23). Certains délégués ont en effet

La problématique du droit des peuples africains à l'autodétermination est ainsi clairement définie dans le cadre de la Charte de l'OUA, et elle ne pouvait être posée en d'autres termes que la décolonisation 'officielle' sans faire renaître l'hydre d'un droit de sécession que tous les Etats africains s'accordent à combattre avec d'autant plus d'acharnement qu'ils se savent vulnérables.[24] La place centrale occupée par les principes d'intégrité territoriale et de respect des frontières coloniales, encore réaffirmé par l'OUA il y a quelques années lors de son Sommet d'Alger,[25] explique certainement le rejet des revendications sécessionnistes et irrédentistes[26] observées dans la pratique, et en fournit l'assise juridique.

2. La pratique de l'OUA

Tant la pratique de l'OUA que celle de ses Etats membres confirment cette conception restrictive du principe d'autodétermination qui a pour

considéré que cette question était déjà suffisamment couverte par l'article III (alinéa 1: 'Egalité souveraine de tous les Etats membres' et alinéa 6: 'Dévouement sans réserve à la cause de l'émancipation totale des territoires africains non encore indépendants'). Il est d'autre part très significatif que la proposition ougandaise visant à inclure le principe d'intangibilité des frontières dans le même article ait été agréée alors qu'il a été avancé par certaines délégations que 'la Charte était très claire sur la question des frontières et qu'un ajout à l'article concerné ne l'enrichirait pas' (*ibid.*).

24 Voir par exemple le mémorandum sur la question Somali présenté par le Kenya à la Conférence d'Addis Abeba en 1963; selon cet Etat, le principe d'autodétermination est pertinent quand il est question de domination étrangère, il n'a pas de sens quand il est question de 'désintégration territoriale par des citoyens dissidents', S. M. Finger et G. Singh, 'Self-Determination: A United Nations Perspective', *in:* Alexander and Friedlander (eds.), *Self-Determination*, p. 339.

25 'Nous chefs d'Etat et de gouvernement des pays membres de l'Organisation de l'unité africaine, réunis à Alger du 12 au 14 juillet 1999, . . . Convaincus que le respect du principe d'intangibilité des frontières héritées lors des indépendances a contribué de façon déterminante à la préservation de la paix et de la stabilité sur notre continent, nous réaffirmons sa validité et sa pérennité comme norme fondamentale applicable au traitement des différends frontaliers'; 35ème session ordinaire de la Conférence de l'OUA, Doc. AHG/Decl. 1 (XXXV), p. 4. Le principe est également réaffirmé par les Etats eux-mêmes dans leurs relations réciproques, comme par exemple dans l'Accord de cessez-le-feu de Lusaka en République démocratique du Congo (RDC), signé le 10 juillet 1999 par 6 Etats africains, y compris la RDC, et deux mouvements politiques congolais, qui '*Réaffirm[e]* en outre la Résolution AHG/16 (I) adoptée par la Conférence des chefs d'Etat et de gouvernement de l'OUA en 1964 au Caire (Egypte) sur l'intégrité territoriale et l'inviolabilité des frontières nationales telles qu'héritées à l'indépendance', et précise que '[r]ien dans cet accord ne devra, en aucune manière, nuire à la souveraineté ni à l'intégrité territoriale de la République démocratique du Congo', *DAI* 19 (1er oct. 1999), pp. 794–5, 3ème considérant et par. 15.

26 Voir dans ce sens, Shaw, *Title to Territory*, pp. 186–7; Christakis, *Le droit à l'autodétermination*, p. 178.

corollaire la condamnation de la sécession. L'échec des sécessions du Katanga[27] et du Biafra,[28] ainsi que la longue et laborieuse marche du peuple érythréen vers l'indépendance, ou encore la vigoureuse réaffirmation par l'OUA de son attachement au principe d'intégrité territoriale des Comores après la proclamation d'indépendance de l'île d'Anjouan, en apportent un éloquent témoignage.

Le cas de l'Erythrée est d'autant plus révélateur de l'attachement des Etats africains et de l'OUA aux principes d'intégrité territoriale et d'intangibilité des frontières héritées de la colonisation qu'il présentait une spécificité par rapport aux exemples katangais ou biafrais. Le statut juridique du peuple érythréen a été l'objet de nombreuses controverses doctrinales. Ancienne colonie italienne, l'Erythrée fut placée sous administration britannique en 1941. En 1950, l'Assemblée générale des Nations Unies recommandait, dans sa résolution 390 A (V), que l'Erythrée constitue 'une unité autonome fédérée avec l'Ethiopie et sous la souveraineté de la couronne éthiopienne'.[29] Deux ans plus tard, l'administration britannique prenait fin après que la fédération de l'Erythrée et de l'Ethiopie ait

[27] La proclamation de l'indépendance du Katanga eut lieu le 11 juillet 1960, quelques jours seulement après l'indépendance de l'Etat congolais. Dans sa résolution du 24 novembre 1961, le Conseil de sécurité des Nations Unies réprouva 'énergiquement les activités sécessionnistes illégalement menées par l'administration provinciale du Katanga avec l'appui de ressources de l'extérieur et secondées par des mercenaires étrangers', et déclara 'que toutes les activités sécessionnistes dirigées contre la République du Congo sont contraires à la Loi fondamentale et aux décisions du Conseil de sécurité' (S/RES/169 (1961), par. 1 et 8). La tentative de sécession du Katanga était en effet largement inspirée par les intérêts économiques étrangers; voir notamment D. N. Gibbs, 'Dag Hammarskjöld, the United Nations, and the Congo Crisis of 1960–1: a Reinterpretation', *The Journal of Modern African Studies* 31 (1993), 1, pp. 164–7.

[28] C'est le 30 mai 1967 que la République du Biafra fut déclarée indépendante et souveraine. Voir à ce sujet, F. Wodie, 'La sécession du Biafra et le droit international public', *RGDIP* 73 (1969), 1019–60; et Fall, *Contribution à l'étude*, pp. 279–316. Les Etats membres de l'OUA avaient adopté une résolution en 1967 dans le cadre de laquelle ils réitéraient 'their condemnation of secession in any Member State'; voir I. Brownlie, *Basic Documents on African Affairs* (1971), p. 364. On se souviendra également de la déclaration de U Thant, Secrétaire général des Nations Unies, faite à Dakar le 4 janvier 1970 à l'issue de la crise du Biafra, selon laquelle l'ONU, en sa qualité d'organisation internationale, n'a jamais accepté, n'accepte pas et n'acceptera jamais le principe de la sécession d'une partie d'un de ses Etats membres; *cf.* Nations Unies, *Chronique Mensuelle* VII (1970), p. 38. Pour une étude des cas katangais et biafrais, voir L. C. Buchheit, *Secession – The Legitimacy of Self-Determination* (New Haven & London: Yale University Press, 1978), respectivement pp. 141–53 et 62–176.

[29] Voir pour une analyse des termes de la résolution, B. Habte-Selassie, 'L'Erythrée et les Nations Unies', *in: Le cas de l'Erythrée*, Documents du Tribunal permanent des peuples de la Ligue internationale pour les droits et la libération des peuples, Session sur l'Erythrée, Milan, 24–6 mai 1980.

été formellement établie.[30] En 1962, le gouvernement éthiopien annonçait l'incorporation de la province érythréenne en son sein en mettant un terme au statut fédéral, en procédant à la dissolution du parlement érythréen et à l'annulation de sa Constitution.[31] Dans la foulée de ces événements, un mouvement de résistance armée s'est formé contre les autorités éthiopiennes. Pour nombre d'observateurs, ce conflit et la lutte du peuple érythréen visait à parachever un processus de décolonisation contrarié;[32] tandis que pour d'autres, l'Erythrée ne réunissait d'autre qualité que celle d'entité sécessionniste.[33]

L'issue du conflit a largement bénéficié du contexte de déliquescence du pouvoir éthiopien du début des années 1990 et du soutien des nouveaux dirigeants du pays. Au cours de la Conférence sur la paix et la démocratie, tenue en juillet 1991 à Addis Abeba, le gouvernement de transition éthiopien a reconnu le droit du peuple érythréen de déterminer son avenir politique par le biais d'un référendum supervisé par des instances internationales. Le président du gouvernement de transition éthiopien a ensuite écrit en ce sens au Secrétaire général des

[30] Voir le recueil des documents des Nations Unies, *The United Nations and the Independence of Eritrea* (New York: United Nations, Department of Public Information, 1996), 275 p.

[31] On soulignera que l'Assemblée érythréenne avait voté l'incorporation de l'Erythrée à l'Ethiopie, le 14 novembre 1962, mais que les circonstances du vote ont toujours été dénoncées par les Erythréens qui invoquaient un consentement obtenu sous la contrainte et qualifiaient le rattachement à l'Ethiopie d'annexion illégale. Voir à ce sujet, A. Cassese, *Self-Determination of Peoples – A Legal Reappraisal* (Cambridge / New York / Melbourne: Cambridge University Press, 1995), pp. 221–2; voir aussi B. Habte-Selassie, 'L'Erythrée et les Nations Unies', pp. 183 et ss.; J. Klabbers et R. Lefeber, 'Africa Lost between Self-determination and Uti Possidetis', *in:* C. Brölmann, R. Lefeber, M. Zieck (eds.), *Peoples and Minorities in International Law* (Dordrecht / Boston / London: Martinus Nijhoff Publishers, 1993), pp. 72–3.

[32] Voir en ce sens, E. Gayim, *The Erithrean Question – The Conflict between the Right of Self-Determination and the Interests of States* (Iustus Förlag: Juridiska Föreningen i Uppsala, 1993), 716 p.; R. Goy, 'L'indépendance de l'Erythrée', *AFDI* (1993), 337–56; B. Habte-Selassie, 'Self-Determination in Principle and Practice: the Ethiopian-Eritrean Experience', *Columbia HRLJ* 29/1 (1997), 92–142. *Contra*, voir M. Haile, 'Legality of Secessions: The Case of Eritrea', *Emory ILR* 8/2 (1994), 479–537. Dans son 'avis consultatif', le Tribunal permanent des peuples estimait que 'ne constituant donc aucune forme de sécession, le droit du peuple érythréen à l'autodétermination ne peut s'exercer aujourd'hui que par l'accès à l'indépendance, la volonté du peuple érythréen étant sur ce point démontrée par la lutte armée menée depuis bientôt vingt ans par les Fronts de libération' (par. 10); Avis consultatif du 3 octobre 1980 sur l'Erythrée, *in: Le cas de l'Erythrée*, p. 472.

[33] Voir H. Quane qui qualifie le cas érythréen de 'non-colonial self-determination claim', in 'The United Nations and the Evolving Right to Self-determination', *ICLQ* 47 (1998), 564.

Nations Unies.[34] La décision des dirigeants érythréens de différer de deux années la déclaration d'indépendance de l'Erythrée, pour laisser place à l'organisation d'un référendum, peut s'expliquer par leur volonté de se conformer au principe d'autodétermination[35] et d'échapper à la qualification d'entité sécessionniste. Elle peut aussi s'expliquer par l'assurance de la création d'un Etat érythréen du fait de l'implication de l'ONU.

L'indépendance de l'Erythrée a été proclamée à l'issue du référendum tenu sous la supervision de l'ONU et de l'OUA, au mois d'avril 1993. Ce sont ces circonstances particulières qui expliquent pourquoi l'exercice par le peuple érythréen de son droit à l'autodétermination externe n'a pas été, dans sa dernière phase, perçu par les Etats africains comme antithétique des sacro-saints principes d'intégrité territoriale et de respect des frontières héritées de la colonisation.[36]

Des réactions à d'autres cas de sécession en Afrique confirment cet attachement du droit international africain à la préservation de l'intégrité et de l'unité nationale d'un Etat déjà constitué. C'est le cas par exemple de l'appel lancé par la Commission africaine des droits de l'homme et des peuples, dans sa résolution sur le processus de paix et de réconciliation nationale en Somalie,[37] 'aux membres de la société civile somalienne, à

[34] Voir *Lettre en date du 13 décembre 1991 adressée au Secrétaire général des Nations Unies par le Président du Gouvernement de transition de l'Ethiopie, concernant les résultats de la Conférence sur la paix et la démocratie, tenue en Ethiopie en juillet 1991*, Annexe II, 29 Octobre 1992.

[35] Voir en ce sens, A. Cassese, *Self-determination*, p. 222.

[36] Le Secrétaire général des Nations Unies, Boutros Boutros-Ghali, a ainsi pu écrire dans l'introduction de l'ouvrage précité sur l'indépendance de l'Erythrée que 'the way in which Eritrean independence was achieved – with the involvement of the United Nations, the Organization of African Unity and the new Government of Ethiopia – eased the concerns expressed in Africa and elsewhere over the revision of the continent's colonial boundaries' (*The UN and Independence of Eritrea*, p. 36).

[37] Le territoire de la Somalie, originairement habité par des clans tribaux sans une structure étatique centrale était divisé pendant la période coloniale entre l'Ethiopie, la France, la Grande Bretagne et l'Italie. A son indépendance en juillet 1960, l'Etat de Somalie réunit les parties italienne et britannique de l'ancien territoire. En mai 1991, la partie britannique fait sécession et proclame la République indépendante de Somaliland. Dans le reste du pays durant la même période, il n'y a plus de gouvernement central, la Somalie étant confrontée à une lutte de clans et de factions guerrières, certains aspirant à accéder au pouvoir pour diriger l'ensemble du territoire, d'autres profitant simplement du chaos pour s'adonner à des activités criminelles. Les Nations Unies sont intervenues en Somalie en 1992 par l'imposition d'un embargo sur les armes qui reste en vigueur jusqu'à présent, et l'envoi des missions de maintien de la paix qui n'ont pas réussi à mettre un terme au conflit et à l'absence d'Etat en Somalie. Voir sur ces points, *Les Nations Unies et la Somalie, 1992–1996*, série Livres bleus (New York: Nations Unies, Département de l'information, 1996), 535 p.; H. McCoubrey, J. Morris, *Regional Peacekeeping in the Post-Cold War Era* (The Hague / Boston / London: Kluwer Law International, 2000), pp. 129–31.

toute la population somalienne, aux chefs traditionnels et leaders politiques de la Somalie afin qu'ils participent au processus de règlement pacifique de leur différend et qu'ils accordent la *priorité au maintien de l'unité nationale et de l'intégrité de la Somalie*'.[38] Cet appel ressemble en effet à une directive concernant le statut politique de la Somalie à la fin du processus de paix. Or, on peut penser que, dans l'exercice de leur droit à l'autodétermination, les représentants du peuple somalien participant à ce processus pourraient opter d'un commun accord pour une autre issue que le maintien du statut actuel, c'est-a-dire une autre issue que l'unité et l'intégrité de la Somalie.[39]

Plus significatif encore est la persistance de la condamnation des sécessions proclamées à une vingtaine d'années d'intervalle par deux îles de la République fédérale islamique des Comores, d'autant plus qu'il y a ici une certaine effectivité de la sécession.[40] La résolution adoptée en 1990 par la Conférence des chefs d'Etat et de gouvernement de l'OUA sur la question du Mayotte[41] est à cet égard probante. Rappelant les

[38] 28ème session ordinaire à Cotonou (Bénin), 23 oct.- 6 nov. 2000, respectivement, 4ème considérant et par. 1; c'est nous qui soulignons.

[39] Voir aussi la décision du Conseil des ministres de l'OUA sur la situation en RDC qui affirme son attachement à l'unité, à la souveraineté et à l'intégrité territoriale de cet Etat. Le Conseil des ministres y réitère en outre l'importance du retrait de la RDC de toutes les forces étrangères, en rappelant les engagements des Etats voisins à respecter la souveraineté et l'intégrité territoriale de la RDC, conformément aux Chartes de l'OUA et de l'ONU ainsi qu'à l'Acte constitutif de l'Union africaine; *Décision relative au rapport du Secrétaire général sur la situation en République démocratique de Congo*, CM/Dec.663 (LXXVI), 2002, par. 2 et 15.

[40] La République fédérale islamique des Comores (RFI des Comores) est composée de quatre îles: Anjouan, la Grande Comore, Mayotte et Moheli. Lors d'un scrutin d'autodétermination tenu le 22 décembre 1974 sur l'ensemble de l'archipel, l'île de Mayotte vota pour le maintien des Comores au sein de la France, tandis que les trois autres optèrent pour l'indépendance. Considérant, île par île, ce résultat, le gouvernement français décida d'octroyer l'indépendance à Anjouan, la Grande Comore et Moheli, et octroya au Mayotte, après une nouvelle consultation populaire du 8 février 1976, le statut *sui generis* de 'collectivité territoriale' en 1976 puis de 'collectivité départementale' à partir de 2001. Allant à l'encontre du principe de l'indivisibilité des Comores, de la Déclaration sur l'octroi de l'indépendance aux pays et aux peuples coloniaux de l'Assemblée générale de l'ONU (A/RES/1514 (XV) du 14 décembre 1960) et du principe du respect des frontières héritées de la colonisation, proclamé par l'OUA en 1964, cette situation a fait l'objet d'une condamnation unanime et continue de la communauté internationale, à l'exception notable de la France. Voir sur cette situation deux études de A. Oraison, 'Le différend franco-comorien sur l'île de Mayotte', *RDISDP* 74/3 (1996), 199–214; et 'Réflexions sur la double conception française du droit des peuples à disposer d'eux-mêmes à la lumière du "cas mahorais"', *RDISDP* 81/1 (2003), 1–94.

[41] AHG/Res. 193 (XXVI), adoptée à la 36ème session ordinaire, Addis-Abeba, du 9 au 11 juillet 1990.

différentes résolutions et décisions de condamnation prises par l'ONU,[42] le Mouvement des pays non-alignés, la Conférence islamique et la Ligue des Etats arabes, la Conférence y réitère la légitimité de la revendication du gouvernement comorien pour la réintégration de l'île de Mayotte à la RFI des Comores. Elle réaffirme ensuite la souveraineté de la République fédérale sur cette île (par. 2), et appelle le gouvernement français à satisfaire la demande légitime de son homologue comorien (par. 3). Allant encore plus loin, la Conférence réaffirme sa solidarité avec le peuple comorien dans sa détermination à recouvrir son intégrité politique et à défendre sa souveraineté et son intégrité territoriales (par. 4). Elle lance un appel à tous les Etats membres et à la communauté internationale de condamner toute initiative qui pourrait être prise par la France pour faire participer l'île de Mayotte à des manifestations au cours desquelles celle-ci serait distinguée de la République fédérale islamique des Comores (par. 7).

Plus de vingt ans après cette première sécession, le 3 août 1997, les habitants de l'île d'Anjouan ont aussi proclamé unilatéralement leur indépendance. Cette sécession s'est matérialisée par l'élection du premier Président de l''Etat' d'Anjouan le 5 août 1997 ainsi que par la déroute des forces militaires envoyées début septembre 1997 par le gouvernement central pour mettre fin à la rébellion. A l'issue d'un référendum d'autodétermination, organisé le 26 octobre 1997, 99,88 pour cent de la population de l'île a voté en faveur de l'indépendance.[43]

Depuis ce verdict des urnes, 'l'Etat d'Anjouan' existe matériellement avec ses différentes autorités législatives, exécutives et judiciaires et l'exercice par celles-ci de tous les attributs de la souveraineté sur l'ensemble du territoire. Il y a donc ici une certaine effectivité, même si aucun Etat n'a jamais reconnu l'indépendance d'Anjouan. Cette effectivité n'a pas en effet amené l'OUA à accepter la sécession de l'île, faite en violation de ses principes fondamentaux, ses organes ayant toujours réaffirmé l'attachement de l'OUA à l'intégrité territoriale et à l'unité nationale des Comores,[44] tout en oeuvrant pour trouver une solution pacifique et durable à la situation prévalant dans ce pays.

[42] Les résolutions pertinentes de l'Assemblée générale de l'ONU en la matière sont rappelées dans la résolution 49/18 du 28 novembre 1994, lesquelles affirment l'unité et l'intégrité territoriale de l'Etat comorien, composé des îles d'Anjouan, de la Grande Comore, de Mayotte et de Mohéli.

[43] Sur cette affaire, voir A. Oraison, 'L'obligation de non-reconnaissance de l'Etat d'Anjouan', *RDISDP* 76/2 (1998), 159–83.

[44] Voir par exemple la décision du Conseil des Ministres de l'OUA sur le Rapport du Secrétaire général relatif à la situation en RFI des Comores, CM/Dec.452 (LXX), *in: CM/Dec.450–484*

Sous la médiation de l'OUA, un accord fut ainsi signé le 23 avril 1999, à Antananarivo (Madagascar), entre le gouvernement central et les autorités d'Anjouan, prévoyant le retour de l'île, avec plus d'autonomie, au sein de la RFI des Comores. Devant le rejet de cet accord par Anjouan, l'OUA lui imposa à partir du 21 mars 2000 un embargo sur les carburants, les denrées alimentaires, les communications maritimes et aériennes ainsi que sur les télécommunications. Les durs effets de cet embargo sur la population et l'économie de l'île ont poussé les autorités anjouanaises à signer, le 17 février 2001 à Fomboni, l'accord-cadre de réconciliation nationale,[45] entraînant la suspension puis la levée de l'embargo le 7 juillet 2001. Ceci marqua le début de la fin de cette crise qui a duré quatre ans, car l'accord-cadre 'vise à assurer une réconciliation nationale durable dans "l'archipel aux parfums" [et] a concrètement pour but de réintégrer Anjouan dans un nouvel ensemble institutionnel comorien de type fédéral attribuant une très large autonomie à chaque île et à restaurer le pouvoir civil ainsi que la démocratie grâce à des élections libres'.[46]

La structure fédérale ainsi configurée préserve l'unité et l'intégrité territoriale de la RFI des Comores tout en permettant au 'peuple' anjouanais d'exercer son droit à l'autodétermination à l'intérieur du 'Nouvel ensemble comorien'. En 2002, le Conseil des ministres de l'OUA a salué la restauration de l'unité et de l'intégrité territoriale des Comores, l'établissement d'un gouvernement d'union nationale, ainsi que les élections du Président de l'Union des Comores et des Présidents des îles autonomes d'Anjouan, de la Grande Comore et de Moheli. Cet organe a également exprimé sa reconnaissance aux Etats et personnalités qui ont œuvré continuellement à la préservation de l'unité et de l'intégrité territoriale des Comores et au rétablissement de l'ordre constitutionnel dans le pays.[47]

A la lumière de cette pratique, il s'avère que les Etats et les organisations régionales africains demeurent en règle générale hostiles à l'exercice d'un droit de sécession en dehors des situations de décolonisation et de domination ou d'occupation étrangères, position qui a été réaffirmée dans

(*LXX*) *Rev.1*, 17ème session ordinaire du Conseil des ministres de l'OUA, Alger, 8–10 juillet 1999, p. 4.

[45] Texte dans *DAI* 9 (1er mai 2001), 331–33.

[46] Oraison, 'Réflexions sur la double conception française', p. 94, note 167.

[47] *Décision relative au rapport du Secrétaire général sur la situation aux Comores*, CM/Dec. 664 (LXXVI), 2002, par. 2, 3 et 5. Il faut tout de même remarquer que cette solution ne règle pas la question de la sécession du Mayotte, l'Union des Comores et des îles autonomes ne concernant que les trois îles d'Anjouan, de Grande Comore et de Moheli.

l'Acte constitutif de l'Union africaine, adopté le 11 juillet 2000 à Lomé (Togo).

B. *L'Acte constitutif de l'Union africaine*

A l'instar de la Charte d'Addis-Abeba de 1963, l'Acte constitutif de l'Union africaine attache une grande importance à la défense de l'intégrité territoriale des Etats, et l'exercice du droit des peuples à disposer d'eux-mêmes ne figure pas non plus parmi les objectifs de l'Union africaine. L'accent semble avoir été mis sur la nécessité de préserver la paix et la stabilité en Afrique, considérées alors comme gages du développement du continent, dans le cadre desquelles peuvent s'exercer les droits de l'homme et des peuples. Ainsi, '[c]onscients du fait que le fléau des conflits en Afrique constitue un obstacle majeur au développement socio-économique du continent, et de la nécessité de promouvoir la paix, la sécurité et la stabilité, comme condition préalable à la mise enœuvre de [leur] agenda dans le domaine du développement et de l'intégration', les chefs d'Etat et de gouvernement africains ont posé comme objectifs primaires de l'Union ceux de:

> a) réaliser une plus grande unité et solidarité entre les pays africains et entre les peuples d'Afrique;
> b) défendre la souveraineté, l'intégrité territoriale et l'indépendance de ses Etats membres.[48]

Pour atteindre ces objectifs, l'article 4 de l'Acte constitutif réaffirme le principe de '[l']égalité souveraine et [de l']interdépendance de tous les Etats membres de l'Union', ainsi que le principe du 'respect des frontières existant au moment de l'accession à l'indépendance' (alinéas *a* et *b*). Il est d'ailleurs significatif de voir ce dernier principe figurer dans l'Acte constitutif, alors qu'il n'était pas dans la Charte de l'OUA, démontrant ainsi l'attachement de l'Union africaine à ce principe proclamé par la Conférence des chefs d'Etat et de gouvernement de l'OUA dans la Déclaration du Caire de 1964.

Possédant un contenu identique à ceux consacrés par l'OUA, ces principes ont la même implication sur la question du droit des peuples africains à la sécession telle qu'on l'a analysée ci-dessus. Il suffira

[48] Respectivement, 8ème considérant et article 3, al. a) et b). L'article 3 énumère 14 objectifs de l'Union africaine.

par conséquent de dire ici qu'au regard de l'Acte constitutif de l'Union africaine, le droit à l'autodétermination des peuples africains se trouvant à l'intérieur d'un même Etat[49] s'efface devant le respect de l'intégrité territoriale et des frontières héritées de la décolonisation – ce qui implique la négation du droit de ces peuples à la sécession. Quant à la pratique, les situations de sécession examinées jusqu'ici par l'Union africaine sont survenues durant l'existence de l'OUA, et la nouvelle organisation a maintenu à l'égard de celles-ci la position adoptée par sa devancière.

En outre, un nouveau principe introduit dans l'Acte constitutif semblerait offrir une possibilité de secours pour un Etat membre de l'Union africaine en proie à des activités sécessionnistes sur son territoire. L'alinéa j de l'article 4 prône en effet le 'droit des Etats membres de solliciter l'intervention de l'Union pour restaurer la paix et la sécurité'. Etant donné qu'une sécession non consentie par l'Etat démembré peut être analysée comme une atteinte à la paix et à la sécurité de cet Etat, on peut alors supposer que celui-ci pourrait, sur la base de l'article 4(j), solliciter l'aide de l'Union pour mettre fin à ces actes de sécession et préserver de la sorte son intégrité territoriale ainsi que la paix et la sécurité sur son territoire.

Si telles sont les positions des Etats africains sur la sécession, consacrées dans la Charte de l'OUA et l'Acte constitutif de l'UA puis confirmées par la pratique subséquente, les dispositions qu'ils ont inclues dans la Charte africaine des droits de l'homme et des peuples recèlent des virtualités qui tempèrent cette négation absolue de la sécession non consentie.

II. Les potentialités de la Charte africaine des droits de l'homme et des peuples: vers la reconnaissance en filigrane d'un droit du peuple à la sécession?

Certaines dispositions relatives aux droits des peuples de la Charte africaine semblent reconnaître à ces derniers un droit de sécession, notamment l'article 19 qui proclame l'égalité des peuples et condamne en conséquence la domination d'un peuple par un autre (A), et l'article 20 qui affirme le droit inaliénable et indescriptible de *tout* peuple à l'autodétermination (B). Afin d'apprécier plus précisément les potentialités de ces deux dispositions, les conclusions tirées de leur

[49] Nous verrons (*infra*, pp. 279 et 290) que l'existence de peuples à l'intérieur d'un Etat déjà constitué est envisagée par certains instruments juridiques africains.

interprétation seront soumises à l'épreuve de la 'jurisprudence' pertinente de la Commission africaine.

A. *L'article 19 de la Charte africaine*

Aux termes de l'article 19 de la Charte africaine:

> Tous les peuples sont égaux; ils jouissent de la même dignité et ont les mêmes droits. Rien ne peut justifier la domination d'un peuple par un autre.

Cette disposition consacre expressément le principe d'égalité des peuples et celui d'égalité de droits des peuples, ces derniers pouvant être *constitués ou non en Etats*.[50] De par cet élargissement du peuple à un groupe non encore constitué en Etat, combiné avec le rejet de toute domination d'un peuple par un autre, on peut se demander si l'article 19 ne permet pas à un peuple dominé de faire sécession.

Cette possibilité ne paraît pas en effet être totalement exclue par le texte de l'article. Déjà, il y a lieu de relever que 'la consécration expresse de l'égalité des peuples par un instrument juridique relatif à la protection des droits de l'homme *"et des peuples"* en Afrique' pourrait s'analyser comme

> *une prise en considération de la réalité sociologique du continent africain, à savoir le fait ethnique, ainsi que comme une réaction à ses vicissitudes passées ou actuelles.* L'article 19 porterait ainsi la condamnation de toute hégémonie – *de jure* ou *de facto* – exercée par une ou plusieurs ethnies sur une ou plusieurs autres.[51]

Toute hégémonie d'une éthnie sur une autre est donc condamnée par l'article 19, et il reste à déterminer les conséquences juridiques de cette hégémonie, que 'rien ne peut justifier' comme le souligne la disposition. Celles-ci peuvent-elles consister en une autorisation à faire sécession? L'article 19 ne précise pas ces conséquences juridiques, mais la Commission africaine a été saisie de communications alléguant la violation de l'article 19 par un Etat partie, celles introduites par certaines organisations non gouvernementales (ONG) contre, respectivement, la République islamique de Mauritanie et la Zambie.

[50] M. Bedjaoui et F. Ouguergouz, 'Commentaire de l'article 19', *in:* K. Mbaye et M. Kamto (dirs.), *La Charte africaine des droits de l'homme et des peuples – Commentaire article par article*, p. 1 (à paraître).

[51] *Ibid.*, p. 3; en italiques dans le texte.

Dans les communications relatives à la Mauritanie,[52] des ONG ont dénoncé des actes de persécution et de marginalisation à l'égard de la population noire de Mauritanie, qui seraient des mesures discriminatoires et une négation du principe d'égalité des peuples énoncé à l'article 19 de la Charte africaine (voir notamment la communication 54/91). Dans sa décision au fond, la Commission reconnaît qu'au cœur des différentes communications examinées se trouve la question de la domination d'une frange de la population par une autre, tout en présisant qu'elle

> se doit cependant d'admettre que les informations mises à sa disposition ne lui permettent pas d'établir avec certitude la violation de l'article 19 de la Charte dans les formes alléguées. Elle a toutefois identifié et condamné l'existence de pratiques discriminatoires à l'encontre de certaines couches de la population mauritanienne.[53]

Par sa conclusion sur l'absence de violation de l'article 19, la Commission n'a pas apporté de précision quant au droit qui serait ouvert au peuple discriminé. L'examen de ses décisions ne permet pas en tout cas de détecter une prédisposition à affirmer un droit de sécession au peuple en question. Au vu de sa pratique dans l'examen des allégations de violations d'autres dispositions de la Charte africaine, on pourrait d'ailleurs douter qu'elle puisse aller jusqu'à là; en effet, elle se borne en général à constater la violation alléguée et à demander à l'Etat concerné de prendre les dispositions législatives et règlementaires nécessaires pour y mettre fin.

Il est à cet égard intéressant d'observer qu'une précision quant au droit d'un peuple discriminé de faire sécession a été apportée par le Comité des Nations Unies pour l'élimination du racisme et de la discrimination (CERD), organe de surveillance de l'application de la Convention du même nom des Nations Unies. Dans sa *Recommandation générale XXI (48)*,[54] le Comité a donné son opinion sur le rapport

[52] Communication 54/91, *Malawi African Association c./ Mauritanie*; Communication 61/91, *Amnesty International c./ Mauritanie*; Communication 98/93, Mme Sarr Diop, *Union Interafricaine des Droits de l'Homme et RADDHO c./ Mauritanie*; Communications 164/97 à 196/97, *Collectif des Veuves et Ayants-droits c./ Mauritanie*; Communication 210/98, *Association Mauritanienne des Droits de l'Homme c./ Mauritanie*, in: *Treizième rapport annuel d'activités de la Commission africaine des droits de l'homme et des peuples – 1999/2000*, Doc. OUA AHG/222 (XXXVI).

[53] Par. 142 de la décision.

[54] Adoptée le 8 mars 1996, lors de sa 48ème session, publiée dans le rapport annuel du CERD à l'Assemblée générale des Nations Unies: doc. ONU A/51/18, Annexe VIII-B, pp. 133–4.

entre autodétermination et discrimination d'une partie de la population compte tenu du fait que

> les groupes ou minorités ethniques ou religieuses mentionnent fréquemment le droit à l'autodétermination comme fondement de la revendication d'un droit à la sécession.[55]

Après avoir rappelé les obligations des Etats à l'égard de ces minorités, il souligne

> [qu']aucune de ses initiatives ne doit être interprétée comme autorisant ou encourageant une action quelconque de nature à porter atteinte, en tout ou en partie, à l'intégrité territoriale ou à l'unité politique d'Etats souverains et indépendants qui se conduisent de façon conforme au principe de l'égalité de droits et de l'autodétermination des peuples et sont dotés d'un gouvernement représentant l'ensemble de la population du territoire, sans distinction de race, de croyance ou de couleur. De l'avis du Comité, le droit international ne reconnaît pas de droit général des peuples de déclarer unilatéralement faire sécession par rapport à un Etat.[56]

Ainsi, la sécession n'est pas la conséquence naturelle du non respect du principe de non-discrimination et de non-domination d'un groupe national par un autre. Une partie du peuple constitutif d'un Etat, discriminée ou dominée par une autre, ne peut donc revendiquer un droit de sécession pour changer cet état de chose, même si la *Recommandation générale* du CERD laisse entrevoir un tel droit dans des circonstances extrêmes et en dernier recours.[57]

Il a du reste été relevé, à propos des communications mentionnées plus haut, que la Commission africaine 'ne ferme pas totalement la porte à une interprétation extensive de l'article 19 de la Charte africaine' et que le principe de l'égalité énoncé par cet article, déjà inscrit dans la Charte des Nations Unies, 'revêt une importance particulière dans le contexte africain où il est en effet potentiellement applicable aux peuples intégrés dans un même Etat . . . Celui-ci servirait alors à prévenir toute discrimination à l'égard d'une ethnie particulière, c'est-à-dire toute pratique discriminatoire qui en viserait les membres sur la seule base de leur appartenance à celle-ci.'[58]

Ce point a été justement précisé par la Commission africaine dans l'examen d'une communication introduite par une autre ONG contre la

[55] Par. 6 de l'Annexe VIII-B du rapport annuel précité. [56] *Ibid.*, par. 11.
[57] Voir sur ce point nos développements dans la dernière partie de ce chapitre.
[58] Bedjaoui et Ouguergouz, 'Commentaire de l'article 19', p. 5.

Zambie.[59] L'ONG en question allègue qu'un amendement de la Constitution zambienne, limitant la candidature à la présidence du pays aux citoyens dont les deux parents sont zambiens par la naissance ou par la descendance, est 'discriminatoire, divisionniste et viole les droits humains de 35% de toute la population', allant ainsi à l'encontre des dispositions de la Charte africaine condamnant de telles formes de discrimination, dont l'article 19.[60] De son côté, la Zambie rétorque que l'amendement ne visait aucun individu ni aucun groupe de personnes, et considère d'ailleurs que l'invocation par l'organisation plaignante d'une violation de l'article 19 ne ressortit pas du domaine de ladite communication, étant donné que cet article se rapporte au peuple et ne présente aucun rapport avec les questions de discrimination d'un individu qui ont été soulevées.[61]

Dans sa décision au fond, la Commission suit en partie cette dernière conclusion de la Zambie, tout en apportant des précisions importantes sur les conditions d'application de l'article 19; elle dispose notamment ce qui suit:

> La Commission est d'avis que le recours à l'article 19 de la Charte Africaine est peu judicieux. Car la section traitant des 'peuples' ne peut pas s'appliquer dans le cas d'espèce. Pour ce faire, il faudrait fournir des preuves que l'effet de la mesure allait affecter de manière négative un groupe identifiable de citoyens zambiens du fait de leur descendance commune, de leur origine ethnique, de leur langue ou de leurs habitudes culturelles. Les dispositions prétendument offensantes de la loi portant modification de la Constitution zambienne (1996) ne visent pas cet objectif.[62]

Ainsi, l'article 19 de la Charte africaine ne s'applique que lorsque les mesures discriminatoires alléguées visent, expressément ou dans leurs effets, un groupe déterminé d'une population d'un Etat, idéntifié selon des critères généalogique, ethnique, linguistique ou culturelle. C'est contre ce groupe, qualifié alors de peuple, que toute discrimination ou domination est condamnée par l'article 19. Il est toutefois difficile de déduire de cet article ou de son interprétation par la Commission africaine un droit de sécession des peuples victimes de discrimination ou de domination. L'article 20 de la Charte africaine, qui accorde un droit à l'autodétermination à *tout* peuple, offre-t-il plus de potentialités en la matière?

[59] Communication 211/98, *Legal Resources Foundation c./ Zambie*, in: *Quatorzième rapport annuel d'activités de la Commission africaine des droits de l'homme et des peuples – 2000/2001*, Doc. OUA AHG/229 (XXXVII), Tripoli (Libye), 7 mai 2001.

[60] Par. 2 et 10. [61] Voir par. 36, 37 et 49. [62] Par. 73.

B. L'article 20 de la Charte africaine

L'article 20 de la Charte africaine est ainsi libellé:

1. Tout peuple a droit à l'existence. Tout peuple a un droit imprescriptible et inaliénable à l'autodétermination. Il détermine librement son statut politique et assure son développement économique selon la voie qu'il a librement choisie.
2. Les peuples colonisés ou opprimés ont le droit de se libérer de leur état de domination en recourant à tous moyens reconnus par la Communauté internationale.
3. Tous les peuples ont droit à l'assistance des Etats parties à la présente Charte, dans leur lutte de libération contre la domination étrangère, qu'elle soit d'ordre politique, économique ou culturelle.

Au paragraphe 1 de cet article, le droit à l'autodétermination est conféré à *tout peuple* et, dans l'exercice de ce droit, un peuple pourrait opter pour la création d'un nouvel Etat par voie de sécession. L'expression 'tout peuple' prend en effet un sens particulier lorsqu'on la lit à la lumière des paragraphes 2 et 3 qui se réfèrent pour leur part explicitement aux peuples colonisés, opprimés ou sous domination étrangère. Le droit à l'autodétermination prévu au paragraphe 1 concernerait ainsi tout peuple, qu'il soit colonisé, sous domination étrangère ou intégré dans un Etat ayant déjà acquis son indépendance.

On retrouve les mêmes potentialités dans l'article premier commun aux deux Pactes internationaux des Nations Unies relatifs aux droits civils et politiques, et aux droits économiques, sociaux et culturels. Rédigé presque dans les mêmes termes que l'article 20(1) de la Charte africaine, l'article premier[63] a été aussi interprété par certains auteurs comme octroyant le droit à l'autodétermination à tous les peuples, quelle que soit leur situation, lesquels pourraient alors choisir la sécession dans l'exercice de ce droit.[64] La majorité de la doctrine a toutefois adopté une interprétation restrictive de cette disposition. Il semblerait que la volonté d'extension de ce droit à tous les peuples, notamment aux communautés infra-étatiques,

[63] '*Tous* les peuples ont le droit de disposer d'eux-mêmes. En vertu de ce droit, ils déterminent librement leur statut politique et assurent librement leur développement économique, social et culturel.'

[64] Certains ont ainsi estimé qu' '[i]l serait paradoxal et contradictoire de parler d'un côté d'un droit de libre disposition des peuples, et de leur nier de l'autre des choix parmi les plus désirés, tels que l'indépendance ou le rattachement à un autre Etat. Les deux Pactes internationaux de l'ONU devraient donc être lus comme incluant un droit à la sécession'; Christakis, *Le droit à l'autodétermination*, p. 147.

ait été le fait des puissances coloniales, dans le cadre de leur résistance à l'adoption de l'article premier commun qui poussait à la décolonisation. Les puissances coloniales avançaient que si le droit à l'autodétermination était consacré, il pourrait mettre en danger l'intégrité territoriale de tous les Etats, et non pas seulement celle des empires coloniaux car il devrait nécessairement s'appliquer à tous les peuples, à tous les groupes ethniques, à toutes les minorités nationales.[65] Selon ce courant doctrinal, le principe de droit des peuples à disposer d'eux-mêmes, dans sa dimension externe, ne devrait donc concerner que les seuls peuples sous domination coloniale ou raciale.[66]

L'article 20 de la Charte africaine pourrait pour sa part militer en faveur d'une interprétation plus large dans la mesure où son paragraphe 2 se réfère aux 'peuples colonisés ou opprimés', ce dernier adjectif pouvant en effet s'analyser comme une référence à d'autres situations que celle de domination dans laquelle se trouvaient il y a quelque temps encore les peuples d'Afrique australe. Une telle interprétation est d'autant moins à exclure qu'en prohibant toute discrimination sur la base de l'ethnie,[67] la Charte africaine fait montre du souci de tenir compte de la pluralité ethnique des Etats africains.[68] Il n'est ainsi pas impossible qu'elle ait également voulu prendre en considération cette réalité et viser l'ethnie tout autant que le peuple constitutif d'un Etat quand elle se réfère au 'peuple'. Le mot 'ethnie'[69] recouvre, en effet, en Afrique une réalité sociale

[65] *Ibid.*, p. 150.

[66] En faveur de cette interprétation étroite, voir E. Bello, 'The African Charter on Human and Peoples' Rights. A Legal Analysis', *Recueil des cours* 194 (1985-V), pp. 169–70; R. Gittleman, 'The African Charter on Human and Peoples' Rights: A Legal Analysis', *VJIL* 22/4 (1980), 680; K. J. Partsch, 'The Enforcement of Human Rights and Peoples' Rights: Observations on their Reciprocal Relations', *in:* R. Bernhardt et J. A. Jolowicz (eds.), *International Enforcement of Human Rights* (Berlin / Heidelberg / New York: Springer-Verlag, 1987), p. 28; B. N'Gom, 'Charte africaine des droits de l'homme et des peuples – Présentation', *in:* A. Fenet (dir.), *Droits de l'homme – Droits des peuples* (Paris: P.U.F., 1982), p. 207. En faveur d'une interprétation large, voir par exemple C. Anyangwe, 'Obligations of States Parties to the African Charter on Human and People's Rights', *RADIC* 10/4 (1998), 653–57.

[67] 8ème considérant du préambule et article 2.

[68] Comparer avec la Charte d'Addis-Abeba du 23 mai 1963 et la Charte Culturelle de l'Afrique du 5 juillet 1976 qui n'y font qu'une brève allusion à travers un considérant de leur préambule rédigé dans des termes identiques et apparemment soigneusement choisis: 'Guidés par une commune volonté de renforcer la compréhension entre nos *peuples* et la coopération entre nos *Etats*, afin de répondre aux aspirations de nos *populations* vers la consolidation d'une fraternité et d'une solidarité intégrées au sein d'une unité plus vaste qui transcende les divergences *ethniques* et *nationales*' (les italiques sont de nous).

[69] Du grec *ethnos*: peuple, le terme désigne un groupement organique d'individus de même culture.

numériquement importante.[70] D'ailleurs, si l'on s'en tient aux traditionnels éléments objectifs et subjectifs proposés pour la définition du peuple – 'forme particulière de communauté humaine unie par la conscience et la volonté de constituer une unité capable d'agir en vue d'un avenir commun'[71] – le concept d'ethnie en épouse sans conteste les contours. En substance, il est à cet égard révélateur que l'Assemblée générale des Nations Unies ait un temps fait de l'élément ethnique un des critères d'identification des peuples des territoires non-autonomes. Celle-ci avait en effet affirmé qu' 'il y a obligation, à première vue, de communiquer des renseignements à l'égard d'un territoire géographiquement séparé et ethniquement ou culturellement distinct du pays qui l'administre'.[72] De par son homogénéité culturelle, son assise territoriale claire, l'identité de groupe et la facilité de recensement de ses membres, rien n'interdirait *a priori* à une entité ethnique de revendiquer la qualité de peuple et de prétendre ainsi au bénéfice de l'article 20 de la Charte africaine.

C'est toutefois là une analyse que ne semble pas partager la Commission africaine des droits de l'homme et des peuples. Celle-ci fait en effet preuve de beaucoup de prudence dans son interprétation de l'article 20(1). En 1992, elle a eu à se prononcer sur une requête introduite sur la base de cette disposition par le président du Congrès du Peuple Katangais, lui demandant de reconnaître ce parti comme un mouvement de libération nationale habilité à recevoir une assistance pour l'accession du Katanga à l'indépendance, de reconnaître l'indépendance de cette province et d'aider à l'évacuation du Zaïre du territoire katangais. Dans sa décision, la Commission indique

> [qu']en l'absence de preuve tangible à l'appui des violations des droits de l'homme à tel point qu'il faille mettre en cause l'intégrité territoriale du Zaïre et en l'absence de toute preuve attestant le refus au peuple Katangais du droit de participer à la direction des affaires publiques conformément

70 Voir par exemple, les principales ethnies des pays suivants: Benin (Fon, Adja, Bariba), Burundi (Hutu, Tutsi), Congo (Bakongo, Bateke, Mboshi, Sangha), Côte d'Ivoire (Baoulé, Bété), Ghana (Akan, Mossi, Ewe), Kenya (Agikuyu, Abaluyia), Nigeria (Yoruba, Hausa, Ibo, Fulani), Rwanda (Hutu, Tutsi), Soudan (Sudanese Arabs, Dinka, Nuba), Senegal (Wolof, Fulani, Tukulor, Serer, Diola, Mandingo).

71 H. Gros Espiell, *Le droit à l'autodétermination – Application des résolutions de l'O.N.U.* (New York: Nations Unies, 1979), Doc. ONU E/CN.4/Sub.2/405/Rev.1, p. 9 (# 56).

72 Principe IV de la résolution A/RES/1541 (XV) du 15 décembre 1960, *Principes qui doivent guider les Etats Membres pour déterminer si l'obligation de communiquer des renseignements prévue à l'alinéa e de l'Article 73 de la Charte, leur est applicable ou non.*

à l'article 13 (1) de la Charte africaine, la Commission maintient que le Katanga est tenu d'user d'une forme d'autodétermination qui soit compatible avec la souveraineté et l'intégrité territoriale du Zaïre.[73]

Elle déclare en conséquence qu'en l'absence de toute violation d'un droit garanti par la Charte africaine, la requête relative à l'indépendance du Katanga n'est pas fondée. On mesure là l'extrême prudence de la Commission africaine qui a préféré insister sur la dimension interne du droit à l'autodétermination et lier son exercice à celui du droit de l'individu de participer à la direction des affaires publiques de son pays.

La Commission a confirmé sa manière de voir à propos de l'examen d'une communication dirigée celle-ci contre le Nigeria.[74] Selon la Commission:

> Le droit d'un peuple à déterminer son 'statut politique' [tel que garanti par l'article 20(1) de la Charte] peut être interprété comme impliquant le droit des Nigérians à choisir librement les personnes ou le parti qui les gouvernent. C'est l'équivalent du droit dont jouit tout individu aux termes de l'article 13.[75]

La Commission poursuit son raisonnement de la manière qui suit:

> Les élections en question ici, tenues dans des conditions considérées comme libres et justes par les observateurs internationaux, étaient l'expression du droit des Nigérians à choisir librement ce statut politique. L'annulation des résultats par l'autorité au pouvoir est une violation de ce droit du peuple nigérian.[76]

La Commission ne tire toutefois pas toutes les conséquences de son raisonnement puisque dans le dispositif de sa décision elle ne mentionne pas l'article 20(1) et conclut à la violation de l'article 13 de la Charte africaine. Par contre, dans une résolution de 1994, la Commission indique clairement que l'article 20 est violé lorsqu'un groupe prend le pouvoir par la force;[77] elle réitérera cette position dans une résolution sur la situation

[73] Communication 75/92, *Congrès du Peuple Katangais c./ Zaïre* (par. 1 et 6), in: *Huitième rapport annuel d'activités de la Commission, 1994–1995.*

[74] Communication 102/93, *Constitutional Rights Project and Civil Liberties Organization c./ Nigeria,* in: *Douzième rapport annuel d'activités de la Commission, 1998–1999.*

[75] Par. 51 de la décision.

[76] Par. 52 de la décision.

[77] CADHP, 16ème session ordinaire, Banjul (Gambie), 25 oct.–3 nov. 1994, *Résolution sur les régimes militaires,* doc. OUA AHG/201 (XXXI), Annexe VII, 4ème considérant.

aux Comores et dans une autre sur la situation au Niger, liant à chaque fois les articles 13(1) et 20(1).[78]

A la lumière de la pratique de la Commission africaine, de l'Organisation de l'Unité africaine et de l'Union africaine, il conviendra donc d'interpréter de façon restrictive l'article 20 de la Charte africaine.[79] Selon cette interprétation, celui-ci ne reconnaît pas le droit à la sécession, qui demeure un mode radical de mise en oeuvre du principe de droit des peuples à disposer d'eux-mêmes qu'il prévoit. Pris dans sa dimension externe et en dehors des situations de colonisation et de domination raciale, le principe de droit des peuples à disposer d'eux-mêmes n'a donc pas la faveur des Etats africains. Ceux-ci semblent plutôt préférer promouvoir le principe dans sa dimension interne, de manière à désamorcer tout mouvement centrifuge. L'autodétermination interne est ainsi conçue comme une alternative aux éventuelles revendications sécessionnistes d'une fraction de la population d'un Etat.

III. La promotion de l'autodétermination interne par l'OUA, la Commission africaine et l'Union africaine, comme alternative au droit à la sécession

La promotion du respect de l'autodétermination interne est une évolution très récente dans l'ordre juridique régional et la pratique africains.[80] Pendant longtemps en Afrique, l'exercice de l'autodétermination, même dans sa dimension interne, et la préservation de l'unité nationale, étaient

[78] 'Reconnaissant que la prise du pouvoir par la force est contraire aux dispositions des articles 13(1) et 20(1) de la Charte Africaine des Droits de l'Homme et des Peuples et que l'accession au pouvoir de régimes militaires par voie de coups d'Etats constitue une atteinte intolérable aux principes démocratiques de l'Etat de Droit; . . . Déclare que le coup d'Etat militaire survenu au Niger est une violation grave et intolérable des droits du Peuple nigérien de choisir librement son gouvernement'; *Résolution sur la situation au Niger* et *Résolution sur la situation aux Comores*, 25ème session ordinaire, Banjul (Gambie), 26 avril – 5 mai 1999, *Douzième rapport annuel d'activités de la Commission, 1998–1999.*

[79] Voir dans ce sens également, R. Kiwanuka, 'The Meaning of "People" in the African Charter on Human and Peoples' Rights', *AJIL* 82 (1988), 88–9.

[80] Il a été ainsi dit qu'au lendemain de la vague des indépendances des Etats africains dans les années 1960 et sa cohorte de problèmes liés au maintien du tracé arbitraire des frontières coloniales, 'nombre de ces nouveaux Etats [ont] été préoccupés par deux tâches simultanées – l'édification de l'État et l'édification de la nation – surtout après la guerre de sécession au Congo. Trop souvent, cela dit, ils ont eu recours, pour assurer l'unité nationale, à une centralisation massive du pouvoir politique et économique et à la suppression du pluralisme politique'; Rapport du Secrétaire général de l'ONU, Kofi Annan, sur *Les causes des conflits et la promotion d'une paix et d'un développement durables en Afrique* (A/52/871–S/1998/318, 13 avril 1998), par. 8.

considérés comme deux objectifs inconciliables.[81] Reflet d'une époque où l'autoritarisme légué par l'administration coloniale n'encourageait pas la représentation ou la participation populaires,[82] la situation va peu à peu évoluer, du moins sur le plan juridique, par l'adoption de plusieurs décisions des organisations internationales ou de conventions internationales en matière de droits de l'homme, mettant en avant le respect de la dimension interne du droit des peuples à disposer d'eux-mêmes (A). Quelles incidences cette insistance sur le respect de la dimension interne du droit à l'autodétermination peut-elle avoir sur l'exercice de la sécession en Afrique? (B).

A. Vers une redynamisation du droit des peuples

La Charte de l'OUA de 1963, comme nous l'avons vu, n'a pas accordé une grande place au droit des peuples à l'autodétermination, pas plus qu'aux droits de la personne humaine en général. Cette attention portée aux droits des peuples date de 1981 avec l'inclusion dans la Charte africaine de six articles y relatifs, et s'est renforcée par l'adoption subséquente de nombreuses résolutions et décisions précisant ces droits, avec en point d'orgue la consécration dans l'Acte constitutif de l'Union africaine, adopté en l'an 2000, d'objectifs et de principes qui n'existaient pas dans la Charte d'Addis Abeba. Ces principes mis en avant par les institutions africaines[83] pour promouvoir le respect de l'autodétermination interne des peuples s'articulent autour du respect des principes démocratiques et de la condamnation des changements anti-constitutionnels de gouvernement.

Plusieurs textes juridiques régionaux africains exigent en effet le respect des principes démocratiques sur le continent, au premier rang desquels figure l'article 20(1) de la Charte africaine, déjà examiné plus haut. Si cet article a pu être interprété comme une voie possible à la sécession, il prévoit surtout la libre détermination par les peuples de leur destinée au moyen

[81] Le professeur T. M. Franck explique à ce propos que 'self-determination, in its African context, was not a doctrine interpreted as creating a populist entitlement to democracy... It seemed that the new governments of the former colonies regarded self-determination as a unique event occurring only at the moment of a colony's independence: what has been called "one man, one vote, one time". It was not widely contemplated that the entitlement of self-determination would continue to empower "peoples" after the decolonization task had been completed'; 'Postmodern Tribalism and the Right to Secession', *in:* C.Brölmann & al. (eds.), *Peoples and Minorities*, p. 10.

[82] Rapport cité du Secrétaire général de l'ONU, doc. A/52/871 – S/1998/318, par. 71.

[83] Voir par exemple, *Résolution sur l'Union africaine et la Charte africaine des droits de l'homme et des peuples*, 29ème session ordinaire tenue à Tripoli (Libye), 23 avril – 7 mai 2001.

d'élections libres, périodiques et transparentes. Dans sa décision du 11 mai 2000 sur la Gambie, la Commission africaine a clairement montré que l'article 20(1) consacre le droit du peuple de désigner ses dirigeants politiques et de choisir son système de gouvernement.[84] A cet égard, cette disposition est le pendant de l'article 13(1) qui prévoit le droit de tous les citoyens de participer librement à la direction des affaires publiques de leur pays, soit directement, soit par l'intermédiaire de représentants librement choisis.[85]

L'intérêt porté par la Commission au respect des principes démocratiques l'a aussi amené à déplorer l'annulation des élections présidentielles dans un Etat lorsque celles-ci ont été jugées libres et démocratiques par des observateurs nationaux et internationaux, ainsi qu'à condamner la détention de militants démocrates et de membres de la presse.[86] Elle a en outre affirmé que les élections représentent le seul moyen par lequel les peuples peuvent démocratiquement mettre en place leur gouvernement, conformément à la Charte africaine, et

> qu'il incombe aux Etats parties à la Charte de prendre les mesures nécessaires pour préserver et protéger la crédibilité du processus électoral. Ces mesures doivent assurer la présence d'observateurs nationaux et internationaux aux élections et garantir à ces observateurs l'accès et les conditions de sécurité nécessaires pour leur permettre de s'acquitter de leur mission et de faire rapport avec précision concernant les élections.[87]

Enfin, il est intéressant de noter que dans une résolution sur le processus de paix en Somalie, la Commission mentionne expressément les articles 19 à 24 de la Charte africaine et affirme que pour promouvoir les droits des peuples garantis par ces dispositions, 'il faut nécessairement

[84] Communications 147/95 et 149/96, *Sir Dawda K. Jawara c./ Gambie*, par. 72 et 73, in: *Treizième rapport annuel d'activités, 1999–2000.*

[85] Voir sur ce point les résolutions sur la situation prévalant aux Comores et au Nigeria citées plus haut (*supra*, p. 281 et note 78) où la Commission africaine associe ces deux dispositions.

[86] *Résolution sur le Nigeria*, 16ème session ordinaire, Banjul, du 25 octobre au 3 novembre 1994.

[87] *Résolution sur le processus électoral et la gouvernance participative*, par. 1 et 3, 19ème session ordinaire, Ouagadougou, du 26 mars au 4 avril 1996. Dans la pratique d'ailleurs, l'OUA a pris part à des observations électorales dont la première en Namibie en 1989, conjointement avec les Nations Unies. Mais c'est en février 1990 qu'elle a débuté sa propre expérience avec l'envoi d'une mission d'observations électorales aux Comores, sur invitation du président de ce pays. Depuis, le processus semble être bien en marche puisqu'à la date de juillet 2003, l'OUA/UA a participé à l'observation de près de 100 élections dans 43 Etats membres. Voir le site web de l'Union africaine, www.africa-union.org (Commission, Affaires politiques).

un gouvernement démocratiquement élu par la population entière de la Somalie'.[88]

On observera que cette implication de la Commission africaine dans le processus de démocratisation de l'Afrique s'inscrit dans le sillage de certaines prises de position formelle de l'OUA, par exemple celles faites en 1990 dans la Déclaration sur les situations politiques et socio-économiques en Afrique et les changements fondamentaux intervenus dans le monde,[89] où la Conférence des chefs d'Etat et de gouvernement met l'accent sur la consolidation des institutions démocratiques à travers la participation populaire; ou, en 2000, dans la Déclaration du même organe sur la Conférence sur la sécurité, la stabilité, le développement et la coopération en Afrique (CSSDCA), où la promotion de la démocratisation et de la bonne gouvernance est présentée comme allant de pair avec la tenue d'élections libres et transparentes.[90]

Dans l'Acte constitutif de l'Union africaine, les dirigeants africains ont confirmé leur attachement à la démocratisation du continent en posant comme l'un des objectifs de la nouvelle organisation régionale celui de 'promouvoir les principes et les institutions démocratiques, la participation populaire et la bonne gouvernance', et comme moyens d'atteindre ce but le 'respect des principes démocratiques, des droits de l'homme, de l'état de droit et de la bonne gouvernance'.[91]

Cette promotion des principes et institutions démocratiques a pour conséquence la condamnation et le rejet des changements anticonstitutionnels de gouvernement. Les textes que nous venons de mentionner condamnent tous de tels changements et l'Acte constitutif de l'Union africaine consacre solennellement leur rejet comme l'un des principes de l'Organisation.[92] Mais c'est là le résultat d'un long processus qui a commencé dans les années 1990, avec notamment l'adoption par la Commission africaine des droits de l'homme et des peuples de résolutions et de décisions condamnant des coups d'Etat militaires survenus en Afrique, invitant 'les régimes militaires africains à respecter les droits de l'homme' et encourageant 'les Etats à reléguer l'ère des interventions militaires au passé afin de préserver l'image de l'Afrique, d'assumer

88 *Résolution sur le processus de paix et de réconciliation nationale en Somalie*, préambule, 27ème session ordinaire, Alger, du 27 avril au 11 mai 2000.

89 AHG/Decl. 1 (XXVI), 26ème session ordinaire, Addis Abeba (Ethiopie), 11 juillet 1990.

90 AHG/Decl. 4 (XXXVI).

91 Respectivement, article 3 (g) et article 4 (m). Voir aussi la Déclaration de l'OUA sur le principes régissant les élections démocratiques en Afrique, adoptée à la 38ème session ordinaire de la Conférence des chefs d'Etat à Durban, 9 juillet 2002.

92 Article 4, al. p).

le progrès et le développement et de favoriser l'instauration d'un climat propice à l'épanouissement des valeurs des droits de l'homme'.[93] La Commission a également estimé que la prise du pouvoir par la force par tout groupe de civils ou militaires est contraire aux prescriptions des articles 13(1) et 20(1) de la Charte africaine des droits de l'homme et des peuples, et constitue une atteinte intolérable aux principes démocratiques de l'Etat de droit.[94]

Cette position de la Commission africaine a été par la suite confirmée par la Conférence des chefs d'Etat et de gouvernement de l'OUA. Condamnant le coup d'Etat du 25 mai 1997 en Sierra Leone, alors qu'elle était en session ordinaire à Harare (Zimbabwe), la Conférence s'est engagée à ne plus tolérer des changements de gouvernement par des voies non constitutionnelles. Au Sommet d'Alger de 1999, une décision sur le rejet des changements anti-constitutionnels de gouvernement et la promotion de la démocratie en Afrique a été prise par le même organe,[95] dans laquelle, entre autres, il lance un ultimatum aux gouvernements des Etats membres qui sont arrivés au pouvoir de manière anti-constitutionnelle depuis le Sommet de Harare de rétablir l'ordre constitutionnel d'ici le prochain Sommet, sous peine de se voir imposer des sanctions.

Des précisions sur les éléments relatifs à ce rejet des coups d'Etats ont été par la suite apportées par la Conférence dans sa Déclaration sur le cadre des réponses de l'OUA aux changements anti-constitutionnels de gouvernement.[96] Devant la résurgence des coups d'Etat en Afrique, les dirigeants africains y reconnaissent que ce phénomène constitue une menace contre la paix et la sécurité sur le continent, est une entrave au processus de démocratisation en Afrique, et entraîne des violations

[93] *Résolution sur les régimes militaires*, 16ème session ordinaire, Banjul (Gambie), 25 oct.–3 nov. 1994.

[94] Voir *Résolution sur la situation aux Comores*, 25ème session ordinaire, Bujumbura, Burundi, 25 avril – 5 mai 1999, *Douzième rapport annuel d'activités, 1998–1999*; également *Résolution sur la Gambie*, dans laquelle la Commission réaffirme que le coup d'Etat du 22 juillet 1994 dans ce pays 'constitue une violation flagrante et grave du droit du peuple gambien de choisir librement son gouvernement', et prie les autorités militaires de remettre le pouvoir aux représentants du peuple librement choisis, 16ème session ordinaire, Banjul, 25 oct. – 3 nov. 1994. Au cours de la même session, une *Résolution sur la situation des droits de l'homme en Afrique* a élargi la condamnation des coups d'Etat à 'la planification ou l'exécution de coup d'Etat et toute tentative d'accéder au pouvoir par des moyens non démocratiques', en même temps qu'elle précise aux Etats les mesures à prendre pour prévenir de tels coups d'Etat, à savoir veiller 'à ce que les élections et les processus électoraux soient transparents et justes'.

[95] Décision AHG/Dec.142 (XXXV).

[96] AHG/Decl.5 (XXXVI), 36ème session ordinaire, Lomé (Togo), 10–12 juillet 2000.

flagrantes des principes fondamentaux de l'OUA et de l'ONU (al. 2).[97] C'est ainsi que dans sa récente décision sur le coup d'Etat en République centrafricaine (RCA), le Conseil exécutif de l'Union africaine:

1. Réaffirme son attachement indéfectible au respect de la décision d'Alger de juillet 1999 et de la déclaration de Lomé de juillet 2000 sur les changements anticonstitutionnels de gouvernement . . .
2. Demande aux autorités centrafricaines de prendre les mesures nécessaires pour la restauration rapide de l'ordre constitutionnel et les encourage à continuer d'œuvrer à la promotion de la réconciliation nationale et du dialogue avec l'ensemble des forces politiques et sociales du pays;
3. Recommande, dans l'intervalle, et conformément à la déclaration de Lomé, la suspension de la participation de la RCA aux activités des organes de décision de l'Union africaine.[98]

Enfin, il est à noter que toutes ces prises de positions s'accompagnent généralement d'un appel à la réconciliation nationale et au dialogue entre les forces politiques. Ces appels, fruits surtout de la pratique, interviennent à la fois au moment de la naissance d'une crise interne et après le règlement de cette crise par un accord de paix ou un Pacte de réconciliation nationale.[99] Ils font partie des moyens destinés à favoriser

[97] La Conférence y énumère ensuite les éléments formant le cadre général des réponses de l'OUA aux changements inconstitutionnels de gouvernement, à savoir un ensemble de principes et valeurs communs pour la gouvernance démocratique; une définition de ce qui constitue un changement anticonstitutionnel; les mesures et actions que l'Organisation pourrait prendre progressivement en réaction à un changement anticonstitutionnel de gouvernement; et un mécanisme d'application au niveau des différents organes de l'OUA. Chacun de ces éléments a été détaillé dans la Déclaration.

[98] *Décision sur la situation en République centrafricaine*, 3ème session ordinaire du Conseil exécutif, Maputo (Mozambique), 4–8 juillet 2003, Doc. EX/CL/42 (III) g). Voir aussi la *Décision sur la situation au Libéria* – Doc. EX/CL/42 (III) i), par. 6 – prise lors de la même session, où le Conseil exécutif 'réitère la *position de l'Union africaine*, tel qu'énoncée dans la décision d'Alger de 1999 et la Déclaration de Lomé de 2000, qui soulignent que l'Union ne reconnaîtra aucun changement inconstitutionnel de Gouvernement' (les italiques sont de nous).

[99] On peut citer, à titre d'exemple, l'appui du Conseil exécutif de l'Union africaine aux efforts de réconciliation en République centrafricaine, par l'intensification du dialogue entre les autorités centrafricaines et les autres acteurs sociaux de ce pays, en vue d'un retour rapide à l'ordre constitutionnel (*Décision sur la situation en République Centrafricaine*, 3ème session ordinaire, Maputo (Mozambique), du 4 au 8 juillet 2003, Doc. EX/CL/42 (III) g). Voir aussi les décisions du Conseil exécutif sur les processus de paix au Soudan (EX/CL/42 (III) c) et en République démocratique du Congo (EX/CL/42 (III) e), sur la situation en Côte d'Ivoire (EX/CL/42 (III) h), et sur la Conférence internationale sur la région des Grands Lacs (EX/CL/43 (III)).

l'exercice du droit du peuple à l'autodétermination à l'intérieur du territoire de l'Etat où il se trouve en permettant la pleine participation de l'ensemble de la population ou de leurs représentants à la direction politique, économique et culturelle de l'Etat, rendant ainsi moins attrayant l'aventure sécessionniste.[100] Ceci nous conduit naturellement à l'examen des incidences de cette nouvelle configuration du droit du peuple à l'autodétermination interne sur la question de la sécession.

B. La relation entre respect de l'autodétermination interne et droit de sécession

L'insistance sur le respect de la dimension interne de l'autodétermination est dictée, rappelons-le, par la volonté de juguler les velléités sécessionnistes des peuples. La question est maintenant de savoir si, en cas de non respect de l'autodétermination interne, une partie de la population d'un Etat pourrait être légitimée à faire sécession.

Sur la base de l'interprétation des textes prévoyant le droit à l'autodétermination, on pourrait envisager des circonstances exceptionnelles dans lesquelles la sécession serait admise, en dernier recours. On soulignera à cet égard que la décision susmentionnée de la Commission africaine sur la question du Katanga[101] suggère fortement que l'exercice du droit de sécession ne serait pas à exclure en cas de violations flagrantes des droits de l'homme et de refus à un peuple intégré dans un Etat de participer à la direction des affaires publiques.[102]

On observera également que l'on peut trouver les germes d'un droit ultime à la sécession dans les termes du paragraphe 7 du cinquième principe de la résolution 2625 (XXV) de l'Assemblée générale des Nations Unies, où il est suggéré qu'un Etat non doté d'un gouvernement représentatif de l'ensemble du peuple, en violation du principe de non-discrimination, pourrait se voir opposer la sécession par cette partie non représentée de sa population. Ce droit à la sécession est toutefois soumis à des conditions strictes, notamment un refus persistant du gouvernement de permettre à l'ensemble de la population

[100] L'encouragement à la réconciliation nationale fait d'ailleurs partie de ce que les Nations Unies appellent la consolidation de la paix après les conflits, telle que développée par le Secrétaire général B. Boutros-Ghali dans son 'Agenda pour la paix', doc. ONU A/50/60 – S/1995/1, 3 janv.1995, par. 47–56.

[101] Voir *supra*, p. 280.

[102] Voir également en ce sens la *Recommandation générale XXI* du CERD, *supra*, p. 276 et note 54.

d'exercer son droit à l'autodétermination interne, des violations graves des droits fondamentaux de l'homme, l'inexistence de solution pacifique du problème dans le cadre de l'Etat concerné, ou encore l'absence de perspective de voir le gouvernement devenir représentatif de la totalité de la population dans un avenir prévisible.[103]

Il existe donc un courant doctrinal en faveur de l'exercice d'un droit de sécession dans des situations exceptionnelles pour assurer: la représentativité de l'Etat, l'égalité des peuples et l'égalité des droits des peuples, ainsi que la protection de leur existence face à des actes de génocide ou autres violations graves des droits de l'homme et des peuples. Le recours à la sécession serait ainsi admis lorsque les moyens juridiques et politiques disponibles pour faire respecter ces droits se sont avérés impuissants; toute la difficulté consistera alors à déterminer qui pourra apprécier la réalité de cet échec.

Pareille interprétation de la résolution 2625 (XXV) susmentionnée n'est pas à écarter totalement dans le cadre particulier du continent africain dans la mesure où l'article 20 de la Charte africaine semble emboîter le pas à cette résolution et codifier le paragraphe 7 de son cinquième principe en des termes à la fois plus vagues et plus généreux.[104] On pourrait en effet imaginer une application de l'article 20 (paragraphes 2 et 3) dans le cas d'une oppression dirigée exclusivement contre les membres d'une portion différenciable d'un peuple constitué en Etat, en l'occurrence une ethnie; une violation systématique des droits politiques des membres de celle-ci correspondrait alors au déni du droit à l'autodétermination interne d'une partie de ce peuple.[105] L'ethnie ne serait pas initialement sujet du droit à l'autodétermination externe mais le deviendrait par le fait même de la violation massive des droits de ses membres.

L'issue des négociations de paix entre le Nord et le Sud du Soudan semble aller dans ce sens. En effet, un des éléments endossés par l'Accord de paix global, signé le 9 janvier 2005 entre le gouvernement du Soudan et le Mouvement/Armée pour la Libération du peuple soudanais (SPLM/A), est de prévoir un droit de sécession de la partie Sud du pays. Ce 'Comprehensive Peace Agreement' parachève et fait entrer en vigueur une série

103 Voir sur ces questions la contribution de Christian Tomuschat dans le présent ouvrage, *supra*, chap. I.

104 La résolution 2625 parle simplement de représentativité du gouvernement alors que l'article 20 parle de domination politique, économique ou culturelle; voir *supra*, p. 278, le texte de l'article 20.

105 C'est alors à la Commission africaine ou de préférence à la future Cour Africaine des Droits de l'Homme et des Peuples qu'il devrait revenir de constater l'inexistence de toute autre alternative.

de six accords et protocoles déjà signés entre les deux parties, sous les auspices de l'Intergovernmental Authority on Development (IGAD).[106] Pour notre propos, ces textes octroient une large autonomie à la partie Sud du Soudan durant une période intérimaire de six ans, à l'issue de laquelle la population de cette partie du territoire sera appelée à choisir, par référendum, entre rester dans l'Etat actuel ou constituer un nouvel Etat indépendant. Cette éventualité de sécession du Sud repose sur les principes de base du processus de paix agréés par les parties dans le Protocole de Machakos du 20 juillet 2002, où elles se sont entendues sur un droit à l'autodétermination 'for the *people* of South Soudan';[107] éventualité qui a été intégrée dans les accords ultérieurs. Par exemple, l'Accord sur le cessez-le-feu permanent prévoit, à la fin de la période intérimaire de six ans, soit la formation d'une 'Sudan National Armed Forces' (SNAF) pour remplacer les unités jointes de l'armée nationale soudanaise et de la Sudan Peoples' Liberation Army (SPLA) – créées durant cette période intérimaire, soit la dissolution de ces unités pour réintégrer leur armée d'origine respective si le Sud opte pour la sécession.[108] Il a été également prévu, entre autres dispositions intéressantes, d'avoir un double système bancaire au Soudan pendant la période transitoire: un système bancaire islamique applicable au Nord et un système bancaire conventionnel pour le Sud, avec une restructuration de la Banque centrale du Soudan pour refléter ce changement.[109] Cette dernière devra ensuite frapper une nouvelle monnaie devant refléter la diversité culturelle du Soudan,[110] qui sera conçue – après l'évaluation

[106] Intergovernmental Authority on Development, organisation sous-régionale regroupant 7 Etats de l'Afrique orientale: Djibouti, Erythrée, Ethiopie, Kenya, Somalie, Soudan et Ouganda (cf. www.igad.org). Les Accords pertinents sont publiés sur ce site, et notamment sur http://www.sudantribune.com <documents>.

[107] 5ème paragraphe (les italiques sont de nous). Ce droit avec les termes 'peuple du Sud du Soudan' a été réitéré dans 'The Nairobi Declaration on the Final Phase of Peace in the Sudan', du 5 juin 2004, par laquelle les parties reconfirment leur accord sur les six textes conclus auparavant.

[108] 'Agreement on Permanent Ceasefire and Security Arrangements Implementation Modalities during the Pre-interim and Interim Periods', 25 sept. 2003, par. 7.1.4, 17.1 à 17.4, 20.1–20.2 et 21.2. A noter toutefois la référence dans le préambule de l'Accord à l'article 3 de l'Acte constitutif de l'Union africaine sur la souveraineté et l'intégrité territoriale des Etats, considérés alors comme 'critical to the peace process, if strictly adhered to'. Il en va de même du par. 1.15 qui stipule que 'Nothing in this agreement shall in any way undermine the sovereignty and territorial integrity of the Sudan.'

[109] 'Agreement on Wealth Sharing during the Pre-interim and Interim Period', 7 Jan. 2004, par. 14.1, 14.2 et 14.3.

[110] *Ibid.*, par. 14.9.

des monnaies circulant dans le pays – par un comité conjoint établi immédiatement après la signature de l'Accord global et sa ratification par les parties.[111]

Réserve faite du cas de l'Erythrée étudié plus haut, qui était une entité séparée de l'Ethiopie durant la période coloniale, c'est la première fois dans l'histoire qu'un accord de paix réglant un conflit interne en Afrique prévoit expressément un droit de sécession d'une partie de territoire d'un Etat[112] et octroie avant le vote du peuple en ce sens une série de prérogatives quasi-étatiques à la partie revendiquant son autonomie, sinon son indépendance. Il s'agit là d'une brèche ouverte à une modification des frontières héritées de la colonisation, dont le maintien est considéré comme un principe sacro-saint par les Etats africains.[113]

Il peut s'agir aussi d'une confirmation de l'idée selon laquelle le droit à la sécession n'est pas à écarter si les circonstances l'exigent. La volonté d'autonomie ou d'indépendance de la population du Sud – noire, chrétienne et animiste – vient en effet, entre autres raisons politiques et économiques, d'un sentiment de sa domination et marginalisation par le pouvoir central issu de la population du Nord, arabe et musulmane. La déclaration de John Garang à son retour dans son fief du Sud pour la ratification de l'Accord de paix est édifiante à cet égard : il dit que l'unité du Soudan est dans les mains de Khartoum. 'You can't be calling for unity and you are asking me to be your inferior', dit-il. Et il continue: 'Should there be a change in attitude, southerners will vote for unity . . . If not, then there is no chance for unity.'[114]

[111] 'The Implementation Modalities of the Protocol on Power Sharing (26 May 2004)', 31 Dec. 2004, pp. 59–60. L'organe législatif du SPLM a ratifié à l'unanimité l'Accord de paix le 24 janvier 2005 (http://www.sudantribune.com/article.php3?id_article = 7690). Le Parlement soudanais a fait de même le 1er février 2005 (http://www.sudantribune.com/article.php3?id_article = 7763).

[112] En ce sens, G. Dyer, 'Sudan deal, a Pandora's box on borders', *The Canberra Times*, 18 Jan. 2005, article publié sur http://www.sudantribune.com/<opinions>, consulté le 24 janvier 2005.

[113] Voir la Déclaration du Caire de 1964, de l'OUA, et l'art. 4(b) de l'Acte constitutif de l'Union africaine.

[114] 'Rebel leader says Sudan unity in Khartoum's hands', *Sudan Tribune*, 23 Jan. 2005, (http://www.sudantribune.com/article_impr.php3?id_article = 7678). Citons aussi la réaction de M. Salah Barqueen, Secrétaire à la communication internationale du Beja Congress (représentant la population de l'Est du Soudan qui a également pris les armes contre le pouvoir central): 'Nous soutenons cet accord. C'est une conquête des sociétés marginalisées contre le pouvoir central au Soudan. Nous pensons que c'est le premier pas vers une paix globale au Soudan'. Regrettant toutefois le caractère bilatéral de l'Accord conclu, il ajoute: 'nous voulons un accord de paix global. Cela inclut toutes les communautés

Il importe à cet égard de noter que le choix de décider de l'avenir du Sud du Soudan en 2011 a été octroyé, non pas à tout le peuple soudanais, mais à la seule population de la partie Sud du territoire. On relèvera aussi l'acceptation par le gouvernement soudanais de ce droit de sécession, surtout lorsque l'on sait que les précédentes négociations, de 1993 à 2002, ont échoué sur la question de l'autonomie du Sud, sans parler encore d'une éventuelle indépendance, et sur celle de l'établissement d'un Etat unitaire laïque et démocratique.[115] Ce changement d'attitude du gouvernement semble traduire, au-delà des motivations économiques (dont l'exploitation du pétrole découvert dans le Sud en 1999), son acceptation du fait qu'il n'y a pas d'autre alternative à la paix dans le pays et à la jouissance du droit du peuple du Sud à l'autodétermination que l'octroi d'une très large autonomie à ce peuple, dans le cadre de l'Etat unitaire actuel, et d'un droit à la sécession si tel est le désir de ce dernier dans six ans.

Et il est significatif que ces Accords aient été conclus sous l'égide d'une organisation régionale africaine (l'IGAD), avec la bienveillance de l'OUA, puis de l'Union africaine. Après la signature de l'Accord global du 9 janvier 2005, le Conseil de paix et de sécurité de l'Union africaine, réuni au niveau des chefs d'Etat et de gouvernement, se félicite de cet 'accord historique', puis 'demande la mise en œuvre scrupuleuse de l'Accord et exprime sa conviction que celui-ci offre un cadre au sein duquel d'autres différends au Soudan, y compris le conflit du Darfour, pourraient être résolus'.[116] Il en va de même du Président de la Commission de l'Union qui rappelle, dans son communiqué de félicitations, les différents accords et protocoles déjà signés entre les parties et dont nous avons vu les dispositions novatrices quant au droit d'un peuple intégré dans un Etat à la sécession.

On pourrait donc voir dans ce bon accueil par l'Union africaine de l'Accord de paix global sur le Soudan un certain fléchissement de sa farouche opposition, héritée de sa devancière – l'OUA, à toute idée d'un

marginalisées au Soudan: l'Est, l'Ouest, le Sud, et même les populations les plus au Nord.' De même, M. Ghazi Suleiman, président de Sudan Human Rights Group dit: 'De mon point de vue, cet accord de paix vient marquer une date importante dans l'histoire du Soudan. Depuis notre indépendance, en 1956, nous ne sommes pas parvenus à identifier notre pays. Est-ce un pays arabe? Un pays africain? Est-ce un pays chrétien ou musulman? Au bout du compte, nous voici capable de dire quelle est l'identité du Soudan: c'est une nation diversifiée'; voir L. Correau, 'Regards croisés sur l'accord de paix', article mis à jour le 10 janvier 2005 sur http://www.rfi.fr/actufr/articles/061/article_33095.asp.

[115] L. Correau, 'Soudan : l'aboutissement d'un processus de dix ans', article publié le 7 janvier 2005 sur http://www.rfi.fr/actufr/articles/061/article_33097.asp.

[116] Communiqué 'sur la situation dans la région du Darfour (Soudan)', 23ème réunion du CPS, 10 janvier 2005, Libreville (Gabon), PSC/AHG/Comm.(XXIII), par. 1.

droit de sécession à un peuple intégré dans un Etat; même si l'on peut comprendre qu'il est difficile pour elle de s'opposer à un texte qui met fin au plus long conflit interne en Afrique, qui a fait deux millions de morts et plus de quatre millions de personnes déplacées, internes ou réfugiées dans les pays voisins.

Ce cas mis à part, l'interprétation généreuse des deux textes sur les droits des peuples susmentionnés n'a pas jusqu'à présent rencontré beaucoup d'écho positif dans la pratique des Etats africains et de l'organisation régionale africaine. Il est toutefois très difficile d'en tirer des conclusions fermes pour l'avenir, comme le montre la pratique soudanaise que l'on vient d'évoquer, et de la même manière qu'il était difficilement prévisible, il y a quelques années encore, de voir l'organisation panafricaine se doter d'un droit d'intervention dans les affaires intérieures de ses membres. La récente consécration dans l'Acte constitutif de l'Union africaine d'un droit d'intervention de cette dernière sur le territoire d'un Etat membre témoigne en effet d'une avancée heureuse mais pour le moins surprenante du droit international régional africain. Pour l'heure, cette consécration, ainsi que celle d'autres principes visant à assurer une participation plus effective des peuples africains à la conduite des affaires publiques, pourraient s'analyser comme l'expression de la volonté des dirigeants africains d'apporter des solutions à moyen ou à long terme à certains problèmes aigus auxquels sont confrontés leurs jeunes Etats, y compris celui de la sécession. L'alinéa h de l'article 4 de l'Acte constitutif de l'Union prévoit ainsi, au rang de ses seize principes,

> [l]e droit de l'Union d'intervenir dans un Etat membre sur décision de la Conférence, dans certaines circonstances graves, à savoir: les crimes de guerre, le génocide et les crimes contre l'humanité.

On peut d'emblée constater que les trois circonstances graves énumérées ici correspondent aux circonstances exceptionnelles qui autoriseraient la sécession selon les critères mentionnés plus haut. On observera également que ce principe d'intervention de l'Union est consacré dans la foulée du principe d'interdiction du recours à la force[117] et du principe de non-ingérence *d'un Etat membre* dans les affaires

[117] Principe affirmé à l'alinéa f de l'article 4. Il s'agirait là d'une quatrième exception au principe de non recours à la force, après la légitime défense, l'autorisation de recours à la force par le Conseil de sécurité des Nations Unies et, dans le contexte de la décolonisation, l'autorisation aux mouvements de libération nationale de recourir à la force pour obtenir l'indépendance. La question de la compatibilité de ce droit d'intervention de l'Union africaine avec le droit international général pourrait se poser, mais l'examen de celle-ci dépasse le cadre de notre étude.

intérieures d'un autre Etat.[118] Il s'agit là de la consécration dans un instrument conventionnel international d'un droit d'intervention humanitaire, dont l'existence coutumière, maintes fois invoquée, demeure très controversée en droit international, comme en témoignent les critiques émises à l'encontre des actions des Etats et organisations régionales qui prétendaient agir sur cette base.[119]

Il y a lieu de noter ici que l'intervention humanitaire prônée par l'Union africaine n'est pas une autorisation générale d'intervenir *unilatéralement* là où sont commises des violations massives des droits de l'homme ou du droit international humanitaire. La rédaction de l'article 4 de l'Acte constitutif montre que cette intervention est au contraire bien circonscrite aux trois cas de crimes de guerre, de génocide et de crimes contre l'humanité, mentionnés limitativement par cette disposition. On sait que les contours juridiques respectifs de ces crimes internationaux ont été bien définis ces derniers temps par les tribunaux pénaux internationaux et le droit international pénal; les risques d'abus de cette intervention humanitaire sont en conséquence limités. En outre, la décision d'intervenir doit émaner de la Conférence des chefs d'Etat et de gouvernement de l'Union (à convoquer éventuellement en session extraordinaire quand la violation massive a lieu en dehors de sa session annuelle) et une intervention peut lui être recommandée par le Conseil de paix et de sécurité de l'Union africaine.[120] On peut encore se demander si la mise en œuvre d'une telle décision nécessite ou non l'autorisation du Conseil de sécurité de l'ONU, conformément à l'article 53(1) de la Charte des Nations Unies.[121]

Cette approche des dirigeants africains, consistant à favoriser l'autodétermination interne par un droit d'intervention collectif en cas

[118] Principe affirmé à l'alinéa g de l'article 4.

[119] Voir à cet égard les analyses juridiques de l'intervention de l'OTAN au Kosovo, conduite sans l'autorisation du Conseil de sécurité de l'ONU et que certains entendaient baser sur le droit d'intervention humanitaire, et ce, pour les mêmes raisons (arrêter un génocide ou des violations graves des droits de l'homme): M. Kohen, 'L'emploi de la force et la crise du Kosovo: vers un nouveau désordre juridique international ?', *RBDI* 1 (1999), 122–48; A. Pellet, "La guerre au Kosovo' – Le fait rattrapé par le droit', *Forum du droit international* 1 (1999), 160–65; B. Simma, 'NATO, the UN and the Use of Force: Legal Aspects', *EJIL* 10 (1999), 1–22; S. Sur, 'L'affaire du Kosovo et le droit international: points et contrepoints', *AFDI* (1999), 280–91; Ph. Weckel, 'L'emploi de la force contre la Yougoslavie ou la Charte fissurée', *RGDIP* 104 (2000), 19–35; D. H. Joyner, 'The Kosovo Intervention: Legal Analysis and a More Persuasive Paradigm', *EJIL* 13/3 (2002), 597–619.

[120] En vertu de l'article 7, par. 1(e), du Protocole relatif à la création du Conseil de paix et de sécurité de l'UA, adopté lors de la 38ème session ordinaire de la Conférence, du 9 au 10 juillet 2002 à Durban (Afrique du Sud).

[121] 'Aucune action coercitive ne sera entreprise en vertu d'accords régionaux ou par des organismes régionaux sans l'autorisation du Conseil de sécurité . . .'

de nécessité, nous paraît être une réponse adéquate aux risques et causes actuels de conflits en Afrique. Comme l'a constaté à la fin des années 1990 le Secrétaire général des Nations Unies,

> [i]l n'y a maintenant pratiquement plus de conflits graves dus à des différends frontaliers [en Afrique], grâce surtout à la décision prise en 1964 par l'Organisation de l'unité africaine d'accepter les frontières que les États d'Afrique avaient héritées des autorités coloniales. Par contre, le problème qui consiste à forger une véritable identité nationale à partir de communautés souvent disparates et rivales existe toujours.[122]

Il serait en conséquence urgent que les dirigeants africains s'attèlent sérieusement à la promotion des principes démocratiques et de participation active des différents groupes ethniques d'un Etat à la direction des affaires publiques, précisément pour développer cette identité nationale, ce sentiment d'appartenance à part entière à l'Etat où ils se trouvent implantés; c'est peut-être là un moyen privilégié de désamorcer en amont toute velléité de sécession desdits groupes.[123]

Conclusion

La composition multi-ethnique et multi-culturelle des Etats africains a obligé ces derniers à une approche très circonspecte de la question de la sécession. Le droit international régional africain ne reconnaît ainsi

[122] Doc. ONU A/52/871 – S/1998/318, par. 8.

[123] L'ajout, dans le Protocole de 2003 sur les Amendements de l'Acte constitutif, d'un droit d'intervention de l'Union en cas de 'menace grave de l'ordre légitime afin de restaurer la paix et la stabilité dans un Etat membre sur la recommandation du Conseil de paix et de sécurité' semble apporter une limite claire aux actions des peuples africains pour l'exercice de cette autodétermination interne. Ces actions ne sauraient en effet menacer l'ordre légitime et la stabilité interne. Une telle limitation a fait dire à certains qu'il devrait s'agir plus d'une intervention pour protéger les régimes en place que pour protéger les droits de l'homme, même si elle est prévue dans le même article 4 (h) relatif au droit d'intervention humanitaire de l'Union (E. Baimu et K. Sturman, 'Amendment to the African Union's Right to Intervene. A Shift from Human Security to Regime Security ?', *ASR* 12/2 (2003), 37–45. Cette intervention conforte ainsi l'opposition de l'ordre juridique régional africain à la sécession. On ne pourrait l'interpréter autrement que si on mettait l'accent sur le terme 'légitime', qui amènerait l'Union africaine à ne pas intervenir dans l'hypothèse d'une menace par un peuple à un ordre *illégitime*, voire à son intervention pour démettre un régime qui a perdu toute légitimité, lorsque cette situation se trouve être la source de la menace grave à la paix et à la stabilité de l'Etat. La difficulté d'application de cette interprétation démontre à quel point le dernier droit d'intervention prôné par l'Union africaine est un rempart contre les diverses menaces au régime en place, dont la sécession. Sur ce droit d'intervention, voir également A. A. Yusuf, 'The Right of Intervention by the African Union: A New Paradigm in Regional Enforcement Action ?', *AADI* 11 (2003), 3–23.

le droit à l'autodétermination externe qu'aux seuls peuples colonisés ou soumis à la domination raciale. La reconnaissance de nombreux droits des peuples par la Charte africaine des droits de l'homme et des peuples est à mettre en balance avec le solide attachement des dirigeants africains aux principes d'unité nationale et d'intégrité territoriale de l'Etat. Bien que le texte des dispositions pertinentes de la Charte africaine n'interdise pas de manière formelle l'exercice de la sécession dans certaines situations extrêmes, il faut reconnaître que, dans son ensemble, l'environnement juridique et politique régional africain ne lui est pas favorable.

En lieu et place de la sécession comme instrument ultime de préservation de l'existence physique, politique ou culturelle d'un peuple intégré dans un Etat, les dirigeants africains ont récemment envisagé l'intervention collective dans le cadre de l'Union africaine. Cette petite 'révolution' dans l'approche des Etats africains est à mettre en parallèle avec l'évolution récente de leurs positions en matière d'autodétermination interne: renforcement de la participation des peuples aux affaires de l'Etat, promotion de la bonne gouvernance, mise en place des conditions pour des élections périodiques, libres et transparentes, et rejet des changements anti-constitutionnels de gouvernement. Un minimum d'autonomie interne,[124] en tant qu'expression de l'autodétermination d'un peuple intégré dans un Etat, pourrait également être envisagé; comme ce fut le cas dans la solution de la crise de sécession de l'île d'Anjouan aux Comores. Toutes ces solutions, qui ne portent aucune atteinte à l'unité politique et territoriale des Etats, constituent les seuls moyens de concilier véritablement le principe du droit des peuples à disposer d'eux-mêmes et le principe de l'intégrité territoriale des Etats, assurant ainsi la libre détermination des peuples africains dans la stabilité et la paix auxquelles ils aspirent.

[124] Pour un examen de la théorie et de la pratique sur les différents degrés de l'autonomie, voir H. Hannum et R. B. Lillich, 'Autonomy in International Law', *AJIL* 74 (1980), 861–89.

10

International law and secession in the Asia and Pacific regions

LI-ANN THIO

I. Introduction

In recent history, the incidence of secessionist movements in the Asia-Pacific region, an area characterised by great ethnic, religious and cultural diversity, is an important area of international practice. Separatist initiatives threaten regional order where spatial and personal autonomy schemes fail to contain ethno-nationalist demands.

A range of claims to independent statehood might be encompassed under the term 'secession', defined as 'the separation of part of the territory of a State carried out by the resident population with the aim of creating a new independent State or acceding to another existing State'.[1] In the post-colonial era, this entails the partition of the territory of a sovereign, independent State, where a group belonging to it seeks to separate itself to create a new State, in contrast with East Timor, previously a non-self-governing territory.[2] This region has seen the emergence of States from non-colonial situations in a consensual and bilateral manner, such as Singapore, which, after two years,[3] peacefully seceded by mutual agreement from the Malaysian Federation in 1965.[4] Indeed, it was the

[1] C. Haverland, 'Secession', *in* Bernhardt, R., (ed.), *Encyclopedia of Public International Law*, vol. IV (Amsterdam, 2000), p. 354.

[2] See C. Drew, 'The East Timor Story: International Law on Trial', *EJIL* 12 (2001), 651.

[3] As a former British colony, Singapore was administered separately from Malaya. It achieved self-government in 1959 and, on 16 September 1963, joined the Federation of Malaysia, formed on 31 August 1957. Insensitive to feelings of Malay nationalism, Singapore notably made a declaration of (temporary) *de facto* independence on 31 August 1963. See M. N. Sopiee, *From Malayan Union to Singapore Separation: Political Unification in the Malaysia Region 1945–65* (Kuala Lumpur: Malaysia, Penerbit Universiti Malaya, 1974), p. 185.

[4] Proclamation of Singapore, Independence of Singapore Agreement (1965), Singapore Government Gazette Extraordinary, 9 August 1965 Vol. VII No. 66. Republic of Singapore Independence Act (Act 9 of 1965): available at http://statutes.agc.gov.sg.

central government's view that Singapore should leave the federation,[5] as the political agitation of Singaporean politicians was perceived as a threat to the inter-ethnic harmony. Separation was effected through the Independence of Singapore Agreement, concluded between the Governments of Malaysia and Singapore on 7 August 1965, whereby the former relinquished sovereignty and jurisdiction over Singapore.[6] Singapore achieved independent statehood on 9 August 1965 and immediately received recognition from the United Kingdom, New Zealand, Australia and the United States of America, gaining UN membership in September 1965.[7]

This region was also witness to a rare, post-1945 example of a 'successful secessionary creation'.[8] The case of Bangladesh, which, despite opposition from Pakistan, issued a unilateral declaration of independence in March 1971.[9] This chapter focuses on such attempts at unilateral secession, involving the creation of States by force without the predecessor State's consent. The main historical and contemporary secessionist movements in the Asia-Pacific region are summarised below:

Region	Country/Secessionist Movement
Central and East Asia	China/Xinjiang Separatists (East Turkistan Question) (Tibet/Taiwan = renegade province?)
South Asia	India: North-eastern Separatists/Assam/Manipur/Nagaland/ Punjab/ Kashmir Pakistan: Bangladesh Sri Lanka: Tamil Eelam
South-East Asia	Federation of Malaysia: Singapore Independence Indonesia: Aceh, West Papua, South Moluccan Republic Philippines: Muslim Mindanao: Moros

5 Correspondence between Tengku Abdul Rahman and Toh Chin Chye, on Singapore's secession from Malaysia (Kuala Lumpur, 1965), available in the Central Library, National University of Singapore.

6 For the view that this Agreement was not international but inter-ministerial since the heads of States did not sign it, see L. C. Green, 'Malaya/Singapore/Malaysia: Comments on State Competence, Succession and Continuity', *CYIL* IV (1966), 3.

7 C. M. Turnbull, *A History of Singapore 1819–1975*, (Singapore: Oxford University Press, 1977), p. 293.

8 J. Crawford, *The Creation of States in International law* (Oxford: Clarendon Press, 1979), p. 247. Others include Indonesia, North Korea, North Vietnam.

9 See Preamble, Bangladesh Constitution (available at http://www.bangladeshgov.org/pmo/constitution/). See generally M. E. Chamberlain, *Longman Companion to European Decolonisation in the Twentieth Century* (London & New York: Longman, 1998), p. 57.

	Myanmar or Burma: Shan States/Karen People; Arakanese Muslims or Rohingya
	Thailand: Malays of Patani
Pacific	USA: Hawaii
	Papua New Guinea: Bougainville
	Solomon Islands

Certain separatist movements, causing civil conflict, date back to the very moment of a country's independence, as was the case in 1947 when India and Pakistan gained Independence, sparking the irredentist[10] Jammu-Kashmir conflict.[11] More recently, a spate of primarily ethno-religious separatist movements, from Aceh to Irian Jaya, reasserted themselves in post-Suharto Indonesia after 1998. The USSR's dissolution in the early 1990s, leading to the creation of various new Central Asian States, heightened China's concerns over its national minorities' separatist ambitions. The intensification of a separatist Islamic agenda, harboured by radical terrorist groups planning to create an Islamic State or *Daulah Islamiyah Nusantara* composed of Malaysia, Indonesia, Mindanao and later Singapore and Brunei,[12] bedevils South-East Asian countries. Sri Lanka and Myanmar both grapple with insurrectionist groups asserting homeland claims.[13] In the face of many failed and continued attempts at unilateral secession, the Asia-Pacific States generally adhere to the principle of territorial integrity.

Positive international law neither prevents nor prohibits secession,[14] treating secessionist conflicts as matters of domestic jurisdiction.[15] A

[10] Other irredentist conflicts in this region relate to China/Taiwan and China/Tibet.

[11] See R. Ganguly, 'Kashmiri Secessionism in India and the Role of Pakistan in Kin State Intervention', *in* R. Ganguly, *Ethnic Conflicts: Lessons from South Asia* (New Delhi: Sage Publications, 1998), p. 38.

[12] *The Jemaah Islamiyah Arrests and the Threats of Terrorism*, White Paper, Cmd. 2 of 2003 (Singapore Ministry of Home Affairs, 2003), at 4, 6. [hereafter, JI White Paper]

[13] The Tamils in Sri Lanka and the Shan and Karen people in Myanmar.

[14] The Committee overseeing the Convention for the Elimination of Racial Discrimination (CERD) considers that international law does not recognise a peoples' right to unilateral secession: 'General Recommendations 21: Right to Self Determination', 23 August 1996, at para. 6.

[15] J. Crawford, 'State Practice and International Law in Relation to Secession', *BYIL* 69 (1998), 85; Musgrave notes that secession is essentially political, though the act produces international legal consequences: T. Musgrave, *Self-Determination and National Minorities* (Oxford: Clarendon Press, 1997), p. 210.

right to 'ethnic' self-determination[16] or Wilsonian 'one nation one State' national self-determination,[17] which would entitle distinct ethno-cultural communities to secede in order to satisfy aspirations of democratic self-governance,[18] is not recognised. However, a State's right to territorial integrity is contingent upon a representative government 'without distinction as to race, creed or colour',[19] respecting the right of peoples to 'internal self-determination',[20] including the right to political participation.[21] The international community is more likely to recognise the realities of secessionist attempts as a remedy where the government of the predecessor State committed gross human rights violations against the seceding unit.[22]

This chapter offers a thematic review and analysis of recent practice in the Asia-Pacific region, identifying the main secessionist claims and the international response thereto; a particular feature will be the role of religion and ethnicity in fuelling secessionist ethnic insurgencies, supported by 'kin' ethnic groups in other countries,[23] and the justification of separatist claims as responses to gross human rights violations or 'internal colonialism'.[24] Part II deals with preliminary issues. Part III briefly

[16] See M. Koskeniemmi, 'National Self-Determination Today: Problems of Legal Theory and Practice', *ICLQ* 43 (1994), 214.

[17] M. Pomerance, 'The United States and Self Determination: Perspectives on the Wilsonian Conceptions', *AJIL* 70 (1976), 1.

[18] T. M. Franck, 'The Emerging Right to Democratic Governance', *AJIL* 86 (1992), 46; G. H. Fox, 'The Right to Political Participation in International Law', *YJIL* 17 (1992), 539.

[19] *Declaration on Principles of International Law concerning Friendly Relations and Co-operation among States in accordance with the Charter of the United Nations*, GA Res. 2625 (XXV), 24 Oct. 1970 [hereafter, 'Friendly Relations Declaration'].

[20] 'Internal' self-determination affirms the continuing nature of the right beyond decolonisation, relating to 'the rights of all peoples to pursue freely their economic, social and cultural development without outside interference': see CERD 'General Recommendations 21: Right to Self Determination'. It is respected through observing human rights obligations in treaties like CERD (660 U.N.T.S. 195), and the 1992 UN Minorities Declaration GA Res. 47/135 of 18 December 1992. See generally A. Rosas, 'Internal Self-Determination', *in* C. Tomuschat, (ed.), *Modern Law of Self-Determination* (Dordrecht/Boston: M. Nijhoff Publishers, 1993), p. 225.

[21] See *Katangese Peoples' Congress vs. Zaire, African Comm. Hum. & Peoples' Rights*, Comm. No. 75/92 and its analysis in chapter 9 of this volume.

[22] Secession itself may not 'cure' majority-minority relations where a former minority becomes an abusive majority. See, *e.g.*, 'Bangladesh attacks on members of the Hindu minority', *Amnesty International*, ASA 13/006/2001 (2001).

[23] *e.g.*, Islam unifies Muslim separatist movements in Indonesia (Aceh), Burma (Rohingya or Arakanese Muslims) and Thailand (Patani Malays): A. Tan, 'Armed Muslim Separatist Rebellion in Southeast Asia: Persistence, Prospects and Implications', *SCT* 23 (2000), 267.

[24] 'Internal colonialism' results where 'an ethnic group in control of a government systematically exploits resources of the regions occupied by minority ethnic groups, resulting in

evaluates the successful instance of Bangladeshi secession and considers its value as a precedent. Part IV examines the grounds which the secessionist movements have advanced and the response of the parent State whose territorial integrity is challenged. Part V considers the response of third States and international organisations to secessionist claims. Part VI offers concluding observations on what regional State practice reveals and the implications for the developing law on secession on a global scale.

II. Preliminary issues

A. *The diversity of the 'Asia Pacific'*

The 'Asia Pacific' is a 'clumsy construct',[25] describing an area lacking shared identity, given the geographical ambiguity of 'Asia', it is a concept of European origins.[26] Spanning an extensive geographical area, it encompasses multi-religious and multi-ethnic[27] States and societies with diverse political cultures, democratic[28] and socialist,[29] secular[30] and religious[31] legal systems, and economic development levels. 'Asia Pacific', thus, is a random grouping of States housing some 3.3 billion people. It includes countries in East Asia (China, Japan, Mongolia, North and South

inequitable distribution of national wealth and social welfare opportunities'. M. Sornarajah, 'Internal Colonialism and Humanitarian Intervention', *Georgia J.I.C.L* 11 (1981), 45. See also D. Brown, 'Internal Colonialism and Ethnic Rebellion in Thailand', *in* D. Brown, *The State and Ethnic Politics in Southeast Asia*, (London/New York: Routledge, 1994), p. 158.

[25] UNESCO Review: 'Social Science Issues in the Asia Pacific Region', 1–25, at 1: available at www.unescobkk.org/rushsap/conf/pdf/UNESCO3.pdf

[26] 'There is no single Asia, there are many Asias.' O. Yasuaki, *In Quest of Intercivilisation Human Rights: Universal v Relative Human Rights Viewed from an Asian Perspective*, *APJHRL* 1 (2000), 53.

[27] The preamble of the Laos Constitution affirms Laos is an indivisible and 'unified country belonging to all multi-ethnic people'. Article 8 prohibits acts 'creating division and discrimination' among ethnics group which the State treats equally.

[28] Art 1(1) of the Cambodia Constitution professes 'liberal democracy and pluralism' as its basis: text available at http://www.cambodia.org/facts/constitution.html.

[29] Art. 1 of the 1992 Vietnamese constitution. Text available at http://www.vietnamembassy-usa.org/learn/gov-constitution1.php3.

[30] Article 100 of the Tajikistan Constitution declares irrevocable and unamendable the 'secular' nature of the State: available at http://www.law.tojikiston.com/english/index.html (accessed 25 Oct. 2003).

[31] For example, Christian principles (Preamble, Western Samoa Constitution, 1 May 1920; Preamble, Vanuatu Constitution of 1980, Constitution of the Independent State of Papua New Guinea): text available at www.vanuatu.usp.ac.fj/paclawmat (Pacific Law Materials, University of the South Pacific). The Brunei Constitution embodies a Malay Islamic Monarchy, after the proclamation of Brunei Independence on 1 January 1984. Article 4 of the 1990 Nepal Constitution serves a Hindu constitutional monarchy.

Korea) Central Asia, (the Central Asian States of the former USSR such as Azerbaijan, Tajikistan, Uzbekistan, Turkmenistan, Kazakhstan and Kyrgyzstan), South Asia (India, Pakistan, Sri Lanka, Bangladesh, Bhutan), South East Asia (Philippines, Indonesia, Singapore, Malaysia, Thailand, Brunei, Vietnam, Laos, Cambodia, Myanmar) and the Pacific (Australia, New Zealand, Hawaii, Papua New Guinea (PNG), Pacific Islands). Some of the smallest countries are found here: Nauru (population 13,048), Tokelau (population 1,405), Cook Islands (population 21,388). The South Pacific Melanesian islands alone display vast ethno-linguistic diversity: Vanautu has 109 languages; PNG, the world's most ethnically diverse State, has around 832 distinct living languages. The indigenous Melanesian inhabitants of West Papua, an Indonesian province, are composed of some 263 separate ethno-linguistic groups.[32] Few societies have a homogenous composition.[33]

Many Asia Pacific countries share a common history of colonisation by the Portuguese, Spanish, Dutch, French and British empires, and later the United States of America, dating from the sixteenth to the early twentieth century.[34] The cause of contemporary secessionist conflict sometimes stems from colonial frontier revisions,[35] resulting in the involuntary incorporation of distinct groups into a territorial unit within which they are a numerical minority, such as the Hindu minority in predominantly Muslim Kashmir[36] or the Punjab Sikhs whose territory was included in India. Consonant with African practice, many newly independent Asian countries in the 1960s retained colonial boundaries as territorial borders, in order to prioritise stability.

[32] J. Fraenkel, 'Minority Rights in Fiji and the Solomon Islands'; Reinforcing Constitutional Protections, Establishing Land Rights and Overcoming Poverty, United Nations, Commission on Human Rights, Sub-Commission on Promotion and Protection of Human Rights, Working Group on Minorities, 9th session, E/CN.4/Sub.2/AC.5/2003/WP.5 (5 May 2003).

[33] Exceptionally, the States of Tonga (whose 104,000 population is almost all Polynesians) and Turkmenistan, composed mainly of Turkmens, are relatively ethnically homogenous States.

[34] Notably, non-Western States like Japan were also involved in colonisation, specifically with respects to the Korean peninsula.

[35] See generally Chamberlain, *Longman Companion to European Decolonisation.*

[36] The divided region of Jammu-Kashmir traces its origins to the autonomous political entity created by the British colonial administration in 1846 when the Punjab State ruler was forced to cede Kashmir to the British as part of war reparations. This was then sold to a Jammu State chieftain and became one of the 560 princely sovereign States with the British as suzerain overlord. Today, 70 per cent of the 12 million people living in Jammu-Kashmir are Muslims while the rest include Hindus, Sikhs and Buddhists. Chamberlain, *Longman Companion to European Decolonisation*, p. 28.

B. *Lack of an overarching institutional regional framework*

There is no Asia Pacific regional organisation of general competence, only topic-specific bodies like the economic-development-oriented Asia Pacific Economic Co-operation (APEC)[37] and sub-regional bodies like the South Asian Association for Regional Co-operation (SAARC)[38] and Association for South-East Asian Nations (ASEAN) whose emphasis on the primacy of territorial borders restricts the contours of an evolving right to self-determination. There is no regional human rights regime. Secessionist issues do not feature on the agenda of the Asia Pacific Forum of National Human Rights Institutions[39] nor do they present a chief security item for the ASEAN Regional Forum.[40] However, the South Pacific Forum[41] does allow its member States to engage in regional co-operation and political dialogue, resulting in, for example, cases such as when Indonesia was commended for introducing an autonomy scheme for West Papua but, at the same time, also asked to address human rights violations.[42]

There is no concerted institutional approach towards self-determination and secession related problems comparable to the European Community's collective response to the dissolution of the former USSR and Yugoslavia.[43] ASEAN countries have not resorted to available conciliatory dispute settlement mechanisms,[44] preferring to settle

[37] APEC was established in 1989 to promote economic development and trade in the Asia-Pacific region. It has 21 members and its website is at: http://www.apecsec.org.sg/apec/about_apec.html.

[38] This was established in 1985 and its members are Bangladesh, Bhutan, India, Maldives, Nepal, Pakistan and Sri Lanka. Its goal is to promote socio-economic development among members and it addresses issues like poverty alleviation, terrorism and drug trafficking, but not self-determination. Its website is at: http://www.saarc-sec.org/.

[39] This was formed in 1996 and has twelve members. Their website is at: http://www.asiapacificforum.net.

[40] See M. C. O. Ortuoste, 'Reviewing the ASEAN Regional Forum and its Role in Southeast Asian Security', Occasional Paper, *Asia-Pacific Centre for Security Studies* 27 (2000), available at http://www.apcss.org/Publications/Ocasional%20Papers/OPAseanForum.htm (visited 2 Sept. 2003).

[41] This was formed in 1971 and comprises sixteen member States.

[42] 33rd Pacific Islands Forum Communiqué, Fiji (August 2002), para. 58: available at http://www.forumsec.org.fj/Home.htm (accessed 25 Oct. 2003).

[43] EC Declaration on Yugoslavia, 16 December 1991, *UKMIL, BYIL* 62 (1991), 559; *EJIL* 4 (1993), 72; EU Guidelines on the Recognition of New States in Eastern Europe and in the Soviet Union, 16 Dec. 1991, *UKMIL*; 62 BYIL (1991), 559; *EJIL* 4 (1993), 72. See the analysis of this practice in chapter 11 of this volume.

[44] Chapter IV of the (Pacific Settlement of Disputes) 1976 Treaty of Amity and Co-Operation in Southeast Asia, provides for a ministerial-level High Council to make recommendations to parties to a dispute and to offer its good offices in negotiation, mediation or inquiry.

disputes, including political situations relating to secessionist claims, through informal modes of diplomacy or mediation. The mediation of the Mindanao-Philippines debacle is one such example. Unlike the North American experience,[45] no major national cases relating to secession have arisen. Self-determination-related matters are raised before UN human rights bodies like the Human Rights and CERD Committee, and monitored by NGOs primarily as human rights violations rather than as structural issues that require attention.

III. Bangladesh – precedent or extraordinary incident?

Bangladesh is 'the only secession after World War II to succeed in its aim of independence'.[46] While appreciating the notion that there is 'no longer one comprehensive test for secessionary independence',[47] this section seeks to identify the factors that influenced the international community's decision to recognise Bangladesh as a State, providing a platform for evaluating other regional secessionist claims.

A. Secession and recognition of statehood

Bangladesh was formerly part of Pakistan, itself a product of Muslim nationalism and the attempt to appease the desire of Indian Muslims for a homeland in this Muslim-majority area after the 1947 partition of India, indeed quite contrary to the vision of an indivisible India. Bangladesh became a sovereign State in 1972,[48] after proclaiming independence from West Pakistan in 1971, facilitated by Indian military intervention.[49]

[45] See S. J. Toope, 'Re Reference by Governor in Council concerning Certain Questions relating to Secession of Quebec from Canada',161 D.L.R. (4th) 385 (20 August 1998), *AJIL* 93 (1999), 519. Issues about Hawaiian sovereignty, related to the right of self determination, have been raised in a series of Hawaiian land rights cases: e.g., *OHA v HCDCH* (94-4207), Circuit Court, Hawaiian State Judiciary, at http://www.state.hi.us/jud/ohavhcdch.pdf; *Ahuna v Department of Hawaiian Home Lands*, 64 Haw. 327, 339, 640 P.2d 1161, 1168–9 (1982).

[46] A. Heraclides, 'Secessionist Movements and External Involvement' *International Organisation* 44/3 (1990), 341, at 349. See Ganguly, 'The Secession of Bangladesh and the Role of India', *in* Ganguly, *Ethnic Conflicts*, p. 96; R. Sisson and L. E. Rose, *War and Secession: Pakistan, India, and the Creation of Bangladesh* (Berkeley: University of California Press, 1990).

[47] Crawford, *The Creation of States*, p. 257.

[48] A. Gauhar, 'Asia: the Experience of the Sub-Continent' *in* B. Kreisky and H. Gauhar, (eds.), *Decolonisation and After: The Future of the Third World* (London: South Publications, 1987), p. 51.

[49] Crawford, *The Creation of States*, p. 115.

The East-Pakistan-based Awami League, which had proposed East Pakistani autonomy from the Pakistani Union in 1966,[50] won the 1970 national elections with an overwhelming majority. The Pakistani military rejected these results, precipitating the 26 March 1971 unilateral declaration of independence of East Pakistan and the ensuing civil war, when Pakistan deployed troops to its eastern province. With 9.5 million refugees pouring across the Indian border, India attacked the Pakistani forces in East Pakistan on 4 December 1971.

These events were initially treated as an internal matter by organisations like the United Nations (UN) and the Organisation of Islamic Conference (OIC)[51] and countries like the United States and the United Kingdom.[52] Pakistan criticised subsequent Indian military intervention as undue interference with its internal affairs.[53] Indeed, the UN was 'conspicuously absent'[54] despite the threat posed to international peace; only the sheer scale of the Indo-Pakistan war compelled the Security Council and General Assembly to address the matter. The UN did not immediately recognise Bangladesh but expressed concern for the gross human rights violations committed,[55] urging both parties to settle the dispute while respecting Pakistan's territorial integrity.

After the defeat of Pakistani forces on 16 December 1971, the Awami League claimed full control, with 47 States recognising Bangladesh by February 1972.[56] Bangladesh's 1972 application for UN membership was not granted until Pakistan changed its policy and recognised Bangladesh

[50] S. H. Hashmi, 'Self-Determination and Secession in Islamic Thought', *in* M. Sellers (ed.), *The New World Order: Sovereignty, Human Rights and the Self-Determination of Peoples*, (Oxford/Washington DC: Berg, 1996), p. 117 at 139.

[51] Initially the OIC supported Pakistan and deemed the secessionist attempt illegal. It failed to arbitrate the dispute but eventually played a bigger role in getting Pakistan to recognise Bangladesh after the civil war and in establishing formal relations between the two States. See Hashmi, 'Self-Determination and Secession', p. 139. Many Muslims regard Bangladesh as a Muslim tragedy and departure from the one Muslim *umma* ideal, *Ibid.* p. 141.

[52] *New York Times*, 3 April 1971, p. 3, col. 1.

[53] *New York Times*, 28 March 1971, p. 3, col. 5, as quoted in V. Nanda, 'Self-Determination in International Law: The Tragic Tale of Two Cities – Islamabad (West Pakistan) and Dacca (East Pakistan)', *AJIL* 66 (1972), 321, at 334.

[54] V. Nanda, 'A Critique of the UN Inaction in the Bangladesh Crisis', *Denver J.I.L.P* 49 (1972), 53.

[55] GA Resolution 2793 of 7 December 1971 called for the withdrawal of Indian forces, with a view to dealing with the cause of the conflict later. Pakistan was charged with human rights violations before an ECOSOC meeting. Nanda, 'A Critique of the UN Inaction', p. 335 quoting the *Indian and Foreign Review* (1971), 3.

[56] *New York Times*, 3 March 1972, p. 2, col. 5, as quoted in V. Nanda, 'Self-Determination in International Law', p. 336.

in 1974.[57] Pakistan's assent provided strong proof that sovereignty was transferred from the predecessor State to the secessionist unit.[58]

B. Causes of the secessionist movement

The geographically non-contiguous eastern wing of Pakistan, where 56 per cent of the total population lived, was separated from the western wing by 1200 miles of Indian territory. Islam was the sole unifying factor, given the cultural and linguistic differences of West and East Pakistanis. Rather than implementing a proposed federal system, military rule was imposed; further, Pakistani nationalism shaped the central policies that were designed to keep East Pakistan under-developed, negating the Bengali cultural identity. This unjust socio-economic and political order bred Bengali armed resistance and the desire to establish a Bengalese nation-State as a curative to the repressive West Pakistani rule.[59]

C. Evaluation

When contrasted with the earlier 'illegal' secessionist attempts[60] of Biafra and Katanga, which never won widespread support,[61] Bangladesh stands as a significant instance of secessionist self-determination from a plural State in the post-colonial Cold War era. Various factors support the view that Bangladeshi secession[62] was more a unique rather than precedent-setting case.

The Bangladesh case bears close analogy with the colonial situation of an 'overseas' non-self-governing territory. As General Assembly Resolution 1514 (XV) defines a territory as prima facie non-self-governing if it is geographically separate and ethnically distinct from its administering country, Crawford opines that East Pakistan could have qualified as a Chapter XI territory in 1971.[63] The analogical colonial conditions

[57] Pakistan recognised Bangladesh on 2 February 1974. Bangladesh had been recognised by more than seventy States between January and May 1972 and received some collective recognition after admission as a Commonwealth member on 18 April 1972. See, GA Res. 3203 of 17 September 1974.

[58] Crawford, *The Creation of States*, p. 219. [59] Gauhar, 'Asia', p. 55.

[60] SC Resolution 169 of 24 November1961 characterised the attempted Katanga secession as illegal.

[61] The Katanga secession started in 1960, ending by 21 January 1963, while the Biafran secession of 30 May 1967 ended on 12 January 1970. Crawford, *The Creation of States*, p. 263. The Organization of African Unity supported the central Nigerian government, while only five States recognised the Biafran secession.

[62] Crawford, *The Creation of States*, p. 115. [63] *Ibid.*, p. 116.

and the other factors influenced the international community's generally supportive response[64] towards what was perceived as a reasonable claim.

First, the geographical separation of East and West Pakistan, unlike Katanga or Biafra, betrayed the 'illogical boundaries'[65] drawn by colonialists, undermining national unity. Second, West Pakistan was unrepresentative and effectively accorded East Pakistan a subordinate political status through oppressive treatment.[66] Its neo-colonial status evidenced in regional economic disparity stemmed from the abuse of the East Pakistani minority.[67] Third, the Bengalis as the 'self' or 'peoples' were concentrated in a defined territory they had occupied since time immemorial.[68] Bengalis had distinct ethnic, cultural and linguistic traits, speaking the Sanskrit-based Bengali, and resented West Pakistan's imposition of assimilating the Arabic-based Urdu.[69] Fourth, the West Pakistani government committed gross human rights violations, involving torture and genocide, imperilling the Bengalis' physical security. Further, the excessive military force deployed against East Pakistan elicited international sympathy, rendering remote the prospect of reunification. Fifth, the secessionist struggle was not instigated by outside electors but enjoyed substantial local support, led by the democratically elected Awami League.[70] Sixth, twenty-four years had passed since 1947 and East Pakistan had tried to co-exist within the Pakistani framework as part of the costs of union, exhausting peaceful reconciliatory efforts while suffering physical insecurity. Seventh, independent Bengali statehood appeared to promote rather than undermine regional security and global order. This was because the Bengali State satisfied the statehood requirements of discrete territory, population and democratically supported political leadership. Furthermore, it was economically viable and would be the world's second largest Islamic State, with a population exceeding that of Great Britain.[71] Secession would not

64 Indeed, the Indian representative before the 1606th meeting of the Security Council (4 December 1971), at paragraph 185, described East Bengal as, 'in reality a non-self governing territory'. See Crawford, *The Creation of States*, p. 116.

65 M. Rafiqul Islam, 'Secessionist Self-Determination: Some Lessons from Katanga, Biafra and Bangladesh' *Journal of Peace Research* 22/3 (1985), 211, at 211.

66 Nanda, 'Self-Determination in International Law', p. 328.

67 In contrast, the Biafran population was only 13 million out of Nigeria's 56 million people.

68 The East Region claimed by the Ibo secessionists (Biafra) excluded Ibos outside the region and included many other non-Ibos; thus secession would not eradicate the minority problem.

69 Nanda, 'Self-Determination in International Law', p. 328.

70 In contrast, Belgium had vested interests in the outcome of the Katangese struggle: Rafiqul Islam, 'Secessionist Self-Determination', p. 213.

71 Nanda, 'Self-Determination in International Law', p. 333.

undermine West Pakistan's political stability or economic wealth, as the West was richer than the East.[72]

In contrast, a successful Biafran or Katangese secession would have destabilised the Congo or Nigeria by depriving the State of a resource-rich province. Finally, the overpowering external intervention by India was decisive in leading to Bangladesh's emergence, producing, in the view of some, a *fait accompli* ratified by the world community,[73] underscoring the special circumstances that were present. India granted political asylum to the exiled provisional government, allowing it to train guerrilla forces on Indian soil. India provided direct and indirect assistance to the Bengali insurgents, including land and air military forces to support the Bangladeshi Liberation Forces.[74] Such intervention in the face of human suffering also blunted criticism of external interference from other States and international bodies on humanitarian grounds.

Although these agglomerations of factors led to the successful secession of Bangladesh, not a single one can account for its success. The West Pakistani government's repressive acts, territorial coherence and distinct Bengali identity 'probably qualified East Bengal as a self-determination unit'.[75] States have been less receptive towards later regional secessionist attempts.

IV. Secessionist claims and reactions

A. *International standards, the right to self-determination and State attitudes towards secession in the Asia Pacific*

1. Constitutional and legal provisions: the priority of indivisibility

Few constitutions contain secession clauses;[76] many stress the importance of locating decentralisation schemes within the framework of national

[72] Rafiqul Islam, 'Secessionist Self-Determination', p. 214. He argues that West Pakistan's dependency on the East stemmed not from resource location but an exploitative economic structure that favoured the West.

[73] Crawford, *The Creation of States*, p. 115.

[74] Rafiqul Islam, 'Secessionist Self-Determination', p. 218.

[75] Crawford, *The Creation of States*, p. 117.

[76] Article 3 of the 1992 Uzbekistan Republic Constitution proclaims the inviolability and indivisibility of its State borders, while Article 74 recognises that the Republic of Karakalpakstan, a sovereign republic having its own constitution but which is part of the Republic of Uzbekistan (Art. 70) 'possesses the right to withdraw': text at http://www.ecostan.org/laws/uzb/uzbekistancon_eng.html (visited 5 Nov. 2003). Chapter X, 1947 Constitution of the Union of Burma recognised the right of constituent

unity.[77] The importance of territorial integrity, State indivisibility[78] and State continuity is emphasised in constitutions[79] and sub-regional charters.[80] Advocating and attempting secession is an offence in certain jurisdictions.[81] There is no State practice, as such, on constitutional secessionist clauses.

States to secede, prescribing procedures to ascertain the will of the people of a concerned State: text at http://shanland.org/History/Publications/consittution_of_the_union_of_bur.htm. This was abolished by the 1974 Constitution.

77 The Papua New Guinea Constitution's preamble calls for popular structures enabling 'effective, meaningful participation by our people' and the 'substantial decentralisation' of government activity, bearing in mind ethno-cultural diversity. See also Preamble, 1978 Solomon Islands Constitution; Section 13, Vanuatu Constitution (1980); Art. III Sect. 3, Federated States of Micronesia Constitution.

78 Art. 3, Cambodia Constitution: text at http://www.embassy.org/cambodia/cambodia/constitu.htm.

79 Art. 1, Turkmenistan Constitution (1992): text at http://www.ecostan.org/laws/turkm/turkmenistancon.html. Art. 7, Tajikistan constitution (prohibits 'agitation and actions aimed at disunity of the State'). Art. 8 (prohibits establishments that encourage 'nationalism' and advocate 'the forcible overthrow of the constitutional structures'). On 'national unity', see Art. 2(2), Kazakhstan Republic Constitution; Art. 13, 1992 Vietnam Constitution; Art. 4, 1992 Mongolia Constitution.

80 The ASEAN Treaty of Amity and Cooperation (1976) (text at http://www.aseansec.org/3631.htm) stresses mutual respect for the 'independence, sovereignty, equality, territorial integrity and national identity of all nations' (Art. 2) and prohibits State parties from engaging in activities threatening another State's territorial integrity (Art. 10). ASEAN comments on the right to self-determination have been confined to cases of foreign occupation: See 'An Appeal for Kampuchea Independence by the ASEAN Foreign Ministers', 20 Sept. 1983, available at http://www.aseansec.org/5180.htm. ASEAN never addressed the East Timor problem as one of self-determination, to avoid offending Indonesian sensitivities, and therefore characterised the issue as the need to promote 'reconciliation, rehabilitation and reconstruction' to stabilise East Timor: Joint Communique, 33rd ASEAN Ministerial Meeting (July 2000), available at http://www.aseansec.org/13413.htm. The Myanmar problem was characterised innocuously as one requiring the promotion of 'national reconciliation and dialogue among all parties' rather than as a violation of the people's choice of government: Joint Communique, 36th ASEAN Ministerial Meeting (June 2003), available at http://www.aseansec.org/14876.htm. On ASEAN attitudes towards self-determination issues, see L. Thio, 'Implementing Human Rights in ASEAN Countries: Promises to Keep and Miles to go before I Sleep', *YHRDLJ* 2 (1999), 1, at 11–13. See also Art. 2, South Asian Association for Regional Co-operation Charter (1985), available at http://www.saarc-sec.org/.

81 *e.g.*, proposed Art. 23, Chapter II, Hong Kong Basic Law, defines speech that incites others to commit secession against the Peoples' Republic of China as seditious: available at http://www.info.gov.hk/basic_law/fulltext. Art. 6, 1997 Cambodia Law of Political Parties prohibits political parties from engaging in secessionist activities: Summary Record, Cambodia, CCPR/C/SR.1759, 29 July 1999, at para. 40.

2. Attitude before international human rights bodies

The reticence of States towards secessionist claims is further evident in how State reports before UN human rights bodies like the Human Rights Committee locate such claims within the individualist framework of the article 27 minority-rights clause in the Covenant on Civil and Political Rights (ICCPR), rather than in article 1, relating to the peoples' right of self-determination.[82] The 1993 Bangkok Declaration, on human rights, representing 'the aspirations and commitments of the Asian region',[83] contemplates a narrow conception of self-determination as inherent in 'peoples under alien or colonial domination and foreign occupation', particularly affirming the Palestinian right to self-determination. However, at the same time, it also stresses that such right should not undermine a State's political independence and territorial integrity.[84] This contemplates self-determination restrictively, as a legal tool designed primarily to achieve decolonisation or emancipation from quasi-colonial subjugation, following the 1960 Declaration on the Granting of Independence to Colonial Countries and Peoples.[85] This pre-empts groups within sovereign, independent States from asserting self-determination as grounds for a legal claim to secession, allaying fears of State fragmentation.

B. The cause of secessionist movements and grounds invoked as the basis of justification

Many secessionist movements in the Asia-Pacific regions have been short-lived and unsuccessful: *e.g.*, the attempted secession of the South Moluccas Republic from Indonesia or the declaration of an East Turkistan Republic

[82] The 1988 Philippines report addressed the autonomy schemes for Muslim Mindanao, over which a long-standing separatist war had been waged, under Article 27. Article 1 was related to its colonial past and overthrowing the authoritarian Marcos regime. CCPR/C/50/Add.1/Rev.1 (1989); II *Human Rights Committee Official Report* (1988–1989), paras. 208–210. Art. X, 1987 Philippines Constitution deals with 'Autonomous Regions', which are to operate within the intra-State framework.

[83] *Report of the Regional Meeting for Asia of the World Conference*, A/CONF.157/ASRM/8 (7 April 1993), Part II, para 6. [hereafter, Bangkok Declaration].

[84] See paras. 12–14, Bangkok Declaration, *ibid.* Notably the 1993 Bangkok NGO Declaration on Human Rights, involving some 240 NGO participants, affirmed that self-determination did not necessarily imply secession or independence but could involve constitutional arrangements based on popular consent. It did not preclude the possibility of secession as an expression of the right: para 8. Text available at http://www.arrc-hre.com/publications/hrepack1/page52.html.

[85] GA Res. 1514 (XV) of 14 Dec. 1960. Paragraph 6 considers acts that partially or totally disrupt a country's national unity and territorial integrity as contravening the UN Charter.

in the Xinjiang Uighur Autonomous Region of Western China (XUAR),[86] a product of Uyghur nationalism motivated by Turkic identity and the Sunni Islam faith in 1933 and 1944, suppressed by the Chinese communist government.[87] Galvanised by the establishment of the former Soviet Central Asian Republics in 1991, Uyghur organisations began to accelerate calls for independence, based on a continuous Uyghur claim to the land, disrupted only by Sino-Soviet intervention, given their belief in having a 6000-year cultural and physical regional history. Other decades-long independence rebellions persist: *e.g.*, the armed Muslim separatist rebellion in South-East Asia, regarding Mindanao (Philippines), or the Muslim Pattani separatists in Southern Thailand.[88] Ambiguous ceasefires have been reached with various secessionist groups (Shan, Karen, Mon) in Myanmar.[89] The independence of Timor Leste in 2002 fanned secessionist movements within the Indonesian provinces of Aceh, Riau and Irian Jaya. Some groups have posed credible military threats to their home States, managing to win the political support of external States.

The configuration of territorial units by the colonial powers brought within the same borders distinct ethnic, religious and cultural communities as well as past kingdoms.[90] The creation of multi-ethnic States in former colonies like India, Indonesia and Sri Lanka, and the attendant problems of promoting co-existence between distinct groups, some with

[86] This was established on 1 Oct. 1953 by the People's Liberation Army which ousted the Chinese Nationalists in 1949, thus consolidating the nationality policy which recognises Uyghurs as a national minority under Chinese rule. 99.8 per cent of Uyghurs, amounting to 8 million people, are located in Xinjiang, constituting half the population in this Northwest Chinese province. Many desire an independent 'Uyghuristan'. See D.C. Gladney, 'China's Minorities: The Case of Xinjiang and the Uyghur People', *WGM*, 9th Sess., E/CN.4/Sub.2/AC.5/2003/WP/16 (5 May 2003).

[87] S. Yom, 'Uighur Muslims in Xinjiang', *Foreign Policy in Focus* (2001), available at http://www.selfdetermine.org/index.html.

[88] A. Tan, 'Armed Muslim Separatist Rebellion in Southeast Asia'; A. Rabasa and P. Chalk, 'Muslim Separatist Movements in the Philippines and Thailand', *in* A. Rabasa and P. Chalk, *Indonesia's Transformation and the Stability of Southeast Asia*, (Santa Monica, CA : Rand, 2001), p. 85, at 94–8; S. S. Islam, 'Independence Movements in Patani of Thailand and Mindanao of the Philippines', *Asian Survey* 38/5 (1998), 441.

[89] Ethnic separatism in Myanmar broke out in 1948 but was brought under control in 1999 with the defeat of the long-running Karen rebellion, dating back to the end of World War Two.

[90] In some cases, importing foreign labour during the colonial era, as when the British imported indentured Indian labourers into Fiji, caused contemporary ethnic tensions. In 1996, 44 per cent of Fijians were Indians while only 51 per cent were indigenous Fijians. T. Hadden, 'Towards a Set of Regional Guidelines or Codes of Practice on the Implementation of the Declaration', *WGM*, 9th Sess. (12–16 May 2003); E/CN.4/Sub.2/AC.5/2003/WP.1 (27 March 2003), para. 29.

antagonistic histories, is partly a legacy of European colonialism.[91] No frontier revisions to reflect pre-colonial ethnic or tribal affiliations were made after their respective independence, in order to maximise the viability of new unitary States. For example, when Papua New Guinea became independent in 1975, some 750 language groups existed within its borders. Indonesia, with a population of 220 million, is ethnically very diverse with at least 300 local languages. Central Asian republics, like Kazakhstan, are ethnically diverse with its population of 15.4 million composed of Kazakhs (50%), Russians (25%), with the remainder being ethnically Ukrainian, German, Chechen, Kurdish and Korean.

Ethnic and religious conflicts fuel contemporary secessionist struggles by groups possessing distinct identities. Growing Islamisation is, for example, reflected in the desire to impose *hudud* laws in Aceh. Although it must also be mentioned that even though most Asia Pacific States have diverse populations, this does not necessarily lead to secessionist claims; there are instances where groups restrict their claims to greater autonomy and political participation rights.

Various unilateral declarations of independence have been made:[92] by the Tamil Tigers (Sri Lanka), Bougainvilleans (Papua New Guinea) and Mindanao Moros (Philippines). Typically, the concerned governments have rejected these secessionist calls. The Indonesian government rejected the independence declaration of 2000 by Irian Jaya activists issued after 2500 delegates, representing 250 tribal groups, met and requested the international recognition of West Papua as a sovereign State.[93] This is not surprising, as Indonesia is extremely sensitive about separatist claims and maintaining internal cohesiveness ever since losing East Timor, which it illegally annexed in 1975. Similarly, India denied secessionist claims by

[91] With respect to India, Gauhar considered that 'the seeds of disintegration' were sown in the colonial era, coming now into 'bitter fruition': 'Asia', p. 58. Prior to independence, two streams of nationalism emerged in the Indian sub-continent. The Hindu majority envisaged a united secular Indian State while Muslim nationalists, fearing Hindu domination, wanted Islam-based 'independent States' in northern Indian regions with Muslim majorities: see Chamberlain, *Longman Companion to European Decolonisation*, p. 51. The departing British administration considered and dismissed the possibility of an Indian partition to placate Muslim anxieties but thought that a sovereign Pakistan State would not solve the 'communal minority problem': 'India, Statement by the Cabinet Mission and His Excellency, the Viceroy', Cmd 6821 (1946), as quoted in Chamberlain, *Longman Companion to European Decolonisation*, p. 53.

[92] M. Rafiqul Islam, 'Status of Unilateral Declaration of Independence in International Law: The Case of Bangladesh', *IJIL* 23 (1983), 1.

[93] 'Irian Jaya declared independent', *BBC News*, 4 June 2000, available at http://news.bbc.co.uk/1/hi/world/asia-pacific/776911.stm.

the Punjabi minority, fearing an autonomous Sikh State would threaten national unity[94] and cause further State fragmentation along ethnic lines.

Secessionist groups tend to articulate the same litany of complaints, drawing from a common pool of grievances examined and illustrated below. These revolve around claims to distinct nationhood, homeland claims and economic and political maltreatment by a dominant ethno-cultural group.

1. Mode of incorporation into existing State and denial of the peoples' right of self-determination in terms of popular consent

A common grievance is the incorporation of various nations by colonial authorities into a common State – in complete disregard of their histories, traditional homeland claims or wishes – in the name of preserving the territorial integrity established at the time of independence. Only exceptionally has the colonial unit's territorial integrity been revised.[95]

a. South East Asia The peoples' right to self-determination regarding their future political destiny is thwarted where the popular will is entirely disregarded or its imperfect expression followed. For example, Irian Jaya activists argue that the 1969 United Nations supervised plebiscite in favour of joining Indonesia was a sham.[96] It was rejected by the Papua Independence Organisation (OPM) which then began to conduct low-level guerrilla warfare[97] against Jakarta's rule, after the Act of Free Choice[98]

[94] Gauhar, 'Asia', p. 57.

[95] *e.g.*, when the Ellice and Gilbert Islands, whose inhabitants were largely Micronesian, subdivided to form the independent States of Tuvalu and Kiribati in 1978 and 1979 respectively: Musgrave, *Self-Determination*, p. 186. Similarly, the strategic Trust Territory of Micronesia yielded the Federated States of Micronesia, Marshall Islands and Palau who entered into a Compact of Free Association in 1986: *ibid.*, at 187.

[96] The question posed to West Irian Papuan inhabitants was whether they preferred 'in an act of free choice' to stay under Indonesian control. Furthermore, the plebiscite was not conducted along the lines of 'one man one vote' but by means of consultative assemblies, involving only 1000 West Irians, where one voted for 800 people. Australian External Affairs Minister Gordon Freeth justified this by arguing a free vote would not necessarily produce the exact wishes of the West Irians, since many lived in primitive, stone-age conditions. See J. van der Kroef, 'Australia and the West Irian Problem', *Asian Survey* 10/6 (1970), 483, at 483.

[97] Chamberlain, *Longman Companion to European Decolonisation*, p. 186.

[98] The call for a Dutch parliamentary review of the Act of Free choice is seen as evidence that the Papua independence movement is gaining international ground: S. Jones, USINDO Open Forum, 'Aceh, Papua and Rising Nationalism in Indonesia', *International Crisis Group*, 3 April 2003, Washington DC, available at http://www.usindo.org/Briefs/2003/Sidney%20Jones%2004-03-03.htm.

which incorporated West Irian into Indonesia came into existence.[99] Formerly, Irian Jaya was retained by the Dutch, even after the independence of Indonesia in 1949. The Netherlands was engaged in the process of entering a separate independence agreement with Irian Jaya but this became moot after Indonesia invaded the copper and gold rich province in 1961. On 1 December 1962, the Free Papua movement proclaimed the State of West Papua. In 1963, Indonesia renamed it, with US support,[100] and the UN formalised it in 1969.[101]

Similarly, the Achinese, constituting 90 per cent of the population in the northern Indonesian island of Sumatra, take pride in their distinct 400-year history as an important Islamic sultanate and reluctant last acquisition of the Dutch East Indian colonies.[102] The contemporary independence demand by the Free Aceh Movement (Gerakan Aceh Merdeka or GAM) is partly founded on the view that the Aceh Kingdom should not have been incorporated into the Republic of Indonesia in 1949, as it was not a formal Dutch possession and because the Achinese were never consulted. Dutch colonialism was followed by Javanese colonialism, with the GAM initiating low-level insurgency against Jakarta since the 1970s.[103] In 1976, Hasan di Tiro, the GAM leader currently exiled in Sweden, proclaimed Aceh as independent. Calls for a referendum on Aceh's future in November 1999 by a student-led coalition were ignored.[104]

b. South Asia After fifty-two years of bloodshed, Kashmir still awaits the holding of an impartial, UN supervised plebiscite.[105] The Hindu Maharaja

[99] 'Irian Jaya declared independent', *BBC News*, 4 June 2000, available at http://news.bbc.co.uk/1/hi/world/asia-pacific/776911.stm.

[100] The US had interests in Irian Jaya, especially the US mining companies like Freeport McMoRan.

[101] See generally 'Indonesia: Human Rights and Pro-Independence Actions in Papua, 1999–2000', *Human Rights Watch*, 12/2(C) (2000), available at http://www.hrw.org/reports/2000/papua/index.htm.

[102] A. L. Smith, 'Aceh, Self Determination Conflict Profile', *Foreign Policy in Focus* (2002), available at http://www.fpif.org.

[103] See 'Indonesia: The War in Aceh', Profile on Aceh's Separatists, *BBC News*; *Human Rights Watch Report* 13/4 (2001), available at http://www.hrw.org/reports/2001/aceh/.

[104] The group is called SIRA (Aceh Referendum Information Centre). A. Rabasa and P. Chalk, 'The Challenge of Separatism and Ethnic and Religious Conflict', *in* A. Rabasa and P. Chalk, *Indonesia's Transformation and the Stability of Southeast Asia* (Santa Monica, CA: Rand, 2001), pp. 27–45.

[105] India brought the Kashmir issue to the Security Council. On 21 April 1948, the Security Council noted that both countries wanted to place the issue before a 'democratic method of a free and impartial plebiscite', which has yet to be held. A. Singh, 'The Right to Self Determination: Is East Timor a Viable Model for Kashmir?' *Human Rights Brief* 8/3 (2001), *Brief*, available at http://www.wcl.american.edu/hrbrief/08/3selfdet.cfm.

of Kashmir had ceded Kashmir, whose people are 77 per cent Muslim, to India on October 26 1947, apparently against popular will. Pakistan immediately disputed India's claim to Kashmir. Currently, the UN truce line places one-third of Kashmir under Pakistani control.[106]

c. The Pacific Papua New Guinea (PNG) was beset with anti-colonial secessionist initiatives. Historically, Papua was Australian territory acquired in 1946 while the previous German possession of New Guinea came under Australian control as a mandate and, later, a trust territory.[107] By a colonial quirk, administrative convenience shaped the decision to grant these two legally separate entities simultaneous independence as a single entity. Papuans, a racially distinct people, protested, demanding a referendum to choose between separate statehood or to join New Guinea. Having been denied this, liberation movements such as the 1970s Papua Besena movement, declared Papua's independence from Australia on 16 March 1975. The desire was to 'wipe out . . . white colonialism and black colonialism', given Australia's economic neglect of Papua.[108] The fear was that forcing Papua to unite with New Guinea, which had more inhabitants, would perpetuate a state of internal colonialism in Papua.[109]

Slated for inclusion in PNG, secessionists from the Bougainville island declared its independence as the 'North Solomons Republic' on 1 September 1975, three weeks before PNG obtained independence.[110] Such inclusion constituted a 'juggling of colonial territories' to serve a 'false unity'.[111] Nineteen distinct language groups co-existed in Bougainville and the Bougainvilleans claimed to have a greater affinity with the Solomon Islanders (West Solomons) who were 'blackskins' as compared to 'red-skins'[112] mainlanders, appealing to the ethno-cultural distinctiveness with long-standing statehood aspirations and geographical distinction to buttress independence claims. Noted popular Boungainville ideologue Leo

106 See generally Chamberlain, *Longman Companion to European Decolonisation*, p. 57.
107 R. P. Premdas, 'Secessionist Politics in Papua New Guinea', *Pacific Affairs* 50/1 (1977), 64.
108 Quoting J. Abaijah, *in* Premdas, *ibid*, at 73.
109 Quoting J. Abaijah, *in* Premdas, *ibid.*, at 68.
110 Premdas, *ibid.*, at 65. See M. Rafiqul Islam, 'Secession Crisis in Papua New Guinea: The Proclaimed Republic of Bougainville in International Law', *U. Haw. L.R* 13 (1991), 453; R. Alley, 'Ethnosecession in Papua New Guinea: The Bougainville Case, *in* R. Ganguly and I. Macduff, (ed.), *Ethnic Conflict and Secessionism in South and Southeast Asia: Causes. Dynamics, Solutions* (New Delhi: Thousand Oaks, London: Sage Publications (2003), p. 225.
111 Premdas, 'Secessionist Politics', p. 67.
112 S. Lawson, 'Self Determination as Ethnocracy: Perspectives from the South Pacific', *in* Sellers, M., (ed.), *The New World Order: Sovereignty, Human Rights and the Self-Determination of Peoples* (Oxford/Washington DC: Berg 1996), p. 153.

Hannett said that Bougainville, subject to white colonialism, had been 'the victim of mad imperial musical chairs',[113] questioning whether 'the arbitrary divisions of the colonial powers that cut across our geographical, historical, racial, ethnic and blood affinity ties'[114] warranted observance. The PNG government's employment of mercenaries against the secessionists was criticised as impeding the Bougainvilleans' right to self-determination.[115]

The technique of using a referendum to decide a territory's status was done in relation to Hawaii, even though the US considers that Hawaii, formerly a non-self-governing territory under the UN Charter, has 'completed acts of self-determination',[116] thus resolving its relational status with the US, consistent with General Assembly Resolution 1469 (XIV) of 1959 which found that the people of Hawaii had exercised their right to self-determination and freely chosen their political status.[117]

Nevertheless, the indigenous people of Hawaii, the *Na Kanaka Maoli*, have asserted before UN bodies[118] the violation of their right to self-determination through the US' invalid annexation[119] of the Hawaiian Kingdom after staging the imperfect 1959 referendum.[120] Craven raised

[113] L. Hannett, 'The Case for Bougainville Secession' *Meanjin Quarterly* (1975), 286, as quoted by Premdas, 'Secessionist Politics', p. 67.

[114] Quoted by Premdas, *ibid.*, p. 68.

[115] The Sandline company had in 1997 signed a contract for US$36 million with the PNG government to carry out offensive military operations in Bougainville: see E. Ballesteros, Report of the Special Rapporteur, 'The Right of Peoples to Self Determination and its Application to Peoples under Colonial or Alien Domination or Foreign Occupation', *Commission on Human Rights (CHR)*, 55th Sess., E/CN.4/1999/11 (13 Jan 1999), at para. 26. See also 'Secessionists in Papua New Guinea say British, South African Mercenaries in action', *Agence France-Press* (1997).

[116] US Report (art. 1 ICCPR), CCPR/C/81/Add. 4 (24 August 1994), para. 13.

[117] GA Res. 1469 (XIV) of 12 December 1959; see 'Human Rights of Indigenous Peoples', *Report of Working Group on Indigenous Populations*, 16th Sess., E/CN.4/Sub.2/1998/16 (19 August 1998).

[118] The Hawaiian Kingdom filed a complaint against the United States with the Security Council in July 2001. Press release and complaint about American Occupation of the Kingdom since the 1898 Spanish-American war, available at http://www.hawaiiankingdom.org/united-nations.shtml.

[119] Hawaiian Queen Lili'uokalani submitted a memorial in 1897, with 21169 signatures, detailing the Hawaiian peoples' protests against annexation: available at Perspectives on Hawaiian Sovereignty: http://www.opihi.com/sovereignty/memoral1897.htm. Hawaii's historical background was detailed in *Office of Hawaiian Affairs v Housing and Community Development Corporation of Hawaii 94-4207*, dealing with State responsibilities over ceded lands and the public trust.

[120] The case for independence and the illegality of US annexation and occupation is extensively made at http://www.hawaiikingdom.org. See also F. A. Boyle, 'Restoration of the Independent Nation of Hawaii under International Law', *St. T.L.R* 7 (1995), 723.

two related concerns,[121] casting doubt on the US' justification to rely on the referendum to perfect its title. First, no distinction was drawn between 'native' Hawaiians from the majority 'colonial' population and non-'native' Hawaiians; second, the choice the plebiscite presented was inadequate for the requirements of a valid exercise of the right of self-determination, as stipulated by General Assembly Resolution 1514 which requires an informed democratic process.

The political status of Hawaii is still being challenged through judicial and political channels. The issue was raised tangentially, in judicial settings, before the Permanent Court of Arbitration in *Lance Paul Larsen v The Hawaiian Kingdom*,[122] where it was argued that the Hawaiian people never relinquished sovereignty to the United States; hence, the Hawaiian Kingdom continued to exist and bore international legal responsibility for protecting Hawaiian subjects.

In 1993, a joint US Congress resolution acknowledged that the United States had overthrown the Kingdom of Hawaii on 17 January 1893, offering an apology to Native Hawaiians, in order to further reconciliation efforts.[123] The State of Hawaii has, through various Acts, recognised the right of the Native Hawaiian People to re-establish an autonomous sovereign government with control over land and resources,[124] passing legislative resolutions supporting the need to recognise an official political relationship between the US government and Native Hawaiian People. The Hawaiian State court in *OHA v HCDCH*[125] took judicial notice that various Hawaiian groups supporting sovereignty were active.

[121] M. Craven, 'Continuity of the Hawaiian Kingdom', a portion of a Legal Brief provided for the acting Council of Regency (12 July 2002), available at http://www.HawaiianKingdom.org., at para. 5.3.6.

[122] 5 Feb. 2001. For a comment, see D. J. Bederman and K. R. Hilbert, 'International Decisions', *AJIL* 95(2001), 927; D. J. Bederman and K. R. Hilbert, 'International Decisions', *CJIL* 1/2 (2002), 655.

[123] 1993 Apology Resolution, Pub. L. 103–150, 107 Stat. 1510. It apologises for 'the deprivation of the rights of Native Hawaiians to self-determination'. Text available at http://www.freehawaii.org/bill103.html.

[124] The State of Hawaii Legislature by Act 359 S. B. No. 1028 (1 July 1993) in relation to Hawaiian Sovereignty found that Native Hawaiians 'are a distinct and unique indigenous people with a historical continuity to the original inhabitants of the Hawaiian archipelago'.

[125] *OHA v HCDCH (94-4207)*, Circuit Court, Hawaiian State Judiciary. While acknowledging the possibility of the creation and recognition of a sovereign Hawaiian government, the Court found that the 1993 Apology Resolution and legislative enactments had not altered the authority of the State of Hawaii as trustee of the ceded lands to sell them for public purposes: available at http://www.state.hi.us/jud/ohavhcdch.pdf.

A descendant of Hawaiian royalty in 1999 issued a global announcement seeking foreign State recognition for the Kingdom of Hawaii, a *de facto* State.[126]

Efforts to meet the concerns of advocates of Hawaiian sovereignty are framed to operate within the existing US federal system. The Hawaii Supreme Court in *Ahuna v Department of Hawaiian Home Lands*[127] acknowledged that Hawaiians had the same special status under State law as Native Americans. The recommended path is to utilise the legislative framework to enhance self-determination rights, through conferring greater control over land, culture and resources to a representative Native Hawaiian governing body, which would establish direct government-to-government relations with Washington DC.[128] At present, the Akaka Bill,[129] introduced in 2000 but not yet passed, seeks to reorganise a Native Hawaiian Government,[130] similar to what American Indians and Native Alaskans enjoy under federal law.[131] It has alternatively been praised as a vehicle to promote self-government and criticised for effectively making Hawaii a wardship of the US Department of Interior and Hawaiians, a new class of subjugated people under Federal Law, precluding the re-emergence of the Hawaiian nation-State.

2. Denying the constitutional promise of secession

Secessionist agendas are pursued where a constitutional guarantee is thwarted, as was the case in the Union of Burma's 1947 Constitution.[132]

[126] Majesty Akahi Nui, 'Re: Truth, Freedom and Justice, Announcement to the World': available at http://www.freehawaii.org/proc2wrld.html. The statement declares the invalidity of the 1839 US overthrow of the Kingdom of Hawaii; hence, the 1840 Constitution and 1839 Declaration of Rights remained in full force.

[127] 64 Haw. 327, 339, 640 P.2d 1161, 1168-69 (1982).

[128] 'From Mauka to Makai: The River of Justice must flow freely', *US Department of Justice Report* (Oct. 2000), Ex. 71.

[129] Latest Version SB 344 – Latest version of the Bill (June 2003): available at http://stopakaka.com/2003/FedRecog.html. See H. Lindsey, 'Akaka Bill: Native Hawaiian, Legal Realities and Politics as Usual', *HLR* 24 (2002), 693; L. M. Kanehe, 'The Akaka Bill: The Native Hawaiians' Race for Federal Recognition', *HLR* 23 (2001), 857.

[130] Section 1(19) of the Bill provides a process 'within the framework of Federal law for the Native Hawaiian people to exercise their inherent rights as a distinct aboriginal indigenous native community to reorganise a Native Hawaiian governing entity for the purpose of giving expression to their rights as native people to self-determination and self government'.

[131] Committee Report Akaka Bill, 107-66, Ex. 28.

[132] Chapter X, sections 201–4, 1947 Constitution of the Union of Burma. The right of secession was only to be exercised ten years after the Constitution's ratification, after holding a plebiscite to ascertain popular will. Text available at http://shanland.org/

This provided various mountain tribes, specifically, the Shans[133] and the Kayahs, the option to secede after ten years.[134] This was the price that convinced groups like the Karens to forgo their desire for a Karenistan, embracing Karen regions spanning the Thai-Burma border, and to enter the Union as a constituent State.[135] Indeed, a 1945 mass meeting of Liberated Karens of Burma, during the time of the Constitutional Progress, passed a resolution asking the UN Conference and the British to add other adjacent Karen areas in Thailand to the Karen territory in Burma as part of a British administered 'United Frontier Karen States'.[136] This was to ensure the Karen nation's future security, given the past history of Burmese enslavement and persecution. The Karens were advised to 'throw your lot with the Burman' but persisted in desiring their own State within a genuine Federal Union, as a safeguard against Burmese assimilation pressures. The Karen National Movement, which has since 1949 sought self-determination to preserve ethnicity and equal rights, remains active.[137]

However, the present Myanmar government considers that '. . . we would not survive if we allowed the tribes to secede', preferring negotiations to solve the issue of the ethnic fighting it has spawned. The 1947 Constitution was suspended in 1962, after a military coup ostensibly to

History/Publications/ constitution_of_the_union_of_bur.htm. On the supporters and opponents of secession, see J. Silverstein, 'Politics in the Shan State: The Question of Secession from the Union of Burma', *Journal of Asian Studies* 18/1 (1958), 43.

133 It was clear that the Shan-Burma alliance did not mean lasting co-operation but was an attempt to form an alliance to expel colonialism. Without abandoning the hope of an independent Shanland, the mass organisation Shan Peoples' Freedom League (SPFL) came into being and stated in its Proclamation No. 4, of 5 February 1947 ('Let us Join Burma to gain Independence') that association with Burma should be on a federal basis, based on equal rights, full internal autonomy for Shan States and a right of secession at any time after the attainment of freedom (para. 3). Quoted in H. Myint of Taunggyi, 'The Shan State Secession Issue' (Thailand: Shan Herald Agency for News, 1957): available at http://www.shanland.org/History/Publications/shan_state_secession_issue_by_ht.htm. For an argument for a more genuine federation, see S. M. Win, 'Secession as an Ethnic Conflict Resolution: The Case of the Shan State': available at http://www.shanland.org/Political/SDU/activities/secession_as_an_ethnic_conflict_.htm.

134 Kachin and Karen States did not have a constitutional right to secede.

135 'Anatomy of a Betrayal: the Karens of Burma', *in* C. J. Christie, *A Modern History of Southeast Asia: Decolonization, Nationalism and Separatism* (London & New York: Tauris Academic Studies, 1996), p. 53.

136 See The Karen Memorial addressed to the British Secretary of State, 26 September 1945, in *ibid.*, Appendix 2, p. 214.

137 M. Zin, 'Karen History: In Their Own Words', *The Irrawaddy* 8/1 (2000): available at http://www.irrawaddy.org/database/2000/vol8.10/culturearts.html.

'save the nation from disintegration'.[138] The rationale was that politicians would cause divisiveness and instability.[139] In noting that Aung San Suu Kyii desires a return to the Constitution that allows secession, Foreign Minister Win Aung cautioned: 'once the process starts it will never stop. Look at Yugoslavia, do you think after Kosovo the problems will end?'[140]

3. Discrimination and maltreatment by dominant group (or 'identity politics')

A central grievance stems from the neglect of groups, united by a strong ethnic or religious identity,[141] who feel discriminated against or politically subordinate to a dominant group of a different ethnicity or religious affiliation.[142] Crudely put, the three decades long Mindanao separatist conflict, costing 120,000 lives, is laced with religious identity issues, setting the Muslim Moros, a distinct cultural community, against the majority Catholic Filipinos. This inter-faith tension is exacerbated where the dominant group seeks to impose its values and culture on the subordinate group, such as the imposition of the assimilation of the Thai language and Buddhist culture on the Patani Malay in south Thailand who, led by the Patani United Liberation Front, demand a separate Islamic territory.[143] Within Myanmar, ethnic tension is sustained by the Burman ethnic dominance led by the military junta, sustaining separatist rebellions with groups like the Muslim Rohingya in the north Arakanese region.[144] Repressive measures by the Chinese government in 1995 to curtail the

[138] S. Wansai, 'Minority Groups: a third force in Burma', *The Nation* (Thailand), 11 Aug. 2003.

[139] 'The Tatmadaw as a preserver of the Union' *Business Times* (Singapore), 4 Aug. 1993, p. 22.

[140] A. Kamil, 'Economic growth, national unity take priority in Myanmar', *New Straits Times* (Malaysia) (1999), p. 10.

[141] A 'peoples' who are entitled to the right of self-determination tend to have a distinct history, ethnic identity, cultural homogeneity, linguistic unity, religious affinity, territorial connection and common economic life: 'International Meeting of Experts on Further Study of the Concept of the Rights of Peoples: Report and Recommendations', *UNESCO* (1990), p. 38.

[142] e.g., Aceh rebels agitate for a Muslim State as they practice a stricter form of Sunni Islam than the majority Muslim Javanese who are considered overly secular in the view of the Aceh rebels. The 1953 Manifesto of the Aceh Rebels asserts a desire for an 'Islamic State' on 'native soil' and rejects allegiance to a Republic based solely on nationalism rather than religion: text *in* Christie, *Modern History of Southeast Asia*, p. 225.

[143] K. Mahmood, 'Thailand perpetuating the Taming of Islam in Patani', *IslamicOnline.net* (2002): available at http://www.islamonline.net/English/Views/2002/03/article9.shtml.

[144] 'The Ethnocratic State and Ethnic Separatism in Burma', *in* D. Brown, *The State and Ethnic Politics in Southeast Asia*, p. 33.

Uyghur cultural institution of the *meshrep*, a congregation of people who sing, recite poetry and play music, and thereby curb Islamic revivalism[145] and Uyghur cultural traditions, also heightened separatist feelings.[146]

Such 'identity politics' is evident in the maltreatment of the minority, predominantly Hindu, Tamil community in Sri Lanka, constituting 18 per cent of the population, by the politically dominant Sinhalese Buddhist majority. The Sinhalas, constituting 75 per cent of the population, 70 per cent of whom are Buddhists, practice an aggressive majoritarianism based on Sinhala nationalism and the Buddhist religious code.[147] This translates into attempts at linguistic assimilation by making Sinhala the official language, according Buddhism constitutional status and privileging Sinhalese with educational and government posts quotas.[148] The Tamil nationalist insurrection is propelled by the desire for Tamil Eelam, a separate State in the northeast, to become a nation possessing its own distinct language, culture and traditional homeland claims.[149] Negotiations for an autonomy scheme have currently stalled.[150] Commentators have argued that Sri Lanka's right to territorial integrity is contingent on the equal treatment of ethnic groups within the State, which has not been observed.[151] The violation of the right to internal self-determination, including the violation of minority and political participation rights, is a precursor to claims for external self-determination through secession.

[145] The Uyghurs, who adopted Islam between the 15th and 17th centuries, were not associated with Islam until 1935 when Chinese nationalists officially defined Uyghurs as an ethnic group of oasis-dwelling Muslims in the Tarim basin. See N. P. Concepcion, 'Human Rights Violations against Muslims in the Xinjiang Uighur Autonomous Region of Western China', *Human Rights Brief* 19, 8/1 (2004): available at http://www.wcl.american.edu/hrbrief/issue.cfm.

[146] Concepcion, *ibid.*

[147] I. A. Rehman, 'Minorities in South Asia', *WGM*, 9th Sess., E/CN.4/Sub.2/AC.5/2003/WP.13, at 19.

[148] M. Young, 'Sri Lanka's Long War', *Foreign Policy in Focus* 5/35 (2000): available at http://www.foreignpolicy-infocus.org.

[149] The Tamil Tigers webpage is at http://www.eelam.com. See 'Tamil Eelam Demand in International Law', *in* 'Towards a Just Peace', presented by International Federation of Tamils, Seminar, 15 February 1992, School of Oriental and African Studies, University of London: available at http://www.eekam.com/introduction/eelam_demand.html.

[150] 'Sri Lanka's rebel leader warns of secession', *Straits Times* (Singapore), 28 Nov. 2003, p. A10.

[151] M. Sornarajah, 'Eelam and the Right to Secession', Speech to the *International Tamil Foundation at London*, 25 June 2000; available at http://www.news.tamilcanadian.com/news/2000/07/20000718_2.shtml.

4. Economic underdevelopment / internal colonialism

Inequitable and exploitative relations between central and provincial governments in managing natural resources and allocating profits can stir political discontent. In relation to Aceh, the Indonesian government has not fairly shared revenue derived from the province's considerable natural resources in oil, gas and forests, constituting 11–15 per cent of the country's total export earnings. Jakarta returns only 5 per cent of this revenue to Aceh through development subsidies, perpetuating widespread poverty, economic under-development and the Achinese view that Western imperialism was merely replaced by internal colonialism.[152]

Similar sentiments exist in relation to Irian Jaya / Indonesia, Xinjiang / China and Bougainville / Papua New Guinea, where the central government economically neglects 'peripheral' regions by favouring central 'core' provinces. For example, inequitable distribution of profits from the Panguna Copper mine in Bougainville, resentment over poverty and outsiders taking jobs, and the impotence of the provincial government to act, fomented secessionist movements which turned violent in 1988.[153]

5. Military maltreatment and violence

Deep-seated antagonisms are further cemented when a government uses brutal military force to suppress insurrections. For example, the gross human rights violations committed by the Indonesian military in Aceh in the 1990s only radicalized independence sentiment, where previously a significant percentage of the population considered enhanced autonomous status sufficient remedy.[154]

C. Reaction of the affected State facing a secessionist claim: opposition and control

Pakistan's eventual recognition of Bangladesh remains the sole regional instance of a predecessor State recognising a secessionist unit.[155] Most affected parent States seek to suppress secessionist movements and

[152] A. Rabasa and P. Chalk, 'The Challenge of Separatism and Ethnic and Religious Conflict', p. 33.

[153] Y. Ghai and A. J. J. Regan, 'Constitutional Accommodation and Conflict Prevention'; available at *Accord*, http://www.c-r.org/accord/boug/accord12/constitutional.shtml.

[154] Tan, 'Armed Muslim Separatist Rebellion in Southeast Asia', at 277–82.

[155] D. Wright, *Bangladesh and the Indian Ocean Area 1971–1975* (New Delhi: Sterling, 1989); available at http://www.une.edu.au/~arts/SouthAsiaNet/publications/bangladesh&indianocean/index.html.

preserve territorial integrity through domestic or bilateral measures, or attempt through intra-State measures to address and ameliorate claims of political and economic exploitation and harsh military operations.

1. Policies of outright rejection

Governments have expressly ruled out secession. While tendering apologies for past human rights abuses, Indonesian President Wahid declared his intolerance of separatist initiatives in mostly Christian Irian Jaya in the east or predominantly Muslim Aceh in the west.[156] Both provinces were to remain 'part of the unitary State of the Republic of Indonesia'.[157] This hard-line stance was considered crucial to quashing secessionist hopes for referenda arising elsewhere after the East Timorese experience.

A 2002 white paper entitled 'China's National Defense', declaring China's political resolve and military capacity to suppress separatist movements to preserve national sovereignty and unity,[158] stood resolute against the oppression of any ethnic group, as a 'unitary multi-ethnic country', as well as against acts 'undermining ethnic harmony and splitting the country'. This included taking action against any independence manoeuvres by Taiwan or military assistance by another country to aid Taiwanese separatism,[159] contrary to the 'one country two systems' or 'peaceful reunification' policy. Senior Chinese officials have argued that China must 'pre-emptively and aggressively' attack ethnic separatist forces in Xinjiang, rather than focus on regional economic development.[160]

2. Crimes against the State: treason and terrorism

To deter secessionist tendencies, States have enacted laws charging separatists with crimes against the State ranging from treason or, in the post-9/11 world, terrorism. Separatist leaders have been tried for treason

[156] 'Indonesia flexes muscle against independence thrusts', *Edmonton Journal (Alberta)*, 1 Dec. 2000, p. A4.

[157] 'Wahid warns Irian Jaya', *Herald Sun* (Melbourne, Australia) 27 Dec. 2000, p. 38; 'Secession bids will be crushed by force', *Straits Times* (Singapore), 2 Jan. 2003, p. A1.

[158] 'Chinese army able to check any separatist act: white paper', *Xinhuanet* (China); available at http://www.humanrights-china.org/news/2002-12-10/China20021210090039.htm.

[159] Crawford, *The Creation of States*, p. 143; W. T. Tie, 'Consolidating Separation: The Lee Teng-hui Administration and the Political Status of Taiwan', *SJEAA* 3/1 (2003), 19; J. I. Charney and J. R. V. Prescott, 'Resolving Cross-Strait Relations between China and Taiwan', *AJIL* 94 (2000), 453; J. Shen, 'Sovereignty, Statehood, Self Determination and the Issue of Taiwan', *AUILR* 15 (2000),1101.

[160] 'Xinjiang's First Priority is to Annihilate the Ethnic Separatist Forces', *Uyghur Information Agency*, 15 Jan. 2003; available at http://coranet.radicalparty.org/pressreview/print_right.php?func=detail&par=4238.

in Thailand,[161] the Indonesian islands of Aceh[162] and the Moluccus,[163] and Papua New Guinea.[164] Supporters of separatist groups can be tried for subversive activities: *e.g.*, GAM supporters under the Anti-Subversion Law, punishable by death.[165]

Labelling separatist groups as 'terrorists' is a strategy employed to delegitimise separatist movements by outlawing them. India outlawed separatist groups in its restive North-East Province, such as the United Liberation Front of Assam, which has been engaged in a violent twenty-year-long independence struggle,[166] as well as the National Liberation Front of Tripula.[167] This legitimises the suppression of local rebellions, undercutting any external support they might otherwise garner. In this regard, States seek to get international organisations and other States to recognise that a particular group is a terrorist one: *e.g.*, the United States, India and Britain consider the Liberation Tigers of Tamil Eelam a terrorist group,[168] while Singapore recognises both the Tamil Tigers and the Moro Islamic Liberation Front as terrorist groups.[169]

[161] Three members of the separatist Pattani United Liberation Organisation were convicted for treason: 'Terrorists Sentenced: Three Separatists Convicted of Treason', *The Nation* (Thailand), 16 Oct. 2002

[162] Treason and terrorism: life and death penalty: 'Aceh negotiations put on trial', R. Harvey, BBC Jakarta, 29 July 2003; available at http://news.bbc.co.uk/2/hi/asia-pacific/3105733.stm; L. McCulloch, 'Fear pain and shame in Aceh', 2 July 2003, *Asia Times Online*; available at http://www.atimes.com/atimes/Southeast_Asia/EG02Ae03.html.

[163] While 80 per cent of Indonesians are Muslim, the inhabitants of the Moluccas are equally divided between Christians and Muslims. A small separatist group, the Maluku Sovereignty Front, seeks an independent State in the southern part of the Maluccan archipelago. 'Christian separatist on trial in Indonesia', *BBC News*, 19 Aug. 2002, and its leader has been tried for a planned rebellion: available at http://news.bbc.co.uk/1/hi/world/asia-pacific/2202709.stm.

[164] 'On Trial In Papua', *Sydney Morning Herald*, 15 May 2001, p. 14

[165] Presidential Decree 11/1963. Article 1 defines 'subversive activities' broadly to include actions which 'distort, stir up trouble or digress' from *Pancasila* or the State or are deemed to be 'spreading feelings of hostility . . . among the population'. See 'The Anti-Subversion Law: A Briefing' *Amnesty International* (ASAASA 21/003/1997), 1 Feb. 1997; available at Amnesty International website: http://web2.amnesty.org/library. Supporters of GAM already on the wanted list include student activists and NGO members. See 'GAM supporters may face death penalty', *Straits Times* (Singapore), 4 June 2003, p. A6.

[166] 'Rocket Attack kills two in Assam', *BBC News*, 25 Dec. 2002; available at http://news.bbc.co.uk/2/hi/south_asia/2605791.stm.

[167] S. Bhaumik, 'Officials abducted in Tripura', *BBC News*, 20 May 2003; available at http://news.bbc.co.uk/1/hi/world/south_asia/0342303.stm.

[168] 'Sri Lanka's rebel leader warns of secession', *Straits Times* (Singapore) 28 Nov. 2003, p. A10. See also 'Philippines may brand MILF a terrorist group', *Straits Times* (Singapore), 11 March 2003, p. A7.

[169] JI White Paper, p. 3.

Certain States such as Indonesia display ambivalence towards the proposal to label separatist groups like GAM as terrorist organisations for fear of 'internationalising' the Aceh conflict. If GAM were placed on the UN list of terrorist groups, UN members would be obliged to arrest GAM members (many in Sweden, Malaysia and the US) and seize their assets. However, this would pressurise Indonesia to allow foreign monitors in to observe the Aceh conflict.[170] The Foreign Affairs Ministry stresses that the international community acknowledges 'that separatism in Aceh is Indonesia's domestic affair'.[171]

Prior to September 2000, the Chinese government had publicly equated Uyghur calls for autonomy or independence with global terrorism, co-ordinating forceful campaigns such as the 'Strike Hard Campaign' of April 2000 targeting 'religious extremists', 'violent terrorists' and 'national splittists' in Xinjiang.[172] The prioritisation of national unity is evident, when using the term 'Eastern Turkenstan' could lead to arrest.[173]

Subsequent attempts after 9/11 have been made to link the Xinjiang groups with Al Qaeda to justify China's brutal anti-separatist campaign.[174] This has elicited concerns from human rights groups that in linking the suppression of Xinjiang dissent with its anti-terrorist campaigns, China obscures the commission of gross human rights violations against ethnic minorities. These ethnic minorities, though peacefully seeking their own national identity in Xinjiang, Tibet and Inner Mongolia, are charged with acts of 'splitting the country', in the name of eradicating separatist organisations.[175] Such 'eradication' efforts include arbitrary arrests, detention, extra-judicial killings, torture, summary executions and unfair

[170] 'Indonesia backs down: No terrorist label for Aceh rebels', *Straits Times* (Singapore), 19 Nov. 2003, p. A8

[171] 'Jakarta wants to tag Aceh rebels as terrorists', *Straits Times* (Singapore), 22 May 2003, p. A1; 'Plan to have GAM listed as terrorist group still on' *Jakarta Post (Indonesia)*, 21 Nov. 2003.

[172] Part IV 'Origin of the East Turkistan Issue', in *History and Development of Xinjiang*, White paper. People's Republic of China (PRC) Information Office of the State Council, May 2003, Beijing, available at http://www.humanrights-china.org/whitepapers/white_c23.htm.

[173] Gladney, 'China's Minorities'; Concepcion, 'Human Rights Violations'.

[174] 'China denounces separatists', Bin Laden 'link', *BBC News*, 21 Jan. 2002: available at http://news.bbc.co.uk/1/hi/world/asia-pacific/1772928.stm. The US and UN have supported China's claims that the East Turkistan Islamic Movement (ETIM), for example, is an international terrorist organisation. E. Eckholm, 'US Labeling of Group in China as Terrorist is Criticized', *New York Times*, 1 Sept. 2002, p. 1.

[175] 'Written Statement', International Federation for Human Rights, E/CN.4/20003/NGO/242, 17 March 2003, *CHR* 59th Sess.

trials. Chinese representatives before UN human rights bodies have dismissed alleged incidences of torture in Tibet and Xinjiang as emanating from anti-China NGOs.[176] Further allegations of torture and the raping of nuns in Tibetan prisons were 'not worth refuting', although it was admitted that imprisoned criminals shouting separatist slogans in May 1998 in the Tibet Autonomous Region were further charged with undermining prison order under the Prison Law, receiving additional punishment for inciting persons to split the State.[177] These harsh measures were justified by saying that 'China was no different from any other country in its lack of tolerance of separatist and terrorist activities'.[178]

3. Counter-insurgency initiatives and the preservation of internal security

States have resorted to forceful military action to quell insurgencies and disorder. India has adopted strong, armed measures against Sikh separatists in the Punjab,[179] and the Indian northeast, deploying a 300–400,000 strong sizeable security force[180] to deal with the Kashmiri Muslim armed insurgency breaking out in 1989. Indonesia has authorised military action in Irian Jaya[181] and imposed martial law in Aceh in May 2003, sending in 40,000 troops to regain order and reclaim GAM-influenced provinces in 13 of Aceh's 233 sub-districts,[182] as a response following the failure of peace talks. After the December 2004 Tsunami disaster, GAM unilaterally declared an unconditional and indefinite ceasefire with government forces[183] to facilitate the delivery of humanitarian assistance; in response, the head of the Indonesian military offered a moratorium to

176 'Summary Record', Committee against Torture, CAT/C/SR.252/Add.1, 16th Sess., 3 May 1996.

177 'Summary Record', Committee against Torture, CAT/C/SR.419, 24th Sess., 12 May 2000.

178 CERD Summary Record, CERD/C/SR.1164, 49th Sess., 14 August 1996.

179 R. Ganguly, 'Coping with Ethnic Insurgencies: View from New Delhi', *Asia Quarterly*, (2000): available at http://www.vuw.ac.nz/asianstudies/publications/quarterly/00january5.html. The author notes that tough counter-insurgency measures adopted from 1988 were viewed as successful, given the return to electoral politics in the Punjab in 1996 and the curbing of Sikh militancy.

180 Ganguly, *ibid.*

181 'Indonesia flexes muscle against independence thrusts', *Edmonton Journal (Alberta)*, 1 Dec. 2000, p. A4

182 'Indonesian officers take over from civilians in some parts of Aceh' 14 July 2003, Agence France-Presse: available at http://www.reliefweb.int.

183 'Aceh tsunami victims await aid', *Reuters*, *ABC News Online*, 28 Dec. 2004.

rebels who laid down their arms to help with the humanitarian effort.[184] Vice President Jusuf Kalla subsequently called for a permanent truce in January 2005.[185] However, the abandonment of the informal ceasefire when the government apparently killed guerrillas to protect tsunami aid deliveries[186] does not bode well for future peace-making efforts.

Alleged human rights abuses committed during harsh counter-insurgency operations has provoked domestic and international concern. For example, Komnas Ham, the Indonesian human rights commission, reported that human rights abuses had been committed by the military since the May 19 presidential decree[187] of emergency in Aceh. An Indonesian parliamentary team was sent to investigate this.[188] The Thai government, while establishing an independent commission[189] to investigate the use of military force by the Southern Border Provinces Peace-Keeping Command (SBPPC) to crush Muslim protestors in an October 2004 incident in Takbai district, Narathiwat province, rejected a call by Commission of Human Rights Special Rapporteur Philip Alston to allow him to visit and investigate the situation.[190] Alston was concerned with the forceful measures adopted which resulted in casualties, including the suffocation of 78 detainees in overloaded trucks, resulting in spiralling acts of reprisal[191] directed against Buddhist monks and other symbols of

[184] M. Moore, 'Aceh ceasefire in doubt as rebels threaten bloodshed', *Sydney Morning Herald*, 12 Jan. 2005.

[185] 'Jakarta calls for Aceh truce', *BCC News Online*, 14 Jan. 2005.

[186] 'Aceh rebels killed "to protect aid"', *The Age (Australia)*, 22 Jan. 2005.

[187] Presidential Decree No. 28/2003, On The Declaration of a state of Emergency with the Status of Martial Law in Nanggroe Aceh Darussalam Province, noted that a series of amicable efforts made by the government, either by means of the stipulation of special autonomy for Aceh as an integrated approach in a comprehensive development plan or as dialogue held overseas, has failed to stop the intention and actions by the Free Aceh Movement (GAM) to secede from the unitary State of the Republic of Indonesia and declare its independence. Text available at http://www.thejakartapost.com/aceh/acehlatestnews2.asp.

[188] 'Soldiers accused of human rights abuses', *Straits Times* (Singapore), 2 Aug. 2003; 'Jakarta to extend Aceh military ops', *Straits Times* (Singapore), 30 Oct. 2003 at A6.

[189] 'Thailand rejects U.N. probe into deaths', *The Washington Times*, 19 Nov. 2004, available at http://www.washtimes.com/upi-breaking/ 20041118-095946-9890r.htm. The Commission produced a report which attributed fault to three senior security officers, leading to disciplinary investigation of these officials by the Defence Ministry: 'Panel finds three senior security officers at fault', *Bangkok Post*, 29 Dec. 2004, available on Lexis.

[190] 'UN expert on extrajudicial killings seeks to visit Thailand', 17 Nov. 2004, available at http://www.unhchr.ch/huricane/huricane.nsf/0/ 3A8567EFA62D7CFCC1256F4F0053F0EA?opendocument.

[191] No separatist groups have specifically claimed responsibility for these recent attacks although the Pattani United Liberation Organisation has posted a message on its website

authority such as teachers and police officials.[192] In November 2004, the Thai Prime Minister, whose heavy-handed military approach towards the separatist problem has been criticised, ruled out negotiations with militants, trying to force the government to discuss secession;[193] in January 2005, 10,000 troops were dispatched to Thailand's southern provinces to fortify efforts to avert Muslim separatism.[194] Implicitly, while governments are entitled to use force to quell separatist insurrections, the manner in which these operations are conducted is subject to some external scrutiny.

4. Diluting claims: population transfers, migrant settler policies and assimilation

In some instances, governments have denied that a secessionist group is a distinct nation. The PNG government said that as the Bougainville secessionists were all of 'Melanesian indigenous stock', there were 'no minorities in PNG' since 'we are one people and one nation.'[195]

To dilute the 'numbers' justification of secessionist groups, central governments programmes relating to population transfers or migrant resettlement are undertaken and perceived as assimilative attempts to make an ethnic group a minority in its traditional homeland. For example, by the 1960s the Moro Muslims had become a minority in Mindanao, given the massive influx of Catholic Filipino settlers from the north, ongoing since the Republic's founding in 1946. As of 1986, Muslims were only a majority in five of the twenty-three provinces in Mindanao and Sulu.[196] The sending of landless Javanese farmers from Java to others parts of the Indonesian archipelago under the transmigration programme has precipitated land disputes with locals, fanning armed separatist movements in Aceh and Irian Jaya and ethnic conflict in Maluku, Central Kalimantan and Central Sulawesi.[197] This programme is also perceived as a

in November 2004 urging Buddhists to leave the Muslim majority South and threatening terrorist attacks in Bangkok: 'Thai PM rules out militant talks', *BBC News Online*, 8 Nov. 2004.

[192] 'Thailand's restive south', *BBC News Online*, 23 Dec. 2004; 'Bloodshed, Mayhem in South', *Bangkok Post*, 26 Oct. 2004 (available on LEXIS).

[193] 'Thai PM rules out militant talks', *BBC News Online*, 8 Nov. 2004.

[194] T. Cheng, 'Thai troops deployed to the south', *BBC News Online*, 3 Jan. 2005.

[195] Letter, PNG Secretary of Foreign Affairs and Trade to CHR Chairman, 25 Feb. 1994, E/CN.4/1994/120 (2 March 1994).

[196] Tan, 'Armed Muslim Separatist Rebellion in Southeast Asia', at 273.

[197] As noted by Indonesia's Permanent Mission before the Committee against Torture, CAT/C/GC/2002/1 (17 Sept. 2002).

veiled attempt at imposing the dominant, more secular Javanese abangan culture.

The Chinese government supports the migration of Han Chinese to its border regions. The resettlement of twenty million Han Chinese in Southern Mongolia, governed by the Chinese-established Inner Mongolian Autonomous Government,[198] which was formed after the 1947 suppression of the Southern Mongolia Independence Movement, has made the Southern Mongols a 14 per cent minority in their homeland. Furthermore, claims of ethnic genocide and extinguishing Mongol ethnic identity have been raised in relation to coercive government measures forcing Mongols to study Chinese history, language and culture, spurring concern about 'ethnic splittists'.[199] The migratory movement of Han Chinese to Xinjiang, aside from threatening Uyghur cultural survival,[200] has caused economic discrimination against its indigenous, predominantly Muslim, inhabitants.[201] In totality, this is an anti-self-determination strategy[202] or an attempt to dilute separatist sentiment. In some instances, forced assimilation and the promotion of a mono-cultural State within a heterogeneous polity[203] in the name of national integration has been adopted. In Bhutan, a citizenship code based on Buddhist or Drupka values operates,[204] the wearing of traditional Drupka dress is compulsory[205] and significant ethnic groups such as the Nepali-speaking Lhotshampas are excluded from representation in the constitutional drafting process.[206] Thus, Drupka communalism is privileged over nationalism, causing alienation and spurring pro-democracy movements (Bhutan's People's Party) and secessionist movements in southern Bhutan where it is feared that the Bhutan Nepalese seek to unite with their kin in Nepal to establish a

198 Open Letter, PRC Government: available at http://members.aol.com/yikhmongol/oltcg.htm.

199 D.C. Gladney, 'Ethnic Separatism in China: Threat or Smoke?', *Wall Street Journal*, 8 July 1996.

200 Concepcion, 'Human Rights Violations'.

201 C. Mackerras, *China's Minorities: Integration and Modernisation in the 20th century* (Hong Kong: Oxford University Press, 1994).

202 Written Statement, International Educational Development Inc., to *CHR* 54th Sess., E/CN.4/1998/NGO/89 (23 March 1998), para. 11.

203 Political Crisis in Bhutan: Nationalism and Other Issues: *Spotlight Magazine*, 30 April 1992. Bhutan is a multi-ethnic State with three distinct ethnic groups: the ruling Ngalong (15%), Sharchops (40%) and Lhotshampas (40%).

204 B. Bhattarai, 'Refugee Talks Deadlocked', *Financial Times*, 16 Sept., 1999. The laws also banned Nepalese dress and language in Bhutanese schools.

205 'Revivalist Drupkas and Fundamentalism' *Kathmandu Post*, 22 Jan. 1998 (Art. No. 18)

206 Rehman, 'Minorities in South Asia', p. 19.

'Greater Nepal'. [207] This conflict has spawned a refugee problem eliciting UN and European Union concern.

5. Characterisation as internal matter and preclusion of external interference

In displaying hostility towards secession, States characterise on-going secessionist movements as civil conflicts or internal matters that preclude external intervention. The PNG government insisted that any political solution to the 1989 secessionist outbreak in Bougainville had to respect PNG territorial integrity. Furthermore, UN or Commonwealth intervention should be minimal and contingent upon the government's invitation,[208] in order to prevent the Bougainville Revolutionary Army (Bougainville Interim Government) from using this as a pretext to 'internationalise' a domestic issue.[209] The official stance was that the Bougainville issue has 'nothing to do with separatism', being the work of criminal elements exploiting an internal matter relating to a 'legitimate resource benefit dispute' between a mining company and traditional landowners; determination was 'an *ex post facto* rationalisation' to legitimate rebel activities.[210]

Similarly, Indonesia angrily responded to foreign criticism over imposing martial law in Aceh in May 2003 after failed peace negotiations, arguing that this was necessary to restore peace for the Achinese people living under the threat of the separatist Free Aceh Movement (GAM). It considered the statement of concern issued by the United States, Japan and the European Union[211] about ending the Emergency expeditiously as 'leading to meddling',[212] urging that 'international support for Indonesia's integrity' should be demonstrated by pressing GAM to disarm and accept as the final solution the offer of special autonomy for Aceh within Indonesia's unitary State framework. A government spokesman characterised the

[207] 'Bhutan: Crackdown on anti-nationals in the east', *Amnesty International*, ASA 14/01/98.

[208] The PNG government considered that external interference would prolong the crisis, maintaining it could handle 'this unfortunate crisis with minimal assistance from outside when it considers necessary'. Letter, PNG Secretary of Foreign Affairs and Trade to CHR Chairman, 25 Feb. 1994, E/CN.4/1994/120 (2 March 1994).

[209] 'Human Rights Violations in the PNG of Bougainville', Report of Secretary-General E/CN.4/1996/58 (15 April 1996), *CHR* 52nd Sess., para. 8.

[210] Letter, PNG Secretary of Foreign Affairs and Trade to CHR Chairman.

[211] The US, Japan and EU had jointly organised a conference as a forum for dialogue between Jakarta and GAM to evaluate implementation of so-called Cessation of Hostilities Agreement in Aceh on 17–18 May 2003 in Tokyo but Indonesia pulled out of these talks: 'War looks likely as Indonesia's Peace talks fail', *The Scotsman*, 19 May 2003, p. 10.

[212] R. Harvey, 'Jakarta angry at Aceh meddling', *BBC News*, 7 Nov. 2003; available at http://news.bbc.co.uk/2/hi/asia-pacific/3249407.stm.

Aceh situation as a 'humanitarian problem', declaring that the government possessed enough resources and confidence to overcome this problem *sans* external intervention.[213]

6. Securing accords respectful of territorial integrity

To buttress internal security, countries such as China entered into accords with neighbouring Central Asian States in the Spring of 1996.[214]China, for example, sought to ensure respect for its territorial integrity and, by promising not to harbour separatist groups, attempted to thwart potential secessionist movements which might receive support from these States.

D. Reaction of the affected State facing a secessionist claim: attempts at diffusion and accommodation

States seeking political solutions to secessionist problems have proposed measures that would, in name at least, vindicate the right of internal self-determination of ethno-nationalists seeking to establish their own State. This is pragmatic and realistic, given that in the context of long-standing civil conflict, some groups are *de facto* in control of certain territories, such as the Tamil Tigers in Sri Lanka and the Moro Islamic Liberation Front (MILF) in Southern Philippines. Such accommodation comes in the form of negotiated territorial and personal autonomy schemes, economic development programmes to mitigate poverty and the recognition of minority rights. Governments have uniformly denied the validity of secessionist claims, even while reconciliatory overtures are made: *e.g.*, allowing Irian Jaya to change its name to West Papua in January 2002 and to fly their Morning Star flag below the Indonesian flag. This concession was later retracted as it came to symbolise the separatist cause.[215]

1. Autonomy schemes

Federalism[216] or autonomy schemes have been offered to placate secessionist sentiments and maintain State cohesion, although it is feared that

[213] 'Martial law in Aceh', *Straits Times* (Singapore), Commentary, 14 Nov. 2003.

[214] 'Kazakhstan Government Deport Political Refugees to China' *Eastern Turkistan Information Center*, Gröbenried (Germany), 15 June 1999; available at http://www.uygur.org/enorg/reports99/9901615.html).

[215] N. D. Somba, 'Over 40 Papuans held for flying separatist flags', *The Jakarta Post*, 28 Nov. 2003; 'Papuans face treason charges over flags', *Straits Times* (Singapore), 29 Aug. 2003, p. A26.

[216] The original agreement in 1949 was that Indonesia should have a federal structure, but this was dissolved in favour of a unitary State in August 1950: see Chamberlain, *Longman Companion to European Decolonisation*, p. 185. The Solomon Islands government is currently negotiating a shift towards federation to appease the secessionist Istabu Freedom

such schemes could be the prelude to independence claims, by weakening the central government. The Tamil insurrectionists in Sri Lanka were offered a devolution package and constitutional autonomy to end a bloody twenty-year-long ethnic conflict, although at present, negotiations have stalled.[217] In 1995, when the Bougainville Revolutionary Army controlled central Bougainville, the UN Secretary-General noted that most of the Bougainvilleans that were interviewed desired that their unique position within the PNG political order be given constitutional status. The government, however, expressed fears that granting concessions might precipitate similar demands in other parts of PNG, 'a country which, given its geography and its myriad tribes and language groups, suffers from strong centrifugal tendencies'.[218] A Peace Agreement was signed in 2001,[219] providing for an independence referendum to be held 10–15 years after the election of the first autonomous Bougainville government,[220] a compromise solution designed to satisfy Bougainvillean autonomy aspirations while simultaneously affirming PNG's territorial integrity.

The Indonesian government also offered special autonomy status to West Papua and Aceh. Law No. 21/2001 on special autonomy for Papua,[221] allowing the name change from Irian Jaya to Papua, was rejected by the Papuan Presidium Council, as the Papuan people were not sufficiently consulted.[222] The Council also criticised Law No. 45/1999, the intent of which was to partition West Papua into three provinces for apparent administrative considerations while effectively controlling the rising separatist sentiment.[223] This was contrary to Law No. 21/2001 which

Movement on Guadalcanal Plains as well. This movement dates back to independence in 1978, spurred by resentment towards the flood of settlers from Malaita islands. Fraenkel, 'Minority Rights in Fiji and the Solomon Islands'.

217 Hadden, 'Towards a Set of Regional Guidelines', para 22.

218 'Report of the Secretary-General': Human Rights Violations in the Papua New Guinea Island of Bougainville, para. 14, E/CN.4/1996/58 (15 April 1996), *Commission on Human Rights*, 52nd Sess., para. 8. [hereafter, Secretary-General Report].

219 See 'Bougainville: The Peace Process and Beyond', Parliament of Australia, *Joint Standing Committee on Foreign Affairs, Defence and Trade* (27 Sept. 1999), available at http://www.aph.gov.au/house/ committee/jfadt/bougainville/BVrepindx.htm.

220 'PNG-Bougainville arms accord', *BBC News.co.uk.*, 23 Feb. 2001.

221 P. Kammerer, 'Lessons of East Timor keep Papua tied down; The province's special status has been reduced to a facade, experts say, as a rising nationalism sways Jakarta's elite', *South China Morning Post*, 4 Dec. 2003, p. 10.

222 'Autonomy troubles Papuans', *Jakarta Post* (Indonesia), 15 April 2002.

223 'Indonesia shelves Papua division', *BBC News*, 27 Aug. 2003; available at http://news.bbc.co.uk/1/hi/world/asia-pacific/3184591.stm. The implementation of Law

had not been fully implemented, especially in relation to establishing a Papuan People's Assembly (MPR) as a powerful legislative oversight body. Activists have found in UN-sponsored meetings a venue to express their views that autonomy plans such as the West Papuan scheme are considered impositions.[224] In the case of West Papua, in their view, these plans failed because pressing issues like past human rights abuses and local-language use were not addressed and because only certain elite community representatives participated in the negotiations.

In the Philippines, a 1995 Peace Agreement was brokered with one of the main secessionist groups, the Moro National Liberation Front (MNLF), after 24 years of separatist conflict.[225] The 1987 Constitution had mandated the creation of an autonomous region in Muslim Mindanao which the MNLF refused to recognise. Under the 1995 accord, a Southern Philippines Council for Peace and Development (SPCPD) was formed to replace the provisional government, chaired by MNLF leader Nur Misuari, who governed an autonomous five-province Muslim region. However, this plan lacked broad-based support and was rejected by an MNLF splinter group, the now dominant Moro Islamic Liberation Front (MILF),[226] which ultimately sought to carve out an independent Islamic country within Mindanao called Bangsamoro which has a large population of non-Muslim indigenous peoples and Catholic settlers.[227]

No. 45 of 1999 resulted in Papua losing almost two-thirds of its territory and annual revenue, being deprived of income from copper and gold mining in Timika and oil and gas mining in Tangguh, Manokwari, West Irian Jaya. Presidential Instruction No.1/2003 calls for acceleration of the province's partition: 'Govt to emasculate Papua's special autonomy', *Jakarta Post* (Indonesia), 2 Sept. 2003.

224 'Regional Seminar on Minority Rights: Cultural Diversity and Development in Southeast Asia', paras. 12–14, E/CN.4/Sub.2/AC.5/2003/WP.14 (5 May 2003).

225 The Moros are one of three main groups in Mindanao, their ancestors being indigenous peoples who converted to Islam in the 13th century, and who resisted Catholicism under Spanish colonial rule. 'Moro' is derived from 'Moors' which forms the source of a distinct national identity centred on the quest for Bangsa Moro, an Islamic republic. Today, Mindanao has 13 Islamic ethno-linguistic groups: E. Montillo-Burton, 'The Quest of the Indigenous Communities in Mindanao, Philippines: Rights to Ancestral Domain', E/CN.4/Sub.2/AC.5/2003/WP.3, *WGM*, 9th Sess., at 14–15.

226 The MILF was formed in the 1970s as an initial separatist movement championing an Islamic Republic in Mindanao-Sulu-Palawan. See L. Baguioro, 'MILF rebels popular in Mindanao despite terror acts; Filipino Muslims, who see themselves as neglected by the government, think of the separatist rebels as their champions', *Straits Times* (Singapore), 1 March 2003.

227 Montillo-Burton, 'The Quest of the Indigenous Communities' , p. 19.

The autonomy experiment failed, owing to poor governance. Misuari was ousted on corruption charges,[228] and fighting resumed in November 2001.[229] The 12,500-person-strong MILF is now the chief advocate for a separate Moro State.

Failure to negotiate peace and to find political solutions protective of internal self-determination with respect to separatist conflicts draws forth State military intervention to quash assertions of external self-determination.

2. National minority status

The People's Republic of China (PRC), founded in 1949, views itself as a multi-ethnic country with a Han majority and a 'big united family of ethnic groups' committed to preserving national unity consonant with the historic 'will of the Chinese nation'. It thereby opposes movements to secure Tibetan independence or the Eastern Turkestan State in Xinjiang, considered to be engineered by a few ethnic separatists and imperialist invaders.[230] It seeks to contain nationalist sentiments in its provinces by creating four autonomous regions enjoying some self-government under centralised State leadership, regulated by the 1984 Law on Ethnic Regional Autonomy.[231]

China also accords official recognition to some fifty-six national minorities.[232] In Xinjiang for example, these schemes afford some protection for Muslim practices, making provision to address grievances over interference with religious/cultural rights and granting citizens who belong to a recognised national minority group some limited representation in regional government.

[228] L. Baguiro, 'Muslim Filipinos no closer to homeland dream', *Straits Times* (Singapore), 26 Feb. 2002.

[229] 'Misuari deported home to face charges', *Straits Times* (Singapore), 8 Jan. 2002, p. 4; 'No objection to Malaysia's prosecuting Misuari – GMA', *BusinessWorld*, 26 Nov. 2001, p. 12.

[230] 'National Minorities Policy and Its Practice in China', *PRC Information Office of the State Council*, Sept. 1999; available at http://www.humanrights-china.org/whitepapers/white_c10.htm.

[231] These are the Xinjiang Uygur Autonomous Region (Oct. 1955); Guangxi Zhuang Autonomous Region (March 1958); Ningxia Hui Autonomous Region (Oct. 1958) and Tibet Autonomous Region (Sept. 1965): Part III, Regional Autonomy for Ethnic Minorities, in *ibid.*

[232] National Minorities Policy and its Practice in China: 'PNG-Bougainville arms accord', *BBC News.co.uk.*, 23 Feb. 2001; Gladney, 'China's Minorities'.

3. Economic development plans

Integration into the national society is facilitated by attempts to redress deep-seated grievances stemming from the inequitable distribution of revenues from provincial resources, between one or another province and the central government.[233] The 29 July 2001 special autonomy law provides[234] that Aceh should receive 70 per cent of the oil revenue rather than the current mere 5 per cent, and 80 per cent of the agriculture and fisheries revenue.[235]

The Philippines and China acknowledge that long-term strategies to eliminate separatism entail eradicating poverty and improving the people's socio-economic welfare, two problems which otherwise fuel unrest. Consequently, President Arroyo has decided to disburse half of a US$55 million US aid package to Mindanao.[236] Deng Xiaoping considered that economic development could best diffuse ethnic conflict, though this was considered insulting to Tibetan theocratic values that viewed 'developmentalism' as contributory to stirring up ethnic competition and materialism.[237] Through its Western Region Development Strategy, China seeks to promote economic growth through government investment in infrastructure and industry, in a region where forty-three of China's fifty-five ethnic minorities are concentrated. This preferential treatment of ethnic minorities[238] is designed to equalise development levels between the 'eastern' and 'western region' and thereby harmoniously integrate national minorities.[239]

233 National Assembly (MPR) chairman Amien Rais noted that frustration stemmed from poverty and economic neglect, stressing the importance that revenue-sharing be more 'just' to ensure the central government did not retain the 'lion's share'. 'Aceh, Irian Jaya may secede, Amien warns', *Straits Times* (Singapore), 18 Oct. 2000, p. 28.

234 'Indonesian neo-patrimonialism and integration: The case of Aceh', *in* D. Brown, *The State and Ethnic Politics in Southeast Asia*, p. 135.

235 'Mega offers Aceh more autonomy', *Straits Times* (Singapore), 16 Aug. 2001, p. 4. See also A. L. Smith, 'Indonesia's Aceh Problems: Measuring International and Domestic Costs', *Asia-Pacific Centre for Security Studies* 2/5, (2003).

236 'Arroyo to inject $50m into Mindanao', *Straits Times* (Singapore), 11 Dec. 2001, p. A6.

237 A. P. L. Liu, 'Ethnic Separatism', in *Mass politics in the People's Republic: State and Society in Contemporary China* (Boulder, Colorado: Westview Press, 1996), p. 189.

238 'History and Development of Xinjiang', White Paper May 2003, Part X : 'State Support for the Development of Xinjiang', *PRC's Information Office of the State Council*: available at http://www.humanrights-china.org/whitepapers/white_c23.htm (accessed 10 Nov. 2003).

239 Li. Baodong, 'Statement (China)', *CHR* 57th Sess., 12 April 2001, available at http://www.china-un.ch/eng/12261.html. See also T. Xiaowen, 'China's Drive to Develop its Western Region: Why Turn to this Region Now?', *East Asia Institute Background Brief*, No. 71, 28 Sept. 2000; available at www.nus.edu.sg/NUSinfo/EAI/es71.doc.

V. Reaction of the international community and third States

A. *Addressing secessionist conflicts in humanitarian and human rights terms*

The international community and third States generally react negatively to secessionist claims, although humanitarian concern is expressed for human rights violations arising out of secessionist conflicts, as was done in the case of Chechnya.

NGOs have called for press restrictions under the current martial law regime in Aceh to be lifted,[240] while the UN Secretary-General, on the basis of reports, has urged both rebels and the military to protect civilians in the face of extra-judicial killings and the burning of schools.[241] Both the Charter[242] and Treaty-based UN human rights bodies regularly address secessionist conflicts in terms of human rights violations rather than through the framework of a purported right to secede. UN Working Groups, such as the one on Enforced or Involuntary Disappearances, have visited countries facing secessionist conflicts.[243]

Some organised groups have presented their cases in terms of human rights violations before international fora.[244] For example, the Uyghurs of north-west China, as represented by the East Turkestan National Congress and Transnational Radical Party (TRP), have complained before the UN Sub-Commission on Human Rights and Fundamental Freedoms of measures tantamount to cultural genocide, including banning the Uyghur language in schools and curtailing Muslim religious activities, systematically violating the 'the civil, political, social, cultural and economic rights

[240] 'International Rights group calls for lifting of press restrictions in Aceh', *Yahoo News*, 26 Nov. 2003; available at http://sg.news.yahoo.com/031126/1/3g7ro.html.

[241] 'UN Fears for Aceh Civilians', *BBC News*, 30 May 2003, available at http://news.bbc.co.uk/1/hi/world/asia-pacifici/2949064.stm.

[242] The Commission of Human Rights has requested that thematic rapporteurs be sent to visit the PNG island of Bougainville to monitor the peace process and report on human rights violations; for example: CHR Res. 1994/81 of 9 March 1994 and CHR Res. 1995/65 of 7 March 1995; 'Special Rapporteur report', mission to PNG Island of Bougainville (Oct. 1995), *CHR*, 52nd Sess., E/CN.4/1996/4/Add.2 (27 Feb. 1996), para 1. [hereafter, 'Special Rapporteur report'].

[243] Report of the Working Group on Enforced or Involuntary Disappearances, E/CN.4/2000/64/Add.1, 21 Dec. 1999; visited SL 1991–1992.

[244] *e.g.*, there are about twenty-five international organisations and websites on 'Eastern Turkistan', a product of Uyghur nationalism, not all of which are separatist, fuelled by 500,000 expatriated Uyghurs based worldwide in Amsterdam, Munich, Istanbul, Melbourne, DC and NY. In 1995, an expatriate Uyghur was elected chair of the Hague-based Unrepresented Nations and People's Organisation (UNPO). This 'cyber-separatism' facilitates information exchanges and large financial transfers. Gladney, 'China's Minorities'.

of... people living in the colonial province Xinjiang Uighur Autonomous Region'.[245] The TRP asked the Sub-Commission to pressure the Chinese government to change the language law and to appoint an East Turkistan special rapporteur to document human rights abuses.

The international community has exerted moderate influence in encouraging the relevant parties to negotiate political solutions and by sponsoring such initiatives. International bodies like the European Parliament have adopted resolutions condemning China's policy of suppressing Islamic practices and eradicating Uyghur culture, urging negotiations.[246] Favouring intact borders, the UN Secretary-General and Western countries have urged Indonesia to resume negotiations with Aceh separatists, not because they support GAM, but to serve the priority of regional stability.[247]

B. Making and keeping peace

1. Mediation and peace-keeping

a. State-driven initiatives Individual States have taken the initiative to mediate talks between secessionist rebels and the affected State, since encouraging national reconciliation promotes both State territorial integrity and regional stability.

Third-party involvement tends to 'internationalise' secessionist issues. For example, Norway acted in a mediatory capacity in relation to the Sri Lankan government and Liberation Tigers of Tamil Eelam, hosting peace talks in Norway in December 2000 and getting both parties to agree to a model of internal self-determination and power-sharing based on a 'federal model within a united Sri Lanka'.[248] The Tamil Tiger leader asserted that if regional self-rule were not accorded, in the face of 'alien military occupation' in the North-East Tamil heartlands, 'we have no alternative other than to secede and form an independent State'.[249] Norway and other Nordic States have participated in Sri Lanka ceasefire monitoring

245 Sub-Commission on Human Rights and Fundamental Freedoms, Geneva, 8 Aug. 2003. 55th Sess., available at http://www.coranet.radicalparty.org/pressreleases/press_release.php?func-detail&part=5971.

246 Resolution on Human Rights Situation in Eastern Turkistan (Region of Xinjiang) 10/04/97; see Gladney, 'China's Minorities'.

247 Smith, 'Indonesia's Aceh Problems'.

248 'Sri Lanka peace breakthrough' *BBC News*, 5 Dec. 2002; available at http://news.bbc.co.uk/2/hi/south_asia/2544553.stm (accessed, 15 Oct. 2003).

249 'Sri Lanka's rebel leader warns of secession', *Straits Times* (Singapore), 28 Nov. 2003, p. A10.

missions.[250] Seeking to further peace talks and solidify the fragile ceasefire, a Norwegian delegation headed by the Foreign Minister served as peace-broker between the government and Tamil Tigers in January 2005, after the Tsunami crisis.[251]

In relation to the Bougainville crisis peaking during 1988–95, New Zealand provided a ship, *Endeavour*, as the venue for talks. Before Canadian, New Zealand and Vanuatu observers, the Endeavour Accord was signed in July 1990, paving the way for further peace conferences and, eventually, installing a transitional government in April 1995.[252]

Complementing peacemaking, States also play a peace-building role in sending ceasefire observers and peacekeeping forces to regions suffering from secessionist civil strife – a reminder of the compliance-pull of an international presence. In July 2003, Malaysia hosted talks between thc MILF and Philippine government,[253] and also deployed ceasefire observers to Mindanao where most MILF rebels, numbering some twelve different 500-member groups, are based.[254] Australia dispatched a peacekeeping force in July 2003 to the Solomon Islands where the Istabu Freedom Movement, drawn from ethnic Melanesian islanders who constitute 90 per cent of the Islanders, sought to force the migrant Maliatans out of Guadacanal.[255] After the signing of the Honiara Commitments, the PNG government and Bougainville secessionists agreed to a ceasefire, to the deployment of a South Pacific Regional Peacekeeping Force and to the convening of a peace conference.[256]

b. Involvement of public international organisations Public international organisations seek to diffuse secessionist conflicts by helping the parties to adopt a political settlement. For example, the fifty-six-member Organisation of Islamic Conference (OIC), formed to foster Muslim solidarity and Muslim peoples' rights,[257] played an important

[250] 'Norway puts Sri Lankan peace bid on backburner', *Straits Times* (Singapore), 15 Nov. 2001, p. A18.

[251] 'Aceh rebels killed "to protect aid"', *The Age* (Australia), 22 Jan. 2005.

[252] Special Rapporteur report, para 64.

[253] 'Manila signs ceasefire with MILF', *BBC News*, 18 July 2003, available at http://news.bbc.co.uk/1/hi/world/asia-pacific/3077137.stm.

[254] 'KL agrees to send peace monitors', *Straits Times* (Singapore), 21 July 2003, p. A7; 'KL sets condition for peace talks', *Straits Times* (Singapore), 5 July 2003, p. A13.

[255] Solomon Islands, *BBC News Country Profile*, available at http://news.bbc.co.uk/1/hi/world/asia-pacific/country_profiles/ 1249307.stm.

[256] Secretary-General Report, 'Human Rights violations in the PNG island of Bougainville', para. 5.

[257] Hashmi, 'Self-Determination and Secession', pp. 117–151.

mediatory role in the Mindanao secessionist imbroglio in the Southern Philippine.

OIC States, especially Libya, helped broker the 1976 Tripoli Agreement, to which the MNLF was a party. Pakistan and Saudi Arabia also publicised separatists' grievances, pressuring the Philippine government, by threats to reduce oil supplies, to negotiate with the MNLF, thereby legitimating this group as representing the Moro voice.[258] The OIC further elevated the status of the MNLF through the granting of official observership in 1977.[259] Under the 1996 Peace Agreement signed between the Philippine government and MNLF, the OIC maintained a monitoring role.[260] This involved overseeing the transitional administrative structure known as the Southern Philippines Council for Peace and Development, which failed due to corruption and funding deficits. The OIC and the Muslim World League[261] also mediated between the Philippine government and the 12,500-man-strong MILF which controls at least seven Mindanao provinces and spearheads the independence cause, largely on funding received from overseas radical groups.[262] The MILF, having rejected the 1996 Agreement, entered into formal peace talks with the Philippine government in 1997 and 1999 facilitated by external mediation.

c. Non-governmental organisations Despite government dislike of external intervention in secessionist conflicts, private bodies such as the Swiss-based NGO, the Henry Dunant Centre (HDC), facilitated a dialogue process between GAM and then Indonesian President Wahid in 2000.[263] It brokered a ceasefire agreement in May 2000 and a cessation of hostilities on 9 December 2002. The Indonesian military was hostile towards HDC involvement, as this legitimised and internationalised an 'internal' separatist conflict.

[258] 'Interview with Prof Thomas McKenna, Question & Answer', *Asia Source Interview*: available at http://www.asiasource.org/news/special_reports/philipiine.cfm.

[259] When the OIC Secretary-General visited Manila in 1993, he snubbed the MILF, which employed violent methods and rejected a ceasefire, and supported the MNLF by commending peace efforts by the sole legitimate representatives of the Muslims of the southern Philippines, Nur Misuari': Tan, 'Armed Muslim Separatist Rebellion in Southeast Asia', p. 274.

[260] 'Misuari to be deported in January to face trial', *Straits Times* (Singapore), 22 Dec. 2001.

[261] 'Manila signs ceasefire with MILF', *BBC News*, 18 July 2003, available at http://news.bbc.co.uk/1/hi/world/asia-pacific/3077137.stm.

[262] The MILF was formed in 1978. A. Tan, 'Armed Muslim Separatist Rebellion in Southeast Asia', p. 275.

[263] 'Southeast Asia and International Law', *SJICL* 7 (2003), 290.

2. Development and stabilisation

In order to stabilise States and strengthen the resilience of autonomy regimes, international organisations and individual States have pledged financial and technical support to promote economic development. For example, the World Bank and US government pledged to finance development projects in Mindanao once a peace deal was signed.[264] The Special Rapporteur visiting the PNG island of Bougainville in 1995 also called for a UN development programme to assist rehabilitation efforts and to meet the economic grievances of Bougainville secessionists. These secessionists felt exploited because Australian companies had been granted copper prospecting licenses, which led to land disputes and the channelling of all mining royalties to the Administration, for the benefit of PNG as a whole.[265] The environmental damage caused by mining in the Panguna area had disrupted traditional lifestyles, which fact, together with the employment of many non-Bougainvilleans by the mine, bred strong antagonism against the central government as well as increasing the desire for independence.[266] Such concerns require attention to preserve long-term State stability.

C. The UN and secessionist movements

1. UN and recognition policy

UN Membership has, to some extent, a 'constitutive' effect insofar as it confers legitimacy upon and helps to consolidate a State. Thus, secessionist groups have attempted to gain UN support and involvement in their cause, such as when the pro-Independence Papua presidium spokesmen asked the UN to mediate relationships between them and Indonesia by deploying UN peace monitors pursuant to their proposed peace plan.[267]

Nevertheless, the UN has underscored its antipathy towards secession in rejecting demands for independence referenda emanating from Indonesian provinces like Aceh, Maluku, Irian Jaya and Riau, inspired by the East Timor model. UN Secretary-General Kofi Annan stated that 'The United

[264] '4 killed in attack on Philippines Mosque', *Straits Times* (Singapore), 4 Oct. 2003, p. A21; 'Arroyo wins promises of military and economic assistance', *Straits Times* (Singapore), 24 Oct. 2003.

[265] Special Rapporteur Report, paras. 1, 19.

[266] *Ibid.* para 21.

[267] 'Irian separatists want UN intervention', 14 Dec. 2000, *BBC News*, available at http://news.bbc.co.uk/1/hi/world/asia-pacific/1070218.stm.

Nations recognizes the unity of Indonesian territory. We will not take any move that will break off the country.'[268]

2. UN recognition of the right to self-determination and UN apathy and incapacity

While recognising specific group rights to self-determination and even calling for referenda to ascertain popular will, the apathy and incapacity of the UN to follow through has resulted in inaction.

For example, the UN was involved in addressing the 'Indonesia question' (1947–1949) when the Netherlands East Indies was undergoing dissolution. The Netherlands, the UN and the then United States of Indonesia, which was to be federally organised, signed the 1949 Round Table Conference Agreements guaranteeing that component parts of former Dutch colonies could exercise their right to self-determination and opt out of joining predominantly Javanese and Muslim Indonesia.[269] The Security Council Committee of Good Offices was replaced by the UN Commission for Indonesia to oversee the implementation of these agreements. In 1950, the mainly Christian Moluccan people decided to opt out, declaring the independence of Republik Maluku Selatan (Republic of South Moluccas).[270] Subsequently, Indonesia invaded the islands and Moluccan forces retreated to Ceram island; the latter were eventually shipped back to the Netherlands. The UN Commission's failure to enforce this agreement, and the Netherlands' inaction, thwarted nationalist aspirations to secede from Indonesia, with Ambonese separatists arguing that crushing the Republic of South Moluccas violated their right to self-determination.[271] Nevertheless, Indonesia's hold on the Moluccas was consolidated during the

[268] 'U.N. Not to Support Separatist Movement in Indonesia: Annan' *Xinhuanet*, 20 May 2002, available at http://www.humanrights-china.org/news/2002-5-20/Inter200252085926.htm.

[269] 'Defining Self Determination: The Republic of Indonesia vs. the South Moluccan Republic', *in* Christie, *A Modern History of Southeast Asia*, p. 108.

[270] *Declaration of Independence of the South Moluccas*, 25 April 1950, Christie, *A Modern History of Southeast Asia*, Appendix 4, p. 224.

[271] Ambon was never part of the provisional United States of Indonesia. At the 1949 Netherlands Conference, the plan was to call the new federal entity 'Republik Indonesia Serikat', with the component States' right of secession firmly entrenched in the provisional constitution. Indonesia ultimately adopted a unitary State structure. Further, as territorial integrity was accorded priority after decolonisation, minority regions in post-colonial States like Indonesia were denied a right to self-determination insofar as former colonial units' borders were retained: 'Defining Self Determination: The Republic of Indonesia vs. the South Moluccan Republic', *in* Christie, *A Modern History of Southeast Asia*, p. 108.

Cold War, where allies like the United States shored up the post-colonial State to prevent the spread of Communist influence.

Similarly, the Security Council called for a UN-supervised plebiscite[272] to determine the Kashmiri peoples' political future after they had suffered two out of three Indo-Pakistan wars since India's Independence in 1947 when it seized Kashmir.[273] Despite separatist sentiments, the choice was restricted to joining either India or Pakistan, precluding the independence option. This plebiscite has yet to be carried out; thus, the long Indian military occupation has forestalled the implementation of the Kashmiri right to self-determination. NGOs have urged the UN to ensure that the plebiscite is carried out.[274] Kashmiri separatists like the Jammu Kashmir Liberation Front (JKLF) continue to campaign for an independent State. Recently, India has engaged the main separatist alliance, the All Party Hurriyat Conference, in direct talks, all the while insisting that this is an internal Indian matter and thus granting Pakistan no role in the talks.[275] India blames Pakistan for fomenting violence in Kashmir, which Pakistan denies, arguing that only diplomatic and moral support is provided to Kashmiri militants. Third-State assistance to a failed secessionist group would constitute intervention in the parent State's domestic affairs.

D. *Supporting the parent State against secessionist movements*

1. States policy on recognition and preference for intra-State solutions

Recognition, conferred by States or international organisations, has a powerful legitimating effect. Unrecognised cultural or religious groups seek to support each other by meeting together regularly, as, for example, the Uyghur leaders and Tibet's Dalai Lama have done since 1981, both of these latter being united in seeking to pressure China politically.[276] However, these non-State actors have found it harder to engage the support of international bodies and other States, protective of territorial integrity,

[272] SC Res. 122 of 24 January 1957.

[273] B. Farrell, 'The Role of International Law in the Kashmir Conflict', *PSILR* 21 (2003), 293.

[274] International Educational Development Inc., Written Statement, *CHR*, 54th Sess., E/CN.4/1998/NGO/89 (23 March 1998), paras. 4–8.

[275] 'Separatists draft Kashmir roadmap', *BBC News*, 21 Nov. 2003, available at http://news.bbc.co.uk/go/pr/fr/-/1/hi/world/south_asia/3226958.stm.

[276] Gladney, 'China's Minorities'.

for their secessionist agendas and may indeed be denied access to such fora.[277]

Other States have sought to buttress the stability of vulnerable newly independent States facing secessionist movements. The Australian, Fijian and Indonesian governments expressed support for the independence of PNG, while rejecting concurrent Bougainville secessionist claims that Suharto feared were Communist-inspired.[278] States have discouraged irredentist ambitions such as those held by Jinnah. States refused to entertain calls by the North Arakan Muslim League in 1946 to include the Muslim-majority area of Arakan within Pakistan, as it was slated for absorption within a Burma-dominated independent State.[279] This type of non-action on the part of States thwart secessionist ambitions, reflecting State preference to maintain good inter-State relations over and above the pull of ethnic and religious loyalties.

Where a government affirms another State's territorial integrity, it delegitimises secessionist movements. Indonesian government officials have claimed that all countries must respect Indonesian borders. For example, while disappointed at the resumption of hostilities and military brutalities in Aceh, the US representative sent a clear diplomatic message affirming support for Indonesian territorial integrity, dashing the hopes of GAM rebels for international recognition.[280] Australia declared its opposition to GAM's independence agenda on grounds that it would impair South-East Asian security by triggering Indonesia's break-up. It urged GAM rebels to return to negotiations and focus on securing autonomy,[281] a call Malaysia echoed.[282] The lack of international support for GAM and the preference for a reconciliatory, intra-State solution for the Aceh question obviously weakens GAM's claim to secession and capacity to secede.

[277] Members from Irian Jaya's Free Papua Movement (OPM) were barred from attending the Pacific Islands forum. Before being deported, a senior official attended the meeting uninvited and asked Australia to relax its opposition to independence and to support negotiations to avoid increasing violence. C. Skehan, 'West Papuan Separatists Warn Of Another Timor', *Sydney Morning Herald*, 15 Aug. 2001, p. 8.

[278] T. Bobola, 'Indonesia's Tough Line on Communism', *Post Courier*, 26 Oct. 1976, p. 3, as quoted *in* Premdas, 'Secessionist Politics in Papua New Guinea', *Pacific Affairs* 50/1 (1977), 64–85.

[279] 'At the Frontier of the Islamic World: the Arakanese Muslims', *in* Christie, *A Modern History of Southeast Asia*, p. 161.

[280] Smith, 'Indonesia's Aceh Problems'.

[281] P. Mercer, 'Asia instability if Aceh rebels win', *BBC News*, 25 May 2003, available at http://news.bbc.co.uk/1/hi/world/asia-pacific/2936264.stm.

[282] 'Separatists threat to regional stability', *Straits Times* (Singapore), 26 May 2003, p. A6.

2. Inter-State co-operation against separatism

States have sometimes entered into mutual commitments to address separatist issues. In 1998, China and Turkmenistan issued a declaration pledging to combat separatism, oppose inter-State and ethnic confrontation, and disallow any organisation on their soil from carrying out subversive activities against each other.[283] No member of the Shanghai Cooperation Organisation, comprising China, Russia and four Central Asian republics, will support Uyghur separatist nationalism at the expense of China's security.[284] Indeed, States act in solidarity when co-operating to thwart separatist activists, as was the case when three alleged Uyghur separatists were deported from Kazakstan to China.[285] Other States like Pakistan, Kyrgyzstan and Uzbekistan[286] have repatriated Uyghur separatists to China upon request.

Not all States respond favourably to extradition requests. Sweden refused to extradite four exiled GAM leaders living in Sweden, as they were Swedish citizens.[287] Sweden refused Indonesia's request to curtail the activities of separatist groups, as Swedish laws had not been contravened.[288] Fellow South-East Asian States have been more co-operative in responding positively to Indonesia's appeal not to afford sanctuary and political asylum to Aceh rebels. Malaysia agreed to deport illegal entrants,[289] despite the objections of the UN High Commissioner for Refugees that immigrants could not be deported to conflict zones.[290] (This contrasts with the more obvious sympathy Achinese co-religionists received in 1991 when rebels fled to Penang after a military crackdown and Malaysia refused to surrender them to Indonesia.)[291] Malaysia similarly did not afford asylum to wanted MNLF head Nur Misuari who was

[283] 'Turkmenistan and China say no to separatism', *BBC News*, 2 Sept. 1998, available at http://news.bbc.co.uk/1/hi/world/asia-pacific/164025.stm (accessed 15 Sept. 2003).

[284] Yom, 'Uighur Muslims in Xinjiang'.

[285] 'Kazakhstan Government Deport Political Refugees to China', Eastern Turkistan Information Center.

[286] 'Fearing unrest, China pressures Muslim Group', *New York Times*, 5 Oct. 2001.

[287] 'UN Fears for Aceh Civilians', *BBC News*, 30 May 2003, available at http://news.bbc.co.uk/1/hi/world/asia-pacifici/2949064.stm.

[288] Smith, 'Indonesia's Aceh Problems'.

[289] 'Southeast Asia and International Law', p. 292; 'GAM supporters may face death penalty', *Straits Times* (Singapore), 4 June 2003, p. A6.

[290] 'Malaysia walks tightrope on Aceh refugees', B. Kuppusamy, *Asia Times*, 9 Sept. 2003, available at http://www.atimes.com/Southeast_Asia/ EI09Ae04.html ; 'KL vows to deport 250 Acehnese despite UN protest', 21 Aug. 2003, p. A5; 'KL and Jakarta cement anti-terror alliance' *Straits Times* (Singapore), 29 Aug. 2003, p. A1.

[291] Tan, 'Armed Muslim Separatist Rebellion in Southeast Asia', p. 278.

arrested in Kuala Lumpur, considering this to be an internal Philippines matter.[292]

3. Regional co-operation against secessionist movements

Despite the existence of secessionist conflicts in many ASEAN States, ASEAN takes no stand on this issue, influenced by its adherence to principles of non-intervention in internal affairs and stress on territorial integrity. This indicates ASEAN's aversion to secessionist claims.[293]

For example, ASEAN affirmed Indonesia's territorial integrity and national unity in the face of secessionist claims.[294] The Philippines invoked the non-intervention principle in relation to the Southern Muslim separatist conflict.[295] The only time ASEAN grappled with self-determination issues was when Vietnam invaded Cambodia in 1979,[296] which related to external intervention.

ASEAN countries, while recognising the regional terrorist threat, are at pains to ensure that this is not conflated with any religion or ethnicity.[297] Collectively and individually, these States are aware of the threat posed by radical Islamisation and a separatist Islamic agenda with links to terrorist groups. Islam is a powerful force in countries with significant Muslim populations, such as the Rohingyas in Burma or the Moros in the Philippines, drawing on the ideal of the united Islamic *umma* based on religious affiliation, in contrast with the Western secular concept of national sovereignty. [298]

A 2003 Singapore white paper detailing visions of a greater Islamic State[299] shows an awareness of separatist Islamic groups networks: *e.g.*, the Moro Islamic Liberation Front (MILF) and Abu Sayyaf who demand independence in South Philippines, and the New Patani United Liberation

[292] 'South East Asia and International Law', 814, at 822; 'Misuari Should be on Terrorist List, says Arroyo', *Straits Times* (Singapore), 7 Dec. 2001.

[293] Art. 2, 1976 ASEAN Treaty of Amity and Cooperation in Southeast Asia, available at http://www.aseansec.org/1217.htm.

[294] Joint Communiqué, 34th ASEAN Ministerial Meeting, (July 2001): available at ASEAN-WEB, http:// www.aseansec.org/newdata/hanoi04.htm.

[295] 'Manila to invoke principle of non-intervention', *Straits Times* (Singapore), 21 July 2000, p. 38.

[296] Thio, 'Implementing Human Rights in ASEAN Countries', pp. 12, 39–44.

[297] 'Special ASEAN Ministerial Meeting on Terrorism', Joint Communiqué (May 2002). Para. 5 states: 'We strongly emphasize that terrorism must not be identified with any religion, race, culture or nationality.' Text available at http://www.aseansec.org/5618.htm.

[298] Christie, *A Modern History of Southeast Asia*, p. 132.

[299] JI White Paper, pp. 4, 6.

Organisation which seeks an Islamic State in southern Thailand.[300] The co-operative links between these radicalised groups were noted, such as when GAM recruits are trained at MILF camps.[301] It is feared that the politicisation of a burgeoning Islamic consciousness will spur Muslim-majority States, such as the Malaysian provinces of Kelantan and Terengganu, to demand a more Islamic form of State. Hence, 'the spectre of a brace of Muslim mini-States espousing fundamentalist Muslim values and having affinities with Libyan-style radicalism' is cause for concern.[302]

Recognising the shared threat of Islamic terrorists and their linkages with South-East Asian Muslim separatists, ASEAN countries have co-operated to curb this threat[303] and to preserve friendly inter-State relations. The Thai military, with Indonesian assistance, also co-operated to investigate links between Patani liberation fighters and GAM rebels.[304]

States have denied helping secessionist movements when criticised. For example, Malaysia was accused of tacitly supporting Aceh secessionists and Islamic militants in southern Thailand. In December 1999, Malaysia denied having a role in the Aceh separatist movement after Indonesia alleged that Aceh rebels were smuggling in weapons from Malaysia, stressing that friendly countries should be neutral *vis-à-vis* an internal Indonesian problem and not seek to undermine the unitary State.[305] In 2000, Malaysia affirmed that 'Aceh should be part of Indonesia', and expressed a willingness to 'play the role of mediator', at Jakarta's request.[306]

Malaysia was responsive to Thai threats to curtail closer economic ties over Malaysia's apparent support for the Malays of Patani in southern Thailand,[307] with whom the Malays of Malaysia share an ethnic and religious 'kin' affiliation. The Patani United Liberation Front (PULO)

300 JI White Paper, p. 3.

301 JI White Paper, pp. 4, 8. MILF rebels apparently trained Indonesian Jemaah Islamiah terrorists in their camps in the Philippines: 'JI trained hundreds of men in Philippine camp', *Straits Times* (Singapore), 19 Nov. 2003, p. A7.

302 Tan, 'Armed Muslim Separatist Rebellion in Southeast Asia', p. 281.

303 Declaration on Terrorism by the 8th ASEAN Summit; available at http://www.aseansec.org/13154.htm;ASEAN Efforts to Counter Terrorism, at http://www.aseansec.org/14396.htm.

304 Mahmood, 'Thailand perpetuating the Taming of Islam'.

305 Tan, 'Armed Muslim Separatist Rebellion in Southeast Asia', p. 280.

306 D. Pereira, 'KL ready to help end Aceh dispute', *Straits Times* (Singapore), 10 March 2000, p. 47.

307 Patani, a former Malay kingdom, was annexed to Thailand in 1902. In 1945 the Malays issued the Patani Petition to the Colony's Secretary of State detailing the measures the Thai kingdom employed to eradicate Malaya nationalism and culture. It requested release from oppressive Siamese rule and to be reunited with peninsula Malays. Appendix 6, Christie,

demands a separate Islamic territory to preserve its culture in the face of Thai measures for assimilation. The Thai government said that Operation 'Falling Leaves' in 1997 must have had the support of the regional government in Malaysian provinces like Kelantan, confronted with the federal government's indifference. Kelantan allegedly provided a safe haven for two secessionist groups. Malaysia acceded to Thai requests to intensify its cross-border co-operation, helping Thai forces to crush PULO in the 1990s and sanctioning joint police raids in 1998 in northern Malaysia, resulting in the arrests of top PULO leaders.[308]

E. Aiding secessionist groups

States may overtly or tacitly support secessionist groups in military and non-military ways. The 1970 Friendly Relations Declaration[309] notes that States are obliged to promote the principle of equal rights and self-determination of peoples in accordance with UN principles. States cannot use force to deprive peoples of their national identity or their right to exercise self-determination and 'to seek and to receive support' in a manner consistent with UN principles. In affording such support, third States may not interfere with another State's civil strife or support subversive armed activities.

1. Sponsored radio services

The US Congress created the Radio Free Asia Uyghur Service in 1994, which regularly broadcast to Xinjiang and other regions from transmitters in Tajikistan and Kyrgyzstan in various local languages. The Chinese government blocked this service, equating it with support for separatists.[310]

2. Providing aid and support

Secessionist groups have received aid from neighbouring States, such as when the Solomon Islands lent assistance, including arms, to Bougainville separatist groups while Australia supplied combat helicopters to the PNG

A Modern History of Southeast Asia, p. 227. See also, 'Ethnicity, Islam and Irredentism: the Malays of Patani', in *ibid.*, p. 173.

308 'Muslim Separatist Movements in the Philippines and Thailand', *in* A. Rabasa, and P. Chalk, *Indonesia's Transformation and the Stability of Southeast Asia* (Santa Monica, CA: Rand, 2001), p. 85; Mahmood, 'Thailand Perpetuating the Taming of Islam'.

309 Friendly Relations Declaration.

310 'The Anti-Separatism Struggle and its Historical Lessons since the Liberation of Xinjiang', translated by Uyghur American Association 1993, 4 Feb. 1998, available at http://www.uyghuramerican.org/researchanalysis/trans.html.

government.[311] The Tamil Tigers of Sri Lanka received external support from South India and North America.[312]

3. Safe havens and training camps

States have openly supported secessionist groups by allowing separatists to establish or have access to training camps within their territory: *e.g.*, GAM members exiled from Aceh reportedly received training in Libya,[313] Abu Sayaff trains its member in camps located in Pakistan and Afghanistan,[314] and Irian Jaya secessionists have been allowed to set up PNG camps. States have harboured governments-in-exile seeking to spearhead a secessionist movement in another State: *e.g.*, the Bougainville Revolutionary Army was based in Honiara, Solomon Islands.[315] Kinship ties and strong cultural affinities between Western Solomon Islanders and Bougainville secessionist rebels partially underscore the former's support for Bougainvilleans.[316]

Malaysia also tacitly supported the Moros insofar as Sabah's Chief Minister, Tun Mustapha, was not restrained from offering them aid.[317] Saudi Arabia, Egypt and other OIC countries also gave aid to the Moros and undertook diplomatic initiatives to promote peaceful settlement with the Philippine government.[318]

4. Conclusions

In the post-9/11 world, neither States nor separatist groups are keen to be labelled as 'terrorists' or perceived as supporting terrorists. In a diplomatic overture, Libya offered military instruction and aid to help Indonesia's fight against separatism. While admitting that Aceh rebels might have joined defence-training programmes for the Libyan people, Gaddafi

[311] Special Rapporteur Report, para. 34.

[312] P. Chalk, 'The Liberation Tigers of Tamil Eelam Insurgency', in *Ethnic Conflict & Secessionism*, p. 128.

[313] Tan, 'Armed Muslim Separatist Rebellion in Southeast Asia', p. 278.

[314] Ibid., p. 275.

[315] Special Rapporteur Report, para 31.

[316] Fraenkel, 'Minority Rights in Fiji and the Solomon Islands'. An 1886 Anglo-German colonial agreement incorporated Bougainville island into PNG (Northern Solomons Provinces), disregarding cultural affiliations with the Western Solomon Islands.

[317] In 1969, the main group was the Union of Islamic Forces and Organisations. Malaysia allowed Moro separatists to train on Sabah, a move crucial to the forming of rebel Moro armies. The Philippines publicly claimed that Malaysia was tolerating secessionist Moro training camps in Sabah and providing a supply base: Tan, 'Armed Muslim Separatist Rebellion in Southeast Asia', p. 272.

[318] Heraclides, 'Secessionist Movements', pp. 350–1.

insisted in August 2003 that his government never intended to support separatist movements.[319]

Recognising shared security interests, inter-State co-operation to thwart separatist movements has intensified, from dialoguing with separatist rebels, repatriating them and co-ordinating counter-insurgency operations,[320] to promising not to allow their territories to be used in a way harmful to another State's national interests.[321] Bhutan has responded to its powerful neighbour's concerns about the location of some 3000 Indian separatist guerrillas seeking independence for North East India in its southern forests, such as the United Liberation Front of Assam (ULGA), National Democratic Front for Bodoland and Kuki Liberation Organisation. From these training camps, low-key guerrilla warfare is conducted against Indian forces, with the aim of winning secession for Assam.[322] Fearing retaliation, Bhutan has avoided taking action against these groups,[323] seeking rather to placate India by holding talks with some thirty Indian secessionist groups[324] in order to persuade peaceful decampment. Bhutan stated that the separatist agenda for Assam constituted 'a threat to India's peace and territorial integrity' and has shown solidarity with India by banning Bhutanese people from selling goods to militants, and punishing people assisting Assamese militants under the national security Act. Bhutan agreed in September 2003, 'if necessary', to undertake joint military action with India[325] against the North-East Indian separatists.

Clearly, Asia-Pacific States uniformly oppose secessionist movements, seeking to manage secessionist aspirations by promoting political

319 'Libya to support and train Jakarta troops,' *Straits Times* (Singapore), 15 Nov. 2003, p. A22. Libya has offered to provide instructors, helicopters and other military vehicles to Indonesia.

320 Burma and India agreed to co-ordinate military operations against separatist armies on their 1500 km shared border. In November 2001 the Burmese army captured 200 separatist rebels from the North Eastern State of Manipur: 'Burma moves against Indian separatists', *BBC News*, 15 Nov. 2001, available at http://news.bbc.co.uk/1/hi/world/south_asia/1658651.stm.

321 N. Banerjee, *Times of India*, 9 Nov. 2003, available at http://timesofindia.indiatimes.com/cms.dll/articleshow?msid = 273924.

322 Available at http://observer.guardian.co.uk/international/story/0,6903,800492,00. html.

323 Available at http://www.alertnet.org/thenews/newsdesk/DEL230579.htm.

324 'Bhutan's king invites Indian separatist rebels for talks', *ABC Radio Australia News*, 16 Sept. 2003, available at http://www.abc.net.au/asiapacific/news/GoAsiaPacificBNA_946476.htm.

325 'India and Bhutan are in close cooperation on militant problem', 20 Sept. 2003, *Kuensel online.com.*

settlement through internal autonomy schemes and mutually respecting territorial sovereignty. While critical of human rights abuses committed in counter-insurgency operations, no State has unequivocally endorsed the legitimacy of a secessionist movement.

VI. Factors buttressing the general anti-secessionist stances of States and the international community

While one might hope that the international law on secession is morally progressive, a minimal realism is warranted, given States' preoccupation with internal security and regional stability. Aside from Bangladesh, no secessionist claim in this region has gained international support, nor is endorsement forthcoming for groups controlling significant amounts of territory and running *de facto* governments: *e.g.* the Tamil Tigers in north-east Sri Lanka and the MILF in Mindanao, which oversees large swathes of territory and runs an 80-person-strong Consultative Assembly. Local authorities make their own arrangements with MILF officials and commanders in MILF-controlled areas, which goes unchallenged by the Philippine government.[326]

Rather, efforts are oriented towards promoting intra-State peace settlements and addressing economic resources distribution, human rights accountability and demilitarisation. Focus is on the internal aspect of self-determination. Governments facing secessionist movements at home are unlikely to promote secessionist claims abroad. Terrorist groups espousing violence, such as the Abu Sayyaf in southern Philippines who oppose religious accommodation with the Catholics, are not broadly supported. An impasse is reached where secessionist groups resist negotiated settlement and refuse to renounce violence leading to counter-insurgency operations.

Aside from the 'domino effect' fear of multiplying and escalating secessionist claims, several other factors militate against their acceptance – most importantly, the economic impact on the truncated parent State. For example, if Indonesia lost Aceh and Irian Jaya, the loss of revenue from the natural resources of these provinces would hamstring Indonesian economic recovery and capacity to meet its massive debts. Notwithstanding the threat to political instability and economic insecurity posed by secessionist claims, arguments for such claims based on gross human

[326] Tan, 'Armed Muslim Separatist Rebellion in Southeast Asia', p. 275.

rights violations and the need to preserve physical survival and cultural identity *per se* have not succeeded in broadening the scope of self-determination to include secession.

In Sri Lanka, where the majority Buddhist Sinhalese and 3.2 million Hindu Tamils concentrated in the northeast have engaged in twenty years of civil war, it has been argued that a bitter, bloody history of antagonistic relations and Tamil resentment against discriminatory treatment as second-class citizens have dimmed the prospects for national reconciliation, in the face of vibrant Tamil separatist nationalism. The declared goal of the radicalised group, the Tamil United Liberation Front[327] (TULF), active since 1976, has been to secede and recreate or reconstitute a secular and socialist State of Tamil Eelam in the area forming the traditional Tamil homeland.[328] In this case, 'territorial integrity', identified as the greatest obstacle to secession, was criticised as an outdated notion which should not stand in the way of necessity, secession having been deemed an 'ineluctable necessity for Tamil national self-preservation' in the face of 'racial subjugation' and 'genocidal repression'.[329] The Liberation Tigers of Tamil Eelam (LTTE), in presenting their case to the world, argued that an 'enlightened and progressive realisation' of self-determination should serve a 'higher cause' like human rights and dignity; further arguing that existing State structures were indefensible where these are oppressive in practicing racial subjugation, internal colonialism and genocidal repression. Sornarajah argues that Tamil Eelam meets all the conditions of statehood, being a *de facto* State as a territorial entity governed by a definite group of people and effective government.[330] Furthermore, the legitimacy of the Sri Lankan government is impugned as undemocratic, arguably forfeiting its right of territorial integrity by persistently treating ethnic groups unequally, violating their human rights without redress. Although there are concerns that it will intensify separatist demands on the Indian sub-continent, with India and Pakistan reportedly likely to oppose secession, it is argued that the sub-continent did not unravel in the aftermath of Bangladesh and that Indian federalism survives.

327 The Tiger movement was born in 1972 and initially called 'The Tamil New Tigers', renamed the 'Liberation Tigers of Tamil Eelam' (LTTE) in 1976. See R. Ganguly, 'The Role of India in the Tamil Secessionist Movement in Sri Lanka', *Ethnic Conflicts: Lessons from South Asia*, p. 193.

328 Liberation Tigers of Tamil Eelam, 'Tamil Eelam Demand in International Law'.

329 'Tamil Eelam demand in International Law', *ibid.*

330 Sornarajah, 'Eelam and the Right to Secession'.

The Sri Lankan government firmly rejects the idea of a negotiated secession with the Tamils,[331] whose appeal for international support to extend the right of self-determination to serve a 'just cause' has received a 'frosty reception'.[332] The lack of broad support for the merits of the Tamil Tigers case may be explained by distinguishing it from the unique Bangladesh precedent and by showing that Katanga and Biafra are more analogical instances of failed secessionism.[333]

First, the claimed Tamil homelands are territorially contiguous and lack clear definition, unlike Bangladesh. Furthermore, the population of 'Tamil Eelam' would not be homogenous in ethnic or religious terms, having Tamil-speaking Muslims and Burgher Malay minorities. In contrast, the Bengalis had a stronger sense of 'self', were more homogenous and resided in a compact area to which they were indigenous, as opposed to the Indian Tamils of South India whom the British imported into Ceylon as cheap labour. The Tamils are a clear minority, constituting some 20.5 per cent of the Sri Lankan population, while the Bengalis in Bangladesh constituted 65.7 per cent of the population in 1947 when India became independent.[334]

Second, in humanitarian terms, the gravity and intensity of suffering flowing from political oppression, economic exploitation and humanitarian deprivation was greater for the Bengalis than it has been for the Tamils in terms of physical insecurity, a chief factor in garnering world support for Bangladeshi secession.[335]

What distinguishes the Bangladesh case is that, similar to the separation of overseas colonies from the metropolitan State, Bangladesh's separation from West Pakistan had relatively less effect on the predecessor State, as secession created two viable States from one. On the contrary, should Sri Lanka lose its Tamil region, not only would it suffer population and territorial loss, it would also lose a region of economic and strategic significance, being a valuable source of raw materials and foreign exchange, imperilling the economic and physical security of rump Sri Lanka.[336] The viability of the two small States, were Sri Lanka carved up, would be in question, as contrasted to Bangladesh whose sizeable territory

[331] 'Tamil Secession ruled out', *BBC News*, 21 July 2000, available at http://news.bbc.co.uk/1/hi/world/south_asia/844780.stm.

[332] M. Rafiqul Islam, 'The Tamil Separatism in Sri Lanka: Some Factors Undermining the Claim', *NILR* 33 (1986), 65, at 66.

[333] *Ibid.*, p. 65. [334] *Ibid.*, p. 69. [335] *Ibid.*, p. 74. [336] *Ibid.*, pp. 69–70.

(55,000 square miles) and large population of 75 million presented better prospects for State survivability and regional order.

VII. Concluding observations

The continuing potency of nationalism-related issues of State formation and fragmentation in the Asia Pacific is apparent from this review. Separatists waging long-standing secessionist movements desire to be majorities in their own State, rather than another State's minorities. Thus, secessionist movements led by oppressed ethno-cultural minority groups within post-colonial States spark fears of political balkanisation.

India has struggled with separatist movements since decolonisation; and China has had to manage unstable regions after the USSR disintegrated, particularly where Muslim separatists in the northwest desire their own State resembling neighbouring Muslim-majority States like Uzbekistan and Tajikistan, reflecting the vital unifying force of religion. East Timor's independence in 2002 revitalised secessionist groups in post-Suharto Indonesia, causing former Indonesian President Megawati Sukarnoputri to warn that should Indonesia dissolve like Yugoslavia and become the 'Balkans of the eastern hemisphere', it would never enjoy national happiness and would threaten regional stability.[337]

Fearing State dismemberment, the problem of securing the co-existence of distinct ethnic or religious communities while preserving social harmony remains a pressing State objective. Efforts are made to diffuse destabilising secessionist movements primarily through offering autonomous regimes operating within existing State frameworks. Clearly, no Asia-Pacific State recognises a post-colonial right of self-determination of ethno-cultural minorities in terms of a collective right of territorial secession against the will of the parent State. Bangladesh has not become a precedent followed or expanded upon. Regional State practice reveals a consistent deference to territorial integrity and rejection of unilateral independence declarations, reflecting the continuing overwhelming State opposition to secessionist claims, undercutting arguments that a legal right to secession exists in international law.

Where ethno-cultural groups are unrepresented and their fundamental human rights denied within existing States, the international

[337] M. Kearney, 'Indonesia Risks Becoming Like Balkans: Mega', *Straits Times* (Singapore), 29 Oct. 2001, p. 3.

community is more likely to recognise retrospectively successful secession. But this is not a determinative factor. Consonant with practice elsewhere, Asia-Pacific States remain cautious about nurturing the idea that the right to secession is granted to ethnic minorities in the name of self-determination. As was noted, this question may arise 'the day that Pakistan or India granted the right of secession to their minorities', but at present, it is 'inadmissible that a country should be asked to do something that no other country was doing'.[338]

[338] Summary Record, CERD Committee, 43rd Sess., 1006th Meeting: Tonga, Yugoslavia, CERD/C/SR.1006, 7 Oct. 1994, para. 42.

11

Secession and international law: the European dimension

PHOTINI PAZARTZIS

This collection of essays comes at a timely moment. Indeed, while the doctrinal debate on the issue of secession appeared to have subsided as the decolonisation period came to an end, a revival of secessionist movements in many parts of the world has brought this issue to the fore again.[1] In fact, secession has been one of the main causes of the proliferation of States in recent years.[2] Moreover, the most striking recent events occurred, not 'across the deep blue sea', but in Europe. In particular, since 1991, the international community has witnessed the disintegration of the former USSR, Yugoslavia and Czechoslovakia, as well as further movements for secession within the newly independent States. Secessionist proclivities have also been witnessed, at times, within some western European States: the Basques in Spain, Corsica in France, South Tyrol or the so-called 'Padania' in Italy.[3] This recent revival of secessionist tendencies once again raises the question of whether there exists a right to secede under international law.

Secession is often viewed more as a problem of politics than one of law.[4] The basic postulate has been that international law neither allows

[1] T. Franck, 'Postmodern Tribalism and the Right to Secession', *in* C. Brölmann, R. Lefeber, M. Zieck (eds.), *Peoples and Minorities in International Law* (Dordrecht: Martinus Nijhoff Publishers, 1993), p. 3; R. Higgins, 'Postmodern Tribalism and the Right to Secession: Comments', *in ibid*, p. 29. P. Moreau Defarges, 'Le droit à la sécession: jusqu'où?', *Defense nationale* 8/9 (1999), 87–93.

[2] A. Tancredi, 'Secessione e diritto internazionale', *Rivista* 3 (1998), 673–768, at 678; P. Boniface, 'The Proliferation of States, *The Washington Quarterly* 21 (1998), 111–27.

[3] See J. Crawford, 'State Practice and International Law in Relation to Secession', *BYIL* (1998), 85–117, at 108, which lists some cases in Europe. In all these particular instances, there has been no formal attempt at unilateral secession, and the cases have been treated as internal to the States involved.

[4] U. Schneckener, 'The Fall of Leviathan. On Self-Determination and Secession', *Law and State* 57 (1998), 81–103; M. Eisner, 'A Procedural Model for the Resolution of Secessionist Disputes', *HILJ* 33 (1992), 407–25.

nor prohibits secession.[5] International law has traditionally acknowledged secession subsequent to a factual state of events, which has led to a situation in which the constitutive elements of a State are present rather than stating the conditions of its legality.[6] This legal neutrality has, to a great extent, been influenced by the tension between two opposing principles, self-determination and territorial integrity.[7] On the one hand, the principle of self-determination[8] has been evoked as constituting a basis for the right to secede. On the other hand, the principle of territorial integrity has constituted a staunch bulwark protecting States from forcible mutations 'coming from within'.[9] It remains to be seen if and to what extent there has been a change or a redefinition of international law on the question of secession.

Recent developments could shed new light on these issues. This chapter will focus, in particular, on events which occurred in Europe during the 1990s. Before examining recent practice in Europe with respect to secession, it could be useful to explore the approach adopted towards the principle of self-determination within the European context.

[5] 'The position is . . . that secession is neither legal nor illegal in international law, but a legally neutral act the consequences of which are, or may be, regulated internationally', J. Crawford, *The Creation of States in International Law* (Oxford: Clarendon Press, 1979), p. 286. See also, 'Sécession' *in* J. Salmon (sous la dir. de); *Dictionnaire de droit international public* (Bruylant: Bruxelles, 2001), p. 1021. However, cf. Marcelo Kohen's introduction and Olivier Corten's contribution to this volume.

[6] C. Haverland, 'Secession', *in* R. Bernhardt (ed.), *Encyclopedia of Public International Law*, vol. IV (Amsterdam: Elsevier/North Holland-2000), p. 354, at 355.

[7] L. Brilmayer, 'Secession and Self-Determination: A Territorial Interpretation', *YJIL* 16 (1991), 177. See the contribution of C. Tomuschat to this volume.

[8] Literature on self-determination is extensive; *inter alia*, A. Cassese, *Self-Determination of Peoples. A Legal Reappraisal* (Cambridge: Cambridge University Press, 1995); C. Tomuschat (ed.), *Modern Law of Self-Determination* (Dordrecht: Martinus Nijhoff, 1993); T. Christakis, *Le droit à l'autodétermination en dehors des situations de decolonisation* (Paris: La documentation française, 1999); H. Hannum, 'Rethinking Self-Determination', *VJIL* 34 (1993), 1–69; M. Kohen, *Possession contestée et souveraineté territoriale* (Paris: PUF, 1997), pp. 407–23; M. Koskenniemi, 'National Self-Determination Today: Problems of Legal Theory and Practice', *ICLQ* 43 (1994), 241–69; A. Cassese, 'Self-Determination Revisited', *in Le droit international dans un monde de mutation. Liber Amicorum en homage au Professeur Eduardo Jiménez de Aréchaga* (Montevideo: Fundación de Cultura Universitaria, 1994, t. I), p. 229; Y. Dinstein, 'Self-Determination Revisited, *in ibid.*, p. 241; A. Pellet, 'Quel avenir pour le droit des peoples à disposer d'eux-mêmes?', *in ibid.*, p. 255; S. Blay, 'Self-Determination: A Reassessment in the Post-Communist Era', *Denver J.I.L.P.* 2–3/22 (1999), 275–315; H. Quane, 'The United Nations and the Evolving Right to Self-Determination', *ICLQ* 47 (1998), 537–72.

[9] H. Ruiz Fabri, 'Genèse et disparition de l'État à l'époque contemporaine', *AFDI* (1992), 153–78.

I. Self-determination in a European context

While the existence of a legal right of self-determination is widely upheld, there remains controversy surrounding the content and scope of this right. Since 1945, there has been a tendency to 'domesticate' this principle by limiting its application to decolonisation and precluding any attempt to use it as a justification for secession.[10] During the decolonisation period, the right of self-determination was recognised as the right to become free from colonial rule (and extended to cover peoples under foreign occupation or racist regimes). The peoples entitled to self-determination were defined as the inhabitants of a colony but not as ethnically distinct groups within the colonial territory or established State.[11]

As self-determination claims did not die with the end of colonialism and a new generation of diverse demands surfaced, attention turned to whether this principle applied outside of a colonial context. Support for an extra-colonial application of this principle was found in an extensive interpretation of international instruments, such as the UN Friendly Relations Declaration[12] and more importantly the two International Covenants of 1966,[13] which refer to self-determination as a right of 'all peoples'.[14]

[10] Koskenniemi, 'National Self-Determination Today', p. 242.

[11] Quane, 'The United Nations', p. 554, M. N. Shaw, 'Peoples, Territorialism and Boundaries', *EJIL* 3 (1997), 478–507, at 480; M. Kohen, *Possession contestée et souveraineté territoriale* (Paris: PUF, 1997), p. 410. This is reflected in GA Resolution 1514 (XV), according to which self-determination was only applicable 'in respect of a territory which is geographically separate and is distinct ethnically and/or culturally from the country administering it'. Some authors have questioned the use of the term 'secession' in the colonial context: '[t]he implementation of the right to independence by colonial societies was not strictly speaking . . . secession. Populations and territories of a metropolis and their colonies constituted neither *de facto* nor even *de jure* the population and territory of one and the same State'; R. Mullerson, 'Self-Determination of Peoples and the Dissolution of the USSR', *in* R. St. J. Macdonald (ed.), *Essays in Honour of Wang Tieya* (Kluwer Academic Publishers, 1993), p. 567, at 574. The 'salt-water' theory in a sense served to sever the concept of secession from the concept of self-determination.

[12] Declaration on Principles of International Law Concerning Friendly Relations and Co-operation among States in Accordance with the Charter of the United Nations, GA Res. 2625 (XXV) of 24 November 1970.

[13] 1966 International Covenant on Civil and Political Rights (art. 1) and 1966 International Covenant on Economic, Social and Cultural Rights (art. 1).

[14] See Dinstein, 'Self-Determination Revisited', p. 246, Hannum, 'Rethinking Self-Determination', p. 18. According to Franck, '[t]he text [of the Covenants] makes clear that the right is not to be limited to colonies but that it is exercisable continuously. It does not make clear what the right will entail in the future, leaving that for new contextual interpretation', 'Postmodern Tribalism', p. 11.

While the debate on the nature and scope of the right of self-determination as developed through UN instruments and decolonisation practice was becoming rather sterile, an important step towards the recognition of the applicability of self-determination beyond the process of decolonisation was achieved within the Conference on (later, Organization for) Security and Co-operation in Europe (CSCE/OSCE) through the Helsinki Final Act of 1975, by affirming the right of self-determination.[15] In fact, the Act recognised that this principle *is* applicable outside a decolonisation context.[16] The Helsinki Act is more expansive than previous instruments regarding self-determination.[17] Principle VIII is viewed as an important confirmation of the right of self-determination as a continuing right of all peoples to determine their internal and external political status. Despite its non-binding status, this provision is seen as an important crystallisation of the right to self-determination.[18] However, the scope of this principle is limited by reference to the preservation of the territorial integrity of States. By virtue of its combining Principle VIII with Principle III on the Inviolability of Frontiers and Principle IV on Territorial Integrity, the Helsinki Act is taken as confirming the existing boundaries of the participating States.

[15] Principle VIII on Equal Rights and Self-Determination of Peoples states:

> The participating States will respect the equal rights of peoples and their right to self-determination, acting at all times in conformity with the purposes and principles of the Charter of the United Nations and with the relevant norms of international law, including those relating to the territorial integrity of States.
> By virtue of the principle of equal rights and self-determination of peoples, all peoples always have the right, in full freedom, to determine, when and as they wish, their internal and external political status, without external interference, and to pursue as they wish their political, economic and social development.
> The participating States reaffirm the universal significance of respect for and effective exercise of equal rights and self-determination of peoples for the development of friendly relations among themselves as among all States; they also recall the importance of elimination of any form of violation of this principle.
>
> Text in *ILM 14* (1975), p. 1292

[16] Koskenniemi, 'National Self-Determination Today', p. 242; Turp considered this clause as opening the way to secessionist self-determination, D. Turp, 'Le droit de secession en droit international public', *CYIL* (1982), 24–78. For a different view, see Cassese, *Self-Determination of Peoples*, p. 287.

[17] H. Hannum, 'Rethinking Self-Determination', p. 29; Cassese, *Self-Determination of Peoples*, p. 285.

[18] C. Gray, 'Self-Determination and the Breakup of the Soviet Union', *YEL* 12 (1992), 466–503, at 469.

More recent references to the right of self-determination seem to limit earlier formulations. Thus, in the Concluding Document of the Vienna Meeting of the CSCE on the Follow Up to the Helsinki Conference (1989), while Principle VIII of the Helsinki Act is reiterated, the obligation to respect territorial integrity is reinforced as well.[19] In addition, the Charter of Paris reinforces the obligation to respect territorial integrity.[20] This confirms the impression that CSCE/OSCE documents posterior to the Helsinki Act have progressively moderated the scope of the original Principle VIII by reinforcing the respect for territorial integrity, perhaps in order to deter secessionist claims, which started appearing in the early 1990s.[21]

Furthermore, any 'secessionist' implications of the right of self-determination have been contained in the CSCE/OSCE process by always supplementing the affirmation of self-determination with the principle of minority protection within States[22] and by the development of *internal* self-determination, namely, the guaranteeing of democratic,

[19] According to Principle V of the Vienna Concluding Document, participating States 'confirm their commitment strictly and effectively to observe the principle of the territorial integrity of States. They will refrain from any violation of this principle and thus from any action aimed by direct or indirect means, in contravening the purposes and principles of the Charter of the United Nations, other obligations under international law or the provisions of the Final Act, at violating the territorial integrity, political independence or the unity of a State. No actions or situations in contravention of this principle will be recognised as legal by the participating States.' Text *in* A. Bloed, *From Helsinki to Vienna: Basic Documents of the Helsinki Process* (Dordrecht: Martinus Nijhoff, 1990), p. 184.

[20] The relevant provision states: 'We reaffirm the equal rights of peoples and their right to self-determination in conformity with the Charter of the United Nations and with the relevant norms of international law, including those related to the territorial integrity of States.' Text *in* 30 *ILM* (1990), p. 197. This trend can be fully witnessed in the Warsaw Declaration of 8 July 1997, adopted at the Sixth Annual Session of the OSCE Parliamentary Assembly, where it is stated: '21 . . . that ensuring the inviolability of State frontiers and their territorial integrity constitutes one of the imperatives of our time, and that its implementation requires a thorough democratisation of domestic relationships in the countries concerned in order to create conditions for full equality and free development of all nations and persons belonging to national minorities; 22 . . . that the implementation of the principle of self-determination in the form of secession may at present create a serious threat to the peace and security of nations, and that this principle should be implemented exclusively by peaceful means and on the basis of democratic decisions adopted within the framework of national legal systems, international norms and possibly under the supervision of the international community; 23 . . . that the right to self-determination cannot be founded upon or be the result of the violation of the territorial integrity of a State'. Text cited *in* Christakis, *Le droit à l'autodétermination*, p. 223.

[21] See Tancredi, 'Secessione e diritto internazionale', p. 694.

[22] The tension between the principles of territorial integrity and self-determination is thus moderated by modifying the substance of the right of self-determination so that it leads to

representative government for all groups residing in the State. Indeed, as it has been held, there is an increasing tendency towards the affirmation of the *internal* aspect of the right to self-determination, implying a right to democracy for a people.[23] Recent practice with respect to the recognition of new States in Central and Eastern Europe has given internal self-determination a leading role.[24]

On the other hand, while there have been significant developments in international minority protection since the end of the Cold War,[25] and in particular, in Europe[26] the status of minorities remains limited. Firstly, the rights are conferred upon 'persons belonging to minorities', not upon minorities as such.[27] Secondly, these rights are centred upon minority members' rights 'to enjoy their own culture, to profess and practice their own religion, or to use their own language'. All international instruments on minorities reaffirm the principles of territorial integrity and inviolability of frontiers.[28]

Furthermore, attempts at the European level to introduce some form of autonomy to territorially concentrated minorities have been envisaged with extreme reluctance and the recent documents remain very moderate

minority protection rather than secession; see Koskenniemi, 'National Self-Determination Today', p. 256.

23 Christakis, *Le droit à l'autodétermination*, p. 23; Franck, 'Postmodern Tribalism', p. 20: 'The probable redefinition of self-determination does recognise an international legal right, but it is not to secession, but to democracy.'

24 *Section* III.

25 P. Thornberry, *International Law and the Rights of Minorities* (Oxford: Clarendon Press, 1991).

26 See for example, the Framework Convention for the Protection of National Minorities adopted by the Council of Europe on 1 February 1995, which entered into force in February 1998, and the European Charter for Regional or Minority Languages adopted by the Council of Europe on 5 November 1992, which entered into force in March 1998. These are the only international treaties devoted entirely to minority issues. Further, of importance to this issue are texts in the CSCE/OSCE process, such as the Copenhagen Declaration adopted in 1990 (*ILM* 29 (1990), p. 1306), which contains a list of rights recognised to members of minorities.

27 Even though a tendency can be discerned in the CSCE/OSCE process towards the recognition of minorities as groups, this is formulated in very cautious terms, see for example, the 1990 Copenhagen Document which states in paragraph 35 that the participating States 'note the efforts undertaken to protect and create conditions for the promotion of the ethnic, cultural, linguistic and religious identity of certain national minorities by establishing, as one of the possible means to achieve these aims, appropriate local or autonomous administrations corresponding to the specific historical and territorial circumstances of such minorities and in accordance with the policies of the State concerned'.

28 Shaw, 'Peoples, Territorialism and Boundaries', p. 487.

in this respect.[29] The cautious formulation of the 1990 OSCE Copenhagen Document whereby States limited themselves to 'take note' of autonomy solutions is but one example.[30] More recently, the *Charter for European Security* adopted at the 1999 Istanbul Summit reaffirms this cautious approach, stating that:

> Full respect for human rights, including the rights of persons belonging to national minorities, besides being an end in itself, may not undermine but strengthen territorial integrity and sovereignty. Various concepts of autonomy as well as other approaches . . . which are in line with OSCE principles, constitute ways to preserve and promote the ethnic, cultural, linguistic and religious identity of national minorities within an existing State.[31]

The emphasis on the territorial framework of States reflects the opposition of States to any 'secessionist' interpretation of minority rights and supports the view that, under current international law, there is no right of secession, in the name of self-determination, for groups living within a State.[32]

II. Recent practice in Europe

The most interesting examples in contemporary practice regarding secession of non-colonial territories relate to Central and Eastern Europe. In fact, it was the events witnessed in Europe in the 1990s[33] that rekindled

[29] See, for example, articles 10(2) and 11(3) of the 1995 Framework Convention for the Protection of National Minorities. The proposal submitted by the Parliamentary Assembly of the Council of Europe of an additional protocol to the European Commission on Human Rights (ECHR) on the rights of national minorities (Recommendation 1201/1993), which provided that (art. 11): 'in a region where they are in a majority the persons belonging to a national minority shall have the right to have at their disposal appropriate local or autonomous authorities or to have a special status, matching the specific historical and territorial situation and in accordance with the domestic legislation of the state', was considered by the member States of the Council of Europe as going too far and was not accepted.

[30] See note 27.

[31] Text *in* http://www.osce.org/docs/english/summite.htm.

[32] Higgins, 'Postmodern Tribalism', p. 29, at 33; see also Franck, 'Postmodern Tribalism', p. 11.

[33] These events have been seen as constituting a separate category of 'cases of self-determination in the post-communist context' (Blay, 'Self-Determination: A Reassessment', p. 277), or a 'third generation' of secession/self-determination claims.

interest in the question of secession.[34] Apart from the special case of Germany's reunification, three multinational States collapsed, namely, the Soviet Union, Czechoslovakia and Yugoslavia. Furthermore, there have been claims for independence that have been witnessed both as attempts to unilaterally secede by groups or territories within independent States, and as simple movements for some form of independence.[35] International responses to independence claims can provide more insight on the question of self-determination and secession in the European context.

A. *Cases of 'successful' secessions*

While the dissolution of the former USSR occurred to a large extent without much resistance on the part of the central authorities[36] and could thus be regarded as creating no precedent for cases of 'contested' secessions,[37] the former Yugoslavia's Republics' declarations of independence were opposed by the federal authorities and have been considered as 'acts of secession'.[38]

1. The former Soviet Union

According to the Constitution of the former USSR (art. 72), the constituent republics had the right to secede, though this right existed only on paper. On 3 April 1990, the Soviet Union passed a law on secession, ostensibly to provide procedures to be followed when a republic sought to secede; in reality, this law entailed such a complicated procedure that it made secession practically impossible; it was therefore not applied in the dissolution process, but was superseded by the events which led to the collapse of the USSR.

[34] In fact, only one 'successful' secession occurred during the Cold War Era, namely, the separation of Bangladesh from Pakistan in 1971. Apart from this one example of true secession, there were also the instances of the peaceful exit of Senegal from the Federation with Mali in 1960 and that of Singapore from Malaysia in 1965.

[35] See, Crawford, 'State Practice and International Law', p. 92.

[36] The central government did initially resist the break-away of the Baltic States and the dissolution of the Soviet Union until it no longer had the political power to do so. The failure of the 1991 August coup provided a catalyst for the dismemberment of the USSR.

[37] The same applies for the 'velvet divorce' of Czechoslovakia. See Hannum, 'Rethinking Self-Determination', p. 51: 'The voluntary division or dissolution of a state is certainly within that state's right of internal self-determination, unless the international community views the division as a fraudulent attempt to prevent real self-determination.'

[38] See, Quane, 'The United Nations', p. 569.

The dissolution of the USSR[39] was spurred on by the declarations of sovereignty, at the time, of the Baltic Republics (Lithuania, Estonia, Latvia).[40] Their legal position was special since they had been forcibly annexed by the Soviet Union in 1940.[41] These Republics thus based their independence claims on the illegality of their annexation to the Soviet Union. Hence their declarations were not articulated as an exercise of a right to self-determination or as a secession, but rather as a reassertion of the independence and *de jure* continuity of these States which had been sovereign from 1918 to 1940. Even so, their declarations of independence initially provoked a cautious response from the international community. Recognition by the international community took place after the attempted coup in the USSR in August 1991 and after the Soviet Union formally recognised the independence of the Baltic States on 6 September 1991.[42]

The twelve remaining Republics of the former USSR achieved independence by means of break-away from the USSR, a process that acquired the support of all the constituent Republics, including the Russian Federation.[43] The emergence of the remaining Republics as independent States was the result of the Minsk Agreement and the Alma Ata Protocol.[44] Central to these agreements was the mutual consent of the constituent Republics to dismantle the Union.[45] It was further agreed that the Russian Federation would continue the legal personality of the former USSR within the United Nations. Shortly thereafter, the international community recognised the new States. The dissolution of the USSR has

[39] On the dissolution of the USSR, see Mullerson, 'Self-Determination of Peoples', p. 567; Cassese *in ibid*, p. 131; Gray, 'Self-Determination', pp. 465–503; Blay, 'Self-Determination: A Reassessment', pp. 287–9.

[40] Lithuania declared its independence on 11 March 1990, Estonia on 20 August 1991, Latvia on 21 August 1991.

[41] R. Yakemtchouk, 'Les républiques baltes en droit international. Échec d'une annexion opérée en violation du droit des gens', *AFDI* (1991), 259–89.

[42] R. Kherad, 'La reconnaissance internationale des États baltes', *RGDIP* (1992), 843–71.

[43] J. Crawford, 'State Practice and International Law', p. 98.

[44] The Minsk Agreement ('Agreement establishing the Commonwealth of Independent States') was signed on 8 December 1991 by Belarus, Ukraine and the Russian Federation, see *ILM* 31 (1992), p. 143. This agreement was modified by the Protocol of Alma Ata of 21 December 1991 signed by eleven of the Republics (but not Georgia), *ibid.*, p. 147.

[45] According to Blay, 'The republics did not secede as such from the union, they dissolved it ... No rule of international law prohibits the mutual dissolution of a state by its component units and the subsequent creation of states out of those units'. See Blay, 'Self-Determination: A Reassessment', pp. 298–9.

been viewed by some authors as a successful exercise of the right to self-determination.[46]

2. The former Socialist Federal Republic of Yugoslavia

The case of Yugoslavia[47] has been considered 'the first test of post-colonial type secessionist conflict in Europe'.[48] The events leading to the dissolution of Yugoslavia and its consequences have been extensively analysed.[49] The situation in Yugoslavia came to a head after a period of constitutional turmoil when, on 25 June 1991, Croatia and Slovenia declared their independence following referendums. The Federal government rejected the declarations of independence by its constituent republics and used force to prevent them from seceding. The escalation of fighting and the widespread human rights violations led to the involvement of the international community. The international response was basically articulated on a European level, in particular within the framework of the Peace Conference for Yugoslavia established by the European Community (EC) on 27 August 1991.

The legal starting point for the position to be adopted towards the former Yugoslavia was set by the Arbitration Commission[50] in its first advisory opinion, in which the Commission stated that Yugoslavia was in a process of dissolution. The basis for this conclusion was that the Socialist Federal Republic of Yugoslavia (SFRY) had been a 'federal-type

[46] See Gray, 'Self-Determination', p. 491.

[47] Yugoslavia was a federation comprising six Republics (Croatia, Slovenia, Bosnia-Herzegovina, Montenegro, Macedonia and Serbia) and including the two autonomous regions of Kosovo and Vojvodina.

[48] Blay, 'Self-Determination: A Reassessment', p. 312.

[49] See M. Weller, 'The International Response to the Dissolution of the Socialist Federal Republic of Yugoslavia', *AJIL* 3/86 (1992), 569–607; A. Cassese, 'Self-Determination of Peoples and the Recent Break-Up of USSR and Yugoslavia', *in* R. St. J. Macdonald (ed.), *Essays in Honour of Wang Tieya* (Dordrecht/Boston [etc.]: Kluwer Academic Publishers, 1993), p. 131; P. Akhavan, 'Self-Determination and the Disintegration of Yugoslavia: What Lessons for the International Community?' *in* D. Clark and R. Williamson (eds.), *Self-Determination. International Perspectives* (London: Macmillan Press Ltd., St. Martin's Press, Inc., 1996), p. 227; B. Bagwell, 'Yugoslavian Constitutional Questions: Self-Determination and Secession of Member Republics', *Georgia J.I.C.L* 3/21 (1991), 489–523; D. F. Orentlicher, 'Separation Anxiety: International Responses to Ethno-Separatist Claims', *YJIL* 1/23 (1998), 1–78; S. Tierney, 'In a State of Flux: Self-Determination and the Collapse of Yugoslavia', *IJMGR* 6 (1999) 197–233.

[50] This Commission was established by the Peace Conference to deal with the legal aspects of the crisis; see M. Craven, 'The European Community Arbitration Commission on Yugoslavia', *BYIL* (1995), 333–413. For the texts of the Commission's opinions see, *ILM* 31 (1992), 1488 and *ILM* 32 (1993), 1586.

State' embracing 'communities that possess a degree of autonomy'; and with the four Republics having claimed independence, federal authorities could 'no longer meet the criteria of representativeness inherent in a federal state'.[51]

Against this background, on 16 December 1991, the EC adopted two declarations, a *Declaration on Yugoslavia* and a *Declaration on the Guidelines on the Recognition of new States in Eastern Europe and the Soviet Union.*[52] According to the latter, recognition would be conditional on respect for the provisions of the UN Charter and the CSCE with regard to the rule of law, democracy, human rights and minority rights, the inviolability of frontiers, the acceptance of commitments with regard to disarmament and nuclear non-proliferation and the peaceful settlement of disputes. The Declaration on Yugoslavia invited the constituent Republics to apply for recognition on the basis of these Guidelines. Subsequently, the Arbitration Commission examined the requests for international recognition by Bosnia and Herzegovina, Croatia, Macedonia and Slovenia. In all opinions, the Commission ascertained, in particular, whether or not a referendum on independence had been held in each Republic, as well as whether each Republic had committed itself to respecting the rights of individuals, groups and minorities.[53] In the case of Croatia, Macedonia and Slovenia, the Commission found that all requirements had been satisfied; in the case of Bosnia and Herzegovina, on the other hand, the Commission opined that the will of the people to constitute this Republic as a sovereign State had not been fully established. The Commission thus recommended a referendum, which took place in March 1992.[54]

Premature recognition of Croatia and Slovenia by European States[55] was based on the conclusion that, as a matter of political fact, the former Yugoslavia was in the process of dissolving.[56] Thus, this did not

[51] Opinion no. 1, *ibid*, p. 1494.

[52] *Ibid.*, p. 1485. See J. Charpentier, 'Les déclarations des Douze sur la reconnaissance des nouveaux États', *RGDIP* 2 (1992), 343–55.

[53] This requirement of the Commission that a referendum be held has, in Cassese's view, a wide significance because, through this requirement, the referendum was elevated 'to the status of a basic requirement for the legitimisation of secession', Casesse, 'Self-Determination of Peoples', p. 143.

[54] Bosnia was recognised on 6 April 1992.

[55] On 15 January 1992, the EC decided to recognise Slovenia and Croatia. For a detailed account of the international community's response, see Weller, 'The International Response', p. 569.

[56] See Opinion no. 1, *ILM* 31 (1992), 1488–1526 and *ILM* 32 (1993), 1586.

create a precedent in favour of a right of secession.[57] But while the question of secession was removed to a large extent, the principle of self-determination remained prominent in the reaction to the Yugoslav crisis.[58]

The Arbitration Commission was specifically asked whether the Serbian populations of Croatia and Bosnia and Herzegovina had a right of self-determination.[59] While prudently observing that international law did not define the precise consequences of that right or its scope of application, the Commission found that the right of self-determination did not involve the modification of borders as they existed at the moment of independence, except by mutual consent. The Commission affirmed that minorities have 'the right to recognition of their identity under international law'. The Commission interpreted the right of self-determination put forth in the two 1966 Covenants as serving to 'safeguard human rights', observing further that 'by virtue of that right every individual may choose to belong to whatever ethnic, religious or language community he or she wishes' and to benefit from all human rights, including, where appropriate, the right to choose his nationality. This, however, did not signify that they could exercise a collective right of territorial secession.[60]

[57] C. Hillgruber, 'The Admission of New States to the International Community', 9 *EJIL* 9 (1998), 491–509, at 507. The ambiguous response in the first phase of the conflict, notably with the rapid recognitions, even before the finding of the Arbitration Commission that the process of dissolution 'is now complete and that the SFRY no longer exists' (Opinion no. 8, *ILM* 31 (1992), p. 1523), has been interpreted as an, at least implicit, recognition of the Republics' right to secede; Blay, 'Self-Determination: A Reassessment', pp. 310–12; D. Murswiek, 'The Issue of a Right of Secession – Reconsidered', *in* Tomuschat, *Modern Law of Self-Determination*, p. 29. This does not however seem to be the prevalent opinion of doctrine: see Pellet, 'Quel avenir pour le droit', p. 263; Crawford, 'State Practice and International Law', p. 103; O. Corten, 'Droit des peuples à disposer d'eux-mêmes et *uti possidetis*: deux faces d'une même médaille?' *in* O. Corten, B. Delcourt, P. Klein, N. Levrat (sous la dir. de), *Démembrement d'États et délimitations territoriales: L'* uti possidetis *en question?)* (Bruxelles: Bruylant, 1999), p. 404, at 425. See also, Christakis, *Le droit à l'autodétermination*, p. 207, 'On pourrait donc conclure que la première phase de la crise yugoslave constitue dans une large mesure une pratique favorable à la secession . . . Il s'agit en tout cas d'une situation isolée.'

[58] And, in a sense, the question of secession re-entered through another door.

[59] Opinion. no. 2, *ILM* 31 (1992), 1497.

[60] Weller, 'The International Response', pp. 592, 606. In strictly applying the principle of *uti possidetis*, which the Commission recognised as a general principle (Opinion. no. 3, *ILM* 31 (1992), 1500), thus applicable beyond a colonial context, the Commission did not depart from a territorial concept of people, Quane, 'The United Nations', p. 566; Hannum, 'Rethinking Self-Determination', p. 55. However, the manner in which this principle was applied, did not take into consideration the ethnic strife existing between the various ethnic groups living on Yugoslav territory, and this resulted in further secessionist attempts (see

The imposition of conditions relating to the respect of the popular will and to the respect of human rights and minority rights – that is, of conditions relating to internal self-determination – before the right to external self-determination is recognised by the international community. It is one of the most significant developments to have emerged from Yugoslavia's collapse.[61] It has indeed been considered that the principle of self-determination was 'modernised', through the extension of its application to Europe.[62]

However, while European recognition policy and practice in Central and Eastern Europe showed some interesting developments with regard to the principle of self-determination,[63] the response to the dismantlement of Yugoslavia as well as the former Soviet Union was not seen as implying any acknowledgment of a right of secession, namely, the right of a people or an ethnic group to break away unilaterally from an existing State and create an independent State of its own.[64] This conclusion is further affirmed by the reaction towards other recent secessionist conflicts.

B. Cases of attempted unilateral secession

The dismantlement of States in Central and Eastern Europe has led to further interrogations on the question of whether and to what extent ethnic groups within the secessionist member units can in turn raise secessionist claims themselves on the basis of self-determination.[65] Reactions towards other secessionist (or sub-secessionist) conflicts in Europe reveal

below). On the *uti possidetis* principle in its extra-colonial context, see G. Nesi, 'L'*uti possidetis* hors du contexte de la decolonisation: le cas de l'Europe', *AFDI* (1998), 1–23; M. Kohen, 'Le problème des frontières en cas de dissolution et de séparation d'États: quelles alternatives?' *in* Corten *et al.*, (eds.), *Démembrement d'États et délimitations territoriales*, p. 265.

61 Cassese, *Self-Determination of Peoples*, p. 268.

62 Tierney, 'In a State of Flux', p. 223; A. Pellet, 'The Opinion of the Badinter Committee. A Second Breath for the Self-Determination of Peoples', *EJIL* 3 (1992), 178–81.

63 See R. Bieber, 'European Community Recognition of Eastern European States: A New Perspective for International Law?', *ASIL Proceedings* (1992), 374–8.

64 Mullerson, 'Self-Determination of Peoples', p. 573; Hannum, 'Rethinking Self-Determination', p. 55; Quane, 'The United Nations', p. 570. In the view of Blay, '. . . acceptance of legitimacy of the secessions was part of the strategy of managing the crisis . . . and not dictated by any legal principle or desire to develop a basis for dealing with similar situations in the future', 'Self-Determination: A Reassessment', p. 312.

65 L. Wildhaber, 'Territorial Modifications and Breakups in Federal States', *CYIL* (1995), 41–74.

the continuing hostility towards claims of secession and the recurring emphasis on territorial integrity.[66]

1. Secessionist conflicts after the break-up of the Soviet Union

The dissolution of the USSR revealed the fragility of its constituent Republics, as many were faced with demands for independence advanced by ethnic groups. After 1991, further secessionist claims were put forth by Nagorno-Karabakh in Azerbaijan, Abkhazia and South Ossetia in Georgia, and the Trans-Dniestr region in Moldova.[67] After the Soviet Republics became independent, these entities proclaimed their own independence. In all these cases, the response by the international community, and by the OSCE and its participating States in particular, has been to reaffirm the sovereignty and territorial integrity of the States concerned.[68] At the same time, the OSCE and its participating States have called upon the parties to negotiate a special status for the secessionist regions, supporting the allocation of autonomy for these regions.[69]

[66] Crawford, 'State Practice and International Law', p. 107; Cristakis, *Le droit à l'autodétermination*; Tancredi, 'Secessione e diritto internazionale'; J. Ringelheim, 'Considerations on the International Reaction to the 1999 Kosovo Crisis', *RBDI* 2 (1999), 475–544 and 520–6.

[67] On these conflicts and reactions to them, see V. Y. Ghebali, *L'OSCE dans l'Europe post-communiste, 1990–1996. Vers une identité paneuropéene* (Bruxelles: Bruylant, 1996); Gray, 'Self-Determination'.

[68] See for example, Lisbon Summit Declaration, 1996; Copenhagen Summit Declaration, 1996; Istanbul Summit Declaration, 1999, in particular, para. 15 ('Reaffirming our strong support for the sovereignty and territorial integrity of Georgia, we stress the need for solving conflicts with regard to the Tskhinvali region / South Ossetia and Abkhazia, Georgia, particularly by defining the political status of these regions within Georgia.'), para. 18 (regarding the Trans-Dniestrian problem, the participating States reaffirm 'that in the resolution of this problem the sovereignty and territorial integrity of the Republic of Moldova should be ensured.'), para. 20 (concerning developments in the Nagorno-Karabakh conflict). For these documents see, http://www.osce.org/docs/english/1990–1999/summits.

[69] Ringelheim, 'Considerations on the International Reaction', p. 523, according to whom 'these repeated calls for a political settlement in different contexts, despite their rhetorical character, suggest that OSCE members increasingly consider that a state affected by an internal conflict is under an obligation to endeavour to settle the problem peacefully, through political accommodation' (p. 526). For a more extensive analysis of international responses to these conflicts, see Ringelheim, *ibid.*, pp. 520–4; T. Cristakis, *Le droit à l'autodétermination*, pp. 225–9; Ghebali, *L'OSCE dans l'Europe post-communiste*; Tancredi, 'Secessione e diritto internazionale', pp. 740–2.

In the Chechnyan conflict,[70] responses were more moderate, in the sense that, while reaffirming the principle of territorial integrity of the Russian Federation and stressing the need for a negotiated solution, there seemed to be no specific proposals towards the granting of autonomy in particular. In fact, while expressing concern over the humanitarian situation in Chechnya, the international community preferred to treat the matter as an 'internal affair' of the Russian Federation. In January 1995, reacting to the offensive launched by the Russian Federation against the separatist Chechen Republic, the OSCE Permanent Council adopted a resolution demanding the cessation of hostilities and the opening of negotiations in order to reach a political settlement. A Joint Declaration of 31 August 1996 referred to the 'universally recognised right of peoples to self-determination' and provided for an agreement on mutual relations 'in accordance with commonly recognised principles and norms of international law', to be achieved by 31 December 2001.[71] The crisis deepened when a new military campaign was launched by the Russian army in September 1999, this time provoking a more vivid reaction, without, however, leading to the adoption of any measures against the Russian Federation. During the Istanbul Summit a few months later, the OSCE participating States reiterated their call for a political solution, while reaffirming the territorial integrity of the Russian Federation.[72] International reactions have generally placed

[70] Chechnya, an autonomous Republic within Russia, claimed independence after the break-up of the former USSR. From 1991, the country was virtually governed by the Chechnyan National Congress headed by Dudayev. On the Chechnyan conflict, see R. Kherad, 'De la nature juridique du conflit tchétchène', *RGDIP* 1 (2000), 143–78; P. Gaeta, 'The Armed Conflict in Chechnya before the Russian Constitutional Court', *EJIL* 7 (1996), 563.

[71] Joint Declaration and Principles for Determining the Basis for Mutual Relations Between the Russian Federation and the Chechen Republic, 31 August 1996. This formulation was interpreted as a victory by the separatist Chechens, who saw it as an acknowledgment of their right to self-determination; but for the Russian side, it meant affirmation of existing borders. See M. Torelli (sous la dir. de), 'Chronique des faits internationaux', *RGDIP* 3 (1997), 774.

[72] See Istanbul Summit Declaration, 1999, para. 21: 'In connection with the recent chain of events in North Caucasus, we strongly reaffirm that we fully acknowledge the territorial integrity of the Russian Federation and condemn terrorism in all its forms . . . We agree that a political solution is essential, and that the assistance of the OSCE would contribute to achieving this goal . . . In this regard, we also welcome the willingness of the Russian Federation to facilitate these steps, which will contribute to creating conditions for stability, security, and economic prosperity in the region.' The only concession made by the Russian Federation was the acceptance, at least in principle, of the involvement of the OSCE in the search for a political solution.

emphasis on the respect for the territorial integrity of the Russian Federation.[73]

2. Conflicts in the territory of the former Yugoslavia: Kosovo

Reactions to secessionist conflicts within the Republics of the former Yugoslavia have been similar. External self-determination was denied to the Serbian population in Bosnia and Herzegovina which, in January 1992, proclaimed the independence of the Srpska Republic.[74]

The Kosovo crisis and its escalation in 1999 is the most recent example portraying the reluctance of the international community to support an independence claim by an ethnic group, even when the members of that group are faced with repressive policies of the State, reaching tragic dimensions.[75] Kosovo's autonomy was terminated by the Serbian government in 1990, leading to large-scale discrimination and prosecution of Kosovar Albanians during the 1990s. The Albanian leadership declared the independence of the Republic of Kosovo in 1991, but this declaration was not recognised by the international community (with the exception of Albania). The escalation of violence resulted in increasing international reaction from 1998 onwards.[76] The international community's response was constant in rejecting Kosovar Albanians' claim to independent statehood, which suggests that in this case, the international community did not recognise any right to secede, even in cases of gross violations of human rights of an ethnic group.[77] Instead, the solution consisted in construing a plan of autonomy for Kosovo.[78] This plan was initially rejected by the Yugoslav authorities. However, after the NATO bombing campaign

[73] At the same time, there has been a shift towards the recognition, explicit or implicit, of the existence of an armed conflict in Chechnya, which in turn implies that the affair is not purely internal; see R. Kherad, 'La reconnaissance internationale', p. 175.

[74] This position was confirmed in the Dayton-Paris Peace Agreement of 1995 (*ILM* 35 (1996) 89), which guarantees the territorial integrity of Bosnia and Hezegovina.

[75] For a thorough analysis of the Kosovo crisis, particularly with regard to questions of self-determination and minorities, see generally, Ringelheim, 'Considerations on the International Reaction'.

[76] See SC Res. 1160 of 31 March 1998 and SC Res. 1199 of 23 September 1998.

[77] See Christakis, *Le droit à l'autodétermination*, p. 208 at 239, who poses the question of whether, by the attitude of the international community towards the situation of the ethnic Albanians and the series of measures taken against the FRY, one might infer a positive reaction by the international community towards a secessionist movement when it becomes the target of gross human rights violations. However, the insistence of the international community on the principle of territorial integrity and the refusal to recognise any independence for Kosovo, do not lend any support to this view.

[78] M. Weller, 'The Rambouillet Conference on Kosovo', *International Affairs* (1999), 163–203.

ended, they accepted an arrangement providing for the deployment of an international force in Kosovo under UN auspices,[79] until its future political status is determined.

Apart from the reaffirmation of territorial integrity, international response to these claims, in particular by the OSCE, has placed emphasis on the need for parties to reach a solution by negotiation.[80] Thus, even while not accepting secessionist claims, some procedural requirements are set for the resolution of secessionist conflicts.

III. Assessing recent practice: some concluding remarks

The events witnessed in Central and Eastern Europe in the decade of the nineties were seen by many internationalists as an ideal opportunity to re-examine the issue of secession in a non-colonial context. It remains to be assessed whether and to what extent recent practice in Europe has contributed towards a clarification of this controversial issue. In the light of developments outside the colonial context, secession today principally refers to 'claims by national groups within the continuous boundaries of independent States to break away from these States'.[81] This meaning corresponds to the new phenomena of secession witnessed recently. The international reaction towards such phenomena gives further insight into the substance of the term, in particular on the question whether there is a right of secession under international law.

State practice with regard to secessionist movements witnessed in Europe does not support the existence of a right of secession as an aspect of self-determination. The strongly prevailing view of the international community is that, beyond the right of peoples under colonial or other comparable alien domination, self-determination support will not be given to secession from an existing State against the will of the government of that State. The dissolution of Czechoslovakia and, to some extent, of the Soviet Union, occurred with the consent of the central authorities, and this aspect was a significant factor in the international recognition that ensued. In the case of Yugoslavia, the course of events initially suggested

[79] UN Security Council Resolution 1244 of 10 June 1999. While reaffirming the 'commitments of all Member States to the sovereignty and territorial integrity of the FRY' and their position in favour of 'substantial and meaningful self-administration for Kosovo', this resolution entrusts the United Nations Interim Administration Mission in Kosovo (UNMIK) with the administration of this territory, pending a final resolution of the future legal status of Kosovo.

[80] See Ringelheim, 'Considerations on the International Reaction', p. 526.

[81] Quane, 'The United Nations', p. 547.

a process of secession that was resisted by the central authorities. Precipitate reactions of the international community, and in particular of the European Union, led to the assumption that a right of the Yugoslav entities to secede unilaterally was actually endorsed. However, the legal justification given to the events by the Arbitration Commission, namely the treatment of the disintegration as an instance of dissolution rather than as an exercise of self-determination, served as the legal basis to international recognition, and thus the international response in this case is not seen as creating a precedent in favour of a right of secession. This can furthermore be deduced from the response to other more recent secessionist conflicts where the international community has refused to recognise any right of secession in cases where the consent of the State involved is lacking, and has consistently referred to the principle of territorial sovereignty (e.g. Chechnya). This has been a consistent reaction, even in cases where there is a systematic discrimination and persecution of an ethnic group by the State from which it is claiming independence (e.g. Kosovo).[82] Responses show that it is extremely difficult to obtain international recognition where the government of the State in question maintains its opposition.[83]

This refusal to extend the right to self-determination in its external aspect to include a right to secede has been counterbalanced, on the other hand, by a shifting focus on the internal aspect of self-determination. Documents and practice in Europe have largely contributed to this development.[84] Indeed, on a European level, respect of internal self-determination – including respect of human and minority rights, representative government, respect for the rule of law – has been elevated to a necessary condition before any right to external self-determination is recognised. An interesting development in this direction might be seen in the proposals tending to the granting of some form of autonomy advanced

[82] It has been held that secession could be accepted as a remedy of last resort in cases where an ethnic group is victim of systematic violations of human rights by the State authorities; see, Franck, 'Postmodern Tribalism', p. 13; Christakis, *Le droit à l'autodétermination*, p. 295. However, reaction towards the Kosovo conflict demonstrates that 'so long as the situation does not threaten international stability, states will remain reluctant to support a special status for an ethnic group in another state, even if members of that group are victims of discrimination and human rights violations': Ringelheim, 'Considerations on the International Reaction', p. 542.

[83] Crawford, 'State Practice and International Law', pp. 115–16.

[84] As it has been held, 'secession is only one of the numerous faces of self-determination': F. Kirgis, 'The Degrees of Self-Determination in the United Nations Era', *AJIL* 88 (1994), 304–10, at 306.

as a potential for initiating resolution of recent secessionist conflicts. While autonomy is not an established right of international law[85] and is only mentioned as a possible option in recent OSCE texts,[86] it has in practice been proffered as a possible solution to recent secessionist conflicts that would permit the accommodation of secessionist aspirations while at the same time maintaining territorial integrity.[87] In many European countries, various forms of self-government have proven capable of reconciling the conflicting needs of minorities and the demands of State integrity.[88] However, autonomy cannot be seen as the only solution, but only one in a range of options offered by the ever-evolving concept of self-determination.

85 See generally, M. Suksi (ed.), *Autonomy: Applications and Implications* (The Hague: Kluwer Law International, 1998); H. Hannum, *Autonomy, Sovereignty, and Self-Determination. The Accommodation of Conflicting Rights* (Philadelphia: University of Pennsylvania Press, 1990).

86 See Section I.

87 Furthermore, according to Hannum, 'A strong commitment to autonomy solutions within states also obviates the need to develop criteria for secession, since secession (except by mutual consent) is simply not available as an internationally sanctioned outcome. This is the approach taken by the international community thus far in Kosovo, for example – although the situation there is far from resolved . . .' 'Territorial Autonomy: Permanent Solution or Step toward Secession?', *Facing Ethnic Conflicts*, Conference, Bonn, Germany, 14–16 December 2000; for text see: www.zef.de/download/ethnic_conflict/hannum.pdf

88 See generally, A. Cassese, *Self-Determination of Peoples.*

12

Secession and international law: Latin American practice

FRIDA ARMAS PFIRTER AND

SILVINA GONZÁLEZ NAPOLITANO

I. Introduction

Prior to the nineteenth century, secession was probably the most typical mode for States to come into existence, especially when we bear the process of independence of the American colonies in mind.[1]

Unlike the case of the Portuguese colony in South America, independence of the Spanish colonies constituted a very complex and unique process. The territory colonised by Spain was considerably vast, with different regions, each with its own characteristics. Consequently, the administrative divisions created by the Spanish Crown enjoyed ample autonomy. Thus, in the case of these colonial territories, the 'secession' or 'emancipation' from the metropolitan State did not always take place in a uniform manner, as opposed to the 'no particular case of dismemberment or secession' in the case of the South American Portuguese colony.

This chapter outlines a general picture of the colonisation, independence and dismemberment of the Spanish colonies in the Americas during the process of independence experienced by the Latin American States.

The Spanish colonies in the Americas declared their independence progressively. In some cases, it took a long time before Spain formally recognised them,[2] in spite of the fact that they had established enduring

[1] J. Crawford, *The Creation of States in International Law* (Oxford: Clarendon Press, 1979), p. 247.

[2] E.g., Spain recognised Mexico in 1836, Venezuela in 1845, Argentina in 1863 and Peru in 1879. See L. A. Podestá Costa and J. M. Ruda, *Derecho Internacional Público*, vol. I (Buenos Aires: Tipográfica Editora Argentina, 1988), p. 63.

control over their territory.[3] They were first recognised by third States such as Portugal and the United States who led the way, followed by Great Britain.[4] The delay on the part of the metropolitan State in recognising new States in cases of secession through a war of independence made some sense, as the secession could constitute a long drawn-out process and one whose results might be reversed. This was actually the case with some Spanish-American colonies.[5]

The term 'secession' has been defined as 'the creation of a State by the use or threat of force and without the consent of the former sovereign'.[6] Although part of the doctrine admits that secession may even occur in the context of colonialism, thus enveloping 'emancipation' as an additional instance of that notion, such an opinion is not universal.[7] Bearing the above-mentioned definition in mind, for the purposes of the present chapter, the term 'secession' will be defined as: the separation of a part of the territory of a State by its population with the purpose of creating an independent State or being subsumed by another existing State, carried out without the consent of the sovereign.

These features have served to draw a distinction between secession and other types of creation or extinction of States: (1) secession vs. separation: the first refers to a violent process while the second relates to a peaceful one;[8] (2) secession vs. dismemberment or

[3] Crawford, *The Creation of States*, p. 248.

[4] Portugal recognised the United Provinces of Rio de la Plata in 1821; US recognised Colombia, the United Provinces of Rio de la Plata and Mexico in 1822; the United Kingdom recognised Colombia and the United Provinces of Rio de la Plata in 1825 and Mexico in 1826.

[5] J. Crawford, 'State Practice and International Law in Relation to Unilateral Secession', *Report to the Government of Canada concerning unilateral secession by Quebec*, 19 February 1997, para. 8.

[6] Crawford, 'State Practice and International Law', para. 8. Other scholars add that this mode necessarily implies the creation of one or more new States without the correlative extinction of the other. See A. Remiro Brotóns, R. M. Riquelme Cortado, J. Díez-Hochleitner, E. Orihuela Calatayud and L. Pérez-Prat Durbán, *Derecho Internacional* (Madrid: McGraw Hill, 1997), p. 49. According to this position, secession 'consiste dans l'amputation du territoire d'un État, dont la partie retranchée constituera l'assiette spatiale de l'État nouveau; la société interétatique est ainsi augmentée d'une unité, ou davantage quand plusieurs collectivités se détachent simultanément du même État', J. Combacau and S. Sur, *Droit international public* (2nd edn, Paris: Montchrestien, 1995), p. 265.

[7] In favour: Crawford, 'State Practice and International Law', Part II; Combacau and Sur, *Droit international public*, p. 266; D. P. O'Connell, *The Law of State Succession* (Cambridge: Cambridge University Press, 1956), p. 32; In contra: J. Barboza, *Derecho Internacional Público* (Buenos Aires: Zavalía, 1999), p. 226.

[8] Remiro Brotóns *et al.*, *Derecho Internacional*, p. 49. However, some authors use the expressions 'separation' and 'secession' as synonyms, disregarding the element of use of force

dissolution[9] (also known as substitution[10]): in the first, the predecessor State survives, while in the second it ceases to exist; (3) secession vs. devolution: in the first, the consent of the metropolitan State is absent since it is a unilateral process, while in the second, the parent State gives its consent and the process is bilateral and consensual;[11] (4) secession vs. annexation: when the separating territory does not become a new State but is integrated with an existing State, we find a connection between secession and annexation.

Again, these terms are not free from ambiguity. Certain authors use the term 'annexation' only to refer to the case in which a State is subsumed in another State by forceful means – which nowadays is considered illegal.[12] On the other hand, others speak of 'annexation' in cases where the portion of territory of a State is subsumed in another State, irrespective of whether the process takes place through the use of force or with the consent of the population of the transferred territory.[13] Therefore, we shall use the term 'annexation' in this latter broader sense, or rather the terms 'incorporation' or 'integration', given their more neutral sense.

Within the decolonisation process, consent by the metropolitan State is not always clear, since in many cases the colonial power granted independence to its colonies when they were already in an advanced stage of secession.[14] Besides, in general terms it can be said that the independence of the Latin American colonies constituted a real case of secession from the colonial power and that, as we shall see, some specific cases of secession within the former colonial divisions also took place.

Nevertheless, the opinion of jurists is not unanimous. Some authors regard the independence of the Latin American Spanish and Portuguese

or violence. See H. Accioly, *Manual de Direito Internacional Público* (11th edn, Sao Paulo: Saraiva, 1991), p. 23; S. Benadava, *Derecho Internacional Público* (4th edn, Santiago de Chile: Ed. Universitaria, 1993), p. 121.

9 Some jurists use the expression 'dissolution' to refer to real unions and confederations. But Remiro Brotóns and others understand that those cases are not, in point of fact, examples of dissolution of States because the new States already had international personality when they were a part of the dissolved entity. See Remiro Brotóns *et al., Derecho Internacional,* p. 49.

10 Combacau and Sur, *Droit international public,* p. 265.

11 Crawford, *The Creation of States,* p. 215.

12 Remiro Brotóns *et al., Derecho Internacional,* p. 49.

13 O'Connell also refers to 'voluntary annexations', *The Law of State Succession,* p. 25. If the metropolitan State (or, in general, the predecessor State) gives its consent to the integration of a colony or a part of its territory with another State, the case is one of cession.

14 C. Haverland, 'Secession', *in* R. Bernhardt (ed.), 4 *Encyclopedia of Public International Law* (Amsterdam: Elsevier/North-Holland, 2000), p. 354.

colonies as instances of 'historical acquisition'[15] or 'emancipation',[16] considering the coming into existence of the Republics of Paraguay, Uruguay and Bolivia to be the consequence of secessions from the territory of the United Provinces of the Rio de la Plata, a position, as will be illustrated, we cannot share.[17]

II. The colonisation of Latin America

Upon the discovery of the New World, Spain and Portugal encouraged travel and exploration, moved by the intention to add territories to their lands and to increase their respective political influence.

In those days it was common practice that the Pope ratified the discovery of territories inhabited by non-Christians through the issuance of a Bull, thus preventing any other Christian Prince from taking possession of them. In previous centuries, Spain and Portugal had relied upon the Bulls with regard to the African territories. After all, even Ireland had been granted to England in 1155 through the *Laudabiliter* Bull issued by Pope Adrian IV. In the case of the Americas, Pope Alexander VI granted all the lands discovered and yet to be discovered west of the meridian, situated at 100 *leguas* (some 301 nautical miles) from the Azores, to the Crown of Castilla. This boundary was later shifted 370 *leguas* (some 1,113.33 nautical miles) to the west by the Treaty of Tordesillas, which was later confirmed by the *Ea quae* Bull, issued by Pope Julius II.[18]

Immediately after the discovery of America by Christopher Columbus in 1492, the Spanish Crown commissioned military officers called '*Adelantados*' to temporarily rule the conquered territories of the Americas on behalf of the Spanish Crown. In time, they were replaced by

[15] J. P. Pancracio, *Droit International des Espaces* (Paris : Armand-Colin, 1997), p. 5.

[16] Accioly, *Manual de Direito Internacional*, p. 23.

[17] C. Díaz Cisneros, *Derecho Internacional Público* (2nd edn., Buenos Aires: Tipográfica Editora Argentina, 1966), p. 473; Moreno L. M. Quintana, *Tratado de Derecho Internacional*, vol. I (Buenos Aires: Sudamericana, 1963), p. 139.

[18] The division between the Spanish and Portuguese possessions in America was the object of Bulls *Inter caetera* (3–4 May 1403) and *Dudum siquidem* (26 September 1493) and of the Treaties of Tordesillas (1494), of Lisboa (1681), of Utrecht (1713), of Madrid (1750) and of San Ildefonso (1777). See texts of the Bulls in F. J. Hernaez (ed.), *Colección de Bulas, Breves y otros Documentos relativos a la Iglesia de América y Filipinas*, vol. I (Brussels: Ed. A. Vromant, 1879), p. 12, and vol. II, p. 838. See texts of the treaties in C. Calvo, *Colección Completa de los Tratados, Convenios, Capitulaciones, Armisticios y otros Actos diplomáticos de Todos los Estados de América Latina*, vol. I (Paris, 1862, repr. Vaduz: Topos), p. 19; see also F. M. Armas Pfirter, 'Le Tribunal arbitral international de Salto Grande et sa jurisprudence', in *AFDI* 39 (1993), 540–66.

'Governors'. Subsequently, the Spanish Crown divided its territories with the purpose of exercising adequate administrative and political control. Thus, in 1534, the first 'viceroyalty' of the Americas was created.[19] It was subject to a 'viceroy', the legitimate representative of the King of Spain. Smaller divisions followed, ruled by a 'captain general', with capacities similar to those of a viceroy.[20]

By the end of the eighteenth century, after the organisation of the American colonies was subjected to several changes introduced by successive kings, 'Spanish' America was comprised of four viceroyalties and four 'general captaincies', which in turn were divided into '*Intendencias*' and military districts called '*Gobernaciones*'. Governors acted as chairmen of the '*Audiencias*', institutions with a competence that was predominantly judicial, although some political and administrative functions were not entirely excluded.[21]

The viceroyalties of Spanish America were:

- Viceroyalty of New Spain, which comprised the territory of Mexico and territories in the south west of the US;
- Viceroyalty of New Granada, which comprised the territories of the present States of Colombia, Panama and Ecuador;
- Viceroyalty of Peru, which comprised mainly the territories of Peru; and
- Viceroyalty of the Rio de la Plata, which comprised the territories of the present States of Argentina, Paraguay, Uruguay and Bolivia.

The general captaincies were:

- General Captaincy of Cuba, which comprised the territories of the present State of Cuba and other dependencies in the Caribbean;
- General Captaincy of Guatemala, which comprised the territories of the present States of Guatemala, Belize, El Salvador, Honduras, Nicaragua and Costa Rica;
- General Captaincy of Venezuela, which comprised the territory of the present Venezuela; and
- General Captaincy of Chile, which comprised mainly what is present-day Chile.

On the other hand, Portugal organised its colonial system in the Americas on the basis of 'captaincies', which resembled the Spanish

[19] It was named 'Viceroyalty of New Spain'.

[20] See V. Tau Anzoategui and E. Martiré, *Manual de Historia de las Instituciones Argentinas* (4th edn, Buenos Aires: Macchi, 1980), p. 69.

[21] Tau Anzoategui and Martiré, *Manual de Historia*, p. 74.

'*adelantados*'.[22] In the eighteenth century, as a result of the re-organisation instituted by Sebastian de Carvalho y Mello,[23] the Portuguese colony (Brazil) was organised as a viceroyalty, with its capital in Rio de Janeiro, and further subdivided into eight general captaincies and eight subordinate administrations.[24] Nevertheless in 1815, the Portuguese Regent Prince João raised Brazil to the status of a kingdom, similar to that of Portugal.[25]

Towards the end of the eighteenth century, revolutionary movements were organised in the Americas, inspired both from the new political, social and economic liberal ideas from Europe and from the repercussions of the American and the French Revolutions. Such movements blossomed in different regions and resulted in the independence of the whole of Spanish America.[26]

Nevertheless, those movements did not give birth to a single newly independent State. Each viceroyalty and each captaincy proclaimed its independence, following the administrative boundaries established by the Spanish Crown. Furthermore, several subordinate administrative dependencies decided to take a path different from the viceroyalties and general-captaincies they depended upon, resulting in the dismemberment of some of them.[27]

The only ones that remained undivided were the Viceroyalty of Peru and the General Captaincy of Chile, although this does not mean that they maintained their original territory, as there had been great fluctuations of boundaries since their establishment.[28] Below, we analyse the cases

22 M. B. Etchart and M. C. Douzón, *Historia de las Instituciones Políticas y Sociales de América hasta 1810* (7th edn, Buenos Aires: Cesarini, 1976), p. 275.

23 He was the Marquis of Pombal and Prime Minister to the Portuguese Monarch José I.

24 The Captaincies were Pará, Maranhão, Bahía, Pernambuco, São Paulo, Ceará, Minas Gerais and Mato Grosso. See Etchart and Douzón, *Historia*, p. 285.

25 B. Keen and K. Haynes, *A History of Latin America* (6th edn, Boston: Houghton Mifflin, 2000), p. 173.

26 See J. E. O. Rodríguez, *La Independencia de la América Española* (México: Fondo de Cultura Económica, 1996); Congreso Hispanoamericano de Historia, *Causas y Caracteres de la Independencia Hispanoamericana* (Madrid: Ediciones Cultura Hispánica, 1953), p. 47. Regarding the differences between the independence of Spanish and Portuguese colonies in America, see T. Halperin Donghi, *Historia Contemporánea de América Latina* (6th edn, Madrid: Alianza, 1977), p. 129; R. Salazar Mallen, *El Pensamiento Político en América*, vol. I (Mexico: Jus, 1973), p. 9.

27 F. M. Armas Pfirter, J. Barberis, A. Beraud and N. Freyre, *Límites de la República Argentina – Cuadernos de Derecho Internacional 2* (Buenos Aires: Abaco-Depalma, 2000), p. 15.

28 See D. Antokoletz, *Tratado de Derecho Internacional Público*, vol. II (5th edn, Buenos Aires: La Facultad, 1951), p. 330.

of emancipation; we will highlight the case in which one administrative dependency was split into several independent States.

The newly independent States considered themselves as successors of Spain with regard to the titles over the West Indies granted by the Bulls issued by Pope Alexander VI. Since those titles legitimated Spanish sovereignty over 'all lands discovered and yet to be discovered', without requiring effective possession, no territory in Americas was *res nullius.* Therefore, the newly independent States in the Spanish America enjoyed full jurisdiction over their respective territories, even in areas not subject to their effective possession.[29] Moreover, the boundaries between the former administrative divisions became international borders.

'*Uti possidetis*'[30] was the concept conceived by the newly independent States of Spanish America to prescribe that no territory in America was *res nullius* and that the former administrative divisions between them had become international borders. Those countries introduced that concept in their boundary treaties, in their national constitutions and in the agreements they concluded for the submission of territorial or boundary disputes to arbitration.[31]

The term '*uti possidetis*' means 'you shall possess as you possess'. It aimed at establishing new boundaries for the newly independent States, having the boundaries established by the Spanish authorities as the point of departure. The principle proved useful since it gave rise to a 'succeeding vocation' in the entire Spanish Empire, denying the existence of any '*res nullius*' territory. However, it caused serious conflicts between the former

[29] Armas Pfirter *et al.*, *Límites de la República Argentina*, p. 15, and J. A. Barberis, *El territorio del Estado y la soberanía territorial*, (Buenos Aires: Abaco, 2003), p. 88. For another view, see M. Kohen, *Possession contestée et souveraineté territoriale* (Paris: Presses universitaires de France, 1997), p. 426.

[30] J. A. Barberis, 'Les règles spécifiques du droit international en Amérique latine', *Recueil des Cours* 235 (1992-IV), 140. Even though it shares the same denomination, there is no connection between this notion and that of possessory injunction in Roman Law. See also S. R. Ratner, 'Drawing a Better Line: *Uti Possidetis* and the Borders of New States', *AJIL* 90 (1996), 590–625, at 593–5.

[31] Armas Pfirter *et al.*, *Límites de la República Argentina*, pp. 16–17. For example, Argentina referred to *uti possidetis* in boundary conflicts with Bolivia, Chile and Paraguay. As to the treaties, the Treaty concluded in 1811 between Venezuela and Cundinamarca might be said to be the first to uphold this juridical theory. Argentina and Chile established, by the treaty signed on 30 August 1855, that they would acknowledge the borders between their respective territories as those existing at the time of the emancipation from Spain in 1810 (art. 39). As to the constitutions, those of Ecuador, Venezuela, Costa Rica and Mexico include this principle. This principle can also be found in agreements to submit their boundary disputes to arbitration signed by Venezuela and Colombia (1891), Honduras and Nicaragua (1906), and Peru and Bolivia (1909).

colonies due to the uncertainties typical of the Spanish administrative divisions and to the dual administrative/ecclesiastic division. On the other hand, Brazil adhered to this principle with a different formulation.[32]

III. Emancipation and dismemberment

A. Viceroyalty of the New Spain

The Viceroyalty of the New Spain was comprised of territories that, at present, form parts of Mexico and the United States. It is an interesting case not only to analyse the emancipation phenomenon which occurred in every viceroyalty and general captaincy but also a short-lived case of the secession of Texas, which will be examined separately.

After several peaceful attempts to emancipate themselves from the Spanish Crown, a war for independence[33] began on 16 September 1810. It was to last eleven years.[34] The key plan of the emancipation process, the 'Iguala Plan', was prompted by Agustín de Iturbide[35] and signed on 24 March 1821.[36] On 24 August of that same year Juan O'Donojú, Captain General of Mexico and last viceroy, accepted to sign an agreement with Iturbide known as the 'Cordoba Treaties', by virtue of which the Mexican Empire was recognised as a sovereign independent nation to be ruled by Ferdinand VII of Spain, except in the event of his abdication or non-acceptance, in which case, other appointments were provided for.[37] In this way, Mexico obtained its political emancipation. On 28 September 1821, the first independent government was established. Henceforth the new State underwent several forms of government: regency, federal

32 M. A. Vieira, 'Relevamiento de Problemas Fronterizos en América Latina', *in* H. Arbuet Vignali (ed.), *Nuestras Fronteras, Situación General y Problemas*, vol. I (Montevideo: Fundación de Cultura Universitaria, 1989), p. 44. See also H. Gros Espiell, *España y la Solución Pacífica de los Conflictos Limítrofes en Hispano-América*' (Madrid: Civitas, 1984). For another perspective, see M. G. Kohen, 'La contribución de América Latina al desarrollo progresivo del Derecho Internacional en materia territorial', *ADI* 27 (2001), 57–77.

33 The Mexican revolution was the result of the formation of a movement led by the priest Miguel Hidalgo. See J. Lynch, *Las Revoluciones Hispanoamericanas 1808–1826* (Barcelona: Ariel, 1976), p. 341; J. Calderón Quijano and F. Morales Padrón, 'Historia de las Naciones Iberoamericanas', *in Enciclopedia Labor*, vol. V (2nd edn, Barcelona: Labor, 1962), p. 585.

34 From 1810 to 1819, the revolution may be characterised as an anarchic civil war that divided the population into two opposing groups. It was not until 1821 that a 'national war' consolidated, aimed at establishing a constitutional monarchy under the reign of Ferdinand VII of Spain or some member of his family.

35 Agustín de Iturbide was a Creole officer.

36 J. Z. Vázquez, 'The Mexican Declaration of Independence', *JAH* 85 (1999), 1362–9, at 1368.

37 E. de la Torre, *La Independencia de México* (Madrid: Mapfre, 1992), p. 130.

republic, unitarian republic, empire, and also anarchy, experiencing war, acquisitions and territorial losses.

Mexico was recognised as an independent State by the United States of America in December 1822. With regard to Spain, although in 1821 it had disavowed all acts carried out by O'Donojú[38] and refused to recognise Mexico, its finally accorded recognition on 28 December 1836.

In 1835, Mexico was established as a republic. In that period, it faced several armed conflicts, including a war against one of its territorial regions, *Tejas* (now Texas),[39] which may be regarded as a case of secession (this case is discussed in the following section).

With regard to the effects of independence on treaties, in 1854 Great Britain expressed, in the context of a treaty with Mexico, that it 'simply stipulates that British Subjects should not be worse off under Mexico independent that under Mexico when a Spanish Province'.[40]

As for the national debt of Mexico, in 1825 the British King's Advocate issued an opinion on the obligation of Mexico to undertake payments of certain ecclesiastical annuities to the late Cardinal of York because the Spanish Government had pledged these annuities on Mexican revenues. The Advocate, undecided on the legal character of the pledge, held that 'a seceding State would not be responsible for such a debt'.[41]

B. *Viceroyalty of New Granada and General Captaincy of Venezuela*

The Viceroyalty of New Granada comprised the territories of the present States of Colombia, Panama and Ecuador, while the General Captaincy of Venezuela comprised the territory of the present Venezuela. Here we find processes of emancipation, union or unification[42] as well as dissolution

38 de la Torre, *La Independencia*, p. 130.

39 Calderón Quijano and Morales Padrón, 'Historia de las Naciones', p.591.

40 And that '(i)t was natural, that Great Britain should make such a stipulation but the fact of her doing so rather proves that she thought a special stipulation necessary, and that she did not conceive that she would have enjoyed under any general principle the privilege she bargained for; and this stipulation, as indeed, the Treaty itself, is a proof that Mexico was not considered as inheriting the obligations or rights of Spain'. See Smith, *Great Britain and the Law of Nations*, vol. I (1932), p. 377, as quoted by O'Connell, *The Law of State Succession*, p. 34.

41 O'Connell, *The Law of State Succession*, p. 34. The Opinion of 5 July 1825 was reproduced at pp. 284–5.

42 The classification as union or unification depends on the status of the member States involved (whether they are independent States or not).

or dismemberment.[43] All of these are useful to highlight their differences from the concept of secession.

On 5 July 1811, the first Venezuelan Republic was proclaimed. It only lasted one year, since in 1812 it was reconquered by Spain, which took advantage of the social divisions the territory was facing at the time.[44] Starting in 1813, the emancipation campaigns of Venezuela and New Granada were interrelated and amalgamated.[45]

At the beginning of the nineteenth century, a number of pro-independence insurrections took place in several regions of the Viceroyalty of New Granada. Starting in 1810, certain provinces proclaimed their independence from Spain, establishing an autonomous administration[46] – for example the dependencies of Antioquia, Cartagena, Pamplona, Neiva and Tunja, which united themselves as the United Provinces of New Granada on 27 November 1811.[47] Nevertheless, on 28 April 1816, Spain recovered control over New Granada and re-established the Viceroyalty.[48]

New Granada and Venezuela were not to be emancipated until 17 December 1819, giving birth to the Republic of Colombia, known as 'Great Colombia'.[49] On 30 August 1821, the National Congress adopted the first constitution of Colombia.

On 28 November 1821, Panama declared its independence and decided to join 'Great Colombia'. On the other side, Ecuador became emancipated

43 Some authors use the expression 'dissolution' to refer to the disintegration of unions of States, e.g. Barboza, *Derecho Internacional Público*, p. 228, whereas others use both terms (dissolution and dismemberment) as synonyms.

44 Lynch, *Las Revoluciones*, p. 223; J. A. de Armas Chitty, *La Independencia de Venezuela* (Madrid: Mapfre, 1992), p. 95.

45 D. Boersner, *Relaciones Internacionales de América Latina*, 5th edn, (Caracas: Nueva Sociedad, 1996), p. 62.

46 On 20 June 1810, in Santafé, a *Junta* was established and replaced the viceroy. On 10 July 1810, in Socorro, the Declaration of Independence was subscribed. On 1 April 1811, in Cundinamarca, the first President was elected, and a few days later – 4 April – the first Constitution was promulgated. On 11 November 1811, Cartagena proclaimed its absolute independence from Spain. See C. Valderrama Andrade, 'Atlas Básico de Historia de Colombia', *Revista Credencial Historia* 9 (1993), 12–14; D. D. Uribe Vargas, *Evolución Política y Constitucional de Colombia* (Madrid: Universidad Complutense, 1996), p. 34.

47 In January 1812, another province, Cundinamarca – already independent from Spain – declared war on the United Provinces, which resulted in the establishment of a single Government named the 'United Provinces of New Granada.'

48 Valderrama Andrade, 'Atlas Básico', p. 12.

49 At the Congress of Angostura, Simón Bolívar, the Liberator, secured the proclamation of the union between Venezuela and New Granada, with the name Republic of Colombia. See Lynch, *Las Revoluciones*, p. 244. The Republic had three departments: Venezuela, Quito and Cundinamarca.

from Spain on 24 May 1822[50] and also joined the federation of 'Great Colombia'.[51] In April 1822, the United States recognised the independence of Colombia. Britain followed in April 1825.

From 1826 onwards, a sequence of events[52] took place in 'Great Colombia' which inevitably led to its dismemberment or dissolution (1829–1831).[53] In 1830, Ecuador and Venezuela left 'Great Colombia', and proclaimed their independence. Only New Granada remained, with Panama being an integral part of it.

On 17 November 1831, a centralist 'Fundamental Act of the State of New Granada' was adopted (the Constitution was later enacted in 1832), according to which the official name became 'Republic of New Granada'. By virtue of the constitutional reform in 1858, the State changed its name to 'Granadina Confederation',[54] which was further changed to 'United States of Colombia' in 1863.[55] It was not until the 1886

[50] This took place after the victory of Sucre – Bolívar's Lieutenant – in the battle of Pichincha.

[51] On 11 July 1822, the Province of Guayaquil became part of the Great Colombia.

[52] Mainly the controversial acts by Bolívar against the Constitution in force and his efforts to impose the Bolivian Constitution over that of Great Colombia, especially since the 1821 Constitution did not allow for its revision before ten years had lapsed from the moment it became binding. The 1828 Constitutional Assembly, summoned by Bolívar, failed as it ended without having approved any amendment. See, Uribe Vargas, *Evolución Política*, p. 80.

[53] O'Connell, *The Law of State Succession*, p. 43.

[54] Throughout the 1850s, due to internal conflicts, the entities that made up New Granada were acquiring more federal prerogatives and increasing legislative autonomy. Provinces took the place of the Departments, and these multiplied to reach the number of thirty-five. In 1855, the sovereign State of Panama was created (comprising the provinces of Panama, Agüero, Veraguas and Chiriquí). Other provinces followed suit, and other States emerged: Antioquia, Santander, Cauca, Cundinamarca, Boyacá, Bolívar and Magdalena. As a result, the Constitution was reformed and the Granadina Confederation came into existence. The eight States mentioned above agreed to become part of a permanent confederation, and surrendered certain competencies to a central authority (e.g. as to government organisation, foreign affairs, defence, determination of international boundaries and other monetary and commercial matters). See Uribe Vargas, *Evolución Política*, p. 125.

[55] Again this new Constitution was adopted after violent internal conflict. The nine federal States (eight from the former Granadina Confederation plus a new one: Tolima, created in 1861) confederated by this Constitution, gave rise to a free, sovereign and independent nation named the 'United States of Colombia'. Foreign affairs and the entering into treaties – with parliamentary approval – were competencies of the President of the Union. Uribe Vargas analysed the differences between a federation and a confederation, concluding that the Constitution of 1863 is federal in spite of its terminology (Confederation), because the Government and the Congress of the Union reserved the management of the international relations to itself. See Uribe Vargas, *Evolución Política*, p. 133, at 136–8. The same could be said regarding the 1858 Granadina Confederation. In contrast, some authors understand that the central power in a confederation is limited to certain

Constitution[56] that the State was re-organised under the name of 'Republic of Colombia'.

Upon the dissolution of 'Great Colombia', Ecuador, Venezuela and New Granada regained their independence (as we have seen, the latter finally took the name of 'Colombia'). These entities had been Spanish dependencies in colonial times, when Ecuador was part of the Presidency of Quito,[57] Venezuela of the General Captaincy of Venezuela and New Granada of the Viceroyalty of New Granada. Thus, the newly independent States established their territorial boundaries accepting the principle of *uti possidetis juris*. The Fundamental Act of the State of New Granada defined its boundaries, which were identical to those of the former Viceroyalty,[58] emphatically rejecting any attempts of territorial aggregation or segregation as a result of the dismemberment of Colombia.[59]

From the above-mentioned, we may conclude that the following different phenomena took place:

1) Two separate administrative dependencies were emancipated from Spain: (a) the Viceroyalty of New Granada, and (b) the General Captaincy of Venezuela. In the case of New Granada, the administrative districts that were part of the Viceroyalty, New Granada, Panama and Ecuador, gained separate independence, on different dates. Thus, we could consider this to be, in principle, the dismemberment of the Viceroyalty into three separate States. The case of Venezuela can be considered simply to be an act of emancipation.
2) A case of union or unification also took place when a former dependency, Venezuela, united with one of the districts of another former dependency, New Granada, and this union later attracted other districts of the latter, namely Panama and Ecuador. In conclusion, the administrative dependencies of the former Viceroyalty of New Granada and

competencies – e.g., defence and foreign representation. See Barboza, *Derecho Internacional Público*, p. 171; C. D. de Albuquerque Mello, *Direito Internacional Público*, vol. I, 9th edn, (Rio de Janeiro: Renovar, 1992), p. 302. See also S. V. Linares Quintana, *Derecho Constitucional e Instituciones Políticas. Teoría Empírica de las Instituciones Políticas*, vol. II, 2nd edn, (Buenos Aires: Plus Ultra, 1976), p. 112.

56 Which established a centralist regime.

57 The Presidency was the regime that replaced the *Audiencia*. It was an intermediate system if compared to the viceroyalty. After successive reforms, the territory under the former Presidency of Quito was transferred to the Viceroyalty of New Granada. See Calderón Quijano and Morales Padrón, 'Historia de las Naciones', p. 540.

58 Uribe Vargas, *Evolución Política*, p. 99.

59 The Republic of Ecuador tried to annex the Pasto region, which was beyond the borders of the former Presidency of Quito. See Uribe Vargas, *Evolución Política*, p. 97.

the former General Captaincy of Venezuela were united in the 'Great Colombia'.

3) Finally, Great Colombia dismembered[60] with the result that the dependencies and districts that had come to independence between 1819 and 1822 resumed their individual sovereignty, with the exception of Panama which remained part of New Granada (later Colombia) until its independence in 1902.

With regard to the effects of the succession of States, it is interesting to note that when Colombia achieved independence, the United States considered it bound 'in honour and justice' by all treaties concluded by Spain with other nations.[61] After the dissolution of 'Great Colombia', the question arose as to whether or not the privileges granted by an 1825 treaty between Great Britain and Colombia (about the operation of British Navigation laws) could be claimed by the several constituent States.[62] In 1851, Great Britain and Ecuador concluded a new

[60] Most of the scholars regard it as a case of dissolution. See T. Halperín Donghi, *Historia de América Latina. Reforma y Disolución de los Imperios Ibéricos 1750–1850*, vol. III (Madrid: Alianza, 1985), p. 229; Vieira, 'Relevamiento de Problemas', pp. 44–7. Yet, others understand that Great Colombia is not a true case of dissolution of States, because the States that were part of the former entity had international personality by themselves. See Remiro Brotóns *et al.*, *Derecho Internacional*, p. 49. Accioly uses the terms 'separation' and 'division'; Accioly, *Manual de Direito Internacional*, p. 23. Others refer to it as a case of dismemberment – e.g. see F. Chevalier, *América Latina de la Independencia a Nuestros Días*, (Barcelona: Labor, 1983), p. 12.

[61] J. B. Moore, *Digest of International Law*, vol. V (Washington, DC: G. P. O., 1906), p. 341, quoted by O'Connell, *The Law of State Succession*, p. 32. As a result, in 1862 the United States made a claim before the Ecuadorian Mixed Claims Commission alleging that 'condemnation as contraband by Colombia of goods carried in a United States ship, at the time when Colombia was engaged in the war of independence with Spain, was contrary to a treaty of 1785 between the United States and Spain'. See J. B. Moore, *International Arbitration*, vol. III (1898), p. 3223, quoted by O'Connell, *ibid.*, pp. 32–3. In a letter sent to the Nicaraguan Government, the United Kingdom explained that when Spanish American Provinces became independent from Spain, 'they neither acknowledged . . . [Spanish obligations] nor were called upon by other States to adopt them. On the contrary, when their political existence as independent States was acknowledged by other Countries, they contracted severally with those Foreign Countries such new Treaties as were applicable to their respective geographical limits and political condition; and neither they nor the foreign Powers with which they treated even thought of considering them as Inheritors of any of the Rights or Obligations arising out of the Treaty Engagements of the Spanish Crown' (O'Connell, *ibid.*, p. 34).

[62] The King's Advocate of Great Britain made a distinction between the treaty itself and the rights and duties created by it. As to the former, 'the Treaty will not be binding upon either of those Provinces, prospectively, after their complete separation from each other, when they will be no longer bound by one common bond of union, but each will form a distinct

agreement which abrogated the 1825 treaty in respect of its application to Ecuador.[63]

With respect to national debts, in December of 1834 the debt which the former Republic of Colombia had incurred was divided according to the following proportions: New Granada 50 per cent, Ecuador 21.5 per cent and Venezuela 28.5 per cent.[64]

C. *Viceroyalty of the Rio de la Plata*

1. Creation

Spain created the Viceroyalty of the Rio de la Plata in 1776[65] for internal political reasons. The Spanish also wanted to restrain Portuguese expansion in the territory of the present Argentine province of Misiones and in the '*Banda Oriental*' ['Eastern Strip', today Uruguay]. In order to legitimise this state of affairs, the following year Spain and Portugal concluded a preliminary boundary treaty wherein they accepted the existing state of territorial occupation.[66]

independent State, and will be at liberty, to form for itself its own engagements'. But he also advised that '(n)otwithstanding the separation of these States . . . the Treaty of 1825 is still binding upon each of them, so far as to entitle His Majesty's Government to require the observance of those rights and privileges, which were secured by it, to His Majesty's Subjects resident in any part of the Territories, which then constituted the Republic of Colombia'. However, he concluded by admitting each of the States to have the right to give 'due and timely notice that they consider themselves no longer bound by the Treaty'. See the Opinions of 3 June 1834 and 12 September 1834, quoted by O'Connell, *The Law of State Succession*, pp. 43–4. In that case, Venezuela claimed the automatic application of the rights granted by that treaty. On the position of the Adviser, O'Connell understands that he 'seems to have believed that a novation of the contract would be necessary to enable Venezuela to derive the benefits of the treaty, and that such novation should be evidenced by an act on the part of Venezuela, "accepted" by Great Britain', and that if his inference is correct, 'it affords a doubtful precedent for the problem under discussion', O'Connell, *ibid.*, p. 44.

63 In regard to Great Colombia, O'Connell considers that '(t)he ordinary principle that a new State does not inherit the treaties of its predecessor does not, it would seem, apply to the case of the emergence to full sovereignty of a semi-sovereign or self-governing community', O'Connell, *The Law of State Succession*, p. 43.

64 For more details, see O'Connell, *The Law of State Succession*, p. 158.

65 It was created provisionally by a *Real Cédula* (Royal Decree) dated 1 August 1776 by King Charles III. See *República Argentina, Tratados, Convenciones, Protocolos, Actos y Acuerdos Internacionales*, vol. XI, (Buenos Aires, 1912), p. 173. Also, Pedro de Cevallos was proclaimed Viceroy by this document and proceeded immediately to regain control of the Colony of Sacramento and other Spanish territories. By a *Real Cédula* dated 27 October 1777, the Viceroyalty became permanent. See also pp. 193–6.

66 Treaty of San Ildefonso, signed on 1 October 1777.

The territories of the present Republics of Argentina, Bolivia, Paraguay and Uruguay, and even a section of the Southern states of Brazil (Rio Grande do Sul, Santa Catarina and Parana) were part of the Viceroyalty of the Rio de la Plata until their emancipation.[67]

2. The dismemberment of the territory

The vast domain of this Viceroyalty began to dismember in 1810, when the emancipation movement started, in spite of the apparent aim to keep 'these domains' – the territory of the Viceroyalty – under King Ferdinand VII of Spain. This dismemberment could not be impeded, either by the invitation by the First National Government ('*Primera Junta*') to all provinces to send representatives to Buenos Aires, or by the actual participation of most of them in the General Constitutional Assembly of 1813,[68] in the Congress which took place in Tucumán in 1816[69] and in the 1825 national Congress.[70]

The dismemberment of the Viceroyalty of the Rio de la Plata gave rise to four newly independent States: the Argentine Republic, which in the beginning was named the 'United Provinces of Rio de la Plata, Uruguay, Paraguay and Bolivia'. The subdivisions that gave rise to this phenomenon were not only large administrative divisions but also smaller districts such as *Intendencias, Gobernaciones* and *Audiencias.*[71]

[67] It encompassed the following territory: (a) North, it reached up to *Desaguadero* River – which was a border with the Viceroyalty of Peru – including the Titicaca Lake region, the upper Beni, Mamore, Guapore and Jaurú rivers and the slopes of the Paraná and Uruguay rivers; (b) East, it reached the slopes of the Uruguay river, including the *guaraní* missions and the Rio de la Plata region, contouring the Portuguese territories and the Atlantic Ocean; (c) West, it extended up to the Pacific Ocean, between the Desaguadero and Salado rivers and the Andes Mountains, its border with the *Gobernación de Chile*; and (d) South, it comprised the *Patagonia* region, and other territories and islands located in the southern end of the continent. Since 1782, it had been divided into eight intendancies: Buenos Aires (comprising the present Argentine provinces of Buenos Aires, Entre Rios, Corrientes and Santa Fe, and including the Patagonia region and the Malvinas Islands); Asuncion del Paraguay, Mendoza (comprising the present Argentine provinces of Cordoba, San Juan, Mendoza, San Luis and La Rioja); San Miguel del Tucumán (comprising the present Argentine provinces of Jujuy, Salta, Tucuman, Santiago del Estero and Catamarca); Santa Cruz de la Sierra (part of the present Republic of Bolivia); La Plata, also called Charcas or Chuquisaca (part of Bolivia), Potosí and La Paz (Bolivia). V. G. Quesada, *Virreinato del Río de la Plata. 1776–1810. Apuntamientos crítico-históricos para servir en la cuestión de límites entre la República Argentina y Chile* (Buenos Aires: Ediciones de la Tipografía M. Biedma 1881), p. 9.

[68] Potosí, Charcas, Mizque and Montevideo.

[69] Tarija, Cochabamba, Charcas and Mizque.

[70] Montevideo and Tarija.

[71] Díaz Cisneros, *Derecho Internacional Público*, p. 232.

The independence of Argentina was recognised in 1821 by Portugal, in 1822 by the United States and in 1825 by Great Britain.[72] The conclusion of the Preliminary Peace Convention between Spain and the United Provinces of Rio de la Plata on 4 July 1823 may be regarded as the recognition of this newly independent State[73] by its former colonial power. But, as it never entered into force, formal recognition was not granted until 1863.

3. Paraguay

The province of Paraguay separated from the Viceroyalty and established its own '*Junta*' (Government) in 1811, maintaining a '*modus vivendi*' of '*de facto*' independence until it was recognised as an independent State by the Argentine Confederation in 1852.

The city of Asuncion, founded in 1536, had been the starting point from which the Spanish colonial process in the Rio de la Plata irradiated, demonstrating a fast-growing development and for a long while surpassing the importance of Buenos Aires. On the other hand, natives that had been colonised by Jesuits held large agricultural ventures and were part of what was then called 'the *Guaraní* Empire'.

Based on this expanding clout of Asuncion, the Governor of Paraguay ignored the invitation by the Buenos Aires *Junta* in 1810 to follow its same policy. The military expedition sent by Buenos Aires failed to make this province embrace the revolution that irradiated from Buenos Aires. The people of Asuncion overthrew the Governor and established a *Junta* that declared independence. Afterwards, a diplomatic mission sent by the Buenos Aires *Junta* failed in its attempt to integrate this territory to the United Provinces of Rio de La Plata, and signed a Convention on 12 October 1811 with the Paraguayan *Junta* whereby the independence of Paraguay from Buenos Aires was recognised until such time as a General Congress could be convened. However, at the time of the Congress, Paraguay refused to send representatives to Buenos Aires.

Finally, in 1842, Paraguay proclaimed its independence from the United Provinces of Rio de La Plata[74] which recognised it through a Declaration

[72] This last recognition was formally made before the Parliament. But as early as 1823 Great Britain had appointed a general consul in Argentina; Díaz Cisneros, *Derecho Internacional Público*, p. 635. Also E. O. Acevedo, *La Independencia de Argentina* (Madrid: Mapfre, 1992).

[73] Díaz Cisneros, *Derecho Internacional Público*, p. 137.

[74] Lynch, *Las Revoluciones*, p. 121.

issued in Asuncion on 17 July 1852[75] and approved by the Congress of Paraná through an Act dated 4 June 1856.[76]

4. Bolivia

In spite of the military campaigns sent by the Government of Buenos Aires, the provinces of the Alto Peru (Cochabamba, La Paz, La Plata and Potosí) remained under Spanish rule until 1824. The United Provinces of Rio de la Plata sent[77] a delegation in order to invite them to send representatives to the General Constitutional Congress, making it clear that even though they had always been a part of the United Provinces, they were 'free to decide their own fate, as they deemed suitable to their interests and their happiness'.[78]

On 25 May 1825, an Assembly of representatives from all four provinces of Alto Peru convened in Chuquisaca, and on 6 August it declared its independence and established the Republic of Bolivia, named after the Liberator Simón Bolívar.[79]

Following the declaration of independence, Bolivia annexed territories such as Tarija that, in the light of *uti possidetis* of 1810, were to belong to the United Provinces of Rio de la Plata.[80] Argentinian diplomats,[81] alleging the *uti possidetis* of 1810, obtained a declaration acknowledging the right of the United Provinces of Rio de la Plata over Tarija from Simón Bolívar.[82] However, even though the United Provinces took diplomatic action, and having gone so far as to threaten Bolivia with the use of force,

75 *República Argentina, Tratados*, p. 84. This Declaration and others similar to it made by the envoy of the Emperor of Brazil at Asuncion, on 14 September 1844, were 'confirmed and ratified' by provision 5 of the Argentine-Brazilian Treaty of Peace, Trade and Navigation signed on 7 March 1856; see its text in *República Argentina, Tratados*, p. 428.

76 *República Argentina, Tratados*, p. 87.

77 By an Act of 9 May 1825, Generals Carlos María de Alvear and José Miguel Díaz Vélez were sent as such a delegation. See *República Argentina, Registro Nacional*, vol. II, pp. 77–8.

78 Art. 4 of the Act of 9 May 1825.

79 V. G. Quesada, *Historia Diplomática Hispano-Americana* (Buenos Aires, 1918), p. 291. See also E. de Gandia, *Nueva Historia de América*, (Buenos Aires: Claridad, 1946); Lynch, *Las Revoluciones*, p. 313.

80 The territories included by article 4 of the Act of 9 May 1825, by which the independence of Bolivia was declared, were exclusively the four provinces of Alto Peru, with their boundaries as fixed by the King of Spain (*uti possidetis* of 1810).

81 Carlos María de Alvear and José Miguel Díaz Vélez were appointed by virtue of the Act passed on 9 May 1825, which authorised them to settle any difficulty that could emerge in relation to the freedom of the four provinces of the Alto Peru with General Bolívar.

82 Letter dated 6 November 1825. See C. Díaz Cisneros, *Límites de la República Argentina* (Buenos Aires: Desalma, 1944), p. 81.

Bolivia maintained control over the territory of Tarija and did not accept the *uti possidetis* of 1810 that it had recognised in other cases.[83]

5. Uruguay

The eastern bank of the Rio de la Plata, the present Eastern Republic of Uruguay, had been occupied by Spain and Portugal successively. A Spanish '*adelantado*', Juan Díaz de Solís had discovered the Rio de la Plata in 1516. However, Spain and Portugal alternatively exercised control in the 'Eastern Strip'. This led to the conclusion of several treaties. Portugal, with the support of Britain and France, sought to establish its southern boundary at the Rio de la Plata instead of the Uruguay River in order to prevent Spanish control over both banks of the river and consequently the right to exclusive navigation.[84]

Altercations followed until 1777 when peace was signed in the treaty of San Ildefonso which granted Spain sole and absolute control over the Rio de la Plata and part of the eastern bank of the Uruguay River. It also returned Colonia del Sacramento to Spain.[85] That was the last boundary treaty signed by both Crowns in South America.[86]

The Spanish control over the Eastern Strip ceased in 1814 when Montevideo capitulated after three years of being under siege by the land and maritime forces of Buenos Aires, who counted on the collaboration of the people in arms who were followers of General Antonio Gervasio de Artigas. Disagreements with the Government of Buenos Aires gave a strong impulse to the Eastern Strip's aspirations for autonomy. Nevertheless in 1816, Portuguese troops invaded the territory which then was annexed to Portugal and Brazil under the name of '*Provincia Cisplatina*' in 1821.

In 1825, the Eastern Strip Congress requested its reincorporation into the United Provinces of Rio de la Plata, which was accepted by the Argentine Congress. This gave rise to a declaration of war by Brazil on 10 December 1825.[87] In spite of its military success, both at land and at sea,

[83] Díaz Cisneros, *Límites de la República*, p. 82.

[84] Treaty of Lisboa, dated 7 May 1681 (see its text in Calvo, *Colección Completa de los Tratados*, Vol. I., p. 183.); Treaty of Madrid, dated 13 January 1750 (see its text in A. Del Cantillo, *Tratados, Convenios y Declaraciones de Paz y Comercio que han hecho con las potencias extranjeras los monarcas españoles de la Casa de Borbón, desde el año 1700 hasta el día* (Madrid: Imp. de Alegria y Charlain, 1843), p. 400; Treaty 'El Pardo', *in* Del Cantillo, *ibid.*, p. 467. See also E. M. Narancio, *La Independencia de Uruguay* (Madrid: Mapfre, 1992).

[85] J. Galvez, *Rosas y la Libre Navegación de Nuestros Ríos* (Buenos Aires, Instituto Inv. J. M. de Rosas, 1944), p. 23.

[86] Text in Del Cantillo, *Tratados, Convenios y Declaraciones*, p. 537.

[87] Lynch, *Las Revoluciones*, p. 104.

the Government of the United Provinces accepted the mediation by the British Government, which resulted in the conclusion of the preliminary Peace Convention of Rio de Janeiro on 27 August 1828.[88] The Peace Convention declared the independence of the Eastern Republic of Uruguay under the guarantee of Argentina and Brazil,[89] which in turn was 'confirmed and ratified' by article 3 of the Treaty of Peace, Friendship, Trade and Navigation between Argentina and Brazil signed in Paraná on 7 March 1856.[90]

The Treaty of 1863 between Spain and Argentina established that local debts had *ipso facto* been transferred to Argentina upon the change of sovereignty.[91]

D. *The General Captaincy of Guatemala*

This General Captaincy was comprised of what is today the territory of Honduras, El Salvador, Costa Rica, Guatemala, Nicaragua, Belize[92] and part of Mexico.[93] At the beginning of the nineteenth century, it was divided in five intendancies for administrative purposes: Leon (Nicaragua), Comayagua (Honduras), San Salvador and Ciudad Real de Chiapas. It also included the provinces of Guatemala and Costa Rica.[94]

Towards the end of the colonial period, the administrative unity disrupted, and the Captaincy was divided into two independent districts,[95] one having its seat in Guatemala City and the other in the city of Leon,

[88] 'Convencion Preliminar de Paz', *in República Argentina, Tratados*, pp. 411–20. See Armas Pfirter, 'Le Tribunal arbitral', pp. 540–66.

[89] Arts. 1–3. [90] *República Argentina, Tratados*, p. 427.

[91] O'Connell, *The Law of State Succession*, p. 176.

[92] The establishment of the British colony of Belize, in northeast Guatemala, was recognised by Spain following the peace treaty of Paris signed on 31 May 1727. In September of 1798, a battle took place where the Spanish ships tried to repel Belize intruders without success. This event was used to justify Britain's right of conquest, even when that State forwent the territories conquered during the war by means of a treaty signed in Amiens in 1802. Starting the moment of its independence in 1821, Guatemala began to claim sovereignty over Belize's territory. See C. Meléndez, *La Independencia de Centroamérica* (Madrid: Mapfre, 1993), p. 21. In 1850, the United States recognised Belize as a British territory by the Clayton-Bulwer Treaty. Finally, in 1859, the United Kingdom and Guatemala defined the existing boundaries between the British possession (Belize) and Guatemala. Nowadays Belize is an independent State recognised by Guatemala. However, there still remains a dispute over a part of that territory. See A. Herrante, *La Cuestión de Belice. Estudio Histórico-Jurídico de la Controversia* (Guatemala, 2000).

[93] Nowadays, the province of Chiapas.

[94] Meléndez, *La Independencia de Centroamérica*, p. 14.

[95] These were called '*diputaciones provinciales*' [provincial deputy administrations].

Nicaragua.[96] This subdivision had consequences at the time of independence, favouring the dismemberment of Central America.[97]

As we shall see, the administrative divisions within the General Captaincy maintained their identities from the start, although they made several attempts to give rise to a single unit: the Federation, the Union (or Confederation), the Republic, the *República Mayor* [Major Republic] and the United States of Central America. Nevertheless, it must be pointed out that some of the associations entailed transferring the conduct of foreign affairs to a central government.[98]

Since the beginning of the nineteenth century, several seditious acts, conspiracies and revolutionary movements took place in Central America aimed at achieving emancipation from Spain and establishing a State which would comprise all the provinces or dependencies that were part of the General Captaincy of Guatemala.[99]

Independence ideals which were spreading throughout all the Spanish dependencies in the Americas, particularly those geographically close to each other,[100] led the General Captaincy of Guatemala to declare its independence on 15 September 1821, with the former Captain General Gabino Gainza as the head of the new government. These developments did not satisfy some intendancies, and thus as a result, decided to unite with Mexico instead.[101]

Upon the proposal made by General Iturbide[102] that all dependencies within the former General Captaincy of Guatemala be integrated into the Mexican Empire, and following a controversial referendum, Gainza agreed on the annexation of Mexico on 5 January 1822. This triggered a

[96] The first one had authority over Chiapas (presently Mexico), Guatemala, El Salvador, Comayagua (Honduras); the second over Nicaragua and Costa Rica.

[97] Meléndez, *La Independencia de Centroamérica*, p. 15.

[98] As a result, none of the aforementioned regimes can be considered as a confederation in the sense accepted by political science. The arguments offered in footnote 55 also apply here. In contra, see Accioly, *Manual de Direito Internacional*, p. 18.

[99] L. Moreno, *Historia de las Relaciones Interestatales de Centroamérica* (Madrid: Compañía Ibero-Americana de Publicaciones, 1928); Calderón Quijano; Morales Padrón, 'Historia de las Naciones', p. 427.

[100] News of the independence of Mexico, proclaimed by Iturbide on 24 February 1821 at Iguala, had attracted the adhesion of certain dependencies from the Captaincy General of Guatemala, mainly Chiapas. As a consequence, supporters of the emancipation from Spain proposed Captain General Gabino Gainza to imitate Mexico's action.

[101] The Governors of Honduras and Nicaragua, Gainza's opponents, did not send delegates to the Constitutional Assembly, and decided that those dependencies would be integrated into Mexico. As Chiapas had adhered to the Iguala Plan, it thus remained a part of Mexico.

[102] Emperor of Mexico.

civil war which resulted in many provinces declaring their own independence. In spite of resistance, integration with the Mexican Empire was imposed on the San Salvador *Intendencia.* However, after the abdication of Iturbide, and as the internal struggle unravelled in certain regions, the provinces of Central America, with the exception of Chiapas (as we explain *infra*) regained their independence on 29 March 1823.[103]

On 1 July 1823, the representatives of the provinces of Central America gathered in a Congress proclaiming their absolute independence from Spain, Mexico and from any other power, and thus establishing themselves as a sovereign nation. The Central America Federation[104] was comprised of five States: Costa Rica, Nicaragua, Honduras, El Salvador and Guatemala.[105]

In August 1824, Mexico recognised the Federation. Colombia did so in March 1825 and United States in December of that year.[106]

The *Intendencia* of Chiapas comprised three dependencies: Ciudad Real, Tuxtla and Soconusco. Ciudad Real was the first to adopt a position in favour of its incorporation into Mexico. For this reason, the Mexican Regency passed an act dated 16 January 1822 deciding the integration of Chiapas into the Empire of Mexico. In 1824, the Government (*Junta*) of Chiapas declared that that province was incorporated into Mexico. Tuxtla and Soconusco followed, albeit with some interruptions. In May of 1824, the inhabitants of Soconusco were in favour of its incorporation into Mexico. However, on 24 July it was reincorporated into Guatemala, and on 18 August, the Federal Congress of Guatemala decreed its reincorporation. This spurred protests by the authorities of Ciudad Real and Mexico. Only in September of 1842, was the whole *Intendencia*, including Soconusco, made a part of the Mexican territory, following its occupation by Mexican armed forces.[107]

The existence of rivalries and jurisdictional disputes between the various dependencies led to the dismemberment of the Federation. Although Costa Rica remained neutral throughout these events, the impossibility of maintaining constitutional relations with the Federal Government forced

[103] Meléndez, *La Independencia de Centroamérica*, p. 18.

[104] In the beginning it was called United Provinces of Central America. By the Constitution of 22 November 1824, the new Republic was named the 'Federation of Central America' and it was also called the 'Federal Republic of Central America.'

[105] Chiapas was considered as a State by the new Constitution, if it decided to join the newly born nation of its own volition. That, however, never happened.

[106] Moreno, *Historia de las Relaciones Interestatales;* Calderón Quijano and Morales Padrón, 'Historia de las Naciones', p. 427.

[107] Meléndez, *La Independencia de Centroamérica*, p. 18.

Costa Rica to resume the exercise of sovereignty on 1 April 1829. This measure was only temporary, as Costa Rica rejoined the Federation in 1831.

In 1830, with a new Head of State, the Federation was recomposed, and a period of stability began which was to last only eight years. In 1838, taking advantage of the political crisis the Government of Guatemala was facing, several departments united in the State of Los Altos, organised under a provisional government. The Federal Congress legitimated this short-lived new political entity.

On the other hand, on 30 April 1838, Nicaragua broke the Federal Pact, declaring itself a free, sovereign and independent State. Honduras and Costa Rica followed, declaring their independence on 18 October and 14 November 1838, respectively. Therefore, by 2 February 1839 and due to the fact that the federal authority could not be re-established, the Federal Government became vacant and the Federal Pact disintegrated. The State of Guatemala regained its independence on 17 April 1839, and on 27 January 1840 it forced the State of Los Altos to re-join Guatemala.

By 1839, the Federal Republic of Central America had disintegrated.[108] In spite of its efforts to uphold the Federation, on 18 February 1841 El Salvador adopted its Constitution, declaring itself sovereign and independent as well.

In 1848, each of the Central American countries assumed their full sovereignty,[109] in spite of continuing attempts by some leaders to reconstruct the Federation.[110]

Thus, on 17 March 1842, the representatives of the Governments of El Salvador, Honduras and Nicaragua met and agreed on the foundations of the union, including perpetual alliance of all three States, and on the creation of a provisional government, leaving it open to the possibility that the

108 Some authors take 30 May 1838 as the date on which the Federation disintegrated. That day the Federal Congress declared that all States part of the Federal Republic of Central America remained free to choose their new constitutions and form of government. See Calderón Quijano and Morales Padrón, 'Historia de las Naciones', p.602. But the International Court of Justice (I.C.J.) refers to the period between 1821–39 as '. . . the time of the Federal Republic of Central America' (*Land, Island and Maritime Frontier Dispute (El Salvador/Honduras: Nicaragua intervening), Judgment of 11 September 1992, I.C.J. Reports 1992*, p. 395, para. 56).

109 C. Meléndez, *La Independencia de Centroamérica*, p. 242. Guatemala was declared an independent Republic by a Decree dated 21 March 1847. See Herrante, *La Cuestión de Belice*, p. 3.

110 One of the main reasons for this was that, upon the dissolution of the Federation, the new republics were afraid of an intervention by foreign armed forces, attracted by the geopolitical interest of the region – the prospect of building an inter-oceanic canal.

States of Guatemala, Costa Rica and Los Altos might follow with voluntary integration. On 27 July 1842, a Constitution (Permanent Pact for a Central America Confederation) was adopted. This established a new political entity named the 'Central American Confederation', which was conformed to by Honduras, El Salvador and Nicaragua.[111]

On 7 October 1842, Guatemala, Honduras, Nicaragua and El Salvador concluded a defence alliance, called the '*Pacto de la Unión*' [Union Pact], whereby the four States recognised their respective sovereignty and independence but also committed themselves to act jointly in the event of foreign invasion or hostilities against the territory of Central America.

On 15 October 1889, the States of Central America (Guatemala, Honduras, El Salvador, Nicaragua and Costa Rica) signed the Pact for the Provisional Union of the States of Central America, declaring the political union of those States under the name of 'Republic of Central America'.[112] However, on 22 June 1890, a *coup d'état* took place in El Salvador, derived from an armed conflict between some of the States, and made it impossible to set up the confederation they had agreed upon.

On 20 June 1895, the presidents of Honduras, Nicaragua and El Salvador signed the Amapala Pact, a union pact whereby a new political entity was created: the 'Major Republic of Central America'. It was decided that the union would be named the 'Republic of Central America', once Guatemala and Costa Rica had voluntarily joined the union. The member States did not withdraw their autonomy and independence in the management of internal affairs, but a Central Government (the '*Dieta*')[113] was empowered to manage the foreign affairs. The first States to recognise the new entity were Costa Rica and the United States.

On 15 June 1897, Costa Rica, Guatemala and the *Dieta*, on behalf of the Major Republic, signed the Central America Union Treaty establishing that the Major Republic, Guatemala and Costa Rica, constituted a single nation, namely the 'Republic of Central America'. Both Guatemala and Costa Rica, as well as the Major Republic member States, retained their independence, with some restrictions provided for in the treaty. Their unification was aimed mainly at harmonising the conduct of foreign relations through a single entity.

[111] Costa Rica adhered later, with many conditions and reservations, which in fact meant the impossibility of effective incorporation. Guatemala never adhered, due to internal opposition to the union.

[112] Article 2 gave the union a provisional character, unifying the external representation of the States so that other nations should treat and recognise it as a single entity.

[113] Its national emblems were the same that those of the former Federation.

In 1898, a Constitutional National Assembly was convened and the new Constitution was adopted, which changed the name to 'United States of Central America'. It was adopted by the representatives of Honduras, Nicaragua and El Salvador. These States established a sovereign and independent Federation while at the same time they remained autonomous in the management of their internal affairs, in all respects not delegated to the national State. The constitution of the United States of Central America entered into force on 1 November 1898; but a military insurrection followed in El Salvador, resulting in the seizure of the presidency and the decision to leave the Federation. After that, the President of Nicaragua announced his decision also to leave the United States of Central America. As only Honduras remained part of the Federation, its dissolution was decreed on 30 November 1898.

Central America is an interesting case, as it presents instances of emancipation, secession, union or unification and dissolution or dismemberment, a phenomenon similar to the case of Great Colombia, as seen above. Shortly after its emancipation, the General Captaincy of Guatemala was broken up, maintaining the previous administrative divisions established by Spain. The emancipation gave rise to five newly independent States, albeit with some territorial losses resulting from incorporation into another State. This can be seen in the case of Chiapas, which could be characterised as an instance of secession followed by incorporation by another State, in the sense that there was the separation of part of the territory of a State (Guatemala) without the consent of its federal government, with the purpose of becoming integrated into another existing State (Mexico). Later on, some of the newly independent States united in confederations (Federation of Central America, Central American Union, Major Republic of Central America, Unites States of Central America), which also, in the end, dissolved.[114]

E. *The Viceroyalty of Peru and the General Captaincy of Chile*

The Viceroyalty of Peru and the General Captaincy of Chile achieved their independence as a result of the emancipation campaign that had begun towards the end of the eighteenth century, giving birth to the

[114] The I.C.J. refers to the 'disintegration' of the Federal Republic of Central America in 1839. *Land, Island and Maritime Frontier Dispute (El Salvador/Honduras: Nicaragua intervening), Judgment of 11 September 1992, I.C.J. Reports 1992*, pp. 380–1, para. 29. Barboza describes the case of the Central American Federation in 1898 as an example of 'dissolution'. Barboza, *Derecho Internacional Público*, p. 171.

newly independent States of Chile (1818) and Peru (1821).[115] Unlike other Viceroyalties and General Captaincies,[116] dismemberment did not take place in either of the two. Nevertheless, territorial changes did occur as a result of acquisitions or losses of territory.

F. Main insular dependencies

1. Haiti and the Dominican Republic

The first vice royalty in Spanish America had its seat in the Caribbean island named '*Hispaniola*' by Columbus and then changed to the 'Island of Santo Domingo'.[117]

In 1679, the French occupied the western sector of the island. As a consequence, in 1777, the boundaries between both colonies were defined by the Aranjuez Treaty. However, Spain finally withdrew from the eastern sector of the island in 1795 through the Basilea Treaty.[118] The conclusion of the Treaty gave rise to incidents among the inhabitants from both sides of the island, due to their deep cultural differences.[119] France did not exercise effective control over its sector for eight years. When it finally tried to take control, it was impeded by the Haitian revolution,[120] conducted by former slaves who were determined to emancipate themselves from France, which had occupied the Spanish Santo Domingo since the beginning of 1801.[121]

The Constitution adopted in 1801 stated that the whole island of Santo Domingo was part of the French Empire, although ruled by special laws.[122]

[115] Lynch, *Las Revoluciones*, p. 159.

[116] On the contrary, we could mention an attempt of unification between Peru and Bolivia, with the constitution of the short-lived Peruvian-Bolivian Confederation in 1836, which was to dissolve in 1839. See Boersner, *Relaciones Internacionales*, p. 102.

[117] It was the seat of the *Real Audiencia* of Santo Domingo.

[118] J. D Balcácer and M. A. García, *La Independencia Dominicana* (Madrid, Mapfre, 1992), p. 21.

[119] The 'Dominicans', of Spanish influence, were the inhabitants of the eastern part of the island.

[120] The revolution was led by Toussaint Louverture, a former slave from the French part of the island.

[121] Their goal was the unification of Santo Domingo so as to face France, in case it tried to regain control of the island. See Balcácer and García, *La Independencia Dominicana*, p. 23.

[122] The Haitian leader Toussaint Louverture proclaimed the unity and indivisibility of the island, against the Dominicans' wishes. Balcácer and García, *La Independencia Dominicana*, p. 29.

The armed forces that were sent by France were able to regain control over only the eastern sector (the Spanish sector) with the support of the Dominicans, while the western sector (the French sector) declared its independence on 1 January 1804 and proclaimed the Republic of Haiti.[123]

The eastern sector of the island underwent numerous changes throughout the nineteenth century: restitution of the Spanish colonial rule (1809),[124] declaration of independence (1821),[125] an attempt to become part of the Colombian Confederation,[126] annexation to the Republic of Haiti (1822–1844),[127] and effective independence and the establishment of the First Republic (1844–1861).[128]

In connection with the notion of secession, the 1844 events are of interest. Until then, Spain had fruitlessly attempted to recover the eastern sector of the island, which was under Haitian domination. Dominicans, afflicted by the graveness of the social and economic situation, organised themselves in order to achieve their separation from the Republic of Haiti and adopted the Dominican Separation Act on 16 January 1844. On 27 February, the separation was made effective, the new Dominican Republic was proclaimed, and a Central Governmental '*Junta*' was established, followed by the appointment of a President.[129]

The declaration of Dominican independence provoked Pierrot, the new Haitian dictator, to instigate an armed invasion as a reaction to the protection that the Dominican Government tried to obtain from the United States, Britain, France and Spain. In 1849, Haiti, under the government of Faustino Soulongue, invaded the Dominican Republic. After strong combats, the Dominicans defeated the Haitian invaders, with the indirect support of France, interested in re-establishing its influence over the Island.[130] Nevertheless, taking into account that Spain also had

[123] After a violent Haitian attempt to seize the Spanish part of the island (1805) and due to domestic trouble, the Republic of Haiti broke into two separate States: a monarchy in the north, and a republic in the south. Balcácer and García, *La Independencia Dominicana*, p. 32.

[124] By the Treaty of Paris of 1814, France returned its former possessions in the eastern side of Santo Domingo Island to Spain; Balcácer and García, *La Independencia Dominicana*, p. 43.

[125] In the eastern side of the island, a new republic was established, called '*Estado Independiente de la Parte Española de Haití*' [Independent State of the Spanish Part of Haiti]. Balcácer and García, *La Independencia Dominicana*, p. 47.

[126] The new State had proclaimed its independence under the protection of Gran Colombia, which was why the flag of that federation was raised in the city of Santo Domingo.

[127] Balcácer and García, *La Independencia Dominicana*, p. 54.

[128] *Ibid.*, p. 67.

[129] *Ibid.*

[130] Boersner, *Relaciones Internacionales*, p. 100.

interests in the Dominican Republic,[131] in 1861 the Dominican Government itself requested its integration with Spain. However, in 1865 the Second Dominican Republic was restored.[132]

With regard to private rights, the General Attorney of the British Crown issued an opinion in 1861 on the mining rights of a British subject in the Dominican part of the Island which they enjoyed before the Spanish annexation.[133] He stated that as the British Government had made no special stipulation in favour of British subjects residing in the Dominican Republic when recognising the annexation of that country by Spain, he was entitled to apply its laws and introduce changes to the use of mineral property as well as tax regulations on imports and exports.[134]

2. Cuba and Puerto Rico

In the early nineteenth century, while all other Spanish dependencies in America were struggling for independence, Puerto Rico maintained its ties with the metropolitan State. Cuba was administered in the form of a General Captaincy while Puerto Rico was ruled by a Governor until the creation of the *Intendencia* of Puerto Rico in 1811. By the Treaty of Paris (1898), Spain withdrew its rights over Cuba, thus legitimising the American intervention, and ceded[135] the island of Puerto Rico to the United States.[136]

However, it was to be only in 1902 that Cuba would achieve its independence and adopt the republican system of government. Although Cuba faced insurrections, invasions, interventions, occupations, attempts to subsume it into some other State (the United States, Mexico and Colombia), and annexation by the United States,[137] it was a case of emancipation, presenting instances of secession or dismemberment.[138]

131 G. Connell-Smith, *Los Estados Unidos y la América Latina* (Mexico: Fondo de Cultura Económica, 1977), p. 116.

132 Balcácer and García, *La Independencia Dominicana*, p. 161.

133 The mentioned rights had been acquired during the existence of the Republic. But after the annexation, the mines were considered to be the property of the State, according to Spanish Law.

134 Opinion of 16 November 1861, reproduced in O'Connell, *The Law of State Succession*, p. 306.

135 In respect of the cession of Puerto Rico, on the nationality of the inhabitants, see O'Connell, *The Law of State Succession*, p. 249.

136 See T. E. Skidmore and P. H. Smith, *Historia Contemporánea de América Latina* (Barcelona: Critica, 1996), p. 331.

137 García, L. Navarro, *La Independencia de Cuba* (Madrid: Mapfre, 1992).

138 It was a controversy between the United States and Spain during the negotiations of the Treaty of Paris of 1898 concerning the loans charged on the Cuban revenues. See

Unlike other cases, Puerto Rico was the result of cession. In 1952, it was given the status of a free associated State by the United States (Commonwealth of Puerto Rico).[139]

G. *The Viceroyalty of Brazil*

After several unsuccessful conspiracies, Brazil declared its independence from Portugal on 7 September 1822, giving rise to a newly independent State[140] that was immediately recognised by third powers.[141] As seen above, the Viceroyalty of Brazil had been, until 1815, divided into general captaincies and subordinate governments. After that date, it was ruled by a dual monarchy. Nevertheless, it must be highlighted that the independence of the Portuguese colony in South America did not give rise to dismemberment. Therefore, the administrative divisions of the former viceroyalty were the basis for the boundaries of the State of Brazil. Secession is a phenomenon that cannot be found[142] in the emancipation from Portugal.

In relation to the above-mentioned, it is interesting to point out that in 1827[143] the Attorney General of the British Crown expressed that 'a treaty of 1785 between Portugal and Algiers "appears to have been framed with special reference to Portugal proper, without including Transatlantic Possessions", and for this reason it "could not be interpreted to extend to Brazil" . . .' Years before, he had held the opinion that 'a treaty of 1810 between England and Portugal respecting the verification of British goods in Brazilian ports did not confer similar rights on the Brazilian customs officials'; but '(a)t a later date he appears to have considered that certain other clauses of the same treaty applied to Brazil since he advised

O'Connell, *The Law of State Succession*, p. 171, and Moore, *Digest of International Law*, p. 355. As to the cession of Cuba, on the economic concessions and the nationality of the inhabitants, see O'Connell, *ibid.*, p. 112.

139 According to some authors, this does not mean separation nor integration, but a federation. See Calderón Quijano and Morales Padrón, 'Historia de las Naciones', p.746.

140 See Keen and Haynes, *A History of Latin America*, p. 174.

141 The first State that recognised Brazil was the United States in 1824. Portugal recognised it in 1825 by a treaty. De Albuquerque Mello, *Direito Internacional Público*, p. 809.

142 In June 1824, a separatist movement called Confederation of Ecuador emerged in Pernambuco, but it was repelled by the Emperor of Brazil. J. A. Calderón Quijano and F. A. Morales Padrón, 'Los Portugueses en América - Brasil', in *Enciclopedia Labor*, vol. V, 2nd edn, (Barcelona: Labor, 1962), p. 751.

143 At this time the sovereignty of Portugal and Brazil were united under the same Emperor, as a consequence of the personal union that had emerged in 1825.

on their interpretation with respect to British goods landed at Rio de Janeiro'.[144]

With regard to public debt, by virtue of the Treaty of Rio de Janeiro of 1825, Brazil succeeded Portugal in a portion of its debt 'as part of a general adjustment of financial arrangements'.[145]

IV. Special secession cases

The following situations do not constitute cases of emancipation of colonies and will be examined as special cases of secession, as they gave rise to the creation of a new State, although in almost every case, the newly independent entity was short-lived.

A. *Buenos Aires*[146]

The case of the Province of Buenos Aires is an interesting one. It was part of the United Provinces of Rio de la Plata until 1852 when it declared its independence. After a few years, on 11 November 1859, it re-joined what at that time was named the 'Argentine Republic', although demanding a revision of the 1853 Constitution in order to provide for the protection of its interests.[147]

1. The Argentine Confederation and the 1853 Constitution

After more than four decades of antagonism and internal struggle, the United Provinces of Rio de la Plata succeeded in establishing the 'Argentine Confederation' in 1852. However, as we have seen, one of the constituent provinces, Buenos Aires, refused from the start to become part of the Confederation and became an independent State.

144 Opinions of 9 February 1827, 7 February 1823 and 1 February 1827, quoted by O'Connell, *The Law of State Succession*, p. 37.

145 O'Connell, *The Law of State Succession*, p. 160.

146 See R. Levene (ed.), *Historia de la Nación Argentina*, vol. VII, 2nd edn., (Buenos Aires: El Ateneo, 1947).

147 See a complete study about the consequences of the annexation and the mode of application of the clauses of safeguard included in the Argentine Constitution in J. A. Barberis, 'Los Tratados Internacionales Celebrados por la Confederación Argentina y la Constitución Nacional', *in* R. E. Vinuesa, (ed.), *Temas de Derecho Internacional – En Homenaje a Frida M. Pfirter de Armas Barea* (Buenos Aires: Fundación del Centro de Estudios Internacionales de Buenos Aires, 1989), p. 25. See also R. E. Vinuesa, 'The Application of Public International Law Rules to the Relations of Member States of a Federal State: The Argentine Case', *in* M. Bothe and R. E. Vinuesa (eds.), *International Law and Municipal Law* (Berlin, Duncker: Humblot, 1982), p. 195.

The Confederation adopted its Constitution in 1853,[148] and several trade and navigation treaties were concluded, some of which still remain in force.

2. The incorporation of Buenos Aires

A desire for unity had always been present and, on 11 November 1859, the State of Buenos Aires re-joined the Confederation through the ratification of the San José de Flores Pact that had been signed the previous day.[149]

Nevertheless, as the State of Buenos Aires disagreed with some clauses of the 1853 Constitution, the Pact provided that Buenos Aires would, in order to become a part of the Argentine Confederation, expressly have to accept and formally swear submission to the National Constitution. Previously, in order to do this, a special Convention would have to be convened to examine the need to introduce amendments. Should the Convention decide the need for amendments, the Government of the Confederation would then convene a Constituent Assembly.

3. The 1860 constitutional reform

The provisions of the National Constitution to which Buenos Aires objected were those concerning the international treaties concluded by the Confederation, in particular those regarding the free navigation of rivers, slavery and nationality.[150]

[148] The Constitution became binding on 1 May 1853. For the present analysis, it is interesting to emphasise those clauses concerning international treaties included in arts. 27 and 31. The first one states that: 'The Federal Government is under the obligation to strengthen its relationships of peace and trade with foreign powers, by means of treaties in accordance with the principles of public law laid down by this Constitution' (unofficial translation). On the other hand, art. 31 provides for a legal hierarchy for national law vs. provincial law: 'This Constitution, the laws of the Confederation enacted by Congress in pursuance thereof, and treaties with foreign powers, are the supreme law of the Nation; and the authorities of each Province are bound thereby, notwithstanding any provision to the contrary included in the provincial laws or constitutions' (unofficial translation). By this provision, international treaties were made a part of the 'supreme law of the Nation' and its standing was above that of the provincial regulations.

[149] *República Argentina, Tratados*, p. 445. See the ratification by the State of Buenos Aires at p. 450.

[150] In this sense, Lucio V. Mansilla, a representative at Santa Fe Constitutional Congress, wrote to Mariano Varela on 19 September 1860 that the issue of treaties signed by the Confederation was 'the most serious obstacle the Convention came upon' and held that the agreements that were 'unfair and onerous from the national point of view', entered into by the Confederation, were not acceptable to Buenos Aires. Universidad Nacional de La Plata, *Reforma Constitucional de 1860 – Textos y Documentos Fundamentales* (La Plata, 1961), p. 555.

As to the abolition of slavery, the Confederation had signed with Brazil, on 14 December 1857, a treaty for the extradition of slaves. The treaty was approved by the Argentine National Congress and ratified by President Urquiza, although the instruments of ratification were never exchanged. With respect to this issue, Buenos Aires proposed the addition of the following phrase to the text of article 15 of the Constitution: 'All slaves who by any means enter the territory of the Nation shall be free due to that mere fact.'[151] The new text of article 15 prevented the extradition Treaty with Brazil from ever coming into force. The exchange of instruments of ratification was never completed.

Apart from that, Buenos Aires disagreed with the Nationality Act passed by the Confederation in 1857, and consequently did not consider that the terms of a treaty signed in 1859 with Spain regarding this issue were appropriate.[152] Therefore, it proposed to amend the constitutional clause which conferred upon the National Congress the power to pass an act on nationality to introduce the requirement that such an act would be 'based on the principle of natural nationality'.[153] The new text contradicted the terms of the 1859 treaty with Spain, so Argentina had to negotiate a new treaty with Spain, which was signed on 21 September 1863.[154] The Preamble to this Treaty made reference to the inconveniences which had arisen from article 7 of the previous Treaty, which made the *jus sanguinis* criterion applicable in some cases. The preamble also stated that the incorporation of Buenos Aires into the Confederation 'renders it necessary to amend' such an article.[155]

4. The interpretation of article 31 of the Constitution

The greatest difficulty to Buenos Aires was posed by article 31 of the Constitution, which established that provincial authorities were bound to conform to treaties as the supreme law of the nation, while Buenos

[151] E. Ravignani, *Asambleas Constituyentes Argentinas*, vol. IV (Buenos Aires: Instituto de Investigaciones Históricas de la Facultad de Filosofía y Letras. Universidad de Buenos Aires, 1937), p. 774.

[152] Ravignani, *Asambleas Constituyentes*, p. 875.

[153] Former art. 64 (para. 11) and present art. 75 (para. 12), Ravignani, *Asambleas Constituyentes*, p. 782.

[154] *República Argentina, Tratados*, p. 71.

[155] '. . . with a spirit to remove all difficulties regarding performance of article 7 of the Recognition, Peace and Friendship Treaty signed in Madrid on 9 July 1859, and bearing in mind that restoration of the Argentine unity, happily achieved by virtue of the reincorporation of the Province of Buenos Aires, renders it necessary to amend that very article . . .' (unofficial translation), *República Argentina, Tratados*, p. 71.

Aires contested the treaties on freedom of navigation signed by the Confederation during the period when Buenos Aires was not a part of it.

Agreement was reached on the inclusion of the following phrase at the end of the article: 'except for the Province of Buenos Aires, the treaties ratified after the Pact of 11th November 1859'.[156] Although the wording is unclear and may be subject to a number of interpretations, the most appropriate interpretation according to the object and purpose of the phrase was given by the Argentine Ministry of Foreign Affairs, which considered that, as to the Province of Buenos Aires, the concept 'supreme law of the Nation' comprises the Constitution, the statutes, and all treaties ratified after the Pact signed on 11 November 1859.

The Province of Buenos Aires not being bound by treaties ratified before that date was thus not under the obligations that resulted from, *inter alia*, the 1853 treaties which provided for freedom of navigation and the agreements signed with Brazil in 1856 and 1857.[157]

It has been argued that this interpretation implies a breach of the *pacta sunt servanda* rule with respect to France, the United Kingdom, the United States of America, Brazil and the other powers that signed treaties with the Confederation.[158] However, this case involves no breach of international law, since those treaties were signed by the Confederation and remained binding with respect to the territory it possessed at the time. As a result of article 31 *in fine*, those treaties would not apply to the territory of the Province of Buenos Aires. Thus, by virtue of this provision, the foreign States that had negotiated with the Confederation could not benefit from the incorporation of the State of Buenos Aires. It must be highlighted that such foreign States would neither benefit nor suffer prejudice from the

[156] Ravignani, *Asambleas Constituyentes*, p. 1048. It is worth remembering that the Pact of San Jose de Flores was signed on 10 November 1859 and ratified the following day. See *República Argentina, Tratados*, p. 445.

[157] This had special significance in the negotiation of the 1973 Treaty of Rio de la Plata between Argentina and Uruguay in relation with the neutralisation of the island Martín García and the freedom of navigation in the river. In relation with Martín García, the Argentine Confederation and Brazil had agreed, in 1856, to try to obtain the neutralisation of the island. But the Province of Buenos Aires did not agree to neutralise it. When the Treaty of Rio de la Plata was negotiated in the 1970s, the Argentine Ministry of Foreign Affairs maintained that the international obligations assumed by the Confederation before the Pact of 11 November 1859 could not be imposed upon Buenos Aires, thus they do not prevail in the territory of this Province, i.e., the Rio de la Plata. The same statement was maintained by the Ministry in relation with the freedom of navigation in the Rio de la Plata and the treaties signed before the Pact of 1859.

[158] M. A. Montes de Oca, *Lecciones de Derecho Constitucional*, vol. I (Buenos Aires: Imprenta y Litografía 'La Buenos Aires', 1927), p. 499.

incorporation of Buenos Aires. As their situation *vis-à-vis* the Confederation was not altered, no breach of the *pacta sunt servanda* rule can be said to have taken place.

The issue raised by the application of treaties signed by the Confederation within the territory of the Province of Buenos Aires was later incorporated into international law under the title of 'moving boundaries'. In principle, when a State expands its territory, treaties signed by that State are binding upon the newly acquired land. However, the rule does not apply when the annexed State (or the one which cedes part of its territory) and the annexing State agree to the contrary, or when the latter makes a unilateral declaration to that effect.[159] Article 31 *in fine* of the Constitution would be precisely the example of a result of an agreement made by virtue of the San Jose de Flores Pact and later expressed in the Constitutional Convention of 1860.[160]

With those amendments, fidelity to the revised Constitution was sworn to on 21 October 1860 by Buenos Aires,[161] thus complying with the agreement contained in the San Jose de Flores Pact. The texts of articles 15 and 31 have not been, in any other way, amended until the present day, and have been continuously in force, not having been affected by the 1949 and 1994 constitutional amendments.

B. Texas

As previously stated, at the time of the emancipation of the Viceroyalty of New Spain (1821), Texas (then *Tejas*) was part of Mexico.

Already in 1815, the United States, in an attempt to weaken the British influence in the area, pressed Spain to cede parts of its contiguous territory.[162] In fact, American President Madison had encouraged a rebellion by the Anglo-American settlers in West Florida, who proclaimed their independence[163] and requested to be annexed to the United States. In

[159] M. Udina, 'La succession des Etats quant aux obligations internationales autres que les dettes publiques', *Recueil des Cours* (1933-II), 699; E. J. Castren, 'Aspects recents de la succession d'Etats', *Recueil des Cours* (1951-I), 448; K. Doehring, 'The Scope of the Territorial Application of Treaties', *ZaöRV* (1967), 483. Also see the contribution of A. Zimmermann to this book.

[160] Barberis, 'Los Tratados Internacionales'; Ravignani, *Asambleas Constituyentes*, p. 33.

[161] *Universidad Nacional de La Plata*, p. 634.

[162] Boersner, *Relaciones Internacionales*, p. 52.

[163] The independence of the short-lived republic of West Florida was proclaimed on 26 September 1810. See I. J. Cox, 'The American Intervention in West Florida', *AHR* 17 (1912), 290–311.

1812, such a request was accepted, by the American Congress. In 1818, the Secretary of State proposed that Spain should sell the integrity of its territory in Florida to the United States. The Spanish Government accepted, subject to the condition that the United States withdraw all claims on Texas and agreed not to recognise the independence of the newly independent countries of Spanish America. The latter was not accepted by the United States but, taking into consideration that Florida had been occupied by an American expedition, Spain chose to cede Florida but with the guarantee of the integrity of Texas left to Spain.[164] Thus, both countries signed the Trans-Continental Treaty (Adams-Onis Treaty) whereby Mexico ceded the integrity of the territory of Florida to the United States and the latter recognised Spanish sovereignty over Texas.[165]

The reasons for the war against *Tejas* can be found both in the territorial expansion of the United States and in the slavery issue.[166] According to the 1820 Missouri Compromise, slavery was allowed in the United States only to the south of 36° N. Consequently, supporters of slavery advocated the annexation of Mexican territories, which would increase the number of representatives of pro-slavery States in the Congress of the Union.

The colonisation of Texas had begun in 1821 when Moses Austin, leader of a group of southern farmers and cattle breeders, negotiated an agreement with Mexico aimed at establishing thirty Anglo-American families in Texas, then inhabited by an indigenous population. In accordance with the terms of the agreement, the new inhabitants were to conform to Mexican laws, including the prohibition of slavery, a condition that was not complied with.[167]

In 1825, the Government of the United States resumed negotiations for the purchase of Texas and made several offers which were rejected by Mexico.

In 1830, the new Mexican Government imposed several measures for the protection of Mexican agriculture and industry and restricted Anglo-American immigration to Texas. It decreed that the region should be united to Coahuila in order to secure control of the territory, which triggered a rebellion among the Texans. Sam Houston organised a secessionist

164 Boersner, *Relaciones Internacionales*, p. 53.

165 The treaty was signed on 22 February 1918 and ratified in 1821. Furthermore, it provided for the release of Spanish debts amounting to the sum of five million dollars; Boersner, *Relaciones Internacionales*, p. 55.

166 See E. C. Barker, 'The Influence of Slavery in the Colonisation of Texas', *MVHR* 11 (1924), 3–36; L. G. Bugbee, 'Slavery in Early Texas II', *Political Science Quarterly* 13 (1898), 648–68.

167 The agreement was ratified in 1823. See Boersner, *Relaciones Internacionales*, p. 91.

revolution with the purpose of separating Texas from Mexico and annexing it to the United States.[168]

In 1836, taking advantage of the chaos reigning in the Mexican Government, originating in the approval of a centralist Constitution, Texans, with the assistance of their American neighbours,[169] rebelled against the Mexican authorities. Mexico tried to withstand the insurrection and sent armed forces commanded by General Santa Anna. On 2 May 1836, after battles in El Alamo, Goliad and San Jacinto, Texas declared its independence from Mexico and proclaimed the Republic of Texas.[170] When captured by the enemy, Santa Anna committed himself to withdrawing from combat, recognised the independence of Texas and accepted that the boundary between Mexico and Texas would be the 'Rio Grande' (Rio Bravo). However, once he was set free, Santa Anna claimed those agreements were null and void, as they had been signed under coercion.[171]

In spite of Houston's intention that Texas be annexed to the United States, the American Congress did not agree. Quite the contrary, in 1837 it decided to recognise Texas as an independent State instead,[172] and France and Britain followed suit.[173] However, the independence of Texas was to last only nine years (1836–1845).[174] Upset about the American rejection of its request for annexation, in October 1838 Texas withdrew such request and established commercial relations with Britain and France. This foreign presence led to a reconsideration of its decision by the United States Congress.[175]

[168] Boersner, *Relaciones Internacionales*, p. 92.

[169] E. C. Barker, 'President Jackson and the Texas Revolution', *AHR* 12 (1907), 788–809.

[170] Boersner, *Relaciones Internacionales*, p. 92. [171] *Ibid.*, pp. 92–3.

[172] Already in 1836, the suggestive pattern and colours of the Texas flag showed a wish for its incorporation into the United States. Even in September of 1836, the issue was submitted to popular referendum, the result being practically unanimous for the incorporation. See G. P. Garrison, 'The First Stage of the Movement for the Annexation of Texas', *AHR* 10 (1904), 72–96.

[173] The European Powers as well as the anti-slavery political party in the Union were against the purchase of Texas by the United States, for they did not want to admit a new State that would accept slavery. In fact, France and England hoped Mexico would sign a treaty with Texas whereby Texas would be bound not to be incorporated into the United States. But no treaty of this kind was signed. See Connell-Smith, *Los Estados Unidos*, p. 102. Furthermore, France and Great Britain tried to influence the Mexican Government to recognise the independence of Texas, but this too failed. See J. Smith, 'The Mexican Recognition of Texas', *AHR* 16 (1910), 36–55.

[174] During that time Texas celebrated many treaties with other countries, e.g. a treaty of commerce with the United States (1840).

[175] Boersner, *Relaciones Internacionales*, p. 93.

In March 1845, due to the victory of the democratic candidate James Polk (from the southern states), the Congress of the United States approved the annexation of Texas.[176] On 29 December 1845, Texas became the 28th State of the United States.

As Mexico was opposed to the annexation,[177] President Polk sent troops to Texas to deter any problem that might arise. Moreover, he unsuccessfully tried to sell the territories of California and New Mexico to Mexico, offering to take responsibility for the compensation to their citizens if Mexico accepted the Rio Grande (Rio Bravo) as the western boundary of Texas.[178] Faced with the American advance and refusing to step back, on 26 April 1846 the new Government of Mexico confronted the United States, giving rise to a war in which the United States would succeed.[179] As a result of the war, on 2 February 1848, both States signed the Guadalupe-Hidalgo Treaty, whereby United States confirmed its title over Texas and obtained the cession of the territory of Alta California and part of the territory of New Mexico.[180]

After examination, one may conclude that in 1836, the separation of Texas from Mexico against the will of the latter constituted a case of secession.[181] This conclusion stands, even though in 1845 the situation turned into incorporation, as Texas was annexed to the United States and then finally confirmed by Mexico, upon the latter's defeat.

With regard to the effects of secession on treaties, it is interesting to note that when the United States recognised the independence of Texas in 1840 it indicated that it considered the Treaty of Amity, Commerce and Navigation of 1831 with Mexico 'as binding on both the United States and the new State'.[182] Nevertheless, Texas did not agree with this view. In respect to the boundaries established by a treaty, it is worthwhile pointing out that in 1840 the boundary established by an 1828 treaty between the

176 Connell-Smith, *Los Estados Unidos*, p. 102.

177 Mexico broke off its relations with the United States to protest the resolution of annexation. See Boersner, *Relaciones Internacionales*, p. 94.

178 Connell-Smith, *Los Estados Unidos*, p. 104.

179 Skidmore and Smith, *Historia Contemporánea*, p. 245.

180 Later, in 1853, the United States consolidated its acquisition of the southern part of New Mexico and Arizona.

181 Boersner, *Relaciones Internacionales*, p. 92.

182 Moore, *Digest of International Law*, p. 343, quoted by O'Connell, *The Law of State Succession*, p. 33. O'Connell considers that this inconclusive precedent is contrary to the current practice over the nineteenth century 'in favour of the proposition that treaties of a parent do not bind a seceding State', O'Connell, *ibid.*, p. 33.

United States and Mexico was recognised as the boundary between the independent Texas and the United States.[183]

After the annexation of Texas in 1845, the United States considered 'that treaties with Texas had lapsed, and that Texas had become absorbed in the treaty system of the United States'.[184] France and Great Britain objected to this position.

Regarding the public debt, the British creditors of Mexico exchanged some correspondence with Texas in 1840. The view of the new State was that 'Mexico had violated its agreement with the settlers and had issued Texan bonds after Texas had declared its independence. But as an issue to be considered in the negotiation of a truce, Texas would as a voluntary concession undertake a fixed proportion of the debt acquired before 1845'.[185]

After the annexation of Texas, the United States discharged the Texan debt.[186] In 1854, Great Britain brought a claim before the Joint Commission established by virtue of the 1853 Claims Convention. Britain presented a claim on behalf of the British nationals who held unpaid Texan bonds.[187] Finally, the Congress of the United States decided that the Treasury would discharge the debt, with a considerable amount of money to be apportioned *pro rata* among the creditors.[188]

[183] *US* v. *Texas*, 143 U.S. 621 at p. 633, quoted by O'Connell, *The Law of State Succession*, p. 50.

[184] The attitude of Great Britain 'was based on a failure to recognise a true incorporation through the veil of quasi-federal union', O'Connell, *The Law of State Succession*, p. 26.

[185] O'Connell, *The Law of State Succession*, pp. 160–1.

[186] Cf. a memorandum of the US Government, quoted by O'Connell, *The Law of State Succession*, p. 156, note 4.

[187] Moore, J. B., *International Arbitrations*, vol. IV (1898), p. 3593.

[188] Moore, *Digest of International Law*, p. 347, quoted by O'Connell, *The Law of State Succession*, p. 156, note 4. With respect to the acquired rights in Texas's territory, in 1849 the British Queen's Advocate gave an opinion about the obligation of the United States to compensate a British company for a confiscation executed in 1836 by the Texan legislature. The confiscated land had been purchased by a company from Mexico. The negative answer given by the adviser was due to his considering that the company had not complied with some statutory requirements concerning land acquisition. See the Opinion of 25 July 1849 reproduced in O'Connell, *ibid.*, p. 299. But later, in another case, the same adviser considered that 'the failure to fulfil the conditions in question was not due to any fault of the claimants, and that the confiscation of their lands upon an alleged failure so to fulfil them would render the British Government competent to intervene on their behalf'. See the Opinion of 23 July 1839, reproduced in O'Connell, *ibid.*, pp. 296–7. See also p. 85.

C. Panama

By the end of the colonial period, Panama was part of the Viceroyalty of New Granada, together with the present territories of Colombia and Ecuador.

The first attempts to become emancipated from Spain were unsuccessful, e.g., those carried on in 1814 and 1819. The manifestations for independence took place in 1820, when Brigadier Ruiz Porras took office as head of the government.[189]

In 1821, representatives of General Iturbide proposed that Panama be annexed to Mexico, a State that had achieved its independence that same year. Advocates for the independence of Panama rejected the proposal and at the same time expressed that Panama would unite with Great Colombia, reiterating Panama's autonomy from all other Central American countries.[190]

After long discussions on whether Panama should become part of Peru or Great Colombia, Panama declared its independence on 28 November 1821,[191] although as part of Great Colombia.

Nevertheless, Panama showed ethnical, cultural and geographical characteristics that differentiated it from all other Colombian provinces.[192] This led to a number of secessionist insurrections throughout the nineteenth century.[193]

The possibility of building an inter-oceanic canal caught the attention of several foreign powers. In 1850, Britain and the United States agreed 'that neither the one nor the other will ever obtain or maintain for itself any exclusive control' over the canal to be built in Central America.[194] However, in 1901 both countries signed a new treaty[195] whereby the United Kingdom accepted that the United States would build and run the canal exclusively, as long as it guaranteed freedom of navigation for all nations.[196] The United States considered two possible sites for the

189 Calderón Quijano and Morales Padrón, 'Historia de las Naciones', p. 516.

190 *Ibid.*, p. 516.

191 D. Uribe Vargas, *Los ltimos Derechos de Colombia en el Canal de Panamá. El Tratado Uribe Vargas-Ozores* (Colombia: Universidad Nacional de Colombia, 1993), p. 16.

192 At that time, Panama was a quasi-autonomous province, given the great distances from Bogota and the poor communications. Skidmore and Smith, *Historia Contemporánea*, p. 352.

193 Boersner, *Relaciones Internacionales*, p. 147.

194 Clayton-Bulwer Treaty.

195 Hay-Pauncefote Treaty.

196 As a result of the Monroe Doctrine, the United States wanted to prevent any European intervention in America. It was then necessary to have the exclusive control over any inter-oceanic canal to be built there. See Boersner, *Relaciones Internacionales*, p. 146.

canal: Nicaragua and Panama. In June 1902, the Congress of the United States authorised the negotiation of concessions on the part of Colombia to build the canal in Panama. Thus, in January 1903, the United States and Colombia signed a treaty[197] which provided for Colombia's indefinite concession of an area surrounding the canal for United States' use, with an amount of money in exchange. In August 1903, the Colombian Congress rejected the treaty, considering it to be in violation of Colombian internal law and the sovereignty of the country.[198]

Faced with such a negative response, the Unites States Government took advantage of the restlessness among the people of Panama, resulting from the Colombian refusal to approve the construction of the canal, and supported a separatist rebellion that burst forth in Panama on 3 November 1903.[199] On 4 November 1903, Panama declared its independence, thus seceding from Colombia.

The United States recognised the newly independent State two days later, and immediately signed the Hay-Bunau-Varilla Treaty with Panama,[200] whereby Panama granted the perpetual use of a strip of territory surrounding the canal which started operations in 1914, in exchange for the payment of regular amounts of money.[201]

Colombia interpreted the American conduct in Panama as intervention. Nevertheless, in 1921 it concluded a treaty with the United States which granted 25 million dollars as reparation to Colombia.[202]

Finally, in 1979, a treaty between Panama and Colombia granted the latter the right of passage across the Panama Canal.[203]

Overall, Panama has undergone diverse scenarios throughout its history: its emancipation from Spain (1821), its integration into Great Colombia (1821) until its dismemberment (1829–1831), when it was incorporated into New Granada (later Colombia). It was in the twentieth century that Panama finally separated from Colombia, an event that may well be considered a true case of secession.

[197] Hay-Herran Treaty. [198] See Boersner, *Relaciones Internacionales*, p. 146.

[199] *Ibid.*, p. 147.

[200] Signed on 18 November 1903 and ratified by both States in February of 1904.

[201] Boersner, *Relaciones Internacionales*, p. 147. For a minute study of treaty regulations in force during the twentieth century, see M. Hartwig, 'Panama Canal', *in* R. Bernhardt (ed.), *Encyclopedia of Public International Law* 12 (Amsterdam: Elsevier/North-Holland, 1990), p. 282. See also J. E. Linares *Tratado concerniente a la Neutralidad Permanente y al Funcionamiento del Canal de Panamá, de un colonialismo rooseveltiano a un neocolonialismo senatorial* (Panama: Instituto de Estudios Políticos e Internacionales, 1983).

[202] Boersner, *Relaciones Internacionales*, p. 148.

[203] See Uribe Vargas, *Los ltimos Derechos*, p. 355.

As to the effects of secession on treaties, it is worth mentioning that in the twentieth century, upon a request made by the United States for the extradition of a fugitive, Panama considered that there was no extradition treaty between the United States and Panama.[204] In this regard, the Department of State issued an Opinion on 6 March 1908, stating that 'a consular convention of 1850 with Colombia was not applicable to Panama'.[205]

Concerning treaties that deal with particular servitudes: by means of an 1846 treaty, New Granada had granted the United States right of passage over the Isthmus of Panama. In 1903, after the independence of Panama, the United States declared that treaty 'to be a burden on the territory in the nature of a covenant running with the land, to the duties and benefits of which, the new state of Panama succeeded'.[206] Therefore, when the United States took control over the Panama Canal area, it declared its own extradition conventions with other States to be applicable to that territory.[207]

With relation to the Colombian public debt, Panama accepted no liability declaring that 'all claims of Colombia in this respect were abandoned as a part of a general settlement'.[208]

V. Conclusions

We may conclude from the preceding analysis that a dual mode of creation of States took place in the case of the Spanish-American colonies: independence of those which constituted the main administrative dependencies, the viceroyalties and general captaincies on the one hand and the dismemberment of the main administrative dependencies into several States, following the former administrative internal borders by operation of the *uti possidetis* principle, on the other.[209]

[204] Nevertheless, the request was accepted by Panama as an act of comity. See O'Connell, *The Law of State Succession*, p. 35.

[205] G. H. Hackworth, *Digest of International Law*, vol. V (Washington DC: 1943), p. 363, quoted by O'Connell, *The Law of State Succession*, p. 35.

[206] O'Connell, *The Law of State Succession*, p. 54. [207] *Ibid.*, p. 71. [208] *Ibid.*, p. 162.

[209] *Land, Island and Maritime Frontier Dispute (El Salvador/Honduras: Nicaragua intervening), Judgment of 11 September 1992, I.C.J. Reports 1992*, p. 380, para. 28; *Affaire des frontières colombo-vénézuéliennes (Colombie/Vénézuéla), 24 March 1922, R.S.A.*, vol. I, p. 228; *Honduras Borders (Guatemala/Honduras), 23 January 1933, R.I.A.A.*, vol. II, p. 1322; *The Boundary Case between Costa-Rica and Panama, 12 September 1914, R.I.A.A.*, vol. XI, p. 531.

Upon the emancipation of Latin American colonies, although there were attempts to preserve the territories of the viceroyalties unchanged, divisions and sub-divisions were not forced to become part of the newly independent States. This becomes visible in the case of the Viceroyalty of Rio de la Plata, where the Government of the United Provinces invited all former dependencies to send representatives to the General Constitutional Congress, making it clear that even though they had always been part of the same administration, as was the case of Bolivia, they enjoyed absolute freedom to take whatever path best served their interests. That was also the case with Uruguay, a State that had been part of the Viceroyalty of Rio de la Plata, later an annexation to Brazil and finally an independent State by virtue of a treaty between the United Provinces and Brazil.

The case of the Viceroyalty of New Spain constituted a case of emancipation. Yet there followed the secession of part the independent country, Texas, which was later annexed to another State, the United States.

As to the Viceroyalty of New Granada, it experienced two emancipation processes, due to the fact that Spain had regained control. However, we also find an instance of dissolution, that of Great Colombia where the former provinces regained their independence, except for Panama which remained part of Colombia until its final secession in 1903.

The case of Central America is of particular interest, as it shows instances of emancipation, secession, union or unification and dissolution or dismemberment and reunification. We also find a particular case of secession in the case of Chiapas, which did not give rise to the creation of a new State but to its incorporation into another State (Mexico).

In other cases, such as the Viceroyalty of Peru and the General Captaincy of Chile, no dismemberment took place, although some territorial alterations occurred due to acquisition or loss of parts of the territory of the newly independent State.

In the case of the Dominican Republic and Panama, secession took place not only as the means of achieving independence from Spain, but also in connection with their annexation to a newly independent State (Haiti and Colombia, respectively).

With regard to the two other secession cases, Texas and the Province of Buenos Aires, they were later integrated into other States (the United States and Argentina, respectively). Therefore, it can be said that among all the special cases of secession, the only one that led to the creation of a new State was Panama at the beginning of the twentieth century.

Regarding the effects of the succession of States through secession, it must be highlighted that, in general terms, the Spanish colonies in South

America that became independent throughout the nineteenth century did not regard themselves bound by treaties concluded by Spain,[210] with the exception of boundary treaties.

In cases where secession later developed into annexation, treaties that had been concluded by the successor State were applicable to the annexed territory (as was the case in the annexations of Texas and the Province of Buenos Aires).

Regarding public local debts, when granting recognition of the independence of its former colonies in the Americas through treaties, Spain 'transferred to the new States debts owed by or charged to the Spanish treasuries in those territories, or debts owed by Spain in respect of their administration'.[211] As to the emancipation of Brazil from Portugal, by virtue of the 1825 Treaty of Rio de Janeiro, Brazil took over a portion of the Portuguese debt 'as part of a general adjustment of financial arrangements'.[212] Unlike these cases, Panama refused to assume part of the Colombian debt, hence the latter ultimately withdrew such aspirations.[213]

[210] O'Connell, *The Law of State Succession*, p. 34. This jurist underlines that in 1826 the British Foreign Office considered that a convention of 1790 concerning fishery rights in the South Seas was not applicable to the present States of South America.

[211] O'Connell, *The Law of State Succession*, p. 176. [212] *Ibid.*, p. 160. [213] *Ibid.*, p. 162.

13

Lessons learned from the *Quebec Secession Reference* before the Supreme Court of Canada*

PATRICK DUMBERRY

Introduction

The present chapter deals with the practice of secession in North America. It is both a bloody story as well as one of virtue. The contrast between the approach adopted by courts in the United States following the attempt by the southern states to secede in 1861, and that adopted by the Supreme Court of Canada in 1998, could not be more striking.[1] Both attempts at secession (one real and the other hypothetical) were firmly opposed by the federal government of the United States.[2] However, one secessionist bid was crushed by war, while the other was discussed in a court of law and became the object of legislative acts. Even when the U.S. Supreme Court discussed the issue of the legality of secession in the famous *Texas v. White Case*, it took the view that:

* This article reflects facts current as of 8 August 2003. I wish to thank Prof. Marcelo G. Kohen (Graduate Institute of International Studies, Geneva), Prof. Vilaysoun Loungnarath (Counselor, WTO Appellate Body), Prof. Daniel Turp (University of Montreal) Mr. François Boudreault (Iran-U.S. Claims Tribunal, The Hague), Dr. Veijo Heiskanen (Attorney, Lalive & Partners, Geneva) and Mr. Karl Tabbakh (Attorney, McCarthy Tétrault, London) for their very useful comments, suggestions and corrections made on an earlier draft of this chapter. All errors that remain are my own.

1 The issue is discussed in: S. V. LaSelva, 'Divides Houses: Secession and Constitutional Faith in Canada and the United States', *VLR* 23 (1999) 771–92.

2 In the context of the secession of the Confederate States, U.S. President Lincoln called the doctrine of the secessionists 'an insidious debauching of the public mind'. For him 'they invented an ingenious sophism, which, if conceded, was followed by perfectly logical steps, through all the incidents, to the complete destruction of the Union. The sophism itself is that any state of the Union may, consistently with the national Constitution, and therefore lawfully, and peacefully, withdraw from the Union, without the consent of the Union, or of any other state': Address to Congress, 4 July 1861, quoted in J. Ostrowski, 'Was the Union Army's Invasion of the Confederate States a Lawful Act? An Analysis of President Lincoln's Legal Arguments Against Secession', in: D. Gordon (ed.), *Secession, State and Liberty* (New Brunswick, N.J.: Transaction Publ., 1998), pp. 155–90, at p. 159.

> [t]he [US] Constitution, in all its provisions, looks to an indestructible Union, composed of indestructible States. When, therefore, Texas became one of the United States, she entered into an indissoluble relation. All the obligations of perpetual union, and all the guaranties of republican government in the Union, attached at once to the State. The act which consummated her admission into the Union was something more than a compact; it was the incorporation of a new member into the political body. And it was final. The union between Texas and the other States was as complete, as perpetual, and as indissoluble as the union between the original States. There was no place for reconsideration, or revocation, except through revolution, or through consent of the States.[3]

This fundamentally contrasts with Canada's highest court's outline of the constitutional procedure for secession in the light of its assessment that 'the Constitution is not a straitjacket'[4] and that 'the continued existence and operation of the Canadian constitutional order could not be indifferent to a clear expression of a clear majority of Quebecers that they no longer wish to remain in Canada'.[5]

This approach also differs considerably from the attempt by the Province of Nova Scotia to secede from Canada just a few years after the enactment of the Constitution Act of 1867, which marked the birth of the Dominion of Canada.[6] In this case, the request for withdrawal from the Federation was rejected by the United Kingdom, the colonial power at the time, which, it determined, had 'no business to inquire into the local arrangements of the North American Provinces'.[7] The matter was

[3] *Texas v. White* (1869) 74 US (7 Wallace) 700, 725 (1868), at 726.

[4] *Reference re Secession of Quebec*, [1998] 2 S.C.R. 217; 37 *ILM*, 1998, 1342, at para. 150 (hereinafter referred to as the *Secession Reference*).

[5] *Ibid.*, para. 151.

[6] The election of September 1867 in Nova Scotia resulted in the victory in both provincial and federal elections of the opponents to the Province's entry in the Dominion. An address to the Queen of England was adopted unanimously at the Provincial Legislative Assembly and a petition by the majority of the members of the same Assembly was also sent to the members of both chambers of the British Parliament. Subsequently, the Premier of the Province led a delegation to the United Kingdom with instructions from his constituents to seek withdrawal of the Province from the Confederation. Finally, 31,000 out of the 48,000 provincial voters also signed a petition to that effect.

[7] The request was rejected by the Colonial Office and the motion presented before the House of Commons defeated: U.K. House of Commons, *Parliamentary Debates*, vol. 192, col. 1658–96. This historical precedent is discussed in the *Secession Reference*, at paras. 242–4, and in H.W. MacLauchlan, 'Accounting for Democracy and the Rule of Law in the Quebec Secession Reference', *Canadian Bar Review* 76 (1997), 155.

not pursued further, as negotiations were subsequently undertaken with Ottawa that led to a satisfactory solution.

This essay will focus on the recent attempt by Quebec to secede from Canada and will leave aside the attempt at secession by the Confederate states. The reason for this focus is that the former case may be more representative of modern State practice on the question. The case of the secession of Nova Scotia will also not be dealt with in this chapter due to the fact that it arose when Canada was still a British colony and not yet an independent State.

In the present chapter, the reasoning of the *Secession Reference* case before the Supreme Court of Canada will be examined and critically discussed from the perspective of international law, bearing in mind the specificities of Canadian constitutional law. The chapter will also deal with other cases before Quebec courts where the issue of the legality of secession has been discussed. Finally, it will address the legal consequences of the *Reference* case and the passing of legislative acts by the Canadian and Quebec parliaments, which regulate the procedural aspects of secession under Canadian law.

I. Historical background

In November 1976, the *Parti Québécois* (a political party in favour of 'sovereignty' of Quebec) was elected into office in the Province of Quebec for the first time. A few years later, the 'sovereignty-association' option (defined as sovereignty combined with an economic association with Canada) was put before the Quebec electorate in a referendum held on 20 May 1980.[8] The 'sovereignty-association' option was defeated in the referendum with 59.6 per cent of the vote against. In 1982, the Constitution was 'repatriated' from the United Kingdom and the Constitution

[8] The referendum question was as follows: 'The government of Quebec has made public its proposal to negotiate a new agreement with the rest of Canada, based on the equality of nations; this agreement would enable Quebec to acquire the exclusive power to make its own laws, administer its taxes and establish relations abroad, in other words, sovereignty and at the same time, to maintain with Canada an economic association including a common currency; any change in political status resulting from these negotiations will be submitted to the people through a referendum; on these terms, do you agree to give the government of Quebec the mandate to negotiate the proposed agreement between Quebec and Canada?'

Act was adopted.[9] The government of Quebec opposed these changes.[10] Negotiations towards the acceptance by Quebec of the 1982 Constitution Act were subsequently held in the context of the Meech Lake Accord of 1987 and the Charlottetown Accord of 1992. Both attempts at constitutional reform failed.

In 1994, the *Parti Québécois* was re-elected. Soon thereafter, a draft bill was introduced in the National Assembly relating to the process of Quebec's accession to sovereignty.[11] The draft bill proclaimed that Quebec was a sovereign country while authorising the Quebec government to conclude an agreement on an 'economic association' with Canada.[12] On 12 June 1995 a 'Tripartite Agreement' was reached between three pro-sovereignty parties (the *Parti Québécois*, the *Bloc Québécois* and the *Action Démocratique du Québec*) whereby, following a favourable vote at the referendum, the National Assembly would proclaim the sovereignty of Quebec *after* having proposed to Canada a treaty on a new 'economic and political Partnership'.[13] Following consultations by several Regional Commissions on the Future of Quebec and the filing of the report of a

[9] Constitution Act, 1982, being Schedule B to the Canada Act 1982 (U.K.), 1982, c. 11. In the present context, the term 'patriation' refers to the repatriation of the Constitution (mainly the 1867 British North America Act, (U.K.), 30 & 31 Vict., c. 3, an Imperial Statute) from the United Kingdom, which until then had retained the formal power to pass amendments to the Constitution. The adoption of the Constitution Act, 1982, which formally put an end to the authority of the United Kingdom Parliament over Canada, included a Charter of Rights and Freedoms and a domestic procedure to amend the Constitution.

[10] In an advisory opinion, *Re Objection by Quebec to a Resolution to Amend the Constitution*, [1982] 2 S.C.R. 793, 817–18, the Supreme Court of Canada refused to acknowledge Quebec's view of the existence of a constitutional convention granting it a veto over constitutional amendments affecting its powers. The federal government, with the assent of the nine other Canadian provinces, then agreed to the patriation of the Constitution and requested the United Kingdom Parliament to adopt the new Constitution without the consent of Quebec. Since then, no subsequent governments in Quebec (not even those formed by the federalist Liberal Party of Quebec in power from 1985 to 1994 and again elected in 2003) have assented to the Constitution Act, 1982.

[11] Draft Bill, An Act Respecting the Sovereignty of Quebec, tabled at the National Assembly on 6 December 1994 (hereinafter referred to as the Draft Bill). For an in-depth analysis of the Draft Bill, see: D. Turp, *L'Avant-projet de loi sur la souveraineté du Québec: texte annoté* (Montreal: Éditions Yvon Blais, 2001).

[12] Draft Bill, arts. 1 and 2.

[13] The Agreement also indicated that if the negotiations (set not to exceed one year) would unfold in a positive fashion, the sovereignty of Quebec would be declared after an agreement is reached with Canada on the Partnership treaty. However, 'if the negotiations prove to be fruitless, the National Assembly will be empowered to declare the sovereignty of Quebec without further delay'.

National Commission on the Future of Quebec, on 7 September 1995, Bill 1, An Act Respecting the Future of Quebec, was tabled in the National Assembly.[14] Bill 1 stated that the proclamation of sovereignty 'must be preceded by a formal offer of economic and political partnership with Canada', but it also authorised the government to proceed with a unilateral declaration of independence.[15] A referendum was held in Quebec on 30 October 1995 and was narrowly defeated with 50.58 per cent of the population voting 'no' and 49.42 per cent voting for the move towards sovereignty.[16]

II. The *Bertrand Case* before the Superior Court of Quebec

Before the October 1995 referendum took place, a citizen of Quebec, Mr. Guy Bertrand, filed an action for declaratory judgment and permanent injunction, as well as for interlocutory measures, in the Superior Court of Quebec, challenging the validity of the draft bill and the legality of holding the upcoming referendum on sovereignty.[17] The Attorney General of Quebec filed a motion to dismiss the case on the ground that the Court would be interfering with the National Assembly's legislative powers.[18] The motion was denied on 31 August 1995 by Justice Lesage of the Superior Court of Quebec, which decided to hear Mr. Bertrand's action

[14] Bill 1, An Act Respecting the Future of Quebec, 1st Sess., 35th Leg., Quebec (hereinafter referred to as Bill 1). The Tripartite Agreement of 12 June 1995 was included as a schedule of Bill 1.

[15] According to Article 26 of Bill 1, *ibid.*, 'the proclamation of sovereignty may be made as soon as the partnership treaty has been approved by the National Assembly or as soon as the latter, after requesting the opinion of the orientation and supervision committee, has concluded that the negotiations have proved fruitless'.

[16] The question put before voters was as follows: 'Do you agree that Quebec should become sovereign, after having made a formal offer to Canada for a new economic and political partnership, within the scope of the bill respecting the future of Quebec and of the agreement signed on June 12, 1995 (i.e. the "Tripartite Agreement")?'.

[17] Action for Declaratory Judgment and Permanent Injunction, and Motion for Interlocutory Measures, *Bertrand v. Bégin*, (10 August 1995), Quebec 200-05-002117-955 (Sup. Ct.). A similar motion for declaratory judgement was filed by a Quebec resident before the Superior Court: Motion for Declaratory Judgment, *Singh* v. *Attorney General of Quebec* (23 October 1995) Montreal 500-05-11275-953 (Sup. Ct.).

[18] The Attorney General indicated that: 'Par les conclusions recherchées, le requérant sollicite de la Cour qu'elle s'ingère dans l'exercice du pouvoir législatif et le fonctionnement de l'Assemblée nationale, ce qui constituerait une atteinte injustifiable aux attributions fondamentales de l'Assemblée nationale, de même qu'une atteinte à ses privilèges les plus essentiels . . . D'autre part, il est clair que le pouvoir judiciaire ne doit pas intervenir relativement à la tenue du référendum et au processus référendaire en cause puisque ceux-ci relèvent essentiellement d'une démarche démocratique fondamentale qui trouve sa sanction dans le droit international public et dont l'opportunité n'a pas à être débattue devant

for interlocutory injunction and declaratory judgment.[19] The Attorney General of Quebec withdrew from further participation in the case. On 8 September 1995, Justice Lesage rendered his judgment and refused to grant an injunction to prevent the holding of the upcoming referendum.[20] He issued, however, a declaratory judgment stating that the Court could not approve a violation of the constitutional order and that the events, which had been set in motion by the draft bill and Bill 1, could lead to such violation.[21] He added that: 'In this regard, the Quebec Government is giving itself a mandate that the Constitution of Canada does not confer on it. The actions taken by the Government of Quebec in view of the secession of Quebec are a repudiation of the Constitution of Canada.'[22]

Despite the result of the 1995 referendum, Mr. Bertrand nevertheless filed in January 1996 a revised action for declaratory judgment and permanent injunction. The Attorney General of Quebec again filed a motion to dismiss the case, arguing that not only was it hypothetical since no new referendum was envisaged, but also that Quebec's accession to sovereignty was a democratic process, which was sanctioned by international law, and that the Superior Court had no jurisdiction over such matters.[23] This position led the Attorney General of Canada to intervene in the case to argue that the Court had jurisdiction over the issue and that:

> Neither international law nor Canadian constitutional law confer on the National Assembly of Quebec the right to proceed to unilateral secession. Disagreement on this important point itself demonstrates that there are substantive *legal* issues in this case that are justiciable in the Superior Court.

les tribunaux.': Motion of Attorney General of Quebec to Dismiss Mr. Bertrand's Motion for Interlocutory Measures, 24 August 1995, *Bertrand* v. *Bégin.*

19 Interlocutory Judgment of J. Lesage, 31 August 1995, *Bertrand* v. *Bégin*: 'La menace que le Gouvernement du Québec ferait porter aux institutions politiques de la fédération canadienne est une question grave et sérieuse, qui de sa nature est justiciable en regard de la Constitution du Canada.'

20 Declaratory Judgment of J. Lesage, 8 September 1995, *Bertrand* v. *Bégin*, [1995] R.J.Q. 2500. An English translation of the case is available in: *Bertrand v. Quebec (A.G.)*, [1995] 127 D.L.R. (4th) 408. The decision is available (in French) at: http://www.uni.ca/bert_lesage95.html.

21 Thus, for Justice Lesage all the actions taken by the Quebec government indicated its intention to proceed with a unilateral declaration of independence and not to accomplish the secession of Quebec by resorting to the amending formula provided for in the Canadian Constitution.

22 *Bertrand* v. *Quebec (A.G.)*, [1995] 127 D.L.R. (4th) 408, at 428. He concluded (at 432) that Bill 1 constituted 'a serious threat to the rights and freedoms of the plaintiff granted by the Canadian Charter of Rights and Freedoms'.

23 Declinatory Motion and Motion to Dismiss Bertrand Action, 12 April 1996, *Bertrand* v. *Bégin*. On 30 April 1996, the Attorney General of Quebec also filed a declinatory motion and a motion to dismiss the *Singh case*: *Singh* v. *Attorney General of Quebec*.

> The Attorney General of Canada does not challenge the right of Quebecers to express democratically their desire to secede or to stay in Canada. However, the secession of any province would need to be done in accordance with the law. The rule of law is not an obstacle to change; rather, it provides the framework within which change can occur in an orderly fashion. While secession is not expressly prohibited in international law, Quebec does not meet the conditions for a right to secede.[24] (Emphasis in the original)

On 30 August 1996 Justice Pidgeon of the Superior Court of Quebec rejected the motion to dismiss the *Bertrand* action.[25] Justice Pidgeon refused to conclude that the case was hypothetical and decided to refer the matter to the judge in the main action finding that constitutional issues raised by the plaintiff deserved a determination on the merits. The questions referred for judgment on the merits were the following: 'Is the right to self-determination synonymous with the right to secession? Can Quebec unilaterally secede from Canada? Is Quebec's process for achieving sovereignty consistent with international law? Does international law prevail over domestic law?' Following this judgment, the Attorney General of Quebec decided not to appeal the case and to no longer participate in the proceedings.

III. The *Quebec Secession Reference* before the Supreme Court of Canada

As a result of the 1995 referendum, the federal government started an aggressive campaign to openly oppose the separatist sentiment in Quebec (the so-called 'Plan B').[26] One aspect of this new strategy was the submission of a reference to the Supreme Court of Canada concerning certain questions relating to the unilateral secession of Quebec from Canada.[27] The three questions of the *Reference* were as follows:

[24] Attorney General of Canada, *Synopsis of the Position of the Attorney General of Canada on the Motion to Dismiss* (22 May 1996), available at: http://canada.justice.gc.ca/en/news/nr/1996/resume7.html.

[25] Judgment of J. Pidgeon, 30 August 1996, *Bertrand* v. *Bégin*, [1996] R.J.Q. 2393. An English translation of the case is available in: *Bertrand v. Quebec (A.G.)*, [1996] 138 D.L.R. (4th) 481, at 507–8.

[26] The so-called, 'Plan B', refers to several initiatives taken by the federal government after the 1995 referendum to identify the consequences of secession and, most importantly, to actively take part in the debate leading to any future referendum on this issue. For a critical legal analysis, see: D. Turp, *La nation bâillonnée: le Plan B ou l'offensive d'Ottawa contre le Québec* (Montréal: VLB éditeur, 2000), at pp. 35–73.

[27] This decision was certainly influenced by the fact that in the *Bertrand Case*, the government of Quebec had decided not to participate in the merits phase of the case, which in effect was leaving many of the contentious issues raised during the case unanswered. Prior to the formal submission of the reference questions to the Supreme Court by the Governor in

1. Under the Constitution of Canada, can the National Assembly, legislature or Government of Quebec effect the secession of Quebec from Canada unilaterally?
2. Does international law give the National Assembly, legislature or Government of Quebec the right to effect the secession of Quebec from Canada unilaterally? In this regard, is there a right to self-determination under international law that would give the National Assembly, legislature or Government of Quebec the right to effect the secession of Quebec from Canada unilaterally?
3. In the event of a conflict between domestic and international law on the right of the National Assembly, legislature or Government of Quebec to effect the secession of Quebec from Canada unilaterally, which would take precedence in Canada?

The government of Quebec refused to take part in the proceedings before the Court, and in accordance with its Statute, the Court appointed an *amicus curiae* to present the position of Quebec.[28]

A. *Introduction: jurisdictional issues and the definition of secession*

The Court rendered its advisory opinion on 20 August 1998.[29] The Court first rejected the jurisdictional objection raised by the *amicus curiae* that

Council on 30 September 1996, Canada's Minister of Justice Allan Rock (in a letter of 26 September 1996) had identified the fundamental legal disagreement between Quebec and Canada in the following terms: 'The Government of Quebec submits that it can determine by itself alone the process of secession and that it is supported in this by international law. The federal government submits that international law does not give this power to the Government of Quebec and that a referendum does not create, as a matter of law, an automatic right of secession. . . . As responsible governments, we have the duty to ensure that this crucial question is clarified.'

[28] The *amicus* was Me Jolicoeur, an attorney with no formal links with the Quebec government. Many Aboriginal groups and interest groups, as well as individuals, also intervened before the Supreme Court.

[29] *Reference re Secession of Quebec*, [1998] 2 S. C. R. 217; 37 *ILM* 1998, 1342. The relevant background materials, the pleadings and the many legal opinions by international law experts are available at the Internet site of Canada's Department of Justice: http://canada.justice.gc.ca/en/ps/const/ref.html. See also: A. F. Bayefsky, *Self-Determination in International Law: Quebec and Lessons Learned* (The Hague: Kluwer, 2000). Good reviews of the historical background and the issues dealt with in the *Reference* can be found in: W. J. Newman, *The Quebec Secession Reference: The Rules of Law and the Position of the Attorney General of Canada* (Toronto: York Univ. Press, 1999); P. Bienvenu, 'Secession by Constitutional Means: Decision of the Supreme Court of Canada in the Quebec Secession Reference', *HJPLP* 23 (2001), 185–224; M. Dawson, 'Reflections on the Opinion of the Supreme Court of Canada in the Quebec Secession Reference', *Nat. J. Const. L.* 11 (1999–2000), 5–48.

the question was strictly political in nature, and that only the population of Quebec could decide it.[30] It also rejected the argument that the case was hypothetical since the referendum had been defeated and no new referendum was scheduled for the future.[31] The Court was also unconvinced by the proposition that, as a domestic court, it had no jurisdiction over a question of 'pure' international law.[32]

The Court described secession as a 'legal act as much as a political one' and defined it as the 'the effort of a group or section of a state to withdraw itself from the political and constitutional authority of that state, with a view to achieving statehood for a new territorial unit on the international plane'.[33] The use of the term 'secession' is thus undifferentiated whether it is achieved with or without the accord of the predecessor state.[34] The Court defines 'unilateral' secession as one 'without prior negotiations with the other provinces and the federal government'.[35]

B. *The obligation to negotiate secession through an amendment to the constitution*

The first question tackled by the Court was whether Quebec could legally secede unilaterally under the Constitution of Canada. For the Court, 'the legality of unilateral secession must be evaluated, at least in the first

30 According to the Court (at para. 27), its judgment would not 'usurp any democratic decision that the people of Quebec may be called to make'.

31 The Court simply indicated that it could answer hypothetical questions in a reference. P. J. Monahan, 'The Public Policy Role of the Supreme Court of Canada in the Secession Reference', *Nat. J. Const. L.* 11 (2000), 65, at 69–73, argues that the Court should have rejected the allegation based on the fact that waiting until secession was achieved for deciding on the issue would have deprived citizens of an effective remedy.

32 The point is further discussed in: Y. Le Bouthillier, 'La Cour suprême du Canada peut-elle répondre à une question de droit dans le cadre du renvoi sur la sécession unilatérale du Québec?', *Revue générale de droit* 28 (1997), 431–48.

33 *Secession Reference*, para. 83.

34 As argued by M. G. Kohen in his conribution, 'Le problème des frontières en cas de dissolution et de séparation d'Etats : quelles alternatives ?', in: O. Corten *et al.* (eds.), *Démembrement d'Etats et délimitations territoriales : L'uti possidetis en question(s)*, (Brussels: Bruylant, 1999), pp. 368–9, the use of the term 'secession' (as opposed to 'separation') is reserved for the situation where the break-up is achieved without the agreement of the predecessor State. Similar distinctions are also made in: J. Brossard, *L'accession à la souveraineté et le cas du Québec: conditions et modalités politico-juridiques*, 2nd edn (Montreal: Presses de l'Univ. de Montréal, 1995), at p. 94, and in: D. Turp, 'Le droit des peuples à disposer d'eux-mêmes, le droit de sécession et son application au cas du Québec', in: D. Turp, *Le droit de choisir: Essais sur le droit du Québec à disposer de lui-même* (Montreal: Thémis, 2001), p. 1, at p. 22.

35 *Secession Reference*, para. 86.

instance, from the perspective of the domestic legal order of the state from which the unit seeks to withdraw'.[36] Later in its opinion, the Court also noted that 'international law . . . by and large, leaves the creation of a new state to be determined by the domestic law of the existing state of which the seceding entity presently forms a part', and that international law is likely to be consistent with the conclusion that a unilateral secession is illegal, only subject to the possibility that such right may be recognised to this entity based on the right of peoples to self-determination.[37]

The Constitution of Canada is silent on this question. Scholars generally agree that the unilateral secession of a province would be unconstitutional under Canadian Law.[38] It has however been argued by some commentators that the Constitution of Canada would nevertheless permit secession, even unilaterally, based on a 'constitutional convention' resulting, *inter alia*, from federal acquiescence in the holding of both 1980 and 1995 referenda.[39] Similar arguments have also been advanced based on the 'compact theory' of confederation, according to which Canada was created by the agreement of pre-existing colonies (or, according to another version, by two 'founding nations': the French- and the English-speaking populations) and that, consequently, they may freely choose to leave the pact if breached.[40] The Court definitively put an end to this debate in concluding that, although the Constitution neither expressly authorises

[36] *Ibid.*, para. 83.

[37] *Ibid.*, para. 112. The Court's direct reference to municipal law to determine the legality of secession under international law has been the object of criticism in doctrine: O. Corten, 'Vers un droit international public canadien', *Canada Watch* 7/1–2 (1999), 39; G. Dufour and A. Morin, 'Le renvoi relatif à la sécession du Québec: critique du traitement que fait la Cour suprême du droit international', *R. Québécoise D.I.* 12 (1999), 184–9, 192–4.

[38] J. Woehrling, 'Les aspects juridiques d'une éventuelle sécession du Québec', *Canadian Bar Review* 74 (1995), 293, at 309–14; P. J. Monahan, 'The Law and Politics of Quebec Secession', *Osgood Hall L. J.* 33 (1995), 2, at 4–19; J. Webber, 'The Legality of a Unilateral Declaration of Independence under Canadian Law', *McGill L. J.* 42 (1996–1997), 281–318; N. Finkelstein and G. Vegh, *The Separation of Quebec and the Constitution of Canada* (North York, Ont.: York Univ. Centre for Public Law and Public Policy, 1992).

[39] This is the position developed by D. Turp, 'Quebec's Democratic Right to Self-Determination', in: S. Hartt *et al.* (eds.), *Tangled Web: Legal Aspects of Deconfederation* (Toronto: Renouf Publ. Co. Ltd./C.D. Howe Inst., 1992), p. 99 at pp. 103–7. It is also supported by: H. Brun and G. Tremblay, *Droit Constitutionnel* (Cowansville: Quebec, Yvon Blais ed., 2002, 4th edn), at p. 248; A. Makovka, 'Les limites territoriales et maritimes d'un Québec souverain', *R. Québécoise D. I.* 8 (1993–1994), 312; C. Beauchamp, 'De l'existence d'une convention constitutionnelle reconnaissant le droit du Québec à l'autodétermination', *RJEUL* 6 (1992), 56. This argument is discussed (and rejected) by Webber, 'The Legality of a Unilateral Declaration of Independence', at 302–4.

[40] This interpretation is advanced by: G. Marchildon and E. Maxwell, 'Quebec's Right of Secession Under Canadian and International Law' *VJIL* 32 (1992), 583 at 593–8; G. Craven,

nor prohibits secession, an act of secession 'would purport to alter the governance of Canadian territory in a manner which undoubtedly is inconsistent with our current constitutional arrangements' and would therefore be illegal.[41] The Court found that secession would require an amendment of the Constitution of Canada.[42] By reaching this decision, the Court also resolved a doctrinal controversy around the question of whether any amendment formula would be appropriate to deal with such a revolutionary change as the secession of a province from the Federation.[43] The Court also rejected a long-time separatist argument that, upon a winning referendum, Quebec would immediately fall outside the scope of the Canadian legal order and be governed by international law.[44] The Court, however, refrained from expressing an opinion on another area of dispute amongst Canadian constitutionalists, namely, which of the constitutional amendment procedures is the most appropriate to effect secession.[45] This silence has been construed by some as proof of the irrelevance

'Of Federalism, Secession, Canada and Quebec', *Dalhousie J.L.S.* 14 (1991), 231, at 258–60; M. Thibodeau, 'The Legality of an Independent Quebec: Canadian Constitutional Law and Self-Determination in International Law', *Boston C.I.C.L.R.* 3 (1979), 99, at 140 (who uses the treaty doctrine of *rebus sic stantibus*). A similar argument is made in: H. Brun and G. Tremblay, *Droit Constitutionnel*, 2nd edn (Cowansville: Quebec, Yvon Blais ed., 1990), at p. 237. Brossard, *L'accession à la souveraineté et le cas du Québec*, at pp. 204–26, believes (in 1976) that many 'clauses' of the original pact have been breached (e.g. the respect of linguistic and education rights of francophone outside Quebec) and that the prevailing circumstances (such as the absence of decentralisation of powers) are now different from the one which led Quebec to join the Federation in 1867. It should be noted that this 'compact theory' is only one of many theories explaining Canadian federalism. This point is further discussed in: Webber, 'The Legality of a Unilateral Declaration of Independence', at 304–6.

41 *Secession Reference*, *supra* note 4, para. 84.

42 *Ibid.* Elsewhere, the Court noted that, 'any attempt to effect the secession of a province from Canada must be undertaken pursuant to the Constitution of Canada, or else violate the Canadian legal order' (para. 104).

43 Several writers had questioned the applicability of the amending procedure of the Constitution and concluded that secession could only be achieved through a 'revolution' in the legal order: MacLauchlan, 'Accounting for Democracy and the Rule of Law', 155; R. Howse and A. Malkin, 'Canadians are a Sovereign People: How the Supreme Court Should Approach the Reference on Quebec Secession', *Canadian Bar Review* 76 (1997), 186, at 210; J. Frémont and F. Boudreault, 'Supracontitutionalité canadienne et sécession du Québec', *Nat. J. Const. L.* 8 (1997), 163, at 203 (also in: *Policy Options*, Dec. 1997, at 36–40).

44 Brun and Tremblay, *Droit Constitutionnel*, at p. 236. The reasoning of the Court on this point is further discussed in: J.-F. Gaudreault-DesBiens, 'The Quebec Secession Reference and the Judicial Arbitration of Conflicting Narratives about Law, Democracy, and Identity', *VLR* 23 (1999), 793, at 821–3.

45 *Secession Reference*, para. 105. On these debates, see: Monahan, 'The Law and Politics of Quebec Secession', at pp. 4–19; P. J. Monahan, *Cooler Heads shall Prevail: Assessing the Costs*

of any amendment procedure in the context of secession.[46] Although the Court clearly did not have to venture into such controversy in order to answer Question no. 1 of the *Reference*, its silence may also be politically motivated.[47]

For the Court, the 'democratic principle' (identified as one of the four fundamental constitutional principles underlying the Constitution) would demand that 'considerable weight be given to a clear expression by the people of Quebec of their will to secede from Canada'.[48] Elsewhere in the *Reference*, the Court speaks of the 'clear expression of a clear majority' of the population of Quebec 'on a clear question to pursue secession'.[49] The Court also indicates that the referendum result 'must be free of ambiguity both in terms of the question asked and in terms of the support it achieves'[50] and that 'a right and a corresponding duty to negotiate secession cannot be built on an alleged expression of democratic will if the expression of democratic will is itself fraught with ambiguities'.[51] By these affirmations, the Court validates the very idea of a

and Consequences of Quebec Separation, (Toronto: C.D. Howe Inst., 1995); Webber, 'The Legality of a Unilateral Declaration of Independence', at 281–318; Woehrling, 'Les aspects juridiques', at 309–14; J. Woehrling, 'L'avis de la Cour suprême du Canada sur l'éventuelle sécession du Québec', *RFDC* 37 (1999), 3 at 19–21 (see also: J. Woehrling, 'The Supreme Court's Ruling on Quebec's Secession: Legality and Legitimacy Reconciled by a Return to Constitutional First Principles', in: H. Mellon and M. Westmacott (eds.), *Political Dispute and Judicial Review* (Scarborough, Ont.: Nelson, 2000), pp. 83–101).

46 For Woehrling, 'L'avis de la Cour suprême du Canada', at pp. 17–19; see also: J. Woehrling, 'Unexpected Consequences of Constitutional First Principles', *Canada Watch* 7/1–2 (1999), 18: the outcome of negotiations (based on the four fundamental constitutional principles identified by the Court) would ultimately prevail over the technical details of any amendment procedure. Of the same view: D. Greschner, 'The Quebec Secession Reference: Goodbye to Part V?', *Constitutional Forum* 10 (1998), 19, at 23. *Contra*: P. Radan, 'Constitutional Law and Secession: the Case of Quebec', *Macarthur Law Review* 2 (1998), 69, at 81–3. The question is also dealt with in: G. Tremblay, 'La procédure implicite de modification de la Constitution du Canada et le cas de la sécession du Québec', *Revue du Barreau* 58 (1998), 423.

47 In the pleading, the Attorney General of Canada emphasised the fact that the Court did not have to determine *how* secession would be constitutionally achieved. This is certainly so for fear that the Court would have concluded (as many writers do, see e.g.: Finkelstein and Vegh, *The Separation of Quebec*) that secession by amendment of the Constitution requires (pursuant to section 41 of the Constitutional Act of 1982) the *unanimous* consent of all 10 provinces legislative assemblies, the federal House of Commons, the federal Senate, as well as, most likely, the Aboriginal peoples. This strict constitutional requirement of unanimity, which Quebec has never formally accepted, would arguably block any attempt by Quebec to pursue secession *legally* under the Constitution. This was certainly not the message that the Court intended to send to Quebec voters.

48 *Secession Reference*, para. 87. 49 *Ibid.*, paras. 92–3.

50 *Ibid.*, para. 87. 51 *Ibid.*, para. 100.

referendum on secession.[52] Thus, the Court acknowledges that a referendum 'undoubtedly may provide a democratic method of ascertaining the views of the electorate', but also that 'in itself and without more, it has no direct legal effect, and could not in itself bring about unilateral secession'.[53]

This expression of democracy 'would confer legitimacy on the efforts of the government of Quebec to initiate the Constitution's amendment process in order to secede by constitutional means'.[54] Under the 'federalism' principle (also identified by the Court as one of the four fundamental constitutional principles) a 'clear repudiation of the existing constitutional order and the clear expression of the desire to pursue secession' by the population of Quebec would confer such legitimacy to which the 'Canadian constitutional order cannot remain indifferent'.[55] Later, the Court not only speaks of the *(political) legitimacy* which would result from an unambiguous vote in favour of independence, but also of the *right* of Quebec to pursue secession through an amendment to the Constitution.[56] This legitimacy would in turn 'give rise to a reciprocal obligation on all parties to the Confederation to negotiate constitutional changes to respond to that desire'.[57] It has been observed in doctrine that the introduction of this innovative obligation to negotiate was not supported by any authority and that the Court provided an unsatisfactory account for

[52] The Court therefore rejects an argument often heard in English Canada that any referendum on secession would be a revolutionary act, which should be prevented by the federal government. However, opponents to secession have also made the argument that the referendum questions of 1980 and 1995 were deliberately unclear and, in that sense, the Court's requirement of a 'clear' question seems to have echoed their concerns.

[53] *Secession Reference*, para. 87. [54] *Ibid.*, para. 87.

[55] *Ibid.*, para. 92. D. Turp, 'The Issue of International Recognition in the Supreme Court of Canada's Reference on Quebec Sovereignty', *Canada Watch* 7/1–2 (1999), at 83–4, 97–8 (see also: D. Turp and G. Van Ert, 'International Recognition in the Supreme Court of Canada's Reference', *CYIL* 35 (1998), 225–346) makes the interesting observation that the 'legitimacy', which the Court believes would result from a winning referendum, is not relevant here since, under the present Constitution, Quebec has in any case the *right* to initiate any constitutional change, including secession. He therefore rejects the Court's observation (at para. 95) that Quebec's refusal to take part in eventual negotiations would 'put at risk the legitimacy' of its existing rights under the Constitution.

[56] The Court (*ibid.*, para. 92) indicates that 'the rights' of other provinces and the federal government 'cannot deny the right of the government of Quebec to pursue secession, should a clear majority of the people of Quebec choose that goal'. This led D. Turp, 'The Right to Choose: Essay on Quebec's Right of Self-Determination', in: Turp, *Le droit de choisir*, p. 801, at p. 821, to conclude that the Court 'acknowledges the existence of a constitutional right of secession which is subjected to an obligation to negotiate'.

[57] *Secession Reference*, para. 88.

its justification.[58] Others have, on the contrary, underlined the wisdom of the Court for coming up with this novel constitutional obligation.[59]

Apart from Quebec and the federal government, the Court also identified that the other provinces as well as 'other participants' would take part in these negotiations. This last reference is probably directed to the Aboriginal peoples, since elsewhere in its opinion the Court acknowledged that 'aboriginal interests would be taken into account' in such negotiations.[60] The question of the participants is nevertheless the object of some controversy in doctrine.[61] The content of this constitutional duty to negotiate is loosely defined by the Court, but it is clear that it should not solely consist of the 'logistical details of secession' since Quebec 'could not purport to invoke a right of self-determination such as to dictate the terms of a proposed secession to the other parties: that would not be a negotiation at all'.[62] However, the other provinces and the federal government

58 This is the opinion of D. P. Haljan, 'Negotiating Quebec Secession', *RBDI* 31 (1998), 190, at 208–10; Turp, 'The Issue of International Recognition', at 83–4, 97–8; D. Usher, 'The New Constitutional Duty to Negotiate', *Policy Options* (Jan.–Feb. 1999), at 41–4; D. Usher, 'Profundity Rampant: Secession and the Court, II', *Policy Options* (Sept. 1999), at 44–9. For P. Hogg, 'The Duty to Negotiate', *Canada Watch* 7/1–2 (1999), at 34–5, 'the vague principles of democracy and federalism, which were relied upon by the court, hardly seem sufficient to require a federal government to negotiate the dismemberment of the country that it was elected to protect'. Relying on earlier cases of secession, Hogg concludes that there is no historical basis for the proposition that a referendum in a province wishing to secede should impose on the federal government an obligation of cooperation and negotiation. For S. Lalonde, 'Quebec's Boundaries in the Event of Secession', *Macquarie Law Journal* 3 (2003), at 139, 'it is difficult to see where the obligation to negotiate has come from'. Other types of criticisms are found in: Monahan, 'The Public Policy Role of the Supreme Court of Canada', at 69, 89–92.

59 Newman, *The Quebec Secession Reference*, at pp. 83–7; Gaudreault-DesBiens, 'The Quebec Secession Reference', at 839–41.

60 *Secession Reference*, paras. 96, 139. This is discussed in: P. Joffe, 'Quebec's Sovereignty Project and Aboriginal Rights', *Canada Watch* 7/1–2 (1999), 6. In the *Reference*, the Court indicated that it was not necessary to explore further questions relating to Aboriginal concerns (such as the boundaries issue) since it had already concluded that there was no right to unilateral secession by Quebec in the first place.

61 Woehrling, 'L'avis de la Cour suprême du Canada', at 20–1, (also in: Woehrling, 'Unexpected Consequences') interprets the Court's findings as a 'bilateralisation' of the negotiation process between Quebec and the government of Canada, which would be speaking as one voice in the name of the 10 provinces and the 'other participants'. Others believe that the Court actually rejected this bilateral model of negotiations: Monahan, 'The Public Policy Role of the Supreme Court of Canada', at 95; D. Greschner, 'What Can Small Provinces Do?', *Canada Watch* 7/1–2 (1999). It seems that it is the latter view which is likely to prevail in light of article 3(1) of the Clarity Act, which will be discussed below; see *infra* note 165.

62 *Secession Reference*, paras. 90, 91. At para. 97, the Court also mentions that Quebec would have 'no absolute legal entitlement' to secession.

could not negotiate 'in such a way as to amount to an absolute denial of Quebec's rights'.[63] Ultimately, the negotiations would have to 'address the interests' of all participants, as well as 'the rights of all Canadians both within and outside Quebec';[64] it would require the 'reconciliation of various rights and obligations by the representatives of two legitimate majorities, namely, the clear majority of the population of Quebec, and the clear majority of Canada as a whole, whatever that may be'.[65]

The Court indicated that negotiations would be difficult and could ultimately fail.[66] The Court was, however, quick to point out that its role in the *Reference* was 'limited to the identification of the relevant aspects of the Constitution', and that in the future it would have 'no supervisory role over the political aspects of constitutional negotiations', such as the determination of what constitutes a clear majority on a clear referendum question, which would be 'subject only to political evaluation', as 'only the political actors would have the information and expertise to make the appropriate judgment'.[67] However, it has been rightly pointed out that this self-imposed secondary role may very well be untenable in the face of the importance of the issue at stake.[68] For the Court, the non-justiciability of this political issue would 'not deprive the surrounding constitutional framework of its binding status' nor would it mean that these 'constitutional obligations could be breached without incurring serious legal repercussions'.[69] Thus, this binding obligation, although not judicially enforceable, would have 'legal repercussions' administered through the political process. The inherent ambiguity of the Court's reasoning has not

[63] *Ibid.*, para. 93. [64] *Ibid.*, para. 92.

[65] *Ibid.*, para. 93. Some of the issues that the Court mentioned as being part of the negotiations are 'national economy and national debts', boundaries, and the protection of linguistic and cultural minorities' rights, including those of Aboriginal peoples.

[66] *Ibid.*, para. 97.

[67] *Ibid.*, para. 100. The Court added that 'the search for truth in a court of law [is] ill-suited to getting to the bottom of constitutional negotiations' and that 'to the extent that the questions are political in nature, it is not the role of the judiciary to interpose its own views on the different negotiating positions of the parties, even were it invited to do so' (para. 101). The Court also indicated that 'the reconciliation of the various legitimate constitutional interests outlined above is necessarily committed to the political rather than the judicial realm, precisely because that reconciliation can only be achieved through the give and take of the negotiation process' (para. 101).

[68] Thus, the Court would probably have to intervene at some point to assess whether the participants in the negotiations are acting in a manner which is consistent with the fundamental constitutional values identified in the *Reference:* Haljan, 'Negotiating Quebec Secession', at 212–13; Monahan, 'The Public Policy Role of the Supreme Court of Canada', at 96.

[69] *Secession Reference*, para. 102.

passed unnoticed.[70] For the Court, the refusal of any party to take part in the negotiations and to pursue them in accordance with the principles of democracy, federalism, the rule of law, and the respect for minority rights (the four fundamental constitutional principles)[71] would 'seriously put at risk the legitimacy of the exercise of its rights, and perhaps the negotiation process as a whole'.[72] Such a breach of this obligation to negotiate 'may have important ramifications at the international level' with respect to the international recognition of the new State.[73] In doing so, the Court undoubtedly internationalised the issue in conferring to other States a key role in indirectly evaluating the negotiation process.[74]

C. *The absence of any legal basis for the unilateral secession of Quebec under international law*

It is widely held in doctrine that Quebec cannot invoke the right of peoples to self-determination to sustain any *right* to secession under international law. Quebec simply does not meet the criteria set by international law: it is neither a colonial nor an oppressed people under the Canadian Federation.[75] Indeed, Quebec undoubtedly has a degree of relative autonomy

[70] See the criticisms of Monahan, 'The Public Policy Role of the Supreme Court of Canada', at 84, who asks, 'if all aspects of these negotiations involve political rather than legal considerations and if the courts will therefore not enforce the duty to negotiate, how can the duty to negotiate be said to be a legal duty?' See also: D. Proulx, 'La sécession du Québec: Principes et mode d'emploi selon la Cour suprême du Canada', *RBDC* 1998, 361, at 376–7; Woehrling, 'L'avis de la Cour suprême du Canada', at 17–19.

[71] *Secession Reference*, paras. 88, 90. [72] *Ibid.*, para. 95.

[73] *Ibid.*, para. 103. This aspect of the *Reference* will be discussed below.

[74] D. Turp, 'Globalising Sovereignty: The International Implications of the Supreme Court of Canada's Advisory Opinion on Quebec Sovereignty', *Canada Watch* 7/1–2 (1999), at 4. Gaudreault-DesBiens, 'The Quebec Secession Reference', at 832, argues that the Court has 'indirectly appointed the international community as the ultimate arbitrator of Canada-Quebec disputes following a clear "yes" vote in a referendum. In fact, it virtually invites the international community's supervisory intervention'.

[75] For instance, see the following: Monahan, 'The Law and Politics of Quebec Secession' at 21; L. Eastwood Jr., 'Secession: State Practice and International Law After the Dissolution of the Soviet Union and Yugoslavia', *Duke J.C.I.L.* 3 (1993), 299 at 342; Marchildon and Maxwell, 'Quebec's Right of Secession', at 618; A. Cassese, *Self-Determination of Peoples: A Legal Reappraisal,* (Cambridge: Cambridge Univ. Press, 1995), at pp. 251, 253; J. D. Van Der Vyver, 'Self-Determination of the People of Quebec under International Law', *Journal of Transnational Law & Policy* 10 (2000), at 27; Woehrling, 'L'avis de la Cour suprême du Canada', at 7; Thibodeau, 'The Legality of an Independent Quebec', at 136; U. O. Umozurike, *Self-Determination in International Law* (Hamden, Conn.: Archon Books, 1972), at pp. 256–9; D. Cameron, *Nationalism, Self-Determination and the Quebec Question,* (Toronto: Macmillan, 1974), at pp. 82–106, 143–57; J. Claydon and J. D. Whyte,

within the Federation, is fully participating and represented in all aspects of Canadian democracy and is not subject to discrimination.[76] Some other (less convincing) grounds have also been advanced by commentators: the Quebec population would not constitute a 'people' under international law;[77] Quebec has already exercised its right to self-determination;[78] secession would not be accepted by the international community because of its negative effect on its stability.[79] Only a minority of scholars are of the opinion that Quebec could invoke the right of peoples to self-determination to secede.[80]

'Legal Aspects of Quebec's Claim for Independence', in: R. Simeon (ed.), *Must Canada Fail?* (Montreal: McGill-Queen's Univ. Press, 1977), at pp. 260–70; L. Wildhaber, 'Territorial Modifications and Break-ups in Federal States', *CYIL* 33 (1995), at 64.

76 This is the position of the following authors: S. A. Williams, *International Legal Effects of Secession by Quebec* (North York: York Univ. Centre for Public Law and Public Policy, 1992), at pp. 20–2; Webber, 'The Legality of a Unilateral Declaration of Independence', at 310; Woehrling, 'Les aspects juridiques', at 317–18; K. MacMillan, 'Secession Perspectives and the Independence of Quebec', *Tulane J. I. C. L.* 7 (1999), 333, at 363–4; Marchildon and Maxwell, 'Quebec's Right of Secession', at 618; K. Finkelstein, G. Vegh and C. Joly, 'Does Quebec Have a Right to Secede at International Law?' *Canadian Bar Review* 74 (1995), 225, at 230–1, 252–6; Howse and Malkin, 'Canadians are a Sovereign People'.

77 Van Der Vyver, 'Self-Determination of the People of Quebec', at 21. This is also the view of M. G. Kohen, 'El individuo y los conflictos territoriales', in: O.E.A., Comité Jurídico Interamericano, *Curso de Derecho Internacional*, 2001, vol. XXVIII, pp. 425–60, who distinguishes between the legal and the sociological notion of people.

78 For F. Crépeau, 'The Law of Quebec's Secession', *American Review of Canadian Studies* 27 (1997), 27–50, such a right was exercised in 1867, at the time of the creation of the Federation, as well in the two referenda of 1980 and 1995. This position is largely rejected in doctrine, which tends to go in the direction that Quebec's agreeable entry into the Canadian Federation cannot have provided support for the claim of the illegality of secession: Marchildon and Maxwell, 'Quebec's Right of Secession', at 610–12; Thibodeau, 'The Legality of an Independent Quebec', at 140; Brossard, *L'accession à la souveraineté et le cas du Québec*, at pp. 199–200.

79 Marchildon and Maxwell, 'Quebec's Right of Secession', at 615–17, 619, for whom the concern of the international community is whether 'general international harmony' will be better served by Quebec remaining in Canada or by its secession. They conclude that Quebec has no right to secede since the disruption that secession would create for Canadian national unity would outweigh the benefit that Quebec would gain in becoming an independent State.

80 These writers have an extensive interpretation of this right which they believe would apply to *all* peoples: Brossard, *L'accession à la souveraineté et le cas du Québec*, at pp. 190, 304–9 (for whom, however, the situation of the Quebec people has, to some extent, analogies with colonial peoples: see pp. 201, 223–6, 230); J. Brossard, 'Le droit du peuple québécois à disposer de lui-même au regard du droit international', *CYIL* 15 (1977), 84; D. Turp, 'Le droit de sécession en droit international public', *CYIL* 20 (1980), 47; D. Turp, 'Le droit à la sécession: l'expression du principe démocratique', in: A.-G. Gagnon and F. Rocher (eds.), *Répliques aux détracteurs de la souveraineté* (Montreal: VLB éditeur, 1992), p. 49 at p. 57; Turp, 'Quebec's Democratic Right to Self-Determination' at 107–115. However, see

Among Quebec supporters of secession, the argument of the *legality* of the process by which secession would be achieved is generally supplanted by reference to its *legitimacy* if corresponding to the expression of the democratic will of the population.[81] This was the approach taken by the Bélanger-Campeau Commission: 'L'expression démocratique d'une volonté claire de la population québécoise de se constituer en État indépendant, associé à l'engagement du Québec de respecter les principes de l'ordre juridique international, fonderait la légitimité politique d'une démarche du Québec vers l'accession à la souveraineté.'[82]

Let us now turn to the reasoning of the Court on the second question of the *Reference*, namely, whether there exists a positive right under international law for the secession of Quebec. The position of the Attorney General of Canada, which was not refuted by the *amicus curiae*, was that no such right exists for Quebec.[83] The Court rightly started its investigation by stating that 'international law contains neither a right of unilateral secession nor the explicit denial of such a right, although such a denial is, to some extent, implicit in the exceptional circumstances required for secession to be permitted under the right of a people to self-determination'.[84] The Court then examined the content of the right of peoples to self-determination, which is 'so widely recognised in international

a more nuanced position adopted by D. Turp, 'Supplément' in: Brossard, *L'accession à la souveraineté et le cas du Québec*, at p. 805. See also: Roger Chaput, 'Du rapport Durham au rapport Brossard: le droit des québécois à disposer d'eux-mêmes', *Cahier de droit* (Univ. Laval) 20 (1979), 289, at 308.

81 This approach is followed by Woehrling, 'Les aspects juridiques', at 296; D. Turp, 'Supplément', in: Brossard, *L'accession à la souveraineté et le cas du Québec*, at 800, 801, 804.

82 *Rapport de la Commission sur l'avenir politique et constitutionnel du Québec*, National Assembly of Quebec, March 1991, at p. 59. The Report is available at: http://www.uni.ca/belangercampeau.html. The non-partisan Commission (known as Bélanger-Campeau) was created in 1990 after the failure of the Meech Lake Accord, and had as its mandate to analyse and make recommendations on the political future of Quebec, within or outside Canada. It commissioned expert reports on several issues of international law likely to arise upon Quebec secession. These reports were published in: *Commission d'étude des questions afférentes à l'accession du Québec à la souveraineté, Exposés et études*, 1992 (hereinafter referred to as '*Commission d'étude*'). The updated 2001 versions of these reports were later published in: *Mise à jour des études originalement préparées pour la Commission parlementaire d'étude des questions afférentes à l'accession du Québec à la souveraineté* (1991–2), vol. III, and are available at: http://www.saic.gouv.qc.ca/institutionnelles_constitutionnelles/mise_a_jour_etudes_1991-1992.htm.

83 This was also the position expressed by the international law experts in their reports filed by both the Attorney General of Canada and the *amicus*. See: Bayefsky, *Self-Determination in International Law*.

84 *Secession Reference*, para. 112.

conventions that [it] has acquired a status beyond "convention" and is considered a general principle of international law'.[85] This right to self-determination must however be exercised 'within the framework of existing sovereign states and consistently with the maintenance of the territorial integrity of those states'.[86] Thus, the right to self-determination of a people 'is normally fulfilled through internal self-determination – people's pursuit of its political, economic, social and cultural development within the framework of an existing state'.[87] For the Court:

> A state whose government represents the whole of the people or peoples resident within its territory, on a basis of equality and without discrimination, and respects the principles of self-determination in its own internal arrangements, is entitled to the protection under international law of its territorial integrity.[88]

The right to external self-determination only arises in the 'most extreme of cases and, even then, under carefully defined circumstances'.[89] Such cases are those of colonial peoples and also 'where a people is subject to alien subjugation, domination or exploitation'.[90] For the Court these different criteria are 'irrelevant' for this *Reference*. The Court also mentioned a possible third case where a people could be entitled, 'as a last resort', to exercise its right to self-determination by secession: when a people is 'blocked from the meaningful exercise' of this right internally.[91] But it concluded that it was unclear whether this last possibility 'actually reflects an established international law standard'.[92] One could hardly refute the soundness of this 'traditional' approach taken by the Court.[93] It should simply be noted that in so deciding, the Court, not surprisingly, disregarded several theories put forward in doctrine to enlarge the right to secession to non-colonial situations:[94] the 'liberal' theory of

[85] *Ibid.*, para. 114. [86] *Ibid.*, para. 122. See also para. 127.

[87] *Ibid.*, para. 126. [88] *Ibid.*, para. 130. [89] *Ibid.*, para. 126. [90] *Ibid.*, paras. 132–3.

[91] *Ibid.*, para. 135. Elsewhere, the Court used a different language to define this third case: 'where a definable group is denied meaningful access to government to pursue their political, economic, social and cultural development' (para. 138).

[92] *Ibid.*, para. 135.

[93] However, see the comments by Corten, 'Vers un droit international public canadien', at 39, who criticises the extension of the right to secession to cases other than colonial ones.

[94] Toope in his work, S. J. Toope, 'Re Reference by the Governor in the Council Concerning Certain Questions Relating to the Secession of Quebec to Canada', *AJIL* 93 (1999), 519, at 524, makes this observation. More generally, he criticised the Court's opinion for its failure to clearly articulate the relationship between municipal law and international law and also for its impoverished treatment of the different sources of international law, like its disregard for custom and State practice. Other criticisms of the treatment of international

secession,[95] the various 'moral' theories,[96] as well as those grounded in the concept of legitimacy.[97]

Applying these criteria to Quebec, the Court concluded that 'the current Quebec context cannot approach such a threshold',[98] and that 'such exceptional circumstances are manifestly inapplicable to Quebec under existing conditions'.[99] Thus:

> The population of Quebec cannot plausibly be said to be denied access to government. Quebecers occupy prominent positions within the government of Canada. Residents of the province freely make political choices and pursue economic, social and cultural development within Quebec, across Canada, and throughout the world. The population of Quebec is equitably represented in legislative, executive and judicial institutions.[100]

The Court finally stated that 'the continuing failure to reach agreement on amendments to the Constitution, while a matter of concern, does not amount to a denial of self-determination' and that Quebecers were not placed in a 'disadvantaged position' under the constitutional arrangements presently in effect.[101] This was in reaction to an argument raised in doctrine whereby the 'patriation' of the Constitution over Quebec's objection in 1982, as well as the failure of the Meech Lake Accord in 1990, would be tantamount to a negation of Quebec's right to *internal* self-determination within Canada, therefore opening the way to a right to secession.[102]

In view of the answers provided to Questions no. 1 and 2 of the *Reference*, the Court did not address Question no. 3.

law by the Court are found in: Corten, 'Vers un droit international public canadien', at 39, 43.

95 R. McGee, 'The Theory of Secession and Emerging Democracies: A Constitutional Solution', *SJIL* 28 (1992), at 451–76; H. Beran, 'A Liberal Theory of Secession', *Political Studies* 32 (1984), 21–31.

96 L. Brilmayer, 'Secession and Self-Determination: A Territorial Interpretation', *YJIL* 16 (1991), 177–202; A. Buchanan, *Secession: The Morality of Political Divorce from Fort Sumter to Lithuania and Quebec* (Boulder: Westview Press, 1991).

97 L. C. Buchheit, *Secession: The Legitimacy of Self-Determination* (New Haven: Yale Univ. Press, 1978).

98 *Secession Reference*, para. 135. 99 *Ibid.*, para. 138. 100 *Ibid.*, para. 136.

101 *Ibid.*, para. 137. For a criticism of this position, see: Turp, *Le droit de choisir*, at 811–12.

102 This argument is developed by Turp, 'Quebec's Democratic Right to Self-Determination', at 114; Turp, 'Le droit à la sécession', at 58. It is, however, largely contested in doctrine: Woehrling, 'Les aspects juridiques', at 317–18; Webber, 'The Legality of a Unilateral Declaration of Independence', at 311; Finkelstein *et al.*, 'Does Quebec Have a Right to Secede', at 255–6.

In answering Question no. 2, the Court avoided the controversial issue of the existence of the Quebec people under international law. The Court simply noted that 'much of the Quebec population certainly shares many of the characteristics (such as a common language and culture) that would be considered in determining whether a specific group is a "people," as do other groups within Quebec and/or Canada'.[103] Although the Court refused to determine whether such people of Quebec would 'encompass the entirety of the provincial population or just a portion thereof', its comments suggest that it was of the opinion that there exists not only one people in Quebec, but a juxtaposition of many. In the opinion of this author, the French-speaking majority in Quebec is a people because of their common language, culture, history, religion, and their 'collective desire to live together'.[104] For the same reasons, the ten Amerindian nations as well as the Inuit nation living in Quebec are also, without a doubt, peoples under international law.[105]

D. *The principle of effectivity and international recognition*

The main argument of the *amicus curiae* was that even if Quebec had no legal right to secession under Canadian or international law (which he admitted), this would not rule out the possibility of a *de facto* successful secession based on the principle of effectivity.

In the context of its assessment of the Canadian constitutional order, the Court concluded that the principle of effectivity had no application: it 'has no constitutional or legal status in the sense that it does not provide an *ex ante* explanation or justification for an act'.[106] Thus, the proposition

[103] *Secession Reference*, para. 125.

[104] Turp, 'Quebec's Democratic Right to Self-Determination'. In 2002, Quebec had a population of 7,455,208, with roughly 6 million French speakers and 590,000 English speakers, as well as some 600,000 immigrants.

[105] There are some 72,430 Native peoples in Quebec, 63,800 of which are Amerindians and 8,625 of which are Inuit.

[106] *Secession Reference*, paras. 107–8. Before arriving at such a conclusion, the Court made a clear distinction between the concept of rights and power: 'A distinction must be drawn between the right of a people to act, and their power to do so. They are not identical. A right is recognised in law: mere physical ability is not necessarily given status as a right. The fact that an individual or group can act in a certain way says nothing at all about the legal status or consequences of the act. A power may be exercised even in the absence of a right to do so, but if it is, then it is exercised without legal foundation. Our Constitution does not address powers in this sense. On the contrary, the Constitution is concerned only with the rights and obligations of individuals, groups and governments, and the structure of our institutions.'

that a unilateral (and illegal) secession of Quebec could be successful based on the principle of effectivity is an 'assertion of fact, not a statement of law'.[107] However, if this principle of effectivity is actually put forward, not merely as an assertion of fact, but as an assertion of *law*, it would then 'simply amount to the contention that the law may be broken as long as it can be broken successfully', which notion is 'contrary to the rule of law, and must be rejected'.[108]

The Court also addressed the argument of effectivity in the context of international law. The Court indicated that 'the existence of a positive legal entitlement is quite different from a prediction that the law will respond after the fact to a then-existing political reality'.[109] The Court decided from the outset that it did not need to explore the issue of effectivity to answer Question no. 2, which only concerns whether a *right* to unilateral secession exists under international law and does not deal with 'speculation about the possible future conduct of sovereign states on the international level' subsequent to such secession.[110]

Later in its opinion, the Court nevertheless acknowledged the importance of effectivity: 'it is true that international law may well, depending on the circumstances, adapt to recognize a political and/or factual reality, regardless of the legality of the steps leading to its creation'.[111] In the context of Quebec, 'legal consequences may flow from political facts' and its secession 'if successful in the streets, might well lead to the creation of a new state'.[112] In that sense, international law, which does not recognise a right for Quebec to secede, does not prohibit secession either. The reasoning of the Court is here in harmony with doctrine, which generally recognises that although Quebec has no *right* to secession under international law, a secession may nevertheless occur by *illegal* means, and could ultimately be successful if, for instance, an independent Quebec were to establish its effective control over its territory (to the exclusion of the predecessor State), and international recognition from other States was soon to follow.[113]

On the question of the recognition of an independent Quebec by third States, the Court adopted the declarative theory, according to which recognition is not necessary to achieve statehood, but added that 'the viability of a would-be State in the international community depends, as a practical

[107] *Ibid.*, para. 108. [108] *Ibid.* [109] *Ibid.*, para. 110.
[110] *Ibid.* This was criticised by Proulx, 'La sécession du Québec', at 382.
[111] *Secession Reference*, para. 141. [112] *Ibid.*, para. 142.
[113] Webber, 'The Legality of a Unilateral Declaration of Independence', at 294–5; Woehrling, 'Les aspects juridiques', at 321–3.

matter, upon recognition by other States'.[114] On this point, the Court first admitted that 'national interest and perceived political advantage to the recognizing state obviously play an important role' in the process of recognition.[115] It also stated, more controversially, that this process 'once considered to be an exercise of pure sovereign discretion, has come to be associated with legal norms'.[116] Here the Court made reference to the European Community Declaration on the Guidelines on the Recognition of New States in Eastern Europe and in the Soviet Union, without, however, providing any explanation as to the scope of such Declaration and its relevance in the context of Quebec's secession.[117] According to the Court, one of those 'legal norms' which may be taken into account in the process of granting or withholding recognition of a new State is the 'legitimacy of the process' of secession.[118] Such legitimacy, which the Court characterises as a 'precondition for recognition by the international community',[119] would include whether there existed a right to self-determination on the part of the seceding State and whether the secession was achieved legally in accordance with the law of the State from which the territorial unit seceded.[120]

These are controversial statements. It is submitted that the criteria identified by the Court (such as the reason for secession and the procedure by which it is achieved) are indeed elements which States will undoubtedly take into account in their political decision whether or not to recognise a new State. However, the 'legitimacy of the process' of secession, as important as it may be, is not a 'precondition' for international recognition and clearly not a 'legal norm' as the Court is suggesting.[121] It is true that the recognition process is becoming increasingly collective (at least in the European context), and that it is also more and more made conditional upon certain guarantees.[122] However, recognition has always been and remains today essentially a *discretionary political act*, which is not

[114] *Secession Reference*, para. 142. [115] *Ibid.*, para. 143. [116] *Ibid.*

[117] *ILM* 31 (1992), 1486, at 1487. The Court reference to this Declaration can only be used by analogy, and would, at any rate, not result in any 'legal norms' binding on Quebec. On this point, see: Proulx, 'La sécession du Québec', at 381–2; Dufour and Morin, 'Le renvoi relatif à la sécession du Québec', at 189.

[118] *Secession Reference*, para. 143. [119] *Ibid.*, para. 103. [120] *Ibid.*, para. 143.

[121] Turp, 'The Issue of International Recognition', at 225–346, takes a similar approach.

[122] This is the conclusion reached by the pilot project of the Council of Europe on State practice on State succession and recognition: J. Klappers (ed.), *State Practice Regarding State Succession and Issues of Recognition* (The Hague: Kluwer Law Int., 1999), at pp. 147–53.

conditioned by any 'precondition' or 'legal norm,' even in the European context.[123]

In its application of these different criteria to the Quebec situation, the Court indicated that 'an emergent state that has disregarded legitimate obligations arising out of its previous situation' such as the obligation to negotiate its secession under municipal law 'can potentially expect to be hindered by that disregard in achieving international recognition', and that, on the contrary, compliance by Quebec 'with such legitimate obligations would weigh in favour of international recognition'.[124] According to the Court:

> [A] Quebec that had negotiated in conformity with constitutional principles and values in the face of unreasonable intransigence on the part of other participants at the federal or provincial level would be more likely to be recognized than a Quebec which did not itself act according to constitutional principles in the negotiation process. Both the legality of the acts of the parties to the negotiation process under Canadian law, and the perceived legitimacy of such action, would be important considerations in the recognition process. In this way, the adherence of the parties to the obligation to negotiate would be evaluated in an indirect manner on the international plane.[125]

These affirmations by the Court are open to criticism. There is undeniable truth in the statement that Quebec's quest for international recognition will somehow be shaped by its general behaviour before, during, and after any eventual negotiations with Canada. It is submitted, however, that the Court's suggestion that States are more likely to hesitate to recognise a new State if the latter has failed to fulfil an obligation *under municipal law* to negotiate with the parent State is merely an *opinion* and certainly not a *statement of law*, as no such principle exists under positive international law. There is also little precedent supporting such a claim, and the Court did not refer to any example where States have actually refused to recognise a new entity based on the fact that it had not complied with the domestic constitutional law of the parent State.[126] The unilateral declarations of

[123] On this point, see: Opinion No. 10 of the Badinter Arbitration Commission, in: 92 *ILR* 1993, at 206, as well as the analysis of chapter 4 of this book.

[124] *Secession Reference*, para. 143.

[125] *Ibid.*, para. 103.

[126] For T. D. Grant, *The Recognition of States: Law and Practice in Debate and Evolution* (Westport, Conn.: Praeger, 1999), at pp. 99–106, the fact that an entity has seceded in a manner contrary to the constitutional laws of its parent State is not a deciding factor in

independence by Croatia and Slovenia, which were blatantly unconstitutional under Yugoslav Law (which only permitted secession upon the prior approval of all other republics),[127] certainly did not prevent third States from recognising them as independent States.[128] It is further submitted that this constitutional duty to negotiate is, strictly speaking, an obligation *under Canadian law* that is a mere 'fact' on the international plane:[129] it could not be invoked by Canada to support any eventual claim that the secession of Quebec is illegal *under international law.*[130] There exists, at any rate, clearly no *obligation* for third States *not* to recognise a new entity based on such breach of municipal law.[131]

Similarly, great doubt remains as to the impact, if any, that Canada's refusal to take part in negotiations or its (perceived or real) 'unreasonable intransigence' in conducting them would have on other States' decision to recognise or not recognise Quebec as an independent State.[132] It is

the decision of third States whether or not to recognise it. He points out the absence of State practice supporting this 'constitutional legitimacy' theory. This view is also shared in earlier writing: T. C. Chen, *The International Law of Recognition, with Special Reference to Practice in Great Britain and the United States* (London: Stevens & Sons, 1951) at p. 271; J. L. Kunz, 'Critical Remarks on Lauterpacht's "Recognition in International Law"', *AJIL* 44 (1950), 713, at 715. It has been argued by G. Burdeau, 'Le droit de sécession en question: l'exemple du Québec', *International Law Forum* 1 (1999), 3, at 5, that the Court's position is somehow idealistic and does not rely on relevant precedents: 'C'est malheureusement plus souvent par la force, voire la violence, que la sécession sera alors réalisée contre la volonté de l'Etat fédéral. Il n'est sûr que l'existence préalable de négociations change quoique ce soit au processus politique de reconnaissance par les Etat tiers.' See also: Dufour and Morin, 'Le renvoi relatif à la sécession du Québec', at 189, 193–194.

127 On this point, see: P. Radan, 'Secession and Constitutional Law in the Former Yugoslavia', *University of Tasmania Law Review* 20 (2001), at 201, who refers to some Yugoslav Constitutional Court decisions.

128 Grant, *The Recognition of States*, at p. 103.

129 Opinion No. 1 of the Badinter Commission, in: 92 *ILR* 1993, 166.

130 T. Christakis, *Le droit à l'autodétermination en dehors des situations de décolonisation* (Marseille: CERIC, 1999), at pp. 242–4: 'Il est donc clair qu'un Etat ne peut invoquer directement sa constitution pour prétendre qu'une sécession est illicite du point de vue du droit international.'

131 Such obligation of non-recognition only exists for secession involving the use of force (e.g., the secession of the 'Turkish Republic of Northern Cyprus' from Cyprus) and when it results in the denial of the right to self-determination (e.g. the declaration of independence of the racist state of Rhodesia in 1965).

132 Monahan, 'The Public Policy Role of the Supreme Court of Canada', at 86–7, makes this point. *Contra*: Haljan, 'Negotiating Quebec Secession', at 214, who suggests that a breach of the duty to negotiate by the federal government would not only undermine the legitimacy of its position on the international plane, but that it could also satisfy the third ground for secession identified by the Court (at para. 138) in so far as it would constitute a denial of Quebec's 'meaningful access to government to pursue their political, economic, social and cultural development'.

quite conceivable that this obligation to negotiate, in itself, will have no impact whatsoever on other States' willingness to recognise an independent Quebec. States are more likely to be guided by other more general, and arguably more important, standards of 'good behaviour', such as the new State's renunciation of the use of force and its respect for the UN Charter, as well as its adherence to principles, such as the respect for minorities and human rights, democracy, and the rule of law.[133] The creation by the Court of this obligation to negotiate secession may ultimately be for internal purposes only, as it could have merely a remote application under international law.[134]

Another interesting question, which the Court refrained from considering, is the likely impact of Canada's (possible, yet not probable) persistent refusal to recognise an independent Quebec after an unambiguous referendum result in favour of sovereignty. This point was made by one expert for the Attorney General of Canada (Professor Crawford) who stressed that no entity attempting to secede unilaterally has been admitted to the United Nations since 1945 against the wishes of the government of the State from which it was trying to secede.[135] Some writers conclude that Quebec's chance for recognition by other States is unlikely without prior

[133] By analogy, the Declaration on the Guidelines on the Recognition of New States in Eastern Europe and in the Soviet Union, affirmed the member States of the European Community's 'readiness to recognize, subject to the normal standards of international practice and the political realities in each case, those new States which, following the historic changes in the region, have constituted themselves on a democratic basis, have accepted the appropriate international obligations and have committed themselves in good faith to a peaceful process and to negotiations'. The requirement for recognition includes *inter alia*: the respect of the Charter of the United Nations, the Final Act of Helsinki, the Charter of Paris 'especially with regard to the rule of law, democracy and human rights'; the guarantees for the rights of ethnic and national groups and minorities; the respect for the inviolability of all frontiers which can only be changed by peaceful means and by common agreement; the acceptance of all relevant commitments with regard to disarmament and nuclear non-proliferation as well as to security and regional stability; the commitment to settle by agreement, including where appropriate by recourse to arbitration, all questions concerning state succession and regional disputes.

[134] For Turp, 'The Issue of International Recognition', at 225–346, the Court's findings as to the issue of international recognition consist mainly of political prognostication rather than legal reasoning. Thus, the threat of non-recognition by the international community seems to be the only 'sanction' the Court adverts to the consequence of an illegal secession. He noted the 'weakness' of such 'sanction', as it will be administered unevenly by different States because of its political discretionary nature. He also believes that the sanction is unsatisfying as it is one-sided and applies only to Quebec.

[135] This report was later published in: J. Crawford, 'State Practice and International Law in Relation to Secession', *BYIL* 69 (1998), 85–117. See also: Williams, *International Legal Effects*, at p. 12.

recognition by Canada.[136] This is quite possible, but nowhere near certain. Recent State practice in the context of the break-up of Yugoslavia has shown, on the contrary, that third States have indeed recognised seceding entities prior to their recognition by the parent State.[137] It is true, however, that this example was in the context of dissolution and that it may be of limited help in dealing with cases of secession.[138]

Other writers have further argued that if third States were to recognise an independent Quebec notwithstanding Canada's refusal to act similarly, such 'premature' recognition would infringe Canada's sovereignty and unlawfully violate its territorial integrity.[139] While this position may find some support in doctrine, it should be noted that some expressions of recognition in the context of the dissolution of Yugoslavia were arguably 'premature', but this has not resulted in any claim by the Federal Republic of Yugoslavia against third States.[140]

The Court concluded that international recognition occurs only *after* a territorial unit has been politically successful in achieving secession,

[136] Monahan, 'The Law and Politics of Quebec Secession', at 28–9; Williams, *International Legal Effects*, at pp. 10–12.

[137] Croatia and Slovenia declared their independence on 25 June 1991 (but suspended it until 8 October 1991). They were first recognised by Germany on 23 December 1991 and soon after by the other Member States of the European Community as well as by other States on 15 January 1992. It was only a few months later that the Federal Republic of Yugoslavia recognised (conditionally) these two ex-republics as independent States: new Constitution of the Federal Republic of Yugoslavia of 27 April 1992. Croatia and Slovenia were admitted to the United Nations on 22 May 1992 (Resolutions 46/236 and 46/238 of the UN General Assembly).

[138] For Lalonde, 'Quebec's Boundaries', at 141, as long as the process unfolding in Yugoslavia in the early 1990s was characterised as one of secession, the international community reaffirmed its commitment to the preservation of Yugoslavia's territorial integrity. It is only once the conflict had been described by the Badinter Commission as one of dissolution (in Opinion No. 1, 29 November 1991, 92 *ILR*, 162, 167) that recognition by third States formally extended to the breakaway republics.

[139] Finkelstein *et al.*, 'Does Quebec Have a Right to Secede', at 230–3; Williams, *International Legal Effects*, at p. 11. See the criticisms of Turp, 'Globalising Sovereignty'.

[140] On 11 October 1991, that is soon after Croatia and Slovenia declared their independence, but *before* they were actually recognised by any third States, the Presidency of the Federal Republic of Yugoslavia clearly indicated that any such recognition by third States would constitute 'a flagrant interference in its internal affairs' and a flagrant violation of its territorial integrity and of many international instruments (such as the UN Charter). The statement also indicated that such recognition by third States 'would be an extremely dangerous precedent with deleterious consequences for the overall international legal system', and that, consequently, 'it [would] resort to all available means recognised in international law' against those States. This document is available in: S. Trifunovka, *Yugoslavia Through Documents – From Its Creation to Its Dissolution* (Dordrecht: Martinus Nijhoff Publ., 1994), at pp. 353–4. It seems that this threat, however, was not followed by any concrete actions by the Federal Republic of Yugoslavia against those third States that have recognised Croatia and Slovenia.

and that it could not 'serve retroactively as a source of a "legal" right to secede in the first place'.[141] In accordance with the principle of effectivity, an illegal act may possibly acquire some form of legal status, but this subsequent condonation of the initially illegal act does not retroactively create a *legal right* to engage in the act in the first place.[142] This point has been contested in doctrine.[143] In the Court's view:

> It may be that a unilateral secession by Quebec would eventually be accorded legal status by Canada and other states, and thus give rise to legal consequences; but this does not support the more radical contention that subsequent recognition of a state of affairs brought about by a unilateral declaration of independence could be taken to mean that secession was achieved under colour of a legal right.[144]

E. An important unresolved contentious issue: the territorial integrity of an independent Quebec and the respect of Aboriginal peoples' rights

In its opinion, the Court noted that eventual negotiations on secession would inevitably address a wide range of issues, including the question of the boundaries of an independent Quebec.[145] This is indeed one of the most contentious issues likely to arise in case of secession. The government of Quebec affirmed that the principle of *uti possidetis juris* would guarantee Quebec its existing borders in the event of secession.[146] This

141 *Secession Reference*, para. 142. 142 *Ibid.*, para. 146.

143 Toope, 'Re Reference by the Governor', at 522: 'recognition, though political in content, could provide retroactive legitimacy to a unilateral declaration of independence by Quebec, bequeathing a gloss of "right"'. This also seems to be the position of Proulx, 'La sécession du Québec', at 606–7.

144 *Secession Reference*, para. 144.

145 *Ibid.*, para. 96. The Court noted that 'nobody seriously suggests that our national existence, seamless in so many aspects, could be effortlessly separated along what are now the provincial boundaries of Quebec'. The issue of eventual negotiations on Quebec's borders is discussed in: Lalonde, 'Quebec's Boundaries', at 144.

146 Government of Quebec, *Quebec and its Territory*, 1997, available at: http://www.saic.gouv.qc.ca/publications/territoire-a.pdf. The conclusions are based on a Report by five international law experts commissioned in 1992 by the Bélanger-Campeau Commission: T. Franck, R. Higgins, A. Pellet, M. Shaw and C. Tomuschat, 'L'intégrité territoriale du Québec dans l'hypothèse de l'accession à la souveraineté', in: *Commission d'étude*, vol. I, pp. 377–461, at pp. 383, 418, 420–5, 443. The Report is available in: Bayefsky, *Self-Determination in International Law*, at pp. 241–303. According to the expert Report by Prof. Pellet (see para. 2.44–6) submitted by the *amicus*, the position of Quebec is further supported by more recent developments in the context of the dissolution of Yugoslavia: Opinion No. 3 of the Badinter Commission, 11 January 1992.

position is also supported in doctrine.[147] However, the government of Canada has increasingly contested this position. The argument is that the northern territories, which were transferred to Quebec in 1898 and 1912, would be 'returned' to Canada upon the change of status of the Province in the Federation.[148] It has been argued that, the principle of *uti possidetis* would not apply to Quebec as its application is limited to cases of dissolution,[149] or of decolonisation.[150] Others have argued that Quebec would only retain the territory over which it has effective control upon its secession,[151] to the exclusion of defined regions of the Province which have voted against secession.[152]

[147] Woehrling, 'Les aspects juridiques', at 326–9; H. Brun, 'Les conséquences territoriales de l'accession du Québec à la souveraineté', in: *Commission d'étude*, vol. I, at pp. 477–90; Makovka, 'Les limites territoriales et maritimes', at 309–23; T. Leroux, 'Les frontières terrestres d'un Québec souverain à la lumière du droit international contemporain', *Revue de droit* (Univ. Sherbrooke) 25 (1994–1995), 239–85 (making an exception for eventual Aboriginal claims, at 279). See also: H. Dorion, 'Les frontières du Québec : l'état de la question', in: *Commission d'étude*, vol. I, pp. 353–74; J. I. Charney, 'The Maritime Boundaries of Québec', in: *Commission d'étude*, vol. I, pp. 493–577. All last three studies, which were updated by the authors in 2001, can be found at: http://www.saic.gouv.qc.ca/institutionnelles_constitutionnelles/mise_a_jour_etudes_1991-1992.htm.

[148] This argument is supported in doctrine, *inter alia*, by these writers: Williams, *International Legal Effects*, at p. 7; Finkelstein *et al.*, 'Does Quebec Have a Right to Secede', at 256–60; S. A. Scott, 'Autodétermination sécession, division, légalité', in: *Commission d'étude*, vol. I, pp. 463–74 (see also the updated 2001 version of this study at: http://www.mce.gouv.qc.ca/e/objets/13-SteophenAScott.pdf); P. Radan, '"You Can't Always Get What You Want": the Territorial Scope of an Independent Quebec', *Osgoode Hall Law Journal* 41/4 (2003).

[149] Woehrling, 'L'avis de la Cour suprême du Canada', at 11; Monahan, 'The Law and Politics of Quebec Secession', at 25–8; Finkelstein *et al.*, 'Does Quebec Have a Right to Secede', at 259–60. See also: D. Sanders, 'If Quebec Secedes from Canada Can the Cree Secede from Quebec?', *UBCLR* 29 (1995), 157. This question is also discussed in: C. Hilling, 'Les frontières du Québec dans l'hypothèse de son accession à l'indépendance: pour une interprétation contemporaine de l'*uti possidetis juris*', in: Corten *et al.* (eds.), *Démembrement d'Etats et délimitations territoriales*; P. Girard, 'L'intégrité du territoire québécois dans l'hypothèse de la souveraineté', *RJEUL* 6 (1992), 25.

[150] P. Radan, 'The Borders of Future Independent Quebec: Does the Principle of *uti possidetis juris* Apply?', *Australian I.L.J.* 1998, 200, at 208–14. See also: P. Radan, 'The Supreme Court of Canada and the Borders of Quebec', *Australian I.L.J.* 1998, 171, at 176.

[151] Monahan, 'The Law and Politics of Quebec Secession', at 24–5; Woehrling, 'Les aspects juridiques', at 323, 328. *Contra*: Franck *et al.*, 'L'intégrité territoriale du Québec', at pp. 410–17. On this point, see also: S. Lalonde, 'Quebec Secession and the Principle of Effectiveness', *Canadian Bar Review* 76 (1997), 258–9.

[152] Monahan, 'The Public Policy Role of the Supreme Court of Canada', at 98, makes this argument.

The question of the territorial integrity of an independent Quebec is undoubtedly linked with that of the Aboriginal peoples' rights under Canadian law, whereby the federal government has a fiduciary obligation towards them.[153] Moreover, Aboriginal peoples have to consent to any amendment to the Constitution which affects their rights.[154] It has been argued that, under Canadian law, the secession of Quebec, which would undoubtedly affect the Aboriginal peoples' rights and terminate their fiduciary relationship with the federal government, would therefore require their prior consent.[155] In any event, some have maintained that if Quebec were to secede, the Aboriginal peoples living in the Province could seek to remain part of Canada.[156] This is also the view of the federal government and some Aboriginal peoples of Quebec.[157] On the contrary,

153 Section 91(24) of the Constitution Act, 1867 gives the federal government jurisdiction over Indians and lands reserved for Indians. Canadian courts have established that there is a fiduciary relationship between the federal Crown and the Aboriginal peoples of Canada, and that the government has a responsibility to protect their interests. On this point, see: Royal Commission on Aboriginal Peoples, *Canada's Fiduciary Obligations to Aboriginal Peoples in the Context of Accession to Sovereignty by Quebec* (Ottawa, 1995), which contains two vols.: R. Dupuis and K. McNeil (eds.), *Domestic Dimensions*, and S. J. Anaya, R. Falk and D. Pharand (eds.), *International Dimensions*.

154 Section 35 of the Constitution Act, 1982. See also: Finkelstein and Vegh, *The Separation of Quebec*, at pp. 25–31; Monahan, 'The Law and Politics of Quebec Secession', at 15–17.

155 Monahan, *ibid.* For B. Miller, 'Quebec's Accession to Sovereignty and its Impact on First Nations', *U. New Brunswick L. J.* 43 (1994), 261, at 263–4, the fiduciary obligation towards the Aboriginal peoples, as well as all treaty rights and constitutional protections, would be automatically transferred to an independent Quebec. All these issues are extensively analysed in: B. Morse, 'How Would Quebec's Secession Affect Aboriginal Peoples and Aboriginal Rights', *Nat. J. Const. L.* 11 (1999–2000), 107–45. See also: G. St. Louis, 'The Tangled Web of Sovereignty and Self-Governance: Canada's Obligation to the Cree Nation in Consideration of Quebec's Threats to Secede', *Berkeley J.I.L.*14 (1996), 380; Radan, '"You Can't Always Get What You Want"'.

156 Williams, *International Legal Effects*, at p. 7; Finkelstein *et al.*, 'Does Quebec Have a Right to Secede', at p. 252; Leroux, 'Les frontières terrestres d'un Québec souverain' at 279; Turp, 'Quebec's Democratic Right to Self-Determination', at 99; Miller, 'Quebec's Accession to Sovereignty', at 261; Radan, '"You Can't Always Get What You Want"'. The issue of the right to self-determination of Aboriginal peoples in an independent Quebec is discussed in: Sanders, 'If Quebec Secedes from Canada'; K. McNeil, 'Aboriginal Nations and Quebec's Boundaries: Canada Couldn't Give What It Didn't Have', in: D. Drache and R. Perrin (eds.), *Negotiating With a Sovereign Quebec* (Toronto: James Lorimer & Co., 1992), p. 107; P. Hutchins, 'And do the Indians Pass With It – Quebec Sovereignty, Aboriginal Peoples and the Treaty Order', paper presented at the Canadian Bar Association Seminar on *The Act Respecting the Sovereignty of Quebec: Legal Perspectives*, Montreal, 6 May 1995.

157 For a detailed account of one Aboriginal perspective on the question, see: *Sovereign Injustice: Forcible Inclusion of the James Bay Crees and Cree Territory into a Sovereign Quebec*, a book published by the Grand Council of the Crees, October 1995, which is also available on-line at: http://www.uni.ca/si_index.html.

Quebec maintains that such a right of self-determination should not be exercised inconsistently with its territorial integrity.[158]

This is no doubt a complex issue that cannot be fully addressed in the present chapter. It may be true that, based on the application of the principle of *uti possidetis*, Aboriginal peoples would have no right to external self-determination once Quebec secedes from Canada.[159] However, notwithstanding the legal soundness of such proposition, its logical consistency leaves something to be desired. Professor Kohen's general assessment of this issue seems particularly accurate in the present context: 'Secessionists are at pains to explain why they claim the respect of their territorial integrity (in so doing, denying the right to self-determination of "peoples" claiming it inside the secessionist entity), rejecting at the same time the right to the territorial integrity of the state from which they want to be separated.'[160] Thus, it remains doubtful to what extent international public opinion will be convinced by the argument that the territorial integrity of Canada can be jeopardised by the secession of Quebec, while the territorial integrity of a new independent Quebec would prevent the external self-determination of the Aboriginal peoples.[161] In any event, an independent Quebec, as an absolute priority, would have to address the legitimate claims, and notably the territorial claims, of the Aboriginal peoples and treat with them on a truly equal basis if it wants to avoid the tremendous problems which would result from their legitimate claims to some kind of external self-determination.[162]

IV. The aftermath of the *Quebec Secession Reference*

Following the Court decision, the federal government was quick to initiate legislation identifying in advance any future referendum the circumstances of which would trigger its constitutional duty to negotiate

[158] Section 3 of An Act Respecting the Future of Quebec.

[159] This is the conclusion reached by Franck *et al.*, 'L'intégrité territoriale du Québec', at 430–43.

[160] M. G. Kohen, 'International Law is the Most Appropriate Moral Answer to Territorial Conflicts', *Geopolitics* 6/2 (2001), 169, at 171.

[161] Woehrling, 'Les aspects juridiques', at 328.

[162] It should be noted that recently the government of Quebec has entered into several comprehensive territorial agreements with different Aboriginal peoples, which do not, however, deal with the question of Quebec boundaries upon its secession.

the secession of Quebec from Canada.[163] In other words, as a result of the Court having refused to venture into the controversy of what would constitute a 'clear majority' on a 'clear question', the federal government decided to act.[164] The federal response came in the form of An Act to Give Effect to the Requirement for Clarity as Set out in the Opinion of the Supreme Court of Canada in the Quebec Secession Reference (Bill C-20).[165]

The Clarity Act provides for a two-fold test. With respect to the clarity of the question (Section 1), it indicates that it is for the Federal House of Commons to determine whether a question 'would result in a clear expression of the will of the population' of a province to secede from Canada.[166] The Clarity Act explicitly indicates that a 'clear' question should focus on secession *per se*, and not be combined with other types of proposals.[167] If the House of Commons determines that the referendum question is not clear, 'the Government of Canada shall not enter into negotiations on the terms on which a province might cease to be part of Canada' (Section 1(6)). Should the referendum question pass this first hurdle, the House

[163] An analysis of these developments can be found in P. Bienvenu, 'The Aftermath of the Quebec Secession Reference: the First Two Years', paper prepared for the Law Society of Upper Canada, Special Lectures 2000, Toronto 8–9 June 2000 (on file with the author). For another analysis, see: P. J. Monahan, M.J. Bryant & N. C. Coté, *Coming to Terms with Plan B: Ten Principles Governing Secession*, (Toronto: C. D. Howe Inst., 1996), available at: http://www.cdhowe.org/pdf/Monahan.pdf; B. Pelletier, 'La loi sur la clarté, sa contrepartie québécoise, et le renvoi relatif à la sécession du Québec', *RBDC* 2001, 513–33.

[164] In doctrine, see: C. L. Ford, 'In Search of the Qualitative Clear Majority: Democratic Experimentalism and the Quebec Secession Reference', *Alberta Law Review*, 39 (2001), 511 at 559; T. Flanagan, 'Should a Supermajority be Required in a Referendum on Separation?', in: J. E. Trent, R. Young and G. Lachapelle (eds.), *Quebec-Canada, What is the Path Ahead?* (Ottawa: Univ. Ottawa Press 1996), at pp. 129–34.

[165] S.C. 2000, Chapter 26 (passed by the House of Commons on 15 March 2000, and in force since 29 June 2000) (hereinafter referred to as the Clarity Act). In doctrine: P. J. Monahan, 'Doing the Rules: An Assessment of the Federal Clarity Act in Light of the Quebec Secession Reference' (Toronto: C.D. Howe Inst., 2000), available at: http://www.cdhowe.org/PDF/monahan-2.pdf.

[166] In accordance with Section 1(5), 'in considering the clarity of a referendum question, the House of Commons shall take into account the views of all political parties represented in the legislative assembly of the province whose government is proposing the referendum on secession, any formal statements or resolutions by the government or legislative assembly of any province or territory of Canada, any formal statements or resolutions by the Senate, and any other views it considers to be relevant'.

[167] Thus, in accordance with Section 1(4), a 'clear' referendum question could not merely focus 'on a mandate to negotiate' without soliciting a direct expression on secession, and it could not envisage 'other possibilities in addition to the secession of the province from Canada, such as economic or political arrangements with Canada'. This aspect of the Bill has been criticised, even by its supporters: Monahan, 'Doing the Rules'.

of Commons would also have to determine, after the referendum took place, whether 'in the circumstances, there has been a clear expression of a will by a clear majority of the population of that province that the province cease to be part of Canada' (Section 2).[168] A negative answer to this second question would also prevent the government of Canada from entering into negotiations with Quebec. Finally, article 3 reiterates some of the Court's findings, namely, that the unilateral secession of a province is illegal under the Constitution of Canada and that it requires an amendment through negotiations 'involving at least the governments of all of the provinces and the Government of Canada'.[169]

The response to the Clarity Act in Quebec was explosive. It has been perceived by the government of Quebec as an illegitimate attempt by the federal government to block any future referendum and deprive the National Assembly of its powers. This view is also widely held in Quebec's legal circles.[170] On the contrary, in English Canada scholars have

[168] Section 2(1). In doing so, the House of Commons will be taking into account factors such as 'the size of the majority of valid votes cast in favour of the secessionist option', 'the percentage of eligible voters voting in the referendum', and 'any other matters or circumstances it considers to be relevant' (Section 2(2)). In accordance with Section 2(3), the House of Commons should take into account the views of different actors in considering the clarity of the majority, the list of which is the same as in Section 1(5) quoted above.

[169] Section 3(2) indicates the (non-exhaustive) 'terms of secession' which will need to be addressed during the negotiations: 'the division of assets and liabilities, any changes to the borders of the province, the rights, interests and territorial claims of the Aboriginal peoples of Canada, and the protection of minority rights'.

[170] The *Bloc Québécois* (a pro-sovereignty political party sitting at the federal House of Commons) commissioned two studies on the conformity of the *Clarity Act* with the Supreme Court's *Reference*. See: H. Brun, *Avis juridique concernant la notion de 'majorité claire' dans le Renvoi relatif à la sécession du Québec*, available at: http://daniel.turp.qc.ca/meteo/actualite_politique/ap_1711.htm (arguing that the Court's use of the words 'clear majority' is a reference to simple majority, and that an eventual refusal by the federal government to enter into negotiations with Quebec based on the position that a majority higher than 50 per cent + 1 is required would breach this obligation to negotiate and would be unconstitutional); A. Pellet, *Avis juridique sommaire sur le projet de Loi donnant effet à l'exigence de clarté formulée par la Cour suprême dans son Renvoi sur la sécession du Québec*; available at: http://daniel.turp.qc.ca/meteo/actualite_politique/ap_1312b.htm (arguing that the Clarity Act gives the federal government a double veto in the process: the first, *ex ante* the referendum with respect to the clarity of the question, and the second, *ex post* on the clarity of the majority. This unilateral (and non-negotiable) approach would be contrary to the spirit of the *Reference*, which has as its cornerstone the principle of negotiation). Other writers have also adopted similar views: Brun and Tremblay, *Droit Constitutionnel*, at p. 246 (arguing the unconstitutionality of the Clarity Act on many grounds); C. Ryan, *Consequences of the Quebec Secession Reference: The Clarity Bill and Beyond*, (Toronto:

acclaimed the wisdom of the federal government and have been quite supportive of the content of the Clarity Act.[171]

The political reply of the government of Quebec came in the form of An Act Respecting the Exercise of the Fundamental Rights and Prerogatives of the Quebec People and the Quebec State (Bill-99), which has a much broader scope than the Clarity Act.[172] The preamble makes an implicit reference to the Clarity Act, described as a 'policy of the federal government designed to call into question the legitimacy, integrity and efficient operation of [Quebec's] national democratic institutions'. In rebuttal to the federal law, the Quebec Fundamental Rights Act declares the existence of a Quebec people, and its 'inalienable right to freely decide' its political regime and its legal status (Section 2).[173] It also provides that simple majority is the rule in any future referendum (Section 4), that 'the territory of Quebec and its boundaries cannot be altered except with the consent of the National Assembly' and that 'the Government must ensure that the territorial integrity of Quebec is maintained and respected' (Section 9). In an obvious reference to the Federal Parliament, Section 13 states that 'no other parliament or government may reduce the powers, authority, sovereignty or legitimacy of the National Assembly, or impose constraint on the democratic will of the Quebec people to determine its own future'. This Bill has, not surprisingly, been the object of different assessments

C. D. Howe Inst., 2000), available at: http://www.cdhowe.org/pdf/ryan.pdf (for whom the Clarity Act is an interference by the House of Commons in a matter considered to be of the exclusive jurisdiction of the Quebec National Assembly); A. Lajoie, *Avis juridique: Le sens de l'expression 'question claire' dans le Renvoi relatif à la sécession du Québec*, 7 December 1999, available at: http://www.action-nationale.qc.ca/00–1/lajoie.html; D. Turp, 'Québec's Right to Secessionist Self-Determination: the Colliding Paths of Canada's Clarity Act and Québec's Fundamental Rights Act', in Turp, *Le droit de choisir*, p. 730, at pp. 738–9; Turp, *Le droit de choisir*, at pp. 822–31 (arguing the non-democratic nature of the Clarity Act which amounts to an obligation *not to negotiate* and represents a threat to the freedom of the Quebec people to determine its future). A different assessment is made by Bienvenu, 'The Aftermath of the Quebec Secession Reference', at 29, for whom the Clarity Act is both respectful of the Court's opinion and an appropriate response by the federal government.

171 P. Hogg, 'La loi sur la clarté est conforme au droit constitutionnel', (Montreal) *Le Devoir*, 25 February 2000; Monahan, 'Doing the Rules' (he criticises, however, the Clarity Act for not establishing in advance the threshold that would have to be achieved for a majority to be deemed 'clear').

172 Revised Statutes of Quebec, Chapter E-20.2 (passed by the National Assembly on 7 December 2000, and in force since 28 February 2001) (hereinafter referred to as the Quebec Fundamental Rights Act).

173 Section 1 states: 'The right of the Québec people to self-determination is founded in fact and in law. The Québec people is the holder of rights that are universally recognised under the principle of equal rights and self-determination of peoples.'

depending on the political views of commentators.[174] The Quebec Fundamental Rights Act has also been contested before the Superior Court of Quebec, where the Court decided that the question was not justiciable.[175]

Conclusion

The Court's opinion is a helpful reminder that, for the assessment of the question of the legality of secession, legal arguments are neither completely decisive of the question nor totally irrelevant.[176] The question is both legal and political. The legacy of the Court's opinion from the perspective of international law is positive. It is an important decision defining the circumstances in which secession in a non-colonial context may be allowed under international law, and as such it is a very useful reference for future disputes involving questions relating to the legality of secession. The emphasis that the Court places on negotiations and the duty it imposes on all parties to undertake them in good faith are valuable standards which could serve as guidelines to other secession processes elsewhere in the world. This is particularly so considering that secession processes are too often plagued with violence, instead of being conducted in accordance with principles such as the rule of law and the respect for minorities' rights.

The one criticism that can be formulated with respect to the reasoning of the Court arises in the context of its assessment of the constitutional

[174] A positive assessment can be found in: Turp, 'Québec's Right to Secessionist Self-Determination', at 738–9; Turp, *Le droit de choisir*, at pp. 831–5. Critical reviews are found in: Monahan, 'Doing the Rules'; Scott, 'Autodétermination sécession'.

[175] A petition was submitted on 9 May 2001 to have arts. 1 to 5, and 13, of the *Quebec Fundamental Rights Act* as '*ultra vires*, declared absolutely null and void, and of no force and effect'. In *Henderson and Equality Party c. P. G. Québec et al.*, [2002] R.J.Q. 2435, (available in English at: *Henderson et al. v. Quebec (A. G.)*, [2003] 220 D. L. R. (4th) 691), Mr. Justice Michel Côté of the Superior Court of Quebec dismissed the case on 16 August 2002 on the ground that the question was not justiciable and also for the following reasons (at paras. 60 and 62): 'La requête des requérants est irrecevable car elle n'est fondée sur aucune difficulté réelle et immédiate, mais qu'elle constitue une demande d'opinion juridique fondée sur des hypothèses et des conjectures. En effet, aucune application concrète de la Loi 99 n'est contestée en l'espèce, mais uniquement une situation hypothétique d'application de cette loi qui n'a aucun fondement factuel. . . . Le Procureur général du Québec fait également valoir, avec raison, que les conclusions (2) et (3), recherchées par les requérants, sont également dénuées de tout fondement concret et, au surplus, elles ne visent aucune action gouvernementale ou législative. Ces conclusions constituent une recherche de déclarations de principe et, à ce titre également, elles sont irrecevables.' The on-line version of the case (in French) is available at: http://www.jugements.qc.ca/.

[176] Craven, 'Of Federalism, Secession, Canada and Quebec', at 256; Webber, 'The Legality of a Unilateral Declaration of Independence', at 283–4; Marchildon and Maxwell, 'Quebec's Right of Secession', at 589.

duty to negotiate and the impact it may have on international recognition. However, to the extent that the Court's (questionable) comments on this point were not decisive of the question posed in the *Reference*, which only dealt with the *legality* of secession and not its possible *effectivity*, and that these observations may therefore be considered as mere *obiter dicta*, this should in no way undermine the general soundness of the Court's opinion.

As for the political consequences of this legal saga, both the government of Canada and the government of Quebec have viewed the opinion of the Court as well-balanced and satisfactory. In reality, the conclusions of the Court seem slightly more favourable to the secessionist movement.[177] Thus, on the one hand, the Court's opinion states the illegality of Quebec secession under the Canadian Constitution and the absence of any legal basis under international law. On the other hand, in the event of an unambiguous vote in favour of sovereignty, the Court, most importantly, imposes the obligation to negotiate such secession through an amendment to the Canadian Constitution.[178] The novelty of this obligation, which certainly came as a surprise for the federal government which had hoped the Court would limit itself to a statement as to the illegality of secession, is principally directed at the federal government insofar as the government of Quebec has long recognised that secession would in any case have to be the object of negotiations with Canada.[179] It is the opinion of this author that the Court's recognition of the legitimacy of secession (under certain conditions), and the resulting duty to negotiate which it imposes on the protagonists, is likely to appeal to – and to reassure – uncertain voters in a future referendum, while the findings that secession is illegal under Canadian law, and the absence of any legal basis under international law, are not likely to discourage separatist sentiment in Quebec.[180]

The federal Clarity Act seems to have, in effect, neutralised the one aspect that the government of Quebec would no doubt have counted on in a future referendum, namely, the fact that the federal government could no longer claim (as it did during the last two referenda) that it would never

177 Turp, 'Globalising Sovereignty'. *Contra*: M. Mandel, 'A Solomonic Judgment?', *Canada Watch* 7 1-2 (1999) 15.

178 Monahan, 'The Public Policy Role of the Supreme Court of Canada', at 94, concludes, 'Quebec has everything to gain and nothing to lose from such negotiation.'

179 See, e.g., Bill 1, which expressly required such negotiations to take place *prior* to any declaration of independence by the Quebec National Assembly. For one constitutional expert, Hogg, 'The Duty to Negotiate', at 34–5, after a winning referendum, the federal government would have to negotiate with Quebec anyway, and therefore, the Court simply converted a political reality into a legal rule.

180 Woehrling, 'Unexpected Consequences', p. 18.

negotiate with 'separatists'.[181] The new Act gives the possibility for the federal government to declare *before* any referendum has actually taken place that the question posed to Quebec voters is not 'clear' and therefore to refuse up-front to enter into any eventual negotiations with Quebec. Such a clear message from the federal government would not, of course, prevent the referendum from taking place, or even its result from being unambiguously in favour of sovereignty. However, this 'threat' that no negotiations would take place in the event of a clear victory of the secessionist option in a referendum (and the implicit message it sends that secession would consequently be messy and chaotic) is likely to influence the way people vote in the referendum. In that sense, the federal government strategy will undoubtedly have a great impact on any future referendum to be held on the question of Quebec secession.

At the same time, the Clarity Act is arguably *quite irrelevant* from the perspective of international law. Thus, to the extent that a referendum would result in the clear expression by the people of Quebec of their will to secede from Canada, the unwillingness of the federal government to undertake negotiations, or even the interdiction to do so under the Clarity Act, would not prevent Quebec from eventually becoming an independent State. As previously observed, secessionist entities do have an obligation to negotiate their secession with the parent State. Yet the absence of any negotiations with the federal government prior to the effective secession of Quebec would not, in itself, prevent it from being internationally recognised by third States. In that sense, the Clarity Act can only prevent Quebec from achieving secession *legally under Canadian law*; it cannot in any way block its accession to sovereignty if it chooses to follow such a path.

[181] J.-Y. Morin, 'A Balanced Judgement?', *Canada Watch* 7/1–2 (1999), 5, had, before the enactment of the Clarity Act, rightly observed that by leaving the content of 'clear' majority and 'clear' question to be determined by politicians, the Court in effect left to the federal government the power 'to raise obstacles and difficulties that are important and numerous enough so as to negate any attempt to achieve sovereignty and to throw off track any negotiation on the issue'.

14

The Secession of the Canton of Jura in Switzerland

CHRISTIAN DOMINICÉ

Switzerland is a federal State. The name 'Confederation' is a historical heritage, but is not accurate. The component members are the Cantons. There are twenty-three. The Canton of Jura is the twenty-third and was created on the 1st of January 1979.

From the adoption of the Federal Constitution in 1848 until the addition of the Canton of Jura in 1979, Switzerland was made up of twenty-two Cantons. The Canton of Jura, whose territory was part of the Canton of Berne, came to birth through a true secession process. Several plebiscites were organized.

The relations between the Cantons are governed by federal law – the federal Constitution and the laws adopted by the federal Parliament. However, when for a specific matter there is no federal rule, international law is applied as a substitute.

In the case of the Canton of Jura, important questions were settled by reference to customary international law under the laws of State succession. This was particularly the case in the area of succession of goods, debts and public institutions, as well as with respect to agreements and treaties concluded by the government in Berne with foreign countries and with other Cantons. In this process, various international instruments and the reports of the International Law Commission of the United Nations were taken into consideration.

Since international law was applied in this particular case of 'cantonal secession' it can be presented as an illustration of State succession.

LA SÉCESSION DU NOUVEAU CANTON SUISSE DU JURA

I. Succession d'Etats et cantons suisses

A. L'Etat fédéral

Quoi qu'en donne à penser l'appellation 'Confédération' qu'elle utilise dans sa Constitution,[1] la Suisse est, depuis 1848, un Etat fédéral.[2] C'est souligner que les entités qui la composent – les cantons – à l'instar des *Länder* allemands ou des *States* américains, ne sont pas des Etats souverains.

Les cantons ont néanmoins, à l'exception de la souveraineté internationale, tous les attributs de l'Etat, notamment un territoire qui, à l'intérieur de l'Etat fédéral, peut faire l'objet de mutations, notamment de cessions entre les cantons, ou encore – mais c'est vraiment exceptionnel – d'une modification plus lourde de conséquences, telle une sécession conduisant à la création d'un nouveau canton. C'est ce qui s'est produit lorsque la République et canton du Jura fut créé en 1978, avec pour territoire une partie de celui du canton de Berne.[3]

L'analogie est ici évidente avec le phénomène de la sécession sur la scène internationale. Celle-ci est caractérisée par l'apparition d'un nouvel Etat sans que l'existence ou l'identité de l'Etat amputé d'une partie de son territoire soient mises en question.[4]

Cette analogie dans les faits peut-elle présenter de l'intérêt pour le droit international? La réponse est affirmative dans la mesure où celui-ci est applicable dans les rapports intercantonaux.

[1] La Constitution du 18 avril 1999, actuellement en vigueur, est intitulée 'Constitution fédérale de la Confédération suisse'. Dans le corps du texte, le terme 'Confédération' signifie l'Etat central. Cf. A. Auer, G. Malinverni, M. Hottelier, *Droit constitutionnel suisse* (Berne: Staempli, 2000), vol. I, p. 305.

[2] Cf. J. F. Aubert, *Traité de droit constitutionnel suisse* (Neuchâtel: Ed. Ides et Calandes, 1967), vol. I., p. 34.

[3] L'histoire du problème jurassien, avec pour aboutissement la création du nouveau canton, est retracée notamment dans le Message du Conseil fédéral sur la création du canton du Jura, du 16 novembre 1977, Feuille fédérale (FF) 1977 III 799; voir aussi P. Boillat, *Jura, naissance d'un Etat: aux sources du droit et des institutions jurassiennes* (Lausanne: Payot, 1989); J.R.G. Jenkins, *Jura Separatism in Switzerland* (Oxford: Clarendon Press, 1986).

[4] Voir les deux cours enseignés à La Haye par D. P. O'Connell, 'Recent Problems of State Succession in Relation to New States' et M. Bedjaoui, 'Problèmes récents de succession d'Etats dans les Etats nouveaux', *Recueil des cours* 130 (1970-II), p. 95 et p. 454.

B. *Le droit international dans les rapports entre les cantons*

Les cantons sont assujettis au premier chef au droit fédéral, qui l'emporte sur les droits cantonaux selon l'adage bien connu 'Bundesrecht bricht kantonales Recht'.[5] Leurs rapports mutuels sont donc à maints égards régis par le droit fédéral.

Cependant, lorsque celui-ci est muet, on applique le droit international public à titre subsidiaire. Le droit des gens devient droit fédéral supplétif.[6]

C'est ainsi que la jurisprudence du Tribunal fédéral suisse donne diverses illustrations de différends entre deux cantons, au sujet par exemple de l'utilisation des eaux d'une rivière, ou de problèmes de voisinage, où le droit international général a servi de guide au juge.[7]

Dans le cas de la création du canton du Jura, diverses questions devaient être résolues dans les rapports entre le prédécesseur (Berne) et le successeur (Jura), notamment le partage des biens et dettes, ainsi que le sort des engagements conventionnels du canton de Berne. Les solutions fournies par le droit international ont joué un rôle dans l'élaboration des règlements. Ceux-ci constituent une pratique intéressante en matière de succession d'Etats.

Après un bref rappel des circonstances qui ont conduit à la sécession du Jura, les principales questions à résoudre, et les solutions qui leur ont été données, seront examinées, avec un regard sur la réglementation du droit international.

II. La naissance du canton du Jura

A. *La procédure de sécession*

A la suite du Congrès de Vienne de 1815, l'ancien Evêché de Bâle fut rattaché au canton de Berne. Ce territoire, désormais Jura bernois, constitua la partie nord-ouest du canton.[8]

L'intégration ne fut jamais pleinement réussie. Elle butait, notamment, sur des obstacles linguistiques et religieux. Des difficultés surgirent sporadiquement. Après la deuxième guerre mondiale, le mouvement séparatiste s'affirma davantage. Il y eut des troubles. Finalement un processus de consultations populaires (plébiscites) 'en cascade' fut instauré, qui ne manque pas d'intérêt du point de vue des principes démocratiques.

[5] Cf. Auer et al., *Droit constitutionnel suisse*, p. 354.

[6] Aubert, *Traité de droit constitutionnel*, vol. II, p. 588.

[7] *Ibid.*, vol. I, p. 343.

[8] Voir les références citées *supra*, note 3.

Il fallut tout d'abord qu'un additif à la Constitution bernoise, du 1er mars 1970, rendît possible une consultation populaire, dans le Jura bernois, sur le principe de l'autodétermination.[9] Une majorité se prononça en faveur de la création d'un nouveau canton. Cependant, sur les sept districts constituant le Jura bernois (six francophones et un germanophone), seuls trois au nord (Porrentruy, Franches-Montagnes et Delémont) donnèrent une majorité positive.[10] Des sous-plébiscites furent organisés dans les quatre autres districts, qui refusèrent de rallier le nouveau canton.[11]

L'ultime phase du processus voit le futur canton, réduit aux trois districts du nord, s'organiser et se doter d'une Constitution (adoptée le 20 mars 1977).[12] Il restait à modifier la Constitution fédérale pour y introduire le Canton du Jura, ce qui fut fait par le référendum constitutionnel, au plan fédéral, du 24 septembre 1978.[13]

L'entrée 'en souveraineté' de la République et canton du Jura fut fixée au 1er janvier 1979.

B. Problèmes juridiques nés de la sécession

Le détachement du territoire du nouveau canton constitue bien une sécession, en ce sens que ce territoire a passé de la 'souveraineté' bernoise à la nouvelle 'souveraineté' jurassienne, sans que pour autant l'identité du Canton de Berne soit affectée.

Les cantons suisses, comme déjà indiqué, ne sont pas des Etats souverains, mais dans le cadre de l'ordre juridique fédéral chacun d'eux exerce sur son territoire les prérogatives de puissance publique, de sorte que dans le vocabulaire constitutionnel suisse il est fait état de la souveraineté des cantons, concept qui, entre autres, est au coeur de la règle de partage des compétences.[14]

[9] Cet additif constitutionnel fut assujetti à la garantie fédérale; voir son texte et le message y relatif, FF 1970 II 557.

[10] Votation du 23 juin 1974; en tout, 36802 'oui' contre 34057 'non' se prononcèrent en faveur de la création d'un nouveau canton.

[11] Votation du 16 mars 1975 par laquelle les districts de Courtelary, Moutier et la Neuveville se prononcèrent pour leur maintien dans le canton de Berne. Quant au district de Laufon, il décida lui aussi de rester dans le canton de Berne (14 septembre 1975), ce qui pouvait lui permettre de rallier ultérieurement un autre canton.

[12] Une Assemblée constituante avait été élue le 21 mars 1976.

[13] Voir l'arrêté fédéral du 9 mars 1978, FF 1978 I 663, et son acceptation en votation constitutionnelle, FF 1978 II 1278.

[14] 'Les cantons sont souverains en tant que leur souveraineté n'est pas limitée par la Constitution fédérale . . .' dit l'article 3 de la Constitution. Cf. Auer et al., *Droit constitutionnel suisse*, p. 324.

Sans préjudice du droit fédéral, applicable dans le territoire du Jura après comme avant la création du nouveau canton, il y a donc bien eu substitution d'une puissance publique à une autre dans l'exercice des fonctions étatiques cantonales sur le territoire du nouveau canton.

Parmi les divers problèmes juridiques auxquels il fallut trouver une solution[15] figuraient ceux que l'on rencontre en droit international en matière de succession d'Etats, plus particulièrement dans le cas spécifique de la sécession. Il s'agit du partage des biens, des dettes, des archives, ainsi que, d'autre part, de la question du sort des engagements conventionnels.

Venaient s'y ajouter d'autres questions concernant les fonctionnaires, les services publics en général, dont il importait d'assurer la continuité, le prélèvement des impôts et les liquidités nécessaires au canton du Jura en phase initiale.

Ces dernières questions ne sont pas prises en considération dans la présente étude, où seules seront examinées les solutions retenues pour le partage des biens, dettes et archives d'une part, et pour la succession aux traités et autres accords, d'autre part.

C. *Les accords de succession*

Il faut retenir que toute la procédure de succession a pris plusieurs années. On peut y voir le souci des parties intéressées d'aboutir à des solutions justes, équilibrées, préservant de bons rapports entre l'ancien et le nouveau canton.

Tout a été réglé par voie d'accords, dont il est intéressant de constater qu'ils ont été négociés en prenant pour repères divers principes empruntés au droit international général, dans la mesure où celui-ci était à même de fournir des indications.

Dès qu'il fut acquis que le nouveau canton allait être créé, et après l'élection de l'Assemblée constituante, les premiers travaux visant la succession furent entrepris. Ils associèrent des délégués de Berne et du Jura, ainsi que des représentants de la Confédération helvétique.

En ce qui concerne les biens, ces travaux furent ponctués par un premier accord de coopération du 27 septembre 1977, un accord de procédure du 17 avril 1978, et un important accord-cadre provisoire du 15 septembre 1978, 'régissant les accords provisoires fixant les conditions du transfert ou de l'utilisation des biens et les conditions d'utilisation de l'infrastructure

[15] Cf. J. Voyame, 'Problèmes juridiques posés par la création d'un nouveau canton', *RSJB* 112 (1976), p. 520.

actuellement commune'. C'est dans le cadre de cet accord que, jusqu'à la fin de l'année 1978, 123 accords particuliers furent conclus.

Comme indiqué ci-après, un concordat vint, en 1984, mettre un terme au partage.[16]

Quant aux engagements conventionnels du canton de Berne, accords internationaux[17] et intercantonaux de droit public,[18] ils firent l'objet de l'attention de l'Assemblée constituante, qui détermina ceux qui devaient conserver leur validité pour le Jura, ou dont la continuité était souhaitée. Elle en fixa la liste dans une loi dite 'Loi sur la reprise des traités', le Gouvernement jurassien étant chargé d'entreprendre toutes démarches utiles.[19]

Le Parlement jurassien adopta ultérieurement, le 20 décembre 1979, une loi sur l'approbation des traités, concordats et autres conventions.[20]

III. Le partage des biens, dettes et archives

A. *Les biens en général*

1. L'accord entre prédécesseur et successeur

Les travaux préliminaires avaient permis de bien avancer sur la voie du partage, mais c'est après l'entrée en souveraineté du canton du Jura, le 1er janvier 1979, que la négociation directe, sous les auspices de la Confédération, conduisit, au cours d'étapes successives,[21] à la mise au point définitive du partage.

Celui-ci fut consigné dans un concordat, assorti de 26 conventions, adopté par les deux Parlements cantonaux le 8 novembre 1984. Le partage fut terminé le 31 décembre 1984.

[16] Voir B. Knapp, 'Le partage des biens lors de la création du Canton du Jura', *RFDA* (1985), p. 852; U. Kohli, *Die vermögensrechtliche Auseinandersetzung zwischen den Kantonen Bern und Jura* (Bern: Staempfli, 1986).

[17] Voir Y. Lejeune, 'La succession du nouveau Canton du Jura aux traités internationaux du Canton de Berne', *RGDIP* (1978), p. 1051.

[18] Voir Y. Lejeune, 'La pratique jurassienne en matière de succession aux traités et concordats intercantonaux', *ASDI* XL (1984), p. 30.

[19] Loi du 30 novembre 1978 sur la succession du Canton du Jura aux traités, concordats et conventions auxquels le Canton de Berne est partie (Loi sur la reprise des traités), *ROJU* 1978/111.1. Cette loi est reproduite en Annexe I à l'article de Y. Lejeune cité dans la note précédente.

[20] RSJU 111.1, reproduite en Annexe II à l'article de Y. Lejeune, 'La pratique jurassienne'. Cette loi a abrogé la loi sur la reprise des traités.

[21] Rapport du 20 mai 1980 définissant les options de base; accord du 27 mars 1981 concernant la procédure de partage définitif; acceptation le 23 décembre 1981 de quatre groupes de conventions.

2. Les principes

Dès le début des travaux relatifs à la succession, l'on s'est préoccupé de prendre appui sur des principes et règles reconnus et susceptibles d'application.

Une consultation du Professeur Blaise Knapp examina attentivement les précédents internationaux et nationaux.[22] Lorsqu'elle fut rédigée, en 1976, la Convention de Vienne du 8 avril 1983 sur la succession d'Etats en matière de biens, archives et dettes d'Etat n'existait pas encore,[23] alors que les travaux de la Commission du droit international fournissaient quelques indications sur l'état du droit des gens, incertain il faut le dire.

Ce fut bien cette incertitude que fit apparaître l'examen des précédents et de la doctrine.

Quelques principes généraux furent néanmoins mis en lumière: le partage des biens devait permettre d'assurer la continuité du service public dans des conditions équivalentes dans toutes les parties de l'ancien canton de Berne; le partage devait porter sur l'ensemble de la fortune du prédécesseur; les biens immobiliers devaient être attribués selon le lieu de leur situation; le principe d'équité devait jouer un rôle.[24]

Ces principes guidèrent la négociation, dont l'aboutissement montre qu'elle a été conduite avec pragmatisme, dans le désir d'aboutir à des solutions équitables et politiquement satisfaisantes.

3. La méthode utilisée et les solutions retenues

Il fut convenu que le partage devait porter sur l'ensemble des biens (fortune) du canton de Berne, comprenant également ceux des entités ou établissements qui participaient à la gestion de tâches publiques cantonales, peu important qu'ils soient dotés ou non de la personnalité juridique.

On procéda à une répartition des biens selon la méthode des 'complexes et paquets', qui permettait notamment de s'en tenir à certaines évaluations générales.

Les complexes furent déterminés sur la base des modèles de la comptabilité publique: patrimoine financier, patrimoine administratif,

[22] L'article déjà cité du Professeur Knapp, 'Le partage des biens', contient une analyse des précédents internationaux et nationaux qui avaient été examinés dans son avis de droit.

[23] A/CONF/14, texte publié dans la *RGDIP* (1984), p. 329. Cette convention, qui esquive le problème des droits acquis, n'a pas eu grand succès. Il est peu probable qu'elle entre jamais en vigueur. Cf. J. Monnier, 'La Convention de Vienne sur la succession d'Etats en matière de biens, archives et dettes d'Etat', *AFDI* (1984), p. 221.

[24] Knapp, 'Le partage des biens', p. 858, par. 43; Kohli, *Die vermögensrechtliche*, p. 55.

établissements avec personnalité, patrimoine à affectation déterminée, dettes, archives et biens culturels.[25]

Les complexes étaient eux-mêmes divisés en paquets, ce qui eut notamment l'avantage, dès lors qu'il était possible de choisir pour chacun d'eux le critère de partage le plus adéquat, d'éviter le recours, peu souhaitable, à un critère unique.

Cette méthode conduisit à la mise au point des 26 conventions partielles susmentionnées, portant chacune sur une catégorie de biens, avoirs ou dettes. Elles couvraient l'ensemble des actifs et passifs du canton de Berne, comprenant des objets aussi divers que les avoirs de la Banque cantonale, ceux des diverses caisses d'assurance, le patrimoine administratif, immobilier, les routes, forêts et cours d'eau, etc.[26]

Les questions concrètes qui devaient être résolues purent l'être, dans le cadre de ces subdivisions, d'une manière différenciée. Ainsi, la procédure d'inventaire, évidemment nécessaire, put être simplifiée pour divers types de biens.[27] De même, en matière d'évaluation, où peuvent surgir des problèmes délicats, les estimations, grâce à la méthode retenue, furent faites au sein des paquets, d'une manière pragmatique. En certains cas, le partage en nature, par exemple, simplifia les choses.

4. Les critères de partage

Les travaux préliminaires avaient mis en évidence l'importance du *critère territorial*, assorti du principe d'équité. Le partage conformément au lieu de situation est intervenu avec ou sans soulte, selon que des biens équivalents se trouvaient, ou non, sur le territoire de chacun des deux cantons.[28]

Le *critère de la population* (93,2 pour cent pour Berne et 6,8 pour cent pour le Jura) a été également utilisé lorsque jugé équitable, par exemple pour partager le patrimoine financier, ou la participation aux Forces motrices bernoises S.A.

D'autres critères spécifiques ont été retenus, parfois en combinaison avec ceux de la territorialité ou de la population, pour opérer le

[25] Knapp, *ibid.*, p. 862, par. 77.

[26] Kohli, *Die vermögensrechtliche*, p. 164.

[27] Un exemple mentionné par Knapp ('Le partage des biens', p. 863) est celui de l'attribution des immeubles et du mobilier des administrations d'arrondissement et de district; elle fut faite, après contrôle, selon le principe que ces administrations étaient équipées de façon équivalente.

[28] Ainsi, par exemple, les biens de l'administration centrale n'avaient pas d'équivalents dans le nouveau canton, de sorte qu'il fallut trouver des modalités satisfaisantes pour calculer un montant compensatoire; cf. Knapp, 'Le partage des biens', p. 866.

partage de certains avoirs particuliers (le capital des banques d'Etat, par exemple, ou celui des établissements d'assurance et des caisses de retraite).[29]

B. Archives et biens culturels

On a recherché ici aussi des solutions pratiques et équitables. Ainsi, les anciennes archives de l'Evêché de Bâle ont été confiées à une fondation commune aux deux cantons, tandis que le canton de Berne a conservé ses archives de la période 1815 à 1978, mais en les administrant aussi pour le compte du Jura, qui y a libre accès. Les archives locales ont été partagées selon le lieu qu'elles concernaient.

Pour les autres biens culturels, le critère de la territorialité a joué un rôle prépondérant, avec celui de l'équivalence.

C. La dette

Le canton de Berne est resté seul débiteur, envers les tiers, de la dette, qui a été divisée en dette affectée ou non affectée. Pour cette dernière, la part supportée par le Canton du Jura, versée par déduction sur les sommes qui lui étaient dues à d'autres titres, a été déterminée selon le critère de la population.

Pour la dette affectée, divers critères ont été retenus, selon l'objet de l'affectation, de manière à parvenir à un résultat équitable.

D. Observations

On ne peut manquer d'être frappé par le caractère très minutieux de la procédure. Elle a pris du temps, car il fallait aboutir à un résultat équitable, tout en assurant la continuité du service public dans le territoire du nouveau canton, ce qui a été réalisé grâce à des transferts provisoires et d'autres mesures temporaires susceptibles d'être confirmés ultérieurement.

Tous les accords ont été consciencieusement négociés. A l'évidence, le consentement mutuel, prenant largement en compte toutes les caractéristiques de la succession, offre des perspectives sensiblement plus prometteuses que l'application de règles rigides.

[29] *Ibid.*, p. 866.

Des négociations de bonne foi et une approche pragmatique doivent cependant être encadrées par quelques principes, appliqués certes avec souplesse, mais qui sont nécessaires en qualité de points de repère.

Comme on l'a vu, le principe de territorialité a joué un rôle important, mais sous le contrôle, si l'on peut dire, du principe d'équité. De plus, les notions d'équivalence et de résultat équitable ont dominé les négociations. Quant aux autres critères de partage, plusieurs ont été utilisés, selon les circonstances, avec le souci de choisir le plus adapté à chaque type de biens ou de dettes.

La sécession du Jura présente-t-elle un précédent intéressant pour le droit international?

Elle confirme certainement la priorité qui doit être accordée à la recherche d'un accord, inspiré de quelques principes appliqués avec souplesse.

A cet égard, le règlement intervenu ne va guère dans le sens de la Convention (mort-née?) de 1983, trop directive. Il correspond en revanche bien davantage à la Résolution adoptée par l'Institut de Droit international lors de sa session de Vancouver, en août 2001, intitulée 'Succession d'Etats en matière de biens et d'obligations'.[30] Celle-ci souligne l'importance du règlement conventionnel, elle insiste sur le critère du résultat équitable, et elle indique que le passage des biens et dettes est sans préjudice, s'il y a lieu, de toute compensation équitable entre l'Etat prédécesseur et l'Etat successeur, entre autres pour rééquilibrer le principe de territorialité, qui est important.

IV. Les engagements conventionnels

A. *Les traités internationaux*

Jusqu'à la création de l'Etat fédéral, en 1848, le canton de Berne (Etat de Berne) était un Etat souverain. Il était à ce titre en mesure de conclure des traités internationaux. Ce qu'il a fait, notamment pour fixer ses frontières avec ses voisins.[31]

Depuis 1848, il a été, comme tous les autres cantons suisses, au bénéfice des dispositions de la Constitution fédérale leur reconnaissant le droit de conclure certains traités avec l'étranger. Il s'agit

[30] Résolution publiée dans *ASDI* 69 (2000–2001).

[31] Cf. Lejeune, 'La succession du nouveau Canton', p. 1061.

de l'article 9 de l'ancienne Constitution,[32] et de l'article 56 de la nouvelle.[33]

Les traités antérieurs à la formation de l'Etat fédéral ne sont pas très nombreux. Ils sont relativement anciens. Ils sont généralement consacrés à la délimitation des territoires respectifs des parties. Ils sont restés en vigueur, à la faveur parfois de deux successions. Ainsi, par exemple, la 'Convention entre le Roi Très Chrétien et le Prince-Evêque et l'Eglise de Bâle concernant les limites de leurs Etats'[34] a fait l'objet d'un transfert au bénéfice de Berne, qui a succédé en 1815 à tous les droits du Prince-Evêque sur le territoire de l'Evêché de Bâle; c'est ensuite le Jura qui a été substitué à Berne pour ce qui concerne son territoire.[35]

A côté des quelques traités territoriaux, Berne avait également d'autres engagements internationaux, rares il est vrai.[36] On peut mentionner, par exemple, l'accord (concordat) entre le Saint-Siège et quelques cantons suisses (dont Berne) du 26 mars 1828 relatif à la réorganisation et nouvelle circonscription de l'Evêché de Bâle,[37] que d'ailleurs le Gouvernement de Berne avait décidé d'accepter uniquement pour la partie du canton cédée par le Congrès de Vienne.

Les accords internationaux du canton de Berne conclus après la formation de l'Etat fédéral en 1848 ne sont pas nombreux non plus. On peut donner l'exemple d'accords fiscaux avec la France.[38]

[32] Article 9, *in fine*: 'Exceptionnellement, les cantons conservent le droit de conclure, avec les Etats étrangers, des traités sur des objets concernant l'économie publique, les rapports de voisinage et de police'; cf. J. F. Aubert, *Traité de droit constitutionnel*, Vol. I., p. 256; également J. F. Aubert et al., *Commentaire de la Constitution fédérale de la Confédération suisse du 29 mai 1874* (Bâle: Helbing & Lichtenhahn, Zurich: Schultess, 1987–95), Article 9 par D. Schindler.

[33] Article 56, par. 1: 'Les cantons peuvent conclure des traités avec l'étranger dans les domaines relevant de leur compétence'; cf. Auer et al., *Droit constitutionnel*, vol. I, p. 436.

[34] Signée à Versailles le 20 juin 1780; cf. Lejeune, 'La succession du nouveau Canton', p. 1062.

[35] Il est vrai que l'on a pu suggérer que, dès 1848, c'est la Suisse en sa qualité d'Etat souverain qui est devenue partie aux traités territoriaux des cantons (cf. Lejeune, *ibid.*, 1066–7), mais il nous paraît que ce sont ceux-ci qui restent les parties contractantes, étant entendu que la Confédération assume, le cas échéant, la responsabilité internationale.

[36] Cf. Lejeune, *Recueil des Accords internationaux conclus par les cantons suisses (en vigueur au 1er janvier 1980)* (Berne, Francfort/Main: P. Lang, 1982), qui recense divers accords en matière d'impôts, de main-d'oeuvre frontalière, etc.

[37] Cf. Lejeune, 'La succession du nouveau Canton', p. 1069.

[38] Convention avec la France concernant l'imposition des frontaliers, du 18 octobre 1935, liant également trois autres cantons frontaliers; Déclaration de réciprocité avec la France en matière de taxes sur les successions et donations relatives aux biens échéant à des établissements et fondations publiques d'utilité générale, voir les ch. 9 et 10 de l'article 3 de la Loi sur la reprise des traités, citée *supra* note 19.

Au moment de la sécession du Jura, les accords internationaux du canton de Berne ont été inclus dans la liste générale des engagements conventionnels établie par l'Assemblée constituante jurassienne avant l'adoption de la Loi sur la reprise des traités. Il en sera question ci-après.

B. Les concordats et autres accords intercantonaux

Les cantons suisses concluent entre eux des accords de droit public, portant sur des objets qui relèvent de leurs compétences.[39] Ils sont généralement appelés 'concordats', mais cette appellation est fréquemment réservée aux accords multilatéraux, alors que les accords bilatéraux sont souvent conclus sous le titre 'convention'. Cependant, il n'y a pas, quant à la terminologie, de pratique vraiment établie, quand bien même la Constitution fédérale parle de 'conventions'.[40]

Les engagements conventionnels intercantonaux du canton de Berne offraient l'exemple, au moment de la sécession jurassienne, des différents cas de figure usuels: concordats multilatéraux ouverts à tous les cantons suisses, ou réunissant un nombre limité de cantons; accords bilatéraux de caractère normatif ou obligationnel; accords concernant particulièrement le territoire qui allait être détaché. On peut observer la diversité des textes en prenant connaissance de la liste qui figure dans les articles 2 et 3 de la Loi sur la reprise des traités.

Après l'élection de l'Assemblée constituante, un avis de droit a été demandé à l'auteur de la présente étude, invité à se prononcer sur la question des conséquences résultant de la création du nouveau canton du Jura pour les concordats auxquels le canton de Berne était partie.

Cet avis de droit, remis en novembre 1976 au Département fédéral de justice et police, rappelle que dans les rapports intercantonaux il y a lieu d'appliquer par analogie, à titre de droit fédéral supplétif, le droit international général, lorsque la matière n'est pas réglée par le droit fédéral lui-même.

Tel était bien le cas pour les accords intercantonaux, de sorte que l'avis de droit s'inspira des travaux de la Commission du droit international des

[39] Voir l'article 7 de l'ancienne Constitution, article 48,1, de la Constitution actuelle: 'Les cantons peuvent conclure des conventions entre eux et créer des organisations et des institutions communes . . .'

[40] Sur les conventions intercantonales, voir notamment Aubert, *Traité de droit constitutionnel*, vol. I, pp. 330–5; Auer et al., *Droit constitutionnel*, vol. I, pp. 547–60.

Nations Unies sur la succession d'Etats en matière de traités, qui avaient abouti à un projet d'articles.[41]

L'avis de droit souligna que le canton de Berne restait partie à tous les accords, bilatéraux et multilatéraux, qu'il avait conclus, sauf ceux qui étaient liés au territoire du nouveau canton.

Il souligna aussi, en ce qui concerne le Jura, qu'il était souhaitable que le sort des accords bernois fût réglé d'entente entre les cantons.

Il rappela que les règles du droit des gens stipulaient le maintien en vigueur et le transfert des traités territoriaux; que pour les traités bilatéraux, dans le cas d'une sécession, et dès lors que le prédécesseur reste partie aux traités qu'il a conclus, le successeur n'a pas l'obligation, vis-à-vis de l'autre partie, de rester lié (ce qui constituerait un deuxième accord bilatéral parallèle), mais qu'il n'a pas non plus un droit à la continuité de l'accord pour lui; qu'en ce qui concerne les traités multilatéraux, le successeur a sans doute un droit à devenir partie à ceux qui sont ouverts (par exemple les concordats ouverts à tous les cantons), mais que pour les traités restreints, une demande d'adhésion doit recueillir l'assentiment des participants; que l'admission dans des institutions communes n'est pas automatique mais exige une requête à cette fin.

L'avis de droit suggérait que des travaux fussent entrepris dès avant l'accession du nouveau canton à la souveraineté, et que, si cela paraissait utile, des solutions transitoires fussent adoptées.

C. Le règlement de la succession

1. La procédure suivie

Sur la base de l'avis de droit précité, un examen attentif des engagements conventionnels du canton de Berne a été entrepris. Il s'agissait d'opérer une sélection, parmi tous les accords internationaux et intercantonaux, pour déterminer ceux dont le canton du Jura entendait assurer la continuité.

L'Assemblée constituante attendit pour agir que la votation fédérale du 24 septembre 1978 eût définitivement consacré la création du canton du Jura, mais elle légiféra avant l'entrée en souveraineté du 1er janvier 1979, de manière à assurer la continuité là où elle était souhaitée.

Ce fut la loi du 30 novembre 1978.[42]

[41] Rapport de la Commission du droit international sur les travaux de sa vingt-sixième session, *ACDI* (1974), vol. II, 1ère partie. Sur la base de ce projet, la Convention du 23 août 1978 sur la succession d'Etats en matière de traités a été conclue. Elle est en vigueur depuis le 6 novembre 1996, *Recueil des traités des Nations Unies*, vol. 1946, p. 3.

[42] *Supra*, note 19.

2. La loi sur la reprise des traités

Cette loi comporte pour notre propos trois articles.[43]

Le premier est une habilitation. Le Gouvernement jurassien est 'habilité à entreprendre toutes démarches utiles en vue de maintenir en application sur le territoire du canton les traités, concordats et conventions auxquels le canton de Berne est partie et qui sont mentionnés aux articles 2 et 3'.

C'est sur cette base que des déclarations de continuité furent notifiées dès les derniers jours de 1978 et en 1979.

L'article 2 de la loi contient une liste de concordats, conventions et accords qui 'sous réserve de l'accord des autres parties, sont reconduits sans restriction quant à leur durée . . .'

Cette liste comprend diverses conventions intercantonales multilatérales (concordats) mais aussi des accords bilatéraux et déclarations de réciprocité.

L'article 3 contient une liste de concordats, conventions et accords qui '[s]ous réserve de l'accord des autres parties, sont reconduits à titre provisoire pour une durée d'une année . . .'

La liste contient elle aussi en majorité des conventions intercantonales multilatérales, ainsi que quelques accords bilatéraux et des accords fiscaux avec la France.

On observe tout d'abord que chacune de ces listes comporte indistinctement des accords de diverses catégories, bilatéraux et multilatéraux. C'est à l'occasion de la mise en oeuvre de la loi dans les démarches entreprises ultérieurement que des différences ont été marquées.

On observe surtout qu'aucun des traités relatifs à la frontière n'est mentionné. Il était évident qu'ils restaient en vigueur et que leur continuité n'était pas subordonnée à l'accord de l'autre partie.

3. Les modalités de la continuité

Sans préjudice des accords territoriaux qui continuaient à le lier, le canton du Jura avait donc fait son choix. Il ne manqua d'ailleurs pas de communiquer aux cantons que cela pouvait concerner sa décision de ne pas reprendre à son compte divers accords conclus par le canton de Berne.[44]

Le Gouvernement jurassien procéda aux démarches qu'il devait entreprendre selon la procédure adéquate. C'est ainsi qu'il s'adressa au Conseil fédéral suisse s'agissant d'accords internationaux et de plusieurs concordats multilatéraux, car c'est le Gouvernement helvétique qui est

[43] Un quatrième article prescrit l'organisation d'un vote populaire, et l'article 5 charge le Gouvernement de fixer la date de son entrée en vigueur (ce fut le 1er janvier 1979).

[44] Voir les détails dans Lejeune, 'La pratique jurassienne', p. 47.

l'organe de communication avec les pays étrangers, d'une part, et, d'autre part, l'autorité qui doit approuver les conventions intercantonales. Cette procédure pouvait concerner aussi bien des accords auxquels le Jura était décidé à devenir partie, que d'autres qu'il préférait maintenir en vigueur à titre provisoire, en attendant de se déterminer définitivement.[45]

D'autres déclarations de continuité, de portée définitive ou provisoire, furent adressées aux cantons concernés, tant pour des accords multilatéraux que pour des accords bilatéraux.[46]

La continuité des accords put être réglée selon les voeux du nouveau canton, mais pour plusieurs d'entre eux à titre provisoire seulement, pour une durée d'une année (article 3 de la loi sur la reprise des traités).

La dernière étape intervint précisément à la fin de l'année 1979, avec l'adoption de la 'Loi sur l'approbation des traités, concordats et autres conventions'.[47] Abrogeant la loi sur la reprise des traités, elle fixe la procédure d'approbation des traités, concordats et autres conventions de droit public. Cette approbation est du ressort du Parlement cantonal, sauf si ces accords portent sur des accords d'ordre mineur, auquel cas le Gouvernement est compétent.

C'est sur cette base qu'après accord avec les parties intéressées, la continuité des accords reconduits provisoirement fut définitivement assurée, à l'exception de quelques cas où l'application provisoire fut jugée préférable, dans l'optique d'une révision des textes.[48]

D. *Observations*

Il est évident que dans le contexte d'un Etat fédéral chacune des parties composantes a un intérêt majeur au maintien de bonnes relations de collaboration. Cela facilite sans doute le règlement de problèmes comme ceux qui nous intéressent ici.

Néanmoins, compte tenu du contentieux émotionnel entre Berne et le Jura, des risques de difficultés existaient.

Le Jura ne voulait pas se voir imposer des obligations qui ne lui convenaient pas, mais il souhaitait aussi pouvoir bénéficier d'un droit conventionnel qui était conforme à ses intérêts.

A cet égard, il était important que les autorités jurassiennes puissent prendre appui sur des principes juridiques relativement solides. Ils furent trouvés dans le droit international général car, même peu nombreux, ils ont une certaine consistance.

[45] *Ibid.*, pp. 36 et 41. [46] *Ibid.*, pp. 37 et 43. [47] Loi du 20 décembre 1979, RSJU 111.1.
[48] Analyse détaillée dans Lejeune, 'La pratique jurassienne', p. 48.

C'est ainsi que la continuité des traités territoriaux fut d'emblée reconnue.

Pour les accords multilatéraux, auxquels Berne restait partie, il était clair que le Jura n'assumait aucune obligation de continuité, mais, comme il avait intérêt à devenir partie à nombre d'entre eux, il fit des déclarations de continuité; comme elles ne se heurtèrent point à des oppositions, la question de savoir si le Jura avait un droit à l'adhésion ne fut pas contentieuse. Une réponse affirmative semblait aller de soi.

Quant aux accords bilatéraux, ils ne donnèrent pas lieu à des difficultés, les contacts directs ayant permis de trouver des solutions.

V. Conclusions

L'assujettissement des cantons suisses au droit fédéral, y compris pour leurs relations mutuelles – relations horizontales – laisse subsister des lacunes, ou, plus exactement dit, des espaces qui ne sont pas couverts par cet ordre juridique interne. C'est sans doute l'analogie que l'on peut établir entre ces relations et celles des Etats souverains entre eux qui explique que l'ordre juridique suisse laisse la place, ici, à l'application des règles du droit des gens à titre de droit fédéral supplétif.

Dans la matière délicate de la succession d'Etats, l'analogie n'est pas entière, car il y a des problèmes qui ne surgissent pas dans les rapports entre cantons, et qui sont susceptibles de créer des difficultés au plan international. On a pu mentionner la question des droits acquis.

Toutefois, l'analogie, à maints égards, est suffisamment étroite pour que la comparaison présente de l'intérêt.

Il résulte de l'analyse de la sécession du Jura que le droit international s'est révélé utile. Quant bien même l'esprit de solidarité confédérale (*Bundestreue*) allait faciliter les relations entre prédécesseur et successeur, on a pu observer que les démarches et négociations ont été rendues plus aisées dès lors qu'elles prenaient place dans le cadre de quelques principes mis en lumière par la doctrine et la pratique du droit des gens, notamment les tentatives de codification. Ce furent des repères utiles.

Peut-on, dans l'ordre inverse, affirmer que le règlement de la question jurassienne a apporté des éléments intéressants à la pratique du droit international? Ce serait probablement beaucoup dire, mais on peut tout de même y trouver la confirmation de la valeur de certaines règles et orientations.

En matière de biens et dettes, s'il importe que l'Etat né d'une sécession reçoive une part équitable des biens du prédécesseur, tout en assumant une partie des dettes, il importe de trouver des solutions adaptées aux circonstances.

Même le principe de territorialité, solidement ancré, ne peut être appliqué mécaniquement. Il doit être interprété selon le principe d'équivalence, et ses effets doivent être compensés, le cas échéant, par une soulte.

Il est frappant que le plus récent essai de codification, la Résolution de 2001 de l'Institut de Droit international, insiste, pour chacun des principes qu'elle énonce, sur la recherche d'un résultat équitable.

L'exemple de la sécession jurassienne montre, entre autres, que les critères de partage doivent être divers, afin que le plus adéquat puisse être retenu pour chaque catégorie de biens ou de dettes.

Quant à la succession en matière de traités, l'exemple jurassien confirme, ce qui est l'évidence même, le maintien en vigueur des traités territoriaux.

Pour les autres accords, et dès lors que le prédécesseur reste lié par eux, le successeur conserve une grande latitude de choix, mais sous réserve, s'il souhaite la continuité, du consentement des autres parties. L'exemple jurassien montre que ce successeur a avantage à prendre les devants et à effectuer les démarches nécessaires, tout en suggérant des solutions provisoires, lorsque cela paraît judicieux.

CONCLUSION

GEORGES ABI-SAAB

I. The State as a primary fact compelling acknowledgement by international law

The contemporary system of international law finds its origins in the new structure of power that emerged at the end of the wars of religion in Europe in the seventeenth century, a structure reflecting the rise of the new subjects of the international community of the time – the States – and their fundamental role in international relations. The legal system ensuing from this structure was thus assigned a precise and limited task: to confer legal sanction on the new basis of distribution of power in that community by legitimising State sovereignty, without, however, encroaching on it in any significant manner.

This explains the position of classical international law when faced with the phenomenon of the birth of a State. And while subsequent developments have changed many things in international law, they have only marginally affected this position, as we shall see further on.

Indeed, the State in the contemplation of international law is not a mere legal or 'juristic' person (*personne morale*), whose process of coming into being is prescribed by law. It is rather a 'primary fact', i.e. a fact that precedes the law, and which the law acknowledges only once it has materialised, by attributing certain effects to it, including a certain legal status. However, the law has no direct hold over the unfolding of the process that leads to the birth of the State; it can encourage or discourage its advent by means of inducement or dissuasion, as it did, for example, in encouraging the creation of an independent State in Namibia or in discouraging the existence of a racist State in Rhodesia – in other words, in acting on the probabilities and the effectivities. But it can neither 'create' nor destroy the primary fact directly (since the law is not in this context an 'efficient cause' in the Aristotelian sense of the term). Here there is a parallel with 'physical persons', in the sense that the law can encourage or discourage natality in general, but it cannot 'cause' the birth of an individual human being, though it acknowledges the existence of that individual once he or she is born.

In short, the creation of the State from the standpoint of international law is always a legal fact and not a legal act, even when this fact is based on a legal act such as a treaty. But this primary fact is not legally self-sufficient, for once it exists, international law takes cognisance of it, by apprehending the State's reality or effectiveness in order to rationalise it. And it is via international law that it acquires its full legal significance and finds its legal fulfilment, through recognition of the scope – which also necessarily implies the limits – of its powers.

The primary fact, as apprehended and rationalised in the abstract model of the State by international law, is the triptych of population, territory and sovereignty, or rather, a population sovereignly organised (or governed by a sovereign authority), on a given territory. And it is the effectiveness of these elements, and above all their integration into an operative whole, which constitutes the 'primary fact' and determines its being taken into consideration by international law or, in other words, compels its acknowledgement by international law as a State, regardless of the process that led to this result.

II. The impact of the constitutive principles of contemporary international law

This position of traditional international law has been qualified by the advent of the constitutive principles of contemporary international law, namely those of the United Nations Charter – in particular, the principle of the equality of peoples and their right to self-determination and the principle of the prohibition of the threat or use of force – and this in two different ways. For, instead of proceeding from the State as primary fact, the effect of these two principles are felt both before as well as after the materialisation of the primary fact, by conditioning the legal advent and existence of the State.

A. The right of peoples to self-determination applies in advance of the primary fact by legitimising the claim of any 'people' that satisfies the conditions that it prescribes to constitute a State (among other options). Its legal effects apply in particular before this option is exercised, by removing the issue from the domestic jurisdiction of the State under whose control 'the people' in question finds itself. In other words, it pierces the sovereignty veil of that State in this regard, by establishing the jurisdiction of the international community – comprising international organisations as well as States acting individually – to concern itself with this matter and to help the people in question, by various means, with a view to enabling it to exercise its right to self-determination, without this being considered as intervention in the internal affairs of the State that formally governs it. It also establishes the international responsibility of that State, if it stands in the way, for the denial of that right, with all the consequences that may ensue.

The right of peoples to self-determination also serves to extend to these peoples – by anticipation, before they actually exercise that right – the application of certain principles protecting the State in international law, such as the principle of prohibition of the use of force, the principle of non-intervention, and the principle of permanent sovereignty over natural resources (as formally and expressly provided in the Declaration on Principles of International Law concerning Friendly Relations and Co-operation among States in accordance with the Charter of the United Nations).[1]

B. The principle of the right of peoples to self-determination as well as the principle of the prohibition of the use of force can also have effects subsequent to the materialisation of the primary fact which condition the legal advent and existence of the State, if the process by which the State comes into being involves an ongoing violation of one of these principles. This would be the case, for example, in the creation of a State whose system of government is based on systematic discrimination against the majority or a particular component of the population, i.e., on the denial of its right to self-determination, or in the creation of a new State on a territory that has been conquered by force from another State. In these cases, third States, as well as international organisations, are under an obligation not to recognise the new State or enter into relations with it that imply such recognition or contribute to the continuation of its illegal existence, as expounded in the contribution of John Dugard and David Raič to this volume.

In other words, international law condemns as illegal the existence of such an entity as a consequence of the process of its creation and its mode of existing which perpetuates the violation that gave rise to it. In such cases, it is illegality, through the reaction that it arouses in the international community, which undermines the effectiveness of the entity already existing *de facto*, ultimately leading to its final collapse. This is illustrated by the case of Rhodesia. It is only in such cases, where a new

[1] GA Res. 2625 (XXV) of 24 October 1970.

State is created having at its foundation a violation of a basic principle of contemporary international law, that the process whereby a new State comes into being is to be taken into account in evaluating the effectiveness of its legal existence after its creation, i.e. after the 'primary fact'.

In all other cases, the position of international law remains the same as before, namely, that the State is considered a 'primary fact' to be acknowledged by international law, once that fact has materialised, regardless of the process by which it came into being. However, if that process results from a clear expression of the will of the people in question, the democratic character of that process may be a positive factor later on, conferring greater political legitimacy on the new State and thus reinforcing its legal existence and facilitating its rapid recognition by other States.

III. The case of secession

The above comments also apply in the case of secession. Here we have in mind a situation in which the conditions for exercising the right to self-determination are not met or at least are disputed and are not recognised by the international community as having all been met. This is the case where a component of a State's population seeks to separate from that State and establish a new State on that part of the State's territory on which it is settled.

Before secession actually becomes an effective reality, and so long as the conditions for exercising the right to self-determination (conditions analysed by Christian Tomuschat in his contribution to this volume) are not met, or so long as the international community – through international organisations and a sizable number of States – does not recognise (or does not yet recognise) that those conditions are met in this particular case, the claim of the component of the population that would like to secede, as well as the dispute that may arise between it and the central government of the State, remain, in the view of international law, an internal matter falling within the domestic jurisdiction of the State in question (Olivier Corten's chapter elaborates on this theme). The other States, as well as international organisations, must treat these matters accordingly, since otherwise they would be violating the principle of non-intervention, as shown in Georg Nolte's contribution.

International law would apply to this situation only insofar as it also applies to other situations falling within the internal sphere of the State, for example through the rules of international protection of human rights; or, if the dispute degenerates into armed conflict, through the rules of international humanitarian law applicable in armed conflicts not of an international character.

Thus, all the essentially interventionist rules and advance protections that come along with the right of peoples to self-determination, once it is considered applicable, remain out of reach in this situation.

However, if international law does not recognise a right of secession outside the context of self-determination (assuming that we can still call the exercise of this option 'secession' in this context), this does not mean that it prohibits secession. Secession thus remains basically a phenomenon not regulated by international law.

Therefore, though in some respects the principle of non-intervention, by its effects, favours the central authority, it would be erroneous to say that secession violates the principle of the territorial integrity of the State, since this principle applies only in international relations, i.e. against other States that are required to respect that integrity and not encroach on the territory of their neighbours; it does not apply within the State. Nevertheless, as Marcelo Kohen points out in his Introduction, the Security Council did not hesitate to invoke respect of the territorial integrity of States in the throes of secessionist attempts, particularly while they are pursued by forcible means, characterising the situations created by those conflicts as threats to international peace and security.

By the same token, if secession is the result of an armed struggle, it would not constitute a violation of the principle of prohibition of the threat or use of force unless it is controlled from outside or is carried out by foreign elements that invade the territory in question in order to separate it from the State to which it belongs and create another State in its place. But if a purely internal conflict results in secession, this does not fall under article 2, paragraph 4 of the United Nations Charter, which calls on member States to refrain from 'the threat or use of force' only 'in their international relations'.

Thus, unless secession is controlled from outside or is carried out by elements that either come from outside or seek to establish a State based on denial of the right of self-determination of the majority or a part of the population, the fact that the process of creation of the new State can be characterised as secession does not affect or in any way condition its legal existence from the standpoint of international law, once the primary fact, i.e. its effectiveness as a State, has materialised. However, politically speaking, forcible attempts at secession are, as noted by different contributors, increasingly condemned on the international level, in view of their effect on the maintenance of international peace and security – condemnation which may, in the final analysis, undermine the effectiveness of a secessionist entity claiming statehood.

IV. State effectiveness

From what point in time can it be legally determined that this primary fact, consisting of an effective State, exists? As already noted, the answer is from the point when the three elements of the State are brought together or coalesce into an operative whole. This depends above all on the element of sovereign organisation of the population over the territory. In other words, the population and the territory must be well-defined and ruled (or controlled) by a sovereign government that depends on no other instance.

But 'well-defined' does not mean totally and absolutely defined. It suffices that the major part or bulk of State population and territory be clearly identifiable, even if a certain ambiguity or controversy persists on the margins.

Thus, as regards the territory, the Permanent Court of International Justice, in its Advisory Opinion of 1924 in the case of the *Monastery of Saint Naoum (Albanian Frontier)*,[2] clearly recognised that a State may come into being and exist before its borders are totally defined, and even if some parts of its territory are subject to claims by other States.

The same applies to the population. What matters is that the new State has a stable population, the mass of which is identifiable, even if controversies persist as to the nationality (loss of the old nationality; automatic acquisition of the new) of some elements of the population residing on the territory of the new State. Unfortunately this is unavoidable in almost all cases of State succession, as Andreas Zimmermann's chapter demonstrates.

However, as noted above, the crucial element in evaluating the effectiveness of the State is the effectiveness of its sovereign organisation, or in other words, the existence of an effective government which rules the people within the territory, and which embodies the sovereignty of the State, in the sense that it does not depend, in so doing, on any other instance. The effectiveness of the government may be called into question owing either to its inability to control the population in the sense of exercising the powers and functions of the State with respect to it, or to its authority being disputed by another instance.

[2] *PCIJ*, series B, No 9.

Such controversies over the effectiveness of secessionist States are bound to arise if secession is pursued by violent means; which necessarily leads to a period of uncertainty before the legal situation is clear – a period during which the position of the international community, both international organisations and States, plays a crucial role that is bound to affect the fate of the secession one way or the other.

Recent practice, since the beginning of the 1990s, is shrouded with some ambiguity, particularly when it comes to the case of Yugoslavia. Still, the traditional attitude of international law that favours the State (in the absence of a valid claim of self-determination), without condemning secession once it has taken place (apart from the exceptional cases mentioned above), finds an added *rationale* and renewed vigour in this age of integration and globalisation; that which may even tip the balance against secession if its pursuit is by violent means, subsuming an additional problem of maintenance of international peace and security.

SELECT BIBLIOGRAPHY*

I. Works and courses

Abi-Saab, G., *The United Nations Operation in the Congo* (Oxford: Oxford University Press, 1978), 206 pp.

Alston, Ph., *Peoples' Rights. Collected courses of the Academy of European Law*, vol. 9/2 (Oxford: Oxford University Press, 2001), 329 pp.

Baer, S., *Der Zerfall Jugoslawiens im Lichte des Völkerrechts* (Frankfurt: P. Lang, 1995), 427 pp.

Bayefsky, A. F., *Self-Determination in International Law: Quebec and Lessons Learned* (The Hague: Kluwer, 2000), 512 pp.

Boillat, P., *Jura, naissance d'un Etat: aux sources du droit et des institutions jurassiennes* (Lausanne: Payot, 1989), 207 pp.

Boutros-Ghali, B., *Les conflits de frontières en Afrique (Etude et documents)* (Paris: Ed. techniques et économiques, 1972), 124 pp.

Brölmann, C.; Lefeber, R. and Zieck, M. (eds.), *Peoples and Minorities in International Law* (Dordrecht/Boston/London: Martinus Nijhoff Publishers, 1993), 364 pp.

Brossard, J., *L'accession à la souveraineté et le cas du Québec: conditions et modalités politico-juridiques*, 2e edn (Montreal: Presses de l'Univ. de Montréal, 1995), 853 pp.

Buchanan, A., *Secession: The Morality of Political Divorce from Fort Sumter to Lithuania and Quebec* (Boulder, Colo.: Westview Press, 1991), 174 pp.

Buchheit, L. C., *Secession – The Legitimacy of Self-Determination* (New Haven & London: Yale University Press, 1978), 260 pp.

Bullion, A. J., *India, Sri Lanka and the Tamil Crisis 1976–1994: an International Perspective* (London, New York: Pinter, 1995), 226 pp.

Carment, D.; Harvey, F. and Stack, J. Jr (eds.), *The International Politics of Quebec Secession: State Making and State Breaking in North America* (Westport CT: Praeger, 2001), 187 pp.

Cassese, A., *Self-Determination of Peoples – A Legal Reappraisal* (Cambridge / New York / Melbourne: Cambridge University Press, 1995), 375 pp.

* Prepared with the collaboration of Djacoba Liva Tehindrazanarivelo.

Castellino, J., *International Law and Self-Determination: the Interplay of the Politics of Territorial Possession with Formulations of Post-Colonial 'National' Identity* (The Hague [etc.]: Nijhoff, 2000), 286 pp.

Chen, T. C., *The International Law of Recognition, with Special Reference to Practice in Great Britain and the United States* (London: Stevens & Sons, 1951), 461 pp.

Chesterman, S., *You, the People – The United Nations, Transitional Administration, and State Building* (Oxford: Oxford University Press, 2004), 296 pp.

Chorbajian, L. (ed.), *The Making of Nagorno-Karabagh: From Secession to Republic* (Basingstoke: Palgrave, 2001), 285 pp.

Christakis, Th., *Le droit à l'autodétermination en dehors des situations de décolonisation* (Paris: La documentation française, 1999), 676 pp.

Conversi, D., *The Basques, the Catalans and Spain: Alternative Routes to Nationalist Mobilisation* (London: Hurst & Co., 1997), 312 pp.

Coppieters, B. and Sakwa, R. (eds.), *Contextualizing Secession: Normative Studies in Comparative Perspective* (Oxford: Oxford University Press, 2003), 286 pp.

Corten, O.; Delcourt, B.; Klein, P. and Levrat, N. (eds.), *Démembrements d'Etats et délimitations territoriales: l'uti possidetis en question(s)* (Bruxelles: ULB, Bruylant, 1999), 455 pp.

Crawford, J., *The Creation of States in International Law* (Oxford: Clarendon Press, 1979), 498 pp.

Crawford, J., *The Rights of Peoples* (Oxford: Clarendon Press, 1988), 236 pp.

Cristescu, A. *The Right to Self-Determination, Historical and Current Development on the Basis of United Nations Instruments* (New York, 1981, UN Doc. E/CN.4/Sub.2/ 404/Rev.1).

Dahlitz, J. (ed.), *Secession and International Law: Conflict Avoidance, Regional Appraisals* (The Hague: T.M.C. Asser Press, 2003), 283 pp.

Degan, V.-D., 'Création et disparition de l'État (à la lumière du démembrement de trois fédérations multiethniques en Europe)', *Recueil des cours* 279 (1999), pp. 195–375.

Delcourt B. and Corten, O., *Ex-Yougoslavie. Droit international, politique et idéologies* (Bruxelles: Bruylant, 1998), 202 pp.

Dugard, J., *Recognition and the United Nations* (Cambridge: Grotius, 1987), 192 pp.

Duursma, *Fragmentation and the International Relations of Micro-States. Self-Determination and Statehood* (Cambridge: Cambridge University Press, 1996), 337 pp.

Elsner, B. R., *Die Bedeutung des Volkes im Völkerrecht. Unter besonderer Berücksichtigung der historischen Entwicklung und der Praxis des Selbstbestimmungsrechts der Völker* (Berlin: Duncker & Humblot, 2000), 375 pp.

Erich, R., 'La naissance et la reconnaissance des Etats', *Recueil des cours* 13 (1926-III), pp. 427–507.

Franck, Th. M. (ed.), *The Legal Aspects of the United Nations Action in the Congo* (New York: Dobbs Ferry, 1963), 137 pp.

Gayim, E., *The Concept of Minority in International Law: A Critical Study of the Vital Elements* (Rovaniemi: University of Lapland Press, 2001), 138 pp.

Gayim, E., *The Erithrean Question – The Conflict Between the Right of Self-Determination and the Interests of States* (Iustus Förlag: Juridiska Föreningen i Uppsala, 1993), 716 pp.

Gérard-Libois, J., *Sécession au Katanga* (Bruxelles: [s.n.], Léopoldville : INEP, 1964), 363 pp.

Gowlland-Debbas, V., *Collective Responses to Illegal Acts in International Law – United Nations Action in the Question of Southern Rhodesia* (Dordrecht [etc.]: Nijhoff, 1990), 753 pp.

Grant, T. D., *The Recognition of States: Law and Practice in Debate and Evolution*, (Westport, Conn.: Praeger, 1999), 257 pp.

Groarke, P., *Dividing the State: Legitimacy, Secession and the Doctrine of Oppression* (Aldershot [etc.]: Ashgate, 2004), 212 pp.

Gros Espiell, H., *Le droit à l'autodétermination. Application des résolutions de l'O.N.U.* (New York: Nations Unies, 1979), Doc. ONU E/CN.4/Sub.2/405/Rev.1.

Halperín Donghi, T., *Historia de América Latina. Reforma y Disolución de los Imperios Ibéricos 1750–1850*, vol. III (Madrid: Alianza, 1985).

Hartt, S. H. *et al.* (eds.), *Tangled Web: Legal Aspects of Deconfederation* (Toronto: Renouf Publ. Co. Ltd./C.D. Howe Inst., 1992), 130 pp.

Heintze, H.-J. (ed.), *Selbstbestimmungsrecht der Völker - Herausforderung der Staatenwelt Zerfällt die internationale Gemeinschaft in Hunderte von Staaten?* (Bonn: Stiftung Entwicklung und Frieden, 1997), 384 pp.

Hillgruber, Ch., *Die Aufnahme neuer Staaten in die Völkergemeinschaft* (Frankfurt: Peter Lang, 1998), 827 pp.

Jenkins, J. R. G., *Jura Separatism in Switzerland* (Oxford: Clarendon Press, 1986), 221 pp.

Klappers, J. (ed.), *State Practice Regarding State Succession and Issues of Recognition* (The Hague: Kluwer, 1999), 521 pp.

Kohen, M. G., 'Création d'Etats en droit international contemporain', *Bancaja Euromediterranean Courses of International Law* 6 (2002), pp. 543–635.

Krieger, H. (ed.), *The Kosovo Conflict and International Law. An Analytical Documentation 1974–1999* (Cambridge: Cambridge University Press, 2001), 601 pp.

Lauterpacht, H., *Recognition in International Law* (Cambridge: Cambridge University Press, 1947), 442 pp.

Lehning, P. B. (ed.), *Theories of Secession* (London [etc.]: Routledge, 1998), 262 pp.

Macedo, S. and Buchanan, A. (eds.), *Secession and Self-Determination* (New York [etc.]: New York University Press, 2003), 323 pp.

McWhinney, E., 'Self-Determination of Peoples and Plural-ethnic States: Secession and State Succession and the Alternative, Federal option', *Recueil des cours* 294 (2002), pp. 167–263.

Moore, M. (ed.), *National Self-Determination and Secession* (Oxford: Oxford Univ. Press, 1998), 285 pp.

Musgrave, Th. D., *Self-Determination and National Minorities* (Oxford: Clarendon Press, 1997), 290 pp.

Les Nations Unies et la Somalie, 1992–1996, série Livres bleus (New York: Nations Unies, Département de l'Information, 1996), 535 pp.

Newman, W. J., *The Quebec Secession Reference: The Rules of Law and the Position of the Attorney General of Canada* (Toronto: York Univ. Press, 1999), 99 pp.

Olukoshi, A. O. and Laakso, L. (eds.), *Challenges to the Nation-State in Africa* (Nordiska Afrikainstituted: Uppsala, in cooperation with The Institute of Development Studies, University of Helsinki, 1996), 213 pp.

Omrcanin Stewart, M., *Norway, Sweden, Croatia: a Comparative Study of State Secession and Formation* (Philadelphia : Dorrance, 1976), 138 pp.

Ouguergouz, F., *La Charte africaine des droits de l'homme et des peuples. Une approche juridique des droits de l'homme entre tradition et modernité* (Paris: P.U.F., 1993), 479 pp.

Ouguergouz, F., *The African Charter on Human and Peoples' Rights – A Comprehensive Agenda for Human Dignity and Sustainable Democracy in Africa* (The Hague / London / New York: Martinus Nijhoff Publishers, 2003), 1016 pp.

Quaye, C., *Liberation Struggles in International Law* (Philadelphia: Temple University Press, 1991), 382 pp.

Raič, D., *Statehood and the Law of Self-Determination* (The Hague [etc.] : Kluwer, 2002), 495 pp.

Salmon, J., *La reconnaissance d'Etat* (*Mandchoukouo, Katanga, Biafra, Rhodésie du sud*) (París: Armand Colin, 1971), 286 pp.

Sáenz de Santa Maria, A., 'La libre determinacíon de los pueblos en la nueva sociedad internacional', *Bancaja Euromediterranean Courses of International Law* 1 (1997), pp. 113–203.

Salmon, J., *La reconnaissance d'Etat* (*Mandchoukouo, Katanga, Biafra, Rhodésie du sud*) (Paris: Armand Colin, 1971), 287 pp.

Schoiswohl, M., *Status and (Human Rights) Obligations of Non-Recognized De Facto Regimes in International Law: the Case of 'Somaliland', the Resurrection of Somaliland against All International 'Odds': State Collapse, Secession, Non-Recognition and Human Rights* (Leiden [etc.] : Martinus Nijhoff, 2004), 351 pp.

Simmonds, R., *Legal Problems Arising from the United Nations Military Operations in the Congo* (The Hague: Martinus Nijhoff, 1968), 356 pp.

Simon, S., *Autonomie im Völkerrecht. Ein Versuch zum Selbstbestimmungsrecht der Völker* (Baden-Baden: Nomos, 2000), 149 pp.

Simpson, G. J, *Right of Secession in International Law: A New Theory of Legitimacy* (Ottawa: National Library of Canada, 1989), 266 pp.

Singh, B., *Autonomy or Secession: Jammu and Kashmir* (New Delhi: Har-Anand, 2001), 144 pp.

Sisson, R. and Rose L. E., *War and Secession: Pakistan, India, and the Creation of Bangladesh* (Berkeley, Calif. : University of California Press, 1990), 338 pp.

Stern, B., *Le Statut des Etats issus de l'ex-Yougoslavie à l'ONU* (Paris: Montchrestien, 1996), 189 pp.

Suksi, M. (ed.), *Autonomy: Applications and Implications* (The Hague: Kluwer, 1998), 370 pp.

Tancredi, A., *La secessione nel diritto internazionale* (Padova: Cedam, 2001), 923 pp.

Terrett, S., *The Dissolution of Yugoslavia and the Badinter Commission: a Contextual Study of Peace-making Efforts in the post-Cold War World* (Aldershot: Ashgate / Darmoth, 2000), 395 pp.

The United Nations and the Independence of Eritrea (New York: United Nations, Department of Public Information, 1996), 275 pp.

Tomuschat, Ch. (ed.), *Modern Law of Self-Determination* (Dordrecht: Martinus Nijhoff, 1993), 347 pp.

Trifunovka, S. (ed.), *Yugoslavia Through Documents – From Its Creation to Its Dissolution* (Dordrecht: Martinus Nijhoff, 1994), 1074 pp.

Trifunovka, S. (ed.), *Yugoslavia Through Documents – From Its Dissolution to the Peace Settlement* (The Hague: Martinus Nijhoff, 1999), 1346 pp.

Turp, D., *Le droit de choisir: Essais sur le droit du Québec à disposer de lui-même* (Montreal: Thémis, 2001), 996 pp.

Verhoeven, J., *La reconnaissance internationale dans la pratique contemporaine. Les relations publiques internationales* (Paris: Pedone, 1975), 861 pp.

Welhengama, G., *Minorities' Claims: from Autonomy to Secession. International Law and State Practice* (Aldershot [etc.] : Ashgate, 2000), 339 pp.

Weller, M. (ed.), *The Crisis in Kosovo 1989–1999. From the Dissolution of Yugoslavia to Rambouillet and the Outbreak of Hostilities* (Cambridge: Documents & Analysis Publ. Ltd, 1999), 502 pp.

Williams, S. A., *International Legal Effects of Secession by Quebec* (North York: York Univ. Centre for Public Law and Public Policy, 1992), 48 pp.

Wilson, H. A., *International Law and the Use of Force by National Liberation Movements* (Oxford: Clarendon Press, 1988), 209 pp.

II. Articles and contributions to collective works

Abdullahi, A. M., 'Article 39 of the Ethiopian Constitution on Secession and Self-Determination: A Panacea to the Nationality Question in Africa?', *VRU* 31 (1999), 440–55.

Abie, M. O., 'Droit des peuples dans la Charte africaine des droits de l'homme et des peuples: quelle réalité dans le contexte africain ?', *ASIL Proceedings* 10 (1998), pp. 230–1.

Akhavan, P., 'Self-Determination and the Disintegration of Yugoslavia: What Lessons for the International Community?', *in:* Clark, D. and Williamson, R. (eds.), *Self-Determination. International Perspectives* (Basingstoke: Macmillan Press, New York: St. Martin's Press, 1996), pp. 227–48.

Alvstad, S., 'The Quebec Secession Issue, with an Emphasis on the "Cultural" Side of the Equation', *Temple I.C.L.J.* 18/1 (2004), 89–130.

Ahrens, Ch. B., 'Chechnya and the Right of Self-Determination', *CJTL* 42 (2004), 575–615.

Atrokov, W. T., 'The Khasavyurt Accords: Maintaining the Rule of Law and Legitimacy of Democracy in the Russian Federation Amidst the Chechen Crisis', *Cornell I.L.J.* 32/2 (1999), 367–92.

Ayres, R. W., 'Strategies and Outcomes in Post-Soviet Nationalist Secession Conflicts', *International Politics* 35/2 (1998), 135–63.

Azadon Tiewul, S., 'Relations between the United Nations Organization and the Organization of African Unity in the Settlement of Secessionist Conflicts', *HIJL* 16 (1975), 259–302.

Baev, P. K, 'Russia's Stance against Secessions: from Chechnya to Kosovo', *International Peacekeeping* 6/3 (1993), 73–94.

Bagwell, B., 'Yugoslavian Constitutional Questions: Self-Determination and Secession of Member Republics', *Georgia J.I.C.L.* 21/3 (1991), 489–523.

Basíc, N; Fleming, D. and Vaughn, W., 'The Right of Secession as a Tool to Protect the Territorial Integrity of State', *Mezdunarodni problemi* 49/4 (1997), 421–40.

Bedjaoui, M. and Ouguergouz, F., 'Commentaire de l'article 19', *in:* Mbaye, K. and Kamto, M. (eds.), *La Charte africaine des droits de l'homme et des peuples – Commentaire article par article* (forthcoming).

Benchikh, M., 'Le terrorisme, les mouvements de libération nationale et de sécession et le droit international', *in:* Bannelier, K. *et al.* (eds.), *Le droit international face au terrorisme: après le 11 septembre 2001* (Paris: Pedone, 2003), pp. 69–81.

Bieber, R., 'European Community Recognition of Eastern European States: A New Perspective for International Law?', *ASIL Proceedings* (1992), pp. 374–8.

Bienvenu, P., 'Secession by Constitutional Means: Decision of the Supreme Court of Canada in the Quebec Secession Reference', *HJPLP* 23 (2001), 185–224.

Blay, S., 'Self-Determination: A Reassessment in the Post-communist Era', *Denver J.I.L.P.* 22/2–3 (1994), 275–315.

Blishchenko, I. P., 'International Law Problems of the CIS Member States', *Moscow J.I.L.* 2/1 (1997), 2–9.

Blum, D. S., 'The Apportionment of Public Debt and Assets during State Succession', *CWRJIL* 29/2 (1997), 263–98.

Boniface, P., 'The Proliferation of States', *The Washington Quarterly* 21/3 (1998), 111–27.

Bookman, M. Z., 'War and Peace: the Divergent Breakups of Yugoslavia and Czechoslovakia', *JPR* 31/2 (1994), 175–87.

Bookman-Zarkovic, M., 'Economic Issues Underlying Secession: the Case of Slovenia and Slovakia', *CEET* 4/1 (1992), 111–34.

Brebner, A., 'Things Fall Apart? NAFTA after Quebec Secession', *D.J.L.S.* 6 (1997), 287–306.

Briffault, R., 'Voting Rights, Home Rule, and Metropolitan Governance: the Secession of Staten Island as a Case Study in the Dilemmas of Local Self-Determination', *CLR* 92 (1992), 775–850.

Brilmayer, L., 'Secession and Self-Determination: a Territorial Interpretation', *YJIL* 16 (1991), 177–202.

Brilmayer, L., 'Secession and Self-Determination: One Decade Later', *YJIL* 25/2 (2000), 283–6.

Brooks, R.-O., 'Introduction: Quebec, Canada and the First Nations: the Problem of Secession (Symposium)', *VLR* 23/4 (1999), 699–707.

Brown-John, C.-L., 'Self-Determination, Autonomy and State Secession in Federal Constitutional and International Law', *STLR* 40/3 (1999), 567–601.

Buchanan, A., 'Federalism, Secession, and the Morality of Inclusion', *ALR* 37 (1995), 53–63.

Buchanan, A., 'Self-Determination and the Right to Secede', *JIA* 45 (1991/92), 347–64.

Burdeau, G., 'Le droit de sécession en question: l'exemple du Québec', *Int'l Law Forum* 1 (1999), 3–5.

Castellino, J., 'The Secession of Bangladesh in International Law: Setting New Standards?', *AsYIL* 7 (1997), 83–104.

Charney, J. I., 'Maritime Jurisdiction and the Secession of States: the Case of Quebec', *Vanderbilt J.T.L.* 25 (1992), 343–427.

Charpentier, J., 'Les décarations des Douze sur la reconnaissance des nouveaux Etats', *RGDIP* (1992), 343–55.

Christiano, Th., 'Secession, Democracy and Distributive Justice', *ALR* 37 (1995), 65–72.

Chufrin, G. I., 'Russia: Separatism and Conflicts in the North Caucasus', *SIPRI Yearbook* (2000), 157–80.

Craven, G. J., 'An Indissoluble Federal Commonwealth? The Founding Fathers and the Secession of an Australian State', *Melbourne U.L.R.* 14 (1983), 281–99.

Craven, G. J., 'Of Federalism, Secession, Canada and Quebec', *DLJ* 14 (1991), 231–65.

Craven, G. J., 'The Constitutionality of the Unilateral Secession of an Australian State', *Federal Law Review* 15 (1985), 123–44.

Crawford, J., 'State Practice and International Law in Relation to Secession', *BYIL* 69 (1998), 85–117.

Dawson, M., 'Reflections on the Opinion of the Supreme Court of Canada in the Quebec Secession Reference', *Nat. J. Const. L.* 11 (1999–2000), 5–48.

Delcourt B. and Corten, O., 'Les ambiguïtés de la position belge sur le droit à l'autodétermination des peuples en Croatie', *RBDI* 30/1 (1997), 357–79.

Demissie, D., 'Self-Determination Including Secession vs. the Territorial Integrity of Nation-States: A Prima Facie Case for Secession', *Suffolk T.L.R.* 20 (1996), 165–92.

Dibas-Franck, E., 'L'O.N.U. et la question du Cabinda', *RJPIC* 49/1 (1995), 57–63.

Dinstein, Y., 'Collective Human Rights of Peoples and Minorities', *ICLQ* 25 (1976), 102–20.

Dinstein, Y., 'Is There a Right to Secede?', *ASIL Proceedings* 90 (1996), 299–303.

Dodge, W.-J., 'Succeeding in Seceding? Internationalizing the Quebec Secession Reference ((1998) 2 S.C.R. 217) under NAFTA', *Texas I.L.J* 34/2 (1999), 287–326.

Dufour, G. and Morin, A., 'Le renvoi relatif à la sécession du Québec: critique du traitement que fait la Cour suprême du droit international', *RQDI* 12/2 (1999), 175–95.

Dugard, J., 'Collective Non-Recognition: The Failure of South Africa's Bantustan States, *in: Boutros Boutros-Ghali Amicorum Discipulorumque Liber*, vol. I (Bruxelles: Bruylant, 1998), pp. 383–403.

Dugard, J., 'Secession: Is the Case of Yugoslavia A Precedent for Africa?', *AfYIL* 5/1 (1993), 163–75.

Dumberry, P. and Turp, D., 'La succession d'Etats en matière de traités et le cas de la sécession: du principe de la table rase à l'émergence d'une présomption de continuité des traités', *RBDI* 36/2 (2003), 377–412.

Eastwood Jr, L. S., 'Secession: State Practice and International Law after the Dissolution of the Soviet Union and Yugoslavia', *Duke J.C.I.L.* 3/2 (1993), 299–349.

Ebenroth, C.-Th. and Kemner, M.-J., 'The Enduring Political Nature of Questions of State Succession and Secession and the Quest for Objective Standards', *U. Penn. JIEL* 17 (1996), 753–819.

Eide, A., 'Peaceful Group Accommodation as an Alternative to Secession in Sovereign States', *in:* Clark, D. and Williamson, R. (eds.), *Self-Determination* (1996), pp. 87–111.

Eisner, M., 'A Procedural Model for the Resolution of Secessionist Disputes', *HILJ* 33 (1992), 407–25.

Emerson, R., 'The Logic of Secession', *YLJ* 29 (1979–1980), 802–24.

Etzioni, A., 'The Evils of Self-Determination', *Foreign Policy* 89 (1992/1993), 21–35.

Ewald, G. J., 'The Kurds' Right to Secede under International Law: Self-Determination Prevails over Political Manipulation', *Denver J.I.L.P.* 22/2–3 (1994), 375–407.

Falkowski, J. E., 'Secessionary Self-Determination: A Jeffersonian Perspective', *Boston U.I.L.J.* 9 (1991), 209–42.

Fawn, R., 'Recognition, Self-Determination and Secession in the Post-Cold War International Society', *in:* R. Fawn (ed.), *International Society after the Cold War* (Basingstoke and London: Macmillan Press, 1996), pp. 193–219.

Feshbach, M. and Simonyan, R., 'Soviet Futures: Union, Federation or Secession?', *Adelphi papers* 257 (1990/91), 19–40.

Finkelstein, K.; Vegh, G. and Joly, C., 'Does Quebec Have a Right to Secede at International Law?', *CBR* 74 (1995), 223–60.

Franck, Th. M. and Rodley, N. S., 'After Bangladesh: The Law of Humanitarian Intervention by Military Force', *AJIL* 67 (1973), 275–305.

Frank, Th.; Higgins, R.; Pellet, A.; Shaw, M. and Tomuschat, Ch., 'L'intégrité territoriale du Québec dans l'hypothèse de l'accession à la souveraineté, Etude commandée par la Commission d'étude des questions afférentes à l'accession du Québec à la souveraineté', *in: Les Attributs d'un Québec souverain* (Québec: Bibliothèque nationale, 1992), Exposés et études, vol. I.

Frankel, L., 'International Law of Secession: New Rules for A New Era', *Houston J.I.L.* 14 (1992), 521–64.

Frémont, J. and Boudreault, F., 'Supracontitutionalité canadienne et sécession du Québec', *Nat. J. Const. L.* 8 (1997), 161–204.

Frey, D., 'Selbstbestimmungsrecht, Sezession und Gewaltverbot', *in:* Seidl-Hohenveldern, Schrötter (eds.), *Vereinte Nationen, Menschenrechte und Sicherheitspolitik. Völkerrechtliche Fragen zu internationalen Konfliktbegrenzungen* (Köln [etc.]: Heymann, 1994), pp. 31–74.

Friel, R. J., 'Secession from the European Union: Checking out of the Proverbial "cockroach motel"', *Fordham International Law Journal* 27/2 (2004), 590–641.

Gaeta, P., 'The Armed Conflict in Chechnya before the Russian Constitutional Court', *EJIL* 7/4 (1996), 563–70.

Ganguly, R., 'The Challenge of Ethnic Insurgency and Secession in South and South-east Asia: Introduction', *in:* R. Ganguly (ed.), *Ethnic Conflict and Secessionism in South and Southeast Asia* (New Delhi: Sage, 2003), pp. 9–22.

Gaudreault-DesBiens, J.-F., 'The Quebec Secession Reference ((1998) 2 S. C. R. 217) and the Judicial Arbitration of Conflicting Narratives about Law, Democracy, and Identity', *VLR* 23/4 (1999), 793–843.

Gazzini, T., 'Some Considerations on the Conflict in Chechnya', *HRLJ* 17 (1996), 93–105.

Gibbs, D. N., 'Dag Hammarskjöld, the United Nations, and the Congo Crisis of 1960–1: A Reinterpretation', *The Journal of Modern African Studies* 31/1 (1993), 164–7.

Goy, R., 'L'indépendance de l'Erythrée', *AFDI* (1993), 337–56.

Grant, Th. D., 'A Panel of Experts for Chechnya: Purposes and Prospects in Light of International law', *FYIL* 9 (1998), 145–248.

Gray, Ch. D., 'Self-Determination and the Breakup of the Soviet Union', *YEL* 12 (1992), 465–503.

Greene, K., 'International Responses to Secessionist Conflicts', *ASIL Proceedings* 90 (1996), pp. 296–318.

Gunter, M. M., 'A De Facto Kurdish State in Northern Iraq', *TWQ* 14/2 (1993), 295–319.

Guyard, M., 'Les puissances occidentales et la crise congolaise: de la sécession du Katanga à l'accord de Kitona (1960–1961)', *Guerres mondiales et conflits contemporains* 49/196 (1999), 53–63.

Habte-Selassie, B., 'Self-Determination in Principle and Practice: the Ethiopian-Eritrean Experience', *Columbia H.R.L.J.* 29/1 (1997), 92–142.

Haile, M., 'Legality of Secessions: the Case of Eritrea', *Emory I.L.R.* 8/2 (1994), 479–537.

Haljan, D. P., 'Negotiating Quebec Secession', *RBDI* 31 (1998), 190–216.

Hanna, R. M., 'Right to Self-Determination in *In re Secession of Quebec* ((1998) 2 S.C.R. 217)', *Maryland J.I.L.T.* 23/1 (1999), 213–46.

Hannum, H., 'The Specter of Secession: Responding to Claims for Ethnic Self-Determination', *Foreign Affairs* 77/2 (1998), 13–18.

Hannum, H. and Lillich, R. B., 'Autonomy in International Law', *AJIL* 74 (1980), 861–89.

Hannum, H., 'Rethinking Self-Determination', *VJIL* 34/1 (1993), 1–69.

Happold, M., 'Independence: In or Out of Europe? An Independent Scotland and the European Union', *ICLQ* 49/1 (2000), 15–34.

Hashmi, S. H., 'Self-Determination and Secession in Islamic Thought', *in:* M. Sellers (ed.), *The New World Order: Sovereignty, Human Rights, and the Self-Determination of Peoples* (Oxford [etc.]: Berg, 1996), pp. 117–51.

Haverland, C., 'Secession', *in:* R. Bernhardt (ed.), *Encyclopedia of Public International Law* 4 (2000), pp. 354–9.

Hennayake, Sh. K., 'The Peace Accord and the Tamils in Sri Lanka', *Asian Survey* 29 (1989), 401–15.

Heraclides, A., 'Secession, Self-Determination and Non-Intervention: In Quest of a Normative Symbiosis', *JIA* 45/2 (1992), 399–420.

Heraclides, A., 'Secessionist Conflagration: What Is to Be Done?', *Security Dialogue* 25/3 (1994), 283–93.

Heraclides, A., 'The Ending of Unending Conflicts: Separatist Ears', *Millennium* 26/3 (1997), 679–707.

Hillgruber, C., 'The Admission of New States to the International Community', *EJIL* 9 (1998), 491–509.

Hilpold, P., 'Sezession und humanitäre Intervention – völkerrechtliche Instrumente zur Bewältigung innerstaatlicher Konflikte?', *ZöR* 54/4 (1999), 529–602.

Hollis, D., 'Accountability in Chechnya. Addressing Internal Matters with Legal and Political International Norms', *Boston C.L.R.* 36/4 (1995), 793–846.

Horowitz, D. L., 'Irredentas and Secessions: Adjacent Phenomena, Neglected Connections', *in:* N. Chazan (ed.), *Irredentism and International Politics* (Boulder: Lynne Rienner Publishers, London: Adamantine Press, 1991), pp. 9–22.

'The International Legal Aspects of the Lithuanian Secession', *Journal of Legislation* 17 (1991), 309–30.

Islam, M. R., 'Secession Crisis in Papua New Guinea: the Proclaimed Republic of Bougainville in International Law', *U.Haw. L.R.* 13 (1991), 453–75.

Islam, M. R., 'Secessionist Self-Determination: Some Lessons from Katanga, Biafra and Bangladesh', *JPR* 22/3 (1985), 211–21.

Islam, M. R., 'Status of Unilateral Declaration of Independence in International Law: The Case of Bangladesh', *IJIL* 23 (1983), 1–16.

Islam, M. R., 'The Tamil Separatism in Sri Lanka: Some Factors Undermining the Claim', *NILR* 33 (1986), 65–83.

Jensen, E. M., 'American Indian Tribes and Secession', *Tulsa Law Journal* 29 (1993), 385–96.

Joireman, S. F., 'Secession and its Aftermath: Eritrea', *in:* Schneckener, U. and Wolff, S. (eds.), *Managing and Settling Ethnic Conflicts* (London: Hurst, 2004), pp. 176–88.

Kay, R. S., 'The Secession Reference and the Limits of Law', *Otago Law Review* 10/3 (2003), 327–44.

Khachikian, A., 'Multilateral Mediation in Intrastate Conflicts: Russia, the United Nations, and the War in Abkhazia', *in:* Greenberg, M. C., Barton, J. H. and McGuinness, M. E. (eds.), *Words Over War, Mediation and Arbitration to Prevent Deadly Conflict* (Lanham, MD: Rowman & Littlefield, 2000), pp. 15–34.

Kherad, R., 'La reconnaissance internationale des Etats baltes', *RGDIP* 96/4 (1992), 843–72.

Kherad, R., 'La reconnaissance des Etats issus de la dissolution de la République socialiste fédérative de Yougoslavie par les membres de l'Union européenne', *RGDIP* 101/3 (1997), 663–93.

Kherad, R., 'De la nature juridique du conflit tchétchène', *RGDIP* 104/1 (2000), 143–79.

King, Ch., 'Moldova and the New Bessarabian Questions', *World Today* 49/7 (1993), 135–9.

Kirgis, F., 'The Degrees of Self-Determination in the United Nations Era', *AJIL* 88/2 (1994), 304–10.

Kirgis, F. L., 'Self-Determination of Peoples and Polities', *ASIL Proceedings* 86 (1992), pp. 369–400.

Kiwanuka, R., 'The Meaning of "People" in the African Charter on Human and Peoples' Rights', *AJIL* 82 (1988), 80–101.

Kohen, M., 'Le problème des frontières en cas de dissolution et de séparation d'Etats: quelles alternatives ?', *RBDI* 31/1 (1998), 129–60.

Kolsto, P., 'The Dniester Conflict: Between Irredentism and Separatism', *Europe-Asia Studies* 45/6 (1993), 973–1000.

Kooijmans, P. H., 'Tolerance, Sovereignty and Self-Determination', *NILR* 43/2 (1996), 211–17.

Koskenniemi, M., 'National Self-Determination Today: Problems of Legal Theory and Practice', *ICLQ* 43 (1994), 241–69.

Lalonde, S., 'Secession: Quebec: (1995) 74 Can. Bar Rev. 225 and 293: addendum: Quebec and the Principle of Effectiveness', *CBR* 76 (1997), 258–61.

LaSelva, S.-V., 'Divided Houses: Secession and Constitutional Faith in Canada and the United States', *VLR* 23/4 (1999), 771–92.

Lattanzi, F., 'La secessione nel diritto internazionale: autodeterminazione dei popoli e delimitazioni di un territorio nazionale nell'esperienza recente', *in: Stato, etnicità e nazionalismo nella transizione tra due ordini mondiali* (Urbino: Università degli studi di Urbino-Facoltà di scienze politiche, 1995), 19–38.

Le-Bouthillier, Y., 'La Cour suprême du Canada peut-elle répondre à une pure question de droit international dans le cadre du renvoi sur la sécession unilatérale du Quebec?', *Revue générale de droit* 28/4 (1997), 431–48.

Lefeber, R. and Raič, D., 'Frontiers of International Law, Part One: The Chechen People', *LJIL* (1996), 1–6.

Leff, C. S., 'Democratization and Disintegration in Multinational States: the Breakup of the Communist Federations', *World Politics* 51/2 (1999), 205–35.

Lejeune, Y., 'La succession du nouveau Canton du Jura aux traités internationaux du Canton de Berne', *RGDIP* (1978), 1051–74.

Lloyd, A. M., 'The Southern Sudan: A Compelling Case for Secession', *CJTL* 32 (1994), 419–54.

Lloyd, D. O., 'Succession, Secession, and State Membership in the United Nations', *NYUJILP* 26 (1994), 761–96.

Luchterhandt, O., 'Integration oder Separation: Bricht das "grosse Reich Russland" auseinander?', *Internationale Politik* 52/1 (1997), 17–24.

MacLauchlan, H. W., 'Accounting for Democracy and the Rule of Law in the Quebec Secession Reference (Supreme Court of Canada, File No. 25506)', *CBR* 76 (1997), 155–85.

MacMillan, K., 'Secession Perspectives and the Independence of Quebec', *Tulane J.I.C.L.* 7 (1999), 333–65.

Majzub, D. B., 'Does Secession Mean Succession? The International Law of Treaty Succession and an Independent Quebec', *QLR* 24/2 (1999), 411–50.

Makovka, A., 'Les limites territoriales et maritimes d'un Québec souverain', *RQDI* 8 (1993–1994), 309–23.

Marchildon, G. and Maxwell, E., 'Quebec's Right of Secession under Canadian and International Law', *VJIL* 32 (1992), 583–623.

Massa, S., 'Secession by Mutual Assent: A Comparative Analysis of the Dissolution of Czechoslovakia and the Separatist Movement in Canada', *WILR* 14 (1995), 183–222.

McCorquodale, R., 'Self-Determination: a Human Rights Approach', *ICLQ* 43/4 (1994), 857–85.

McGee, R. W. and Lam, D. K. K., 'Hong Kong's Option to Secede', *HILJ* 33 (1992), 427–40.

McGee, R. W., 'A Third Liberal Theory of Secession', *Liverpool L.R.* 14 (1992), 45–66.

McGee, R. W., 'Secession as a Tool for Limiting the Growth of State and Municipal Government and Making it more Responsive: A Constitutional Proposal', *WSULR* 21 (1994), 499–513.

McGee, R. W., 'The Theory of Secession and Emerging Democracies: A Constitutional Solution', *SJIL* 28 (1992), 451–76.

McIntosh, S. C. R., 'The St. Kitts-Nevis Question: Secession or Constitutional Reform?', *Caribbean L.R.* 7/2 (1997), 419–63.

Millard, G., 'The Secession Reference and National Reconciliation: A Critical Note', *Canadian J. L.S.* 14/2 (1999), 1–19.

Moffa, C., 'L'ethnicité en Afrique: l'implosion de la "question nationale" après la décolonisation', *Politique africaine* 66 (1997), 101–14.

Monaco, R., 'Observations sur le droit des peuples dans la communauté internationale', *in: El derecho internacional en un mondo en transformación: liber amicorum en homenaje al profesor Eduardo Jiménez de Aréchaga* (Montevideo: Fundación de Cultura Universitaria, 1994), pp. 217–27.

Monahan, P.-J., 'The Law and Politics of Quebec Secession', *OHLJ* 33 (1995), 1–33.

Moreau Defarges, Ph., 'Le droit de sécession: jusqu'où?', *Défense nationale* 55/8–9 (1999), 87–93.

Morse, H. N., 'The Foundations and Meaning of Secession', *Stetson L.R.* 15 (1986), 19–36.

Mouskhély, M., 'La naissance des Etats en droit international public', *RGDIP* (1962), 469–85.

Mousson-Lestang, J. P., 'Négociation ou intervention: la Suède et la sécession de la Norvège en 1905', *in: Enjeux et puissances. Pour une histoire des relations internationales au XXe siècle. Melanges en l'honneur de Jean-Baptiste Duroselle* (Paris: Publications de la Sorbonne, 1986), pp. 257–70.

Mullerson, R., 'Self-Determination of Peoples and the Dissolution of the USSR', *in:* R. St. J. Macdonald (ed.), *Essays in Honour of Wang Tieya* (The Hague: Kluwer, 1993), pp. 567–85.

Murswiek, D., 'Das Problematik eines Rechts auf Sezession neu betrachtet', *Archiv des Völkerrechts* 31 (1993), 307–32.

Naldi, G., 'Separatism in the Comoros: Some Legal Aspects', *LJIL* 11 (1998), 247–56.

N'Kolombua, A., 'L'ambivalence des relations entre le droit des peuples à disposer d'eux-mêmes et l'intégrité territoriale des Etats en droit international contemporain', *in: Le droit des peuples à disposer d'eux-mêmes: méthodes d'analyse du droit international: mélanges offerts à Charles Chaumont* (Paris: Pedone, 1984), 443–61.

Nanda, P., 'Self-Determination under International Law: Validity of Claims to Secede', *CWRJIL* 13 (1981), 257–80.

Nanda, V. P., 'Self-Determination and Secession under International Law', *Denver J.I.L.P.* 29/3–4 (2001), 305–26.

Nesi, G., 'L' "*uti possidetis*" hors du contexte de la décolonisation: le cas de l'Europe', *AFDI* 44 (1998), 1–23.

Nielsen, K., 'Liberal Nationalism, Liberal Democracies, and Secession', *UTLJ* 48/2 (1998), 253–95.

Oeter, S., 'Selbstbestimmungsrecht im Wandel: Überlegungen zur Debatte um Selbstbestimmung, Sezessionsrecht und 'vorzeitige' Anerkennung', *ZaöRV* 52/3–4 (1992), 741–80.

Okoronkwo, P. L., 'Self-Determination and the Legality of Biafra's Secession under International Law', *Loyola L.A.I.C.L.R.* 25/1 (2002), 63–115.

Oraison, A., 'L'obligation de non-reconnaissance de l'Etat d'Anjouan', *RDISDP* 76/2 (1998), 159–83.

Oraison, A., 'Réflexions sur la double conception française du droit des peuples à disposer d'eux-mêmes à la lumière du "cas mahorais"', *RDISDP* 81/1 (2003), 1–94.

Orentlicher, D. F., 'Separation Anxiety: International Responses to Ethno-separatist Claims', *YJIL* 23/1 (1998), 1–78.

Osterland, H.-A., 'National Self-Determination and Secession: the Slovak Model', *Case Western Reserve J. of Int'l Law* 25 (1993), 655–702.

Ostrowski, J., 'Was the Union Army's Invasion of the Confederate States a Lawful Act? An Analysis of President Lincoln's Legal Arguments against Secession',: *in:* D. Gordon (ed.), *Secession, State and Liberty* (New Brunswick, N.J.; Transaction Publ., 1998), pp. 155–90.

Pabst, M., 'Partition: Still an Issue in South Africa?', *Aussenpolitik: German Foreign Affairs Review* 47/3 (1996), 300–10.

Pellet, A., 'Quel avenir pour le droit des peuples à disposer d'eux-mêmes?', *in: El derecho internacional en un mondo en transformación: liber amicorum en homenaje al profesor Eduardo Jiménez de Aréchaga* (Montevideo: Fundación de Cultura Universitaria, 1994), pp. 255–76.

Pellet, A., 'The Opinion of the Badinter Committee. A Second Breath for the Self-Determination of Peoples', *EJIL* 3 (1992), 178–81.

Pelletier, B., 'Le face à face entre le projet sécessionniste québécois et la Constitution du Canada', *Revue du Barreau* 57 (1997), 341–95.

Perouse de Montclos, M.-A., 'Le Somaliland, de l'Etat virtuel et la gestion pratique du pouvoir', *Cultures et conflits* 31/32 (1998), 205–23.

Plawker, K. R., 'The Soviet Contradiction: Socialist Federalism and the Freedom of Secession', *WILJ* 10 (1991), 169–83.

Premdas, R. R., 'Decentralisation, Development and Secession: the Case of Papua New Guinea', *Marga* 9/3–4 (1988), 1–14.

Proulx, D., 'La sécession du Québec: Principes et mode d'emploi selon la Cour suprême du Canada', *RBDC* (1998), 361–84.

Quane, H., 'The United Nations and the Evolving Right to Self-Determination', *ICLQ* 47 (1998), 537–72.

'Quebec, Canada, and First Nations: The Problem of Secession. Symposium', *VLR* 23/4 (1999), 699–859.

Radan, P., 'Post-Secession International Borders: A Critical Analysis of the Opinions of the Badinter Arbitration Commission', *Melbourne U.L.R.* 24/1 (2000), 50–76.

Radan, P., 'Secessionist Self-Determination: The Cases of Slovenia and Croatia', *Australian J.I.A.* 48/2 (1994), 183–95.

Rao, K. M., 'Right of Self-Determination in the Post-Colonial Era: A Survey of Juristic Opinion and State Practice', *IJIL* 28/1 (1988), 58–71.

Rayfuse, R., 'Reference re Secession of Quebec ((1998) 2 S.C.R. 217) from Canada: Breaking Up is Hard to Do', *UNSWLJ* 21/3 (1998), 834–44.

Rice, J., 'Culture, Postmodernism, and Canadian Legal Hermeneutics: A Comment on Reference re Secession of Quebec ((1998) 2 S.C.R. 217)', *DJLS* 8 (1999), 183–206.

Ringelheim, J., 'Considerations on the International Reaction to the 1999 Kosovo Crisis', *RBDI* (1999/2), 475–544.

Roosens, C., 'Les Etats-Unis et la sécession du Katanga 1960–1963', *Studia diplomatica* 35 (1982), 371–415.

Rowlands, D., 'Negotiating Debt under Secession: the Case of Quebec and Canada', *in:* Carment, D.; Harvey, F. and Stack, J. Jr (eds.), *The International Politics of Quebec Secession* (2001), pp. 91–104.

Rubin, A. P., 'Secession and Self-Determination: A Legal, Moral and Political Analysis', *in:* A. Jokíc (ed.), *War Crimes and Collective Wrongdoing: A Reader* (Malden, MA: Blackwell, 2001), pp. 176–97.

Rudrakumaran, V., 'The Legitimacy of Lithuania's Claim for Secession', *Boston U.I.L.J.* 10 (1992), 33–60.

Ruiz Fabri, H., 'Genèse et disparition de l'Etat à l'époque contemporaine', *AFDI* (1992), 153–78.

Salmon, J., 'Le droit des peuples à disposer d'eux-mêmes. Aspects juridiques et politiques', *in: Le nationalisme, facteur belligène. Etudes de sociologie de la guerre* (Bruxelles: Bruylant, 1972), pp. 347–70.

Salmon, J., 'Naissance et reconnaissance du Bangla-Desh: quelques réflexions sur l'application des principes du droit international touchant les relations amicales entre États', *in:* J. Tittel (ed.), *Multitudo legum ius unum: Festschrift für Wilhelm Wengler zu seinem 65. Geburtstag* (Berlin: Inter Recht, 1973), vol. I, pp. 467–90.

Sanders, D., 'If Quebec Secedes from Canada Can the Cree Secede from Quebec?', *UBCLR* 29/1 (1995), 143–58.

Schachter, O., 'Micronationalism and Secession', *in:* Beyerlin, U. *et al.* (eds.), *Recht zwischen Umbruch und Bewahrung: Festschrift fur Rudolf Bernhardt* (Berlin: Springer-Verlag, 1995), pp. 179–86.

Scharf, M. P., 'Musical Chairs: The Dissolution of States and Membership in the United Nations', *Cornell I.L.J* 28/1 (1995), 29–69.

Schneckener, U., 'The Fall of Leviathan: On Self-Determination and Secession', *Law and State* 57 (1998), 81–103.

Schrijver, N., 'Can the Cause of Human Rights Justify Breaking up a State? Reflections on Secession and the Ban on the Use of Force', *in:* Arts, K. and Mihyo, P. (eds.), *Responding to the Human Rights Deficit* (The Hague: Kluwer, 2003), pp. 49–57.

Schwartz, B. and Waywood, S., 'A Model Declaration on the Right of Secession', *New York ILR* 11/2 (1998), 1–53.

'Secession: State Practice and International Law after the Dissolution of the Soviet Union and Yugoslavia', *Duke J.C.I.L.* 3 (1993), 299–349.

Seidel, G., 'A New Dimension of the Right of Self-Determination in Kosovo?', *in:* Ch. Tomuschat (ed.), *Kosovo and the International Community. A Legal Assessment* (The Hague: Kluwer Law, 2002), pp. 203–15.

Sheppard, Cl.-A., 'The Cree Intervention in the Canadian Supreme Court Reference on Quebec Secession ((1998) 2 S.C.R. 217): A Subjective Assessment', *VLR* 23/4 (1999), 845–59.

Simpson, G. J., 'The Diffusion of Sovereignty: Self-Determination in the Post-Colonial Age', *SJIL* 32 (1996), 255–86.

Stahn, C., 'Constitution without a State? Kosovo under the United Nations Constitutional Framework for Self-Government, *LJIL* 14 (2001), pp. 531–61.

Stahn, C., 'The Agreement on Succession Issues of the Former Socialist Federal Republic of Yugoslavia', *AJIL* 96/2 (2002), 379–97.

Stairs, D., 'Canada and Quebec after Quebec Secession: "Realist" Reflections on an International Dilemma', *in:* Carment, D.; Harvey, F. and Stack, J. Jr (eds.), *The International Politics of Quebec Secession* (2001), pp. 33–56.

Stanovcic, V., 'National Self-Determination and Secession: Ideas and Problems', *Arhiv za Pravne i Drustvene Nauke* 79 (1993), 747–62.

Starushenko, G. B., 'Self-Determination without Separatism', *International Affairs* 3/4 (1994), 50–56.

Stein, E., 'Peaceful Separation: "a New Virus"?', *CJTL* 36/1–2 (1997), 25–39.

Stromseth, J., 'Self-Determination, Secession and Humanitarian Intervention by the United Nations', *ASIL Proceedings* (1992), pp. 370–4.

Sunstein, C. R., 'Constitutionalism and Secession', *UCLR* 58 (1991), 633–70.

Svoboda, K., 'No Success in Secession: 135 Years Ago the United States of America Experienced Civil War, now Canada Grapples with the Possible Secession of Quebec', *St Louis U.L.J.* 44/2 (2000), 747–88.

Szayna, Th. S., 'The Breakup of Czechoslovakia: Some Thoughts about its Implications', *Polish Q.I.A.* 2/1 (1993), 55–72.

Tancredi, A., 'Secessione e diritto internazionale', *Rivista* 81/3 (1998), 673–768.

Tappe, T.-N., 'Chechnya and the State of Self-Determination in a Breakaway Region of the former Soviet Union: Evaluating the Legitimacy of Secessionist Claims', *CJTL* 34 (1995), 255–95.

Thibodeau, M., 'The Legality of an Independent Quebec: Canadian Constitutional Law and Self-Determination in International Law', *Boston C.I.C.L.R.* 3 (1979), 99–142.

Thomas, R. G. C., 'Secessionist Movements in South Asia', *Survival* 36/2 (1994), 92–114.

Thornberry, P., 'Self-Determination, Minorities, Human Rights: A Review of International Instruments', *ICLQ* 38 (1989), 867–89.

Tierney, S., 'In a State of Flux: Self-Determination and the Collapse of Yugoslavia', *IJMGR* 6 (1999), 197–233.

Tir, J. *et al.*, 'Territorial Changes, 1816–1996: Procedures and Data', *Conflict Management and Peace Science* 16/1 (1998), 89–97.

Tomuschat, Ch., 'Yugoslavia's Damaged Sovereignty over the Province of Kosovo', *in: State, Sovereignty and International Governance. Liber Amicorum Judge Kooijmans* (Oxford, 2002), pp. 323–47.

Toope, S. J., 'Self-Determination, Canada-Quebec Right to Secede under Constitutional Law and Public International Law, Role of International Law in Canadian Courts', *AJIL* 93/2 (1999), 519–25.

Treisman, D. S., 'Russia's "Ethnic Revival": the Separatist Activism of Regional Leaders in a Postcommunist Order', *World Politics* 49/2 (1997), 212–49.

Tremblay, R. Ch., 'Nation, Identity and the Intervening Role of the State: A Study of the Secessionist Movement in Kashmir', *Pacific affairs* 69/4 (1996/1997), 471–97.

Turp, D., 'Le droit de sécession en droit international public', *CYIL* 20 (1982), 24–78.

Valentine, D. A., 'The Logic of Secession', *YLJ* 89/4 (1980), 802–24.

Vázquez, J. Z., 'The Mexican Declaration of Independence', *JAH* 85 (1999), 1362–9.

Verhoeven, J., 'La reconnaissance internationale: déclin ou renouveau ?', *AFDI* (1993), 7–40.

Viteritti, J.-P., 'Municipal Home Rule and the Conditions of Justifiable Secession', *FULJ* 23 (1995), 1–68.

Walters, M. D., 'Nationalism and the Pathology of Legal Systems: Considering the Quebec Secession Reference ((1998) 2 S.C.R. 217) and its Lessons for the United Kingdom', *MLR* 62/3 (1999), 371–96.

Wangsgard, S.-A., 'Secession, Humanitarian Intervention, and Clear Objectives: when to Commit United States Military Forces', *Tulsa J.C.I.L.* 3 (1996), 313–34.

Webber, J., 'The Legality of a Unilateral Declaration of Independence under Canadian Law', *McGill L.J.* 42 (1996–7), 281–318.

Weinstock, D. M., 'Toward a Proceduralist Theory of Secession', *Canadian J.L.J.* 13/2 (2000), 251–64.

Weller, M., 'The International Response to the Dissolution of the Socialist Federal Republic of Yugoslavia', *AJIL* 86/3 (1992), 569–607.

Whelan, A., 'Wilsonian Self-Determination and the Versailles Settlement', *ICLQ* 43 (1994), 99–115.

Whites, Ch., 'Reference re Secession of Quebec ((1998) 2 S.C.R. 217): Secession by Quebec is a Nearly Impossible Task', *NYLSJICL* 19/2 (1999), 323–45.

Wildhaber, L., 'Territorial Modifications and Breakups in Federal States', *CYIL* 33 (1995), 41–74.

Wiltanger, E., 'Sound the trumpets! Quebec is shouting, "Victory!" despite the Canadian Supreme Court's denial of unilateral secession', *Dickinson J.I.L.* 17/3 (1999), 505–29.

Wippman, D., 'Secession, Territorial Claims, and the Indeterminacy of Self-Determination', *YJIL* 25/2 (2000), 287–9.

Wodie, F., 'La sécession du Biafra et le droit international public', *RGDIP* 73 (1969), 1019–60.

Woehrling, J., 'Les aspects juridiques d'une éventuelle sécession du Quebec', *CBR* 74 (1995), 292–329.

Woehrling, J., 'Unexpected Consequences of Constitutional First Principles', *Canada Watch* 7/1–2 (1999), 18–20.

Wood, J. R., 'Secession: A Comparative Analytical Framework', *Canadian J.P.S.* 14/1 (1981), 107–34.

Wroth, L.-K., 'Quebec, Canada, and the First Nations: the Problem of Secession', *VLR* 23/4 (1999), 709–19.

Yakemtchouk, R., 'Les républiques baltes en droit international. Échec d'une annexion opérée en violation du droit des gens', *AFDI* (1991), 259–89.

Young, R.A, 'How Do Peaceful Secessions Happen?', *in:* Carment, D. and James, P. (eds.), *Wars in the Midst of Peace* (Pittsburg, PA: University of Pittsburgh Press, 1997), pp. 45–60.

Yusuf, A. A., 'The Right of Intervention by the African Union: A New Paradigm in Regional Enforcement Action ?', *AfYIL* 11 (2003), 3–23.

INDEX

For EU product safety concerns, contact us at Calle de José Abascal, 56–1°, 28003 Madrid, Spain or eugpsr@cambridge.org.

www.ingramcontent.com/pod-product-compliance
Lightning Source LLC
LaVergne TN
LVHW011533200926
848484LV00001B/250

* 9 7 8 0 5 2 1 8 4 9 2 8 9 *